# THE
# ENDURING DEBATE

## CLASSIC AND CONTEMPORARY READINGS
## IN AMERICAN POLITICS

Fourth Edition

# THE
# ENDURING DEBATE

## CLASSIC AND CONTEMPORARY READINGS
## IN AMERICAN POLITICS

### Fourth Edition

Edited by
David T. Canon
John J. Coleman
Kenneth R. Mayer

W. W. NORTON & COMPANY
NEW YORK   LONDON

Copyright © 2006, 2003, 2000, 1997 by W. W. Norton & Company, Inc.

All rights reserved.
Printed in the United States of America.

Manufacturing by the Courier Companies.
Production manager: Diane O'Connor.

Library of Congress Cataloging-in-Publication Data

**ISBN 0–393–92618-4 (pbk.)**

W. W. Norton & Company, Inc., 500 Fifth Avenue, New York, N.Y. 10110
www.wwnorton.com

W. W. Norton & Company Ltd., Castle House,
75/76 Wells Street, London W1T 3QT

2   3   4   5   6   7   8   9   0

# Contents

# PART II   Institutions

## PART  IV    Public Policy

# PART I

# The Constitutional System

# CHAPTER 1

# Political Culture

## 1

## From *The Liberal Tradition in America: An Interpretation of American Political Thought Since the Revolution*

### LOUIS HARTZ

*Political culture refers to the orientation of citizens toward the political system and toward themselves as actors in it. This includes the basic values, beliefs, attitudes, predispositions, and expectations that citizens bring to political life. Given the great diversity of the American population, one might expect a similarly diverse array of thought within political culture, with rival sets of political values challenging each other. In his classic and influential work, Louis Hartz argues that in fact there is broad agreement in the United States around a set of political beliefs. Hartz refers to this as the "liberal tradition"; the terms "liberal consensus" and "American Creed" have also been used. "Liberal" here means a focus on the individual and minimizing government intervention in daily life. Within the liberal tradition, the values of equality, private property, liberty, individualism, protection of religious freedom, and democracy are especially powerful. There is certainly debate over what these terms mean or how much to emphasize one versus another, and these clashes animate party politics, but we do not see successful political movements in the United States that directly challenge these values. On the contrary, most movements seek to show how their beliefs and principles are highly consistent with these basic American values. Hartz argues that it is the nature of American history that led to this unusual uniformity. Not having had a feudal stage, Americans also did not witness the revolutionary stages and ideologies that challenged feudalism in Europe. As Hartz puts it, "no feudalism, no socialism." This historical path does present some problems, in Hartz's view. Americans view liberalism as natural, as obvious. Indeed, to some extent, we are hardly aware of it as an ideology because it has been unchallenged. To Hartz, writing in the 1950s, this sometimes blinds Americans to policy alternatives, heightens our fears of social disharmony and "foreign" ideas, and makes it hard for Americans to understand other societies where a liberal tradition is not so dominant.*

## 1. America and Europe

The analysis which this book contains is based on what might be called the storybook truth about American history: that America was settled by men who fled from the feudal and clerical oppressions of the Old World. If there is anything in this view, as old as the national folklore itself, then the outstanding thing about the American community in Western history ought to be the non-existence of those oppressions, or since the reaction against them was in the broadest sense liberal, that the American community is a liberal community. We are confronted * * * with * * * America skipping the feudal stage of history * * *. "Feudalism" refers technically to the institutions of the medieval era, and it is well known that aspects of the decadent feudalism of the later period, such as primogeniture, entail, and quitrents, were present in America even in the eighteenth century. "Liberalism" is an even vaguer term, clouded as it is by all sorts of modern social reform connotations, and even when one insists on using it in the classic Lockian sense, as I shall insist here, there are aspects of our original life in the Puritan colonies and the South which hardly fit its meaning.[1] But these are the liabilities of any large generalization, danger points but not insuperable barriers. What in the end is more interesting is the curious failure of American historians, after repeating endlessly that America was grounded in escape from the European past, to interpret our history in the light of that fact. * * *

*   *   *

## 2. "Natural Liberalism": The Frame of Mind

One of the central characteristics of a nonfeudal society is that it lacks a genuine revolutionary tradition, the tradition which in Europe has been linked with the Puritan and French revolutions: that it is "born free," as Tocqueville said. And this being the case, it lacks also a tradition of reaction * * *. Its liberalism is * * * a "natural" phenomenon. But the matter is curiously broader than this, for a society which begins with Locke, and thus transforms him, stays with Locke, by virtue of an absolute and irrational attachment it develops for him, and becomes as indifferent to the challenge of socialism in the later era as it was unfamiliar with the heritage of feudalism in the earlier one. It has within it, as it were, a kind of self-completing mechanism, which insures the universality of the liberal idea. * * * It is not accidental that America which has uniquely lacked a feudal tradition has uniquely lacked also a socialist tradition. The hidden origin of socialist thought everywhere in the West is to be found in the feudal ethos. * * *

America has presented the world with the peculiar phenomenon, not of a frustrated middle class, but of a *"frustrated aristocracy"*—of men, Aristotelian-like, trying to break out of the egalitarian confines of middle-class life but suffering guilt and failure in the process. The South before the Civil War is the case par excellence of this, though New England of course exemplifies it also. * * * The Southerners were thrown into fantastic contradictions by their iconoclastic conservatism, by what I have called the "Reactionary Enlightenment," and after the Civil War for good historical reasons they fell quickly into oblivion. The South, as John Crowe Ransom has said, has been the part of America closest to Old World Europe, but it has never really been Europe. It has been an alien child in a liberal family, tortured and confused, driven to a fantasy life which, instead of disproving the power of Locke in America, portrays more poignantly than anything else the tyranny he has had.

* * * Here we have one of the great and neglected relationships in American history: the common fecklessness of the Southern "feudalists" and the modern socialists. It is not accidental, but something rooted in the logic of all of Western history, that they should fail alike to leave a dent in the American liberal intelligence. * * * Socialism arises not only to fight capitalism but remnants of feudalism itself, so that the failure of the Southern [feudalists], in addition to setting the pattern for the failure of the later Marxists, robbed them in the process of a normal ground for growth. * * *

Surely, then, it is a remarkable force: this fixed, dogmatic liberalism of a liberal way of life. It is the secret root from which have sprung many of the most puzzling of American cultural phenomena. Take the unusual power of the Supreme Court and the cult of constitution worship on which it rests. Federal factors apart, judicial review as it has worked in America would be inconceivable without the national acceptance of the Lockian creed, ultimately enshrined in the Constitution, since the removal of high policy to the realm of adjudication implies a prior recognition of the principles to be legally interpreted. * * * If in England a marvelous organic cohesion has held together the feudal, liberal, and socialist ideas, it would still be unthinkable there that the largest issues of public policy should be put before nine Talmudic judges examining a single text. But this is merely another way of saying that law has flourished on the corpse of philosophy in America, for the settlement of the ultimate moral question is the end of speculation upon it. Pragmatism, interestingly enough America's great contribution to the philosophic tradition, does not alter this, since it feeds itself on the Lockian settlement. It is only when you take your ethics for granted that all problems emerge as problems of technique. Not that this is a bar in America to institutional innovations of highly non-Lockian kind. Indeed, as the New Deal shows, when you simply "solve problems" on the basis of a submerged and absolute liberal faith, you can depart from Locke with a kind of inventive freedom that European Liberal reformers and even European socialists, dominated by ideological systems, cannot duplicate. * * *

Here is a Lockian doctrine which in the West as a whole is the symbol of rationalism, yet in America the devotion to it has been so irrational that it has not even been recognized for what it is: liberalism. There has never been a "liberal movement" or a real "liberal party" in America: we have only had the American Way of Life, a nationalist articulation of Locke which usually does not know that Locke himself is involved; and we did not even get that until after the Civil War when the Whigs of the nation, deserting the Hamiltonian tradition, saw the capital that could be made out of it. This is why even critics who have noticed America's moral unity have usually missed its substance. Ironically, "liberalism" is a stranger in the land of its greatest realization and fulfillment. But this is not all. Here is a doctrine which everywhere in the West has been a glorious symbol of individual liberty, yet in America its compulsive power has been so great that it has posed a threat to liberty itself. * * *

I believe that this is the basic ethical problem of a liberal society: not the danger of the majority which has been its conscious fear, but the danger of unanimity, which has slumbered unconsciously behind it: the "tyranny of opinion" that Tocqueville saw unfolding as even the pathetic social distinctions of the Federalist era collapsed before his eyes. But in recent times this manifestation of irrational Lockianism, or of "Americanism," to use a favorite term of the American Legion, * * * has neither slumbered nor been unconscious. It has been very much awake in a red scare hysteria which no other nation in the West has really been able to understand. And this suggests a very significant principle: that when a liberal community faces military and ideological pressure from without it transforms eccentricity into sin, and the irritating figure of the bourgeois gossip flowers into the frightening figure of an A. Mitchell Palmer or a Senator McCarthy. * * *

The decisive domestic issue of our time may well lie in the counter resources a liberal society can muster against this deep and unwritten tyrannical compulsion it contains. They exist. Given the individualist nature of the Lockian doctrine, there is always a logical impulse within it to transcend the very conformitarian spirit it breeds in a Lockian society * * *.

But the most powerful force working to shatter the American absolutism is, paradoxically enough, the very international involvement which tensifies it. This involvement is complex in its implications. If in the context of the Russian Revolution it elicits a domestic redscare, in the context of diplomacy it elicits an impulse to impose Locke everywhere. * * * Thus to say that world politics shatters "Americanism" at the moment it intensifies it is to say a lot: it is to say that the basic horizons of the nation both at home and abroad are drastically widened by it. * * * [W]hen has the nation appreciated more keenly the limits of its own cultural pattern as applied to the rest of the world? * * * [W]hen has the meaning of civil liberties been more ardently understood than now? * * * The outcome of the battle between intensified "Americanism" and new enlightenment is still an open question.

\* \* \*

### 3. The Dynamics of a Liberal Society

So far I have spoken of natural liberalism as a psychological whole, embracing the nation and inspiring unanimous decisions. We must not assume, however, that this is to obscure or to minimize the nature of the internal conflicts which have characterized American political life. * * * What we learn from the concept of a liberal society, lacking feudalism and therefore socialism and governed by an irrational Lockianism, is that the domestic struggles of such a society have all been projected with the setting of Western liberal alignments. * * *

\* \* \*

That society has been a triumph for the liberal idea, but we must not assume that this ideological victory was not helped forward by the magnificent material setting it found in the New World. The agrarian and proletarian strands of the American democratic personality, which in some sense typify the whole of American uniqueness, reveal a remarkable collusion between Locke and the New World. Had it been merely the liberal spirit alone which inspired the American farmer to become capitalistically oriented, to repudiate save for a few early remnants the village organization of Europe, to produce for a market and even to enter capitalist occupations on the side such as logging and railroad building, then the difficulties he encountered would have been greater than they were. But where land was abundant and the voyage to the New World itself a claim to independence, the spirit which repudiated peasantry and tenantry flourished with remarkable ease. Similarly, had it merely been an aspect of irrational Lockianism which inspired the American worker to think in terms of the capitalist setup, the task would have been harder than it was.

But social fluidity was peculiarly fortified by the riches of a rich land, so that there was no small amount of meaning to Lincoln's claim in 1861 that the American laborer, instead of "being fixed to that condition for life," works for "a while," then "saves," then "hires another beginner" as he himself becomes an entrepreneur. And even when factory industrialism gained sway after the Civil War, and the old artisan and cottage-and-mill mentality was definitely gone, it was still a Lockian idea fortified by material resources which inspired the triumph of the job mentality of Gompers rather than the class mentality of the European worker. The "petit-bourgeois" giant of America, though ultimately a triumph for the liberal idea, could hardly have chosen a better material setting in which to flourish.

\*    \*    \*

One cannot say of the liberal society analysis that by concentrating on national unities it rules out the meaning of domestic conflict. Actually it discovers that meaning \* \* \*. The argument over whether we should "stress" solidarity or conflict in American politics misleads us by advancing a false set of alternatives.

\*    \*    \*

## DISCUSSION QUESTIONS

1. Do you agree with Hartz that Americans have a hard time understanding other societies because of ideological uniformity in the United States?

2. Do you think Hartz is correct in saying that Americans are in agreement on the values of the liberal tradition? Are there parts of American history or society today that make you doubt his thesis?

3. Without limiting yourself to Hartz's observations, what do you think might be some of the advantages and disadvantages of a high degree of agreement on basic values for American society and politics?

## NOTES

1. Ed. note: "Lockian" refers to John Locke, a British political theorist. Locke's ideas of individualism, liberty, property rights, and limited government were among those that influenced political leaders at the time of the American Revolution.

# 2

# From *The Creation of the American Republic, 1776–1787*

## Gordon S. Wood

*In the 1960s, a group of historians took issue with the depiction of American society as fundamentally and uniformly liberal. Perhaps American society in the twentieth century was dominated by the liberal tradition, historians such as Gordon Wood argued, but in the colonial and revolutionary period, it was classical republicanism that most shaped public thought about politics. The liberal consensus emphasizes the primacy of the individual in society; classical republicanism draws individuals' attention to society and the community. A contemporary term for this approach is "commmunitarianism." To classical republicans, individuals are not self-made—society makes individuals what they are and individuals owe something to society in return. The classical republican approach doesn't disagree that individuals have personal responsibility and need to work hard and diligently. It would, however, suggest that the point of self-improvement is to better serve the community and society. Wood notes that in this view, politics is not primarily about achieving your self-interest. Rather, the focus is on civic duty. Participation is expected, for the social good. Individuals are to be motivated not by self-interest, but by morality and virtue. Although Wood argues elsewhere that classical republicanism failed in the 1780s and made the way for liberal politics to become dominant and embraced by the Constitution, other historians suggest that the classical republican ideals continued to influence American politics through various reform movements over the course of U.S. history.*

\* \* \*

### The Public Good

The sacrifice of individual interests to the greater good of the whole formed the essence of republicanism and comprehended for Americans the idealistic goal of their Revolution. From this goal flowed all of the Americans' exhortatory literature and all that made their ideology truly revolutionary. This republican ideology both presumed and helped shape the Americans' conception of the way their society and politics should be structured and operated—a vision so divorced from the realities of American society, so contrary to the previous century of American experience, that it alone was enough to make the Revolution one of the great utopian movements of American history. By 1776 the Revolution came to represent a final attempt, perhaps—given the nature of American society— even a desperate attempt, by many Americans to realize the traditional Commonwealth ideal of a corporate society, in which the common good would be the only objective of government.

\* \* \*

To make the people's welfare—the public good—the exclusive end of government became for the Americans, as one general put it, their "Polar Star," the central tenet of the Whig faith, shared not only by Hamilton and Paine at opposite ends of the Whig spectrum, but by any American bitterly opposed to a system which held "that a Part is greater than its Whole; or, in other Words, that some Individuals ought to be considered, even to the Destruction of the Community, which they compose." No phrase except "liberty" was invoked more often by the Revolutionaries than "the public good." It expressed the colonists' deepest hatreds of the old order and their most visionary hopes for the new. \* \* \*

From the logic of belief that "all government . . . is or ought to be, calculated for the general good and safety of the community," for which end "the most effectual means that human wisdom hath ever been able to devise, is frequently appealing to the body of the people," followed the Americans' unhesitating adoption of republicanism in 1776. The peculiar excellence of republican government was that it was "wholly characteristical of the purport, matter, or object for which government ought to be instituted." By definition it had no other end than the welfare of the people: *res publica*, the public affairs, or the public good. "The word *republic*," said Thomas Paine, "means the *public good*, or the good of the whole, in contradistinction to the despotic-form, which makes the good of the sovereign, or of one man, the only object of the government." \* \* \*

Since in a free government the public good was identical with the people's welfare, a "matter of COMMON FEELING" and founded on the "COMMON CONSENT" of the people, the best way of realizing it in the Whig mind was to allow the people a maximum voice in the government. "That the great body of the people," as even the Tory William Smith of Philadelphia admitted, "can have any interest separate from their country, or (when fairly understood) pursue any other, is not to be imagined," "unless," as John Sullivan said, "we suppose them idiots or self-murderers." Therefore any government which lacked "a proper representation of the people" or was in any way even "independent of the people" was liable to violate the common good and become tyrannical. Most Whigs had little doubt of the people's honesty or even of their ability to discern what was good for themselves. It was a maxim, declared a New York patriot, "that whatever may be the particular opinions of Individuals, the bulk of the people, both mean, and think right." Was there ever any fear, James Burgh had gone so far as to ask, that the people might be *"too free* to consult the general good?" Of course even the most radical English Whigs admitted that the people might sometimes mistake their own interest and might often be unable to effect it even when they did correctly perceive it. Most Americans therefore assumed that the people, in their representational expression of their collective liberty in the houses of representatives, could not run the whole government. "Liberty, though the most essential requisite in government," Richard Price had written, "is not the only one; wisdom, union, dispatch, secrecy, and vigour are likewise requisite"—qualities best supplied by a magistracy and a senate.

Yet such governors and upper houses, however necessary, must be electively dependent on the people. Republicanism with its elective magistracy would not eliminate the problems of politics and the threat of power, but it did promise a new era of stability and cooperation between rulers and ruled. * * * For decades, and especially in recent years, the Crown's presence in America had played havoc with the colonists' political life and was the real source of that factious behavior of which royal officials had so repeatedly and unjustly accused them. "Every man that has lived any time in America, under regal government, knows what frequent, and almost continual opposition there is between the country interest and those in power." "By keeping clear of British government," the Americans could at last be rid of those "jars and contentions between Governors and Assemblies." By allowing the people to elect their magistracy, republicanism would work to "blend the interests of the people and their rulers" and thus "put down every animosity among the people." In the kind of states where *"their governors shall proceed from the midst of them"* the people could be surer that their interests exclusively would be promoted, and therefore in turn would "pay obedience to officers properly appointed" and maintain "no discontents on account of their advancement."

What made the Whig conception of politics and the republican emphasis on the collective welfare of the people comprehensible was the assumption that the people, especially when set against their rulers, were a homogeneous body whose "interests when candidly considered are one." Since everyone in the community was linked organically to everyone else, what was good for the whole community was ultimately good for all the parts. The people were in fact a single organic piece (*"for God hath so tempered the body that there should be no Schism in the body, but that the Members should have the same care for one another"*) with a unitary concern that was the only legitimate objective of governmental policy. This common interest was not, as we might today think of it, simply the sum or consensus of the particular interests that made up the community. It was rather an entity in itself, prior to and distinct from the various private interests of groups and individuals. As Samuel Adams said in 1776, paraphrasing Vattel, the state was "a moral person, having an interest and will of its own." Because politics was conceived to be not the reconciling but the transcending of the different interests of the society in the search for the single common good, the republican state necessarily had to be small in territory and generally similar in interests. Despite sporadic suggestions in the press for "a simple government" of a strong continental congress chosen "by the people, (not by their representatives)," and uniting all the people "in one great republick," few Americans thought that such an extensive continental republic, as distinct from a league of states, was feasible in 1776—however much they may have differed over the desirable strength of the expected confederation.

No one, of course, denied that the community was filled with different, often clashing combinations of interests. But apart from the basic conflict between governors and people these were not to be dignified by their incorporation into formal political theory or into any serious discussion of what ought to be. In light of the assumption that the state was "to be considered as one moral whole" these interests and parties were regarded as aberrations or perversions, indeed signs of sickness in the body politic. Although some eighteenth-century thinkers were in fact beginning to perceive the inevitability, even the desirability, of faction in a free state, most continued to regard division among the people as "both dangerous and destructive," arising "from false ambition, avarice, or revenge." Men lost control of their basest passions and were unwilling to sacrifice their immediate desires for the corporate good. Hence, "party differences," however much they may infect the society, could never ideally be admitted into the institutions of government, but "would be dropped at the threshold of the state house." The representatives of the people would not act as spokesmen for private and partial interests, but all would be "disinterested men, who could have no interest of their own to seek," and "would employ their whole time for the public good; then there would be but one interest, the good of the people at large."

\*   \*   \*

Yet ironically it was precisely internal discord and conflict for which republics were most widely known. Throughout history "free republican governments have been objected to, as if exposed to factions from an excess of liberty." But this was because liberty had been misunderstood and falsely equated with licentiousness or the liberty of man in a state of nature which was "a state of war, rapine and murder." True liberty was "natural liberty restrained in such manner, as to render society one great family; where every one must consult his neighbour's happiness, as well as his own." In a republic "each individual gives up all private interest that is not consistent with the general good, the interest of the whole body." For the republican patriots of 1776 the commonweal was all-encompassing—a transcendent object with a unique moral worth that made partial considerations fade into insignificance. "Let regard be had only to the good of the whole" was the constant exhortation by publicists and clergy. Ideally, republicanism obliterated the individual. "A Citizen," said Samuel Adams, "owes everything to the Commonwealth." "Every man in a republic," declared Benjamin Rush, "is public property. His time and talents—his youth—his manhood—his old age—nay more, life, all belong to his country." "No man is a true republican," wrote a Pennsylvanian in 1776, "that will not give up his single voice to that of the public."

Individual liberty and the public good were easily reconcilable because the important liberty in the Whig ideology was public or political liberty. In 1776 the solution to the problems of American politics seemed to rest not so much in emphasizing the private rights of individuals against the general will as it did in stressing the public rights of the collective people against the supposed privileged interests of their rulers. "Civil Liberty," as one colonist put it, was not primarily individual; it was "the freedom of bodies politic, or States." Because, as Josiah Quincy said, the people "as a body" were "never interested to injure themselves," and were "uniformly desirous of the general welfare," there could be no real sense of conflict between public and personal liberty. Indeed, the private liberties of individuals depended upon their collective public liberty. * * *

Thus in the minds of most Whigs in 1776 individual rights, even the basic civil liberties that we consider so crucial, possessed little of their modern theoretical relevance when set against the will of the people. This is why, for example, throughout the eighteenth century the Americans could contend for the broadest freedom of speech against the magistracy, while at the same time punishing with a severe strictness any seditious libels against the representatives of the people in the colonial assemblies. Anyone who tried to speak against the interests of the people "should be held in execration. . . . Every word, that tends to weaken the hands of the people is a crime of devilish dye"; indeed, "it is the *unpardonable Sin* in politics." Thus it was "no *Loss of Liberty*, that court-minions can complain of, when they are silenced. No man has a right to say a word, which may lame the liberties of his country." * * *

*    *    *

Even at the beginning, however, there were some good Whigs who perceived the inherent conflict between individual liberty and traditional republican theory. Ancient Sparta, William Moore Smith told the members of the Continental Congress in the spring of 1775, had demonstrated the problem. Knowing that luxury was the great enemy of republicanism and liberty, Lycurgus had sought to avoid the evil by eliminating wealth itself. But in doing so he undermined the very basis of freedom. "He seems not to have reflected that there can be no true liberty without security of property; and where property is secure, industry begets wealth; and wealth is often productive of a train of evils naturally destructive to virtue and freedom!" "Here, then," said Smith, "is a sad dilemma in politics." If the people "exclude *wealth*, it must be by regulations intrenching too far upon civil *liberty*." But if wealth is allowed to flourish, "the syren *luxury*" soon follows at its heels and gradually contaminates the whole society. "What is to be done in this case?" Must the society, "to secure the first of blessings, *liberty*," strangle wealth, the first offspring of liberty, in its birth and thus in effect destroy liberty as well? "Or, is there no proper use of *wealth* and *civil happiness*, the genuine descendants of *civil liberty*, without abusing them to the nourishment of *luxury* and *corruption*?" Smith, like other Whigs in 1776, thought there was an answer to the dilemma in the more enlightened policy and "purer system of *religion*" of this modern age—"to regulate the use of wealth, but not to exclude it."

*   *   *

### The Need for Virtue

Perhaps everyone in the eighteenth century could have agreed that in theory no state was more beautiful than a republic, whose whole object by definition was the good of the people. * * * The very greatness of republicanism, its utter dependence on the people, was at the same time its source of weakness. In a republic there was no place for fear; there could be no sustained coercion from above. The state, like no other, rested on the consent of the governed freely given and not compelled. In a free government the laws, as the American clergy never tired of repeating, had to be obeyed by the people for conscience's sake, not for wrath's.

*   *   *

In a monarchy each man's desire to do what was right in his own eyes could be restrained by fear or force. In a republic, however, each man must somehow be persuaded to submerge his personal wants into the greater good of the whole. This willingness of the individual to sacrifice his private interests for the good of the community—such patriotism or love of country—the eighteenth century termed "public virtue." A republic was such a delicate polity precisely because it demanded an extraordinary moral character in the people. Every state in which the people participated needed a degree of virtue; but a republic which rested solely on the people absolutely required it. * * * The eighteenth-century mind was thoroughly convinced that a popularly based government "cannot be supported without *Virtue*." Only with a public-spirited, self-sacrificing people could the authority of a popularly elected ruler be obeyed, but "more by the virtue of the people, than by the terror of his power." Because virtue was truly the lifeblood of the republic, the thoughts and hopes surrounding this concept of public spirit gave the Revolution its socially radical character—an expected alteration in the very behavior of the people, "laying the foundation in a constitution, not without or over, but within the subjects."

This public virtue, "this endearing and benevolent passion," was "the noblest which can be displayed" and represented all that men of the eighteenth century sought in social behavior. "Its grand source" lay in the attitudes and actions of the individuals who made up the society, "in that charity which forms every social connection." In other words, public virtue, the willingness of the people to surrender all, even their lives, for the good of the state, was primarily the consequence of men's individual private virtues. * * * For most Americans in 1776 vicious behavior by an individual could have only disastrous results for the community. A man racked by the selfish passions of greed, envy, and hate lost his conception of order; "his sense of a connection with the *general* system—his benevolence—his desire and freedom of *doing good*, ceased." It seemed obvious that a republican society could not "be maintained without justice, benevolence and the social virtues." * * * Somehow, as a Boston writer argued * * * the individual's widening and traditionally weakening circles of love—from himself to his family to the community—must be broken into; men must be convinced that their fullest satisfaction would come from the subordination of their individual loves to the greater good of the whole. It was man's duty and interest to be benevolent. "The happiness of every individual" depended "on the happiness of society." * * * Once men correctly perceived their relation to the commonwealth they would never injure what was really their personal interest to protect and sustain.

*Equality*

* * *

Even the most radical republicans in 1776 admitted the inevitability of all natural distinctions: weak and strong, wise and foolish—and even of incidental distinctions: rich and poor, learned and unlearned. Yet, of course, in a truly republican society the artificial subsidiary distinctions would never be extreme, not as long as they were based solely on natural distinctions. It was widely believed that equality of opportunity would necessarily result in a rough equality of station, that as long as the social channels of ascent and descent were kept open it would be impossible for any artificial aristocrats or overgrown rich men to maintain themselves for long. With social movement founded only on merit, no distinctions could have time to harden. * * * And projected public educational systems would open up the advantages of learning and advancement to all.

Great consequences were expected to flow from such an egalitarian society. If every man realized that his associations with other men and the state depended solely on his merit, then, as former Massachusetts Governor Thomas Pownall told the Americans, there would be an end to the jealousy and the contentions for "unequal Dominion" that had beset communities from time immemorial. Indeed, equality represented the social source from which the anticipated harmony and public virtue of the New World would flow. "It is this principle of equality . . . ," wrote one Virginian in 1776, "which alone can inspire and preserve the virtue of its members, by placing them in a relation to the publick and to their fellow-citizens, which has a tendency to engage the heart and affections to both."

It was a beautiful but ambiguous ideal. The Revolutionaries who hoped for so much from equality assumed that republican America would be a community where none would be too rich or too poor, and yet at the same time believed that men would readily accede to such distinctions as emerged as long as they were fairly earned. But ironically their ideal contained the sources of the very bitterness and envy it was designed to eliminate. For if the promised equality was the kind in which "one should consider himself as good a man as another, and not be brow beaten or intimidated by riches or supposed superiority," then their new republican society would be no different from that in which they had lived, and the Revolution would have failed to end precisely what it was supposed to end. Indeed, although few Americans could admit it in 1776, it was the very prevalence of this ambivalent attitude toward equality that had been at the root of much of their squabbling during the eighteenth century.

* * *

## DISCUSSION QUESTIONS

1. Do classical republican values sound impractical for contemporary American politics? Or do you think these values have more influence in politics than someone like Louis Hartz would acknowledge?

2. What are the key components of the classical republican outlook, as presented by Wood? How do they differ from the liberal tradition?

3. Wood notes at several points that some of the strengths of republican thought would also prove to contain seeds of difficulty for republicanism. Identify and describe these strengths.

4. How would you define "the public good"?

# 3

# "Beyond Tocqueville, Myrdal, and Hartz: The Multiple Traditions in America"

## Rogers M. Smith

*Where liberalism and republicanism both point to notions of equality, Rogers Smith argues that there is another tradition in American political thought that has been influential. Not denying the significance of liberalism or republicanism, Smith contends that an equally significant strain of thought, "ascriptive hierarchy," has been important across U.S. history. In this way of thinking, society is a hierarchy, where some groups are on top and others are below. Those on top are deserving of all the rights and benefits the liberal tradition can offer; those below are not. The most glaring examples of this throughout American history were the treatment of racial minorities, especially blacks, and the treatment of women. Smith notes that those holding these illiberal views were not on the fringes of society but, rather, were probably the majority view. We cannot, Smith argues, marginalize the impact of "ascriptive American" hierarchy or those who held these views. American public policy at the highest levels was influenced by its premises. Moreover, the same individuals often held these illiberal views in tandem with their liberal or republican views and expended great intellectual energy to make these views seem acceptable in the light of fundamental American beliefs.*

Since the nation's inception, analysts have described American political culture as the preeminent example of modern liberal democracy, of government by popular consent with respect for the equal rights of all. They have portrayed American political development as the working out of liberal democratic or republican principles, via both "liberalizing" and "democratizing" socioeconomic changes and political efforts to cope with tensions inherent in these principles. Illiberal, undemocratic beliefs and practices have usually been seen only as expressions of ignorance and prejudice, destined to marginality by their lack of rational defenses. * * *

[Alexis de] Tocqueville's thesis—that America has been most shaped by the unusually free and egalitarian ideas and material conditions that prevailed at its founding—captures important truths. Nonetheless, the purpose of this essay is to challenge that thesis by showing that its adherents fail to give due weight to inegalitarian ideologies and conditions that have shaped the participants and the substance of American politics just as deeply. For over 80% of U.S. history, its laws declared most of the world's population to be ineligible for full American citizenship solely because of their race, original nationality, or gender. For at least two-thirds of American history, the majority of the domestic adult population was also ineligible for full citizenship for the same reasons. * * *

The Tocquevillian story is thus deceptive because it is too narrow. It is centered on relationships among a minority of Americans (white men, largely of northern European ancestry) analyzed via reference to categories derived from the hierarchy of political and economic statuses men have held in Europe: monarchs and aristocrats, commercial burghers, farmers, industrial and rural laborers, and indigents. Because most European observers and British American men have regarded these categories as politically fundamental, it is understandable that they have always found the most striking fact about the new nation to be its lack of one type of ascriptive hierarchy. There was no hereditary monarchy or nobility native to British America, and the revolutionaries rejected both the authority of the British king and aristocracy and the creation of any new American substitutes. Those features of American political life made the United States appear remarkably egalitarian by comparison with Europe.

But the comparative moral, material, and political egalitarianism that prevailed at the founding among moderately propertied white men was surrounded by an array of other fixed, ascriptive systems of unequal status, all largely unchallenged by the American revolutionaries. Men were thought naturally suited to rule over women, within both the family and the polity. White northern Europeans were thought superior culturally—and probably biologically—to black Africans, bronze Native Americans, and indeed all other races and civilizations. Many British Americans also treated religion as an inherited condition and regarded Protestants as created by God to be morally and politically, as well as theologically, superior to Catholics, Jews, Muslims, and others.

These beliefs were not merely emotional prejudices or "attitudes." Over time, American intellectual and political elites elaborated distinctive justifications for these ascriptive systems, including inegalitarian scriptural readings, the scientific racism of the "American school" of ethnology, racial and sexual Darwinism, and the romantic cult of Anglo-Saxonism in American historiography. All these discourses identified the true meaning of *Americanism* with particular forms of cultural, religious, ethnic, and especially racial and gender hierarchies. Many adherents of ascriptive Americanist outlooks insisted that the nation's political and economic structures should formally reflect natural and cultural inequalities, even at the cost of violating doctrines of universal rights. Although these views never entirely prevailed, their impact has been wide and deep.

Thus to approach a truer picture of America's political culture and its characteristic conflicts, we must consider more than the familiar categories of (absent) feudalism and socialism and (pervasive) bourgeois liberalism and republicanism. The nation has also been deeply constituted by the ideologies and practices that defined the relationships of the white male minority with subordinate groups, and the relationships of these groups with each other. When these elements are kept in view, the flat plain of American egalitarianism mapped by Tocqueville and others suddenly looks quite different. We instead perceive America's initial conditions as exhibiting only a rather small, recently leveled valley of relative equality nestled amid steep mountains of hierarchy. And though we can see forces working to erode those mountains over time, broadening the valley, many of the peaks also prove to be volcanic, frequently responding to seismic pressures with outbursts that harden into substantial peaks once again.

To be sure, America's ascriptive, unequal statuses, and the ideologies by which they have been defended have always been heavily conditioned and constrained by the presence of liberal democratic values and institutions. The reverse, however, is also true. Although liberal democratic ideas and practices have been more potent in America than elsewhere, American politics is best seen as expressing the interaction of multiple political traditions, including *liberalism, republicanism*, and *ascriptive forms of Americanism*, which have collectively comprised American political culture, without any constituting it as a whole. Though Americans have often struggled over contradictions among these traditions, almost all have tried to embrace what they saw as the best features of each.

Ascriptive outlooks have had such a hold in America because they have provided something that neither liberalism nor republicanism has done so well. They have offered creditable intellectual and psychological reasons for many Americans to believe that their social roles and personal characteristics express an identity that has inherent and transcendant worth, thanks to nature, history, and God. Those rationales have obviously aided those who sat atop the nation's political, economic, and social hierarchies. But many Americans besides elites have felt that they have gained meaning, as well as material and political benefits, from their nation's traditional structures of ascribed places and destinies.

Conventional narratives, preoccupied with the absence of aristocracy and socialism, usually stress the liberal and democratic elements in the rhetoric of even America's dissenters. These accounts fail to explain how and why liberalizing efforts have frequently lost to forces favoring new forms of racial and gender hierarchy. Those forces have sometimes negated major liberal victories, especially in the half-century following Reconstruction; and the fate of that era may be finding echoes today.

My chief aim here is to persuade readers that many leading accounts of American political culture are inadequate. * * * This argument is relevant to contemporary politics in two ways. First, it raises the possibility that novel intellectual, political, and legal systems reinforcing racial, ethnic, and gender inequalities might be rebuilt in America in the years ahead. That prospect does not seem plausible if the United States has always been essentially liberal democratic, with all exceptions marginal and steadily eliminated. It seems quite real, however, if liberal democratic traditions have been but contested parts of American culture, with inegalitarian ideologies and practices often resurging even after major enhancements of liberal democracy. Second, the political implications of the view that America has never been completely liberal, and that changes have come only through difficult struggles and then have often not been sustained, are very different from the complacency—sometimes despair—engendered by beliefs that liberal democracy has always been hegemonic.

*   *   *

*The Multiple-Traditions Thesis of American Civic Identity*

It seems prudent to stress what is not proposed here. This is not a call for analysts to minimize the significance of white male political actors or their conflicts with each other. Neither is it a call for accounts that assail "Eurocentric" white male oppressors on behalf of diverse but always heroic subjugated groups. The multiple-traditions thesis holds that Americans share a *common* culture but one more complexly and multiply constituted than is usually acknowledged. Most members of all groups have shared and often helped to shape all the ideologies and institutions that have structured American life, including ascriptive ones. A few have done so while resisting all subjugating practices. But members of every group have sometimes embraced "essentialist" ideologies valorizing their own ascriptive traits and denigrating those of others, to bleak effect. Cherokees enslaved blacks, champions of women's rights disparaged blacks and immigrants, and blacks have often been hostile toward Hispanics and other new immigrants. White men, in turn, have been prominent among those combating invidious exclusions, as well as those imposing them.

Above all, recognition of the strong attractions of restrictive Americanist ideas does not imply any denial that America's liberal and democratic traditions have had great normative and political potency, even if they have not been so hegemonic as some claim. Instead, it sheds a new—and, in some respects, more flattering—light on the constitutive role of liberal democratic values in American life. Although some Americans have been willing to repudiate notions of democracy and universal rights, most have not; and though many have tried to blend those commitments with exclusionary ascriptive views, the illogic of these mixes has repeatedly proven a major resource for successful reformers. But we obscure the difficulty of those reforms (and thereby diminish their significance) if we slight the ideological and political appeal of contrary ascriptive traditions by portraying them as merely the shadowy side of a hegemonic liberal republicanism.

At its heart, the multiple-traditions thesis holds that the definitive feature of American political culture has been not its liberal, republican, or "ascriptive Americanist" elements but, rather, this more complex pattern of apparently inconsistent combinations of the traditions, accompanied by recurring conflicts. Because standard accounts neglect this pattern, they do not explore how and why Americans have tried to uphold aspects of all three of these heterogeneous traditions in combinations that are longer on political and psychological appeal than on intellectual coherency.

A focus on these questions generates an understanding of American politics that differs from Tocquevillian ones in four major respects. First, on this view, purely liberal and republican conceptions of civic identity are seen as frequently unsatisfying to many Americans, because they contain elements that threaten, rather than affirm, sincere, reputable beliefs in the propriety of the privileged positions that whites, Christianity, Anglo-Saxon traditions, and patriarchy have had in the United States. At the same time, even Americans deeply attached to those inegalitarian arrangements have also had liberal democratic values. Second, it has therefore been typical, not aberrational, for Americans to embody strikingly opposed beliefs in their institutions, such as doctrines that blacks should and should not be full and equal citizens. But though American efforts to blend aspects of opposing views have often been remarkably stable, the resulting tensions have still been important sources of change. Third, when older types of ascriptive inequality, such as slavery, have been rejected as unduly illiberal, it has been normal, not anomalous, for many Americans to embrace new doctrines and institutions that reinvigorate the hierarchies they esteem in modified form. Changes toward greater inequality and exclusion, as well as toward greater equality and inclusiveness, thus can and do occur. Finally, the dynamics of American development cannot simply be seen as a rising tide of liberalizing forces progressively submerging contrary beliefs and practices. The national course has been more serpentine. The economic, political, and moral forces propelling the United States toward liberal democracy have often been heeded by American leaders, especially since World War II. But the currents pulling toward fuller expression of alleged natural and cultural inequalities have also always won victories. In some eras they have predominated, appearing to define not only the path of safety but that of progress. In all eras, including our own, many Americans have combined their allegiance to liberal democracy with beliefs that the presence of certain groups favored by history, nature, and God has made Americans an intrinsically "special" people. Their adherents have usually regarded such beliefs as benign and intellectually well founded; yet they also have always had more or less harsh discriminatory corollaries.

To test these multiple-traditions claims, consider the United States in 1870. By then the Civil War and Reconstruction had produced dramatic advances in the liberal and democratic character of America's laws. Slavery was abolished. All persons born in the United States and subject to its jurisdiction were deemed citizens of the United States and the states in which they resided, regardless of their race, creed or gender. None could be denied voting rights on racial grounds. The civil rights of all were newly protected through an array of national statutes. The 1790 ban on naturalizing Africans had been repealed, and expatriation declared a natural right. Over the past two decades women had become more politically engaged and had begun to gain respect as political actors.

*   *   *

[Neither liberal or republican analyses] would have had the intellectual resources to explain what in fact occurred. Over the next fifty years, Americans did not make blacks, women, and members of other races full and equal citizens, nor did racial and gender prejudices undergo major erosion. Neither, however, were minorities and women declared to be subhuman and outside the body politic. And although white Americans engaged in extensive violence against blacks and Native Americans, those groups grew in population, and no cataclysm loomed. Instead, intellectual and political elites worked out the most elaborate theories of racial and gender hierarchy in U.S. history and partially embodied them in a staggering array of new laws governing naturalization, immigration, deportation, voting rights, electoral institutions, judicial procedures, and economic rights—but only partially. The laws retained important liberal and democratic features, and some were strengthened. They had enough purchase on the moral and material interests of most Americans to compel advocates of inequality to adopt contrived, often clumsy means to achieve their ends.

The considerable success of the proponents of inegalitarian ideas reflects the power these traditions have long had in America. But after the Civil War, * * * evolutionary theories enormously strengthened the intellectual prestige of doctrines presenting the races and sexes as naturally arrayed into what historians have termed a "raciocultural hierarchy," as well as a "hierarchy of sex." Until the end of the nineteenth century, most evolutionists * * * thought acquired characteristics could be inherited. Thus beliefs in biological differences were easily merged with the * * * historians' views that peoples were the products of historical and cultural forces. Both outlooks usually presented the current traits of the races as fixed for the foreseeable future. Few intellectuals were shy about noting the implications of these views for public policy. Anthropologist Daniel

G. Brinton made typical arguments in his 1895 presidential address to the American Association for the Advancement of Science. He contended that the "black, brown and red races" each had "a peculiar mental temperament which has become hereditary," leaving them constitutionally "recreant to the codes of civilization." Brinton believed that this fact had not been adequately appreciated by American lawmakers. Henceforth, conceptions of "race, nations, tribes" had to "supply the only sure foundations for legislation; not *a priori* notions of the rights of man."

As Brinton knew, many politicians and judges had already begun to seize on such suggestions. In 1882, for example, California senator John Miller drew on the Darwinian "law of the 'survival of the fittest'" to explain that "forty centuries of Chinese life" had "ground into" the Chinese race characteristics that made them unbeatable competitors against the free white man. They were "automatic engines of flesh and blood," of "obtuse nerve," marked by degradation and demoralization, and thus far below the Anglo-Saxon, but were still a threat to the latter's livelihood in a market economy. Hence, Miller argued, the immigration of Chinese laborers must be banned. His bill prevailed, many expressing concern that these Chinese would otherwise become American citizens. The Chinese Exclusion Act was not a vestige of the past but something new, the first repudiation of America's long history of open immigration; and it was justified in terms of the postwar era's revivified racial theories.

Yet although men like Miller not only sustained but expanded Chinese exclusions until they were made virtually total in 1917 (and tight restrictions survived until 1965), they never managed to deny American citizenship to all of the "Chinese race." Until 1917 there were no restrictions on the immigration of upper-class Chinese, and in 1898 the Supreme Court declared that children born on U.S. soil to Chinese parents were American citizens (*United States* v. *Wong Kim Ark* 1898). Birthplace citizenship was a doctrine enshrined in common law, reinforced by the Fourteenth Amendment, and vital to citizenship for the children of *all* immigrant aliens. Hence it had enough legal and political support to override the Court's recognition of Congress's exclusionary desires. Even so, in other cases the Court sustained bans on Chinese immigration while admitting the racial animosities behind them, as in the "Chinese Exclusion Case" (*Chae Chan Ping* v. *United States* 1889); upheld requirements for Chinese-Americans to have certificates of citizenship not required of whites (*Fong Yue Ting* v. *United States* 1893); and permitted officials to deport even Chinese persons who had later been judged by courts to be native-born U.S. citizens (*United States* v. *Ju Toy* 1905).

The upshot, then, was the sort of none-too-coherent mix that the multiple-traditions thesis holds likely. Chinese were excluded on racial grounds, but race did not bar citizenship to those born in the United States; yet Chinese ancestry could subject some American citizens to burdens, including deportation, that others did not face. The mix was not perfect from any ideological viewpoint, but it was politically popular. It maintained a valued inclusive feature of American law (birthplace citizenship) while sharply reducing the resident Chinese population. And it most fully satisfied the increasingly powerful champions of Anglo-Saxon supremacy.

From 1887 on, academic reformers and politicians sought to restrict immigration more generally by a means that paid lip service to liberal norms even as it aimed at racist results—the literacy test. On its face, this measure expressed concern only for the intellectual merits of immigrants. But the test's true aims were spelled out in 1896 by its sponsor, Senator Henry Cabot Lodge, a Harvard Ph.D. in history and politics. Committee research, he reported, showed that the test would exclude "the Italians, Russians, Poles, Hungarians, Greeks, and Asiatics," thereby preserving "the quality of our race and citizenship." Citing "modern history" and "modern science," Thomas Carlyle and Gustave le Bon, Lodge contended that the need for racial exclusion arose from "something deeper and more fundamental than anything which concerns the intellect." Race was above all constituted by moral characteristics, the "stock of ideas, traditions, sentiments, modes of thought" that a people possessed as an "accumulation of centuries of toil and conflict." These mental and moral qualities constituted the "soul of a race," an inheritance in which its members "blindly believe," and upon which learning had no effect. But these qualities could be degraded if "a lower race mixes with a higher"; thus, exclusion by race, not reading ability, was the nation's proper goal.

When the literacy test finally passed in 1917 but proved ineffective in keeping out "lower races," Congress moved to versions of an explicitly racist national-origins quota system. It banned virtually all Asians and permitted European immigration only in ratios preserving the northern European cast of the American citizenry. Congressman Albert Johnson, chief author of the most important quota act in 1924, proclaimed that through it, "the day of indiscriminate acceptance of all races, has definitely ended." The quota system, repealed only in 1965, was a novel, elaborate monument to ideologies holding that access to American citizenship should be subject to racial and ethnic limits. It also served as the prime model for similar systems in Europe and Latin America.

\*   \*   \*

But despite the new prevalence of such attitudes on the part of northern and western elites in the late nineteenth century, the Reconstruction amendments and statutes were still on the books, and surviving liberal sentiments made repealing them politically difficult. Believers in racial inequality were, moreover, undecided on just what to do about blacks. \* \* \* "Radical" racists \* \* \* argued that blacks, like other lower races, should be excluded from American society and looked hopefully for evidence that they were dying out. Their position was consistent with Hartz's claim that Americans could not tolerate permanent unequal statuses; persons must either be equal citizens or outsiders. But * * * "Conservatives" believed * * * that blacks and other people of color might instead have a permanent "place" in America, so long as "placeness included hierarchy." Some still thought that blacks, like the other "lower races," might one day be led by whites to fully civilized status, but no one expected progress in the near future. Thus blacks should instead be segregated, largely disfranchised, and confined to menial occupations via inferior education and discriminatory hiring practices—but not expelled, tortured, or killed. A few talented blacks might even be allowed somewhat higher stations.

* * * The result was a system closest to Conservative desires, one that kept blacks in their place, although that place was structured more repressively than most Conservatives favored. And unlike the ineffective literacy test, here racial inegalitarians achieved much of what they wanted without explicitly violating liberal legal requirements. Complex registration systems, poll taxes, and civics tests appeared race-neutral but were designed and administered to disfranchise blacks. This intent was little masked. * * * These efforts succeeded. Most dramatically, in Louisiana 95.6% of blacks were registered in 1896, and over half (130,000) voted. After disfranchising measures, black registration dropped by 90% and by 1904 totaled only 1,342. The Supreme Court found convoluted ways to close its eyes to these tactics.

By similar devices, blacks were virtually eliminated from juries in the south, where 90% of American blacks lived, sharply limiting their ability to have their personal and economic rights protected by the courts. "Separate but equal" educational and business laws and practices also stifled the capacities of blacks to participate in the nation's economy as equals, severely curtailed the occupations they could train for, and marked them—unofficially but clearly—as an inferior caste. Thus here, as elsewhere, it was evident that the nation's laws and institutions were not meant to confer the equal civic status they proclaimed for all Americans; but neither did they conform fully to doctrines favoring overt racial hierarchy. They represented another asymmetrical compromise among the multiple ideologies vying to define American political culture.

So, too, did the policies governing two groups whose civic status formally improved during these years: Native Americans and women. * * *

*    *    *

This period also highlights how the influence of inegalitarian doctrines has not been confined to white male intellectuals, legislators, and judges. The leading writer of the early twentieth-century women's movement, Charlotte Perkins Gilman, was a thoroughgoing Darwinian who accepted that evolution had made women inferior to men in certain respects, although she insisted that these differences were usually exaggerated and that altered social conditions could transform them. And even as he attacked Booker T. Washington for appearing to accept the "alleged inferiority of the Negro race," W. E. B. DuBois embraced the widespread Lamarckian view that racial characteristics were socially conditioned but then inherited as the "soul" of a race. He could thus accept that most blacks were "primitive folk" in need of tutelage. * * *

The acceptance of ascriptive inegalitarian beliefs by brilliant and politically dissident female and black male intellectuals strongly suggests that these ideas had broad appeal. Writers whose interests they did not easily serve still saw them as persuasive in light of contemporary scientific theories and empirical evidence of massive inequalities. It is likely, too, that for many the vision of a meaningful natural order that these doctrines provided had the psychological and philosophical appeal that such positions have always had for human beings, grounding their status and significance in something greater and more enduring than their own lives. * * *

In sum, if we accept that ideologies and institutions of ascriptive hierarchy have shaped America in interaction with its liberal and democratic features, we can make more sense of a wide range of inegalitarian policies newly contrived after 1870 and perpetuated through much of the twentieth century. Those policies were dismantled only through great struggles, aided by international pressures during World War II and the Cold War; and it is not clear that these struggles have ended. The novelties in the policies and scientific doctrines of the Gilded Age and Progressive Era should alert us to the possibility that new intellectual systems and political forces defending racial and gender inequalities may yet gain increased power in our own time.

*   *   *

The achievements of Americans in building a more inclusive democracy certainly provide reasons to believe that illiberal forces will not prevail. But just as we can better explain the nation's past by recognizing how and why liberal democratic principles have been contested with frequent success, we will better understand the present and future of American politics if we do not presume they are rooted in essentially liberal or democratic values and conditions. Instead, we must analyze America as the ongoing product of often conflicting multiple traditions.

## DISCUSSION QUESTIONS

1. According to Smith, what are some examples of how Americans in the late nineteenth century simultaneously held liberal and ascriptive Americanist views?

2. Do you believe that ascriptive hierarchy is still a powerful strain of thought in American political culture? If so, what are some examples?

3. How would you know if ascriptive hierarchy was as widespread as Smith contends? What kind of evidence would you look for?

## DEBATING THE ISSUES: THE ROLE OF RELIGION IN AMERICAN POLITICS

In recent American history, religious belief has been central to political discourse. Reverend Martin Luther King, Jr. often invoked religious language and principles in support of the civil rights movement, and religious belief has motivated many activists in the anti-abortion movement. Political party coalitions have differed historically in their religious composition—most recently, in the 1980s and 1990s, Americans with more conservative religious beliefs became an important part of the Republican party coalition. Presidents and presidential candidates have also wrestled with the place of religion in politics. Presidential candidate John F. Kennedy, a Catholic, defended himself against accusations that he had "divided loyalties" and that his decision making would be directed from Rome. Speaking to a group of Protestant ministers in Houston in September 1960, Kennedy stated that he believed firmly in the separation of church and state. "I do not speak for my church on public matters—and the church does not speak for me," he declared. At the same time, Kennedy pointed out that he wouldn't simply abandon his beliefs: "I do not intend to apologize for these views . . . nor do I intend to disavow either my views or my church in order to win this election." In November, he was narrowly elected president, and was the first Catholic elected to that office.

More than thirty years later, religious references in public life were commonplace. President Bill Clinton, by one accounting, was not only personally a believer who often included religious references in his speeches, but his administration enacted a number of laws intended to strengthen religious institutions. President George W. Bush has spoken openly about his turn to faith at around age forty and the importance of religious belief in his life and views. He has continued and expanded former President Clinton's efforts to increase the role of religious institutions in American public life. One of his chief proposals was the Faith-Based Initiative. The goal of this program was to allow faith-based organizations more access to federal funds in the area of social service provision. Bush had difficulty passing his initiative through Congress, so in December 2002 he signed an executive order that directed federal agencies to treat faith-based organizations equally to secular organizations.

How should a politician's religious views affect his public duties? In their third presidential debate, Democratic candidate John F. Kerry responded that "everything you do in public life has to be guided by your faith, affected by your faith, but without transferring it in any official way to other people." President Bush, the Republican candidate, agreed that he did not seek to impose his religion on anyone, "but when I make decisions, I stand on principle, and the principles are derived from who I am. I believe we ought to love our neighbors as ourselves, as manifested in the Faith-Based Initiative where we've unleashed the armies of compassion to help heal people who hurt. I believe that God wants everyone to be free . . . And that's been part of my foreign policy." Robert Wright and Steven Waldman continue the debate. Wright worries that Bush's religious outlook leads him to overlook evidence that his policies might be unsuccessful: "in the longest run, divinely guided decisions will be vindicated, and any gathering mountains of evidence to the contrary may themselves be signs of God's continuing involvement." Waldman presents the opposite view, stating bluntly that "it is perfectly appropriate to force one's religious beliefs on others." After an election, the candidate who wins gets to impose his religious views just as he gets to impose his other views—it is not valid, from Waldman's perspective, to say that only religious views are to be kept from political discourse. This does not mean, he contends, that a politician's job is to convert you to his or her particular religious worldview, only that it is perfectly acceptable if his positions are determined largely by religion.

# 4

# The Third Bush-Kerry Presidential Debate
# October 13, 2004

## GEORGE W. BUSH AND JOHN F. KERRY

* * *

SCHIEFFER: Senator Kerry, a new question for you. The *New York Times* reports that some Catholic archbishops are telling their church members that it would be a sin to vote for a candidate like you because you support a woman's right to choose an abortion and unlimited stem-cell research. What is your reaction to that?

KERRY: I respect their views. I completely respect their views. I am a Catholic. And I grew up learning how to respect those views. But I disagree with them, as do many.

I believe that I can't legislate or transfer to another American citizen my article of faith. What is an article of faith for me is not something that I can legislate on somebody who doesn't share that article of faith.

I believe that choice is a woman's choice. It's between a woman, God and her doctor. And that's why I support that. Now, I will not allow somebody to come in and change *Roe v. Wade*. The president has never said whether or not he would do that. But we know from the people he's tried to appoint to the court he wants to. I will not. I will defend the right of *Roe v. Wade*.

Now, with respect to religion, you know, as I said, I grew up a Catholic. I was an altar boy. I know that throughout my life this has made a difference to me. And as President Kennedy said when he ran for president, he said, "I'm not running to be a Catholic president. I'm running to be a president who happens to be Catholic."

My faith affects everything that I do, in truth. There's a great passage of the Bible that says, "What does it mean, my brother, to say you have faith if there are no deeds? Faith without works is dead." And I think that everything you do in public life has to be guided by your faith, affected by your faith, but without transferring it in any official way to other people.

That's why I fight against poverty. That's why I fight to clean up the environment and protect this earth. That's why I fight for equality and justice. All of those things come out of that fundamental teaching and belief of faith.

But I know this, that President Kennedy in his inaugural address told all of us that here on Earth, God's work must truly be our own. And that's what we have to—I think that's the test of public service.

SCHIEFFER: Mr. President?

BUSH: I think it's important to promote a culture of life. I think a hospitable society is a society where every being counts and every person matters. I believe the ideal world is one in which every child is protected in law and welcomed to life. I understand there's great differences on this issue of abortion, but I believe reasonable people can come together and put good law in place that will help reduce the number of abortions.

Take, for example, the ban on partial birth abortion. It's a brutal practice. People from both political parties came together in the halls of Congress and voted overwhelmingly to ban that practice. It made a lot of sense. My opponent, in that he's out of the mainstream, voted against that law.

What I'm saying is, is that as we promote life and promote a culture of life, surely there are ways we can work together to reduce the number of abortions: continue to promote adoption laws—it's a great alternative to abortion—continue to fund and promote maternity group homes; I will continue to promote abstinence programs.

The last debate, my opponent said his wife was involved with those programs. That's great. I appreciate that very much. All of us ought to be involved with programs that provide a viable alternative to abortion.

*   *   *

SCHIEFFER: Mr. President, let's go to a new question.

You were asked before the invasion, or after the invasion, of Iraq if you'd checked with your dad. And I believe, I don't remember the quote exactly, but I believe you said you had checked with a higher authority. I would like to ask you, what part does your faith play on your policy decisions?

BUSH: First, my faith plays a lot—a big part in my life. And that's, when I was answering that question, what I was really saying to the person was that I pray a lot. And I do. And my faith is a very—it's very personal. I pray for strength. I pray for wisdom. I pray for our troops in harm's way. I pray for my family. I pray for my little girls.

But I'm mindful in a free society that people can worship if they want to or not. You're equally an American if you choose to worship an almighty and if you choose not to. If you're a Christian, Jew or Muslim, you're equally an American. That's the great thing about America, is the right to worship the way you see fit.

Prayer and religion sustain me. I recieve calmness in the storms of the presidency. I love the fact that people pray for me and my family all around the country. Somebody asked me one time, "Well, how do you know?" I said, "I just feel it."

Religion is an important part. I never want to impose my religion on anybody else.

But when I make decisions, I stand on principle, and the principles are derived from who I am.

I believe we ought to love our neighbor like we love ourself, as manifested in public policy through the Faith-Based Initiative where we've unleashed the armies of compassion to help heal people who hurt. I believe that God wants everybody to be free. That's what I believe. And that's been part of my foreign policy. In Afghanistan, I believe that the freedom there is a gift from the Almighty. And I can't tell you how encouraged I am to see freedom on the march.

And so my principles that I make decisions on are a part of me, and religion is a part of me.

SCHIEFFER: Senator Kerry?

KERRY: Well, I respect everything that the president has said and certainly respect his faith. I think it's important and I share it.

I think that he just said that freedom is a gift from the Almighty. Everything is a gift from the Almighty. And as I measure the words of the Bible—and we all do; different people measure different things—

the Koran, the Torah, or, you know, Native Americans who gave me a blessing the other day had their own special sense of connectedness to a higher being. And people all find their ways to express it.

I was taught—I went to a church school and I was taught that the two greatest commandments are: Love the Lord, your God, with all your mind, your body and your soul, and love your neighbor as yourself. And frankly, I think we have a lot more loving of our neighbor to do in this country and on this planet. We have a separate and unequal school system in the United States of America. There's one for the people who have, and there's one for the people who don't have. And we're struggling with that today.

And the president and I have a difference of opinion about how we live out our sense of our faith. I talked about it earlier when I talked about the works and faith without works being dead.

I think we've got a lot more work to do. And as president, I will always respect everybody's right to practice religion as they choose—or not to practice—because that's part of America.

\* \* \*

# 5

# "Faith, Hope and Clarity"

## ROBERT WRIGHT

The Bush administration is suddenly taking pains to calibrate the president's devoutness: yes, Mr. Bush is very religious, but he's not too religious—not hearing-voices religious.

Last week several White House aides insisted that, contrary to the witness of the televangelist Pat Robertson, the president never said God had guaranteed him a low casualty count in Iraq. And as for those reports about Mr. Bush feeling summoned to the presidency: Laura Bush denies that her husband sees himself as a divine instrument. "It's not a faith where he hears from God," she said a few days ago.

It's hard to settle "he said, she said" questions, let alone "he said, He said" questions. But there is a way to get a clearer picture of religion's role in this White House. Every morning President Bush reads a devotional from "My Utmost for His Highest," a collection of homilies by a Protestant minister named Oswald Chambers, who lived a century ago.

As Mr. Bush explained in an interview broadcast on Tuesday on Fox News, reading Chambers is a way for him "on a daily basis to be in the Word."

Chambers's book continues to sell well, especially an updated edition with the language tweaked toward the modern. Inspecting the book—or the free online edition—may give even some devout Christians qualms about America's current guidance.

Chambers was Scottish, and he conforms to the stereotype of Scots as a bit dour (as in the joke about the Scot who responds to "What a lovely day!" by saying, "Just wait.") In the entry for Dec. 4, by way of underscoring adversity, Chambers asserts, "Everything outside my physical life is designed to cause my death."

So whence the optimism that Republicans say George Bush possesses and John Kerry lacks? There's a kind of optimism in Chambers, but it's not exactly sunny. To understand it you have to understand the theme that dominates "My Utmost": committing your life to Jesus Christ—"absolute and irrevocable surrender of the will"—and staying committed. "If we turn away from obedience for even one second, darkness and death are immediately at work again." In all things and at all times, you must do God's will.

But what exactly does God want? Chambers gives little substantive advice. There is no great stress on Jesus' ethical teaching—not much about loving your neighbor or loving your enemy. (And Chambers doesn't seem to share Isaiah's hope of beating swords into plowshares. "Life without war is impossible in the natural or the supernatural realm.") But the basic idea is that, once you surrender to God, divine guidance is palpable. "If you obey God in the first thing he shows you, then he instantly opens up the next truth to you," Chambers writes.

And you shouldn't let your powers of reflection get in the way. Chambers lauds Abraham for preparing to slay his son at God's command without, as the Bible put it, conferring "with flesh and blood." Chambers warns: "Beware when you want to 'confer with flesh and blood' or even your own thoughts, insights, or understandings—anything that is not based on your personal relationship with God. These are all things that compete with and hinder obedience to God."

Once you're on the right path, setbacks that might give others pause needn't faze you. As Chambers noted in last Sunday's reading, "Paul said, in essence, 'I am in the procession of a conqueror, and it doesn't matter what the difficulties are, for I am always led in triumph.'" Indeed, setbacks may have a purpose, Chambers will tell Mr. Bush this Sunday: "God frequently has to knock the bottom out of your experience as his saint to get you in direct contact with himself." Faith "by its very nature must be tested and tried."

Some have marveled at Mr. Bush's refusal to admit any mistakes in Iraq other than "catastrophic success." But what looks like negative feedback to some of us—more than 1,100 dead Americans, more than 10,000 dead Iraqi civilians and the biggest incubator of anti-American terrorists in history—is, through Chambers's eyes, not cause for doubt. Indeed, seemingly negative feedback may be positive feedback, proof that God is there, testing your faith, strengthening your resolve.

This, I think, is Mr. Bush's optimism: In the longest run, divinely guided decisions will be vindicated, and any gathering mountains of evidence to the contrary may themselves be signs of God's continuing involvement. It's all good.

Of course, all religions have ways of explaining bad news, and the Abrahamic faiths, with one omnipotent God, must explain it as part of God's plan. But lots of Christians do that without going the Oswald Chambers route—abandoning rational analysis and critical reevaluation for ineffable intuition and iron certainty. For example: maybe God gave people rational minds so they would use them; and this plan meant letting people make mistakes that, however painful, at least lead to better decision-making and the edification of humankind—so long as they pay attention.

I was raised a Southern Baptist, and I still remember going to Calvary Baptist Church in Midland, Tex., my family's hometown as well as Mr. Bush's (though, because my father was a career soldier, I lived there only one year). I also remember the only theological pronouncement I ever heard from my father: "I don't think God tells you which car to buy."

People unfamiliar with a certain strain in evangelical tradition may have trouble seeing the point of Chambers's emphasis on utter surrender. But in the Baptist churches of my youth, it went without saying (though it was often said) that surrender was in no small part about self-control. Because human nature is subtly corrupt, with every temptation concealing a slippery slope, complete commitment was the only path to virtue. Chambers stresses this binary nature of devotion more than some contemporary evangelicals, and that may explain his appeal for Mr. Bush, who became a born-again Christian when he quit drinking and has stayed off the bottle ever since.

Some people who find moderation easy can't understand why for others abstinence is necessary—and still less why it would demand a spiritual framework. I don't find moderation easy, and, even leaving that issue aside, I find being human so deeply challenging that I can't imagine it without an anchoring spirituality in some sense of the word. So I respect Mr. Bush's religious impulse, and I even find Chambers's Scottish austerity true and appealing in a generic way.

Still, it's another question whether Chambers's worldview, as mediated by Mr. Bush, should help shape the world's future. People who take drastic action based on divine-feeling feelings, and view ensuing death and destruction with equanimity, have in recent years tended to be the problem, not the solution.

Chambers himself eventually showed some philosophical flexibility. By and large, the teachings in "My Utmost for His Highest" were written before World War I (and compiled by his wife posthumously). But the war seems to have made him less sanguine about the antagonism that, he had long stressed, is inherent in life.

Shortly before his death in 1917, Chambers declared that "war is the most damnably bad thing," according to *Christianity Today* magazine. He added: "If the war has made me reconcile myself with the fact that there is sin in human beings, I shall no longer go with my head in the clouds, or buried in the sand like an ostrich, but I shall be wishing to face facts as they are." Amen.

*6*

# "Religious, and Right: Faith Belongs in Politics"

### STEVEN WALDMAN

In his speech at the Democratic Convention, Ron Reagan complained that, in the case of embryonic-stem-cell research, "the theology of the few" was dictating policy. This echoes a sentiment expressed by John Kerry earlier, when he explained how he could believe life begins at conception but still be pro-choice. "I can't take my Catholic belief, my article of faith, and legislate it on a Protestant or a Jew or an atheist." Both those on the left and libertarian right suggest that it's O.K. for religious conservatives to have their beliefs, but that they shouldn't "impose" their theology on others. This is frightening, the argument goes, because we have freedom of religion here in America and no one should be compelled to adopt the religious beliefs of someone else.

But it is perfectly appropriate to force one's religious beliefs on others.

Let's say a Senator A opposes the Iraq war on practical grounds. He thinks it's a distraction from fighting al Qaeda that erodes our credibility overseas. He votes no on the war. Senator B also opposes the war. He's a Catholic and has read up on just-war theory and concluded that this war is immoral because it was preemptive and could have been avoided through peaceful means. He votes no, too.

They both voted no—and yet one did so for reasons practical, and the other for reasons moral and theological. Is one an appropriate vote and the other not? Slice it further. Let's say Senator C also voted against the war and, like Senator B, did so primarily for moral reasons. But in his case, Senator C read no Catholic just-war theory; instead, he came to view it as immoral after seeing *Fahrenheit 9/11*. So Senators B and C both voted against for moral reasons: in one case, from having seen a secular movie, and in the other, from having read a religious document.

Are we really saying that *only* Senators A and C, the ones who didn't draw upon religion, used legitimate thought processes?

What people really mean when they say so-and-so is imposing his religious beliefs on me is that they don't happen to agree with those beliefs. Because most of these big issues are decided democratically, it is by definition impossible to impose one's religious views on someone else. Actually, strike that: It's impossible to impose one's religious views any more than we impose any other kind of views. The candidate who wins 51 percent gets to impose his views on all those people who voted for the candidate who got 49 percent.

The Founding Fathers were quite clear that, while they wanted separation of church and state, they also wanted religion to play a major role in shaping political morality. In his farewell address, George Washington said, "Reason and experience both forbid us to expect that national morality can prevail in exclusion of religious principle."

The Left and Right have both followed the advice of the Founding Fathers at different points in history. Abolitionism and the civil-rights movement—two moral highpoints of our history—were driven by people attempting to impose their religious views on others. So is the right-to-life movement.

There is, however, a problem with the way some religious conservatives approach the political sphere. The problem is not dogmatism, but laziness. Someone who rests the argument for a certain position entirely on the fact that his religion told him to is not really attempting to persuade. Even if one is motivated by faith, one still has to convince others using secular, or at least broad-gauge, moral arguments. It is fine for someone to oppose gay marriage because Leviticus frowns on homosexuality. It's neither appropriate nor smart to say Leviticus calls homosexuality an abomination and so you should too. *That* is demanding that other people accept your religion. Some religious conservatives forget to persuade because they live in a political cloister, speaking mostly with others who agree with them, and for whom Leviticus is an effective shorthand. One of the reasons the Founding Fathers thought religion important to a functioning democracy is that it would tamp down passions and ensure that people would listen to each other. Religious conservatives need to understand that part of the Founding Fathers' wisdom, too.

So, Senator Kerry, it's appropriate for religious conservatives to try to impose their religious views. As for those who merely assert religious dogma, you shouldn't worry—since they're likely to lose.

## DISCUSSION QUESTIONS

1. How would you define "imposing one's religious views on others"?

2. Where would you draw the line between the appropriate and inappropriate use of religious belief and religious references by an elected public official? Are you comfortable with the use of religious language and imagery in public debate? Is it any more problematic if a public official defends his or her actions by referring to religious beliefs rather than by secular references to "the values" that drive his or her decision making?

3. Supporters argue that the Faith-Based Initiative is primarily about providing effective government services. If studies were to find that a particular organization was exceptionally effective in combating drug use, should the government be prevented from assisting this organization because it does not hire individuals from other faiths or because of the possibility that certain theological messages would be conveyed to program beneficiaries?

4. Wright worries that the content of President Bush's religious beliefs have made for poor choices in public policy. Assuming he or she does not want to seem critical of the beliefs of the president and like-minded citizens, how might a political opponent raise this issue? Is it too divisive to raise such a concern?

# CHAPTER 2

# Constructing the Government: The Founding and the Constitution

7

## "The Nature of American Constitutionalism" from *The Origins of the American Constitution*

### MICHAEL KAMMEN

*The Constitution is a remarkably simple document that has provided a frame-work of governance for the United States for more than 215 years. It establishes a shared sovereignty between the states and the federal government, a separation and checking of powers between three branches of government, qualifications for citizenship and holding office, and a delineation of the rights considered so fun-damental that their restriction by government requires extensive due process and a compelling national or state concern. Yet the Constitution's simple text pro-duces constant controversy over its interpretation, and efforts to bend, twist, and nudge its application to changing economic markets, technology, social trends, and family structures. The document's durability and flexibility amid conflict and social change are a tribute not only to the men who drafted the Constitution in 1787, but also to the American people and their willingness to embrace the challenges of self-governance at the time of the Revolution and today.*

*In the following article Michael Kammen argues that in order to begin to un-derstand the Constitution and the continuous debate surrounding its interpreta-tion, we must look to the history of American constitutionalism. Informed by John Locke's* Second Treatise of Government, *the British constitution, and a colonial experience deemed an affront to basic liberties and rights, Americans plunged into the writing of the Constitution as a means of delegating power from the sovereign people to their elected and appointed agents. It is, as Kammen notes, quite remarkable that the American states chose to draft state consti-tutions in the midst of a revolutionary battle for independence, rather than establish provisional governments. It is similarly remarkable that these state*

*constitutions have grown significantly in length over the years and are so read-
ily amended and even rewritten, in contrast to the relatively succinct and diffi-
cult-to-amend Constitution of the United States.*

*Kammen suggests that the Constitution's simplicity and durability lies in
both the historic need for compromise between conflicted interests and the surprising common ground that nevertheless existed over basic principles: the need
to protect personal liberty, the commitment to a republican form of government,
and the importance of civic virtue for preserving citizen sovereignty. This embrace of basic governing principles could explain the deeper devotion to the U.S.
Constitution, in contrast to the state documents, as well as the fear that an
amended or completely altered Constitution might prove less malleable and accommodating for the governance of a diverse nation.*

## The Nature of American Constitutionalism

"Like the Bible, it ought to be read again and again." Franklin Delano
Roosevelt made that remark about the U.S. Constitution in March
1937, during one of those cozy "fireside chats" that reached millions of
Americans by radio. "It is an easy document to understand," he added.
And six months later, speaking to his fellow citizens from the grounds
of the Washington Monument on Constitution Day—a widely noted
speech because 1937 marked the sesquicentennial of the Constitution,
and because the President had provoked the nation with his controversial plan to add as many as six new justices to the Supreme Court—
Roosevelt observed that the Constitution was "a layman's document, not
a lawyer's contract," a theme that he reiterated several times in the
course of this address.

It seems fair to say that Roosevelt's assertions were approximately half
true. No one could disagree that the Constitution ought to be read and
reread. Few would deny that it was meant to be comprehended by lay-
men, by ordinary American citizens and aspirants for citizenship. Nevertheless, we must ponder whether it is truly "an easy document to
understand." Although the very language of the Constitution is neither technical nor difficult, and although it is notably succinct—one
nineteenth-century expert called it "a great code in a small compass"—
abundant evidence exists that vast numbers of Americans, ever since
1787, have not understood it as well as they might. Even the so-called
experts (judges, lawyers, political leaders, and teachers of constitutional
law) have been unable to agree in critical instances about the proper
application of key provisions of the Constitution, or about the intentions
of those who wrote and approved it. Moreover, we do acknowledge that
the Constitution developed from a significant number of compromises,
and that the document's ambiguities are, for the most part, not accidental.

Understanding the U.S. Constitution is essential for many reasons.
One of the most urgent is that difficult issues are now being and will

continue to be settled in accordance with past interpretations and with our jurists' sense of what the founders meant. In order to make such difficult determinations, we begin with the document itself. Quite often, however, we also seek guidance from closely related or contextual documents, such as the notes kept by participants in the Constitutional Convention held at Philadelphia in 1787, from the correspondence of delegates and other prominent leaders during the later 1780s, from *The Federalist* papers, and even from some of the Anti-Federalist tracts written in opposition to the Constitution. In doing so, we essentially scrutinize the origins of American constitutionalism.

If observers want to know what is meant by constitutionalism, they must uncover several layers of historical thought and experience in public affairs. Most obviously we look to the ideas that developed in the United States during the final quarter of the eighteenth century—unquestionably the most brilliant and creative era in the entire history of American political thought. We have in mind particularly, however, a new set of assumptions that developed after 1775 about the very nature of a constitution. Why, for example, when the colonists found themselves nearly in a political state of nature after 1775, did they promptly feel compelled to write state constitutions, many of which contained a bill of rights? The patriots were, after all, preoccupied with fighting a revolution. Why not simply set up provisional governments based upon those they already had and wait until Independence was achieved? If and when the revolution succeeded, there would be time enough to write permanent constitutions.

The revolutionaries did not regard the situation in such casual and pragmatic terms. They shared a strong interest in what they called the science of politics. They knew a reasonable amount about the history of political theory. They believed in the value of ideas applied to problematic developments, and they felt that their circumstances were possibly unique in all of human history. They knew with assurance that their circumstances were changing, and changing rapidly. They wanted self-government, obviously, but they also wanted legitimacy for their newborn governments. Hence a major reason for writing constitutions. They believed in the doctrine of the social contract (about which Jean-Jacques Rousseau had written in 1762) and they believed in government by the consent of the governed: two more reasons for devising written constitutions approved by the people or by their representatives.

The men responsible for composing and revising state constitutions in the decade following 1775 regarded constitutions as social compacts that delineated the fundamental principles upon which the newly formed polities were agreed and to which they pledged themselves. They frequently used the word "experiment" because they believed that they were making institutional innovations that were risky, for they seemed virtually unprecedented. They intended to create republican governments and assumed that to do so successfully required a fair amount of social homogeneity, a high degree of consensus regarding moral values, and a pervasive capacity for virtue, by which they meant unselfish, public-spirited behavior.

Even though they often spoke of liberty, they meant civil liberty rather than natural liberty. The latter implied unrestrained freedom—absolute liberty for the individual to do as he or she pleased. The former, by contrast, meant freedom of action so long as it was not detrimental to others and was beneficial to the common weal. When they spoke of *political* liberty they meant the freedom to be a participant, to vote and hold public office, responsible commitments that ought to be widely shared if republican institutions were to function successfully.

The colonists' experiences throughout the seventeenth and eighteenth centuries had helped to prepare them for this participatory and contractual view of the nature of government. Over and over again, as the circles of settlement expanded, colonists learned to improvise the rules by which they would be governed. They had received charters and had entered into covenants or compacts that may be described as proto-constitutional, i.e., cruder and less complete versions of the constitutional documents that would be formulated in 1776 and subsequently. These colonial charters not only described the structure of government, but frequently explained what officials (often called magistrates) could or could not do.

As a result, by the 1770s American attitudes toward constitutionalism were simultaneously derivative as well as original. On the one hand, they extravagantly admired the British constitution ("unwritten" in the sense that it was not contained in a single document) and declared it to be the ultimate achievement in the entire history of governmental development. On the other hand, as Oscar and Mary Handlin have explained, Americans no longer conceived of constitutions in general as the British had for centuries.

> In the New World the term, constitution, no longer referred to the actual organization of power developed through custom, prescription, and precedent. Instead it had come to mean a written frame of government setting fixed limits on the use of power. The American view was, of course, closely related to the rejection of the old conception that authority descended from the Crown to its officials. In the newer view—that authority was derived from the consent of the governed—the written constitution became the instrument by which the people entrusted power to their agents.[1]

\* \* \*

*Issues, Aspirations, and Apprehensions in 1787–1788*

The major problems that confronted the Constitution-makers, and the issues that separated them from their opponents, can be specified by the key words that recur so frequently in the documents that follow in this collection. The Federalists often refer to the need for much more energy, stability, and efficiency in the national government. They fear anarchy and seek a political system better suited to America's geographical expanse: "an extensive sphere" was Madison's phrase in a letter to Jefferson.

The Anti-Federalists were apprehensive about "unrestrained power" (George Mason's words), about the great risk of national "consolidation" rather than a true confederation, about the failure to include a bill of rights in the new Constitution, about the prospect of too much power in the federal judiciary, about the "tendency to aristocracy" (see the "Federal Farmer"*), about insufficient separation of powers, and a government unresponsive to the needs of diverse and widely scattered people.

Because the two sides disagreed so strongly about the nature of the proposed government—was it genuinely federal or really national?—it is all too easy to lose sight of the common ground that they shared, a common ground that made it possible for many Anti-Federalists to support the Constitution fully even before George Washington's first administration came to a close in 1793. Both sides felt an absolute commitment to republicanism and the protection of personal liberty, as we have already seen. Both sides acknowledged that a science of politics was possible and ought to be pursued, but that "our own experience" (Madison's view, though held by "Brutus"† also) ought to be heeded above all. A majority on both sides accepted the inevitable role that interests would play in public affairs and recognized that public opinion would be a powerful force. The phrase "public opinion" appears eleven times explicitly in *The Federalist* papers, and many other times implicitly or indirectly.

The desire for happiness was invoked constantly. Although admittedly a vague and elusive concept, it clearly meant much more than the safeguarding of property (though the protection of property belonged under the rubric of happiness in the minds of many). For some it simply meant personal contentment; but increasingly there were leaders, such as George Washington, who spoke of "social happiness," which referred to harmony among diverse groups. David Humphreys's "Poem on the Happiness of America" (1786) provides an indication that this notion had national as well as individual and societal connotations.

Although both sides believed that the preservation of liberty was one of the most essential ends of government, the continued existence of chattel slavery in a freedom-loving society created considerable awkwardness for the founders. In 1775–1776, when the revolutionaries had explained the reasons for their rebellion, they frequently referred to a British plot to "enslave" Americans. The constant invocation of that

* [The pen name of Richard Henry Lee of Virginia, a noted Anti-Federalist.]
† [The pen name of Robert Yates, an Anti-Federalist.]

notion has puzzled many students because whatever the wisdom or un-wisdom of imperial policy in general, there most certainly was no con-spiracy in London to enslave America.

There really should be no mystery about the colonists' usage, how-ever, because as good Lockeans they knew full well the argument in chapter four of John Locke's *Second Treatise of Government*, entitled "Of Slavery" (an argument reiterated in Rousseau's *Social Contract*). "The lib-erty of man in society," Locke wrote, "is to be under no other legislative power but that established by consent in the commonwealth, nor under the dominion of any will or restraint of any law but what that legislative shall enact according to the trust put in it." The denial of *full* freedom quite simply meant "slavery."

Slavery and the international slave trade were discussed extensively in 1787 at the Constitutional Convention. By then, however, "slavery" was not often used as a theoretical and general synonym for unfreedom. It meant the permanent possession of one person (black) by another (white), usually for life, the slaveowner being entitled to own the chil-dren of his or her chattel as well. We must remember that the Convention met in secret session, and that the delegates agreed not to divulge infor-mation about their proceedings for fifty years. Consequently not very much was said publicly about slavery in 1787–1788 in connection with the Constitution. Not until 1840, when the U.S. government published James Madison's detailed notes on the Convention debates, did Ameri-cans learn just how much had been compromised at Philadelphia in or-der to placate South Carolina and Georgia. The Constitution essentially protected slavery where it existed, and remained mute about the legality of slavery in territories that might one day become additional states. Accommodation had prevailed in 1787, which meant, as it turned out, postponing for seventy-four years the moral and political crisis of the Union.

### Legacies of American Constitutionalism

Although it is difficult for us fully to imagine the complexities of interest group politics, regional rivalries, and ideological differences in 1787, the instrumental achievement of that extraordinary Convention has gener-ally been appreciated over the years. Even such a sardonic mind as H. L. Mencken's conceded as much. "The amazing thing about the Con-stitution," he wrote, "is that it is as good as it is—that so subtle and complete a document emerged from that long debate. Most of the Fram-ers, obviously, were second-rate men; before and after their session they accomplished nothing in the world. Yet during that session they made an almost perfect job of the work in hand."

Their accomplishment was, indeed, remarkable. The distribution and separation of powers among three branches at the national level, and the development of federalism as a means of apportioning sovereignty between the nation and the states, have received broad recognition and the compliment of imitation by many other nations.

Equally appreciated is the fact that the U.S. Constitution is the oldest written national constitution in the world. (The Massachusetts Constitution of 1780, although amended and revised many times, is even older.) Its endurance is genuinely remarkable. We should therefore note that the framers deserve much of the credit for that endurance, not simply because they transcended their own limitations, * * * but because they contrived to restrict the ease with which the Constitution might be revised or reconsidered. There was considerable talk in 1787–1788 about holding a second convention in order to refine the product of the first. Anti-Federalists and many who were undecided wanted such a course of action. George Washington, however, regarded that idea as impractical. Hamilton, despite his dissatisfaction with many aspects of the Constitution, doubted whether a second convention could possibly be as successful as the first; and Madison feared a serious erosion of what had been accomplished in 1787.

It is easy to forget that the Philadelphia Convention vastly exceeded its authority, and that the men who met there undertook what amounted to a usurpation of legitimate authority. As [President] Franklin Delano Roosevelt pointed out on Constitution Day in 1937, contemporaries who opposed the newly drafted document "insisted that the Constitution itself was unconstitutional under the Articles of Confederation. But the ratifying conventions overruled them." The right of revolution had been explicitly invoked in 1776 and implicitly practiced in 1787. Having done their work, however, most of the delegates did not believe that it ought to be repealed or casually revised.

The complexity of changing or adding to the original document had profound implications for the subsequent history of American constitutionalism. First, it meant that in order to gain acceptance of their handiwork, the Federalists had to commit themselves, unofficially, to the formulation of a bill of rights when the first Congress met in 1789, even though many Federalists felt that such a list of protections was superfluous. They protested that a finite list of specified safeguards would imply that numerous other liberties might not be protected against encroachment by the government. The point, ultimately, is that promulgation of the U.S. Constitution required two sets of compromises rather than one: those that took place among the delegates to the Convention, and the subsequent sense that support for ratification would be rewarded by the explicit enumeration of broad civil liberties.

Next, the existence of various ambiguities in the Constitution meant that explication would subsequently be required by various authorities, such as the Supreme Court. The justices' interpretations would become part of the total "package" that we call American constitutionalism; but the justices did not always agree with one another, and the rest of the nation did not always agree with the justices. Those realities gave rise to an ongoing pattern that might be called conflict-within-consensus.

Some of those disputes and ambiguities involved very basic questions: What are the implications and limits of consent? Once we have participated in the creation of a polity and agreed to abide by its rules, then what? How are we to resolve the conflict that arises when the wishes or needs of a majority diminish the liberties or interests of a minority? This last question was the tough issue faced by the New England states in 1814, when they contemplated secession, and by South Carolina in 1828–1833 when a high tariff designed to protect northern manufacturing threatened economic distress to southern agricultural interests. And that, of course, was the thorny issue that precipitated southern secession and the greatest constitutional crisis of all in 1860–1861.

There is yet another ambiguity, or contradiction, in American constitutional thought—though it is less commonly noticed than the one described in the previous paragraph. As we have observed, the founders were not eager for a second convention, or for easy revisions or additions to their handiwork. They did provide for change; but they made the process complicated and slow. They did not believe that the fundamental law of a nation should be casually altered; and most Americans have accepted that constraint.

Nevertheless, on the *state* level Americans have amended, expanded, revised, and totally rewritten their constitutions with some frequency. A great deal of so-called positive law (i.e., legislative enactments) finds its way into state constitutions, with the result that many modern ones exceed one hundred pages in length. There is no clear explanation for this striking pattern of divergence between constitutionalism on the national and state levels. The curious pattern does suggest, however, that Americans have regarded the U.S. Constitution of 1787 as more nearly permanent than their state constitutions. Perhaps the pattern only tells us that achieving a national consensus for change in a large and diverse society is much more difficult than achieving a statewide consensus for change.

Whatever the explanation for this dualism in American constitutionalism, the paradox does not diminish the historical reality that writers of the federal as well as the first state constitutions all tried to establish charters clearly suited to the cultural assumptions and political realities of the American scene. Even though the founders explored the history of political thought in general and the history of republics in particular, they reached the commonsense conclusion that a constitution must be adapted to the character and customs of a people. Hence the debate in 1787–1788 over the relative merits of "consolidation" versus "confederation." Hence the concern about what sort of governmental system would work most effectively over a large geographical expanse. James

Madison conveyed this sense of American exceptionalism several times in a letter to Thomas Jefferson (then U.S. minister to France) in 1788, when a bill of rights was under consideration.

On August 28, 1788, a month after New York became the eleventh state to ratify the Constitution, George Washington sent Alexander Hamilton a letter from his temporary retirement at Mount Vernon. The future president acknowledged that public affairs were proceeding more smoothly than he had expected. Consequently, he wrote, "I hope the political Machine may be put in motion, without much effort or hazard of miscarrying." As he soon discovered, to put the new constitutional machine in motion would require considerable effort. It did not miscarry because the "machine" had been so soundly designed. A concerted effort would be required, however, to keep the machine successfully in operation. That should not occasion surprise. The founders had assumed an involved citizenry; and the governmental system they created functions best when their assumption is validated. That is the very essence of democratic constitutionalism.

## Discussion Questions

1. In your view, what would Kammen think about recent efforts to amend the Constitution to ban abortion, ban gay marriage, mandate a balanced budget, protect the flag against "desecration," and protect victims' rights?

2. Although the flexibility of the Constitution helps explain its longevity, that flexibility comes at a price: ambiguity and gaps in constitutional language. What are some examples of constitutional language that is ambiguous?

## Notes

1. Mary Handlin, *The Dimensions of Liberty* (Cambridge, Mass., 1961), p. 55.

# *The Federalist,* No. 15

## Alexander Hamilton

*Despite the deference given the Constitution today, it did not command instant respect in 1787. The fight for ratification was bitter between the Federalists (those who supported the Constitution) and the Anti-Federalists (who feared that the new national government would become too powerful).*

*The Federalist Papers, originally written as a series of newspaper editorials intended to persuade New Yorkers to ratify the Constitution, remains the most valuable exposition of the political theory underlying the Constitution. In* The Federalist, *No. 15, reprinted below, Alexander Hamilton is at his best arguing for the necessity of a stronger central government than that established under the Articles of Confederation. He points out the practical impossibility of engaging in concerted action when each of the thirteen states retains virtual sovereignty, and the need for a strong central government to hold the new country together politically and economically.*

In the course of the preceding papers I have endeavored, my fellow-citizens, to place before you in a clear and convincing light the importance of Union to your political safety and happiness. * * * [T]he point next in order to be examined is the "insufficiency of the present Confederation to the preservation of the Union." * * * There are material imperfections in our national system and * * * something is necessary to be done to rescue us from impending anarchy. The facts that support this opinion are no longer objects of speculation. They have forced themselves upon the sensibility of the people at large, and have at length extorted . . . a reluctant confession of the reality of those defects in the scheme of our federal government which have been long pointed out and regretted by the intelligent friends of the Union.

We may indeed with propriety be said to have reached almost the last stage of national humiliation. There is scarcely anything that can wound the pride or degrade the character of an independent nation which we do not experience. Are there engagements to the performance of which we are held by every tie respectable among men? These are the subjects of constant and unblushing violation. Do we owe debts to foreigners and to our own citizens contracted in a time of imminent peril for the preservation of our political existence? These remain without any proper or satisfactory provision for their discharge. * * * Are we in a condition to resent or to repel the aggression? We have neither troops, nor treasury, nor government. * * * Is public credit an indispensable resource in time of public danger? We seem to have abandoned its cause as desperate and irretrievable. Is commerce of importance to national wealth? Ours is at the lowest point of declension. Is respectability in the eyes of foreign powers a safeguard against foreign encroachments? The imbecility of our government even forbids them to treat with us. . . . Is private credit the friend and patron of industry? That most useful kind which relates to borrowing and lending is reduced within the narrowest limits, and this still more from an opinion of insecurity than from a scarcity of money. * * *

This is the melancholy situation to which we have been brought by those very maxims and counsels which would now deter us from adopting the proposed Constitution; and which, not content with having conducted us to the brink of a precipice, seem resolved to plunge us into the abyss that awaits us below. Here, my countrymen, impelled by every motive that ought to influence an enlightened people, let us make a firm stand for our safety, our tranquility, our dignity, our reputation. Let us at last break the fatal charm which has too long seduced us from the paths of felicity and prosperity.

* * * While [opponents of the Constitution] admit that the government of the United States is destitute of energy, they contend against conferring upon it those powers which are requisite to supply that energy. * * * This renders a full display of the principal defects of the Confederation necessary in order to show that the evils we experience do not proceed from minute or partial imperfections, but from fundamental errors in the structure of the building, which cannot be amended otherwise than by an alteration in the first principles and main pillars of the fabric.

The great and radical vice in the construction of the existing Confederation is in the principle of LEGISLATION FOR STATES OR GOVERNMENTS, in their CORPORATE OR COLLECTIVE CAPACITIES, and as contradistinguished from the INDIVIDUALS of whom they consist. Though this principle does not run through all the powers delegated to the Union, yet it pervades and governs those on which the efficacy of the rest depends. Except as to the rule of apportionment, the United States have an indefinite discretion to make requisitions for men and money; but they have no authority to raise either by regulations extending to the individual citizens of America. The consequence of this is that though in theory their resolutions concerning those objects are laws constitutionally binding on the members of the Union, yet in practice they are mere recommendations which the States observe or disregard at their option. * * *

There is nothing absurd or impracticable in the idea of a league or alliance between independent nations for certain defined purposes precisely stated in a treaty regulating all the details of time, place, circumstance, and quantity, leaving nothing to future discretion, and depending for its execution on the good faith of the parties. * * *

If the particular States in this country are disposed to stand in a similar relation to each other, and to drop the project of a general DISCRETIONARY SUPERINTENDENCE, the scheme would indeed be pernicious and would entail upon us all the mischiefs which have been enumerated under the first head; but it would have the merit of being, at least, consistent and practicable. Abandoning all views towards a confederate government, this would bring us to a simple alliance offensive and defensive; and would place us in a situation to be alternate friends and enemies of each other, as our mutual jealousies and rivalships, nourished by the intrigues of foreign nations, should prescribe to us.

But if we are unwilling to be placed in this perilous situation; if we still will adhere to the design of a national government, or, which is the same thing, of a superintending power under the direction of a common council, we must resolve to incorporate into our plan those ingredients which may be considered as forming the characteristic difference between a league and a government; we must extend the authority of the Union to the persons of the citizens—the only proper objects of government.

Government implies the power of making laws. It is essential to the idea of a law that it be attended with a sanction; or, in other words, a penalty or punishment for disobedience. If there be no penalty annexed to disobedience, the resolutions or commands which pretend to be laws will, in fact, amount to nothing more than advice or recommendation. This penalty, whatever it may be, can only be inflicted in two ways: by the agency of the courts and ministers of justice, or by military force; by the COERCION of the magistracy, or by the COERCION of arms. The first kind can evidently apply only to men; the last kind must of necessity be employed against bodies politic, or communities, or States. * * * In an association where the general authority is confined to the collective bodies of the communities that compose it, every breach of the laws must involve a state of war; and military execution must become the only instrument of civil obedience. Such a state of things can certainly not deserve the name of government, nor would any prudent man choose to commit his happiness to it.

There was a time when we were told that breaches by the States of the regulations of the federal authority were not to be expected; that a sense of common interest would preside over the conduct of the respective members, and would beget a full compliance with all the constitutional requisitions of the Union. This language, at the present day, would appear as wild as a great part of what we now hear from the same quarter will be thought, when we shall have received further lessons from that best oracle of wisdom, experience. It at all times betrayed an ignorance of the true springs by which human conduct is actuated, and belied the original inducements to the establishment of civil power. Why has government been instituted at all? Because the passions of men will not conform to the dictates of reason and justice without constraint. * * *

In addition to all this * * * it happens that in every political association which is formed upon the principle of uniting in a common interest a number of lesser sovereignties, there will be found a kind of eccentric tendency in the subordinate or inferior orbs by the operation of which there will be a perpetual effort in each to fly off from the common center. This tendency is not difficult to be accounted for. It has its origin in the love of power. Power controlled or abridged is almost always the rival and enemy of that power by which it is controlled or abridged. This simple proposition will teach us how little reason there is to expect that the persons intrusted with the administration of the affairs of the particular members of a confederacy will at all times be ready with perfect good humor and an unbiased regard to the public weal to execute the resolutions or decrees of the general authority. * * *

If, therefore, the measures of the Confederacy cannot be executed without the intervention of the particular administrations, there will be little prospect of their being executed at all. * * * [Each state will evaluate every federal measure in light of its own interests] and in a spirit of interested and suspicious scrutiny, without that knowledge of national circumstances and reasons of state, which is essential to a right judgment, and with that strong predilection in favor of local objects, which can hardly fail to mislead the decision. The same process must be repeated in every member of which the body is constituted; and the execution of the plans, framed by the councils of the whole, will always fluctuate on the discretion of the ill-informed and prejudiced opinion of every part. * * *

In our case the concurrence of thirteen distinct sovereign wills is requisite under the Confederation to the complete execution of every important measure that proceeds from the Union. It has happened as was to have been foreseen. The measures of the Union have not been executed; and the delinquencies of the States have step by step matured themselves to an extreme, which has, at length, arrested all the wheels of the national government and brought them to an awful stand. Congress at this time scarcely possess the means of keeping up the forms of administration, till the States can have time to agree upon a more substantial substitute for the present shadow of a federal government. * * * Each State yielding to the persuasive voice of immediate interest or convenience has successively withdrawn its support, till the frail and tottering edifice seems ready to fall upon our heads and to crush us beneath its ruins.

PUBLIUS

## DISCUSSION QUESTIONS

1. Do you think the national government is sufficiently held in check, as Hamilton argues, or is the exercise of its authority so vast as to give credence to the Anti-Federalist fears? To put it another way, would the Framers be distressed or pleased with the scope of government powers today?

2. According to Hamilton, what are the weaknesses of a "league" compared to a government?

3. What is the significance of Hamilton's statement that "we must extend the authority of the Union to the persons of the citizens"?

# The Federalist, No. 51

## JAMES MADISON

*Such well-known patriots as Patrick Henry—"give me liberty or give me death!"—opposed the new Constitution. The proposed national government was stronger than its predecessor, but this was precisely the problem for the Anti-Federalists. A stronger national government could act in a more concerted manner in matters of foreign affairs and interstate commerce, but it also held the power to oppress the very people who gave it sovereignty. Arguments over this delicate balance of power animated debates over constitutional ratification.*

*James Madison concurred with Hamilton on the need for a stronger national government, but also recognized the importance of a limited government. In one of the most famous passages of* The Federalist Papers, *Madison notes in* The Federalist, No. 51, *"If men were angels, no government would be necessary. If angels were to govern men, neither external nor internal controls on government would be necessary." But because angels do not govern us, Madison argued for the importance of controls on government. Here is where Madison attempts to address the concerns of the Anti-Federalists by arguing for a "double security" against majority tyranny. To achieve this security, the power of government must be divided across (between state and national governments) and within levels of government (among the courts, the president, and Congress). Such a division insured that if any one institution tried to become too powerful, the others would step in to counteract it. This essay remains one of the most eloquent defenses of our system of checks and balances and separation of powers.*

*To the People of the State of New York:*

To what expedient, then, shall we finally resort for maintaining in practice the necessary partition of power among the several departments as laid down in the Constitution? The only answer that can be given is, that as all these exterior provisions are found to be inadequate, the defect must be supplied by so contriving the interior structure of the government as that its several constituent parts may, by their mutual relations, be the means of keeping each other in their proper places. Without presuming to undertake a full development of this important idea, I will hazard a few general observations, which may perhaps place it in a clearer light, and enable us to form a more correct judgment of the principles and structure of the government planned by the convention.

In order to lay a due foundation for that separate and distinct exercise of the different powers of government, which to a certain extent is admitted on all hands to be essential to the preservation of liberty, it is evident that each department should have a will of its own; and consequently should be so constituted that the members of each should have as little agency as possible in the appointment of the members of the others. Were this principle rigorously adhered to, it would require that all the appointments for the supreme executive, legislative, and judiciary magistracies should be drawn from the same fountain of authority, the people, through channels having no communication whatever with one another. Perhaps such a plan of constructing the several departments would be less difficult in practice than it may in contemplation appear. Some difficulties, however, and some additional expense would attend the execution of it. Some deviations, therefore, from the principle must be admitted. In the constitution of the judiciary department in particular, it might be inexpedient to insist rigorously on the principle: first, because peculiar qualifications being essential in the members, the primary consideration ought to be to select that mode of choice which best secures these qualifications; secondly, because the permanent tenure by which the appointments are held in that department must soon destroy all sense of dependence on the authority conferring them.

It is equally evident, that the members of each department should be as little dependent as possible on those of the others for the emoluments annexed to their offices. Were the executive magistrate or the judges not independent of the legislature in this particular, their independence in every other would be merely nominal.

But the great security against a gradual concentration of the several powers in the same department, consists in giving to those who administer each department the necessary constitutional means and personal motives to resist encroachments of the others. The provision for defence must in this, as in all other cases, be made commensurate to the danger of attack. Ambition must be made to counteract ambition. The interest of the man must be connected with the constitutional rights of the place. It may be a reflection on human nature, that such devices should be necessary to control the abuses of government. But what is government itself, but the greatest of all reflections on human nature? If men were angels, no government would be necessary. If angels were to govern men, neither external nor internal controls on government would be necessary. In framing a government which is to be administered by men over men, the great difficulty lies in this: you must first enable the government to control the governed; and in the next place oblige it to control itself. A dependence on the people is, no doubt, the primary control on the government; but experience has taught mankind the necessity of auxiliary precautions.

This policy of supplying, by opposite and rival interests, the defect of better motives might be traced through the whole system of human affairs, private as well as public. We see it particularly displayed in all the subordinate distributions of power, where the constant aim is to divide and arrange the several offices in such a manner as that each may be a check on the other—that the private interest of every individual may be a sentinel over the public rights. These inventions of prudence cannot be less requisite in the distribution of the supreme powers of the State.

But it is not possible to give to each department an equal power of self-defence. In republican government the legislative authority necessarily predominates. The remedy for this inconveniency is to divide the legislature into different branches; and to render them, by different modes of election and different principles of action, as little connected with each other as the nature of their common functions and their common dependence on the society will admit. It may even be necessary to guard against dangerous encroachments by still further precautions. As the weight of the legislative authority requires that it should be thus divided, the weakness of the executive may require, on the other hand, that it should be fortified. An absolute negative on the legislature appears, at first view, to be the natural defence with which the executive magistrate should be armed. But perhaps it would be neither altogether safe nor alone sufficient. On ordinary occasions it might not be exerted with the requisite firmness, and on extraordinary occasions it might be perfidiously abused. May not this defect of an absolute negative be supplied by some qualified connection between this weaker department and the weaker branch of the stronger department, by which the latter may be led to support the constitutional rights of the former, without being too much detached from the rights of its own department?

If the principles on which these observations are founded be just . . . and they be applied as a criterion to the several State constitutions and to the federal Constitution, it will be found that if the latter does not perfectly correspond with them, the former are infinitely less able to bear such a test.

There are, moreover, two considerations particularly applicable to the federal system of America, which place that system in a very interesting point of view.

*First.* In a single republic, all the power surrendered by the people is submitted to the administration of a single government; and the usurpations are guarded against by a division of the government into distinct and separate departments. In the compound republic of America, the power surrendered by the people is first divided between two distinct governments, and then the portion allotted to each subdivided among distinct and separate departments. Hence a double security arises to the rights of the people. The different governments will control each other, at the same time that each will be controlled by itself.

*Second.* It is of great importance in a republic not only to guard the society against the oppression of its rulers, but to guard one part of the society against the injustice of the other part. Different interests necessarily exist in different classes of citizens. If a majority be united by a common interest, the rights of the minority will be insecure. There are but two methods of providing against this evil: the one by creating a will in the community independent of the majority—that is, of the society itself; the other by comprehending in the society so many separate descriptions of citizens as will render an unjust combination of a majority of the whole very improbable, if not impracticable. The first method prevails in all governments possessing an hereditary or self-appointed authority. This, at best, is but a precarious security; because a power independent of the society may as well espouse the unjust views of the major, as the rightful interests of the minor party, and may possibly be turned against both parties. The second method will be exemplified in the federal republic of the United States. Whilst all authority in it will be derived from and dependent on the society, the society itself will be broken into so many parts, interests and classes of citizens, that the rights of individuals or of the minority will be in little danger from interested combinations of the majority. In a free government the security for civil rights must be the same as that for religious rights. It consists in the one case in the multiplicity of interests and in the other in the multiplicity of sects. The degree of security in both cases will depend on the number of interests and sects; and this may be presumed to depend on the extent of country and number of people comprehended under the same government. This view of the subject must particularly recommend a proper federal system to all the sincere and considerate friends of republican government, since it shows that in exact proportion as the territory of the Union may be formed into more circumscribed Confederacies or States, oppressive combinations of a majority will be facilitated; the best security under the republican forms for the rights of every class of citizens will be diminished; and consequently the stability and independence of some member of the government, the only other security, must be proportionally increased. Justice is the end [that is, the goal] of government. It is the end of civil society. It ever has been and ever will be pursued until it be obtained, or until liberty be lost in the pursuit. In a society under the forms of which the stronger faction can readily unite and oppress the weaker, anarchy may as truly be said to reign as in a state of nature, where the weaker individual is not secured against the violence of the stronger; and, as in the latter state even the stronger individuals are prompted, by the uncertainty of their condition, to submit to a government which may protect the weak as well as themselves; so, in the former state will the more powerful factions or parties be gradually induced by a like motive to wish for a government which will protect all parties, the weaker as well as the more powerful. It can be little doubted that if the State of Rhode Island was separated from the Confederacy and left to itself, the insecurity of rights under the popular form of government within such narrow limits would be displayed by such reiterated oppressions of factious majorities that some power altogether independent of the people would soon be called for by the voice of the very factions whose misrule had proved the necessity of it. In the extended republic of the United States and among the great variety of interests, parties, and sects which it embraces, a coalition of a majority of the whole society could seldom take place on any other principles than those of justice and the general good; whilst there being thus less danger to a minor from the will of a major party, there must be less pretext, also, to provide for the security of the former, by introducing into the government a will not dependent on the latter, or, in other words, a will independent of the society itself. It is no less certain than it is important, notwithstanding the contrary opinions which have been entertained, that the larger the society, provided it lie within a practical sphere, the more duly capable it will be of self-government. And happily for the *republican cause*, the practicable sphere may be carried to a very great extent by a judicious modification and mixture of the *federal principle*.

Publius

## Discussion Questions

1. According to Madison, the principles of "separation of powers" and "checks and balances" operate to limit the authority of the national government. How? Discuss at least one current issue involving these two principles. What constitutional issues are at stake?

2. Is the system of "separation of powers" and "checks and balances" able to handle the challenges of the modern and dangerous world? Would the United States be better off with a more efficient form of government that would allow for quicker action and more centralized accountability?

DEBATING THE ISSUES: AN ECONOMIC INTERPRETATION OF
THE CONSTITUTION

> One of the longest-running debates over the Constitution focuses on
> the motivation of the Founders in drafting the document. Was the
> motivation ideological, based on beliefs about self-governance, the na-
> ture of a social contract, and the role of representation? Or was the
> motivation primarily economic, based on a need to preserve economic
> interests that were threatened under the system of governance of the
> Articles of Confederation? And if the motivation was economic, what
> economic interests divided the Anti-Federalists from the Federalists
> in their opposition to or support for the Constitution?
>
> One of the earliest and most controversial efforts to answer the
> question was written by Charles A. Beard in 1913. Beard argued that
> those who favored the Constitution and played the primary role in its
> drafting were motivated by the need to better protect their substantial
> "personalty" interests—money, public securities, manufactures, and
> trade and shipping (or commerce)—in contrast to its opponents who
> were primarily small farmers (with small real estate holdings) and
> debtors. Not only was its motivation less than democratic, Beard ar-
> gued, but the Constitution was ratified by only one-sixth of the male
> population because voting was limited to property owners.
>
> Robert E. Brown takes strong opposition to Beard's thesis. His criti-
> cism focuses mainly on Beard's use of historical data and its inter-
> pretation, leaving the door open for other interpretations of the
> motivations behind the Constitution as well as the base of public sup-
> port for the document.

# 10

# From *An Economic Interpretation of the Constitution of the United States*

## CHARLES A. BEARD

The requirements for an economic interpretation of the formation and adoption of the Constitution may be stated in a hypothetical prop-osition which, although it cannot be verified absolutely from ascertain-able data, will at once illustrate the problem and furnish a guide to research and generalization.

It will be admitted without controversy that the Constitution was the creation of a certain number of men, and it was opposed by a certain number of men. Now, if it were possible to have an economic biography of all those connected with its framing and adoption,—perhaps about 160,000 men altogether,—the materials for scientific analysis and classification would be available. Such an economic biography would include a list of the real and personal property owned by all of these men and their families: lands and houses, with incumbrances, money at interest, slaves, capital invested in shipping and manufacturing, and in state and continental securities.

Suppose it could be shown from the classification of the men who supported and opposed the Constitution that there was no line of property division at all; that is, that men owning substantially the same amounts of the same kinds of property were equally divided on the matter of adoption or rejection—it would then become apparent that the Constitution had no ascertainable relation to economic groups or classes, but was the product of some abstract causes remote from the chief business of life—gaining a livelihood.

Suppose, on the other hand, that substantially all of the merchants, money lenders, security holders, manufacturers, shippers, capitalists, and financiers and their professional associates are to be found on one side in support of the Constitution and that substantially all or the major portion of the opposition came from the non-slaveholding farmers and the debtors—would it not be pretty conclusively demonstrated that our fundamental law was not the product of an abstraction known as "the whole people," but of a group of economic interests which must have expected beneficial results from its adoption? Obviously all the facts here desired cannot be discovered, but the data presented in the following chapters bear out the latter hypothesis, and thus a reasonable presumption in favor of the theory is created.

\*   \*   \*

The purpose of such an inquiry is not, of course, to show that the Constitution was made for the personal benefit of the members of the Convention. Far from it. Neither is it of any moment to discover how many hundred thousand dollars accrued to them as a result of the foundation of the new government. The only point here considered is: Did they represent distinct groups whose economic interests they understood and felt in concrete, definite form through their own personal experience with identical property rights, or were they working merely under the guidance of abstract principles of political science?

\*   \*   \*

*The Disfranchised*

In an examination of the structure of American society in 1787, we first encounter four groups whose economic status had a definite legal expression: the slaves, the indentured servants, the mass of men who could not qualify for voting under the property tests imposed by the state constitutions and laws, and women, disfranchised and subjected to the discriminations of the common law. These groups were, therefore, not represented in the Convention which drafted the Constitution, except under the theory that representation has no relation to voting.

How extensive the disfranchisement really was cannot be determined. In some states, for instance, Pennsylvania and Georgia, propertyless mechanics in the towns could vote; but in other states the freehold qualifications certainly excluded a great number of the adult males.

In no state, apparently, had the working class developed a consciousness of a separate interest or an organization that commanded the attention of the politicians of the time. In turning over the hundreds of pages of writings left by eighteenth-century thinkers one cannot help being impressed with the fact that the existence and special problems of a working class, then already sufficiently numerous to form a considerable portion of society, were outside the realm of politics, except in so far as the future power of the proletariat was foreseen and feared.

When the question of the suffrage was before the Convention, Madison warned his colleagues against the coming industrial masses: "Viewing the subject in its merits alone, the freeholders of the Country would be the safest depositories of Republican liberty. In future times a great majority of the people will not only be without landed [property], but any other sort of property. These will either combine under the influence of their common situation; in which case, the rights of property and the public liberty will not be secure in their hands, or, which is more probable, they will become the tools of opulence and ambition; in which case there will be equal danger on another side."

\* \* \*

It is apparent that a majority of the states placed direct property qualifications on the voters, and the other states eliminated practically all who were not taxpayers. Special safeguards for property were secured in the qualifications imposed on members of the legislatures in New Hampshire, Massachusetts, New York, New Jersey, Maryland, North Carolina, South Carolina, and Georgia. Further safeguards were added by the qualifications imposed in the case of senators in New Hampshire, Massachusetts, New Jersey, New York, Maryland, North Carolina, and South Carolina.

While these qualifications operated to exclude a large portion of the adult males from participating in elections, the wide distribution of real property created an extensive electorate and in most rural regions gave the legislatures a broad popular basis. Far from rendering to personal property that defence which was necessary to the full realization of its rights, these qualifications for electors admitted to the suffrage its most dangerous antagonists: the small farmers and many of the debtors who were the most active in all attempts to depreciate personalty [private property] by legislation. Madison with his usual acumen saw the inadequacy of such defence and pointed out in the Convention that the really serious assaults on property (having in mind of course, personalty) had come from the "freeholders."

Nevertheless, in the election of delegates to the Convention, the representatives of personalty in the legislatures were able by the sheer weight of their combined intelligence and economic power to secure delegates from the urban centres or allied with their interests. Happily for them, all the legislatures which they had to convince had not been elected on the issue of choosing delegates to a national Convention, and did not come from a populace stirred up on that question. The call for the Convention went forth on February 21, 1787, from Congress, and within a few months all the legislatures, except that of Rhode Island, had responded. Thus the heated popular discussion usually incident to such a momentous political undertaking was largely avoided, and an orderly and temperate procedure in the selection of delegates was rendered possible.

\*　　\*　　\*

A survey of the economic interests of the members of the Convention presents certain conclusions:

A majority of the members were lawyers by profession.

Most of the members came from towns, on or near the coast, that is, from the regions in which personalty was largely concentrated.

Not one member represented in his immediate personal economic interests the small farming or mechanic classes.

The overwhelming majority of members, at least five-sixths, were immediately, directly, and personally interested in the outcome of their labors at Philadelphia, and were to a greater or less extent economic beneficiaries from the adoption of the Constitution.

1. Public security interests were extensively represented in the Convention. Of the fifty-five members who attended no less than forty appear on the Records of the Treasury Department for sums varying from a few dollars up to more than one hundred thousand dollars. [A list of their names follows.]

It is interesting to note that, with the exception of New York, and possibly Delaware, each state had one or more prominent representatives in the Convention who held more than a negligible amount of securities, and who could therefore speak with feeling and authority on the question of providing in the new Constitution for the full discharge of the public debt: [list of names]

2. Personalty invested in lands for speculation was represented by at least fourteen members: [list of names]

3. Personalty in the form of money loaned at interest was represented by at least twenty-four members: [list of names]

4. Personalty in mercantile, manufacturing, and shipping lines was represented by at least eleven members: [list of names]

5. Personalty in slaves was represented by at least fifteen members: [list of names]

It cannot be said, therefore, that the members of the Convention were "disinterested." On the contrary, we are forced to accept the profoundly significant conclusion that they knew through their personal experiences in economic affairs the precise results which the new government that they were setting up was designed to attain. As a group of doctrinaires, like the Frankfurt assembly of 1848, they would have failed miserably; but as practical men they were able to build the new government upon the only foundations which could be stable: fundamental economic interests.

*    *    *

*Conclusions*

At the close of this long and arid survey—partaking of the nature of catalogue—it seems worthwhile to bring together the important conclusions for political science which the data presented appear to warrant.

[1.] The movement for the Constitution of the United States was originated and carried through principally by four groups of personalty interests which had been adversely affected under the Articles of Confederation: money, public securities, manufactures, and trade and shipping.

[2.] The first firm steps toward the formation of the Constitution were taken by a small and active group of men immediately interested through their personal possessions in the outcome of their labors.

[3.] No popular vote was taken directly or indirectly on the proposition to call the Convention which drafted the Constitution.

[4.] A large propertyless mass was, under the prevailing suffrage qualifications, excluded at the outset from participation (through representatives) in the work of framing the Constitution.

[5.] The members of the Philadelphia Convention which drafted the Constitution were, with a few exceptions, immediately, directly, and personally interested in, and derived economic advantages from, the establishment of the new system.

[6.] The Constitution was essentially an economic document based upon the concept that the fundamental private rights of property are anterior to government and morally beyond the reach of popular majorities.

[7.] The major portion of the members of the Convention are on record as recognizing the claim of property to a special and defensive position in the Constitution.

[8.] In the ratification of the Constitution, about three-fourths of the adult males failed to vote on the question, having abstained from the elections at which delegates to the state conventions were chosen, either on account of their indifference or their disfranchisement by property qualifications.

[9.] The Constitution was ratified by a vote of probably not more than one-sixth of the adult males.

[10.] It is questionable whether a majority of the voters participating in the elections for the state conventions in New York, Massachusetts, New Hampshire, Virginia, and South Carolina, actually approved the ratification of the Constitution.

[11.] The leaders who supported the Constitution in the ratifying conventions represented the same economic groups as the members of the Philadelphia Convention; and in a large number of instances they were also directly and personally interested in the outcome of their efforts.

[12.] In the ratification, it became manifest that the line of cleavage for and against the Constitution was between substantial personalty interests on the one hand and the small farming and debtor interests on the other.

[13.] The Constitution was not created by "the whole people" as the jurists have said; neither was it created by "the states" as Southern nullifiers long contended; but it was the work of a consolidated group whose interests knew no state boundaries and were truly national in their scope.

# From *Charles Beard and the Constitution: A Critical Analysis of "An Economic Interpretation of the Constitution"*

ROBERT E. BROWN

*Conclusions*

At the end of Chapter XI Beard summarized his findings in fourteen paragraphs under the heading of "Conclusions" (pp. 60–61). Actually, these fourteen conclusions merely add up to the two halves of the Beard thesis. One half, that the Constitution originated with and was carried through by personalty interests—money, public securities, manufactures, and commerce—is to be found in paragraphs two, three, six, seven, eight, twelve, thirteen, and fourteen. The other half—that the Constitution was put over undemocratically in an undemocratic society—is expressed in paragraphs four, five, nine, ten, eleven, and fourteen. The lumping of these conclusions under two general headings makes it easier for the reader to see the broad outlines of the Beard thesis.

\* \* \*

If historical method means the gathering of data from primary sources, the critical evaluation of the evidence thus gathered, and the drawing of conclusions consistent with this evidence, then we must conclude that Beard has done great violation to such method in this book. He admitted that the evidence had not been collected which, given the proper use of historical method, should have precluded the writing of the book. Yet he nevertheless proceeded on the assumption that a valid interpretation could be built on secondary writings whose authors had likewise failed to collect the evidence. If we accept Beard's own maxim, "no evidence, no history," and his own admission that the data had never been collected, the answer to whether he used historical method properly is self-evident.

\* \* \*

Finally, the conclusions which he drew were not justified even by the kind of evidence which he used. If we accepted his evidence strictly at face value, it would still not add up to the fact that the Constitution was put over undemocratically in an undemocratic society by personalty. The citing of property qualifications does not prove that a mass of men were disfranchised. And if we accept his figures on property holdings, either we do not know what most of the delegates had in realty and personalty, or we know that realty outnumbered personalty three to one (eighteen to six). Simply showing that a man held public securities is not sufficient to prove that he acted only in terms of his public securities. If we ignore Beard's own generalizations and accept only his evidence, we would have to conclude that most of the property in the country in 1787 was real estate, that real property was widely distributed in rural areas, which included most of the country, and that even the men who were directly concerned with the Constitution, and especially Washington, were large holders of realty.

Perhaps we can never be completely objective in history, but certainly we can be more objective than Beard was in this book. Naturally the historian must always be aware of the biases, the subjectivity, the pitfalls that confront him, but this does not mean that he should not make an effort to overcome these obstacles. Whether Beard had his thesis before he had his evidence, as some have said, is a question that each reader must answer for himself. Certain it is that the evidence does not justify the thesis.

So instead of the Beard interpretation that the Constitution was put over undemocratically in an undemocratic society by personal property, the following fourteen paragraphs are offered as a possible interpretation of the Constitution and as suggestions for future research on that document.

1. The movement for the Constitution was originated and carried through by men who had long been important in both economic and political affairs in their respective states. Some of them owned personalty, more of them owned realty, and if their property was adversely affected by conditions under the Articles of Confederation, so also was the property of the bulk of the people in the country, middle-class farmers as well as town artisans.

2. The movement for the Constitution, like most important movements, was undoubtedly started by a small group of men. They were probably interested personally in the outcome of their labors, but the benefits which they expected were not confined to personal property or, for that matter, strictly to things economic. And if their own interests would be enhanced by a new government, similar interests of other men, whether agricultural or commercial, would also be enhanced.

3. Naturally there was no popular vote on the calling of the convention which drafted the Constitution. Election of delegates by state legislatures was the constitutional method under the Articles of Confederation, and had been the method long established in this country. Del-

egates to the Albany Congress, the Stamp Act Congress, the First Continental Congress, the Second Continental Congress, and subsequent congresses under the Articles were all elected by state legislatures, not by the people. Even the Articles of Confederation had been sanctioned by state legislatures, not by popular vote. This is not to say that the Constitutional Convention should not have been elected directly by the people, but only that such a procedure would have been unusual at the time. Some of the opponents of the Constitution later stressed, without avail, the fact that the Convention had not been directly elected. But at the time the Convention met, the people in general seemed to be about as much concerned over the fact that they had not elected the delegates as the people of this country are now concerned over the fact that they do not elect our delegates to the United Nations.

4. Present evidence seems to indicate that there were no "propertyless masses" who were excluded from the suffrage at the time. Most men were middle-class farmers who owned realty and were qualified voters, and, as the men in the Convention said, mechanics had always voted in the cities. Until credible evidence proves otherwise, we can assume that state legislatures were fairly representative at the time. We cannot condone the fact that a few men were probably disfranchised by prevailing property qualifications, but it makes a great deal of difference to an interpretation of the Constitution whether the disfranchised comprised ninety-five per cent of the adult men or only five per cent. Figures which give percentages of voters in terms of the entire population are misleading, since less than twenty per cent of the people were adult men. And finally, the voting qualifications favored realty, not personalty.

5. If the members of the Convention were directly interested in the outcome of their work and expected to derive benefits from the establishment of the new system, so also did most of the people of the country. We have many statements to the effect that the people in general expected substantial benefits from the labors of the Convention.

6. The Constitution was not just an economic document, although economic factors were undoubtedly important. Since most of the people were middle-class and had private property, practically everybody was interested in the protection of property. A constitution which did not protect property would have been rejected without any question, for the American people had fought the Revolution for the preservation of life, liberty, and property. Many people believed that the Constitution did not go far enough to protect property, and they wrote these views into the amendments to the Constitution. But property was not the only concern of those who wrote and ratified the Constitution, and we would be doing a grave injustice to the political sagacity of the Founding Fathers if we assumed that property or personal gain was their only motive.

7. Naturally the delegates recognized that the protection of property was important under government, but they also recognized that personal

rights were equally important. In fact, persons and property were usually bracketed together as the chief objects of government protection.

8. If three-fourths of the adult males failed to vote on the election of
delegates to ratifying conventions, this fact signified indifference, not
disfranchisement. We must not confuse those who could *not* vote with
those who *could* vote but failed to exercise their right. Many men at the
time bewailed the fact that only a small portion of the voters ever exercised their prerogative. But this in itself should stand as evidence that
the conflict over the Constitution was not very bitter, for if these people
had felt strongly one way or the other, more of them would have voted.

Even if we deny the evidence which I have presented and insist that
American society was undemocratic in 1787, we must still accept the fact
that the men who wrote the Constitution believed that they were writing
it for a democratic society. They did not hide behind an iron curtain of
secrecy and devise the kind of conservative government that they
wanted without regard to the views and interests of "the people." More
than anything else, they were aware that "the people" would have to
ratify what they proposed, and that therefore any government which
would be acceptable to the people must of necessity incorporate much
of what was customary at the time. The men at Philadelphia were practical politicians, not political theorists. They recognized the multitude of
different ideas and interests that had to be reconciled and compromised
before a constitution would be acceptable. They were far too practical,
and represented far too many clashing interests themselves, to fashion a
government weighted in favor of personalty or to believe that the people
would adopt such a government.

9. If the Constitution was ratified by a vote of only one-sixth of the
adult men, that again demonstrates indifference and not disfranchisement. Of the one-fourth of the adult males who voted, nearly two-thirds
favored the Constitution. Present evidence does not permit us to say
what the popular vote was except as it was measured by the votes of
the ratifying conventions.

10. Until we know what the popular vote was, we cannot say that it
is questionable whether a majority of the voters in several states favored
the Constitution. Too many delegates were sent uninstructed. Neither
can we count the towns which did not send delegates on the side of
those opposed to the Constitution. Both items would signify indifference
rather than sharp conflict over ratification.

11. The ratifying conventions were elected for the specific purpose of
adopting or rejecting the Constitution. The people in general had anywhere from several weeks to several months to decide the question. If
they did not like the new government, or if they did not know whether
they liked it, they could have voted *no* and there would have been no
Constitution. Naturally the leaders in the ratifying conventions represented the same interests as the members of the Constitutional Con-

vention—mainly realty and some personalty. But they also represented their constituents in these same interests, especially realty.

12. If the conflict over ratification had been between substantial personality interests on the one hand and small farmers and debtors on the other, there would not have been a constitution. The small farmers comprised such an overwhelming percentage of the voters that they could have rejected the new government without any trouble. Farmers and debtors are not synonymous terms and should not be confused as such. A town-by-town or county-by-county record of the vote would show clearly how the farmers voted.

13. The Constitution was created about as much by the whole people as any government could be which embraced a large area and depended on representation rather than on direct participation. It was also created in part by the states, for as the *Records* show, there was strong state sentiment at the time which had to be appeased by compromise. And it was created by compromising a whole host of interests throughout the country, without which compromises it could never have been adopted.

If the intellectual historians are correct, we cannot explain the Constitution without considering the psychological factors also. Men are motivated by what they believe as well as by what they have. Sometimes their actions can be explained on the basis of what they hope to have or hope that their children will have. Madison understood this fact when he said that the universal hope of acquiring property tended to dispose people to look favorably upon property. It is even possible that some men support a given economic system when they themselves have nothing to gain by it. So we would want to know what the people in 1787 thought of their class status. Did workers and small farmers believe that they were lower-class, or did they, as many workers do now, consider themselves middle-class? Were the common people trying to eliminate the Washingtons, Adamses, Hamiltons, and Pinckneys, or were they trying to join them?

As did Beard's conclusions, these suggestions really add up to two major propositions: the Constitution was adopted in a society which was fundamentally democratic, not undemocratic; and it was adopted by a people who were primarily middle-class property owners, especially farmers who owned realty, not just by the owners of personalty. At present these points seem to be justified by the evidence, but if better evidence in the future disproves or modifies them, we must accept that evidence and change our interpretation accordingly.

After this critical analysis, we should at least not begin future research on this period of American history with the illusion that the Beard thesis of the Constitution is valid. If historians insist on accepting the Beard thesis in spite of this analysis, however, they must do so with the full knowledge that their acceptance is founded on "an act of faith," not an analysis of historical method, and that they are indulging in a "noble dream," not history.

## Discussion Questions

1. Based on these readings, do you think the Framers were governed by self-interest or a commitment to principle, or some combination, when they drafted the Constitution? Explain your answer.

2. What does the debate between Beard and Brown say about the use of historical evidence to support an argument? How can historical evidence be misused? How can historians, or even readers of history, sort out what "really" happened in any specific context?

# CHAPTER 3

# Federalism

## 12

## *The Federalist*, No. 46

JAMES MADISON

*Some of the most divisive and bitter political battles in our nation's history have occurred over interpretations of the constitutional principle of federalism, or the division of powers and functions between the state governments and the national government. The struggle for desegregation and the civil rights of minorities, the legalization of abortion, the selective incorporation of the Bill of Rights into the Fourteenth Amendment, slavery and the Civil War, all ultimately turned on this question: Who has the authority to govern, the states or the national government? Our federal system is a delicate balance of power and shared responsibility between nation and states, each with constitutional authority to pass laws, levy taxes, and protect the interests and rights of citizens. It is a dynamic balance of power, easily destabilized by economic crises, political initiatives, and Supreme Court rulings, but often resolved in more recent years by the question: Who will pay the price for implementing and enforcing government policy?*

*The "double security," which James Madison discussed in* The Federalist, *No. 51 in the previous chapter, did not satisfy those who feared that the national powers would encroach on state sovereignty. In* The Federalist, *No. 46, Madison went to great lengths to reassure the states that they would continue to wield a high degree of power, arguing that "the first and most natural attachment of the people will be to the governments of their respective states." Although recognizing the potential for conflicts between state and federal governments, Madison concluded that the power retained by the states would be sufficient to resist arrogation by the newly established national government.*

I proceed to inquire whether the federal government or the State governments will have the advantage with regard to the predilection and support of the people. Notwithstanding the different modes in which they are appointed, we must consider both of them as substantially dependent on the great body of the citizens of the United States. * * * The federal and State governments are in fact but different agents and trustees of the people, constituted with different powers and designed for different purposes. The adversaries of the Constitution seem to have lost sight of the people altogether in their reasonings on this subject; and to have viewed these different establishments not only as mutual rivals and enemies, but as uncontrolled by any common superior in their efforts to usurp the authorities of each other. These gentlemen must here be reminded of their error. They must be told that the ultimate authority, wherever the derivative may be found, resides in the people alone, and that it will not depend merely on the comparative ambition or address of the different governments whether either, or which of them, will be able to enlarge its sphere of jurisdiction at the expense of the other. Truth, no less than decency, requires that the event in every case should be supposed to depend on the sentiments and sanction of their common constituents.

Many considerations * * * seem to place it beyond doubt that the first and most natural attachment of the people will be to the governments of their respective States. Into the administration of these a greater number of individuals will expect to rise. From the gift of these a greater number of offices and emoluments will flow. By the superintending care of these, all the more domestic and personal interests of the people will be regulated and provided for. With the affairs of these, the people will be more familiarly and minutely conversant. And with the members of these will a greater proportion of the people have the ties of personal acquaintance and friendship, and of family and party attachments; on the side of these, therefore, the popular bias may well be expected most strongly to incline.

The remaining points on which I propose to compare the federal and State governments are the disposition and the faculty they may respectively possess to resist and frustrate the measures of each other.

It has been already proved that the members of the federal will be more dependent on the members of the State governments than the latter will be on the former. It has appeared also that the prepossessions of the people, on whom both will depend, will be more on the side of the State governments than of the federal government. So far as the disposition of each towards the other may be influenced by these causes, the State governments must clearly have the advantage. But in a distinct and very important point of view, the advantage will lie on the same side. The prepossessions, which the members themselves will carry into the federal government, will generally be favorable to the States; whilst it will rarely happen that the members of the State governments will carry into the public councils a bias in favor of the general government. A local spirit will infallibly prevail much more in the members of Congress than a national spirit will prevail in the legislatures of the particular States.

\* \* \* What is the spirit that has in general characterized the proceedings of Congress? A perusal of their journals, as well as the candid acknowledgments of such as have had a seat in that assembly, will inform us that the members have but too frequently displayed the character rather of partisans of their respective States than of impartial guardians of a common interest; that where on one occasion improper sacrifices have been made of local considerations to the aggrandizement of the federal government, the great interests of the nation have suffered on a hundred from an undue attention to the local prejudices, interests, and views of the particular States. I mean not by these reflections to insinuate that the new federal government will not embrace a more enlarged plan of policy than the existing government may have pursued; much less that its views will be as confined as those of the State legislatures; but only that it will partake sufficiently of the spirit of both to be disinclined to invade the rights of the individual States, or the prerogatives of their governments.

Were it admitted, however, that the federal government may feel an equal disposition with the State governments to extend its power beyond the due limits, the latter would still have the advantage in the means of defeating such encroachments. If an act of a particular State, though unfriendly to the national government, be generally popular in that State, and should not too grossly violate the oaths of the State officers, it is executed immediately and, of course, by means on the spot and depending on the State alone. The opposition of the federal government, or the interposition of federal officers, would but inflame the zeal of all parties on the side of the State, and the evil could not be prevented or repaired, if at all, without the employment of means which must always be resorted to with reluctance and difficulty. On the other hand, should an unwarrantable measure of the federal government be unpopular in particular States, which would seldom fail to be the case, or even a warrantable measure be so, which may sometimes be the case, the means of opposition to it are powerful and at hand. The disquietude of the people; their repugnance and, perhaps, refusal to co-operate with the officers of the Union; the frowns of the executive magistracy of the State; the embarrassments created by legislative devices, which would often be added on such occasions, would oppose, in any State, difficulties not to be despised; would form, in a large State, very serious impediments; and where the sentiments of several adjoining States happened to be in unison, would present obstructions which the federal government would hardly be willing to encounter.

But ambitious encroachments of the federal government on the authority of the State governments would not excite the opposition of a single State, or of a few States only. They would be signals of general alarm. Every government would espouse the common cause. A correspondence would be opened. Plans of resistance would be concerted.

One spirit would animate and conduct the whole. The same combinations, in short, would result from an apprehension of the federal, as was produced by the dread of a foreign yoke; and unless the projected innovations should be voluntarily renounced, the same appeal to a trial of force would be made in the one case as was made in the other.

The only refuge left for those who prophesy the downfall of the State governments is the visionary supposition that the federal government may previously accumulate a military force for the projects of ambition. The reasonings contained in these papers must have been employed to little purpose indeed, if it could be necessary now to disprove the reality of this danger. That the people and the States should, for a sufficient period of time, elect an uninterrupted succession of men ready to betray both; that the traitors should, throughout this period, uniformly and systematically pursue some fixed plan for the extension of the military establishment; that the governments and the people of the States should silently and patiently behold the gathering storm and continue to supply the materials until it should be prepared to burst on their own heads must appear to everyone more like the incoherent dreams of a delirious jealousy, or the misjudged exaggerations of a counterfeit zeal, than like the sober apprehensions of genuine patriotism. Extravagant as the supposition is, let it, however, be made. Let a regular army, fully equal to the resources of the country, be formed; and let it be entirely at the devotion of the federal government: still it would not be going too far to say that the State governments with the people on their side would be able to repel the danger.

Besides the advantage of being armed, which the Americans possess over the people of almost every other nation, the existence of subordinate governments, to which the people are attached and by which the militia officers are appointed, forms a barrier against the enterprises of ambition, more insurmountable than any which a simple government of any form can admit of.

Let us not insult the free and gallant citizens of America with the suspicion that they would be less able to defend the rights of which they would be in actual possession than the debased subjects of arbitrary power would be to rescue theirs from the hands of their oppressors. Let us rather no longer insult them with the supposition that they can ever reduce themselves to the necessity of making the experiment by a blind and tame submission to the long train of insidious measures which must precede and produce it.

The argument under the present head may be put into a very concise form, which appears altogether conclusive. Either the mode in which the federal government is to be constructed will render it sufficiently dependent on the people, or it will not. On the first supposition, it will be restrained by that dependence from forming schemes obnoxious to their constituents. On the other supposition, it will not possess the confidence of the people, and its schemes of usurpation will be easily defeated by the State governments, who will be supported by the people.

On summing up the considerations stated in this and the last paper, they seem to amount to the most convincing evidence that the powers proposed to be lodged in the federal government are as little formidable to those reserved to the individual States as they are indispensably necessary to accomplish the purposes of the Union; and that all those alarms which have been sounded of a meditated and consequential annihilation of the State governments must, on the most favorable interpretation, be ascribed to the chimerical fears of the authors of them.

Publius

## Discussion Questions

1. Is Madison right that people are more attached to their state governments than to the national government? Why or why not? Does the democratic process work better if people are more attached to state governments?

2. Would your answer change at all during different political times? For example, are people more attached to the national government in the wake of the terrorist attacks on the United States than they were before September 11, 2001?

3. What reasons does Madison offer to explain why states should not fear the proposed Constitution?

# 13

# From *The Price of Federalism*

## Paul Peterson

*In this concise overview of American federalism, Paul Peterson argues that both the early and the more modern systems of shared sovereignty between the national government and the states have had their disadvantages. From the early period of "dual federalism" to the more modern system of a dominant national government, the battle over national and state government jurisdiction and power has led to bloodshed and war; the denial of political, social, and economic rights; and regional inequalities among the states.*

*Nevertheless, Peterson argues, there are advantages to federalism. Federalism has also facilitated capital growth and development, the creation of infrastructures, and social programs that greatly improved the quality of life for millions of Americans. Once the national government took responsibility for guaranteeing civil rights and civil liberties, the states "became the engines of economic development." Not all states are equally wealthy, but the national government has gradually diminished some of these differences by financing many social and economic programs. One recent battle over the proper form of federal relations involved welfare policy. Republicans in Congress wanted to give back to states the power to devise their own programs, while most Democrats and President Clinton initially wanted to retain a larger degree of federal government control. However, President Clinton eventually agreed to end welfare as an entitlement and return substantial control over the program to the states. The long-term verdict on this landmark legislation is still an open question and there is considerable debate over the proper balance between federal and state funding for the state-level welfare programs.*

### The Price of Early Federalism

As a principle of government, federalism has had a dubious history. It remains on the margins of political respectability even today. I was recently invited to give a presentation on metropolitan government before a United Nations conference. When I offered to discuss how the federal principle could be used to help metropolitan areas govern themselves more effectively, my sponsors politely advised me that this topic would be poorly received. The vast majority of UN members had a unified form of government, I was told, and they saw little of value in federalism. We reached a satisfactory compromise. I replaced "federal" with "two-tier form of government."

Thomas Hobbes, the founder of modern political thought, would have blessed the compromise, for he, too, had little room for federalism in his understanding of the best form of government. Hobbes said that people agreed to have a government over them only because they realized that in a state of nature, that is, when there is no government, life becomes a war of all against all. If no government exists to put malefactors in jail, everyone must become a criminal simply to avoid being a victim. Life becomes "nasty, brutish and short." To avoid the violent state of nature, people need and want rule by a single sovereign. Division of power among multiple sovereigns encourages bickering among them. Conflicts become inevitable, as each sovereign tries to expand its power (if for no other reason than to avoid becoming the prey of competing sovereigns). Government degenerates into anarchy and the world returns to the bitter state of nature from which government originally emerged.

The authors of *The Federalist* papers defended dual sovereignty by turning Hobbes's argument in favor of single sovereignty on its head. While Hobbes said that anything less than a single sovereign would lead to war of all against all, *The Federalist* argued that the best way of preserving liberty was to divide power. If power is concentrated in any one place, it can be used to crush individual liberty. Even in a democracy there can be the tyranny of the majority, the worst kind of tyranny because it is so stifling and complete. A division of power between the national and state governments reduces the possibility that any single majority will be able to control all centers of governmental power. The national government, by defending the country against foreign aggression, prevents external threats to liberty. The state governments, by denying power to any single dictator, reduce threats to liberty from within. As James Madison said in his defense of the Constitution, written on the eve of its ratification,

> The power surrendered by the people is first divided between two distinct governments, and then the portion allotted to each subdivided among distinct and separate departments. Hence a double security arises to the rights of the people. The different governments will control each other, at the same time that each will be controlled by itself. [*The Federalist*, No. 51]

Early federalism was built on the principle of dual sovereignty. The Constitution divided sovereignty between state and nation, each in control of its own sphere. Some even interpreted the Constitution to mean that state legislatures could nullify federal laws. Early federalism also gave both levels of government their own military capacity. Congress was given the power to raise an army and wage war, but states were allowed to maintain their own militia.

The major contribution of early federalism to American liberties took place within a dozen years after the signing of the Constitution. Liberty is never established in a new nation until those in authority have peacefully ceded power to a rival political faction. Those who wrote the Constitution and secured its ratification, known as the Federalists, initially captured control of the main institutions of the national government: Congress, the presidency, and the Supreme Court. Those opposed to the new constitutional order, the antifederalists, had to content themselves with an opposition role in Congress and control over a number of state governments, most notably Virginia's.

The political issues dividing the two parties were serious. The Federalist party favored a strong central government, a powerful central bank that could facilitate economic and industrial development, and a strong, independent executive branch. Federalists had also become increasingly disturbed by the direction the French Revolution had taken. They were alarmed by the execution of thousands, the confiscation of private property, and the movement of French troops across Europe. They called for the creation of a national army and reestablished close ties with Britain.

The antifederalists, who became known as Democratic-Republicans, favored keeping most governmental power in the hands of state governments. They were opposed to a national bank, a strong presidency, and industrial government. They thought the United States would remain a free country only if it remained a land of independent farmers. They bitterly opposed the creation of a national army for fear it would be used to repress political opposition. Impressed by the French Revolution's commitment to the rights of man, they excused its excesses. The greater danger, they thought, was the reassertion of British power, and they denounced the Federalists for seeming to acquiesce in the seizure of U.S. seamen by the British navy.

The conflict between the two sides intensified after George Washington retired to his home in Mount Vernon. In 1800 Thomas Jefferson, founder of the Democratic-Republican party, waged an all-out campaign to defeat Washington's Federalist successor, John Adams. In retrospect, the central issue of the election was democracy itself. Could an opposition party drive a government out of power? Would political leaders accept their defeat?

So bitter was the feud between the two parties that Representative Matthew Lyon, a Democratic-Republican, spit in the face of a Federalist on the floor of Congress. Outside the Congress, pro-French propagandists relentlessly criticized Adams. To silence the opposition, Congress, controlled by the Federalists, passed the Alien and Sedition Acts. One of the Alien Acts gave President Adams the power to deport any foreigners "concerned in any treasonable or secret machinations against the government." The Sedition Act made it illegal to "write, print, utter, or publish . . . any false, scandalous and malicious writing . . . against . . . the Congress of the United States, or the President."

The targets of the Sedition Acts soon became clear. Newspaper editors supporting the Democratic-Republicans were quickly indicted, and ten were brought to trial and convicted by juries under the influence of Federalist judges. Matthew Lyon was sentenced to a four-month jail term for claiming, presumably falsely, that President Adams had an "unbounded thirst for ridiculous pomp, foolish adulation, and selfish avarice." Even George Washington lent his support to this political repression.

Federalism undoubtedly helped the fledgling American democracy survive this first constitutional test. When the Federalists passed the Alien and Sedition Acts, Democratic-Republicans in the Virginia and Kentucky state legislatures passed resolutions nullifying the laws. When it looked as if Jefferson's victory in the election of 1800 might be stripped away by a Federalist-controlled House of Representatives, both sides realized that the Virginia state militia was at least as strong as the remnants of the Continental Army. Lacking the national army they had tried to establish, the Federalists chose not to fight. They acquiesced in their political defeat in part because their opponents had military as well as political power, and because they themselves could retreat to their own regional base of power, the state and local governments of New England and the mid-Atlantic states.

Jefferson claimed his victory was a revolution every bit as comprehensive as the one fought in 1776. The Alien and Sedition Acts were discarded, nullified not by a state legislature but by the results of a national election. President Adams returned to private life without suffering imprisonment or exile. Many years later, he and Jefferson reconciled their differences and developed through correspondence a close friendship. They died on the same day, the fiftieth anniversary of the Declaration of Independence. To both, federalism and liberty seemed closely intertwined.

The price to be paid for early federalism became more evident with the passage of time. To achieve the blessings of liberty, early federalism divided sovereign power. When Virginia and Kentucky nullified the Alien and Sedition Acts, they preserved liberties only by threatening national unity. With the election of Jefferson, the issue was temporarily rendered moot, but the doctrine remained available for use when southerners once again felt threatened by encroaching national power.

The doctrine of nullification was revived in 1830 by John C. Calhoun, sometime senator from South Carolina, who objected to high tariffs that protected northern industry at the expense of southern cotton producers. When Congress raised the tariff, South Carolina's legislature threatened to declare the law null and void. Calhoun, then serving as Andrew Jackson's vice president, argued that liberties could be trampled by national majorities unless states could nullify tyrannical acts. Andrew Jackson, though elected on a state's rights ticket, remained committed to national supremacy. At the annual Democratic banquet honoring the memory of

Thomas Jefferson, Calhoun supporters sought to trap Jackson into endorsing the doctrine. But Jackson, aware of the scheme, raised his glass in a dramatic toast to "Our federal union: it must be preserved!" Not to be outdone, Calhoun replied in kind: "The union, next to our liberty, most dear!"

A compromise was found to the overt issue, the tariff, but it was not so easy to resolve the underlying issue of slavery. In the infamous Dred Scott decision, the Supreme Court interpreted federalism to mean that boundaries could not be placed on the movements of masters and slaves. Northern territories could not free slaves that came within their boundaries; to do so deprived masters of their Fifth Amendment right not to be deprived of their property without due process of law. The decision spurred northern states to elect Abraham Lincoln president, which convinced southern whites that their liberties, most dear, were more important than federal union.

To Lincoln, as to Jackson, the union was to be preserved at all costs. Secession meant war. War meant the loss of 1 million lives, the destruction of the southern economy, the emancipation of African Americans from slavery, the demise of the doctrine of nullification, and the end to early federalism. Early federalism, with its doctrine of dual sovereignty, may have initially helped to preserve liberty, but it did so at a terrible price. As Hobbes feared, the price of dual sovereignty was war.

Since the termination of the Civil War, Americans have concluded that they can no longer trust their liberties to federalism. Sovereignty must be concentrated in the hands of the national government. Quite apart from the dangers of civil war, the powers of state and local governments have been used too often by a tyrannical majority to trample the rights of religious, racial, and political minorities. The courts now seem a more reliable institutional shelter for the nation's liberties.

But if federalism is no longer necessary or even conducive to the preservation of liberty, then what is its purpose? Is it merely a relic of an outdated past? Are the majority of the members of the United Nations correct in objecting to the very use of the word?

*The Rise of Modern Federalism*

The answers to these questions have been gradually articulated in the 130 years following the end of the Civil War. Although the states lost their sovereignty, they remained integral to the workings of American government. Modern federalism no longer meant dual sovereignty and shared military capacity. Modern federalism instead meant only that each level of government had its own independently elected political leaders and its own separate taxing and spending capacity. Equipped with these tools of quasi-sovereignty, each level of government could take all but the most violent of steps to defend its turf.

Although sovereignty and military capacity now rested firmly in the hands of the national government, modern federalism became more complex rather than less so. Power was no longer simply divided between the nation and its states. Cities, counties, towns, school districts, special districts, and a host of additional governmental entities, each with its own elected leaders and taxing authority, assumed new burdens and responsibilities.

Just as the blessings bestowed by early federalism were evident from its inception, so the advantages of modern federalism were clear from the onset. If states and localities were no longer the guarantors of liberty, they became the engines of economic development. By giving state and local governments the autonomy to act independently, the federal system facilitated the rapid growth of an industrial economy that eventually surpassed its European competitors. Canals and railroads were constructed, highways and sewage systems built, schools opened, parks designed, and public safety protected by cities and villages eager to make their locality a boomtown.

The price to be paid for modern federalism did not become evident until government attempted to grapple with the adverse side effects of a burgeoning capitalist economy. Out of a respect for federalism's constitutional status and political durability, social reformers first worked with and through existing components of the federal system, concentrating much of their reform effort on state and local governments. Only gradually did it become clear that state and local governments, for all their ability to work with business leaders to enhance community prosperity, had difficulty meeting the needs of the poor and the needy.

It was ultimately up to the courts to find ways of keeping the price of modern federalism within bounds. Although dual sovereignty no longer meant nullification and secession, much remained to be determined about the respective areas of responsibility of the national and state governments. At first the courts retained remnants of the doctrine of dual sovereignty in order to protect processes of industrialization from governmental intrusion. But with the advent of the New Deal, the constitutional power of the national government expanded so dramatically that the doctrine of dual sovereignty virtually lost all meaning. Court interpretations of the constitutional clauses on commerce and spending have proved to be the most significant.

According to dual sovereignty theory, article 1 of the Constitution gives Congress the power to regulate commerce "among the states," but the regulation of intrastate commerce was to be left to the states. So, for example, in 1895 the Supreme Court said that Congress could not break up a sugar monopoly that had a nationwide impact on the price of sugar, because the monopoly refined its sugar within the state of Pennsylvania. The mere fact that the sugar was to be sold nationwide was only "incidental" to its production. As late as 1935, the Supreme Court, in a 6 to

3 decision, said that Congress could not regulate the sale of poultry because the regulation took effect after the chickens arrived within the state of Illinois, not while they were in transit.

Known as the "sick chicken" case, this decision was one of a series in which the Supreme Court declared unconstitutional legislation passed in the early days of President Franklin Roosevelt's efforts to establish his New Deal programs. Seven of the "nine old men" on the Court had been appointed by Roosevelt's conservative Republican predecessors. By declaring many New Deal programs in violation of the commerce clause, the Supreme Court seemed to be substituting its political views for those of elected officials. In a case denying the federal government the right to protect workers trying to organize a union in the coal industry, the Republican views of the Court seemed to lie just barely below the surface of a technical discussion of the commerce clause. Justice George Sutherland declared, "The relation of employer and employee is a local relation . . . over which the federal government has no legislative control."

The Roosevelt Democrats were furious at decisions that seemed to deny the country's elected officials the right to govern. Not since Dred Scott* had judicial review been in such disrepute. Roosevelt decided to "pack the court" by adding six new judges over and above the nine already on the Court. Although Roosevelt's court-packing scheme did not survive the political uproar on Capitol Hill, its effect on the Supreme Court was noticeable. In the midst of the court-packing debate, Justices Charles Hughes and Owen Roberts, who had agreed with Sutherland's opinion in the coal case, changed their mind and voted to uphold the Wagner Act, a new law designed to facilitate the formation of unions. In his opinion, Hughes did not explicitly overturn the coal miner decision (for which he had voted), but he did say: "When industries organize themselves on a national scale, . . . how can it be maintained that their industrial labor relations constitute a forbidden field into which Congress may not enter?" Relations between employers and their workers, once said to be local, suddenly became part of interstate commerce.

The change of heart by Hughes and Roberts has been called "the switch in time that saved nine." The New Deal majority that emerged on the court was soon augmented by judges appointed by Roosevelt. Since the New Deal, the definition of interstate commerce has continued to expand. In 1942 a farmer raising twenty-three acres of wheat, all of which might be fed to his own livestock, was said to be in violation of the crop quotas imposed by the Agricultural Adjustment Act of 1938. Since he was feeding his cows himself, he was not buying grain on the open market, thereby depressing the worldwide price of grain. With such a definition of interstate commerce, nothing was local.

*[In *Dred Scott v. Sanford* (1857), the Court declared the anti-slavery provision of the Missouri Compromise of 1820 to be unconstitutional.]

The expansion of the meaning of the commerce clause is a well-known part of American political history. The importance to federalism of court interpretations of the "spending clause" is less well known. The constitutional clause in question says that Congress has the power to collect taxes to "provide for the . . . general welfare." But how about Congress's power to collect taxes for the welfare of specific individuals or groups?

The question first arose in a 1923 case, when a childless woman said she could not be asked to pay taxes in order to finance federal grants to states for programs that helped pregnant women. Since she received no benefit from the program, she sued for return of the taxes she had paid to cover its costs. In a decision that has never been reversed, the Supreme Court said that she had suffered no measurable injury and therefore had no right to sue the government. Her taxes were being used for a wide variety of purposes. The amount being spent for this program was too small to be significant. The court's decision to leave spending issues to Congress was restated a decade later when the social security program was also challenged on the grounds that monies were being directed to the elderly, not for the general welfare. Said Justice Benjamin N. Cardozo for a court majority: "The conception of the spending power . . . [must find a point somewhere] between particular and general. . . . There is a middle ground . . . in which discretion is large. The discretion, however, is not confided to the Court. The discretion belongs to Congress, unless the choice is clearly wrong."

The courts have ever since refused to review Congress's power to spend money. They have also conceded to Congress the right to attach any regulations to any aid Congress provides. In 1987 Congress provided a grant to state governments for the maintenance of their highways, but conditioned 5 percent of the funds on state willingness to raise the drinking age from eighteen to twenty-one. The connection between the appropriation and the regulation was based on the assumption that youths under the age of twenty-one are more likely to drive after drinking than those over twenty-one. Presumably, building more roads would only encourage more inebriated young people to drive on them. Despite the fact that the connection between the appropriation and the regulation was problematic, the Supreme Court ruled that Congress could attach any reasonable conditions to its grants to the states. State sovereignty was not violated, because any state could choose not to accept the money.

In short, the courts have virtually given up the doctrine of judicial review when it comes to matters on which Congress can spend money. As a consequence, most national efforts to influence state governments come in the form of federal grants. Federal aid can also be used to influence local governments, such as counties, cities, towns, villages, and school districts. These local governments, from a constitutional point of view, are mere creatures of the state of which they are part. They have no independent sovereignty.

*The Contemporary Price of Federalism*

If constitutional doctrine has evolved to the point that dual sovereign theory has been put to rest, this does not mean that federalism has come to an end. Although ultimate sovereignty resides with the national government, state and local governments still have certain characteristics and capabilities that make them constituent components of a federal system. * * * Two characteristics of federalism are fundamental. First, citizens elect officials of their choice for each level of government. Unless the authority of each level of government rests in the people, it will become the agent of the other. Second, each level of government raises money through taxation from the citizens residing in the area for which it is responsible. It is hard to see how a system could be regarded as federal unless each level of government can levy taxes on its residents. Unless each level of government can raise its own fiscal resources, it cannot act independently.

Although the constitutional authority of the national government has steadily expanded, state and local governments remain of great practical significance. Almost half of all government spending for domestic (as distinct from foreign and military) purposes is paid for out of taxes raised by state and local governments.

The sharing of control over domestic policy among levels of government has many benefits, but federalism still exacts its price. It can lead to great regional inequalities. Also, the need for establishing cooperative relationships among governments can contribute to great inefficiency in the administration of government programs.

## DISCUSSION QUESTIONS

1. What is the constitutional basis for federalism?

2. How has the relationship between state governments and the national government changed since the early years of the Republic?

3. Does a federal system serve our needs today? Does the federal government have too much power relative to the states? What would be the advantages and disadvantages of a reduced federal presence in state matters?

# "The Framers' Design"

## Jonathan H. Adler

*Starting with the landmark case* United States v. Lopez *in 1995, the Supreme Court has become increasingly activist in the area of federalism. In overruling precedents and striking down laws passed by Congress, the Court is substantially circumscribing the powers of Congress and protecting the sovereignty of the states. By significantly revising the interpretation of the complex constitutional mix of commerce clause powers and the Tenth, Eleventh, and Fourteenth Amendments, the Court has altered the balance of power between Congress and the states across a broad range of issues: guns in schools (as mentioned by Adler), the Violence Against Women Act, the Religious Freedom Restoration Act, the Americans with Disabilities Act, age discrimination, patents, gun control, and English as a state's official language. In each instance the power of the national government was limited or the power of the states was enhanced.*

*Jonathan Adler summarizes this as the "most important doctrinal shift during Chief Justice William Rehnquist's tenure" and labels it a return to "dual sovereignty." In the wake of the terrorist attacks on the United States, many commentators have argued that this version of federalism is "obsolete" or a "luxury of peaceful times." Not so, Adler says. Although it is true that the federal government has been thrust into the center of many policy debates after the terrorist attacks and taken the lead in protecting the homeland, Adler argues that this is perfectly consistent with "dual sovereignty." The national government* should *be taking the lead in protecting our nation, and, obviously, in fighting the war on terrorism overseas. However, he also notes that the terrorist attacks may actually strengthen the model of dual sovereignty by forcing the national government to focus on its central responsibilities and leave the rest to the states.*

The most important doctrinal shift during Chief Justice William Rehnquist's tenure has been the revival of federalism. In a series of decisions over the past decade, a slim majority on the Court has resurrected the principle of "dual sovereignty" embedded in the Constitution's text and structure. At the same time, the Court has begun to reaffirm that our federal government is one of limited and enumerated powers.

The Rehnquist Court's federalism jurisprudence has not been well received in all quarters. Many legal commentators have derided the Court's effort to restore the proper federal-state balance. In the wake of

September 11, some even claim concern for federalism is obsolete. "The Supreme Court's federalism revolution has been overtaken by events," declared Linda Greenhouse of the *New York Times*. "Federalism was a luxury of peaceful times," commented Walter Dellinger, acting solicitor general for the Clinton administration. (Note his use of the past tense.) Federalist arguments today "seem as out of date as a John C. Calhoun speech advocating battle with the Northern states," editorialized the Newark *Star-Ledger*. Others label the Rehnquist Court's federalist jurisprudence as "unrealistic" or "quaint." To at least one legal historian, federalism is "dangerous" in the wake of terrorist attacks on American soil. These criticisms evince a misunderstanding of the Court's federalist revival and, more fundamentally, of the principles at the heart of our Constitutional structure. Federalism is not about state sovereignty, as such, nor is federalist jurisprudence inherently hostile to the national government. Rather, the Constitution creates a system of "dual sovereignty." The Constitution explicitly enumerates those powers which may be exercised by Congress, such as coining money, declaring war, raising armies, issuing patents, and regulating commerce "among the several States." In each of these areas, the federal government's power is supreme. In virtually all others, however, state authority is plenary, limited only by an obligation to observe constitutionally guaranteed rights. As the Tenth Amendment reminds us, "The powers not delegated to the United States by the Constitution, nor prohibited by it to the States, are reserved to the States respectively, or to the people." There is nothing wrong with a vigorous federal government so long as its efforts are confined to the proper sphere.

Much as the separation of powers within the federal government limits the accumulation of excessive power in any single branch, the division of authority between the federal and state government further protects liberty from government encroachment. As James Madison explained in *The Federalist* No. 51, the division of power between "two distinct governments"—federal and state—creates a "double security" for individual liberty. "The different governments will control each other, at the same time that each will be controlled by itself." State power is limited further by interjurisdictional competition. State governments that impose excessive burdens on their own citizens will lose out to those that do not. If a state raises taxes too high or fails to control crime, its citizens will migrate elsewhere.

The most important federalism decision was probably *United States v. Lopez*, in which the Court struck down the national Gun-Free School Zones Act (GFSZA). Congress claimed that GFSZA was a proper exercise of its power to regulate interstate commerce. A majority of the Court rightly disagreed. Carrying a gun to school is neither commercial nor is it interstate. Treating the GFSZA as a regulation of commerce would obliterate the very notion of limited and enumerated powers. School safety is not a federal responsibility. It, like defining and enforcing most criminal law, is the province of the states. Striking down the GFSZA does not risk the safety of our children. State and local officials are no less capable of protecting children than are the Feds. Indeed, federal interference can cause affirmative harm, both by obstructing local efforts as well as by diverting federal resources from truly national concerns.

Admittedly the Rehnquist Court has been more aggressive protecting state sovereignty than policing the outer bounds of Congress's constitutional authority. The Supreme Court has been particularly resolute about protecting state sovereign immunity from private lawsuits under the Eleventh Amendment, but more reluctant to hold Congress to the limits of its constitutionally enumerated powers. The Court's majority has invalidated only the most egregious examples of federal overreaching, while reinforcing federalist principles by adopting narrow interpretations of federal statutes. It is understandably reluctant to wage a frontal assault on congressional authority.

Legal prognosticators may foresee an end to the Supreme Court's devotion to federalism in the World Trade Center rubble. Yet they may be projecting nothing more than their own political preferences. There is no reason why an aggressive federal response to foreign and domestic terrorist threats requires reconsidering the balance of federalism. Protecting the nation from foreign threats, whether through diplomacy or military force, is quintessentially a federal responsibility. Rooting out cave dwelling thugs in the mountains of Afghanistan is a proper exercise of federal power, notes Michael Greve of AEI's Federalism Project; regulating private land-use to protect cave bugs in Texas is not. If anything is a "luxury of peaceful times" it is an unserious Congress that wastes their time and our money on symbolic exercises of federal power, from the promotion of school uniforms to the federal prosecution of deadbeat dads.

The importance of not overburdening the federal government with parochial concerns is not lost on some in the Bush administration. Recent reports suggest a reorientation of FBI resources toward counter-terrorism and national security, and away from run-of-the-mill criminal prosecutions. The bureau will devote less attention to bank robbers and carjackers so that it may focus on foreign operatives and terrorist threats. In other words, the national police force will focus on truly national threats, leaving traditional crime fighting to state and local officials. This is federalism in action.

Critics of the Rehnquist Court scoff at adhering to a document written over 200 years ago, and are particularly hostile to the notion that federal power is limited by the constitutional text. Federalism may have been great back then, we hear, but national "emergencies" from the Great Depression to the new terrorist threat justify departures from the Framers' design. To the contrary, the post–September 11 challenges facing

America show our constitutional structure is as important and relevant as ever.

## DISCUSSION QUESTIONS

1. Adler covers some of the key cases in arguing that the national government is playing its appropriate role in fighting terrorism ("protecting the nation from foreign threats" and "rooting out cave-dwelling thugs in the mountains of Afghanistan"), but he omits some of the other policy areas in which debates over national governmental power and federalism have become central in the wake of the terrorist attacks: airport security, public health, law enforcement, and civil liberties. To what extent should the federal government take over in these areas, and to what extent should these responsibilities be left to the states (or the free market)?

2. More specifically, does the threat of anthrax or smallpox or other dangers posed by biological and chemical weapons mean that the federal government needs to coordinate many aspects of our decentralized public health system? Or should management of the public health system still be left to the states or the free market?

3. In general, where should one draw the line in terms of the appropriate boundaries between national and state control over policy?

## DEBATING THE ISSUES: THE FUTURE OF FEDERALISM

"Devolution," the shift in power from the national government to the states, has been very popular in Washington, D.C., and among state governors in the past decade. Supporters of the concept point to the Tenth Amendment to the Constitution, which says that all powers not granted to the federal government are reserved to the states. They also argue that state and local government is "closer to the people," is a good source of new policy ideas, and provides for a range of policy options across the states. State governments have sought more control over public policy within their borders over a broad range of issues, including welfare reform, health care, educational funding, and inner-city redevelopment. In the 1990s, this view had strong support from a Republican Congress, which favored greater state control, and a Democratic president who was eager to improve the delivery of public services. The previous reading explored the impact of the terrorist attacks on the balance of power between the state and national governments in the current administration, and the three authors in this section explore many aspects of the future of federalism.

Justice Clarence Thomas is one of the strongest supporters on the bench of state-centered federalism. As noted in other readings in this chapter, the Supreme Court has limited the power of Congress and enhanced the position of the states over a broad range of issues. Justice Thomas provides some insight into why the Court has moved in this direction. In a speech in honor of James Madison at James Madison University, Thomas applauds Madison's defense of the "double security" that was necessary to protect people from the tyranny of the majority. Federalism, Thomas argues, is the forgotten half of this double security (with the system of checks and balances and separation of powers being the "security" at the national level that receives all the attention). Not only does state-centered federalism protect individual liberty, but it promotes healthy competition between the states (allowing people to "vote with their feet" in terms of which mix of policies they like best). Perhaps most importantly, federalism also provides a check on national power.

Martha Derthick has a different take on the balance of power between the national government and the states. She argues that much of the devolution of power to the states is not as significant as it seems. She examines three aspects of the political system—recent Supreme Court decisions on federalism, elections, and policy—and concludes that there is strong evidence that the national government is still at the center of these concerns. Even after considering the three policy areas in which devolution was supposed to be the most pronounced (welfare, education, and criminal justice), Derthick concludes that evidence in support of devolution is "murky" at best. For example, the widely cited welfare reform in 1996 *did* return power to the states on that specific policy, but annual spending on welfare, shortly after the plan was implemented, was only $22 billion a year, compared to the $431 billion that was still spent on income support programs at the national level. There is no reason to think that the disparity in these relative sizes is likely to change.

Donold F. Kettl has a much more pragmatic view of the future of federalism. He argues that it is a "quixotic quest" (and basically a waste of time) to try to figure out which level of government should take on which tasks. Instead, he lists eight specific recommendations on how to shift from "inputs and formulas" to "outcomes and results." This focus is an attempt to move the debate over federalism to less partisan grounds and to "modernize the American system of governmental relations."

# 15

# Speech at James Madison University

## CLARENCE THOMAS

What is it about our Constitution that has allowed this great nation to enjoy unprecedented political stability and economic and social prosperity for more than two centuries? There are two things that stand above all else: First, the principles upon which the American Constitutional order is based are universal principles, applicable to all people at all times. Second, Madison and other Framers made a significant advance in politics and political theory, an advance that allowed them to create a government strong enough to defend itself and the liberties of its people, yet limited enough, that it would itself not become the destroyer of the self same liberties. * * *

*[After discussing freedom, liberty, and the potential tyranny of government, Justice Thomas turned his attention to federalism]*

* * * But what has escaped notice of late, and perhaps once for very good reason, is that the Framers established another structural safeguard for individual liberty, and I'm speaking here of federalism. Federalism sometimes has been used to justify what I would consider the most terrible tragedies ever inflicted by Americans on Americans—slavery and segregation. I might add that slavery was the glaring contradiction to

the core principles underlying the Constitution. For that reason, the idea of state sovereignty has rightly earned a negative connotation. Nonetheless, federalism, in and of itself, is not an evil or a good. It is just a construct, just as the separation of powers is a construct. They are both means that serve certain ends. They are not ends in and of themselves. It was slavery and segregation, not federalism; the men and women who perpetuated both slavery and segregation were those who committed the wrongs and who perverted the American system of government for their own ends and their own prejudices. It was not federalism. Rightly understood, federalism can advance the same goal as that pursued by the separation of powers or the enumeration of limited federal powers or the Bill of Rights.

I suggest that all of these mechanisms have the same purpose: to protect individual liberty and the private ordering of social life, what we sometimes call today, a civil society. The Framers did not believe that separating powers alone would be sufficient to guard against tyrannical government. They saw, for example, that the three branches of the national government could collude in an unconstitutional exercise of power. In order to protect against this possibility, the Framers created a federal, not purely national, system of government. And federalism was to play a purpose similar to that of the separation of powers. As Madison wrote in *Federalist* No. 51, "In the compound republic of America, the power surrendered by the people is first divided between two distinct governments, and then the portion alloted to each, subdivided among distinct and separate departments. Hence, a double security arises to the rights of the people. The different governments will control each other at the same time that each will be controlled by itself." In other words, federalism provides a check on the national government when the separation of legislative from executive from judicial powers alone cannot do the job or does not do it. Madison does not say that federalism necessarily exists to protect the states as institutions, although, that's a subsidiary effect. Rather, federalism, like the separation of powers exists to protect the rights of the people.

This is a theme that has gone unnoticed but which underlies the Court's current federalism jurisprudence. The Court has not always fully explained the larger purposes behind this resurrection of federalism. This is only to be expected. As judges, the members of the Court are more focused on deciding the cases before us, as presented by the facts and as shaped by precedent, rather than articulating broad principles from the outset. Nonetheless, the Court has come in for some sharp criticism, in part, because the restoration of federalism seems to some to be senseless or without purpose. They can't see the overall picture. For me, however, federalism promotes the same purpose as that served by other broad structures of our federal constitution, such as the enumeration of limited federal powers, the Bill of Rights and the separation of powers.

This multiplicity of constitutional mechanisms checks and controls governmental power, so that a sphere of private activity and individual freedom can flourish free and independent from state interference.

Federalism helps accomplish this goal in a number of ways: it enhances self-government by creating a local decision-making system that is closer to the people and, hence, more responsive to their wishes. States will retain jurisdiction over most of the policies that affect the daily lives of their citizens and so they can play a creative role in defining individual rights. States not only tailor national programs to local conditions and needs, the rather bleak role assigned to them by some. They also provide innovation in creating and protecting new rights, an insight that Justice Brennan recognized, urging states to create rights that went beyond the federal Bill of Rights. At a broader level, the existence of numerous states, each making certain decisions concerning the allocation of resources and the balance between public power and private rights creates a beneficial marketplace of policies. Since people can vote with their feet by moving to states with whose policies they agree, they force the states into a competition to offer policies that best protect individuals and their rights. States can even virtuously compete with the federal government to better protect the individual rights of their citizens.

But federalism provides more than just a decentralized decision-making system. One might think that federalism serves a purpose in protecting individual liberties simply by defusing power among many different political centers, such as states. That could be achieved just as easily by creating administrative subdivisions with a larger national government, as is the case with many European nations with strong centralized governments. And these nations, to say the least, have not demonstrated a history of protection for individual liberties that has characterized the American experience. Our system of federalism does more than that. It not only defuses power, it also creates independent sovereigns. The state of Virginia, for example, is sovereign in a way that an administrative division of France is not. Virginia has its own government, it has plenary control over certain areas, it administers areas such as criminal law and education, with substantial, if not complete, policy-making freedom. Its governmental operations cannot be commandeered or taxed by another sovereign.

Yet, states do not have sovereignty for sovereignty's sake. Instead, the Framers believed that these sovereigns would have an interest in monitoring the activities of the federal government and ensuring that it lives within its enumerated authorities. Keeping the government within the written limits on its power is not a goal in and of itself. Rather, the Framers believed that controlling the federal government through the recognition and protection of independent state sovereigns was necessary to protect, once again, individual liberty. These state sovereigns would provide both constitutional and political checks upon the powers of the national government. In helping to constrain the federal government, the states would supplement the protections for individual rights as surely as did the Bill of Rights and judicial review. As James Madison declared when he introduced the Bill of Rights in Congress:

> If these amendments are incorporated into the Constitution, independent tribunals of justice will consider themselves in a peculiar manner the guardians of those rights. They will be an impenetrable bulwark against every assumption of powers in the legislature or executive. They will be naturally led to resist every encroachment upon rights expressly stipulated for in the Constitution by the declaration of rights.

Judicial protection of individual rights, however, would not be the only protection. Madison went on to say:

> Besides this security, there is a great probability that such a declaration in the federal system would be enforced because the state legislatures will jealously and closely watch the operations of this government and be able to resist with more effect every assumption of power than any other power on earth can do. And the greatest opponents to a federal government admit the state legislatures to be sure guardians of the people's liberty.

Madison's comments reveal the last, and perhaps most important, way federalism protects individual liberty. States do not serve individual rights by allowing the decentralization of power. They do not protect them merely by being laboratories of democracy, as Justice Brandeis so famously argued. They also exist as the organizers of resistance to the unwarranted exercise of federal powers. As Publius wrote in *Federalist* No. 26, "the state legislature who will always be, not only vigilant, but suspicious and jealous guardians of the rights of the citizens against encroachments by the federal government, from the federal government, will constantly have their attention awake to the conduct of the national rulers and will be ready enough if anything improper appears to sound the alarm to the people and not only be they the voice, but if necessary, the arm of their discontent."

States provide an alternate source of political loyalty and a training ground for future political leaders. The Framers certainly foresaw the possibility that the nation's leaders someday might stray from their duty and seek to expand federal powers for their own benefit. To guard against this, they believed that federalism, by protecting the sovereignty of the states, would create centers of political opposition that could control the excesses of the national government. It is this very sovereignty that the Court continues to protect today. Take away that sovereignty and you undermine the ability of the federalist structure to maintain multiple centers of legal and political power.

Now, some see all these Constitutional checks and balances as bothersome or cumbersome or inconvenient impediments to majority rule. Every age has its important policies that some people believe must be enacted at any cost, regardless of the cost to the constitutional structure.

Far from being a vise though, these checks and balances—the "double security," as Madison called them, double security for our liberties—are the genius of our system of government, and I might add, the genius of James Madison. For what is an impediment to majority will is equally an impediment to governmental tyranny. Surely, no one would contend that the majority itself can do no wrong. Our history is replete with all too many instances in which a temporary majority has pursued its own interest at the expense of the individual rights of the minority. Indeed, perhaps we need even more checks on government. But, at the very least, let us retain and reinvigorate the ones we have. Surely, the lives and the liberty of more than 250 million citizens of this great nation warrant that double security. For our liberties designed by our James Madison and the other Founders should be in working order so that, in the words of Abraham Lincoln, "Government of the people, by the people and for the people shall not perish from the face of this earth." That, my friends, would be a worthy birthday present for Mr. Madison. Thank you.

## 16

## "American Federalism: Half-Full or Half-Empty?"

### Martha Derthick

Last August the *Wall Street Journal* noted that some taxpayers were claiming that they did not have to pay federal income tax because they were residents of a state, not the United States. A few weeks earlier the *New York Times* carried a story describing Vice President Albert Gore's plan to have detailed positions on a wide range of issues in his quest for the Democratic presidential nomination in 2000. At the top of his list was education, a function not long ago considered a preserve of state and local governments.

Gore's "blizzard of positions" included preschool for all children, a ban on gang-style clothing, teacher testing, "second-chance" schools for trouble-prone students, back-to-school parent-teacher meetings where a strict discipline code would be signed, and "character education" courses in the schools. Gore proposed to amend the Family and Medical Leave Act to permit parents to attend the parent-teacher meetings during working hours.

As these contrasting conceptions suggest, American federalism is a highly protean form, long on change and confusion, short on fixed, generally accepted principles. In the event, a tax court judge fined the tax-payers who claimed not to be citizens of the United States. And the *Times* reporter hinted that many actions Gore planned to "require" would need local school board cooperation to take effect.

As the 20th century ends, public commentators often suggest that this is a time of decentralization in the federal system. The view derives mainly from a series of Supreme Court decisions that have sought to rehabilitate the states in constitutional doctrine and from passage of a welfare reform act in 1996 that office-holders and analysts alike inter-preted as radically devolutionary.

But matters are more complicated than that. American federalism was born in ambiguity, it institutionalizes ambiguity in our form of govern-ment, and changes in it tend to be ambiguous too.

To sort out what is happening, I will distinguish among three spheres of activity: constitutional interpretation by the Supreme Court; electoral politics; and the everyday work of government as manifested in policies and programs.

*The Supreme Court*

A narrow majority of the Rehnquist Court led by the chief justice attaches importance to preserving federalism. To that end, it has made a series of daring and controversial decisions that purport to limit the powers of Congress or secure constitutional prerogatives of the states.

In *Printz v. U.S.* (1997) the Court invalidated a provision of the Brady Handgun Violence Prevention Act that required local law enforcement officers to conduct background checks on all gun purchasers. The Court objected that the provision impermissibly violated the Tenth Amend-ment by commandeering the state government to carry out a federal law. An earlier opinion, *New York v. U.S.* (1992), had begun to lay the ground for the anticommandeering principle. In another leading case, *U.S. v. Lopez* (1995), the Court held that Congress had exceeded its commerce clause power by prohibiting guns in school zones. Still other decisions signaled a retreat from federal judicial supervision of school desegre-gation, prison administration, and the judgments of state courts. Another line of cases has secured the state governments' immunity from certain classes of suits under federal law.

Some analysts profess to see a revolutionary development here, but qualifications are in order. The Court decides many cases in which it does not give primacy to federalism, as for example a 7–2 ruling in 1999 that state welfare programs may not restrict new residents to the welfare benefits they would have received in the states from which they moved. This ruling struck down a California law and by implication a provision of federal law that had authorized it. Moreover, the majority that has decided the leading federalism cases is narrow (often 5–4) and tenuous, inasmuch as it includes some of the oldest members of the Court. The decisions have not exactly been hailed by legal scholars, even some who might be thought sympathetic. Charles Fried of the Harvard Law School, a former solicitor general in the Reagan administration, denounced the series of decisions last June on immunity from suits as "bizarre" and "absurd."

If this is a revolution, it is one that may not last.

*Electoral Politics*

Speaker Thomas P. O'Neill's famous aphorism that "all politics is local" applied to virtually all structural aspects of U.S. electoral politics for a very long time. Determining electoral districts and voter qualifications, mobilizing voters, and financing campaigns were the province mainly of state laws and customs and were locally rooted well into this century. But that has ceased to be true under the impact of 20th-century constitutional amendments extending the electorate, as well as federal statutes and judicial decisions governing apportionment and voting rights. Federal supervision now extends even to such matters as ward-based versus at-large elections in local governments. And changes in technology and in social and economic structures mean that candidates for congressional seats or even lesser offices do not depend exclusively on funds raised from local constituencies. Candidates may get help from party committees and interest groups organized on a national scale.

Nationalization of electoral practices proceeds apace at century's end. The Motor Voter Act of 1993 requires states to allow all eligible citizens to register to vote when they apply for or renew a driver's license. It also requires states to allow mail-in registration forms at agencies that supply public assistance, such as welfare checks or help for the disabled. The costs are borne by the states.

Nevertheless, one hesitates to insist that our electoral processes are being comprehensively nationalized at a time when governors seem to have gained an advantage in access to the presidency, growing, arguably, out of the public's now chronic distrust of the national government. Of the four last presidents in this century, three were governors before they were elected, and in the run-up to the 2000 election, a governor, George W. Bush of Texas, has secured a large and early advantage over other Republican candidates. He owes his success partly to other Republican governors—of whom there were 32 after the election of 1998 —who have backed him under the lead of Michigan's John Engler. To find a presidential nomination that originated in the action of elected state officials, one must go all the way back to 1824, when several state legislatures put forth candidates.

*Policies and Programs*

It is necessary to be selective because there are so many policies and programs. I will concentrate on three sets—welfare, schools, and criminal justice—that have traditionally been regarded as quite decentralized. Indeed, for decades they constituted the bedrock of local government activity.

The welfare reform legislation of 1996 is everyone's leading example of decentralization in action. The law converted what had been an open-ended matching grant, with federal funds tied to the number of cases, to a fixed-sum ("block") grant and explicitly ended individuals' entitlements to welfare. States gained freedom to design their own programs, a change already largely effectuated by White House decisions during the Reagan, Bush, and Clinton administrations to grant waivers of certain federal requirements to individual states. The decentralization of program authority in this case was an important change in intergovernmental relations. Still, its significance must be put in perspective.

Whatever may have happened with welfare in 1996, income support, which is the core function of the modern welfare state, has been largely federalized in the United States in the six decades since 1935. Social Security, Supplemental Security Income (SSI), and food stamps accounted for $431 billion in federal spending in 1998, compared with $22 billion for welfare, now known as TANF (or Temporary Assistance for Needy Families). I pass over the earned income tax credit, weighing in at a volume comparable to that for welfare, a use of federal tax law for income support that would take us too far afield here.

Welfare could be decentralized in 1996 in large part because, unlike income support for the aged and the disabled, it had never been fully centralized. The main change in 1996 was a national policy change that strongly discouraged dependency and certain behavior, especially out-of-wedlock pregnancies and lack of child support from fathers, that had come to be associated with welfare. To carry out this policy change, the new law imposed some stringent federal requirements, such as time limits for receipt of welfare, on the states. Surprisingly, a liberal president and conservative members of the new Republican majority in Congress coalesced in support of legislation, but the national coalition was so frail and incomplete that it became necessary to lodge discretion in the states to achieve a result.

That is one of the traditional functions of American federalism: in the absence of agreement at the national level, discretion can be left to the states. Typically, through inaction by Congress, matters are left with the states, which have initial jurisdiction. What was new in 1996 was that AFDC (Aid to Families with Dependent Children) had become sufficiently centralized in the generation since the mid-1960s that giving discretion to the states required an affirmative act. It required giving back some portion of what had been taken away, as much by federal courts as by Congress. "No more individual entitlement," the most arresting phrase in the act, was directed at altering relations between Congress and the federal judiciary. I would argue that the law had at least as much significance for what it said about interbranch relations at the federal level as about relations among governments in the federal system.

Elementary and secondary education, far from being off-limits to national politicians as a local matter, has risen to the top of their rhetorical agenda. It took a year for Congress to reauthorize the Elementary and Secondary Education Act in 1993–94. The resulting law consumed 14 titles and 1,200 pages, covering subjects as wide-ranging as academic standards, racial desegregation, language assessments, migrant education, teacher training, math and science equipment, libraries, hate-crime prevention, vouchers, school prayer, sex education, gay rights, gun control, the handicapped, English as a second language, telecommunications, pornography, single-sex schools, national tests, home schooling, drugs, smoking—and more. The level of detail was minute. Any state receiving federal funds had to require that any student who brought a gun to school would be expelled for at least a year. Local officials could, however, modify the requirement on a case-by-case basis. School districts also had to refer offenders to local law enforcement officials. Developmentally disabled students were subject to the expulsion rule, but if school officials established that their behavior was related to their disability, the students could be placed in an alternative educational setting for up to 45 days instead.

In 1999, when the act was again up for reauthorization, Congress by wide margins enacted "Ed-Flex," the Educational Flexibility Partnership Demonstration Act, which authorized the Secretary of Education to implement a nationwide program under which state educational agencies could apply for waivers of certain federal rules. To be eligible for Ed-Flex, states had to develop educational content and performance standards and procedures for holding districts and schools accountable for meeting educational goals. One could point to this law, of course, as an example of decentralization; members of Congress naturally did so. But in education as in welfare, the subject of waivers would never have arisen had not a vast body of law and regulation developed from which relief had to be sought.

In criminal justice, it remains true that most police and prosecutors are state and local officials. Ninety-five percent of prosecutions are handled by state and local governments. Yet federal criminal law has grown explosively as Congress has taken stands against such offenses as carjacking and church burning, disrupting a rodeo and damaging a livestock facility. A 1999 task force report of the American Bar Association documented and decried this development but is unlikely to stop, let alone reverse it.

*The "Mores" of Intergovernmental Relations*

In everyday affairs, how do we and our officials think and talk about governments in the federal system? Without having any evidence to support my point, I would argue that citizens and journalists routinely refer to "the government" as if there were only one—the Big One. That this is a country of many governments, though a patent fact, is nonetheless a fact that it takes a pedant or a lawyer to insist on.

Moreover, we are now accustomed to reading that Washington is giving orders to the states, or at least exhorting them to act in regard to one or another matter in which they have been found deficient. Some sample headlines from end-of-century stories in the *New York Times* would appear very odd to a student of American government who had gone to sleep in, say, 1955 and just awakened: "Clinton to Require State Efforts to Cut Drug Use in Prisons" (January 12, 1998); "White House Plans Medicaid Coverage of Viagra by States" (May 28, 1998); "Clinton to Chide States for Failing to Cover Children" (August 8, 1999). None of this is to say that the states promptly act on orders or admonitions from Washington, only that Washington is accustomed to giving them, without pausing to question the appropriateness of doing so—as is evident from an executive order on federalism that the Clinton administration issued, suspended when state officials angrily protested, and then issued in much revised form.

The offending order, issued in May 1998, contained a set of criteria for policymaking by federal agencies that was broad and inclusive enough invariably to justify federal government action: "(1) When the matter to be addressed by federal action occurs interstate as opposed to being contained within one State's boundaries. (2) When the source of the matter to be addressed occurs in a State different from the State (or States) where a significant amount of the harm occurs. (3) When there is a need for uniform national standards. (4) When decentralization increases the costs of government thus imposing additional burdens on the taxpayer. (5) When States have not adequately protected individual rights and liberties. (6) When States would be reluctant to impose necessary regulations because of fears that regulated business activity will relocate to other States. . . ." Only the most obtuse and indolent federal administrator could not have put this list to use.

The revised executive order, issued following consultation with state officials, was completely different. The section on policymaking criteria called for "strict adherence to constitutional principles," avoiding limits on policymaking discretion of the states except with constitutional and statutory authority, granting "maximum administrative discretion" to the states, encouraging states to "develop their own policies to achieve program objectives," where possible deferring to the states to "establish standards," consulting with appropriate state and local officials "as to the need for national standards," and consulting with them in developing national standards when such were found to be necessary.

It is hard to imagine a more complete about-face. It is also hard to know how to interpret the event. One can cite the original order as evidence of the imperious attitudes that high federal officials actually bring to intergovernmental relations, or one can cite the revision as evidence of the continuing power of the states. In studying American federalism, the analyst is forever asking whether the glass is half-empty or half-full. That is the appropriate question as the century turns, and the answers are to be found more in the day-to-day operations of intergovernmental relations than in either Supreme Court decisions or executive orders. It requires a blind eye to call ours an era of devolution. But even with two sharp eyes, it is hard to detect a plain answer. Everywhere one looks, the answer remains murky and many-sided.

# 17

# "Real-Life Federalism"

## Donald F. Kettl

Suppose you were writing a new initiative to modernize the American system of intergovernmental relations. And suppose you wanted to escape the old tactics and arguments and get down to a strategy for an effective federal system in the age of information. How would you go about it?

Since the Bush administration happens to be engaged in such a project right now, these are more than just academic questions. Let me see if I can offer a few tentative answers. One thing not to do is resurrect the ageless debate about "sorting out" government functions. This has long been like the medieval search for the philosopher's stone: It assumes a mystical vision of just which level of government ought to perform which functions, and a corresponding flow of both money and power.

But it's a quixotic quest. There never was a time when Americans clearly sorted out which public entities ought to do what. Even if they had, the "sorting out" approach is a poor match for 21st-century burdens. Rigid roles and functions won't fit new problems that insist on spilling over every boundary.

Another thing not to do is focus on the old debates about cash and formulas. Except for Medicaid and a few other entitlement programs, federal aid to states and localities topped off in the Carter administration. The crucial issues these days are regulatory, not fiscal.

The real dilemma is that state and local problems vary enormously around the country, and uniform federal policy has rarely taken this into account. Congress and the president expect national policies to be applied nationally, when in fact this has frequently become almost impossible.

That's a brief outline of strategies to avoid. Here's a list of better ideas that need to be considered:

1. Use federal aid to fund results, not programs. Too much of the intergovernmental aid system is hung up on formulas and inputs, not outcomes and benefits. Bush's education proposals stirred a host of battles, but at least they were over the right issue: How can we use the funding to achieve national goals without undermining local flexibility?

2. Employ performance measurement to cement cross-agency partnerships. The Government Performance and Results Act requires federal agencies to measure their progress in achieving outcomes. The Office of Management and Budget could use its powers of review to insist that federal agencies break out of their "stovepipe" mentalities and work together.

3. Use the federal "bully pulpit" to galvanize action. The Federal Emergency Management Agency has quietly transformed itself from a bureaucracy that arrives after a disaster to write checks into one that tries to reduce or eliminate the damage in advance. It's better, FEMA officials smartly reasoned, to work with homeowners and builders to keep roofs from blowing off in a hurricane than to deal with the consequences after a storm. More of this could reduce costs and improve service.

4. Create the presumption of "yes." One of the big irritants for state and local officials is the presumption of federal officials that the feds know best in every situation. Whenever states or localities propose new ideas, the burden of proof is placed on them. What if that burden were reversed—and federal officials decided that they would approve any plausible request as long as state and local officials could promise performance gains?

5. Launch "Reverse RFPs [Request for Proposals]." Most federal aid programs work by putting out the money and setting forth the rules. Instead, Congress could earmark a percentage of current aid money for state, local and regional governments to devise their own innovative rules and solutions to problems that cross existing boundaries.

6. Transform federal regional offices into service coordination centers. Although they have long been a backwater in federal management,

beefed-up federal regional offices could be the places where functionally organized federal agencies link their programs to make effective place-based action. This step, however, requires that top federal officials make regional offices important players in the management system.

7. Create real incentives and consequences for partnership. Everyone salutes the intergovernmental flag, but the system imposes few penalties for failing to live up to the principles. OMB could use the performance measurement law and the annual budget process to enforce coordination.

8. Develop a new navigation principle to guide the partnerships. This means a change of focus at the very top, from managing programs to producing and assessing results. It means a federal government committed to steering the system instead of controlling it. Someone will have to be at the helm. It makes the most sense to build and operate the system within the OMB.

No doubt a federalism strategy such as this one would attract substantial flak from many different quarters. But if we're serious about crafting federalism for the information age, this is roughly what it will have to look like. It's time to shift from inputs and formulas to outcomes and results.

## DISCUSSION QUESTIONS

1. Consider the original version of President Clinton's executive order concerning federalism that is discussed by Derthick. What would the impact of this executive order have been on intergovernmental relations if President Clinton had not revised the order?

2. Do you agree with Justice Thomas's arguments about the advantages of devolving power to the states and maintaining federalism as a check on national power?

3. There are important empirical and normative questions concerning the devolution of power to the states. Derthick tackles the empirical question (Has power really shifted that much?), without directly addressing the normative issues. Thomas, on the other hand, is primarily focused on the normative side (The shift of power to the states is good). A critic of devolution would point to the wide variation among states in terms of both resources and policy responses. Some states are extremely poor and cannot tackle policy problems in innovative ways. In terms of welfare, for example, some states, such as Idaho, have simply cut social welfare programs, while others, such as Wisconsin, have aggressively experimented in a variety of new areas. Does the variation in resources across states raise significant concerns for devolution? Critics of devolution would also

raise the following questions: Will states protect the civil rights of racial and political minorities? Are all states capable of administering complex programs such as job training, child-care services, and other welfare-reform initiatives? Are states inherently better able to serve the needs of their residents than Washington officials?

4. What would be the impact of adopting Kettl's suggestions in terms of the balance of power between the state and national governments? Who do you think would be more likely to support these proposals—state governors, the U.S. Congress, or the national bureaucracy? Who would be most likely to oppose them?

# CHAPTER 4

# The Constitutional Framework and the Individual: Civil Liberties and Civil Rights

*In the next two selections, Abraham Lincoln and Martin Luther King, Jr., take opposing points of view about how to achieve peaceful change in a civil society. What happens when the fight for justice and equality comes into conflict with the rule of law? Are people ever justified in breaking laws for what they perceive to be the greater good? Is civil disobedience justified in some contexts?*

*In a speech that he delivered twenty-three years before becoming president, Lincoln argues that the laws must be followed, as without adherence to laws we have no civil society. Change, Lincoln stresses, must come from working within the system. King disagrees, arguing that while people have a moral obligation to follow just laws, they have an equally compelling duty to break unjust laws through nonviolent means. In his "Letter from Birmingham Jail," which he addressed to more-conservative religious leaders in the civil rights movement who were concerned about his tactics, King outlined procedures for distinguishing between just and unjust laws, and for resisting those laws that are unjust. It is ironic that despite Lincoln's admonitions about working within the system, it was under his leadership that the nation fought its bloodiest war precisely because the central issues of states' rights and slavery could not be solved within the system. King, on the other hand, who argued in favor of breaking unjust laws, was actually instrumental in putting pressure on Congress (the "system") to change those laws that he and others in the civil rights movement considered unjust.*

*Current battles over abortion and the environment show the debate between Lincoln and King to be timeless. Activists in both policy areas have been decried as "radical" or "extremist" because of occasional civil disobedience against legal activities. Some environmentalists have prevented lumber harvesting by putting spikes in trees; some pro-life activists have blocked women's access to abortion clinics. And in the abortion case, as with the Lincoln-King debate, issues of civil rights and civil liberties intersect.*

# 18

# "The Perpetuation of Our Political Institutions"

### Abraham Lincoln

In the great journal of things happening under the sun, we, the American People, find our account running, under date of the nineteenth century of the Christian era. We find ourselves in the peaceful possession, of the fairest portion of the earth, as regards extent of territory, fertility of soil, and salubrity of climate. We find ourselves under the government of a system of political institutions, conducing more essentially to the ends of civil and religious liberty, than any of which the history of former times tells us. We, when mounting the stage of existence, found ourselves the legal inheritors of these fundamental blessings. We toiled not in the acquirement or establishment of them—they are a legacy bequeathed us, by a *once* hardy, brave, and patriotic, but *now* lamented and departed race of ancestors. Theirs was the task (and nobly they performed it) to possess themselves, and through themselves, us, of this goodly land; and to uprear upon its hills and its valleys, a political edifice of liberty and equal rights; 'tis ours only, to transmit these, the former, unprofaned by the foot of an invader; the latter, undecayed by the lapse of time and untorn by usurpation, to the latest generation that fate shall permit the world to know. This task of gratitude to our fathers, justice to ourselves, duty to posterity, and love for our species in general, all imperatively required us faithfully to perform.

How then shall we perform it? At what point shall we expect the approach of danger? By what means shall we fortify against it? Shall we expect some transatlantic military giant, to step the ocean, and crush us at a blow? Never! All the armies of Europe, Asia and Africa combined, with all the treasure of the earth (our own excepted) in their military chest; with a Buonaparte for a commander, could not by force take a drink from the Ohio, or make a track on the Blue Ridge, in a trial of a thousand years.

At what point then is the approach of danger to be expected? I answer, if it ever reach us, it must spring up amongst us. It cannot come from abroad. If destruction be our lot, we must ourselves be its author and finisher. As a nation of freemen, we must live through all time, or die by suicide.

I hope I am over wary; but if I am not, there is, even now, something of ill-omen amongst us. I mean the increasing disregard for law which pervades the country; the growing disposition to substitute the wild and furious passions, in lieu of the sober judgment of Courts; and the worse than savage mobs, for the executive ministers of justice. This disposition is awfully fearful in any community; and that it now exists in ours, though grating to our feelings to admit, it would be a violation of truth, and an insult to our intelligence, to deny. Accounts of outrages committed by mobs, form the everyday news of the times. They have pervaded the country, from New England to Louisiana; they are neither peculiar to the eternal snows of the former, nor the burning suns of the latter; they are not the creature of climate—neither are they confined to the slaveholding, or the non-slaveholding States. Alike, they spring up among the pleasure hunting masters of Southern slaves, and the order loving citizens of the land of steady habits. Whatever, then, their cause may be, it is common to the whole country.

It would be tedious, as well as useless, to recount the horrors of all of them. Those happening in the State of Mississippi, and at St. Louis, are, perhaps, the most dangerous in example and revolting to humanity. In the Mississippi case, they first commenced by hanging the regular gamblers; a set of men, certainly not following for a livelihood, a very useful, or very honest occupation; but one which, so far from being forbidden by the laws, was actually licensed by an act of the Legislature, passed but a single year before. Next, negroes, suspected of conspiring to raise an insurrection, were caught up and hanged in all parts of the State: then, white men, supposed to be leagued with the negroes; and finally, strangers, from neighboring States, going thither on business, were, in many instances, subjected to the same fate. Thus went on this process of hanging, from gamblers to negroes, from negroes to white citizens, and from these to strangers; till, dead men were seen literally dangling from the boughs of trees upon every road side; and in numbers almost sufficient, to rival the native Spanish moss of the country, as a drapery of the forest.

Turn, then, to that horror-striking scene at St. Louis. A single victim was only sacrificed there. His story is very short; and is, perhaps, the most highly tragic, of anything of its length, that has ever been witnessed in real life. A mulatto man, by the name of McIntosh, was seized in the street, dragged to the suburbs of the city, chained to a tree, and actually burned to death; and all within a single hour from the time he had been a freeman, attending to his own business, and at peace with the world.

Such are the effects of mob law; and such are the scenes, becoming more and more frequent in this land so lately famed for love of law and order; and the stories of which have even now grown too familiar, to attract any thing more than an idle remark.

But you are, perhaps, ready to ask, "What has this to do with the perpetuation of our political institutions?" I answer, it has much to do with it. Its direct consequences are, comparatively speaking, but a small evil; and much of its danger consists, in the proneness of our minds, to regard its direct as its only consequences. Abstractly considered, the hanging of the gamblers at Vicksburg was of but little consequence. They constitute a portion of population that is worse than useless in any community; and their death, if no pernicious example be set by it, is never matter of reasonable regret with anyone. If they were annually swept from the stage of existence by the plague or small pox, honest men would, perhaps, be much profited by the operation. Similar too, is the correct reasoning, in regard to the burning of the negro at St. Louis. He had forfeited his life, by the perpetration of an outrageous murder, upon one of the most worthy and respectable citizens of the city; and had he not died as he did, he must have died by the sentence of the law, in a very short time afterwards. As to him alone, it was as well the way it was, as it could otherwise have been. But the example in either case was fearful. When men take it in their heads today, to hang gamblers, or burn murderers, they should recollect, that, in the confusion usually attending such transactions, they will be as likely to hang or burn someone who is neither a gambler nor a murderer as one who is; and that, acting upon the example they set, the mob of tomorrow, may, and probably will, hang or burn some of them by the very same mistake. And not only so; the innocent, those who have ever set their faces against violations of law in every shape, alike with the guilty, fall victims to the ravages of mob law; and thus it goes on, step by step, till all the walls erected for the defence of the persons and property of individuals, are trodden down, and disregarded. But all this even, is not the full extent of the evil. By such examples, by instances of the perpetrators of such acts going unpunished, the lawless in spirit are encouraged to become lawless in practice; and having been used to no restraint, but dread of punishment, they thus become absolutely unrestrained. Having ever regarded Government as their deadliest bane, they make a jubilee of the suspension of its operations; and pray for nothing so much as its total annihilation. While, on the other hand, good men, men who love tranquility, who desire to abide by the laws, and enjoy their benefits, who would gladly spill their blood in the defence of their country; seeing their property destroyed; their families insulted, and their lives endangered; their persons injured; and seeing nothing in prospect that forebodes a change for the better; become tired of, and disgusted with, a Government that offers them no protection; and are not much averse to a change in which they imagine they have nothing to lose. Thus, then, by the operation of this mobocratic spirit, which all must admit is now abroad in the land, the strongest bulwark of any Government, and particularly of those constituted like ours, may effectually be broken down and destroyed—I mean the *attachment* of the People. Whenever this effect shall be produced among us, whenever the vicious portion of population shall be permitted to gather in bands of hundreds and thousands, and burn churches, ravage and rob provision-stores, throw printing presses into rivers, shoot editors, and hang and burn obnoxious persons at pleasure, and with impunity, depend on it, this Government cannot last. By such things, the feelings of the best citizens will become more or less alienated from it; and thus it will be left without friends, or with too few, and those few too weak, to make their friendship effectual. At such a time and under such circumstances, men of sufficient talent and ambition will not be wanting to seize the opportunity, strike the blow, and overturn that fair fabric which for the last half century has been the fondest hope of the lovers of freedom, throughout the world.

I know the American People are *much* attached to their Government; I know they would suffer *much* for its sake; I know they would endure evils long and patiently, before they would ever think of exchanging it for another. Yet, notwithstanding all this, if the laws be continually despised and disregarded, if their rights to be secure in their persons and property are held by no better tenure than the caprice of a mob, the alienation of their affections from the Government is the natural consequence; and to that, sooner or later, it must come.

Here then, is one point at which danger may be expected.

The question recurs, "how shall we fortify against it?" The answer is simple. Let every American, every lover of liberty, every well-wisher to his posterity, swear by the blood of the Revolution never to violate in the least particular the laws of the country; and never to tolerate their violation by others. As the patriots of seventy-six did to the support of the Declaration of Independence, so to the support of the Constitution and Laws, let every American pledge his life, his property, and his sacred honor; let every man remember that to violate the law is to trample on the blood of his father, and to tear the character of his own, and his children's liberty. Let reverence for the laws be breathed by every American mother to the lisping babe that prattles on her lap—let it be taught in schools, in seminaries, and in colleges; let it be written in Primers, spelling books, and in Almanacs; let it be preached from the pulpit, proclaimed in legislative halls, and enforced in courts of justice. And, in short, let it become the *political religion* of the nation; and let the old and the young, the rich and the poor, the grave and the gay, of all sexes and tongues, and colors and conditions, sacrifice unceasingly upon its altars.

While ever a state of feeling, such as this, shall universally, or even, very generally prevail throughout the nation, vain will be every effort, and fruitless every attempt, to subvert our national freedom.

When I so pressingly urge a strict observance of all the laws, let me not be understood as saying there are no bad laws, nor that grievances may not arise, for the redress of which, no legal provisions have been made. I mean to say no such thing. But I do mean to say that, although bad laws, if they exist, should be repealed as soon as possible, still while they continue in force, for the sake of example they should be religiously observed. So also in unprovided cases. If such arise, let proper legal provisions be made for them with the least possible delay; but, till then, let them, if not too intolerable, be borne with.

There is no grievance that is a fit object of redress by mob law. In any case that arises, as for instance, the promulgation of abolitionism, one of two positions is necessarily true; that is, the thing is right within itself, and therefore deserves the protection of all law and all good citizens; or, it is wrong, and therefore proper to be prohibited by legal enactments; and in neither case, is the interposition of mob law, either necessary, justifiable, or excusable.

\* \* \*

But this state of feeling *must fade, is fading, has faded,* with the circumstances that produced it.

I do not mean to say, that the scenes of the revolution *are now* or *ever will* be entirely forgotten; but that like everything else, they must fade upon the memory of the world, and grow more and more dim by the lapse of time. In history, we hope, they will be read of, and recounted, so long as the bible shall be read; but even granting that they will, their influence *cannot be* what it heretofore has been. Even then, they *cannot be* so universally known, nor so vividly felt, as they were by the generation just gone to rest. At the close of that struggle, nearly every adult male had been a participator in some of its scenes. The consequence was, that of those scenes, in the form of a husband, a father, a son or a brother, *a living history* was to be found in every family—a history bearing the indubitable testimonies of its own authenticity, in the limbs mangled, in the scars of wounds received, in the midst of the very scenes related— a history, too, that could be read and understood alike by all, the wise and the ignorant, the learned and the unlearned. But *those* histories are gone. They *can* be read no more forever. They *were* a fortress of strength; but, what invading foeman could *never do,* the silent artillery of time *has done*; the leveling of its walls. They are gone. They *were* a forest of giant oaks; but the all-resistless hurricane has swept over them, and left only, here and there, a lonely trunk, despoiled of its verdure, shorn of its foliage; unshading and unshaded, to murmur in a few more gentle breezes, and to combat with its mutilated limbs, a few more ruder storms, then to sink, and be no more.

They *were* the pillars of the temple of liberty; and now that they have crumbled away, that temple must fall, unless we, their descendants, supply their places with other pillars, hewn from the solid quarry of sober reason. Passion has helped us; but can do so no more. It will in future be our enemy. Reason, cold, calculating, unimpassioned reason, must furnish all the materials for our future support and defence. Let those

materials be molded into *general intelligence, sound morality,* and, in particular, *a reverence for the constitution and laws:* and, that we improved to
the last; that we remained free to the last; that we revered his name to
the last; that, during his long sleep, we permitted no hostile foot to pass
over or desecrate his resting place; shall be that which to learn the last
trump shall awaken our WASHINGTON.

Upon these let the proud fabric of freedom rest, as the rock of its
basis; and as truly as has been said of the only greater institution, *"the
gates of hell shall not prevail against it."*

*19*

# "Letter from Birmingham Jail"

## Martin Luther King, Jr.

Source: *Christian Century*, June 12, 1963.

My Dear Fellow Clergymen:

While confined here in the Birmingham City Jail, I came across your recent statement calling my present activities "unwise and untimely." Seldom do I pause to answer criticism of my work and ideas. If I sought to answer all the criticism that cross my desk, my secretaries would have little time for anything other than such correspondence in the course of the day, and I would have no time for constructive work. But since I feel that you are men of genuine goodwill and that your criticisms are sincerely set forth, I want to try to answer your statement in what I hope will be patient and reasonable terms.

I think I should indicate why I am here in Birmingham, since you have been influenced by the view which argues against "outsiders coming in." I have the honor of serving as president of the Southern Christian Leadership Conference, an organization operating in every Southern state, with headquarters in Atlanta, Georgia. We have some eighty-five affiliate organizations across the South, and one of them is the Alabama Christian Movement for Human Rights. Frequently, we share staff, educational, and financial resources with our affiliates. Several months ago the affiliate here in Birmingham asked us to be on call to engage in a nonviolent direct-action program if such were deemed necessary. We readily consented, and when the hour came we lived up to our promise. So I, along with several members of my staff, am here because I was invited here. I am here because I have organizational ties here.

But more basically, I am in Birmingham because injustice exists here. Just as the prophets of the 8th century B.C. left their villages and carried their "thus saith the Lord" far afield, and just as the apostle Paul left his village of Tarsus and carried the gospel of Jesus Christ to the far corners of the Greco-Roman world, so am I compelled to carry the gospel of freedom beyond my own hometown. Like Paul, I must constantly respond to the Macedonian call for aid.*

* [See Acts 16:9.]

Moreover, I am cognizant of the interrelatedness of all communities and states. I cannot sit idly by in Atlanta and not be concerned about what happens in Birmingham. Injustice anywhere is a threat to justice everywhere. We are caught in an inescapable network of mutuality, tied in a single garment of destiny. Whatever affects one directly affects all indirectly. Never again can we afford to live with the narrow, provincial "outside agitator" idea. Anyone who lives inside the United States can never be considered an outsider anywhere within its bounds.

You deplore the demonstrations taking place in Birmingham. But your statement, I am sorry to say, fails to express a similar concern for the conditions that brought about the demonstrations. I am sure that none of you would want to rest content with the superficial kind of social analysis that deals merely with effects and does not grapple with underlying causes. It is unfortunate that demonstrations are taking place in Birmingham, but it is even more unfortunate that the city's white power structure left the Negro community with no alternative.

*  *  *

You may well ask, "Why direct action? Why sit-ins, marches, etc.? Isn't negotiation a better path?" You are quite right in calling for negotiation. Indeed, this is the very purpose of direct action. Nonviolent direct action seeks to foster such a tension that a community which has constantly refused to negotiate is forced to confront the issue. It seeks so to dramatize the issue that it can no longer be ignored. My citing the creation of tension as part of the work of the nonviolent resister may sound rather shocking. But I readily acknowledge that I am not afraid of the word "tension." I have earnestly opposed violent tension, but there is a type of constructive, nonviolent tension which is necessary for growth. Just as Socrates felt that it was necessary to create a tension in the mind so that individuals could shake off the bondage of myths and half-truths and rise to the realm of creative analysis and objective appraisal, so must we see the need for nonviolent gadflies to create the kind of tension in society that will help men rise from the dark depths of prejudice and racism to the majestic heights of understanding and brotherhood.

The purpose of our direct-action program is to create a situation so crisis-packed that it will inevitably open the door to negotiation. I therefore concur with you in your call for negotiation. Too long has our beloved Southland been bogged down in a tragic effort to live in monologue rather than dialogue.

*  *  *

We have waited for more than 340 years for our constitutional and God-given rights. The nations of Asia and Africa are moving with jetlike speed toward gaining political independence, but we still creep at horse-

and-buggy pace toward gaining a cup of coffee at a lunch counter. Perhaps it is easy for those who have never felt the stinging darts of segregation to say "Wait." But when you have seen vicious mobs lynch your mothers and fathers at will and drown your sisters and brothers at whim; when you have seen hate-filled policemen curse, kick, and even kill your black brothers and sisters with impunity; when you see the vast majority of your 20 million Negro brothers smothering in an air-tight cage of poverty in the midst of an affluent society; when you suddenly find your tongue twisted as you seek to explain to your six-year-old daughter why she can't go to the public amusement park that has just been advertised on television, and see tears welling up when she is told that Funtown is closed to colored children, and see ominous clouds of inferiority beginning to form in her little mental sky, and see her beginning to distort her personality by unconsciously developing a bitterness toward white people; when you have to concoct an answer for a five-year-old son asking, "Daddy, why do white people treat colored people so mean?"; when you take a cross-country drive and find it necessary to sleep night after night in the uncomfortable corners of your automobile because no motel will accept you; when you are humiliated day in and day out by nagging signs reading "white" and "colored"; when your first name becomes "nigger," your middle name becomes "boy" (however old you are), and your last name becomes "John," and your wife and mother are never given the respected title "Mrs."; when you are harried by day and haunted by night by the fact that you are a Negro, never quite knowing what to expect next, and are plagued with inner fears and outer resentments; when you are forever fighting a degenerating sense of "nobodiness"—then you will understand why we find it difficult to wait. There comes a time when the cup of endurance runs over, and men are no longer willing to be plunged into an abyss of injustice where they experience the bleakness of corroding despair. I hope, sirs, you can understand our legitimate and unavoidable impatience.

You express a great deal of anxiety over our willingness to break laws. This is certainly a legitimate concern. Since we so diligently urge people to obey the Supreme Court's decision of 1954 outlawing segregation in the public schools, at first glance it may seem rather paradoxical for us consciously to break laws. One may well ask, "How can you advocate breaking some laws and obeying others?" The answer lies in the fact that there are two types of laws: just and unjust. I agree with St. Augustine that "an unjust law is no law at all."

\* \* \*

Let us consider some of the ways in which a law can be unjust. A law is unjust, for example, if the majority group compels a minority group to obey the statute but does not make it binding on itself. By the same token, a law in all probability is just if the majority is itself willing to obey it. Also, a law is unjust if it is inflicted on a minority that, as a result of being denied the right to vote, had no part in enacting or devising the law. Who can say that the legislature of Alabama which set up that state's segregation laws was democratically elected? Throughout Alabama all sorts of devious methods are used to prevent Negroes from becoming registered voters, and there are some counties in which, even though Negroes constitute a majority of the population, not a single Negro is registered. Can any law enacted under such circumstances be considered democratically structured?

Sometimes a law is just on its face and unjust in its application. For instance, I have been arrested on a charge of parading without a permit. Now there is nothing wrong in having an ordinance which requires a permit for a parade. But such an ordinance becomes unjust when it is used to maintain segregation and to deny citizens the First Amendment privilege of peaceful assembly and protest.

I hope you are able to see the distinction I am trying to point out. In no sense do I advocate evading the law, as would the rabid segregationist. That would lead to anarchy. One who breaks an unjust law must do so *openly*, *lovingly*, and with a willingness to accept the penalty. I submit that an individual who breaks a law that conscience tells him is unjust and who willingly accepts the penalty of imprisonment in order to arouse the conscience of the community over its injustice is in reality expressing the highest respect for law.

\*   \*   \*

I must make two honest confessions to you, my Christian and Jewish brothers. First, I must confess that over the past few years I have been gravely disappointed with the white moderate. I have almost reached the regrettable conclusion that the Negro's great stumbling block in his stride toward freedom is not the White Citizen's Counciler or the Ku Klux Klanner but the white moderate who is more devoted to "order" than to justice; who prefers a negative peace which is the absence of tension to a positive peace which is the presence of justice; who constantly says "I agree with you in the goal you seek, but I cannot agree with your methods"; who paternalistically believes he can set the timetable for another man's freedom; who lives by a mythical concept of time and who constantly advises the Negro to wait for a "more convenient season." Shallow understanding from people of goodwill is more frustrating than absolute misunderstanding from people of ill will. Lukewarm acceptance is much more bewildering than outright rejection.

I had hoped that the white moderate would understand that law and order exist for the purpose of establishing justice and that when they fail in this purpose they block social progress. I had hoped that the white moderate would understand that the present tension in the South is a necessary phase of the transition from an obnoxious negative peace, in which the Negro passively accepted his unjust plight, to a substantive and positive peace, in which all men will respect the dignity and worth of human personality. Actually, we who engage in nonviolent direct action are not the creators of tension. We merely bring to the surface the hidden tension that is already alive. We bring it out in the open where it can be seen and dealt with. Like a boil that can never be cured so long as it is covered up but must be opened with all its pus-flowing ugliness to the natural medicines of air and light, injustice must be exposed, with all the tension its exposure creates, to the light of human conscience and the air of national opinion before it can be cured.

\*   \*   \*

You speak of our activity in Birmingham as extreme. At first I was rather disappointed that fellow clergymen would see my nonviolent efforts as those of an extremist. I began thinking about the fact that I stand in the middle of two opposing forces in the Negro community. One is a force of complacency made up of Negroes who, as a result of long years of oppression, are so completely drained of self-respect and a sense of "somebodiness" that they have adjusted to segregation, and of a few middle-class Negroes who, because of a degree of academic and economic security and because in some ways they profit by segregation, have unconsciously become insensitive to the problems of the masses. The other force is one of bitterness and hatred, and it comes perilously close to advocating violence. It is expressed in the various black nationalist groups that are springing up across the nation, the largest and best-known being Elijah Muhammad's Muslim movement. Nourished by the Negro's frustration over the continued existence of racial discrimination, this movement is made up of people who have lost faith in America, who have absolutely repudiated Christianity, and who have concluded that the white man is an incorrigible "devil."

I have tried to stand between these two forces, saying that we need emulate neither the "do-nothingism" of the complacent nor the hatred of the black nationalist. For there is the more excellent way of love and nonviolent protest. I am grateful to God that, through the influence of the Negro church, the way of nonviolence became an integral part of our struggle.

If this philosophy had not emerged, by now many streets of the South would, I am convinced, be flowing with blood. And I am further convinced that if our white brothers dismiss as "rabble-rousers" and "outside agitators" those of us who employ nonviolent direct action and if they refuse to support our nonviolent efforts, millions of Negroes will, out of frustration and despair, seek solace and security in black nationalist ideologies—a development that would inevitably lead to a frightening racial nightmare.

*  *  *

Let me take note of my other major disappointment. Though there are some notable exceptions, I have also been disappointed with the white church and its leadership. I do not say this as one of those negative critics who can always find something wrong with the church. I say this as a minister of the gospel, who loves the church; who was nurtured in its bosom; who has been sustained by its spiritual blessings and who will remain true to it as long as the cord of life shall lengthen.

When I was suddenly catapulted into the leadership of the bus protest in Montgomery, Alabama, a few years ago, I felt we would be supported by the white church. I felt that the white ministers, priests, and rabbis of the South would be among our strongest allies. Instead, some have been outright opponents, refusing to understand the freedom movement and misrepresenting its leaders; all too many others have been more cautious than courageous and have remained silent and secure behind stained-glass windows.

In spite of my shattered dreams I came to Birmingham with the hope that the white religious leadership of this community would see the justice of our cause and with deep moral concern would serve as the channel through which our just grievances could reach the power structure. But again I have been disappointed.

I have heard numerous Southern religious leaders admonish their worshipers to comply with a desegregation decision because it is the *law*, but I have longed to hear white ministers declare, "Follow this decree because integration is morally *right* and because the Negro is your brother." In the midst of blatant injustices inflicted upon the Negro I have watched white churchmen stand on the sideline and mouth pious irrelevancies and sanctimonious trivialities. In the midst of a mighty struggle to rid our nation of racial and economic injustice I have heard many ministers say, "Those are social issues with which the gospel has no real concern," and I have watched many churches commit themselves to a completely otherworldly religion which makes a strange, unbiblical distinction between body and soul, between the sacred and the secular.

We are moving toward the close of the twentieth century with a religious community largely adjusted to the status quo—a taillight behind other community agencies rather than a headlight leading men to higher levels of justice.

*  *  *

But the judgment of God is upon the church as never before. If today's church does not recapture the sacrificial spirit of the early church, it will lose its authenticity, forfeit the loyalty of millions, and be dismissed as an irrelevant social club with no meaning for the twentieth century. Every day I meet young people whose disappointment with the church has turned into outright disgust.

Perhaps I have once again been too optimistic. Is organized religion too inextricably bound to the status quo to save our nation and the world? Perhaps I must turn my faith to the inner spiritual church, the church within the church, as the true *ecclesia* and the hope of the world. But again I am thankful to God that some noble souls from the ranks of organized religion have broken loose from the paralyzing chains of conformity and joined us as active partners in the struggle for freedom. They have left their secure congregations and walked the streets of Albany, Georgia, with us. They have gone down the highways of the South on torturous rides for freedom. Yes, they have gone to jail with us. Some have been kicked out of their churches, have lost the support of their bishops and fellow ministers. But they have acted in the faith that right defeated is stronger than evil triumphant. Their witness has been the spiritual salt that has preserved the true meaning of the gospel in these troubled times. They have carved a tunnel of hope through the dark mountain of disappointment.

I hope the church as a whole will meet the challenge of this decisive hour. But even if the church does not come to the aid of justice, I have no despair about the future. I have no fear about the outcome of our struggle in Birmingham, even if our motives are at present misunderstood. We will reach the goal of freedom in Birmingham and all over the nation, because the goal of America is freedom.

*   *   *

Before closing I feel impelled to mention one other point in your statement that has troubled me profoundly. You warmly commended the Birmingham police force for keeping "order" and "preventing violence." I doubt that you would have so warmly commended the police force if you had seen its angry dogs sinking their teeth into six unarmed, non-violent Negroes. I doubt that you would so quickly commend the policemen if you were to observe their ugly and inhuman treatment of Negroes here in the City Jail; if you were to watch them push and curse old Negro women and young Negro girls; if you were to see them slap and kick old Negro men and young boys; if you were to observe them, as they did on two occasions, refuse to give us food because we wanted to sing our grace together. I cannot join you in your praise of the Birmingham Police Department.

It is true that the police have exercised discipline in handling the demonstrators. In this sense they have conducted themselves rather "non-violently" in public. But for what purpose? To preserve the evil system of segregation. Over the past few years I have consistently preached that nonviolence demands that the means we use must be as pure as the ends we seek. I have tried to make clear that it is wrong to use immoral means to attain moral ends. But now I must affirm that it is just as wrong, or perhaps even more so, to use moral means to preserve immoral ends.

Perhaps Mr. Connor and his policemen have been rather nonviolent in public, as was Chief Pritchett in Albany, Georgia, but they have used the moral means of nonviolence to maintain the immoral end of racial injustice. As T. S. Eliot has said, there is no greater treason than to do the right deed for the wrong reason.

I wish you had commended the Negro sit-inners and demonstrators of Birmingham for their sublime courage, their willingness to suffer and their amazing discipline in the midst of great provocation. One day the South will recognize its real heroes. . . . One day the South will know that when these disinherited children of God sat down at lunch counters they were in reality standing up for what is best in the American dream and for the most sacred values in our Judeo-Christian heritage, thereby bringing our nation back to those great wells of democracy which were dug deep by the founding fathers in their formulation of the Constitution and the Declaration of Independence.

## DISCUSSION QUESTIONS

1. What are the main points of disagreement between the King and Lincoln views?

2. Many of those involved in social protest movements (from anti-abortion protestors to environmental activists) draw parallels between their efforts and King's legacy of civil disobedience, in an effort to establish their right to disobey laws they find unjust. Are such applications of King's argument legitimate? Why or why not?

# 20

# "In Defense of Prejudice"

## Jonathan Rauch

*Some political theorists argue that democracies must not only prevent the intrusion of government upon basic liberties, but must play a positive role in bolstering and protecting the rights of all their citizens. The challenge is admirable, but difficult, as governments in practice are often faced with trade-offs between the two values.*

*Consider free speech, a right enshrined in the First Amendment. The right to speak freely is fundamental to democratic governance. Yet it is not absolute. Is there a line where my right to speak freely impinges upon your wish not to hear what I have to say, particularly when my words are perceived as offensive, harmful, and prejudicial? What role should the government play in drawing the line, if any? Should it limit speech in order to protect others from the insult words can bring? If there is such a line, who decides where it is drawn?*

*In the following article Jonathan Rauch stands "in defense of prejudice" and in opposition to those who call for government regulation of speech that is insulting to or stigmatizes individuals based on their sex, race, color, handicap, religion, sexual orientation or national and ethnic origin. In the workplace, universities, public school curricula, the media, and criminal law, speech is increasingly regulated by codes aimed at eradicating prejudice. Rauch argues that regulating speech this way is foolish. In his view, the only way to challenge and correct prejudice is through the free flow of speech, some of which we might not want to hear. Government best protects liberty when it works to preserve rather than prevent the free flow of speech, no matter how distasteful or hurtful that speech may be.*

The war on prejudice is now, in all likelihood, the most uncontroversial social movement in America. Opposition to "hate speech," formerly identified with the liberal left, has become a bipartisan piety. In the past year, groups and factions that agree on nothing else have agreed that the public expression of any and all prejudices must be forbidden. On the left, protesters and editorialists have insisted that Francis L. Lawrence resign as president of Rutgers University for describing blacks as "a disadvantaged population that doesn't have that genetic, hereditary background to have a higher average." On the other side of the ideological divide, Ralph Reed, the executive director of the Christian Coalition, responded to criticism of the religious right by calling a press conference to denounce a supposed outbreak of "name-calling, scapegoating, and religious bigotry." Craig Rogers, an evangelical Christian student at California State University, recently filed a $2.5 million sexual-harassment suit against a lesbian professor of psychology, claiming that anti-male bias in one of her lectures violated campus rules and left him feeling "raped and trapped."

In universities and on Capitol Hill, in workplaces and newsrooms, authorities are declaring that there is no place for racism, sexism, homophobia, Christian-bashing, and other forms of prejudice in public debate or even in private thought. "Only when racism and other forms of prejudice are expunged," say the crusaders for sweetness and light, "can minorities be safe and society be fair." So sweet, this dream of a world without prejudice. But the very last thing society should do is seek to utterly eradicate racism and other forms of prejudice.

I suppose I should say, in the customary I-hope-I-don't-sound-too-defensive tone, that I am not a racist and that this is not an article favoring racism or any other particular prejudice. It is an article favoring intellectual pluralism, which permits the expression of various forms of bigotry and always will. Although we like to hope that a time will come when no one will believe that people come in types and that each type belongs with its own kind, I doubt such a day will ever arrive. By all indications, *Homo sapiens* is a tribal species for whom "us versus them" comes naturally and must be continually pushed back. Where there is genuine freedom of expression, there will be racist expression. There will also be people who believe that homosexuals are sick or threaten children or—especially among teenagers—are rightful targets of manly savagery. Homosexuality will always be incomprehensible to most people, and what is incomprehensible is feared. As for anti-Semitism, it appears to be a hardier virus than influenza. If you want pluralism, then you get racism and sexism and homophobia, and communism and fascism and xenophobia and tribalism, and that is just for a start. If you want to believe in intellectual freedom and the progress of knowledge and the advancement of science and all those other good things, then you must swallow hard and accept this: for as thickheaded and wayward an animal as us, the realistic question is how to make the best of prejudice, not how to eradicate it.

Indeed, "eradicating prejudice" is so vague a proposition as to be meaningless. Distinguishing prejudice reliably and nonpolitically from non-prejudice, or even defining it crisply, is quite hopeless. We all feel we know prejudice when we see it. But do we? At the University of Michigan, a student said in a classroom discussion that he considered homosexuality a disease treatable with therapy. He was summoned to a formal disciplinary hearing for violating the school's policy against speech that "victimizes" people based on "sexual orientation." Now, the evidence is abundant that this particular hypothesis is wrong, and any American homosexual can attest to the harm that the student's hypothesis has inflicted on many real people. But was it a statement of prejudice or of misguided belief? Hate speech or hypothesis? Many Americans who do not regard themselves as bigots or haters believe that homosexuality is a treatable disease. They may be wrong, but are they all bigots? I am unwilling to say so, and if you are willing, beware. The line between a prejudiced belief and a merely controversial one is elusive, and the harder you look the more elusive it becomes. "God hates homosexuals" is a statement of fact, not of bias, to those who believe it; "American criminals are disproportionately black" is a statement of bias, not of fact, to those who disbelieve it.

Who is right? You may decide, and so may others, and there is no need to agree. That is the great innovation of intellectual pluralism . . . We cannot know in advance or for sure which belief is prejudice and which is truth, but to advance knowledge we don't need to know. The genius of intellectual pluralism lies not in doing away with prejudices and dogmas but in channeling them—making them socially productive by pitting prejudice against prejudice and dogma against dogma, exposing all to withering public criticism. What survives at the end of the day is our base of knowledge.

*    *    *

Pluralism is the principle that protects and makes a place in human company for that loneliest and most vulnerable of all minorities, the minority who is hounded and despised among blacks and whites, gays and straights, who is suspect or criminal among every tribe and in every nation of the world, and yet on whom progress depends: the dissident. I am not saying that dissent is always or even usually enlightened. Most of the time it is foolish and self-serving. No dissident has the right to be taken seriously, and the fact that Aryan Nation racists or Nation of Islam anti-Semites are unorthodox does not entitle them to respect. But what goes around comes around. As a supporter of gay marriage, for example, I reject the majority's view of family, and as a Jew I reject its view of God. I try to be civil, but the fact is that most Americans regard my views on marriage as a reckless assault on the most fundamental of all institutions, and many people are more than a little discomfited by the statement "Jesus Christ was no more divine than anybody else" (which is why so few people ever say it). Trap the racists and anti-Semites, and you lay a trap for me too. Hunt for them with eradication in your mind, and you have brought dissent itself within your sights.

The new crusade against prejudice waves aside such warnings. Like earlier crusades against antisocial ideas, the mission is fueled by good (if cocksure) intentions and a genuine sense of urgency. Some kinds of error are held to be intolerable, like pollutants that even in small traces poison the water for a whole town. Some errors are so pernicious as to damage real people's lives, so wrongheaded that no person of right mind or goodwill could support them. Like their forebears of other stripe—the Church in its campaigns against heretics, the McCarthyites in their campaigns against Communists—the modern anti-racist and anti-sexist and anti-homophobic campaigners are totalists, demanding not that misguided ideas and ugly expressions be corrected or criticized but that they be eradicated. They make war not on errors but on error, and like other totalists they act in the name of public safety—the safety, especially, of minorities.

The sweeping implications of this challenge to pluralism are not, I think, well enough understood by the public at large. Indeed, the new brand of totalism has yet even to be properly named. "Multiculturalism," for instance, is much too broad. "Political correctness" comes closer but is too trendy and snide. For lack of anything else, I will call the new antipluralism "purism," since its major tenet is that society cannot be just until the last traces of invidious prejudice have been scrubbed away. Whatever you call it, the purists' way of seeing things has spread through American intellectual life with remarkable speed, so much so that many people will blink at you uncomprehendingly or even call you a racist (or sexist or homophobe, etc.) if you suggest that expressions of racism should be tolerated or that prejudice has its part to play.

The new purism sets out, to begin with, on a campaign against words, for words are the currency of prejudice, and if prejudice is hurtful then so must be prejudiced words. "We are not safe when these violent words are among us," wrote Mari Matsuda, then a UCLA law professor. Here one imagines gangs of racist words swinging chains and smashing heads in back alleys. To suppress bigoted language seems, at first blush, reasonable, but it quickly leads to a curious result. A peculiar kind of verbal shamanism takes root, as though certain expressions, like curses or magical incantations, carry in themselves the power to hurt or heal—as though words were bigoted rather than people. "Context is everything," people have always said. The use of the word "nigger" in *Huckleberry Finn* does not make the book an "act" of hate speech—or does it? In the new view, this is no longer so clear. The very utterance of the word "nigger" (at least by a non-black) is a racist act. When a *Sacramento Bee* cartoonist put the word "nigger" mockingly in the mouth of a white supremacist, there were howls of protest and 1,400 canceled subscriptions and an editorial apology, even though the word was plainly being invoked against racists, not against blacks.

Faced with escalating demands of verbal absolutism, newspapers issue lists of forbidden words. The expressions "gyp" (derived from "Gypsy") and "Dutch treat" were among the dozens of terms stricken as "offensive" in a much-ridiculed (and later withdrawn) *Los Angeles Times* speech code. The University of Missouri journalism school issued a *Dictionary of Cautionary Words and Phrases*, which included "*Buxom*: Offensive reference to a woman's chest. Do not use. See 'Woman.' *Codger*: Offensive reference to a senior citizen."

As was bound to happen, purists soon discovered that chasing around after words like "gyp" or "buxom" hardly goes to the roots of the problem. As long as they remain bigoted, bigots will simply find other words. If they can't call you a kike then they will say Jewboy, Judas, or Hebe, and when all those are banned they will press words like "oven" and "lampshade" into their service. The vocabulary of hate is potentially as rich as your dictionary, and all you do by banning language used by cretins is to let them decide what the rest of us may say. The problem, some purists have concluded, must therefore go much deeper than laws: it must go to the deeper level of ideas. Racism, sexism, homophobia, and the rest must be built into the very structure of American society and American patterns of thought, so pervasive yet so insidious that, like water to a fish, they are both omnipresent and unseen. The mere existence of prejudice constructs a society whose very nature is prejudiced.

This line of thinking was pioneered by feminists, who argued that pornography, more than just being expressive, is an act by which men construct an oppressive society. Racial activists quickly picked up the argument. Racist expressions are themselves acts of oppression, they said. "All racist speech constructs the social reality that constrains the liberty of nonwhites because of their race," wrote Charles R. Lawrence III, then a law professor at Stanford. From the purist point of view, a society with even one racist is a racist society, because the idea itself threatens and demeans its targets. They cannot feel wholly safe or wholly welcome as long as racism is present. Pluralism says: There will always be some racists. Marginalize them, ignore them, exploit them, ridicule them, take pains to make their policies illegal, but otherwise leave them alone. Purists say: That's not enough. Society cannot be just until these pervasive and oppressive ideas are searched out and eradicated.

And so what is now under way is a growing drive to eliminate prejudice from every corner of society. I doubt that many people have noticed how far-reaching this anti-pluralist movement is becoming.

*In universities:* Dozens of universities have adopted codes proscribing speech or other expression that (this is from Stanford's policy, which is more or less representative) "is intended to insult or stigmatize an individual or a small number of individuals on the basis of their sex, race, color, handicap, religion, sexual orientation or national and ethnic origin." Some codes punish only persistent harassment of a targeted individual, but many, following the purist doctrine that even one racist is too many, go much further. At Penn, an administrator declared: "We at the University of Pennsylvania have guaranteed students and the community that they can live in a community free of sexism, racism, and homophobia." Here is the purism that gives "political correctness" its distinctive combination of puffy high-mindedness and authoritarian zeal.

*In school curricula:* "More fundamental than eliminating racial segregation has to be the removal of racist thinking, assumptions, symbols, and materials in the curriculum," writes theorist Molefi Kete Asante. In practice, the effort to "remove racist thinking" goes well beyond striking egregious references from textbooks. In many cases it becomes a kind of mental engineering in which students are encouraged to see prejudice everywhere; it includes teaching identity politics as an antidote to internalized racism; it rejects mainstream science as "white male" thinking; and it tampers with history, installing such dubious notions as that the ancient Greeks stole their culture from Africa or that an ancient carving of a bird is an example of "African experimental aeronautics."

*In criminal law:* Consider two crimes. In each, I am beaten brutally; in each, my jaw is smashed and my skull is split in just the same way. However, in the first crime my assailant calls me an "asshole"; in the second he calls me a "queer." In most states, in many localities, and, as of September 1994, in federal cases, these two crimes are treated differently: the crime motivated by bias—or deemed to be so motivated by prosecutors and juries—gets a stiffer punishment. "Longer prison terms for bigots," shrilled Brooklyn Democratic Congressman Charles Schumer, who introduced the federal hate-crimes legislation, and those are what the law now provides. Evidence that the assailant holds prejudiced beliefs, even if he doesn't actually express them while committing an offense, can serve to elevate the crime. Defendants in hate-crimes cases may be grilled on how many black friends they have and whether they have told racist jokes. To increase a prison sentence only because of the defendant's "prejudice" (as gauged by prosecutor and jury) is, of course, to try minds and punish beliefs. Purists say, Well, they are dangerous minds and poisonous beliefs.

*In the workplace:* Though government cannot constitutionally suppress bigotry directly, it is now busy doing so indirectly by requiring employers to eliminate prejudice. Since the early 1980s, courts and the Equal Employment Opportunity Commission have moved to bar workplace speech deemed to create a hostile or abusive working environment for minorities. The law, held a federal court in 1988, "does require that an employer take prompt action to prevent . . . bigots from expressing their opinions in a way that abuses or offends their co-workers," so as to achieve "the goal of eliminating prejudices and biases from our society." So it was, as UCLA law professor Eugene Volokh notes, that the EEOC charged that a manufacturer's ads using admittedly accurate depictions of samurai, kabuki, and sumo were "racist" and "offensive to people of Japanese origin"; that a Pennsylvania court found that an employer's printing Bible verses on paychecks was religious harassment of Jewish employees; that an employer had to desist using gender-based job titles like "foreman" and "draftsman" after a female employee sued.

On and on the campaign goes, darting from one outbreak of prejudice to another like a cat chasing flies. In the American Bar Association, activists demand that lawyers who express "bias or prejudice" be penalized. In the Education Department, the civil-rights office presses for a ban on computer bulletin board comments that "show hostility toward a person or group based on sex, race or color, including slurs, negative stereotypes, jokes or pranks." In its security checks for government jobs, the FBI takes to asking whether applicants are "free of biases against any class of citizens," whether, for instance, they have told racist jokes or indicated other "prejudices." Joke police! George Orwell, grasping the close relationship of jokes to dissent, said that every joke is a tiny revolution. The purists will have no such rebellions.

The purist campaign reaches, in the end, into the mind itself. In a lecture at the University of New Hampshire, a professor compared writing to sex ("You and the subject become one"); he was suspended and required to apologize, but what was most insidious was the order to undergo university-approved counseling to have his mind straightened out. At the University of Pennsylvania, a law lecturer said, "We have ex-slaves here who should know about the Thirteenth Amendment"; he was banished from campus for a year and required to make a public apology, and he, too, was compelled to attend a "sensitivity and racial awareness" session. Mandatory re-education of alleged bigots is the natural consequence of intellectual purism. Prejudice must be eliminated!

. . . "Nobody escapes," said a Rutgers University report on campus prejudice. Bias and prejudice, it found, cross every conceivable line, from sex to race to politics: "No matter who you are, no matter what the color of your skin, no matter what your gender or sexual orientation, no matter what you believe, no matter how you behave, there is somebody out there who doesn't like people of your kind." Charles Lawrence writes: "Racism is ubiquitous. We are all racists." If he means that most of us think racist thoughts of some sort at one time or another, he is right. If we are going to "eliminate prejudices and biases from our society," then the work of the prejudice police is unending. They are doomed to hunt and hunt and hunt, scour and scour and scour.

What is especially dismaying is that the purists pursue prejudice in the name of protecting minorities. In order to protect people like me (homosexual), they must pursue people like me (dissident). In order to bolster minority self-esteem, they suppress minority opinion. There are, of course, all kinds of practical and legal problems with the purists' campaign: the incursions against the First Amendment; the inevitable abuses by prosecutors and activists who define as "hateful" or "violent" whatever speech they dislike or can score points off of; the lack of any evidence that repressing prejudice eliminates rather than inflames it. But minorities, of all people, ought to remember that by definition we cannot prevail by numbers, and we generally cannot prevail by force. Against the power of ignorant mass opinion and group prejudice and superstition, we have only our voices. If you doubt that minorities' voices are powerful weapons, think of the lengths to which Southern officials went to silence the Reverend Martin Luther King, Jr., (recall that the city commissioner of Montgomery, Alabama, won a $500,000 libel suit, later overturned in *New York Times v. Sullivan* [1964], regarding an advertisement in the *Times* placed by civil-rights leaders who denounced the Montgomery police). Think of how much gay people have improved their lot over twenty-five years simply by refusing to remain silent. Recall the Michigan student who was prosecuted for saying that homosexuality is a treatable disease, and notice that he was black. Under that Michigan speech code, more than twenty blacks were charged with racist speech, while no instance of racist speech by whites was punished. In Florida, the hate-speech law was invoked against a black man who called a policeman a "white cracker"; not so surprisingly, in the first hate-crimes case to reach the Supreme Court, the victim was white and the defendant black.

In the escalating war against "prejudice," the right is already learning to play by the rules that were pioneered by the purist activists of the left. Last year leading Democrats, including the President, criticized the Republican Party for being increasingly in the thrall of the Christian right. Some of the rhetoric was harsh ("fire-breathing Christian radical right"), but it wasn't vicious or even clearly wrong. Never mind: when Democratic Representative Vic Fazio said Republicans were "being forced to the fringes by the aggressive political tactics of the religious right," the chairman of the Republican National Committee, Haley Barbour, said, "Christian-bashing" was "the left's preferred form of religious bigotry." Bigotry! Prejudice! "Christians active in politics are now on the receiving end of an extraordinary campaign of bias and prejudice," said the conservative leader William J. Bennett. One discerns, here, where the new purism leads. Eventually, any criticism of any group will be "prejudice."

## DISCUSSION QUESTIONS

1. Do you agree or disagree that some groups need to be protected against offensive or hurtful ideas or speech? How do you define "hurtful" or "offensive"? What is the basis for your position? Where is the First Amendment in this debate?

2. Several campus administrations have shut down "affirmative action bake sales," protests against affirmative action in which white students are charged more for cookies than minorities. Critics argue that such events are racist and disrespectful, while defenders note that this is precisely the kind of symbolic speech at the core of the First Amendment. What do you think?

3. Would a campus newspaper be justified in rejecting a paid advertisement from (a) a group or individual that denied the Holocaust had occurred; (b) a group or individual that argued against any sort of affirmative action; or (c) an environmental group that advocated violence against the property of corporations that polluted the environment? Would you support a "speech code" that prohibited someone from making these arguments on campus? Defend your answer.

## DEBATING THE ISSUES: CIVIL LIBERTIES AND THE FIGHT AGAINST TERROR

Civil liberties and community safety often exist in tension; the difficulty of balancing the two becomes exponentially greater during war or other national crises. The September 11 attacks clearly exposed some key vulnerabilities in our society: the attackers had blended into the background in several communities, and although law-enforcement authorities came tantalizingly close to connecting the dots in advance, the hijackers were clearly able to exploit the openness of American society.

In a reflection of this tension, no domestic element of the fight against terrorism has been more controversial than the USA PATRIOT Act. The debate has been so sharp that it is difficult even to describe the law in terms that both sides can agree upon. Where supporters of the law see a sensible relaxing of walls between the nation's intelligence and law-enforcement agencies, opponents see a shocking erosion of long-cherished civil liberties. Supporters see enhanced secrecy as crucial to the effective investigation of potential terror activity; opponents claim that the new powers are certain to be abused.

The readings in this debate section are examples of the scope of the disagreement. Pearlstein addresses the liberty-security tension directly, arguing that it is wrong to even describe the problem in these terms. In her view, cracking down on liberties—the inevitable result of the post-9/11 policies—makes the security problem worse, not better. Government intrusion into personal activities, rough interrogations, and detentions without trial or charge, are unlikely to produce results. Instead, Pearlstein advocates measures that do not pose any risk to liberty—more searches of cargo containers, increased public health surveillance, securing nuclear materials in Russia. Moreover, she argues that there is a fundamental value in maintaining fidelity to the rule of law.

McCarthy, a former federal prosecutor who secured convictions in the 1993 World Trade Center bombing, sees most PATRIOT Act criticism as histrionic overreaction. Critics of the law have, in his view, fundamentally misrepresented what it actually does. The law does not threaten civil liberties, or give police carte blanche to thumb through medical or library records. Instead, it does little more than make it easier for intelligence agencies and domestic law-enforcement organizations to share information (something that was extremely hard to do under the wall that had existed prior to the act) and allow law enforcement to catch up to technological developments that had rendered existing tools useless.

# 21

# "Rights in an Insecure World: Why National Security and Civil Liberty Are Complements"

## Deborah Pearlstein

A lmost as soon as the planes crashed into the twin towers, scholars, pundits, and politicians began asserting that our most important challenge as a democracy now is to reassess the balance between liberty and security. As Harvard human-rights scholar Michael Ignatieff wrote in *The Financial Times* on September 12, "As America awakens to the reality of being at war—and permanently so—with an enemy that has as yet no face and no name, it must ask itself what balance it should keep between liberty and security in the battle with terrorism."

Long before anyone had a clear idea of what went wrong—much less how to make sure it never happened again—public debate began with the assumption that something about the current "balance" was partially to blame for the attacks' success. As the attorney general testified in December 2001, "al-Qaeda terrorists are told how to use America's freedom as a weapon against us." In embracing the USA PATRIOT Act just weeks after the attacks, congressional member after congressional member stood to explain, as then-Senate Majority Leader Trent Lott put it, "When you're at war, civil liberties are treated differently." Minority Leader Dick Gephardt embraced the assumption as well, saying, "[W]e're not going to have all the openness and freedom we have had."

Our open society had made us less secure. The converse was as clear: A less free society would be safer. We had posited a solution before we had identified the problem. And we had based the solution on the premise that liberty and security are a zero-sum game.

While the drive to think about September 11 in terms of its implications for personal liberties was understandable, the balance metaphor is badly flawed. As the commission report itself demonstrates, the fundamental freedoms of our open society were not the primary (or even secondary) reason the terrorists succeeded on September 11. FBI agents in Minneapolis failed to search terrorist suspect Zacarias Moussaoui's computer before the attacks, not because constitutional restrictions against unreasonable searches and seizures prevented them from doing so but because they misunderstood the tools the law provided. The vast majority of the September 11 hijackers were able to enter the United States not because equal-protection provisions prevented border officials from targeting Arab and Muslim men for special scrutiny but because, according to the commission, "[b]efore 9/11, no agency of the U.S. government systematically analyzed terrorists' travel strategies" to reveal how terrorists had "detectably exploit[ed] weaknesses in our border security."

It is also not the case that a society less concerned with human rights is per se better protected from terrorism. On the contrary, some of our most rights-damaging measures since September 11 have had a neutral or even negative effect on counterterrorism. Most important, it is not the case that enhanced security invariably requires a compromise of human rights.

The balance metaphor has made crafting a security policy response to September 11 easy—and often misguided. It has also made policy unduly prone to undermine human rights. Three years after the fact, both rights and security are the worse for wear.

### Caught in the Balance

The PATRIOT Act became an important first example: It allows the FBI to secretly access Americans' personal information (library, medical, telephone, and financial records, among other things) without needing to show to an independent authority (like a judge) that the target is particularly suspected of terrorist activity. Yet the September 11 commission's report and other studies done since the attacks suggest that our primary intelligence failure on September 10 was not having too little information; our problem was failing to understand, analyze, and disseminate the significant quantity of information we had. For example, Minneapolis FBI agents did not understand what "probable cause" meant (the level of evidence required to obtain a regular criminal search warrant)—so they did not understand that they could have secured a run-of-the-mill search warrant on Moussaoui. This failure is a problem not remedied by the PATRIOT provision that gives the FBI power to trawl secretly through Americans' records. That power is all about gathering more data; it does nothing to address the problem of analysis that we still have. Still, changing the law was fast and easy—far easier than changing culture, competence, or overarching foreign policy. Imposing upon rights could become a policy substitute for enhancing security.

A similar approach was evident in the FBI's "voluntary" interview programs in certain immigrant and minority communities—a process that expended enormous resources and deeply alienated the communities whose cooperation in intelligence gathering may be needed most. After September 11, hundreds of foreign nationals in the United States were wrongly detained, unfairly deported, and subject to mistreatment and abuse under government programs, from special registration requirements to voluntary interviews to the detention of those seeking political asylum from a list of predominantly Arab and Muslim countries. Yet an April 2003 Government Accounting Office report on the effects of these interviews revealed that none of the information gathered from the interviews had yet been analyzed for intelligence, and there were "no specific plans" to do so. Indeed, from a security point of view, information overload can make matters worse. Instead of looking for a needle in a haystack, we must now find a needle in a field full of hay.

And just as our security needs for more careful intelligence assessments, thorough analysis, and greater information sharing are at their height, the executive-branch impulse has been to crack down on information shared not only with the public but with Congress itself. In 2003, the executive branch classified 25 percent more information (based on the number of executive-agency determinations that certain information should be classified) than the year before, which itself had seen a large rise. The CIA's numbers went up 41 percent, the Justice Department's 89 percent. At the same time, the amount of information being declassified fell to half what it had been in 2000, and one-fifth of 1997 levels. And this is not just about traditionally classified information. Last December, for example, the Defense Department announced a new policy preventing its own inspector general from posting *unclassified* information that was, in the Pentagon's estimation, "of questionable value to the general public." At the same time, despite repeated congressional requests over a period of years for complete statistics on how the PATRIOT Act has been used by the Justice Department, information available to Congress remains incomplete.

### Paradigms Lost

Aggressive or humiliating interrogation is the most pointed example of counterproductive policy. If the most important issue we face in the treatment of a suspect who knows the location of a ticking bomb is "what balance" to keep between security and liberty, of course liberty will lose. Saving the lives of 3,000 innocents weighs far heavier in the balance than the rights of any one individual.

But how does aggressive interrogation improve security? Set aside the fact that the certainty of the ticking-bomb scenario never exists in the real world. When John Ashcroft argued that terrorists were trained to "use our freedoms against us," he pointed to an al-Qaeda training-manual instruction that terrorists, if captured, should lie in response to questions from authorities. However, neither the manual nor the attorney general explained how a denial of human rights can overcome the instruction to lie. Are terrorists less likely to lie if we humiliate them in violation of

Geneva Convention protections—which we are, after all, bound to obey by law?

To the extent that the United States is able to answer this question—and compared with the counterterrorism expertise in Israel and the United Kingdom, our knowledge is limited at best—published accounts point to the opposite conclusion. As one Army interrogator put it in testimony related to the investigation of Abu Ghraib, "Embarrassment as a technique would be contradictory to achieving results." That is an important reason why the Army field manual has for decades instructed soldiers to avoid such tactics. They of course violate rights. They also do not reliably work. On the other hand, the widespread use and public revelation of such tactics has been powerfully effective in fueling anger and resentment that may feed anti-American terrorism for some time.

Now compare these tactics with security-enhancing measures that require essentially no balancing of security with human rights. For example, a bipartisan array of counterterrorism experts continues to criticize as inadequate inspection regimes for the 7 million cargo containers that arrive in U.S. ports each year—yet all acknowledge the danger of attack through such containers as a significant ongoing threat. The same may be said for the threat of bioterrorist attack, but the largely rights-neutral improvement of international public-health surveillance (which could help identify infectious-disease agents before they enter the United States) has also taken a backseat. And many in Congress have resisted entirely rights-neutral programs that would help the former Soviet Union secure stockpiles of fissile material to prevent it from becoming available on the global black market. And on and on.

This is not to suggest that balancing security interests against liberty interests is never required. It is to emphasize that taking a stone away from the rights side of the scale does not necessarily give the security side an advantage any more than taking a stone away from the security side strengthens rights. It is to underscore that viewing the issue of security post-September 11 as an exercise where rights and security are opposed is likely to produce both poor security policy and rights-damaging results.

### The Moral Equivalent of Law

If escaping the balancing framework is important to making good judgments about security policy, it is essential to preserving a regime of human rights under law. The dangers of this have been acutely evident in the new U.S. approach to detention and interrogation. Since early 2002, the White House has insisted that the president has the power to designate American citizens "enemy combatants," and thereby deprive them of the constitutional protections of the U.S. criminal-justice system, or, indeed, any legal rights at all. More or less the same position has applied to the U.S. detention of thousands of foreign nationals held indefinitely in a global system from Iraq to Afghanistan to Guantanamo Bay.

As White House Counsel Alberto Gonzales put it in a speech defending the combatant-detention policy to the American Bar Association's Standing Committee on Law and National Security, at issue in these cases was "the balance struck by this administration between protecting our country and preserving our freedoms." This balance had to be struck by the chief executive as "a matter of prudence and policy"—not one fixed in some more permanent domestic or international framework of rights, or one unduly constrained by law. "You have to realize," the president's lawyer told the Supreme Court, "that in situations where there is a war . . . you have to trust the executive to make the kind of quintessential military judgments that are involved" in interrogating detainees under U.S. control. This was not just about a particular entitlement—to a lawyer, to confidentiality, or to due process. This was about the idea of rights itself.

This argument took center stage this past spring when the Supreme Court heard its first three cases arising in the war on terrorism. In each of these cases—two involving the detention of U.S. citizens as "enemy combatants," one involving the detention of hundreds of foreign nationals beyond U.S. borders—the president argued that we should abandon reliance on law according to standards known to all and fixed in advance (the very definition of the rule of law) and move toward a more "flexible" anti-terrorism system where the rule of the road is not law but (in every case, at any moment) balance. Would an enemy-combatant detainee ever be able to assert his innocence to someone other than his interrogator? one justice asked during oral arguments. "As I understand it," the president's lawyer answered, "the plan on a going-forward basis, reflecting the unique situation of this battle, is to provide individuals like [Yaser Esam] Hamdi, like [Jose] Padilla, with the equivalent" of some review. "We don't know for sure."

By most accounts, the Court's decisions in these cases were a victory for human rights. In the case of U.S. citizen Hamdi, eight of the nine justices rejected the White House assertion that the president alone determined what rights Hamdi was entitled to receive. The federal courts will also have a role now in checking presidential power to detain foreign nationals at Guantanamo Bay. And while U.S. citizen Padilla may have to jump through additional procedural hoops, Hamdi's case put the handwriting for him on the wall: There would be no such thing as a rights-less citizen of the United States.

Nonetheless, these cases presented questions about government power and law that were staggeringly fundamental. And judging by the United States' ongoing detention of individuals in uncertain status around the world, and its ongoing resistance to allowing Guantanamo Bay detainees to challenge their detention in federal courts, the administration's basic position remains: Rules can be made "going forward"; on any given day, those rules may not be available for consideration by a court; and the rights available in each situation are "unique." In the rush to adjust the balance, we are abandoning the idea at the core of international human-rights law that some measures are fixed.

Conceiving our primary post-September 11 challenge as what balance to keep between liberty and security leaves us prone to see links between liberty and security where they need not exist, and prone to see rights under law as just another weight that can be readily removed from the scale. In fact, the basic balance between liberty and security in U.S. law was established in some detail centuries ago, at a time when the United States as an enterprise had never been more vulnerable or less secure. It included a commitment to the idea that people should be able to know in advance what the law is, and that if circumstances—like pressing new challenges to national security—required the laws to be changed, the people would have a say in how to change them. We have called that commitment the rule of law. And human rights are meaningless without it.

# 22

# "The PATRIOT Act Without Tears: Understanding a Mythologized Law"

## Andrew C. McCarthy

It was mid-August 2001, the last desperate days before the 9/11 terrorist attacks. Desperate, that is, for an alert agent of the FBI's Foreign Counterintelligence Division (FCI); much of the rest of America, and certainly much of the rest of its government, blithely carried on, content to assume, despite the number and increasing ferocity of terrorist attacks dating back nearly nine years, that national security was little more than an everyday criminal-justice issue.

Since 1995, a "wall" had been erected, presumptively barring communications between FCI agents and their counterparts in law enforcement—the FBI's criminal agents and the assistant U.S. attorneys who collectively, after a string of successful prosecutions through the 1990s, had become the government's best resource for information about the threat of militant Islam. This wall was not required by law; it was imposed as policy. Justice Department lawyers, elevating litigation risk over national security, designed it to forestall accusations that the federal government had used its intelligence-eavesdropping authority to build criminal cases.

This FCI agent collided, head-on, with the wall; and strewn in the wreckage was the last, best hope of stopping 9/11. Putting disconnected clues together, the agent had deduced that two Qaeda operatives, Khalid al-Midhar and Nawaf al-Hazmi, had probably gotten into the U.S. Alarmed; he pleaded with the FBI's criminal division to help him hunt down the terrorists—but they refused: For agents to fuse their information and efforts would be a transgression against the wall. The prescient agent rued that, one day soon, people would die in the face of this paralyzing roadblock. Al-Midhar and al-Hazmi remained undetected until they plunged Flight 77 into the Pentagon on 9/11.

*Facing Reality*

By October 2001, the world had changed—and the USA PATRIOT Act was passed. So patent was the need for this law that it racked up massive support: 357–66 in the House, 98–1 in the Senate. In the nearly three years since, however, it has been distorted beyond recognition by a coalition of anti-Bush leftists and libertarian extremists, such that it is now perhaps the most broadly maligned—and misunderstood—piece of meaningful legislation in U.S. history. If our nation is serious about national security, the Patriot Act must be made permanent; instead, it could soon be gone—and the disastrous "intelligence wall" rebuilt.

Contrary to widespread calumny, PATRIOT is not an assault on the Bill of Rights. It is, basically, an overhaul of the government's antiquated counter-terror arsenal, which had been haplessly fighting a 21st-century war with 20th-century weapons. Indeed, PATRIOT's only obvious flaw is its cloying acronym, short for "The Uniting and Strengthening America by Providing Appropriate Tools to Intercept and Obstruct Terrorism Act of 2001." But once you get past the title, PATRIOT is all substance, and crucial to national security.

The most essential improvement wrought by PATRIOT has been the dismantling of the intelligence wall. The bill expressly amended the government's national-security eavesdropping-and-search authority (under the Foreign Intelligence Surveillance Act or FISA) to clarify that intelligence agents, criminal investigators, and prosecutors not only may but should be pooling information and connecting dots. This is common sense: Along the way toward mass murder, terrorists inevitably commit numerous ordinary crimes, everything from identity theft to immigration fraud to bombing. One could not surveil them as agents of a foreign power (as FISA permits) without necessarily uncovering such crimes, and this, far from being a problem, is a bonus since these lay the groundwork for prosecutions that can both stop terrorists before they strike and pressure them to turn state's evidence.

Yet, as has been detailed in a decisive 2002 opinion by the Foreign Intelligence Surveillance Court of Review, FISA had for decades been misinterpreted by the government and the courts, which, owing to their obsession over the "rights" of enemy operatives, erroneously presumed that national-security intelligence was somehow separate and severable from criminal evidence. This false dichotomy culminated in the wall built by the Clinton Justice Department (and substantially maintained by Bush's DOJ), with awful consequences.

Tearing down the wall—as well as repealing legislation that had barred criminal investigators from sharing with intelligence agents the fruits of grand-jury proceedings and criminal wiretaps—has paid instant dividends. For example, while the wall once caused intelligence and criminal agents in Buffalo to believe they could not be in the same room together during briefings to discuss their parallel investigations of an apparent sleeper cell in Lackawanna, N.Y., the PATRIOT Act allowed the criminal investigators to learn that a theretofore anonymous letter to one of their subjects had, as intelligence agents knew, been penned by a Qaeda operative. This and other fact-sharing broke an investigative logjam, revealing a history of paramilitary training at al-Qaeda's Afghan proving grounds, and directly resulted in guilty pleas and lengthy sentences for six men who had provided material support to the terror network.

In a similar way, in 2002 law-enforcement agents in Oregon learned through an informant that Jeffrey Battle was actively scoping out Jewish schools and synagogues for a terrorist attack. It later emerged that Battle was among a group that set out to train with al-Qaeda in Afghanistan (they never made it). Battle was plainly a time bomb, but his confederates had not yet been fully revealed—and there naturally was fear that if Battle were arrested and removed from the scene the investigators would lose their best hope of identifying other terrorists. Because the wall was down, the criminal investigators had the confidence to delay the arrest and continue the investigation, knowing the intelligence agents using FISA were now free to share what they were learning. As a result, not only Battle but six others, collectively known as the "Portland 7," were identified, convicted on terrorism-support charges, and sentenced to between three and 18 years in prison.

Thanks to PATRIOT's removal of the blinders, action—sometimes long overdue—has been taken against many other accused and convicted terrorists. Criminal investigators won access to a historic trove of intelligence demonstrating that Prof. Sami al Arian had been using his University of South Florida redoubt as an annex of the deadly Palestinian Islamic Jihad group responsible for over 100 murders, including that of Alisa Flatow, a young American woman killed in an Israeli bus bombing. The sharing provisions also ensured the convictions of nine other defendants in Virginia, on charges ranging from support of the Qaeda-affiliated Lashkar-e-Taiba to conspiracy to levy war against the U.S.; the conviction in Chicago of bin Laden intimate Enaam Arnaout for using his Benevolence International Foundation as a conduit to fund terrorist cells in Bosnia and Chechnya, and of Khaled Abdel Latif Dumeisi for working in the U.S. for Saddam Hussein's brutal Iraqi Intelligence Service; the indictment of a University of Idaho graduate student, Sami Omar al-Hussayen, for using his computer skills to support the recruiting and fundraising of Hamas and Chechnyan terror groups; the indictment in Brooklyn of two Yemeni nationals who bragged about having raised millions of dollars for bin Laden; and the smashing of a drugs-for-weapons plot in San Diego that solicited Stinger anti-aircraft missiles for the Taliban in exchange for heroin and hashish. Moreover, while much information provided by criminal investigators to the intelligence community must remain classified, the Justice Department also credits the sharing provisions with the revocation of visas for suspected terrorists, tracking and choking off of terrorist funding channels, and identifying of terrorists operating overseas.

## 21st-Century Tactics

Besides paving the way for agents to pool critical information, PATRIOT has been invaluable in modernizing investigative tools to ensure that more information is actually captured. While the critics' persistent caviling misleadingly suggests that these tools are a novel assault on privacy rights, for the most part they merely extend to national-security intelligence investigations the same methods that have long been available to law-enforcement agents probing the vast array of federal crimes, including those as comparatively innocuous as health-care fraud.

Among the best examples is the so-called "roving" (or multi-point) wiretap. As the telephony revolution unfolded, criminals naturally took advantage, avoiding wiretap surveillance by the simple tactic of constantly switching phones—which became especially easy to do once cell phones became ubiquitous. Congress reacted nearly 20 years ago with a law that authorized criminal agents to obtain wiretaps that, rather than aim at a specific telephone, targeted persons, thus allowing monitoring to continue without significant delay as criminals ditched one phone for the next. Inexplicably, this same authority was not available to intelligence agents investigating terrorists under FISA. PATRIOT rectifies this anomaly.

On the law-enforcement side, PATRIOT expands the substance of the wiretap statute to account for the realities of terrorism. Most Americans would probably be surprised to learn that while the relatively trivial offense of gambling, for example, was a lawful predicate for a criminal wiretap investigation, chemical-weapons offenses, the use of weapons of mass destruction, the killing of Americans abroad, terrorist financing, and computer fraud were not. Thanks to PATRIOT, that is no longer the case.

Analogously, PATRIOT revamped other telecommunications-related techniques. Prior law, for example, had been written in the bygone era when cable service meant television programming. Owing to privacy concerns about viewing habits, which the government rarely has a legitimate reason to probe, federal law made access to cable-usage records practically impossible—creating in service providers a fear of being sued by customers if they complied with government information requests. Now, of course, millions of cable subscribers—including no small number of terrorists—use the service not only for entertainment viewing but for e-mail services.

While e-mail-usage records from dial-up providers have long been available by subpoena, court order, or search warrant (depending on the sensitivity of the information sought), cable providers for years delayed complying with such processes, arguing that their services fell under the restrictive umbrella of prior cable law. This was not only a potentially disastrous state of affairs in terrorism cases, where delay can cost lives, but in many other contexts as well—including one reported case in which a cable company declined to comply with an order to disclose the name of a suspected pedophile who was distributing child pornography on the Internet even as he bragged online about sexually abusing a young girl. (Investigators, forced to pursue other leads, needed two extra weeks to identify and apprehend the suspect.) Recognizing that it made no sense to have radically different standards for acquiring the same information, PATRIOT made cable e-mail available on the same terms as dial-up.

PATRIOT also closed other gaping e-mail loopholes. Under prior law, for example, investigators trying to identify the source of incriminating e-mail were severely handicapped in that their readiest tool, the grand-jury subpoena, could be used only to compel the service provider to produce customers' names, addresses, and lengths of service—information often of little value in ferreting out wrongdoers who routinely use false names and temporary e-mail addresses. PATRIOT solved this problem by empowering grand juries to compel payment information, which can be used to trace the bank and credit-card records by which investigators ultimately establish identity. This not only makes it possible to identify potential terrorists far more quickly—and thus, it is hoped, before they can strike—but also to thwart other criminals who must be apprehended with all due speed. Such subpoenas, for example, have been employed repeatedly to identify and arrest molesters who were actively abusing children. The Justice Department reports that, only a few weeks ago, the new authority prevented a Columbine-like attack by allowing agents to identify a suspect, and obtain his confession, before the attack could take place.

Further, PATRIOT clarified such investigative matters as the methods for lawful access by investigators to stored e-mail held by third parties (such as AOL and other service providers). And it cured the incongruity that allowed agents to access voice messages stored in a suspect's own home answering machine by a simple search warrant but anomalously forced them to obtain a far more cumbersome wiretap order if the messages were in the form of voicemail stored with a third-party provider.

### A Library of Red Herrings

One PATRIOT reform that has been irresponsibly maligned is Section 215 of the act, which merely extends to national-security investigations conducted under FISA the same authority to subpoena business records that criminal investigators have exercised unremarkably for years. Indeed, even under Section 215, intelligence agents remain at a comparative disadvantage since they must get the approval of a FISA court before compelling records production while prosecutors in criminal cases simply issue grand-jury subpoenas. Nonetheless, this commonsense provision came under blistering, disingenuous assault last year when the ACLU and others raised the red herring of library records—which are not even mentioned in the statute. In 2002, for example, the *Hartford Courant* was compelled to retract in full a story that falsely accused the FBI of installing software on computers in the Hartford Public Library to monitor the public's use of the Internet. (In fact, the FBI had obtained a court-ordered search warrant to copy the hard drive of a single computer that had been used criminally to hack into a business computer system in California.)

In 2003, the ACLU issued a warning that Section 215 would allow federal "thought police" to "target us for what we choose to read or what Websites we visit." In reality, Section 215 (unlike criminal-grand-jury subpoena authority) expressly contains safeguards protecting First Amendment rights, and further provides that the attorney general must, twice a year, "fully inform" Congress about how the provision has been implemented. As of September 2003, the provision had not been used a single time neither for library records nor, indeed, for records of any kind.

Unlike reading habits, financing—the lifeblood of terrorist networks—actually is a PATRIOT target. The act has significantly crimped the ability of overseas terrorists to use foreign banks and nominees to avoid seizures of their funds; it cracked down on the so-called "hawalas" (that is, unlicensed money-transmitting businesses) that have been used to funnel millions of dollars to terror groups; it extended the reach of civil money-laundering penalties—which loom large in the minds of financial institutions—against those who engage in transactions involving the proceeds of crime. And it further choked the funding channels by making currency smuggling itself (rather than the mere failure to file a report about the movement of currency) a crime, an initiative that bolsters the legal basis for seizing all, rather than a portion, of the smuggled funds. These and other PATRIOT finance provisions have enabled the government to obtain over 20 convictions to date and freeze over $130 million in assets worldwide.

Mention should also be made of another PATRIOT improvement that has been speciously challenged: the codification of uniform procedures for so-called sneak-and-peek warrants, which allow agents to conduct a search without seizing items, and delay notification to the person whose premises have been searched—thus ensuring that an investigation can proceed and agents can continue identifying other conspirators. Such warrants have been used for many years, and delayed notification has been commonplace—just as it is in other areas, such as wiretap law, where alerting the subject would prematurely end the investigation.

Sneak-and-peek delayed notification, however, evolved through federal case law rather than by statute, and consequently there was a jumble of varying requirements depending on which federal circuit the investigation happened to be in. All PATRIOT did in this regard was impose a uniform national standard that permits delay if notification could cause endangerment to life, facilitation of flight, destruction of evidence, intimidation of witnesses, or similar substantial jeopardizing of investigations. Yet critics drummed up outrage by portraying sneak-and-peek as if it were a novel encroachment on privacy rather than a well-established tool that requires prior court approval. So effective was this campaign that the House of Representatives responded by voting to deny funding for the delayed notification warrants. Inability to delay notification, of course, would defeat the purpose of using sneak-and-peek in the first place. The Senate has not seemed inclined to follow suit, but that so prudent a provision could become the subject of controversy illustrates how effectively the opposition has discredited the PATRIOT Act.

Palpably, the PATRIOT Act, far from imperiling the Constitution, went a long way toward shoring up the perilous state of national security that existed on the morning of 9/11. That is why it is so excruciating to note that, despite all we have been through, we will be transported right back to that precarious state if Congress fails to reauthorize PATRIOT. Because of intense lobbying by civil liberties groups instinctively hostile to anything that makes government stronger—even in the arena of national defense, where we need it to be strong if we are to have liberties at all—PATRIOT's sponsors had to agree, to secure passage, that the act would effectively be experimental. That is, the information sharing, improved investigative techniques, and several other provisions were not permanently enacted into law but are scheduled to "sunset" on December 31, 2005. Dismayingly, far from grasping the eminent sense in making these improvements permanent, the alliance of Democratic Bush-bashers and crusading Republican libertarians is actually pushing a number of proposals to extend the sunset provision to parts of PATRIOT that were not originally covered.

At a time when the 9/11 Commission's public hearings highlight intelligence lapses and investigative backwardness—and when al-Qaeda publicly threatens larger-than-ever attacks while continuing to fight our forces and allies on the battlefield and in murderous attacks throughout the world—it is remarkable that elected officials would have any priority other than making the PATRIOT Act permanent.

## DISCUSSION QUESTIONS

1. Is Pearlstein correct in arguing that it is possible to enhance security without sacrificing liberty? Would the measures she supports—public health surveillance, cargo inspections, and soon affect *other* forms of liberty, such as property rights or economic freedom?

2. Is the slippery-slope argument—that we put up with small restrictions on civil liberties only to find further incremental restrictions acceptable, until they add up to significant curtailments—persuasive? How about the inverse of the slippery-slope argument—if we *don't* take steps to protect ourselves, we risk more attacks that could lead to real restrictions on civil liberties?

# PART II

# Institutions

# CHAPTER 5

# Congress: The First Branch

## 23

## From *Congress: The Electoral Connection*

### David R. Mayhew

*Are members of Congress motivated by the desire to make good public policy that will best serve the public and national interest? Political scientist David R. Mayhew argues that the motivation is not so idealistic or complex. Members of Congress simply want to be reelected, and most of their behavior—advertising, credit claiming, and position taking—is designed to make reelection easier. Further, Mayhew argues that the structure of Congress is ideally suited to facilitate the reelection pursuit. Congressional offices and staff advertise member accomplishments, committees allow for the specialization necessary to claim credit for particularistic benefits provided to the district, and the political parties in Congress do not demand loyalty when constituent interests run counter to the party line.*

*Mayhew's argument is not universally accepted. Many political scientists accept his underlying premise as a given: elected officials are self-interested, and this is manifest in their constant pursuit of reelection. But others disagree with the premise. Motivations, they argue, are far more complex than allowed for by such a simple statement or theory. People often act unselfishly, and members of Congress have been known to vote with their consciences even if it means losing an election. Others have pointed out that parties now serve as a stronger constraint on congressional behavior than they did when Mayhew was writing in the early 1970s.*

[1.] The organization of Congress meets remarkably well the electoral needs of its members. To put it another way, if a group of planners sat down and tried to design a pair of American national assemblies with the goal of serving members' electoral needs year in and year out, they would be hard pressed to improve on what exists. * * * [2.] Satisfaction of electoral needs requires remarkably little zero-sum conflict among members. That is, one member's gain is not another member's loss; to a remarkable degree members can successfully engage in electorally useful activities without denying other members the opportunity successfully to engage in them. In regard to credit claiming, this second point requires elaboration further on. Its application to advertising is perhaps obvious. The members all have different markets, so that what any one member does is not an inconvenience to any other. There are exceptions here— House members are sometimes thrown into districts together, senators have to watch the advertising of ambitious House members within their states, and senators from the same state have to keep up with each other—but the case generally holds. With position taking the point is also reasonably clear. As long as congressmen do not attack each other —and they rarely do—any member can champion the most extraordinary causes without inconveniencing any of his colleagues.

*    *    *

A scrutiny of the basic structural units of Congress will yield evidence to support both these * * * points. First, there are the 535 Capitol Hill *offices*, the small personal empires of the members. * * * The Hill office is a vitally important political unit, part campaign management firm and part political machine. The availability of its staff members for election work in and out of season gives it some of the properties of the former; its casework capabilities, some of the properties of the latter. And there is the franking privilege for use on office emanations. * * * A final comment on congressional offices is perhaps the most important one: office resources are given to all members regardless of party, seniority, or any other qualification. They come with the job.

Second among the structural units are the *committees.* * * * Committee membership can be electorally useful in a number of different ways. Some committees supply good platforms for position taking. The best example over the years is probably the House Un-American Activities Committee (now the Internal Security Committee), whose members have displayed hardly a trace of an interest in legislation. [Theodore] Lowi has a chart showing numbers of days devoted to HUAC public hearings in Congresses from the Eightieth through the Eighty-ninth. It can be read as a supply chart, showing biennial volume of position taking on subversion and related matters; by inference it can also be read as a measure of popular demand (the peak years were 1949–56). Senator Joseph McCarthy used the Senate Government Operations Committee as his investigative base in the Eighty-third Congress; later on in the 1960s Senators Abraham Ribicoff (D., Conn.) and William Proxmire (D., Wis.) used subcommittees of this same unit in catching public attention respectively on auto safety and defense waste. With membership on the Senate Foreign Relations Committee goes a license to make speeches on foreign policy. Some committees perhaps deserve to be designated "cause committees"; membership on them can confer an ostentatious identification with salient public causes. An example is the House Education and Labor Committee, whose members, in Fenno's analysis, have two "strategic premises": "to prosecute policy partisanship" and "to pursue one's individual policy preferences regardless of party." Committee members do a good deal of churning about on education, poverty, and similar matters. In recent years Education and Labor has attracted media-conscious members such as Shirley Chisholm (D., N.Y.), Herman Badillo (D., N.Y.), and Louise Day Hicks (D., Mass.).

Some committees traffic in particularized benefits.

\* \* \*

Specifically, in giving out particularized benefits where the costs are diffuse (falling on taxpayer or consumer) and where in the long run to reward one congressman is not obviously to deprive others, the members follow a policy of universalism. That is, every member, regardless of party or seniority, has a right to his share of benefits. There is evidence of universalism in the distribution of projects on House Public Works, projects on House Interior, projects on Senate Interior, project money on House Appropriations, project money on Senate Appropriations, tax benefits on House Ways and Means, tax benefits on Senate Finance, and (by inference from the reported data) urban renewal projects on House Banking and Currency. The House Interior Committee, in Fenno's account, "takes as its major decision rule a determination to process and pass *all* requests and to do so in such a way as to maximize the chances of passage in the House. Succinctly, then, Interior's major strategic premise is: *to secure House passage of all constituency-supported, Member-sponsored bills.*"

\* \* \*

Particularism also has its position-taking side. On occasion members capture public attention by denouncing the allocation process itself; thus in 1972 a number of liberals held up some Ways and Means "members' bills" on the House floor. But such efforts have little or no effect. Senator Douglas used to offer floor amendments to excise projects from public works appropriations bills, but he had a hard time even getting the Senate to vote on them.

Finally, and very importantly, the committee system aids congressmen simply by allowing a division of labor among members. The parceling out of legislation among small groups of congressmen by subject area has two effects. First, it creates small voting bodies in which membership may be valuable. An attentive interest group will prize more highly the favorable issue positions of members of committees pondering its fortunes than the favorable positions of the general run of congressmen. Second, it creates specialized small-group settings in which individual congressmen can make things happen and be perceived to make things happen. "I put that bill through committee." "That was my amendment." "I talked them around on that." This is the language of credit claiming. It comes easily in the committee setting and also when "expert" committee members handle bills on the floor. To attentive audiences it can be believable. Some political actors follow committee activities closely and mobilize electoral resources to support deserving members.

\*   \*   \*

The other basic structural units in Congress are the *parties*. The case here will be that the parties, like the offices and committees, are tailored to suit members' electoral needs. They are more useful for what they are not than for what they are.

\*   \*   \*

What is important to each congressman, and vitally so, is that he be free to take positions that serve his advantage. There is no member of either house who would not be politically injured—or at least who would not think he would be injured—by being made to toe a party line on all policies (unless of course he could determine the line). There is no congressional bloc whose members have identical position needs across all issues. Thus on the school busing issue in the Ninety-second Congress, it was vital to Detroit white liberal Democratic House members that they be free to vote one way and to Detroit black liberal Democrats that they be free to vote the other. In regard to these member needs the best service a party can supply to its congressmen is a negative one; it can leave them alone. And this in general is what the congressional parties do. Party leaders are chosen not to be program salesmen or vote mobilizers, but to be brokers, favor-doers, agenda-setters, and protectors of established institutional routines. Party "pressure" to vote one way or another is minimal. Party "whipping" hardly deserves the name. Leaders in both houses have a habit of counseling members to "vote their constituencies."

## Discussion Questions

1. Is it necessarily bad that some members of Congress are motivated by the desire to be reelected? After all, shouldn't members of Congress do things that will keep the voters happy? Does the constant quest for reelection have a positive or negative impact on "representation"?

2. How could the institutions of Congress (members' offices, committees, and parties) be changed so that the collective needs of the institution would take precedence over the needs of individual

members? What might be the negative consequences of making these changes?

3. Some have argued that term limits are needed to break the never-ending quest for reelection. Do you think that a three-term limit for members of Congress is a good idea?

# 24

# "Reelection Tips for Legislators"

RON FAUCHEUX

*If the primary goal of elected officials is to be reelected, what's the best strategy? Ron Faucheux, editor-in-chief of* Campaigns and Elections *magazine, offers a nine-point checklist of actions legislators can take to be reelected. The checklist builds upon Mayhew's observations on the importance of advertising, credit claiming, and position taking, and places particular emphasis on the need to communicate clearly, visibly, and frequently with close supporters as well as opponents. Many of his bits of advice are good common sense, but others are things that a member of Congress could easily forget, such as "speak the right language." By this Faucheux means that members need to communicate in simple, clear language rather than legislative jargon. Other suggestions, like "reach out to political opponents," would be useful antidotes to the political polarization discussed in chapter 11.*

An overwhelming majority of legislators—federal, state and local—are reelected every election. Lawmakers who are defeated are usually those who are embroiled in scandal, reapportioned into an unfavorable new district or perceived to have lost touch with their constituents. There's not much that can be done about a scandal or a reapportionment once the deed is done, but the third risk is one that every member of Congress needs to guard against.

The best way to prepare for reelection is to immediately focus upon a plan of action to keep you in close touch with the voters. The following nine tips will go a long way to accomplishing that goal:

*1. Keep your perspective.* The world looks different from behind the high marble walls and big bronze doors of the state capitol or city hall. Smart incumbents, especially in swing districts and states, need to keep that in mind as they delve into the minutiae of legislation.

Insiders may think in terms of bills, resolutions and amendments, but voters think in terms of problems and solutions. While administrative bureaucrats, committee staffers, professional lobbyists and colleagues from both parties are all vitally important to your role as legislator, don't forget that these people—no matter how knowledgeable or powerful—are highly unrepresentative of the electorate that sent you there.

If you forget the folks back home, they may return the favor.

*2. Speak the right language.* If you want to communicate with English-speaking people, you don't speak Russian. If you want to get something across to Germans, you don't tell it to them in Chinese.

The same is true about legislative dialect. Language used in the law-making process—just like language used in court rooms or in operating rooms—is foreign to outsiders.

So, if you want to communicate with your constituents, directly or through the press, talk to them in language they understand—and that ain't Legislativese.

New legislators, federal and state, are prone to becoming so impressed with themselves as they learn insider lingo that they can't wait to show it off. Beware of that, because it happens slowly and naturally. Though an occasional use of a technical term may be OK, make sure you always couple it with everyday language.

For example, when doing media interviews and making speeches at home, avoid excessive use of bill numbers and committee names and stay away from bureaucratic words like "finalize," "establish" and "supplemental." Instead, use terms like "end," "start" and "extra."

*3. Immediately after your election, quickly solidify an impression that you're reaching out to your constituents and keeping your promises.* First impressions are critically important to voters and news reporters. Early efforts that show you're working overtime to stay in contact with the people of your district or state will quickly establish a highly favorable—and enduring—image that will serve you well for your entire career.

Once you're perceived as an effective, tireless, in-touch legislator, it'll be extremely difficult for a future challenger to destroy that impression.

Here's a useful tip: The first time you go back home after you've been sworn in, make a big deal over it. Arrange numerous meetings with supporters, talk to the press, hold town meetings, send streams of mail. Your first visit home is a window of opportunity that doesn't last long, maybe only a few weeks. So do it up right. It'll create a first impression that will last forever.

*4. Don't forget your friends.* Go home with the one who brought you. Translation: Keep your political base happy.

This doesn't mean you have to give every interest group that supported you everything they want—they'll often overreach and ask for more than they'll expect you to give them—but it does mean keeping bonds of friendship and trust strong and lines of communication open.

This requires a two-pronged strategy: First, stay in touch with the organizational leadership of your support base both at the capitol and city hall (lobbyists) and at home (association officers, citizen activists, local PAC directors). Consider them part of your political family. Keep in touch. Ask their advice on a range of issues, even those that may not be on their agenda. Don't mislead or lie to friends in a sneaky effort to curry favor with the other side; they'll catch you as sure as the day is long—and then you'll be left without friends or respect.

Second, make direct appeals to the grassroots base of friendly constituencies. Don't just talk to the leaders. Communicate with their membership—through mailers, invitations, questionnaires—and let them know that you're looking out for them. This ensures that cross-pressured voters who have multiple affiliations—the Chamber of Commerce AND the NRA; the Women's Political Caucus AND the Sierra Club—relate to your overall approach to representation above and beyond your voting record on a single issue.

5. *Reach out to political opponents.* After getting elected, some politicians can't wait to cut out their opponents. Doing so may make you feel good temporarily, but it can also solidify a base of opposition that, if allowed to fester and grow, could ultimately kill you.

The wisest course is to go to your political opponents after the election is over and let them know that you're respectful of their views—even when contrary to your own—and will work with them in a cooperative way. In fact, go further and ask them for their ideas; let them know you're sincere about wanting to include them.

Of course, this doesn't mean you should put your enemies above your friends or sell out your principles. Stick to your guns—and your base—in terms of policy and the casting of roll call votes. But as you do, be careful how you treat the people on the other side. Don't add insult to injury.

Be kind and civil to people who supported your opponent in the last election. Let them know that you will make a real effort to find out what they think and attempt to find common ground that affords them real input.

6. *Send out newsletters that solicit citizen views.* Don't just tell your constituents what you think, ask them their opinions. Use your newsletters not just to disseminate information but to seek it.

In preparing a survey questionnaire for citizens, make sure the questions are not so slanted and biased that it will frustrate or needlessly offend them.

Once you get the returned questionnaires, immediately send each citizen a thank you letter for responding. Keep track of the issues they raised in their surveys, put the information in a database and as legislative action is taken, write to them about what you're doing.

Make it clear on the front page of your newsletter that you're sending this mailing to keep in touch with voters—the way you promised you would do.

Also, put your newsletter on the Internet and use the Web to seek voter views and to provide helpful information about various public services and government agencies.

7. *Hold town hall meetings.* Voters like access. Town hall meetings provide a popular vehicle for public interaction.

Town hall meetings should be promoted through your newsletter as well as local press outlets. A good format for a town hall meeting is to open with a 15- to 20-minute "report to the people" summarizing recent news and to give your views on the issues of the day. If there is a particularly important matter of concern to the public—i.e., the construction of a new highway or the closing of a nearby military base—you may want to have people from the relevant agencies on hand to provide background and to answer technical questions. You may also want to develop a format that gives each side a chance to have a say.

After the initial presentation, it should be opened to questions. But before you ask for audience questions, make it clear that you will stay after the public meeting to handle individual or private questions.

The key is to be a good listener. Make it clear from the outset that you respect every point of view expressed and will take each citizen's input seriously. "You may not always agree with me on every detail on every issue, but at least I listen, at least I'm open-minded and at least I'll tell you straight where I stand"—that should be your motto.

You can also put your town meeting on a local cable TV channel and run ads in the TV section of the local newspaper promoting the programs. Of course, keep in mind that if you allow a telecast of the meeting it provides a videotaped record of any gaffes or mistakes you make that could find their way into the hands of future opponents.

After the meeting, send each attendee a thank you letter.

*8. Build a database.* You should keep an active database of all the registered voters in your constituency. The list should include every piece of information legally available: address, phone number, e-mail address, party identification, age, issue interests, group membership and political involvement. Newly registered voters should be added on a monthly basis and should be sent a letter welcoming them into your area.

Voters who were identified as being favorable or unfavorable in your last campaign should be entered into the database. Volunteers, contributors, sign locations, issue activists and interest group affiliations should also be entered. As voters call or write you, note that contact on the master list; as they express their views on issues—pro or con—keep track of that, too.

If you maintain your database carefully and always enhance it with new information, you will have a powerful grassroots contact tool when it comes to reelection time.

Of course, be careful that you don't improperly use public property to build and maintain this data bank. Play it safe. Don't risk getting into trouble. It may be tempting to use free government facilities and equipment at your disposal to conduct political activities, but don't fall into that trap. Many elected officials have crossed the line and paid a dear price for their indiscretions.

*9. Rebuild your press relations.* You believe that some reporters treated you unfairly at least a time or two in your last campaign. But once you're elected, the best thing to do about those slights—however painful and harmful they may have been—is to forget about them. Start fresh. Make it clear to reporters, editors, news directors and publishers that you're going to be accessible to them and treat them as professionals doing a job.

You want to have a reputation among the news media as being open and accessible. Let reporters know that you're not only a quote source but a good, honest clearinghouse of governmental and congressional information.

## DISCUSSION QUESTIONS

1. Do these tips for legislators provide a sound strategy for reelection? Do they do anything else except secure reelection? Can you think of circumstances when a legislator would not want to take Faucheux's advice?

2. Given Mayhew's assessment of legislative efforts to be representative, how should we assess Faucheux's reelection tips? Might his reelection tips actually increase problems? Or can they be applied in ways that productively alter constituents' expectations for legislative performance?

3. If you were a campaign manager for a member of Congress, which of Faucheux's tips would you particularly emphasize? Which would you avoid? Are there any bits of advice that you would add?

# 25

# "Too Much of a Good Thing: More Representative Is Not Necessarily Better"

## John R. Hibbing and Elizabeth Theiss-Morse

*David Mayhew describes an institution that should be highly responsive to voters. If members of Congress want to get reelected, they need to do what their constituents want them to do. However, John Hibbing and Elizabeth Theiss-Morse argue that having institutions that are* too *representative may be "too much of a good thing." That is, it may not be in the nation's interest to always do what the public wants, especially when it comes to issues of institutional reform. On questions of reform, the public is usually convinced that the only thing that is preventing ideal policies is that "the people in power" are serving their own interests rather than the public's interests. According to this view, the obvious— but wrong, according to Hibbing and Theiss-Morse—solution is to weaken political institutions through "reforms" such as term limits, reducing the salaries of members of Congress, and requiring that Congress balance the federal budget every year. Hibbing and Theiss-Morse argue that these reforms might make people even more disillusioned when they discover that weakening Congress will not solve our nation's problems.*

*The authors also argue that the public generally does not have a very realistic understanding of the inherent nature of conflict in the political process. The public believes that there is substantial consensus on most issues and only small "fringe" groups disagree on a broad range of issues. If this is true, it is certainly understandable why people are frustrated with Congress. But in reality, as the authors point out, the nation is deeply divided about the proper course of action. This makes conflict and compromise an inherent part of the legislative process, and at the same time dims the prospects for simple reforms.*

Reform sentiments are much in evidence on the American political scene as we approach the end of the [twentieth] century, and improving the way public opinion is represented in political institutions is often the major motivation of reformers. This is clear * * * from the activities of contemporary political elites, and from the mood of ordinary people. Gross dissatisfaction exists with the nature of representation perceived to be offered by the modern political system. People believe the political process has been commandeered by narrow special interests and by political parties whose sole aim is to contradict the other political party. Given the centrality of representation in the U.S. polity, the organizers and contributors to this symposium are to be commended. It is laudable to want to consider ways of improving the system and, thereby, making people happier with their government. Many of the ideas described in the accompanying essays have considerable merit.

We do, however, wish to raise two important cautions: one briefly and the second in greater detail. Perhaps these cautions are not needed; the authors of the accompanying pieces are almost certainly aware of them. Still, general debate often neglects these two points. Therefore, quite apart from whether it is a good idea or a bad idea, say, to reform campaign finance, enact term limits, or move toward proportional representation and away from single-member districts, it is important * * * to keep in mind that 1) "because the people want them" is not a good justification for adopting procedural reforms and 2) actual enactment of the reforms craved by the people will not necessarily leave us with a system that is more liked even by the people who asked for the reforms in the first place. We take each point in turn.

### Ignoring the People's Voice on Process Matters Is Not Evil

It would be easy at this point to slip into a discussion of the political acumen possessed by the American public and, relatedly, of the extent to which elected officials and political institutions should listen to the people. But such a discussion has been going on at least since the time of Plato and it is unlikely we would add much to it here. Instead, we merely wish to point out that, whatever the overall talents of the rank and file, political change in the realm of process should *not* be as sensitive to the public's wishes as political change in the realm of policy.

It is one thing to maintain that in a democracy the people should get welfare reform if they want it. It is quite another to maintain that those same people should get term limits if they want them. Process needs to have some relative permanence, some "stickiness." This is the *definiens* of institutional processes. Without this trait, policy legitimacy would be compromised. The U.S. Constitution (like all constitutions) drives home this contention by including much on process (vetoes, impeachments, representational arrangements, terms of officials, minimum qualifications for holding particular offices, etc.) and precious little about policy. What policy proclamations *are* to be found in the Constitution have faced a strong likelihood of being reversed in subsequent actions (slavery and the 13th Amendment; tax policy and the 16th Amendment; prohibition and the 21st Amendment). Constitutions are written not to enshrine policy but to enshrine a system that will then make policy. These systemic structures should not be subjected lightly to popular whimsy.

The Framers took great efforts to insulate processes from the momentary fancies of the people; specifically, they made amending the Constitution difficult. It is not unusual for reformers, therefore, to run up against the Constitution and its main interpreters—the courts. Witness recent decisions undermining the ability of citizens to impose legislative term limits on members of Congress save by constitutional amendment. This uphill battle to enact procedural reform is precisely what the founders intended—and they were wise to do so.

It may be that the people's will should be reflected directly in public policy, perhaps through initiatives or, less drastically, through the actions of citizen-legislators who act as delegates rather than Burkean trustees. But this does not mean that the rules of the system themselves should change with public preferences in the same way health care policy should change with public preferences.

There may be many good reasons to change the processes of government—possibly by making government more representative—but a persuasive defense of process reforms is *not* embedded in the claim that the people are desirous of such reform. Just as the Bill of Rights does not permit a simple majority of the people to make decisions that will restrict basic rights, so the rest of the Constitution does not permit a simple majority of the people to alter willy-nilly the processes of government. There are good reasons for such arrangements.

## Be Careful What You Wish For

One important reason we should be glad ordinary people are not in a position to leave their every mark on questions of political process and institutional design is the very good possibility that people will not be happy with the reforms they themselves advocate. The people generally clamor for reforms that would weaken institutions and strengthen the role of the people themselves in policy decisions. They advocate people's courts, an increased number of popular initiatives and referenda, devolution of authority to institutions "closer" to the people, term limits, staff cuts, emaciating the bureaucracy, elimination of committees, cessation of contact between interest groups and elected officials, and a weakening of political parties. These changes would clear the way for people to have greater influence on decisions, and this is what the people want, right?

Actually, our research suggests this is *not* what the people really want. The public does not desire direct democracy; it is not even clear that people desire democracy at all, although they are quite convinced they do. People want no part of a national direct democracy in which they would be asked to register their preferences, probably electronically, on important issues of the day. Proposals for such procedures are received warmly by a very small minority of citizens. Observers who notice the public's enthusiasm for virtually every populist notion sometimes go the next step of assuming the public wants direct democracy. This is simply an inaccurate assumption.

However, the public *does* want institutions to be transformed into something much closer to the people. The public sees a big disconnect between how they want representation to work and how they believe it is working. Strong support of populist government (not direct democracy) has been detected in innumerable polls conducted during the last couple of decades. That the public looks favorably upon this process agenda is beyond dispute. A national survey we conducted in 1992 found strong support for reforms that would limit the impact of the Washington scene on members of Congress.[1] For example, seven out of 10 respondents supported a reduction in congressional salaries, eight out of 10 supported term limitations, and nine out of 10 supported a balanced-budget amendment. What ties these reforms together is the public's desire to make elected officials more like ordinary people. In focus groups we conducted at the same time as the survey, participants stated many times that elected officials in Washington had lost touch with the people. They supported reforms believed to encourage officials to start keeping in touch. Elected officials should balance the budget just like the people back home. Elected officials should live off modest salaries just like the people back home. And elected officials should face the prospect of getting a real job back home rather than staying in Washington for years and years. These reforms would force elected officials to understand the needs of their constituents rather than get swept up in the money and power that run Washington.

If these reforms were put into place, would the public suddenly love Congress? We do not think so. Certain reforms, such as campaign finance reform, may help, since they would diminish the perception that money rules politics in Washington. But the main reason the public is disgruntled with Congress and with politics in Washington is because they are dissatisfied with the processes intrinsic to the operation of a democratic political system—debates, compromises, conflicting information, inefficiency, and slowness. This argument may seem odd on its face, so in the next few paragraphs we provide our interpretation of why the public questions the need for democratic processes.

The public operates under the erroneous assumption that the majority of the American people agrees on policy matters. In focus groups we conducted in 1997, participants adamantly stated that "80 percent of the American people agree on what needs to be done [about serious societal problems], but it's the other 20 percent who have the power." This pervasive and persistent belief in the existence of popular consensus on tough policy issues is, of course, grossly mistaken. Virtually every well-worded survey question dealing with salient policy issues of the day reveals deep divisions in the American public. From welfare reform to health care; from remaining in Bosnia to the taxes-services trade-off; from a constitutional amendment on flag desecration to the situations in which abortion is believed to be properly permitted, the people are at odds with each other.

This level of popular disagreement would be quite unremarkable except for the fact that the people will not admit that the disagreement actually exists. Instead, people project their own particular views, however ill-formed, onto a clear majority of other "real" people. Those (allegedly) few people who allow it to be known that they do not hold these views are dismissed as radical and noisy fringe elements that are accorded far too much influence by polemical parties, self-serving special interests, and spineless, out-of-touch elected officials. Thus, the desire to move the locus of decision making closer to the people is based on a faulty assumption right off the bat. Many believe that if decisions emanated from the people themselves, we would get a welcome break from the fractious politics created by politicians and institutions. Pastoral, common-sensical solutions will instead quietly begin to find their way into the statute books. The artificial conflict to which we have unfortunately become accustomed will be no more and we can then begin to solve problems.

Given people's widespread belief in popular consensus, it is no wonder they despise the existing structure of governmental institutions. All that these institutions—and the people filling them—do is obscure the will of the people by making it look as though there is a great deal of divisiveness afoot. Who then can condone debate and compromise among elected officials if these processes only give disproportionate weight to nefarious fringe elements that are intent upon subverting the desires of healthy, red-blooded Americans? Who then can condone inefficiency and slowness when we all agree on what needs to be done and politicians ought just to do it? Democratic processes merely get in the way. People react positively to the idea that we ought to run government like a business—it would be efficient, frugal, and quick to respond to problems. Of course, what people tend not to realize is that it would also be undemocratic.

Too many people do not understand political conflict: they have not been taught to deal with it; they have not come to realize it is a natural part of a culture such as ours. When they are confronted with it, they conclude it is an indication something is woefully amiss and in need of correction. They jump at any solution perceived to have the potential of reducing conflict; solutions such as giving authority over to potentially autocratic and hierarchical business-like arrangements or to mythically consensual ordinary people.

Our fear is that, if the people were actually given what they want, they might soon be even more disillusioned with the political system than ever. Suppose people *were* made to feel more represented than they are now; suppose authority *were* really pushed toward the common person. The first thing people would learn is that these changes will have done nothing to eliminate political conflict. The deep policy divisions that polls now reveal among the citizenry would be of more consequence since these very views would now be more determinative of public policy. Conflict would still be pervasive. Popular discontent would not have been ameliorated. Quite likely, people would quickly grow ever more cynical about the potential for reform to accomplish what they want it to accomplish.

Instead of allowing the people to strive for the impossible—an open and inclusive democracy that is devoid of conflict—we need to educate the people about the unrealistic nature of their desires. Instead of giving the people every reform for which they agitate, we need to get them to see where their wishes, if granted, are likely to lead them. The people pay lip service to democracy but that is the extent of it. They claim to love democracy more than life itself, but they only love the concept. They do not love the actual practice of democracy because it suggests differences, because it is ponderous, because it revolves around debate (bickering) and compromise (selling out) and divisions (gridlock).

*Conclusion*

We hasten to point out that we are not opposed to reforms. For what it is worth, we believe the United States polity could certainly benefit from selective modifications to current institutional arrangements. But we *are* opposed to the tendency of many ordinary people to try to enact reforms intended to weaken political institutions even though these same people evince no real plan describing where that power should be transferred. It is often assumed that the people are populists and that they therefore want power in their own hands. As we have indicated, they do not in actuality want power. They only want to know that they could have this power if they wanted it. They only want to know that this power is not being exercised by those who are in a position to use it to their own advantage. They only want decisions to be made nonconflictually. And they are willing to entertain a variety of possible structures (some far from democratic) if those reforms appear to offer hope of bringing about all these somewhat contradictory desires.

Altering representational arrangements should be considered. The current system can and must be improved. The campaign finance system is an embarrassment and the dispute over drawing oddly-shaped districts for the purpose of obtaining majority-minority districts lays bare the very real problems of single member districts. But we should not jump to enact all reforms simply because people think they want them. No one said that in a democracy the people would get to shape processes however they wanted. It is not inconsistent to have democratic governmental structures that are themselves rather impervious to popular sentiments for change in those procedures. What makes the system democratic is the ability of people to influence policy, not the ability of people to influence process.

This is fortunate because the people's ideas about process are fundamentally flawed. People (understandably) think well of the American public writ large, and people (understandably) dislike conflict, so people (nonsensically) assume the two cannot go together in spite of the impressive array of factual evidence indicating that conflict and the American people—indeed any free people, as Madison so eloquently related in *Federalist 10*—go hand in hand. As a result of their misconception, the people will undoubtedly be quite dissatisfied with the actual consequences of most attempts to expand representation via campaign finance reform, term limits, or proportional representation. There may be good reasons to enact such reforms, but, we submit, neither a public likely to be suddenly pleased with the post-reform political system nor a public that is somehow deserving of a direct voice in process reform is one of them.

## DISCUSSION QUESTIONS

1. In one of the more provocative claims in their article, Hibbing and Theiss-Morse say "the public does not desire direct democracy; it is not even clear that people desire democracy at all, although they are quite convinced they do." Do you agree? What evidence do the authors provide to support this claim?

2. If people had a more complex understanding of the political process, what types of reforms would they favor?

3. Is it possible to have a political system that is too responsive?

## NOTE

1. John R. Hibbing and Elizabeth Theiss-Morse. 1995. *Congress as Public Enemy: Public Attitudes Toward American Political Institutions*. Cambridge: Cambridge University Press.

## DEBATING THE ISSUES: PORK BARREL POLITICS

Each article in this chapter highlights the importance legislators place on serving their constituents. The strategy might work for reelection, but it may undermine the capacity of Congress to deal effectively with national problems and priorities. The debate over pork barrel politics captures this institutional tension, and illustrates the difficulties of defining "national" interests rather than parochial, or local, interests.

The emergency spending bill that was passed early in 1999 is one recent example of "pork barrel politics": localized benefits that are tacked onto larger "must pass" bills (in this instance the larger bill provided money for the war in Kosovo and disaster relief for flood and hurricane victims). Even more recently, the war against terrorism and "homeland security" led Congress to quickly spend through the budget surplus late in 2001. The bill that received the most negative attention was the airline bailout, which sailed through Congress without much debate in the weeks after the terrorist attacks. Similar charges of wasteful spending have been made concerning the rebuilding of Iraq as contractors received "no-bid" contracts for securing and restoring oil fields, among other lucrative projects.

The "Citizens Against Government Waste" (CAGW) is an interest group that identifies the pork barrel spending in the federal budget. The first selection is drawn from their *Pig Book*, which they publish every year. CAGW defines the criteria that it uses to identify pork and attributes much of the problem of the balooning federal deficit and debt to Congress's addiction to what CAGW defines as wasteful spending.

Sean Paige and Jonathan Cohn view pork barrel politics from different perspectives. For Paige, the $520 billion spending bill passed in late 1998 tossed aside the "hard-won gains" of budget balancing achieved in 1997 and was "larded . . . with heapings of pork barrel projects." Paige recognizes the difficulties of practicing fiscal discipline when all members of Congress want and need to provide something for their home districts. Nevertheless, he criticizes the practice of attaching last-minute pork barrel riders to the budget, something done even by members who built their careers on deficit reduction. The national interest in a balanced budget, according to Paige, should take priority over parochial projects.

Where Paige sees waste and abuse of the nation's resources, however, Cohn views pork as the "glue" of legislating. If it takes a little pork for the home district or state to get important legislation through Congress, so be it. Cohn also questions the motives of budget-reform groups that call for greater fiscal discipline in Congress; most of these groups, in his view, are not truly concerned over waste, but are simply against government spending in general. The policies they identify as pork, he argues, can have important national implications: military readiness, road improvements for an Olympic host city, or the development of new agricultural and food products. National interests can be served, in other words, by allowing local interests to take a dip into the pork barrel. Finally, Cohn argues that pork, even according to the critics' own definition, constitutes less than one percent of the overall federal budget.

# 26

# From *The Pig Book*

## CITIZENS AGAINST GOVERNMENT WASTE

During election years, politicians make speeches about how concerned they are with wasteful spending, the deficit, and the fiscal woes of the nation. But as soon as the television cameras are turned off, they brag about the pork that they are bringing home to their state or district. This hypocrisy has helped to create a $521 billion deficit and a $7.1 trillion national debt.

While $200,000 for recreation improvements in North Pole, Alaska, or $100,000 to renovate a Coca-Cola building in Macon, Georgia, may seem insignificant in the grand fiscal scheme of the country, such projects represent a corruption of the budget process. Too many members of Congress are more concerned about bringing home the bacon for their reelection than they are about the fiscal future of this country. To make the American people more aware of the connection between pork and the deficit, each earmark should bear a sticker on it that reads, "This project helped contribute to the $521 billion deficit." Maybe then Members of Congress wouldn't be so proud of their pork and taxpayers would demand greater accountability on Capitol Hill.

This year's total reveals that Congress porked out at record levels. For fiscal 2004, appropriators stuck 10,656 projects in the 13 appropriations bills, an increase of 13 percent over last year's total of 9,362. In the last two years, the total number of projects has increased 28 percent. The cost of these projects in fiscal 2004 was $22.9 billion, or 1.6 percent more than last year's total of $22.5 billion. In fact, the total cost of pork has increased by 14 percent since fiscal 2004. Total pork identified by Citizens Against Government Waste (CAGW) since 1991 adds up to $185 billion.

The top three increases in pork from fiscal 2003 to fiscal 2004 were: Foreign Operations from $181.4 million to $449 million (148 percent); Transportation/Treasury from $3.3 billion to $4.4 billion (33 percent); and Interior from $344 million to $446 million (29 percent).

Alaska again led the nation with $808 per capita ($524 million), or 26 times the national pork average of $31. The runners up were Hawaii with $393 per capita ($494 million) and the District of Columbia with $321 per capita ($181 million). The common thread in the top two states is that they are represented by powerful senators and appropriators—Senate Appropriations Committee Chairman Ted Stevens (R, Alaska), and the number-two Democrat on that committee, Sen. Daniel Inouye (D, Hawaii).

Unless Congress enacts serious and meaningful budget reform, there could be another record level of pork in fiscal 2005. Tax dollars should be focused on protecting the nation, instead of being used to protect the incumbency of members of Congress. The 630 projects, totaling $3.1 billion, in this year's Congressional Pig Book Summary symbolize the most egregious and blatant examples of pork. As in previous years, all of the items in the Congressional Pig Book Summary meet at least one of CAGW's seven criteria, but most satisfy at least two:

- Requested by only one chamber of Congress;
- Not specifically authorized;
- Not competitively awarded;
- Not requested by the President;
- Greatly exceeds the President's budget request or the previous year's funding;
- Not the subject of congressional hearings; or
- Serves only a local or special interest.

\* \* \*

Examples of pork from this year's Pig Book:

- $50 million for an indoor rainforest project in Coralville, Iowa.
- $18.5 million for the International Fund for Ireland.
- $15 million for dairy development programs overseas under the U.S. Agency of [International] Development.
- $6.8 million in YMCA funding.
- $6.1 million for wood utilization research (Alaska, Idaho, Maine, Michigan, Minnesota, Mississippi, North Carolina, Oregon, Tennessee, Washington, and West Virginia).
- $3 million for the First Tee Program in St. Augustine, Florida.
- $2.7 million for the Wood Education and Resource Center in West Virginia.
- $2.25 million in various Shakespeare-related funding.
- $2.2 million for North Pole, Alaska (pop. 1,570).
- $1.7 million for the International Fertilizer Development Center headquartered in Muscle Shoals, Alabama.
- $1.3 million for the Western Heritage Center in Billings, Montana.

- $725,000 for the Please Touch Museum in Philadelphia, Pennsylvania, to develop educational programs focusing on hands-on learning experiences.
- $538,000 for the National Wild Turkey Federation in Edgefield, South Carolina.
- $500,000 for Anaheim Resort Transit (including Disneyland) buses in California.
- $300,000 for Rock and Roll-related pork including $200,000 for the Rock and Roll Hall of Fame and Museum in Cleveland, Ohio, and $100,000 for the Kids Rock Free Educational Program.
- $225,000 to rehabilitate the Deer Park Pool in Sparks, Nevada.
- $175,000 for the Wichita Art Museum.
- $100,000 to restore the historic Coca-Cola building in Macon, Georgia.
- $100,000 for the Institute of International Sport to prevent youth crime.
- $50,000 for the Alaska Moving Image Preservation Association in Anchorage to digitize files, photos, and videos of Alaska history.
- $50,000 for the Imaginarium Science Center in Anchorage, Alaska, to develop science exhibits and distance delivery modules.
- $50,000 for the Saint Tikhon's Theological Seminary in South Canaan, Pennsylvania, for the care and preservation of Russian artifacts in Pennsylvania.

CAGW is a nonpartisan, nonprofit organization dedicated to eliminating waste, fraud, mismanagement and abuse in government.

# 27

# "Rolling Out the Pork Barrel"

## SEAN PAIGE

The fall of 1997 was a triumphant time for deficit hawks in Congress: Step by laborious step they finally had maneuvered President Clinton into signing the first balanced-budget bill in two decades, a long-sought political grail. Yet only a year later, as Congress rushed to cram a year's worth of budget writing into the waning weeks before the midterm elections, the hard-won gains of 1997 vanished like a mirage and the madness of budget seasons past made a triumphant return.

"There's a lot of little things tucked away there that I wish weren't," the president said, talking not about the latest batch of White House interns but rather the $520 billion omnibus spending bill he was signing into law. "But on balance, it honors our values and strengthens our country and looks to the future."

Critics, however, say the values it honors most are political expediency, fiscal opportunism and the scruples of the horse trader—while the only future to which its politician authors looked was their own.

All but a few members of Congress claimed to hate the damned thing.

However, a majority in both chambers held their noses and voted for it, larded as it was with heapings of pork barrel projects, the distribution of which remains a staple of the incumbency-protection racket, and some breathtaking acts of budget wizardry. The more than $21 billion in spending that exceeded budget caps set only a year earlier was declared "emergency" spending, as members continued to exploit a loophole that threatens to make the U.S. Treasury a federal disaster area. And some $9.1 billion in additional spending was "forward funded"—which means that Congress will spend it now and figure out how to pay for it later.

Criticism of the bill was rancorous and bipartisan. But even the opposition was divided: One faction hated what it saw as a retreat from fiscal restraint and responsibility; the other was appalled by the opacity of the process, in which a handful of negotiators from the White House and Congress worked out the horse trades behind closed doors. "This is a sham," cried Republican Rep. Jon Christensen of Nebraska. "This Congress ought to be ashamed of itself," scolded Wisconsin Democrat Rep. David Obey.

Retiring Speaker Newt Gingrich, who hasn't been quite the same since the federal-government brownout of 1995, a game of chicken with the White House that went badly for Republicans—found himself fending off a rearguard action from the right, of all places, and had to put the ingrates (he called them "petty dictators" and the "perfectionist caucus") in their place. "It is easy to get up and say, 'Vote No!' Then what would you do?" shrugged a world-wizened Gingrich. "Those of us who have grown up and matured . . . understand that we have to work together on the big issues."

Even the old sausage-maker himself, Democratic Sen. Robert Byrd of West Virginia, was shocked at what he saw. Renowned for his own cagey use of the budget process to bring billions of dollars in pork back to the Mountain State (and perhaps a bit peeved at finding himself excluded from all the behind-the-scenes horse trading), Byrd condemned the bill as a "gargantuan monstrosity"—a "Frankenstein monster patched together from old legislative body parts that don't quite fit."

Members of both parties chafed at having to vote on legislation crafted in such haste that few actually knew what was inside the 40-pound, 16-inch, 4,000-page end product (except, of course, for that quick peek at page 2,216, Part B, subsection 3[a], just to be sure that a wastewater-treatment facility and $4 million grant for the alma mater made it in). But by now a bit more is known about how this particular sausage was made and what ingredients went into it. The measure included funding for eight unfinished spending bills, a $21 billion emergency-spending measure and a cornucopia of legislative riders ranging from the substantial (one resulted in a major reorganization of the State Department) to the trivial (another extended duck-hunting season in Mississippi for 11 days) to the ludicrous (still another bans nude sunbathing at a beach near Cape Canaveral, Fla.).

Fiscal conservatives, led by House Budget Committee Chairman John Kasich of Ohio, had entertained the notion of dusting off the old budget battle-ax. But perennial targets for their imagined whacks, such as the National Endowment for the Arts and the Tennessee Valley Authority, sailed through unscathed. Moreover, even some old budget bogeymen—such as the wool, mohair and sugar subsidies—came roaring back from the brink of extinction.

If and when disputes arose between Democrats and Republicans, they invariably hinged not on where the ax might fall but on whom would be supping upon the larger ladle of gravy.

Clinton and the Democrats got $1.2 billion to begin hiring 30,000 of 100,000 new teachers (meaning much more money will be needed in the future); an $18 billion bailout for the International Monetary Fund; $1.7 billion in new home-health-care money for Medicare (reversing changes to the program made in 1996); and more than most Republicans wanted in farm aid (which even Senate Agriculture Committee Chairman Richard Lugar of Indiana said would "undermine" recent efforts to wean farmers off federal aid). Democrats also prevailed on a measure expanding coverage of the federal-employee health-insurance plan to include oral contraceptives; restored $35 million in food and oil shipments to North Korea; and turned back the Republican push for tax relief.

Republicans got $6.8 billion in increased military spending (some of which is classified), $1 billion for antimissile defense (although the Pentagon already is spending $3 billion annually on missile defense, with no deployment in sight) and $690 million for antidrug efforts (including the purchase of $40 million gulf-stream jets for law-enforcement agencies reportedly surprised by the windfall and $90 million for helicopters for Columbia). The GOP also was successful in its push to increase visa quotas for high-tech workers and, striking a blow for peduncles everywhere, blocked a Department of Transportation move that would have mandated peanut-free zones on commercial airliners.

The standoff continued on the question of how the year-2000 census will be conducted—whether by actual head count, as Republicans and the Constitution demand, or statistical sampling, as Democrats prefer—with a settlement postponed until after the Supreme Court rules on the case early next year. Other interesting bill provisions, without any known partisan parentage, include: a cut in foreign aid to countries that haven't paid parking tickets in the District of Columbia; a measure allowing the secretary of Agriculture to lend Russia money, which the Russians then can use to buy frozen chickens from Mississippi; $325 million inserted to buy enriched uranium from Russia; and $1 billion during the next five years to help the Tennessee Valley Authority refinance its debt.

Some of the $21.4 billion in "emergency" spending extras included: $3.35 billion to tackle the Y2K computer problem; $2.4 billion for anti-terrorism activities; $6.8 billion to improve military readiness; and $5.9 billion in additional aid to farmers. Many items among them drew fire from budgetwatchers, including $100 million for a new visitors center for the U.S. Capitol—an idea entertained for years which received a boost following last summer's fatal shootings there—and $100 million for a buyout of fishermen working in the Bering Sea, where pollock stocks have plummeted.

Singled out for particular opprobrium, however, was the $5.9 billion in emergency farm relief. Citizens Against Government Waste President Tom Schatz called it a "bipartisan and cynical attempt to buy the farm vote before this fall's election," pointing to studies showing that actual farm losses because of drought or other disasters were much lower. The group also condemned increased subsidies to sugar, peanuts and mohair producers contained in the Agriculture appropriations bill. Such subsidies, said CAGW, represented "a first step toward dismantling the 1996 farm bill"; which made history by beginning to phase out farm price supports that have been in place since the 1930s.

Of course, more pedestrian and parochial kinds of pork projects also were packed into the bill, a random sampling of which includes: $37.5 million for a ferry and docking facilities at King Cove, Alaska; $2 million for the National Center for Cool and Cold Water Aquaculture in West Virginia ("The seafood capital of Appalachia!" one wag said); $1 million for peanut quality research in Georgia; $1.4 million for the Jimmy Carter National Historical Site; a $200,000 grant to Vermont's Center for Rural Studies; $1 million to restore a German submarine at a museum in Chicago (the project received $900,000 last year); $1.2 million for a project called "Building America"; $400,000 for another called "Rebuilding America"; and $67,000 for the New Orleans Jazz Commission.

Christmas came early to the nation's capital this year. The party was a hoot-and-a-half while it lasted, but the inevitable hangover followed as its fuller consequences have become clear.

The 1998 spending spree "has made it almost impossible to stay within the budget caps set in the 1997 [budget] agreement," Senate Budget Committee staff director G. William Hoagland told a gathering just weeks after the bill became law. The committee estimates that when everything is factored in, the extra spending in the omnibus bill will drain $38.2 billion from any future budget surplus. And as the bills for its "forward-funding" mechanisms come due, deep and painful cuts in next year's discretionary spending will be necessary. And that, Hoagland says, is "unlikely unless we can come up with more user fees or some quick gimmicks in the budget."

But even if such a plan fails and the fiscal restraint that took decades to muster caves in on itself like a black hole, sucking the rest of the republic in after it, one thing will be said of the ludicrous budget battle of 1998: At least the duck hunters of Mississippi are happy.

## 28

# "Roll Out the Barrel:
# The Case Against the Case Against Pork"

### Jonathan Cohn

On most days, the lobby of the U.S. Chamber of Commerce's Washington, D.C., headquarters has a certain rarefied air. But on this Tuesday morning it is thick with the smell of greasy, grilled bacon. The aroma is appropriate, since the breakfast speaker is Republican Representative Bud Shuster of Pennsylvania, chairman of the House Transportation Committee and, his critics say, one of the most shameless promulgators of pork barrel spending in all of Congress. The odor seems even more fitting given that the topic of Shuster's address is the Building Efficient Surface Transportation and Equity Act, the six-year, $217 billion highway-spending package about to pass Congress—and, according to these same critics, the single biggest hunk of pork Washington has seen in a decade.

The critics, of course, are absolutely right. The House version of BESTEA, which hit the floor this week, contains at least $18 billion in so-called "demonstration" and "high-priority" projects. Those are the congressional euphemisms for pork—public works programs of dubious merit, specific to one congressional district, designed to curry favor with its voters. And Shuster's record for bringing home the bacon is indeed legendary. BESTEA's predecessor, which passed in 1991, included $287 million for 13 projects in Shuster's central Pennsylvania district. Today, visitors can see these and other shrines to his legislative clout by driving along the newly built Interstate 99, a shimmering stretch of asphalt the state has officially christened the Bud Shuster Highway.

None of this much bothers the suits at the Chamber of Commerce, who savor every line of Shuster's pitch as if it were just so much more fat-soaked sausage from the buffet table. Money for roads—whether in Shuster's district or anybody else's—means more ways to transport goods and more work for construction companies. But, outside the friendly confines of groups like this, a relentless chorus of high-minded watchdog groups and puritanical public officials complains that pork barrel spending wastes government money. These critics also protest the way pork becomes law in the first place, as last-minute amendments designed to bypass the hearings and debate bills normally require.

To be sure, these arguments are not exactly novel. The very term "pork barrel" is a pre–Civil War term, derived from what was then a readily understandable (but, to modern ears, rather objectionable) analogy between congressmen gobbling up appropriations and slaves grabbing at salt pork distributed from giant barrels. "By the 1870s," William Safire writes in his *Political Dictionary*, "congressmen were regularly referring to 'pork,' and the word became part of the U.S. political lexicon." Criticizing pork, meanwhile, is just as venerable a tradition. Virtually every president from Abraham Lincoln to Ronald Reagan has promised to eliminate pork from the federal budget, and so have most congressmen, much to the satisfaction of muckraking journalists and similarly high-minded voters.

But rarely have the politicians actually meant it, and even more rarely have they succeeded. Until now. Thanks to an endless parade of media exposés on government waste, and a prevailing political consensus in favor of balanced budgets, pork critics have been gaining momentum. In 1994, anti-pork fervor nearly killed President Clinton's crime bill; in 1995, the same sentiment lay behind enactment of the line-item veto, something budget-balancers had sought in vain for more than a decade. A few years ago, a handful of anti-pork legislators took to calling themselves "pork-busters." Thanks to their vigilance, says the nonprofit group Citizens Against Government Waste, the amount of pork in the budget declined by about nine percent in 1998.

The influence of pork-busters reached a new peak in 1997, when they helped defeat a preliminary attempt at BESTEA. They probably won't be able to duplicate the feat this year—Shuster has nearly 400 votes behind his new pork-laden bill, which House Budget Chairman John Kasich has called an "abomination." But pork-busters won a major public relations victory last week when four House Republicans turned on Shuster and accused him of trying to buy them off with pet projects. "I told them my vote was not for sale," said Steve Largent of Oklahoma. "Shuster bought just about everyone," David Hobson of Ohio told *The Washington Post*. Three weeks ago, Republican Senator John McCain of Arizona, Capitol Hill's most determined pork-buster, won passage of an amendment that could cut at least some of the bill's pork. President Clinton has since joined the chorus, saying he too deplores the parochial waste Shuster and his cronies added to the measure.

In the popular telling, episodes like these represent epic struggles of good versus evil—of principled fiscal discipline versus craven political self-interest—with the nation's economic health and public faith in government at stake. But this narrative, related time and again by purveyors of elite wisdom and then repeated mindlessly by everyday citizens, has it exactly backward. The pork-busters are more anti-government than anti-waste. As for pork-barrel spending, it's good for American citizens and American democracy as well. Instead of criticizing it, we should be celebrating it, in all of its gluttonous glory.

Nearly a week has passed since Shuster made his appearance before the Chamber of Commerce, and now it is the pork-busters' turn to be making headlines. In what has become an annual rite of the budget process, Citizens Against Government Waste is staging a press conference near Capitol Hill to release its compilation of pork in the 1997 federal budget—a 40-page, pink-covered booklet it calls the *Pig Book*. (Actually, the pocket-sized, 40-page version is just a summary of the unabridged *Pig Book*, which weighs in at a hefty 170 pages, in single-sided, legal-sized computer printouts.)

CAGW has been fighting this fight for more than a decade, and its steady stream of propaganda, reports, and testimony is in no small part responsible for pork-busting's Beltway resonance. Republican Representative Christopher Cox calls CAGW "the premier waste-fighting organization in America"; the 1995–1996 Congress sought CAGW testimony 20 times. The interest in today's press conference—attended by more than 60 reporters and a dozen television crews—is testimony to the group's high esteem among the Washington press corps, although it doesn't hurt that CAGW has also provided the TV crews with a good photo opportunity.

Like many press conferences in this city, this one features several members of Congress, including McCain and Democratic Senator Russell Feingold. Unlike many press conferences in this city, this one also features a man dressed in a bright pink pig's suit, rubber pig masks free for the media to take, plus a live, charcoal-gray potbellied pig named Porky. For the duration of the event, Porky does little except scarf down some vegetable shreds. But the beast's mere presence gets a few laughs, which is more than can be said for the puns that CAGW's president, Tom Schatz, makes as he rattles off the recipients of this year's "Oinker Awards."

Senator Daniel Inouye of Hawaii secured $127,000 in funding for research on edible seaweed; for this and other appropriations, Schatz says, Inouye (who is of Japanese ancestry) wins "The Sushi Slush Fund Award." Senator Ted Stevens of Alaska sponsored $100,000 for a project called Ship Creek, so he gets "The Up Ship's Creek Award." (Stevens is a double winner: for his other pork, totaling some $477 million since 1991, CAGW also presents him with "The Half Baked Alaska Award.") The Pentagon budget included $3 million for an observatory in South America: "It's supposed to peer back millions of years in time," Schatz says, his deadpan poker face now giving way to a smarmy, half-cocked smile. "Maybe they're looking for a balanced budget." This dubious-sounding project Schatz dubs "The Black Hole Award." And on. And on.

You might think cornball humor like this would earn CAGW the disdain of the famously cynical Washington press corps. But, when Schatz is done, and the question-and-answer period begins, the reporters display barely any skepticism. Instead, that evening, and during the following days, they will heap gobs of attention on the group. They don't flatter or endorse the organization per se, but the coverage shares a common assumption that the group's findings are evidence of political malfeasance. CNN, for example, will use the *Pig Book*'s release as a peg for stories bemoaning the persistence of pork in the federal budget. A story out of Knight Ridder's Washington bureau, which will run in nearly a dozen of the chain's newspapers, basically recapitulates the report. And all this comes on the heels of a front-page *Wall Street Journal* feature—sparked by a similar report from the Tax Foundation—highlighting the profligate pork barreling of the Senate majority leader, Trent Lott of Mississippi. Its headline: "MISSISSIPPI'S SENATORS CONTINUE A TRADITION: GETTING FEDERAL MONEY."

This is typical. Normally jaded Washingtonians, journalists especially, tend to view pork-busters not as ideologues but as politically disinterested watchdogs. Television producers, in particular, regularly summon CAGW experts to validate stories for such waste-focused segments as NBC's "The Fleecing of America" and ABC's "Your Money, Your Choice." While this image has a basis in reality—CAGW truly goes after pork-barreling Republicans with the same fervor it pursues Democrats—it is also a product of the organization's concerted attempt to wrap itself in the flag of nonpartisanship. "No matter how you slice it, pork is always on the menu in the halls of Congress," Schatz said at the press conference. "Some members of Congress simply couldn't resist the lure of easy money and putting partisan political interests over the best interest of taxpayers."

But it's not as if the pork-busters have no partisan or ideological agenda of their own. Some, like the Cato Institute, are explicit about their anti-government predisposition. CAGW is a little more cagey, but it remains true to the spirit of its past chairman, perennial right-wing Republican candidate Alan Keyes, as well as its cofounder, J. Peter Grace, who headed President Reagan's 1984 commission on government waste and whose antipathy to government in general was widely known. "The government is the worst bunch of stupid jerks you've ever run into in your life," he said once at a CAGW fund-raising dinner. "These people just want to spend money, money, money all the time."

That is, of course, a forgivable overstatement of a plausible argument. But it is also an overtly ideological one, and it calls into question the group's reliability when it comes to making delicate distinctions about what is truly wasteful. After all, CAGW is not just against pork, but against much of what the mainstream conservative movement considers bad or overly intrusive public policy—which encompasses an awful lot. In 1995, CAGW was not bashful about embracing the Contract With America, whose expansive definition of waste included many regulatory programs Americans deem quite worthwhile. "Taxpayers . . . demonstrated in two consecutive elections of a Republican Congress that the Washington establishment at its peril ignores the taxpayers' voice," the group's annual report boasts. "CAGW stood shoulder to shoulder with the reformers and enjoyed a sense of accomplishment at this burst of energy from revitalized taxpayers." CAGW's contributor list, not surprisingly, reads like a who's who of conservative interests, from Philip Morris Companies Inc. to the Columbia/HCA Healthcare Foundation Inc.

To be sure, CAGW is not the only Beltway organization whose partisan allegiances belie its nonprofit, nonpartisan status. At least a dozen other groups on both the left and the right do the exact same thing. Anyway, the fact that an argument may be ideologically motivated hardly means it's wrong.

But that doesn't mean it's right, either. Listen closely the next time some smug good-government type starts criticizing pork: it's an awful lot of fuss over what is, in fact, a very small amount of money. In the *Pig Book*, for example, CAGW claims last year's budget included pork worth about $13.2 billion—or, as a pork-buster would say, "$13.2 billion!" Yes, you could feed quite a few hungry people with that much money, or you could give a bigger tax cut. But it's less than one percent of the federal budget.

And it's not even clear that all of the $13.2 billion of waste is really, well, waste. A good chunk of CAGW's $13.2 billion in pork comes from a few dozen big-ticket items, costing tens of millions of dollars each, scattered through various appropriations measures, particularly the Pentagon's. Among the programs: research of a space-based laser ($90 million), transportation improvements in Utah ($14 million), and military construction in Montana ($32 million).

But it's hardly self-evident that these all constitute waste, as the pork-busters suggest. At least some national security experts believe the space-based laser is a necessary defense against rogue nations that might get their hands on nuclear missiles. A lot of that Utah money is to help Salt Lake City prepare for Olympic traffic. And, if you've ever been to Montana, you know that there are a lot of military bases scattered across that vast state—which means a lot of soldiers who need buildings in which to live, eat, and work. In other words, all of these serve some credible purpose.

The wastefulness of the smaller items is similarly open to interpretation. Remember Senator Inouye's "Sushi Slush Fund Award"—the $127,000 for research on edible seaweed in Hawaii? It turns out that aquaculture is an emerging industry in Hawaii and that edible seaweed—known locally as "limu," "ogo," or "sea sprouts"—is "rich in complex carbohydrates and protein and low in calories," according to the *Honolulu Advertiser.* "It's a good source of vitamin A, calcium, and potassium, too."

Yes, the federal government is paying $3 million for a telescope in South America. But it has to, because the telescope is part of a U.S. effort to explore the southern hemisphere sky—which, of course, is only visible from the southern hemisphere. Although the telescope will be located in Chile, it will be operated remotely from the University of North Carolina at Chapel Hill. "When completed, the telescope will hold tremendous promise for scientists and the federal government," the university chancellor said when Republican Senator Lauch Faircloth of North Carolina announced the appropriation. "We at the university also have high hopes for what the project will mean for the North Carolina economy as well as for students of all ages—on this campus, across our state, and beyond."

And Senator Stevens's "Up Ship's Creek Award"? The Ship Creek water project was part of a bill authorizing studies of environmental cleanup across the country. Some $100,000 went to the U.S. Army Corps of Engineers to assess the impact of development on Ship Creek, which is Anchorage's primary source of freshwater. Ironically, according to the Corps of Engineers, the study is exploring not only what kind of environmental precautions are necessary, but whether the federal government really has to pay for them, and whether local private entities might be convinced to foot part of the bill. In other words, one objective of the Ship Creek appropriation was to reduce government waste.

You could argue, as pork-busters do, that, while projects like these may serve some positive function in society—perhaps even deserving of government money—they should not be on the federal dime. Let the Hawaiians pay for their own calcium-rich dinners! Let Alaskans foot the bill for their own water study! But there's a respectable argument that sometimes parochial needs are in fact a legitimate federal interest, particularly when it involves things like pollution and commerce that cross state lines.

Certainly, that's the way a lot of people outside of Washington understand it. Last month, while the national media was busy flogging unthrifty lawmakers, several local newspapers rose to their defense. "We elect people to Congress not only to see to the nation's defense and keep the currency sound but also to bring home some pork," editorialized *The Fort Worth Star-Telegram*. "Pork can mean local jobs, local beautification, local pride, etc." The *Dayton Daily News* defended one project, a museum on the history of flight, that appeared on CAGW's hit list: "It is at the heart of a community effort that has been painstakingly nurtured for years by all manner of Daytonians. It combines the legitimate national purpose of recognizing the history of flight with the top-priority local purpose of getting Dayton recognized as a center of the history of flight." Other papers were more critical: they wanted to know why their congressmen hadn't brought home *more* bacon. "Alaskans aren't going to sit still for being No. 2 for long," *Anchorage Daily News* columnist Mike Doogan wrote in a spirited defense of pork. "We need the money. And we have our pride."

This is not to say that all or even most of what gets called pork is defensible on its own terms. (Did Bedford County, Pennsylvania, which happens to be smack in the middle of Shuster's rural district, really need a new airport when there were two others nearby?) Nor is it to say that the local interest in getting federal money should always trump the national interest in balancing the budget and distributing the federal largesse fairly. (Couldn't the state of Pennsylvania have paid for the Bedford County airport instead?) Nor is it even to say that local interests defending pork aren't being incredibly hypocritical—no one thinks an appropriation is pork when it's his.

No, the point is simply that you can't call something waste just because it makes a clever pun. "From what we can tell," says John Raffetto, communications director for the Senate Transportation Committee, "CAGW does no research to determine what purpose the project serves other than to flip through the pages of the bill and find projects that sound funny. If it sounds funny, that's pork. I have not heard from any member's office that has told me they've received a call from CAGW to ask what purpose that project has served."

Pork-busters concede they lack the time or resources to investigate items thoroughly. "Some may be worthy of consideration," says CAGW media director Jim Campi. "Our concern is that, if the projects went through the process the way they were supposed to, there would be a [better] opportunity to judge them on their merits."

This is the same argument that most animates McCain, Feingold, and other pork-busting lawmakers. But what constitutes a fair appropriations process? CAGW would have everyone believe that a project is pork if it is "not requested by the president" or if it "greatly exceeds the president's budget request or the previous year's funding." Huh? The whole point of the appropriations process is to give Congress a chance to make independent judgments about spending priorities. Particularly when Republicans control one branch of government and Democrats the other—

as is the case today—differences will exist. The Republican Congress used to routinely declare the president's budget "dead on arrival." Did this mean the entire congressional budget was pork?

Two other criteria for defining pork are equally shaky. Invoking the familiar pork-busting wisdom, CAGW says a program is pork if it was "not specifically authorized"—meaning it wasn't in the original budget which contains general spending limits, but rather added on as part of the subsequent appropriations process, in which money is specifically allocated to each item. But the rationale for a separate budget and appropriations process is to allow Congress (and, for that matter, the president) an opportunity to change their minds about smaller items, as long as they stay within the broad guidelines of the budget agreement. CAGW also damns any projects "requested by only one chamber of Congress." But, just as Congress can disagree with the president over a project's merit, so the House can disagree with the Senate—that's the reason the architects of the Constitution created two houses in the first place. (Also, keep in mind that one reason the Senate doesn't propose as much pork is that senators—wary of getting stung in the national press for lacking frugality—will often wait to see how much pork the House passes. That way, they end up with the best of both worlds: they can quietly tell supporters that they backed the measure without ever incurring the wrath of pork-busting watchdogs.)

Make no mistake, though: Many pork-barrellers are trying to evade the scrutiny bills get when they move through the normal appropriations process. They stick in small bits of pork after hearings end because they know that nobody is going to vote against a multibillion-dollar bill just because it has a few million dollars of pork tucked in. And they can do so safe in the knowledge that, because there's very little in the way of a paper trail, they will not suffer any public consequences—unless, of course, a watchdog group or enthusiastic reporter manages to find out.

Pork-busters call this strategy sleazy, and it is. But remember, the whole point of our Constitution is to harness mankind's corrupt tendencies and channel them in constructive directions. In an oft-quoted passage of *The Federalist Number 51*, James Madison wrote, "if men were angels, no government would be necessary," and "the private interest of every individual may be a sentinel over the public rights." The Founders believed that sometimes local interests should trump national interests because they recognized it was a way to keep federal power in check. It's true this process lends itself to a skewed distribution of benefits, with disproportionate shares going to powerful lawmakers. But, again, pork is such a small portion of the budget that "equalizing" its distribution would mean only modest funding changes here and there.

Which brings us to the final defense of pork, one Madison would certainly endorse. Even if every single pork-barrel project really were a complete waste of federal money, pork still represents a very cheap way to keep our sputtering legislative process from grinding to a halt. In effect, pork is like putting oil in your car engine: it lubricates the parts and keeps friction to a minimum. This is particularly true when you are talking about controversial measures. "Buying off potential coalition members with spending programs they favor is exactly what the Founders not only expected, but practiced," political scientist James Q. Wilson has argued. He has also written: "If you agree with Madison, you believe in pork."

Think of the NAFTA battle in 1993. Contentious to the bitter end, the fate of the agreement ultimately fell on the shoulders of a handful of congressmen, all of whom privately supported it but feared the political backlash if they voted for it. Clinton gave each of them a little pork— for example, a development bank in border states that ostensibly would provide start-up money for entrepreneurs who had lost jobs because of NAFTA. The bank was just another way to pump some federal money into these districts, but that was the whole point. Thanks to that money, NAFTA became politically viable; these lawmakers could tell their constituents, plausibly and truthfully, that there was something in it for their districts.

To take a more current example, just look at BESTEA. U.S. transportation infrastructure is famously inadequate; the Department of Transportation says unsafe roads cause 30 percent of all traffic fatalities. But, when fiscal conservatives questioned the pork in the original BESTEA last year, the measure failed, forcing Congress to pass an emergency extension. This year, a more permanent, six-year version will likely pass, largely because the appearance of a budget surplus has tipped the scales just enough so that the pork seems tolerable. As John W. Ellwood and Eric M. Patashnik wrote in *The Public Interest* several years ago (in what was the best defense of pork in recent memory): "Favoring legislators with small gifts for their districts in order to achieve great things for the nation is an act not of sin but of statesmanship."

Last week, of course, BESTEA's high pork content had fiscal conservatives downright apoplectic. "Frankly, this bill really is a hog," Kasich said. "It is way over the top." But, without the pork, there might be no highway bill at all. As one highway lobbyist told *National Journal* last year, "The projects are the glue that's going to hold the damn thing together." A former transportation official said: "I've always taken the point of view that every business has some overhead. If that's what it costs to get a significant or a good highway bill, it's worth the price." Kasich would surely be aghast at such logic, but someday he and other fiscal conservatives might find it useful for their own purposes. Remember, they are the ones who say that balancing the budget will likely be impossible without severe and politically risky reforms of entitlements like Medicare. When the time comes to make those tough choices—and they need to pry a few extra votes from the opposition—you can bet they will gladly trade a little pork for *their* greater cause. They might feel guilty about it, but they shouldn't. Pork is good. Pork is virtuous. Pork is the American way.

## DISCUSSION QUESTIONS

1. How would you define pork barrel projects? Are all pork barrel projects contrary to the national interest? How do we distinguish between local projects that are in the national interest and those that are not?

2. Consider the criteria that CAGW uses to define pork. Do they seem reasonable to you? Should anything be added or deleted? Is the list objective enough that a liberal Democratic group and conservative Republican group using the criteria would come up with roughly the same list of projects? Is any policy area conspicuously absent?

3. Again, considering the list of examples in the press release, if you were a member of Congress, which of these would you clearly support? Which would you clearly oppose? Which would you need to learn more about before deciding? In general, does the list support Paige's or Cohn's arguments?

4. As Mayhew argues, members of Congress face strong incentives to serve constituent needs and claim credit for delivering federal dollars. Pork barrel projects provide the means to do just that. What changes in Congress or the political process might alter legislative behavior or change the incentives members of Congress face for securing reelection? Do we want members of Congress to be focused primarily on broad national issues rather than local priorities?

# CHAPTER 6

# The President: From Chief Clerk to Chief Executive

## 29

## "The Power to Persuade"
## from *Presidential Power*

### RICHARD NEUSTADT

*An enduring theme in analyses of the presidency is the gap between what the public expects of the office and the president's actual powers. Neustadt, who wrote the first edition of* Presidential Power *in 1960, offered a new way of looking at the office. Neustadt's main point is that the formal powers of the presidency (the constitutional powers set out in Article II and the statutory powers that Congress grants) are not the most important resource. The president cannot, Neustadt concluded, expect to get his way by command—issuing orders to subordinates and other government officials with the expectation of immediate and unquestioning compliance. In a system of "separate institutions sharing power," other political actors have their own independent sources of power and therefore can refuse to comply with presidential orders. Nobody, Neustadt argues, sees things from the president's perspective (or "vantage point"). Legislators, judges, cabinet secretaries, all have their own responsibilities, constituencies, demands of office, and resources, and their interests and the president's will often differ. The key to presidential power is the power to persuade—to convince others that they should comply with the president's wishes because doing so is in their interest. Presidents persuade by bargaining: making deals, reaching compromise positions; in other words, the give and take that is part of politics. The question remains, as the following selection points out, whether our method of selecting presidents is appropriate to the job the winner must do.*

The limits on command suggest the structure of our government. The constitutional convention of 1787 is supposed to have created a gov-

ernment of "separated powers." It did nothing of the sort. Rather, it
created a government of separated institutions *sharing* powers. "I am part
of the legislative process," Eisenhower often said in 1959 as a reminder
of his veto. Congress, the dispenser of authority and funds, is no less
part of the administrative process. Federalism adds another set of separated institutions. The Bill of Rights adds others. Many public purposes
can only be achieved by voluntary acts of private institutions; the press,
for one, in Douglass Cater's phrase, is a "fourth branch of government."
And with the coming of alliances abroad, the separate institutions of a
London, or a Bonn, share in the making of American public policy.

What the Constitution separates our political parties do not combine.
The parties are themselves composed of separated organizations sharing
public authority. The authority consists of nominating powers. Our national parties are confederations of state and local party institutions, with
a headquarters that represents the White House, more or less, if the party
has a President in office. These confederacies manage presidential nominations. All other public offices depend upon electorates confined within
the states. All other nominations are controlled within the states. The
President and congressmen who bear one party's label are divided by
dependence upon different sets of voters. The differences are sharpest at
the stage of nomination. The White House has too small a share in nominating congressmen, and Congress has too little weight in nominating
Presidents for party to erase their constitutional separation. Party links
are stronger than is frequently supposed, but nominating processes assure the separation.

The separateness of institutions and the sharing of authority prescribe
the terms on which a President persuades. When one man shares authority with another, but does not gain or lose his job upon the other's
whim, his willingness to act upon the urging of the other turns on
whether he conceives the action right for him. The essence of a President's persuasive task is to convince such men that what the White
House wants of them is what they ought to do for their sake and on
their authority.

Persuasive power, thus defined, amounts to more than charm or reasoned argument. These have their uses for a President, but these are not
the whole of his resources. For the men he would induce to do what he
wants done on their own responsibility will need or fear some acts by
him on his responsibility. If they share his authority, he has some share
in theirs. Presidential "powers" may be inconclusive when a President
commands, but always remain relevant as he persuades. The status and
authority inherent in his office reinforce his logic and his charm.

*   *   *

A President's authority and status give him great advantages in dealing with the men he would persuade. Each "power" is a vantage point

for him in the degree that other men have use for his authority. From the veto to appointments, from publicity to budgeting, and so down a long list, the White House now controls the most encompassing array of vantage points in the American political system. With hardly an exception, the men who share in governing this country are aware that at some time, in some degree, the doing of *their* jobs, the furthering of *their* ambitions, may depend upon the President of the United States. Their need for presidential action, or their fear of it, is bound to be recurrent if not actually continuous. Their need or fear is his advantage.

A President's advantages are greater than mere listing of his "powers" might suggest. The men with whom he deals must deal with him until the last day of his term. Because they have continuing relationships with him, his future, while it lasts, supports his present influence. Even though there is no need or fear of him today, what he could do tomorrow may supply today's advantage. Continuing relationships may convert any "power," any aspect of his status, into vantage points in almost any case. When he induces other men to do what he wants done, a President can trade on their dependence now *and* later.

The President's advantages are checked by the advantages of others. Continuing relationships will pull in both directions. These are relationships of mutual dependence. A President depends upon the men he would persuade; he has to reckon with his need or fear of them. They too will possess status, or authority, or both, else they would be of little use to him. Their vantage points confront his own; their power tempers his.

\* \* \*

The power to persuade is the power to bargain. Status and authority yield bargaining advantages. But in a government of "separated institutions sharing powers," they yield them to all sides. With the array of vantage points at his disposal, a President may be far more persuasive than his logic or his charm could make him. But outcomes are not guaranteed by his advantages. There remain the counter pressures those whom he would influence can bring to bear on him from vantage points at their disposal. Command has limited utility; persuasion becomes give-and-take. It is well that the White House holds the vantage points it does. In such a business any President may need them all—and more.

\* \* \*

This view of power as akin to bargaining is one we commonly accept in the sphere of congressional relations. Every textbook states and every legislative session demonstrates that save in times like the extraordinary Hundred Days of 1933—times virtually ruled out by definition at midcentury—a President will often be unable to obtain congressional action on his terms or even to halt action he opposes. The reverse is equally accepted: Congress often is frustrated by the President. Their formal powers are so intertwined that neither will accomplish very much, for very long, without the acquiescence of the other. By the same token, though, what one demands the other can resist. The stage is set for that great game, much like collective bargaining, in which each seeks to profit from the other's needs and fears. It is a game played catch-as-catch-can, case by case. And everybody knows the game, observers and participants alike.

\*    \*    \*

Like our governmental structure as a whole, the executive establishment consists of separated institutions sharing powers. The President heads one of these; Cabinet officers, agency administrators, and military commanders head others. Below the departmental level, virtually independent bureau chiefs head many more. Under mid-century conditions, Federal operations spill across dividing lines on organization charts; almost every policy entangles many agencies; almost every program calls for interagency collaboration. Everything somehow involves the President. But operating agencies owe their existence least of all to one another—and only in some part to him. Each has a separate statutory base; each has its statutes to administer; each deals with a different set of subcommittees at the Capitol. Each has its own peculiar set of clients, friends, and enemies outside the formal government. Each has a different set of specialized careerists inside its own bailiwick. Our Constitution gives the President the "take-care" clause and the appointive power. Our statues give him central budgeting and a degree of personnel control. All agency administrators are responsible to him. But they *also* are responsible to Congress, to their clients, to their staffs, and to themselves. In short, they have five masters. Only after all of those do they owe any loyalty to each other.

"The members of the Cabinet," Charles G. Dawes used to remark, "are a President's natural enemies." Dawes had been Harding's Budget Director, Coolidge's Vice-President, and Hoover's Ambassador to London; he also had been General Pershing's chief assistant for supply in the First World War. The words are highly colored, but Dawes knew whereof he spoke. The men who have to serve so many masters cannot help but be somewhat the "enemy" of any one of them. By the same token, any master wanting service is in some degree the "enemy" of such a servant. A President is likely to want loyal support but not to relish trouble on his doorstep. Yet the more his Cabinet members cleave to him, the more they may need help from him in fending off the wrath of rival masters. Help, though, is synonymous with trouble. Many a Cabinet officer, with loyalty ill-rewarded by his lights and help withheld, has come to view the White House as innately hostile to department heads. Dawes's dictum can be turned around.

\*    \*    \*

The more an officeholder's status and his "powers" stem from sources independent of the President, the stronger will be his potential pressure *on* the President. Department heads in general have more bargaining power than do most members of the White House staff; but bureau chiefs may have still more, and specialists at upper levels of established career services may have almost unlimited reserves of the enormous power which consists of sitting still. As Franklin Roosevelt once remarked:

> The Treasury is so large and far-flung and ingrained in its practices that I find it almost impossible to get the action and results I want—even with Henry [Morgenthau] there. But the Treasury is not to be compared with the State Department. You should go through the experience of trying to get any changes in the thinking, policy, and action of the career diplomats and then you'd know what a real problem was. But the Treasury and the State Department put together are nothing compared with the Na-a-vy. The admirals are really something to cope with—and I should know. To change anything in the Na-a-vy is like punching a feather bed. You punch it with your right and you punch it with your left until you are finally exhausted, and then you find the damn bed just as it was before you started punching.[1]

\*   \*   \*

There is a widely held belief in the United States that were it not for folly or for knavery, a reasonable President would need no power other than the logic of his argument. No less a personage than Eisenhower has subscribed to that belief in many a campaign speech and press-conference remark. But faulty reasoning and bad intentions do not cause all quarrels with Presidents. The best of reasoning and of intent cannot compose them all. For in the first place, what the President wants will rarely seem a trifle to the men he wants it from. And in the second place, they will be bound to judge it by the standard of their own responsibilities, not his. However logical his argument according to his lights, their judgment may not bring them to his view.

The men who share in governing this country frequently appear to act as though they were in business for themselves. So, in a real though not entire sense, they are and have to be. When Truman and MacArthur fell to quarreling, for example, the stakes were no less than the substance of American foreign policy, the risks of greater war or military stalemate, the prerogatives of Presidents and field commanders, the pride of a pro-consul and his place in history. Intertwined, inevitably, were other stakes, as well: political stakes for men and factions of both parties; power stakes for interest groups with which they were or wished to be affiliated. And every stake was raised by the apparent discontent in the American public mood. There is no reason to suppose that in such circumstances men of large but differing responsibilities will see all things through the same glasses. On the contrary, it is to be expected that their views of what ought to be done and what they then should do will vary with the differing perspectives their particular responsibilities evoke.

Since their duties are not vested in a "team" or a "collegium" but in themselves, as individuals, one must expect that they will see things *for* themselves. Moreover, when they are responsible to many masters and when an event or policy turns loyalty against loyalty—a day by day occurrence in the nature of the case—one must assume that those who have the duties to perform will choose the terms of reconciliation. This is the essence of their personal responsibility. When their own duties pull in opposite directions, who else but they can choose what they will do?

\*   \*   \*

Outside the Executive Branch the situation is the same, except that loyalty to the President may often matter *less*. . . . And when one comes to congressmen who can do nothing for themselves (or their constituents) save as they are elected, term by term, in districts and through party structures *differing* from those on which a President depends, the case is very clear. An able Eisenhower aide with long congressional experience remarked to me in 1958: "The people on the Hill don't do what they might *like* to do, they do what they think they *have* to do in their own interest as *they* see it. . . ." This states the case precisely.

The essence of a President's persuasive task with congressmen and everybody else, *is to induce them to believe that what he wants of them is what their own appraisal of their own responsibilities requires them to do in their interest, not his.* Because men may differ in their views on public policy, because differences in outlook stem from differences in duty— duty to one's office, one's constituents, oneself—that task is bound to be more like collective bargaining than like a reasoned argument among philosopher kings. Overtly or implicitly, hard bargaining has characterized all illustrations offered up to now. This is the reason why: persuasion deals in the coin of self-interest with men who have some freedom to reject what they find counterfeit.

Let me introduce a case . . . : the European Recovery Program of 1948, the so-called Marshall Plan. This is perhaps the greatest exercise in policy *agreement* since the cold war began. When the then Secretary of State, George Catlett Marshall, spoke at the Harvard commencement in June of 1947, he launched one of the most creative, most imaginative ventures in the history of American foreign relations. What makes this policy most notable for present purposes, however, is that it became effective upon action by the 80th Congress, at the behest of Harry Truman, in the election year of 1948.

Eight months before Marshall spoke at Harvard, the Democrats had lost control of both Houses of Congress for the first time in fourteen years. Truman, whom the Secretary represented, had just finished his second troubled year as President-by-succession. Truman was regarded with so little warmth in his own party that in 1946 he had been urged *not* to participate in the congressional campaign. At the opening of Congress in January 1947, Senator Robert A. Taft, "Mr. Republican," had somewhat the attitude of a President-elect. This was a vision widely shared in Washington, with Truman relegated, thereby, to the role of caretaker-on-term. Moreover, within just two weeks of Marshall's commencement address, Truman was to veto two prized accomplishments of Taft's congressional majority: the Taft-Hartley Act and tax reduction. Yet scarcely ten months later the Marshall Plan was under way on terms to satisfy its sponsors, its authorization completed, its first-year funds in sight, its administering agency in being: all managed by as thorough a display of executive-congressional cooperation as any we have seen since the Second World War. For any President at any time this would have been a great accomplishment. In years before mid-century it would have been enough to make the future reputation of his term. And for a Truman, at this time, enactment of the Marshall Plan appears almost miraculous.

How was the miracle accomplished? How did a President so situated bring it off? In answer, the first thing to note is that he did not do it by himself. Truman had help of a sort no less extraordinary than the outcome. Although each stands for something more complex, the names of Marshall, Vandenberg, . . . Bevin, Stalin, tell the story of that help.

In 1947, two years after V-J Day, General Marshall was something more than Secretary of State. He was a man venerated by the President as "the greatest living American," literally an embodiment of Truman's ideals. He was honored at the Pentagon as an architect of victory. He was thoroughly respected by the Secretary of the Navy, James V. Forrestal, who that year became the first Secretary of Defense. On Capitol Hill Marshall had an enormous fund of respect stemming from his war record as Army Chief of Staff, and in the country generally no officer had come out of the war with a higher reputation for judgment, intellect, and probity. Besides, as Secretary of State, he had behind him the first generation of matured foreign service officers produced by the reforms of the 1920's, and mingled with them, in the departmental service, were some of the ablest of the men drawn by the war from private life to Washington.

*   *   *

Taken together, these are exceptional resources for a Secretary of State. In the circumstances, they were quite as necessary as they obviously are relevant. The Marshall Plan was launched by a "lame duck" Administration "scheduled" to leave office in eighteen months. Marshall's program faced a congressional leadership traditionally isolationist and currently intent upon economy. European aid was viewed with envy by a Pentagon distressed and virtually disarmed through budget cuts, and by domestic agencies intent on enlarged welfare programs. It was not viewed with liking by a Treasury intent on budget surpluses. The plan had need of every asset that could be extracted from the personal position of its nominal author and from the skills of his assistants.

Without the equally remarkable position of the senior Senator from Michigan, Arthur H. Vandenberg, it is hard to see how Marshall's assets could have been enough. Vandenberg was chairman of the Senate Foreign Relations Committee. Actually, he was much more than that. Twenty years a senator, he was the senior member of his party in the Chamber. Assiduously cultivated by F.D.R. and Truman, he was a chief Republican proponent of "bipartisanship" in foreign policy, and consciously conceived himself its living symbol to his party, to the country, and abroad. Moreover, by informal but entirely operative agreement with his colleague Taft, Vandenberg held the acknowledged lead among Senate Republicans in the whole field of international affairs. This acknowledgement meant more in 1947 than it might have meant at any other time. With confidence in the advent of a Republican administration two years hence, most of the gentlemen were in a mood to be responsive and responsible. The war was over, Roosevelt dead, Truman a caretaker, theirs the trust. That the Senator from Michigan saw matters in this light, his diaries make clear. And this was not the outlook from the Senate side alone; the attitudes of House Republicans associated with the Herter Committee and its tours abroad suggest the same mood of responsibility. Vandenberg was not the only source of help on Capitol Hill. But relatively speaking, his position there was as exceptional as Marshall's was downtown.

\* \* \*

At Harvard, Marshall had voiced an idea in general terms. That this was turned into a hard program susceptible of presentation and support is due, in major part, to Ernest Bevin, the British Foreign Secretary. He well deserves the credit he has sometimes been assigned as, in effect, co-author of the Marshall Plan. For Bevin seized on Marshall's Harvard speech and organized a European response with promptness and concreteness beyond the State Department's expectations. What had been virtually a trial balloon to test reactions on both sides of the Atlantic was hailed in London as an invitation to the Europeans to send Washington a bill of particulars. This they promptly organized to do, and the American Administration then organized in turn for its reception without further argument internally about the pros and cons of issuing the "invitation" in the first place. But for Bevin there might have been trouble from the Secretary of the Treasury and others besides.

If Bevin's help was useful at that early stage, Stalin's was vital from first to last. In a mood of self-deprecation Truman once remarked that without Moscow's "crazy" moves "we would never have had our foreign policy . . . we never could have got a thing from Congress." George Kennan, among others, had deplored the anti-Soviet overtone of the case made for the Marshall Plan in Congress and the country, but there is no doubt that this clinched the argument for many segments of American opinion. There also is no doubt that Moscow made the crucial contributions to the case.

\* \* \*

The crucial thing to note about this case is that despite compatibility of views on public policy, Truman got no help he did not pay for (except Stalin's). Bevin scarcely could have seized on Marshall's words had Marshall not been plainly backed by Truman. Marshall's interest would not have comported with the exploitation of his prestige by a President who undercut him openly, or subtly, or even inadvertently, at any point. Vandenberg, presumably, could not have backed proposals by a White House which begrudged him deference and access gratifying to his fellow-partisans (and satisfying to himself). Prominent Republicans in private life would not have found it easy to promote a cause identified with Truman's claims on 1948—and neither would the prominent New Dealers then engaged in searching for a substitute.

Truman paid the price required for their services. So far as the record shows, the White House did not falter once in firm support for Marshall and the Marshall Plan. Truman backed his Secretary's gamble on an invitation to all Europe. He made the plan his own in a well-timed address to the Canadians. He lost no opportunity to widen the involvements of his own official family in the cause. Averell Harriman the Secretary of Commerce, Julius Krug the Secretary of the Interior, Edwin Nourse the Economic Council Chairman, James Webb the Director of the Budget—all were made responsible for studies and reports contributing directly to the legislative presentation. Thus these men were committed in advance. Besides, the President continually emphasized to everyone in reach that he did not have doubts, did not desire complications and would foreclose all he could. Reportedly, his emphasis was felt at the Treasury, with good effect. And Truman was at special pains to smooth the way for Vandenberg. The Senator insisted on "no politics" from the Administration side; there was none. He thought a survey of American resources and capacity essential; he got it in the Krug and Harriman reports. Vandenberg expected advance consultation; he received it, step by step, in frequent meetings with the President and weekly conferences with Marshall. He asked for an effective liaison between Congress and agencies concerned; Lovett and others gave him what he wanted. When the Senator decided on the need to change financing and administrative features of the legislation, Truman disregarded Budget Bureau grumbling and acquiesced with grace. When, finally, Vandenberg desired a Republican to head the new administering agency, his candidate, Paul Hoffman, was appointed despite the President's own preference for another. In all of these ways Truman employed the sparse advantages his "powers" and his status then accorded him to gain the sort of help he had to have.

\* \* \*

Had Truman lacked the personal advantages his "powers" and his status gave him, or if he had been maladroit in using them, there probably would not have been a massive European aid program in 1948. . . . The President's own share in this accomplishment was vital. He made his contribution by exploiting his advantages. Truman, in effect, lent Marshall and the rest the perquisites and status of his office. In return they lent him their prestige and their own influence. The transfer multiplied *his* influence despite his limited authority in form and lack of strength politically. Without the wherewithal to make this bargain, Truman could not have contributed to European aid.

\* \* \*

## DISCUSSION QUESTIONS

1. Considering recent presidents (Bush and Clinton), identify and discuss some examples of Neustadt's argument that presidents cannot get their way by "command," that they must bargain to get what they want.

2. Can you think of any recent examples where a president has been able to get what he wants *by* giving a command?

## NOTE

1. Reprinted from Marriner S. Eccles, *Beckoning Frontiers* (New York: Knopf, 1951), p. 336.

# 30

# "Perspectives on the Presidency"
## from *The Presidency in a Separated System*

### CHARLES O. JONES

*Just how powerful is the president? Have the fears of some of the Framers—that the president would degrade into an imperial despot—been realized, or does the separation of powers effectively check the president's ability to misuse the powers of office? Charles Jones argues that we should view the president as only one of the players in American government; the presidency exists only as one part of a set of institutions where responsibility is diffused, where the bulk of political activity takes place independent of the presidency, and where the different players and institutions learn to adjust to the others. Consider, for example, that the Republican 104th Congress (elected in the 1994 midterms) and President Clinton managed to reach compromises on a number of important issues despite early predictions that they would never agree on anything. Or that President George H. W. Bush managed to find a way to work with the Democratic Congress to get some major legislation through during 1991. Ultimately, Jones argues, the president is only a part of a larger "separated system," in which Congress, the courts, and the bureaucracy can shape policy.*

The president is not the presidency. The presidency is not the government. Ours is not a presidential system.

I begin with these starkly negative themes as partial correctives to the more popular interpretations of the United States government as presidency-centered. Presidents themselves learn these refrains on the job, if they do not know them before. President Lyndon B. Johnson, who had impressive political advantages during the early years of his administration, reflected later on what was required to realize the potentialities of the office:

> Every President has to establish with the various sectors of the country what I call "the right to govern." Just being elected to the office does not guarantee him that right. Every President has to inspire the confidence of the people. Every President has to become a leader, and to be a leader he must attract people who are willing to follow him. Every President has to develop a moral underpinning to his power, or he soon discovers that he has no power at all.[1]

To exercise influence, presidents must learn the setting within which it has bearing. [Then] President-elect Bill Clinton recognized the complexities of translating campaign promises into a legislative program during a news conference shortly after his election in 1992:

> It's all very well to say you want an investment tax credit, and quite another thing to make the 15 decisions that have to be made to shape the exact bill you want.
>    It's all very well to say . . . that the working poor in this country . . . should be lifted out of poverty by increasing the refundable income tax credit for the working poor, and another thing to answer the five or six questions that define how you get that done.[2]

For presidents, new or experienced, to recognize the limitations of office is commendable. Convincing others to do so is a challenge. Presidents become convenient labels for marking historical time: the Johnson years, the Nixon years, the Reagan years. Media coverage naturally focuses more on the president: there is just one at a time, executive organization is oriented in pyramidal fashion toward the Oval Office, Congress is too diffuse an institution to report on as such, and the Supreme Court leads primarily by indirection. Public interest, too, is directed toward the White House as a symbol of the government. As a result, expectations of a president often far exceed the individual's personal, political, institutional, or constitutional capacities for achievement. Performance seldom matches promise. Presidents who understand how it all works resist the inflated image of power born of high-stakes elections and seek to lower expectations. Politically savvy presidents know instinctively that it is precisely at the moment of great achievement that they must prepare themselves for the setback that will surely follow.

Focusing exclusively on the presidency can lead to a seriously distorted picture of how the national government does its work. The plain fact is that the United States does not have a presidential system. It has a *separated* system. It is odd that it is so commonly thought of as otherwise since schoolchildren learn about the separation of powers and checks and balances. As the author of *Federalist* 51 wrote, "Ambition must be made to counteract ambition." No one, least of all presidents, the Founders reasoned, can be entrusted with excessive authority. Human nature, being what it is, requires "auxiliary precautions" in the form of competing legitimacies.

The acceptance that this is a separated, not a presidential, system, prepares one to appraise how politics works, not to be simply reproachful and reformist. Thus, for example, divided (or split-party) government is accepted as a potential or even likely outcome of a separated system, rooted as it is in the separation of elections. Failure to acknowledge the authenticity of the split-party condition leaves one with little to study and much to reform in the post–World War II period, when the government has been divided more than 60 percent of the time.

Simply put, the role of the president in this separated system of governing varies substantially, depending on his resources, advantages, and strategic position. My strong interest is in how presidents place themselves in an ongoing government and are fitted in by other participants, notably those on Capitol Hill. The central purpose of this book is to explore these "fittings." In pursuing this interest, I have found little value in the presidency-centered, party government perspective, as I will explain below. As a substitute, I propose a separationist, diffused-responsibility perspective that I find more suited to the constitutional, institutional, political, and policy conditions associated with the American system of governing.

\* \* \*

### The Dominant Perspective

The presidency-centered perspective is consistent with a dominant and well-developed perspective that has been highly influential in evaluating the American political system. The perspective is that of party government, typically one led by a strong or aggressive president. Those advocating this perspective prefer a system in which political parties are stronger than they normally can be in a system of separated elections.

\* \* \*

The party government perspective is best summarized in the recommendations made in 1946 by the Committee on Political Parties of the American Political Science Association.

> The party system that is needed must be democratic, responsible and effective. . . .
> An effective party system requires, first, that the parties are able to bring forth programs to which they commit themselves and, second, that the parties possess sufficient internal cohesion to carry out these programs. . . .
> The fundamental requirement of such accountability is a two-party system in which the opposition party acts as the critic of the party in power, developing, defining, and presenting the policy alternatives which are necessary for a true choice in reaching public decisions.[3]

Note the language in this summary: party in power, opposition party, policy alternatives for choice, accountability, internal cohesion, programs to which parties commit themselves. As a whole, it forms a test that a separated system is bound to fail.

I know of very few contemporary advocates of the two-party responsibility model. But I know many analysts who rely on its criteria when judging the political system. One sees this reliance at work when reviewing how elections are interpreted and presidents are evaluated. By this standard, the good campaign and election have the following characteristics:

- Publicly visible issues that are debated by the candidates during the campaign.

- Clear differences between the candidates on the issues, preferably deriving from ideology.
- A substantial victory for the winning candidate, thus demonstrating public support for one set of issue positions.
- A party win accompanying the victory for the president, notably an increase in the presidential party's share of congressional seats and statehouses so that the president's win can be said to have had an impact on other races (the coattail effect).
- A greater than expected win for the victorious party, preferably at both ends of Pennsylvania Avenue.
- A postelection declaration of support and unity from the congressional leaders of the president's party.

The good president, by this perspective, is one who makes government work, one who has a program and uses his resources to get it enacted. The good president is an activist: he sets the agenda, is attentive to the progress being made, and willingly accepts responsibility for what happens. He can behave in this way because he has demonstrable support.

It is not in the least surprising that the real outcomes of separated elections frustrate those who prefer responsible party government. Even a cursory reading of the Constitution suggests that these demanding tests will be met only by coincidence. Even an election that gives one party control of the White House and both houses of Congress in no way guarantees a unified or responsible party outcome. And even when a president and his congressional party leaders appear to agree on policy priorities, the situation may change dramatically following midterm elections. Understandably, advocates of party government are led to propose constitutional reform.

*    *    *

*An Alternative Perspective*

The alternative perspective for understanding American national politics is bound to be anathema to party responsibility advocates. By the rendition promoted here, responsibility is not focused, it is diffused. Representation is not pure and unidirectional; it is mixed, diluted, and multidirectional. Further, the tracking of policy from inception to implementation discourages the most devoted advocate of responsibility theories. In a system of diffused responsibility, credit will be taken and blame will be avoided by both institutions and both parties. For the mature government (one that has achieved substantial involvement in social and economic life), much of the agenda will be self-generating, that is, resulting from programs already on the books. Thus the desire to propose new programs is often frustrated by demands to sustain existing programs, and substantial debt will constrain both.

Additionally there is the matter of who *should* be held accountable for what and when. This is not a novel issue by any means. It is a part of the common rhetoric of split-party government. Are the Democrats responsible for how medicare has worked because it was a part of Lyndon Johnson's Great Society? Or are the Republicans responsible because their presidents accepted, administered, and revised the program? Is President Carter responsible for creating a Department of Energy or President Reagan responsible for failing to abolish it, or both? The partisan rhetoric on deficits continues to blame the Democrats for supporting spending programs and the Republicans for cutting taxes. It is noteworthy that this level of debate fails to treat more fundamental issues, such as the constitutional roadblocks to defining responsibility. In preventing the tyranny of the majority, the founders also made it difficult to specify accountability.

Diffusion of responsibility, then, is not only a likely result of a separated system but may also be a fair outcome. From what was said above, one has to doubt how reasonable it is to hold one institution or one party accountable for a program that has grown incrementally through decades of single- and split-party control. Yet reforming a government program is bound to be an occasion for holding one or the other of the branches accountable for wrongs being righted. If, however, politics allows crossing the partisan threshold to place both parties on the same side, then agreements may be reached that will permit blame avoidance, credit taking, and, potentially, significant policy change. This is not to say that both sides agree from the start about what to do, in a cabal devoted to irresponsibility (though that process is not unknown). Rather it is to suggest that diffusion of responsibility may permit policy reform that would have been much less likely if one party had to absorb all of the criticism for past performance or blame should the reforms fail when implemented.

Institutional competition is an expected outcome of the constitutional arrangements that facilitate mixed representation and variable electoral horizons. In recent decades this competition has been reinforced by Republicans settling into the White House, the Democrats comfortably occupying the House of Representatives, and, in very recent times, both parties hotly contending for majority status in the Senate. Bargains struck under these conditions have the effect of perpetuating split control by denying opposition candidates (Democratic presidential challengers, Republican congressional challengers) both the issues upon which to campaign and the means for defining accountability.

The participants in this system of mixed representation and diffused responsibility naturally accommodate their political surroundings. Put otherwise, congressional Democrats and presidential Republicans learn how to do their work. Not only does each side adjust to its political circumstances, but both may also be expected to provide themselves with the resources to participate meaningfully in policy politics.

Much of the above suggests that the political and policy strategies of presidents in dealing with Congress will depend on the advantages they have available at any one time. One cannot employ a constant model of the activist president leading a party government. Conditions may encourage the president to work at the margins of president-congressional interaction (for example, where he judges that he has an advantage, as with foreign and defense issues). He may allow members of Congress to take policy initiatives, hanging back to see how the issue develops. He may certify an issue as important, propose a program to satisfy certain group demands, but fail to expend the political capital necessary to get the program enacted. The lame-duck president requires clearer explication. The last months and years of a two-term administration may be one of congressional initiative with presidential response. The point is that having been relieved of testing the system for party responsibility, one can proceed to analyze how presidents perform under variable political and policy conditions.

*    *    *

In a separated system of diffused responsibility, these are the expectations:

- Presidents will enter the White House with variable personal, political, and policy advantages or resources. Presidents are not equally good at comprehending their advantages or identifying how these advantages may work best for purposes of influencing the rest of the government.
- White House and cabinet organization will be quite personal in nature, reflecting the president's assessment of strengths and weaknesses, the challenges the president faces in fitting into the ongoing government, and the political and policy changes that occur during the term of office. There is no formula for organizing the presidency, though certain models can be identified.
- Public support will be an elusive variable in analyzing presidential power. At the very least, its importance for any one president must be considered alongside other advantages. "Going public" does not necessarily carry a special bonus, though presidents with limited advantages otherwise may be forced to rely on this tactic.
- The agenda will be continuous, with many issues derived from programs already being administered. The president surely plays an important role in certifying issues and setting priorities, but Congress and the bureaucracy will also be natural participants. At the very least, therefore, the president will be required to persuade other policy actors that his choices are the right ones. They will do the same with him.
- Lawmaking will vary substantially in terms of initiative, sequence, partisan and institutional interaction, and productivity. The challenge is

to comprehend the variable role of the president in a government that is designed for continuity and change.
- Reform will be an especially intricate undertaking since, by constitutional design, the governmental structure is antithetical to efficient goal achievement. Yet many, if not most, reforms seek to achieve efficiency within the basic separated structure. There are not many reforms designed to facilitate the more effective working of split-party government.

## DISCUSSION QUESTIONS

1. The conventional wisdom is that presidential power increases (often dramatically) during war and other national crises. How has President George W. Bush's ability to exercise power changed since September 11? What accounts for this change—is it the rise in his approval ratings, an unwillingness of Congress to oppose him, or something else?

2. How can Jones's view of the presidency be squared with the popular view that the president is the most powerful person in the world?

## NOTES

1. Lyndon Baines Johnson, *The Vantage Point: Perspectives on the Presidency, 1963–1969* (New York: Holt, Rinehart and Winston, 1971), p. 18.
2. Ruth Marcus, "In Transition Twilight Zone, Clinton's Every Word Scrutinized," *Washington Post*, November 22, 1992, p. A1.
3. American Political Science Association, *Toward a More Responsible Two-Party System* (New York: Rinehart, 1950), pp. 1–2.

## DEBATING THE ISSUES: PRESIDENTIAL MANDATES

After every presidential election, presidents, reporters, other politicians, and members of the Washington political community debate the question of whether the president-elect has a "mandate." "I earned capital in the campaign—political capital—and now I intend to spend it," declared Bush in a post-election news conference. Supporters pointed to the record number of votes Bush received in 2004—just shy of 60 million—as evidence that he has a solid mandate. Opponents of this notion argued that although Kerry lost, he still received 1.5 million more votes than did Ronald Reagan in his 1984 landslide victory, and a 52–48-percent margin hardly constitutes a landslide. Moreover, they say those who trumpet Bush's 3.5-million-vote margin had a decidedly different view of the meaning of the popular vote in 2000.

Rarely is anyone clear about what is meant by a mandate. Is it a president's presumed right to implement his agenda? A warning to members of Congress not to obstruct? A degree of public support, or willingness to go along, with the president? Is a mandate like a light switch—you either have one or you do not—or is it more of a continuous measure of legitimacy and public support? To many political scientists, the concept is fuzzy at best. It is certainly true that under a system of majority rule and winner-take-all elections, the winner has at least some presumption of public approval of his or her policy positions. After all, elections are the central element of public accountability.

At the same time, it can be difficult to argue that campaign support should translate directly into policy. The structure of the federal government purposely separates the different branches of government on the basis of electoral calendar and constituency. People vote for different offices—House, Senate, President—for different reasons, and split-ticket voting is common. Historically, even landslide victories rarely translate into major policy successes. True, Lyndon Johnson did come out of the 1964 election with enough influence to pass the Civil Rights Act of 1964, the Voting Rights Act, and Medicare. But FDR's notable 1936 landslide did not produce similar results, and Reagan's major second-term success, tax reform, was led by Congress. Scholars who study the issue conclude, mostly, that the conditions for significant mandates rarely, if ever, occur.

The three readings in this section address the mandate question. In "Why Bush Won," three political observers—Democratic pollster Peter Hart, former presidential adviser David Gergen, and scholar Ruy Teixeira—analyze the meaning of the 2004 presidential vote. The discussion reveals the ambiguity in interpreting election results, as it's hard to know how the likability of the candidates, mobilization of the youth vote, or conservative social issues, drove the outcome. The one area of consensus is the importance of national security and concerns about terrorism.

Does that mean that Bush had a mandate? Hacker and Pierson argue that Bush's victory should not be viewed as such. Nobody, they maintain, can argue that Bush's supporters liked every aspect of his agenda. They object in particular to the notion that Bush's win gives him the legitimacy to push through a dramatic domestic agenda, because Bush campaigned as a war president, not a domestic reformer. Congressional gains were driven not by popular support but by redistricting, which produced nearly all of the Republican wins. Bush may claim to have won a mandate, but that doesn't make it so.

Nonsense, William Kristol responds. Opposition to the idea of a mandate is simply a continuation of Democratic efforts to oppose and undermine the president. Bush, Kristol points out, won a majority of the popular vote for the first time since 1988; won 8 million more votes than he won in 2000; and is the first president since Lyndon Johnson to be reelected while increasing his majorities in both the House and Senate. Democrats, Kristol concludes, can deny that a mandate exists all they want (let them "pull their hair till they're bald"), but that doesn't make it so.

# 31

# "Why Bush Won: A Look at the Numbers, What They Really Mean and What Happens Next"

## JANN S. WENNER

It was an outcome that took even the President's closest advisers by surprise. George W. Bush emerged from the election with fifty-one percent of the popular vote—the first outright majority for any presidential candidate since his father in 1988, and the first president since Franklin D. Roosevelt in 1936 to be reelected while gaining seats in both the House and the Senate. To get away from the battle of the ideological elites and make sense of the election, *Rolling Stone* met with Ruy Teixeira and Peter Hart—two analysts deeply grounded in public-opinion research—and David Gergen, a man we consider one of the most dispassionate observers of modern political history.

Teixeira, a joint fellow at the Center for American Progress and the Century Foundation, is co-author of *The Emerging Democratic Majority*, selected as one of the best books of 2002 by *The Economist*. Hart, known for his nonpartisan poll for NBC and *The Wall Street Journal*, has conducted public-opinion research for thirty governors and forty U.S. senators, from Hubert Humphrey to Jay Rockefeller. Gergen, director of the Center for Public Leadership in the Kennedy School of Government at Harvard University, has served in the White House as an adviser to presidents Nixon, Ford, Reagan and Clinton.

RS: Let's start with the major factors in Bush's victory.

RUY TEIXEIRA: If you want to look at ground zero of how Bush expanded his coalition, the key change from 2000 was that he did a lot better among white voters. His margin of victory among whites widened from twelve to seventeen points—and almost all of that was among white working-class women.

DAVID GERGEN: The decrease in the gender gap alone was enough to give him the victory. But he also increased his margin among Hispanics. And I don't think there's any doubt that in some key states, such as Ohio, he rallied his base through a strong organization and symbolic politics—especially the ban on gay marriage.

PETER HART: The other thing that's really important to understand is the Mississippi River: Since 1912, whoever has won a plurality of states along the Mississippi has won the presidency. This year, a sense of Republicanism crept up the river. The president won Missouri—which was always a toss-up state—by more than seven percent. Iowa flipped in his direction, and in Minnesota and Wisconsin, we waited all night to find out that Kerry had just barely carried each of those states. In state legislatures, the story is even more dramatic: going from huge Democratic majorities in the seventies to watching the GOP dominate in Missouri and Wisconsin. Only Illinois remains solidly in Democratic hands.

TEIXEIRA: I don't think it's quite as gruesome in some of the battleground states as Peter is portraying it. If you look at Wisconsin and Minnesota, the Democratic margin actually widened slightly. According to an analysis I did of Bush's increased margin, about half of it came from solid red states—states that Bush won by six points or more in 2000. And about half of that increase came from just four states: Tennessee, Georgia, Texas, and Alabama. Only a fifth of the increase in Bush's margin came from the battleground states, and about half of that increase came just from Florida. So Bush actually made comparatively modest gains in the battleground states.

RS: Nobody mentioned the Christian right. Karl Rove's strategy was to turn out 4 million evangelicals who didn't vote last time. Did he succeed in doing that?

TEIXEIRA: Because of the way exit polls were conducted this year, we can't know exactly how much evangelical turnout went up.

HART: That's right. But polls of likely voters indicate that it was up vastly—and that voters cared tremendously. We also know that half of all the votes that George Bush got this year came from people who go to religious services on a weekly basis. We're not just talking about fundamentalists—we're talking about Catholics, Jews, black Baptists, everyone.

GERGEN: What strikes me is that the Republicans are building a different sort of alliance system. For decades, Democrats have built alliances of voters through government programs such as Social Security and Medicare. Support from believers in those programs has enabled the Democrats to dominate national politics for a long time. The Republicans, in shrinking government, have increasingly turned to churches as a way to build alliances and to do their recruiting in quiet ways; it often takes place below the radar screen of the media. That's one of the reasons the election presented some surprises for us.

RS: Are there places beyond churches that the Republicans are building alliances?

GERGEN: They've been highly successful at building alliances through the military. Not only the people who are in uniform now, but those who have worn a uniform in the past tend to rally to the Republicans in ways beyond what we would have seen, say, forty years ago. That's become a reliable source of voting strength for them.

RS: Did the ballot initiatives in eleven states banning same-sex marriage have an effect?

TEIXEIRA: It helped create an environment, nationally, that was favorable for the Republicans.

GERGEN: My impression is that the country was moving toward a much greater tolerance of gays—and, indeed, an embrace of alternative lifestyles—that went far beyond what we saw, say, twenty years ago. Many voters were perfectly happy in their communities with gays living next door. Had that been left undisturbed, we would have seen far more support for gay unions ten years from now. But the decisions to approve gay marriages in Massachusetts and San Francisco may have spurred voters to make a decision about the issue before they were ready.

HART: I would subscribe to exactly what David said. It was a tactical victory for the Republicans—I don't think it should be interpreted as a referendum on the broader social and constitutional question. In periods of uncertainty and insecurity, the public reaches toward what is safe—and this is definitely a period of insecurity.

TEIXEIRA: That's right. But as we go forward, younger voters are gradually going to move the country in the direction of greater acceptance of gay marriage—whether Karl Rove wants it or not.

RS: Let's talk about the youth vote. What happened with young voters?

TEIXEIRA: One of the misperceptions about the election is that young people didn't turn out. In fact, the number of voters under the age of thirty increased substantially. And they went for Kerry by nine points in an election in which the country as a whole went for the other side by three points. That's the biggest difference between youth and the country as a whole that we've seen in the last four elections—even greater than in 1996, when Bill Clinton carried the youth by nineteen points and carried the country as a whole by eight points. I think there's real potential there for the future.

RS: So why are we hearing the youth vote put down by the media? Everyone says they didn't turn out—they failed to elect John Kerry.

TEIXEIRA: Goodness gracious—they tried their best. To have actually won the election for Kerry, they would have had to vote for him by twenty-five points. So I don't think you can blame it on the youth.

HART: Just the opposite. As Ruy suggests, the youth vote is a tremendous hope for the Democratic Party. I mean, here's a group that in previous elections said, "It doesn't make any difference." This year, all of a sudden they said, "It makes a lot of difference—it's important, and we care." And they turned out—they were active and involved. The way in which youth were communicated to was also a lot wider and broader than before. For the youth, Jon Stewart and Comedy Central made a huge difference in defining an awful lot of the agenda in this election.

GERGEN: There's another reason the youth vote should be encouraging for Democrats. When people enter the voting process and vote for two or three elections in a row for the same party, they tend to vote that way the rest of their lives. So this is a cohort that's going to be more Democratic—and that should give hope to the Democrats as they look ahead.

RS: So should Democrats emphasize the youth vote more as a strategy for the future?

TEIXEIRA: No. To rely on getting much more out of the youth vote would be foolish. If you want to solve the problem of why you lost this election, that's probably not where you want to go. You want to go more toward the middle. You've got to figure out how to get back some of the Hispanic votes you lost, and, most important, how to shore up your support among whites of modest income and education.

GERGEN: I agree that the Democrats can't rely upon the youth vote to increase much more as a way to win future elections. But they have to make the younger generation a foundational piece of their coalition. And that means that they've got to keep people mobilized and interested in the next four years. There's going to be a tendency among some of the young to become cynical after this election—to throw up their hands and walk away from the process. Some of them have gone through enormous psychological pain at the end of this and would just as soon not think about it anymore. How you convince them that this is just one battle lost in a bigger war—in a longer war—is one of the primary challenges Democrats face. They have to keep the turnout up. Doing that, in itself, is going to be hard.

TEIXEIRA: The bigger question is: What do the Democrats stand for? Democrats in this election ran against Bush. Kerry's program was never very clear to voters. They didn't get where he was coming from. Democrats have to have large and good ideas that people can recognize—ideas voters can summarize in a couple of sentences.

GERGEN: There's a tendency now for Democrats to say, "Who can we find to run next time? Should it be Hillary, of Evan Bayh, or XYZ?" I think that's a terrible mistake—it's a trap. It's far more important, as Ruy just said, for them to focus on what their ideas are, and what they believe in, before they decide who should carry the banner. The conservative movement was first built around a series of ideas and principles—then they went out and found Reagan to ride that wave into the White House. The Democrats have got some soul-searching to do about what they believe in.

TEIXEIRA: We should keep a bit of perspective on this. The last three elections, the Democrats got, respectively, forty-nine, forty-eight and forty-eight percent of the vote. That's not that far off a majority. I mean, you shift a point and a half of the vote and you're just about there. They just need to figure out a way to put their natural constituencies, and growing constituencies, together with a more respectable performance among whites of moderate income. Democrats are not in the position that the Republicans were in after Goldwater was defeated in 1964.

GERGEN: I would argue the contrary. I think they may be in a more dangerous position. The Goldwater coalition was in a deep, deep hole. They were a distinct minority, but they could build from the ground up. The Democrats are in danger of sliding down. They haven't won a majority of the white vote since 1964. They haven't won fifty percent of the national vote since 1976. And in the last six congressional elections—starting with 1994—they haven't cracked 48.5 percent of the national vote. This is a party that needs to have some deep rethinking—not simply go out and turn a few dials.

HART: David's right. To win, we need to build a coalition differently from before. It doesn't mean selling out on the coalition that has helped to establish the Democratic Party. It means that if we look at this loss just as a small tactical loss, we'll end up digging a deeper hole. The narrowness of the presidential loss hides the fact that the Republicans are the majority party in Congress; Democrats have a steep road ahead in both Congress and state legislatures.

RS: We haven't discussed the war on terrorism. Wasn't the deck kind of stacked against Kerry—challenging an incumbent president during a time of terrible uncertainty?

HART: That certainly is key. I have no doubt in my mind: If there had not been the terrorism threat, George Bush would have lost this election, and lost it decisively. It enabled him to run as the war president. Voters felt it was about safety.

GERGEN: Peter is absolutely right. Prior to 9/11, George Bush was on the arc of a difficult presidency. He would have been a one-term president. The way he rose to the occasion during the weeks after 9/11 was what convinced voters that he would be the safer choice. He did not win because of Iraq—he won despite Iraq.

RS: How much of this goes to Kerry's inability to connect with voters?

HART: Kerry always thought it was about IQ. But it was really about "I like." He never connected. I asked people, "What would it be like to have John Kerry as your next-door neighbor?" You know what they said? "High hedges" [*laughter*].

TEIXEIRA: Not a good sign.

RS: What were Kerry's strategic mistakes?

GERGEN: His biggest blunder was refusing to say that he would have changed his vote on Iraq had he known then what he knows now. That left him in a position of near incoherence on Iraq for several weeks and cost him precious time in trying to gain an advantage on Bush.

Having said that, I think it would be too easy for Democrats to say, "We lost because of some tactical mistakes Kerry made or because of his lack of likability." Yes, he made some mistakes—but he also ran one heck of a good campaign. He won all three debates, which no challenger has ever done. He raised more money than any Democrat in history and made the Democrats more competitive financially than ever before. And he raised the number of votes at the final election. John Kerry didn't lose this election; George Bush won it—and there's a difference. Democrats would be deluding themselves if they said, "If we just get a better candidate, we'll start winning all the time." That's why it goes back to the notion that they've got to reexamine their ideas—and whether they've got something fresh, interesting and compelling to offer the country.

TEIXEIRA: I agree with David that Kerry ran a solid campaign. But he never really managed to get his program across to the average voter. The Democratic program on the economy, on health care, on how to get out of Iraq—all these things were practically incomprehensible to voters. In one exit poll, voters were asked, "Do you trust Bush to handle the economy?" Fifty-one percent said no. That's not so good for an incumbent president. But voters rated Kerry even worse—fifty-three percent said they didn't trust him to run the economy. That means he never managed to get across what he would do, and how he *would* do it better.

HART: Ruy is right. Kerry kept talking about the plan, the plan, the plan, the plan—but the public never knew what the plan was. It would be equivalent to Martin Luther King, Jr., saying, "I have a dream," but never spelling out the dream that he went on to describe so vividly. I asked voters, "How much confidence do you have in Kerry making the right decisions on domestic issues?" Forty-one percent said a great deal or quite a bit of confidence. Then I asked the same question about George Bush—and the response was forty-one percent. I figured, God, if the Democrats can't dominate on domestic issues, it's because they never got the specifics across.

GERGEN: Bruce Reed wrote a very interesting piece in *The Washington Post* pointing out something I did not know. It suggests that we're entering a new period of politics. Of the twenty-eight states with the lowest per-capita income, Bush carried twenty-six. In the past, we would all have assumed that low-income states would mostly go Democratic. The fact that their income status does not seem to be tied to how they vote is a major advance for Republicans—and something Democrats have to think a lot about. It's conceivable that Republicans, in continuing to emphasize small government, may have left themselves in a position where Bush was not held as accountable for the loss of jobs, say, in Ohio as he would have been twenty years ago. That, to me, is a big change.

There is also an irony in this. Kerry won all the states with the highest per-capita income. States such as New York, with high per-capita incomes, are the ones that send more tax money to Washington and get less back than the rest of the country. So the Democrats win in blue states that are essentially for bigger government but that get less back from government, while Republicans win in red states that stand for smaller government and are getting more money from the government than they send in.

RS: So you think the Republicans are now the party of the workingman?

GERGEN: To the degree that the Republican Party is discovering that you can reach out to lower-income working people, whose lives are in huge flux. As Peter was pointing out, those voters are looking for something beyond an economic boost. They don't have much faith in government producing for them anymore, and they're looking for security. And they find it in a wartime president, and in their cultural beliefs. They're looking for anchors. The Republicans have learned how to reach out to those people and offer them some anchors—while Democrats find it harder to talk to them in those terms than they did in the past. There are some big shifts going on. The Republicans are not picking up the majority of working people, but they're picking up significant chunks in rural America who would have voted Democratic twenty years ago. And that, for Democrats, has to be worrisome.

# 32

# "Popular Fiction"

## Jacob S. Hacker and Paul Pierson

No sooner had the red and blue ink dried on the maps of election commentators than triumphant Republicans began talking about their clear mandate for an ambitious domestic agenda. The people have spoken, Republicans proclaimed, and what they have said is that they favor the conservative agenda on taxes, Social Security, health care, gay marriage, and abortion. The administration, their humble servant, has a solemn duty to execute their wishes. And so President Bush has promised to move forward with ambitious but still only vaguely outlined plans for Social Security privatization, tax simplification, and restrictions on lawsuits. "I have political capital and I intend to spend it," he declared.

Amazingly, much of the media seems to be buying the Republicans' mandate line. Just a day after the election, a front-page *New York Times* article, entitled "PRESIDENT SEEMS POISED TO CLAIM A NEW MANDATE," argued that President Bush "can claim that an apparently insurmountable lead in the popular vote vindicated his policies, his persistence, his personal qualities and his political strategy." *U.S. News & World Report* was more blunt: Bush, according to one headline, is the "MAN WITH THE MANDATE."

This is patently absurd. Leave aside for a moment the sheer brazenness of Republicans' claims in light of their contempt for the vote total in the 2000 election. (When the Bush campaign lost the popular vote in 2000, Dick Cheney reported that the "notion of sort of a restrained presidency because it was such a close election, that lasted maybe thirty seconds. It was not contemplated for any length of time. We had an agenda, we ran on that agenda, we won the election—full speed ahead.")

Leave aside as well the inherent implausibility of suggesting a vote for Candidate A over Candidate B implies support for each item on a laundry list of specific initiatives. Students of elections know well that voters don't choose candidates solely because of their positions on particular issues, much less their complete roster of stances.

And leave aside the fact that this election was the opposite of decisive. Although many pundits are saying that Bush trounced Kerry, the election was in fact exceedingly close by historical standards. In October, the American Political Science Association released the predictions of seven leading models of presidential elections. As an incumbent president running at a time of decent economic growth, Bush's average predicted vote was around 54 percent, meaning he significantly underperformed historical expectations.

Put aside all that. There is a more fundamental objection to Republicans' claim of a clear mandate for an ambitious domestic agenda: It is, put simply, a bait and switch. If one can bear to recall events of only a week ago, the Republican campaign was based on two main pillars: fear and mud. Overwhelmingly, the "positive" case for Bush's reelection rested on the relentless drumbeat of the war on terror. Cheney's remarks typically focused not on domestic issues but on veiled or explicit references to the lurking threat of nuclear incineration. Meanwhile the second pillar of the Bush campaign was to destroy Kerry's image as a credible alternative through any means necessary. Gross distortions of his record and proposals, shameless efforts to rip his words out of context, and the lowest forms of surrogate-based character assassination were central to the campaign. The GOP may well have waged the most negative campaign by an incumbent president in modern political history. As *The Washington Post* reported back in May: "Scholars and political strategists say the ferocious Bush assault on Kerry this spring has been extraordinary, both for the volume of attacks and for the liberties the president and his campaign have taken with the facts. Though stretching the truth is hardly new in a political campaign, they say the volume of negative charges is unprecedented—both in speeches and in advertising."

Karl Rove would not have needed to campaign that way if he believed he had a popular domestic agenda. He knew that he did not. Indeed, in the one setting—the three presidential debates—where popular attention was focused on the major issues of the day and the differences between the candidates, the popular verdict was clear: Kerry defeated Bush decisively.

In fact, everything we know about American opinion suggests that Bush is out of step with the public on all the issues he is now putting at the top of his "to do" list. During the election campaign, polls found that most Americans continue to be highly skeptical of the Republican tax-cut agenda and convinced that they have not benefited from it. In the final debate, Bush had to resort to the fudge of pointing out that the majority of his tax cuts went to "low- and middle-income Americans"—and while they did, the majority of *benefits* from his tax cuts did not.

On Social Security, administration officials have had *four years* to develop specific proposals. They have held back precisely because once an actual proposal is outlined it becomes clear what a dreadful deal it will be for most Americans. Indeed, when surveys mention the potential downsides of private individual accounts, public opinion has remained rock solid against privatization—and there is no evidence of a strong shift in favor of Bush's stance. A year ago, for example, the *Los Angeles Times* found that only a quarter of Americans supported private investment ac-

counts in Social Security if it meant a reduction in guaranteed benefits—
a feature of all leading privatization plans. The same basic story holds for
other domestic policy issues. The point isn't that the majority of Americans aren't conservative on some topics—they are. The point is that their
views have not changed fundamentally, and they remain overwhelmingly hostile to the top domestic priorities on which the administration is
now claiming a mandate.

But what about Republican gains in Congress? Here, the argument for
a mandate is equally dubious. Tracking polls that looked at which congressional party voters preferred showed consistently that average voters
favored the Democrats. In fact, this year Democrats led every one of the
final ten daily preelection tracking polls conducted by Rasmussen Reports—by an average margin of between two and three points. But the
views of middle-of-the-road voters mean less and less in congressional
races. Incumbency continues to provide an enormous advantage. Moreover, thanks to sophisticated partisan gerrymandering, more than 90 percent of House seats are now completely uncompetitive. In Texas, Tom
DeLay engineered an abnormally timed redistricting that cost Democrats
five seats. Without it, House Republicans wouldn't have gained at all.
Meanwhile, in the Senate, five retiring Democrats from the South left the
field clear for Republican pick-ups in the one part of the country the GOP
clearly dominates. Outside the South, Democrats actually gained one net
seat.

Against the backdrop of September 11, the Republican strategy
worked well enough to gain a narrow victory. Yet winning narrowly on a
campaign of mud and fear, and a strategy of hard-nosed partisan gerrymandering, does not a popular mandate for the conservative policy
agenda make. Republicans like to compare the current president with
Ronald Reagan. But in 1980, Reagan made clearly specified tax cuts the
centerpiece of his campaign. And when he won a decisive victory, he
could credibly claim a mandate to implement his pledge. That is simply
not the case today.

Given how conservative the modern Republican Party has become, it's
hardly surprising that administration officials are planning to go after the
key pillars of the domestic social contract. And given Bush's long trail of
similarly audacious rhetorical leaps, his claim to an agenda that represents the "will of the people" is also predictable. What it's not, however,
is credible.

# 33

# "Misunderestimated"

## William Kristol

It has happened again. Here at home, a great many people who fashion themselves his moral and intellectual superiors turn out once more—as he might put it—to have misunderestimated George W. Bush. And it has happened abroad, as well, where the president's opponents and enemies—which is to say America's opponents and enemies—must now be pulling their hair and gnashing their teeth with frustration and resentment. The exit polls said Kerry would win. The *New Yorker* had endorsed him. And *still* those idiot Americans reelected Bush!

How sweet it is to contemplate the misery of people who think like this. And how doubly sweet the joy felt by the president's supporters after those same (misleading) exit polls had plunged them—us—into 12 long hours of anxious gloom. "Nothing in life is so exhilarating as to be shot at without result," Churchill quipped. This week millions of Republicans know just what he was talking about.

But they should know something else, as well. Exit polls aside, the election was not, in fact, a "squeaker."

On November 2, 2004, George W. Bush won more American votes than any other presidential candidate in history—8 million more than he won in 2000, as a matter of fact. He was the first presidential candidate since 1988 to win more than 50 percent of the popular vote. He was the first incumbent since 1964 to win reelection while simultaneously expanding his party's representation in both houses of Congress. He had coattails, in other words; Republicans were elected to no fewer than six Senate seats that had previously been occupied by Democrats, for example, and in all six of those states, Bush ran well ahead of the rest of his party's ticket.

The hair-pullers and teeth-gnashers won't like it, of course, but we're nevertheless inclined to call this a Mandate. Indeed, in one sense, we think it an even larger and clearer mandate than those won in the landslide reelection campaigns of Nixon in 1972, Reagan in 1984, and Clinton in 1996. Needless to say, the Nixon, Reagan, and Clinton victory margins were much, much bigger. But that's in no small part because each of those preceding presidents could plausibly claim to be stage-directing a Morning in America, or building a Bridge to the Twenty-First Century.

George W. Bush could run no such smiley-face campaign. He is a war president. So he has run a war president's remarkably serious and substantive campaign. That campaign was not without its flaws; Bush had his bad moments, especially in the first debate. But he won the overall campaign debate. And because he won that overall debate—not because the visuals were nifty; not because it was the economy, stupid—he won the right to lead the United States for another four momentous years. George W. Bush's 2004 election is an accomplishment of ideological confirmation not unlike—obvious box-score distinctions notwithstanding— the one Franklin Roosevelt achieved in 1936.

Except that Roosevelt's, if anything, was easier. Bush chose the steepest possible climb. A year ago, when the president announced the July 1 transfer of power in Iraq, it was the consensus of cynics everywhere that Karl Rove had informed his boss that politics required him to slither away from Baghdad. Everyone who was anyone, here and in Europe, "knew" that this transfer of sovereignty would be an exit strategy in disguise. Everyone "knew" that Rove would never place his client president before the electorate while 150,000 American troops were still taking daily casualties—and considerable criticism—in the Middle East. Whatever mistakes the administration has made these past 18 months—and there've been more than a few too many—President Bush deserves enormous credit simply for staying the course, for rejecting bad advice to cut and run from purported friends and foes alike. On this central question of national security and principle, George W. Bush has proved himself an extraordinarily courageous president.

And the American people deserve enormous credit for backing up and ratifying his resolve. Let those who would dispute the point pull their hair till they're bald.

Now, the day after Election Day, is not the time to begin debating what sort of ambitious second-term agenda the president should adopt. It is enough to say that its ambitiousness will prove the key to its success. In his elegant Boston concession speech on Wednesday, John Kerry made a public plea for bipartisanship in the Washington, D.C., of a second Bush administration. And the president would be well advised to take Kerry up on the offer; bipartisanship is a fine thing, and nuance is a useful and admirable political grace.

But true statesmanship, and the landmark achievements that attend it, demand something more. *L'audace, toujours l'audace* [audacity, always audacity], said Danton.

Who says George W. Bush doesn't understand the French?

## DISCUSSION QUESTIONS

1. Are claims for or against a mandate purely instrumental? That is, is it true that if you oppose the president, you argue against a mandate, and if you support the president, you argue for one? Are there any concrete standards that we can apply?

2. How useful is it to think of political influence as "capital" that can be spent like a bank balance? Where does the capital come from? Can it be replenished? How, exactly, does one spend it?

3. If a mandate is so important, how did Bush manage to govern after the 2000 election? Is Bush's experience in his first term evidence that the concept is not very useful? Where does a president obtain legitimacy, if not from the popular vote?

# CHAPTER 7

# Bureaucracy in a Democratic System

## 34

## "The Study of Administration"

### WOODROW WILSON

*Until the late nineteenth century, almost no one paid attention to how the government actually worked. Administrative positions were generally filled by political appointees who were supporters of elected officials, and there was little that resembled "management" in the contemporary sense. There was, however, a great deal of money distributed at the national level, and as scandals mounted over the manner in which the money was distributed, the demand for government accountability grew.*

*Reformers argued that government employees should be hired on the basis of their merit, rather than because of their political allegiance to one candidate or another. Others called for reforms in the administration of public programs. Nearly thirty years before he was president, Wilson, then a professor at Bryn Mawr College, wrote an article for the* Political Science Quarterly *arguing that political scientists had neglected the study of public administration (or the problems involved in managing public programs). He argued that public administration should be carried out in accordance with scientific principles of management and efficiency, an argument that can be heard in contemporary debates over the need to "reinvent" government.*

It is the object of administrative study to discover, first, what government can properly and successfully do, and, secondly, how it can do these proper things with the utmost possible efficiency and at the least possible cost either of money or of energy. On both these points there is obviously much need of light among us; and only careful study can supply that light.

\* \* \*

The science of administration is the latest fruit of that study of the science of politics which was begun some twenty-two hundred years ago. It is a birth of our own century, almost of our own generation.

Why was it so late in coming? Why did it wait till this too busy century of ours to demand attention for itself? Administration is the most obvious part of government; it is government in action; it is the executive, the operative, the most visible side of government, and is of course as old as government itself. It is government in action, and one might very naturally expect to find that government in action had arrested the attention and provoked the scrutiny of writers of politics very early in the history of systematic thought.

But such was not the case. No one wrote systematically of administration as a branch of the science of government until the present century had passed its first youth and had begun to put forth its characteristic flower of systematic knowledge. Up to our own day all the political writers whom we now read had thought, argued, dogmatized only about the *constitution* of government; about the nature of the state, the essence and seat of sovereignty, popular power and kingly prerogative; about the greatest meanings lying at the heart of government, and the high ends set before the purpose of government by man's nature and man's aims. * * * The question was always: Who shall make law, and what shall that law be? The other question, how law should be administered with enlightenment, with equity, with speed, and without fiction, was put aside as "practical detail" which clerks could arrange after doctors had agreed upon principles.

*    *    *

[However,] if difficulties of government action are to be seen gathering in other centuries, they are to be seen culminating in our own.

This is the reason why administrative tasks have nowadays to be so studiously and systematically adjusted to carefully tested standards of policy, the reason why we are having now what we never had before, a science of administration. The weightier debates of constitutional principle are even yet by no means concluded; but they are no longer of more immediate practical moment than questions of administration. It is getting to be harder to *run* a constitution than to frame one.

*    *    *

There is scarcely a single duty of government which was once simple which is not now complex; government once had but a few masters; it now has scores of masters. Majorities formerly only underwent government; they now conduct government. Where government once might follow the whims of a court, it must now follow the views of a nation.

And those views are steadily widening to new conceptions of state duty; so that at the same time that the functions of government are every day becoming more complex and difficult, they are also vastly multiplying in number. Administration is everywhere putting its hands to new undertakings. * * * Seeing every day new things which the state ought to do, the next thing is to see clearly how it ought to do them.

This is why there should be a science of administration which shall seek to straighten the paths of government, to make its business less businesslike, to strengthen and purify its organization, and to crown its dutifulness. This is one reason why there is such a science.

But where has this science grown up? Surely not on this side [of] the sea. Not much impartial scientific method is to be discerned in our administrative practices. The poisonous atmosphere of city government, the crooked secrets of state administration, the confusion, sinecurism, and corruption ever and again discovered in the bureaus at Washington forbid us to believe that any clear conceptions of what constitutes good administration are as yet very widely current in the United States.

* * *

American political history has been a history, not of administrative development, but of legislative oversight—not of progress in governmental organization, but of advance in law-making and political criticism. Consequently, we have reached a time when administrative study and creation are imperatively necessary to the well-being of our governments saddled with the habits of a long period of constitution-making. * * * We have reached * * * the period * * * when the people have to develop administration in accordance with the constitutions they won for themselves in a previous period of struggle with absolute power.

* * *

It is harder for democracy to organize administration than for monarchy. The very completeness of our most cherished political successes in the past embarrasses us. We have enthroned public opinion; and it is forbidden us to hope during its reign for any quick schooling of the sovereign in executive expertness or in the conditions of perfect functional balance in government. The very fact that we have realized popular rule in its fullness has made the task of *organizing* that rule just so much the more difficult. * * * An individual sovereign will adopt a simple plan and carry it out directly: he will have but one opinion, and he will embody that one opinion in one command. But this other sovereign, the people, will have a score of differing opinions. They can agree upon nothing simple: advance must be made through compromise, by a compounding of differences, by a trimming of plans and a suppression of too straightforward principles. There will be a succession of resolves running through a course of years, a dropping fire of commands running through a whole gamut of modifications.

* * *

Wherever regard for public opinion is a first principle of government, practical reform must be slow and all reform must be full of compromises. For wherever public opinion exists it must rule.

* * *

The field of administration is a field of business. It is removed from the hurry and strife of politics; it at most points stands apart even from the debatable ground of constitutional study. It is a part of political life only as the methods of the counting-house are a part of the life of society; only as machinery is part of the manufactured product. But it is, at the same time, raised very far above the dull level of mere technical detail by the fact that through its greater principles it is directly connected with the lasting maxims of political wisdom, the permanent truths of political progress.

The object of administrative study is to rescue executive methods from the confusion and costliness of empirical experiment and set them upon foundations laid deep in stable principle.

* * *

[A]dministration lies outside the proper sphere of *politics*. Administrative questions are not political questions. Although politics sets the tasks for administration, it should not be suffered to manipulate its offices.

* * *

There is another distinction which must be worked into all our conclusions, which, though but another side of that between administration and politics, is not quite so easy to keep sight of: I mean the distinction between *constitutional* and administrative questions, between those governmental adjustments which are essential to constitutional principle and those which are merely instrumental to the possibly changing purposes of a wisely adapting convenience.

* * *

A clear view of the difference between the province of constitutional law and the province of administrative function ought to leave no room for misconception; and it is possible to name some roughly definite criteria upon which such a view can be built. Public administration is detailed and systematic execution of public law. Every particular application of general law is an act of administration. The assessment and raising of taxes, for instance, the hanging of a criminal, the transportation and delivery of the mails, the equipment and recruiting of the army, and navy, etc., are all obviously acts of administration; but the general laws which direct these things to be done are as obviously outside of and above administration. The broad plans of governmental action are not administrative; the detailed execution of such plans is administrative. Constitutions, therefore, properly concern themselves only with those instrumentalities of government which are to control general law. Our federal constitution observes this principle in saying nothing of even the greatest of the purely executive offices, and speaking only of that President of the Union who was to share the legislative and policy-making functions of government, only of those judges of highest jurisdiction who were to interpret and guard its principles, and not of those who were merely to give utterance to them.

*    *    *

There is, [however,] one point at which administrative studies trench on constitutional ground—or at least upon what seems constitutional ground. The study of administration, philosophically viewed, is closely connected with the study of the proper distribution of constitutional authority. To be efficient it must discover the simplest arrangements by which responsibility can be unmistakably fixed upon officials; the best way of dividing authority without hampering it, and responsibility without obscuring it. And this question of the distribution of authority, when taken into the sphere of the higher, the originating functions of government, is obviously a central constitutional question.

*    *    *

To discover the best principle for the distribution of authority is of greater importance, possibly, under a democratic system, where officials serve many masters, than under others where they serve but a few. All sovereigns are suspicious of their servants, and the sovereign people is no exception to the rule; but how is its suspicion to be allayed by *knowledge*? If that suspicion could be clarified into wise vigilance, it would be altogether salutary; if that vigilance could be aided by the unmistakable placing of responsibility, it would be altogether beneficent. Suspicion in itself is never healthful either in the private or in the public mind. *Trust is strength* in all relations of life; and, as it is the office of the constitutional reformer to create conditions of trustfulness, so it is the office of the administrative organizer to fit administration with conditions of clear-cut responsibility which shall insure trustworthiness.

And let me say that large powers and unhampered discretion seem to me the indispensable conditions of responsibility. Public attention must be easily directed, in each case of good or bad administration, to just the man deserving of praise or blame. There is no danger in power, if only it be not irresponsible. If it be divided, dealt out in shares to many, it is obscured; and if it be obscured, it is made irresponsible. But if it be centered in heads of the service and in heads of branches of the service, it is easily watched and brought to book. If to keep his office a man must achieve open and honest success, and if at the same time he feels himself intrusted with large freedom of discretion, the greater his power the less likely is he to abuse it, the more is he nerved and sobered and elevated by it. The less his power, the more safely obscure and unnoticed does he feel his position to be, and the more readily does he relapse into remissness.

Just here we manifestly emerge upon the field of that still larger question—the proper relations between public opinion and administration.

To whom is official trustworthiness to be disclosed, and by whom is it to be rewarded? Is the official to look to the public for his meed of praise and his push of promotion, or only to his superior in office? Are the people to be called in to settle administrative discipline as they are called in to settle constitutional principles? These questions evidently find their root in what is undoubtedly the fundamental problem of this whole study. That problem is: What part shall public opinion take in the conduct of administration?

The right answer seems to be, that public opinion shall play the part of authoritative critic.

But the *method* by which its authority shall be made to tell? Our peculiar American difficulty in organizing administration is not the danger of losing liberty, but the danger of not being able or willing to separate its essentials from its accidents. Our success is made doubtful by that besetting error of ours, the error of trying to do too much by vote. Self-government does not consist in having a hand in everything, any more than housekeeping consists necessarily in cooking dinner with one's own hands. The cook must be trusted with a large discretion as to the management of the fires and the ovens.

*   *   *

The problem is to make public opinion efficient without suffering it to be meddlesome. Directly exercised, in the oversight of the daily details and in the choice of the daily means of government, public criticism is of course a clumsy nuisance, a rustic handling delicate machinery. But as superintending the greater forces of formative policy alike in politics and administration, public criticism is altogether safe and beneficent, altogether indispensable. Let administrative study find the best means for giving public criticism this control and for shutting it out from all other interference.

But is the whole duty of administrative study done when it has taught the people what sort of administration to desire and demand, and how to get what they demand? Ought it not to go on to drill candidates for the public service?

*   *   *

If we are to improve public opinion, which is the motive power of government, we must prepare better officials as the *apparatus* of government. * * * It will be necessary to organize democracy by sending up to the competitive examinations for the civil service men definitely prepared for standing liberal tests as to technical knowledge. A technically schooled civil service will presently have become indispensable.

I know that a corps of civil servants prepared by a special schooling and drilled, after appointment, into a perfected organization, with appropriate hierarchy and characteristic discipline, seems to a great many very thoughtful persons to contain elements which might combine to make an offensive official class—a distinct, semi-corporate body with sympathies divorced from those of a progressive, free-spirited people, and with hearts narrowed to the meanness of a bigoted officialism.

*    *    *

But to fear the creation of a domineering, illiberal officialism as a result of the studies I am here proposing is to miss altogether the principle upon which I wish most to insist. That principle is, that administration in the United States must be at all points sensitive to public opinion. A body of thoroughly trained officials serving during good behavior we must have in any case: that is a plain business necessity. But the apprehension that such a body will be anything un-American clears away the moment it is asked, What is to constitute good behavior? For that question obviously carries its own answer on its face. Steady, hearty allegiance to the policy of the government they serve will constitute good behavior. That *policy* will have no taint of officialism about it. It will not be the creation of permanent officials, but of statesmen whose responsibility to public opinion will be direct and inevitable. Bureaucracy can exist only where the whole service of the state is removed from the common political life of the people, its chiefs as well as its rank and file. Its motives, its objects, its policy, its standards, must be bureaucratic.

*    *    *

The ideal for us is a civil service cultured and self-sufficient enough to act with sense and vigor, and yet so intimately connected with the popular thought, by means of elections and constant public counsel, as to find arbitrariness or class spirit quite out of the question.

Having thus viewed in some sort the subject-matter and the objects of this study of administration, what are we to conclude as to the methods best suited to it—the points of view most advantageous for it?

Government is so near us, so much a thing of our daily familiar handling, that we can with difficulty see the need of any philosophical study of it, or the exact point of such study, should it be undertaken. We have been on our feet too long to study now the art of walking. We are a practical people, made so apt, so adept in self-government by centuries of experimental drill that we are scarcely any longer capable of perceiving the awkwardness of the particular system we may be using, just because it is so easy for us to use any system. We do not study the art of governing: we govern. But mere unschooled genius for affairs will not save us from sad blunders in administration. Though democrats by long inheritance and repeated choice, we are still rather crude democrats. Old as democracy is, its organization on a basis of modern ideas and conditions is still an unaccomplished work. The democratic state has yet to be equipped for carrying those enormous burdens of administration which the needs of this industrial and trading age are so fast accumulating.

* * *

We can borrow the science of administration [developed elsewhere] with safety and profit if only we read all fundamental differences of condition into its essential tenets. We have only to filter it through our constitutions, only to put it over a slow fire of criticism and distil away its foreign gases.

* * *

Our own politics must be the touchstone for all theories. The principles on which to base a science of administration for America must be principles which have democratic policy very much at heart. And, to suit American habit, all general theories must, as theories, keep modestly in the background, not in open argument only, but even in our own minds—lest opinions satisfactory only to the standards of the library should be dogmatically used, as if they must be quite as satisfactory to the standards of practical politics as well. Doctrinaire devices must be postponed to tested practices. Arrangements not only sanctioned by conclusive experience elsewhere but also congenial to American habit must be preferred without hesitation to theoretical perfection. In a word, steady, practical statesmanship must come first, closet doctrine second. The cosmopolitan what-to-do must always be commanded by the American how-to-do-it.

Our duty is to supply the best possible life to a *federal* organization, to systems within systems; to make town, city, county, state, and federal governments live with a like strength and an equally assured healthfulness, keeping each unquestionably its own master and yet making all interdependent and co-operative, combining independence with mutual helpfulness. The task is great and important enough to attract the best minds.

This interlacing of local self-government with federal self-government is quite a modern conception. * * * The question for us is, how shall our series of governments within governments be so administered that it shall always be to the interest of the public officer to serve, not his superior alone but the community also, with the best efforts of his talents and the soberest service of his conscience? How shall such service be made to his commonest interest by contributing abundantly to his sustenance, to his dearest interest by furthering his ambition, and to his highest interest by advancing his honor and establishing his character? And how shall this be done alike for the local part and for the national whole?

If we solve this problem we shall again pilot the world.

## DISCUSSION QUESTIONS

1. Do you agree with Wilson's central proposition that politics and administration are separate things? Can you think of any examples where the two overlap?

2. In 2002, the Bush administration announced that it would extend government child health care benefits to fetuses; in effect, pregnant women would become eligible for prenatal care under a program designed to provide health care to children. Some critics argued that this was a veiled attempt to redefine a fetus as a child, a step that would have implications for the abortion debate. What do you think of this decision? Does it alter the view that politics and administration are separate?

# 35

# From *Bureaucracy: What Government Agencies Do and Why They Do It*

## JAMES Q. WILSON

*Woodrow Wilson was merely the first in a long line of reformers to suggest that government might be more efficient if it ran more like a business. The sentiment remains today. Perhaps a more "businesslike" government would issue our income tax refunds more promptly, protect the environment at lower cost, and impose fewer burdens on citizens. The catch is, we want all this at low cost and minimal intrusiveness in our lives, yet we want government bureaucracies to be held strictly accountable for the authority they exercise.*

*James Q. Wilson argues that government will never operate like a business, nor should we expect it to. His 1989 comparison of the Watertown, Massachusetts, Registry of Motor Vehicles (representing any government bureaucracy) with a nearby McDonald's (representing any private profit-seeking organization) shows that the former will most likely never service its clientele as well as the latter. The problem is not bureaucratic laziness, or any of the conventional criticisms of government agencies, but is instead due to the very different characteristics of public versus private enterprises. In order to understand "what government agencies do and why they do it," Wilson argues we must first understand that government bureaucracies operate in a political marketplace, rather than an economic one. The annual revenues and personnel resources of a government agency are determined by elected officials, not by the agency's ability to meet the demands of its customers in a cost-efficient manner. The government agency's internal structure and decision-making procedures are defined by legislation, regulation, and executive orders, while similar decisions in a private business are made by executive officers and management within the organization. And, perhaps most critically, a government agency's goals are often vague, difficult if not impossible to measure, and even contradictory. In business, by contrast, the task is simpler. The basic goal of a private business has always been to maximize the bottom line: profit. Although he suggests we cannot reform government agencies the way we might a private bureaucracy, Wilson notes that we should nevertheless try to make government bureaucracies operate more effectively and efficiently.*

By the time the office opens at 8:45 A.M., the line of people waiting to do business at the Registry of Motor Vehicles in Watertown, Massachusetts, often will be twenty-five deep. By midday, especially if it is near the end of the month, the line may extend clear around the building. Inside, motorists wait in slow-moving rows before poorly marked windows to get a driver's license or to register an automobile. When someone gets to the head of the line, he or she is often told by the clerk that it is the wrong line: "Get an application over there and then come back," or "This is only for people getting a new license; if you want to replace one you lost, you have to go to the next window." The customers grumble impatiently. The clerks act harried and sometimes speak brusquely, even rudely. What seems to be a simple transaction may take 45 minutes or even longer. By the time people are photographed for their driver's licenses, they are often scowling. The photographer valiantly tries to get people to smile, but only occasionally succeeds.

Not far away, people also wait in line at a McDonald's fast-food restaurant. There are several lines; each is short, each moves quickly. The menu is clearly displayed on attractive signs. The workers behind the counter are invariably polite. If someone's order cannot be filled immediately, he or she is asked to step aside for a moment while the food is prepared and then is brought back to the head of the line to receive the order. The atmosphere is friendly and good-natured. The room is immaculately clean.

Many people have noticed the difference between getting a driver's license and ordering a Big Mac. Most will explain it by saying that bureaucracies are different from businesses. "Bureaucracies" behave as they do because they are run by unqualified "bureaucrats" and are enmeshed in "rules" and "red tape."

But business firms are also bureaucracies, and McDonald's is a bureaucracy that regulates virtually every detail of its employees' behavior by a complex and all-encompassing set of rules. Its operations manual is six hundred pages long and weighs four pounds. In it one learns that french fries are to be nine-thirty-seconds of an inch thick and that grill workers are to place hamburger patties on the grill from left to right, six to a row for six rows. They are then to flip the third row first, followed by the fourth, fifth, and sixth rows, and finally the first and second. The amount of sauce placed on each bun is precisely specified. Every window must be washed every day. Workers must get down on their hands and knees and pick up litter as soon as it appears. These and countless other rules designed to reduce the workers to interchangeable automata were inculcated in franchise managers at Hamburger University located in a $40 million facility. There are plenty of rules governing the Registry, but they are only a small fraction of the rules that govern every detail of every operation at McDonald's. Indeed, if the DMV manager tried to impose on his employees as demanding a set of rules as those that govern the McDonald's staff, they would probably rebel and he would lose his job.

It is just as hard to explain the differences between the two organizations by reference to the quality or compensation of their employees. The Registry workers are all adults, most with at least a high-school education; the McDonald's employees are mostly teenagers, many still in school. The Registry staff is well-paid compared to the McDonald's workers, most of whom receive only the minimum wage. When labor shortages developed in Massachusetts during the mid-1980s, many McDonald's stores began hiring older people (typically housewives) of the same sort who had long worked for the Registry. They behaved just like the teenagers they replaced.

Not only are the differences between the two organizations not to be explained by reference to "rules" or "red tape" or "incompetent workers," the differences call into question many of the most frequently mentioned complaints about how government agencies are supposed to behave. For example: "Government agencies are big spenders." The Watertown office of the Registry is in a modest building that can barely handle its clientele. The teletype machine used to check information submitted by people requesting a replacement license was antiquated and prone to errors. Three or four clerks often had to wait in line to use equipment described by the office manager as "personally signed by Thomas Edison." No computers or word processors were available to handle the preparation of licenses and registrations; any error made by a clerk while manually typing a form meant starting over again on another form.

Or: "Government agencies hire people regardless of whether they are really needed." Despite the fact that the citizens of Massachusetts probably have more contact with the Registry than with any other state agency, and despite the fact that these citizens complain more about Registry service than about that of any other bureau, the Watertown branch, like all Registry offices, was seriously understaffed. In 1981, the agency lost 400 workers—about 25 percent of its work force—despite the fact that its workload was rising.

Or: "Government agencies are imperialistic, always grasping for new functions." But there is no record of the Registry doing much grasping, even though one could imagine a case being made that the state government could usefully create at Registry offices "one-stop" multi-service centers where people could not only get drivers' licenses but also pay taxes and parking fines, obtain information, and transact other official business. The Registry seemed content to provide one service.

In short, many of the popular stereotypes about government agencies and their members are either questionable or incomplete. To explain why government agencies behave as they do, it is not enough to know that they are "bureaucracies"—that is, it is not enough to know that they are big, or complex, or have rules. What is crucial is that they are *government* bureaucracies. As the preceding chapters should make clear, not all government bureaucracies behave the same way or suffer from the same problems. There may even be registries of motor vehicles in other states that do a better job than the one in Massachusetts. But all government agencies have in common certain characteristics that tend to make their management far more difficult than managing a McDonald's. These common characteristics are the constraints of public agencies.

The key constraints are three in number. To a much greater extent than is true of private bureaucracies, government agencies (1) cannot lawfully retain and devote to the private benefit of their members the earnings of the organization, (2) cannot allocate the factors of production in accordance with the preferences of the organization's administrators, and (3) must serve goals not of the organization's own choosing. Control over revenues, productive factors, and agency goals is all vested to an important degree in entities external to the organization—legislatures, courts, politicians, and interest groups. Given this, agency managers must attend to the demands of these external entities. As a result, government management tends to be driven by the *constraints* on the organization, not the *tasks* of the organization. To say the same thing in other words, whereas business management focuses on the "bottom line" (that is, profits), government management focuses on the "top line" (that is, constraints). Because government managers are not as strongly motivated as private ones to define the tasks of their subordinates, these tasks are often shaped by [other] factors.

\* \* \*

*Revenues and Incentives*

In the days leading up to September 30, the federal government is Cinderella, courted by legions of individuals and organizations eager to get grants and contracts from the unexpended funds still at the disposal of each agency. At midnight on September 30, the government's coach turns into a pumpkin. That is the moment—the end of the fiscal year—at which every agency, with a few exceptions, must return all unexpended funds to the Treasury Department.

Except for certain quasi-independent government corporations, such as the Tennessee Valley Authority, no agency may keep any surplus revenues (that is, the difference between the funds it received from a congressional appropriation and those it needed to operate during the year). By the same token, any agency that runs out of money before the end of the fiscal year may ask Congress for more (a "supplemental appropriation") instead of being forced to deduct the deficit from any accumulated cash reserves. Because of these fiscal rules agencies do not have a material incentive to economize: Why scrimp and save if you cannot keep the results of your frugality?

Nor can individual bureaucrats lawfully capture for their personal use any revenue surpluses. When a private firm has a good year, many of its officers and workers may receive bonuses. Even if no bonus is paid, these employees may buy stock in the firm so that they can profit from any growth in earnings (and, if they sell the stock in a timely manner, profit from a drop in earnings). Should a public bureaucrat be discovered trying to do what private bureaucrats routinely do, he or she would be charged with corruption.

We take it for granted that bureaucrats should not profit from their offices and nod approvingly when a bureaucrat who has so benefited is indicted and put on trial. But why should we take this view? Once a very different view prevailed. In the seventeenth century, a French colonel would buy his commission from the king, take the king's money to run his regiment, and pocket the profit. At one time a European tax collector was paid by keeping a percentage of the taxes he collected. In this country, some prisons were once managed by giving the warden a sum of money based on how many prisoners were under his control and letting him keep the difference between what he received and what it cost him to feed the prisoners. Such behavior today would be grounds for criminal prosecution. Why? What has changed?

Mostly we the citizenry have changed. We are creatures of the Enlightenment: We believe that the nation ought not to be the property of the sovereign; that laws are intended to rationalize society and (if possible) perfect mankind; and that public service ought to be neutral and disinterested. We worry that a prison warden paid in the old way would have a strong incentive to starve his prisoners in order to maximize his income; that a regiment supported by a greedy colonel would not be properly equipped; and that a tax collector paid on a commission basis would extort excessive taxes from us. These changes reflect our desire to eliminate moral hazards—namely, creating incentives for people to act wrongly. But why should this desire rule out more carefully designed compensation plans that would pay government managers for achieving officially approved goals and would allow efficient agencies to keep any unspent part of their budget for use next year?

Part of the answer is obvious. Often we do not know whether a manager or an agency has achieved the goals we want because either the goals are vague or inconsistent, or their attainment cannot be observed, or both. Bureau chiefs in the Department of State would have to go on welfare if their pay depended on their ability to demonstrate convincingly that they had attained their bureaus' objectives.

But many government agencies have reasonably clear goals toward which progress can be measured. The Social Security Administration, the Postal Service, and the General Services Administration all come to mind. Why not let earnings depend importantly on performance? Why not let agencies keep excess revenues?

* * *

But in part it is because we know that even government agencies with clear goals and readily observable behavior only can be evaluated by making political (and thus conflict-ridden) judgments. If the Welfare Department delivers every benefit check within 24 hours after the application is received, Senator Smith may be pleased but Senator Jones will be irritated because this speedy delivery almost surely would require that the standards of eligibility be relaxed so that many ineligible clients would get money. There is no objective standard by which the trade-off between speed and accuracy in the Welfare Department can be evaluated. Thus we have been unwilling to allow welfare employees to earn large bonuses for achieving either speed or accuracy.

The inability of public managers to capture surplus revenues for their own use alters the pattern of incentives at work in government agencies. Beyond a certain point additional effort does not produce additional earnings. (In this country, Congress from time to time has authorized higher salaries for senior bureaucrats but then put a cap on actual payments to them so that the pay increases were never received. This was done to insure that no bureaucrat would earn more than members of Congress at a time when those members were unwilling to accept the political costs of raising their own salaries. As a result, the pay differential between the top bureaucratic rank and those just below it nearly vanished.) If political constraints reduce the marginal effect of money incentives, then the relative importance of other, nonmonetary incentives will increase. . . .

That bureaucratic performance in most government agencies cannot be linked to monetary benefits is not the whole explanation for the difference between public and private management. There are many examples of private organizations whose members cannot appropriate money surpluses for their own benefit. Private schools ordinarily are run on a nonprofit basis. Neither the headmaster nor the teachers share in the profit of these schools; indeed, most such schools earn no profit at all and instead struggle to keep afloat by soliciting contributions from friends and alumni. Nevertheless, the evidence is quite clear that on the average, private schools, both secular and denominational, do a better job than public ones in educating children. Moreover, as political scientists John Chubb and Terry Moe have pointed out, they do a better job while employing fewer managers. Some other factors are at work. One is the freedom an organization has to acquire and use labor and capital.

## Acquiring and Using the Factors of Production

A business firm acquires capital by retaining earnings, borrowing money, or selling shares of ownership; a government agency (with some exceptions) acquires capital by persuading a legislature to appropriate it. A business firm hires, promotes, demotes, and fires personnel with considerable though not perfect freedom; a federal government agency is told by Congress how many persons it can hire and at what rate of pay, by the Office of Personnel Management (OPM) what rules it must follow in selecting and assigning personnel, by the Office of Management and Budget (OMB) how many persons of each rank it may employ, by the Merit Systems Protection Board (MSPB) what procedures it must follow in demoting or discharging personnel, and by the courts whether it has faithfully followed the rules of Congress, OPM, OMB, and MSPB. A business firm purchases goods and services by internally defined procedures (including those that allow it to buy from someone other than the lowest bidder if a more expensive vendor seems more reliable), or to skip the bidding procedure altogether in favor of direct negotiations; a government agency must purchase much of what it uses by formally advertising for bids, accepting the lowest, and keeping the vendor at arm's length. When a business firm develops a good working relationship with a contractor, it often uses that vendor repeatedly without looking for a new one; when a government agency has a satisfactory relationship with a contractor, ordinarily it cannot use the vendor again without putting a new project out for a fresh set of bids. When a business firm finds that certain offices or factories are no longer economical it will close or combine them; when a government agency wishes to shut down a local office or military base often it must get the permission of the legislature (even when formal permission is not necessary, informal consultation is). When a business firm draws up its annual budget each expenditure item can be reviewed as a discretionary amount (except for legally mandated payments of taxes to government and interest to banks and bondholders); when a government agency makes up its budget many of the detailed expenditure items are mandated by the legislature.

All these complexities of doing business in or with the government are well-known to citizens and firms. These complexities in hiring, purchasing, contracting, and budgeting often are said to be the result of the "bureaucracy's love of red tape." But few, if any, of the rules producing this complexity would have been generated by the bureaucracy if left to its own devices, and many are as cordially disliked by the bureaucrats as by their clients. These rules have been imposed on the agencies by external actors, chiefly the legislature. They are not bureaucratic rules but *political* ones. In principle the legislature could allow the Social Security Administration, the Defense Department, or the New York City public school system to follow the same rules as IBM, General Electric, or Harvard University. In practice they could not. The reason is politics, or more precisely, democratic politics.

\* \* \*

*Public versus Private Management*

What distinguishes public from private organizations is neither their size nor their desire to "plan" (that is, control) their environments but rather the rules under which they acquire and use capital and labor. General Motors acquires capital by selling shares, issuing bonds, or retaining earnings; the Department of Defense acquires it from an annual appropriation by Congress. GM opens and closes plants, subject to certain government regulations, at its own discretion; DOD opens and closes military bases under the watchful guidance of Congress. GM pays its managers with salaries it sets and bonuses tied to its earnings; DOD pays its managers with salaries set by Congress and bonuses (if any) that have no connection with organizational performance. The number of workers in GM is determined by its level of production; the number in DOD by legislation and civil-service rules.

What all this means can be seen by returning to the Registry of Motor Vehicles and McDonald's. Suppose you were just appointed head of the Watertown office of the Registry and you wanted to improve service there so that it more nearly approximated the service at McDonald's. Better service might well require spending more money (on clerks, equipment, and buildings). Why should your political superiors give you that money? It is a cost to them if it requires either higher taxes or taking funds from another agency; offsetting these real and immediate costs are dubious and postponed benefits. If lines become shorter and clients become happier, no legislator will benefit. There may be fewer complaints, but complaints are episodic and have little effect on the career of any given legislator. By contrast, shorter lines and faster service at McDonald's means more customers can be served per hour and thus more money can be earned per hour. A McDonald's manager can estimate the marginal product of the last dollar he or she spends on improving service; the Registry manager can generate no tangible return on any expenditure he or she makes and thus cannot easily justify the expenditure.

Improving service at the Registry may require replacing slow or surly workers with quick and pleasant ones. But you, the manager, can neither hire nor fire them at will. You look enviously at the McDonald's manager who regularly and with little notice replaces poor workers with better ones. Alternatively, you may wish to mount an extensive training program (perhaps creating a Registration University to match McDonald's Hamburger University) that would imbue a culture of service in your employees. But unless the Registry were so large an agency that the legislature would neither notice nor care about funds spent for this purpose—and it is not that large—you would have a tough time convincing anybody that this was not a wasteful expenditure on a frill project.

If somehow your efforts succeed in making Registry clients happier, you can take vicarious pleasure in it; in the unlikely event a client seeks you out to thank you for those efforts, you can bask in a moment's worth of glory. Your colleague at McDonald's who manages to make customers happier may also derive some vicarious satisfaction from the improvement but in addition he or she will earn more money owing to an increase in sales.

In time it will dawn on you that if you improve service too much, clients will start coming to the Watertown office instead of going to the Boston office. As a result, the lines you succeeded in shortening will become longer again. If you wish to keep complaints down, you will have to spend even more on the Watertown office. But if it was hard to persuade the legislature to do that in the past, it is impossible now. Why should the taxpayer be asked to spend more on Watertown when the Boston office, fully staffed (naturally, no one was laid off when the clients disappeared), has no lines at all? From the legislature's point of view the correct level of expenditure is not that which makes one office better than another but that which produces an equal amount of discontent in all offices.

Finally, you remember that your clients have no choice: The Registry offers a monopoly service. It and only it supplies drivers' licenses. In the long run all that matters is that there are not "too many" complaints to the legislature about service. Unlike McDonald's, the Registry need not fear that its clients will take their business to Burger King or to Wendy's. Perhaps you should just relax.

If this were all there is to public management it would be an activity that quickly and inevitably produces cynicism among its practitioners. But this is not the whole story. For one thing, public agencies differ in the kinds of problems they face. For another, many public managers try hard to do a good job even though they face these difficult constraints.

## DISCUSSION QUESTIONS

1. Wilson argues that McDonald's and the Department of Motor Vehicles operate differently because of the inherent differences between public and private organizations. Apply his reasoning to other cases, for instance, the U.S. Postal Service and UPS, or any other area where the government and the private sector compete for business. Think about the goals of the organizations, who controls them, how they distinguish success from failure, and the consequences of failure.

2. What are the advantages and disadvantages of trying to run the government more like a business? How would you define the basic parameters of a "businesslike" government (who are the "customers"?)?

3. Some critics of government inefficiency argue that nearly every domestic government function—from schools to road building—could be run more efficiently if it were "privatized" (turned over to private contractors). Do you agree? Are there any government functions that do not lend themselves to privatization?

## DEBATING THE ISSUES: REFORMING THE NATIONAL SECURITY BUREAUCRACY

One of the key recommendations to emerge from the various studies and commissions on the 9/11 attacks is a substantial reform of the intelligence community—the various agencies that collect and analyze information from foreign governments and adversaries. The fact that nineteen hijackers could live in the U.S. while planning and then carrying out multiple hijackings was seen as a titanic intelligence failure, with investigators unable to connect dots that were right in front of them. Different threads of warnings—reports from FBI agents about Middle Eastern men receiving suspicious flight training; intelligence alerts that were not passed on to law-enforcement agencies; requests for information that were denied—were never connected, even though during the summer of 2001 the system was "blinking red," according to then CIA director George Tenet.

All of the various reform proposals—and there are many—share the fundamental goal of increasing the efficiency with which information is collected, analyzed, and shared. "Integration" is the key concept. As it exists now, the intelligence community consists of over a dozen separate organizations in multiple agencies. As the Commission Report notes, each of these units has its own organizational culture, methods, and standards. They do not like to share information. To fight this, the Commission recommends the establishment of a National Intelligence Directorate that would reorganize many of the separate intelligence agencies into a single organization, and strengthen oversight of the entire community.

Such a plan seems sensible enough. But not everyone agrees. The military and civilian leadership in the Pentagon, notes Joe Pappalardo, worries that the new structure might make it harder to integrate intelligence into military operations. The services view intelligence and operations as part of the same process, and leaders have expressed concern that reform might disrupt existing lines of communication. In addition, the Pentagon controls a large portion of the existing intelligence budget, and the leadership there is inclined to oppose reforms that will redistribute power.

Siobhan Gorman's article provides a sense of how agencies develop their own organizational cultures. The FBI and CIA have different missions and methods, and it has proven difficult to get them to cooperate. The FBI is a law-enforcement agency, and it is structured to support domestic judicial proceedings; until recently, its main focus was on federal crimes, not counterterrorism. The CIA is an intelligence agency barred by law from domestic spying, and it is structured to collect (often covertly) and analyze information that will be used by political leaders. Where the FBI might want to raid and shut down a domestic terror cell, the CIA might want to "turn" one of the members into a spy. These different outlooks turn into a federal government version of the famous self-help book, *Men Are from Mars, Women Are from Venus.*

# 36

# From *The 9/11 Commission Report*

## NATIONAL COMMISSION ON TERRORIST ATTACKS UPON THE UNITED STATES

*13.2 Unity of Effort in the Intelligence Community*

In our first section, we concentrated on counterterrorism, discussing how to combine the analysis of information from all sources of intelligence with the joint planning of operations that draw on that analysis. In this section, we step back from looking just at the counterterrorism problem. We reflect on whether the government is organized adequately to direct resources and build the intelligence capabilities it will need not just for countering terrorism, but for the broader range of national security challenges in the decades ahead.

### The Need for a Change

During the Cold War, intelligence agencies did not depend on seamless integration to track and count the thousands of military targets—such as tanks and missiles—fielded by the Soviet Union and other adversary states. Each agency concentrated on its specialized mission, acquiring its own information and then sharing it via formal, finished reports. The Department of Defense had given birth to and dominated the main agencies for technical collection of intelligence. Resources were shifted at an incremental pace, coping with challenges that arose over years, even decades.

We summarized the resulting organization of the intelligence community in chapter 3. It is outlined below.

## Members of the U.S. Intelligence Community

Office of the Director of Central Intelligence, which includes the Office of the Deputy Director of Central Intelligence for Community Management, the Community Management Staff, the Terrorism Threat Integration Center, the National Intelligence Council, and other community offices

The Central Intelligence Agency (CIA), which performs human source collection, all-source analysis, and advanced science and technology

National intelligence agencies:

- National Security Agency (NSA), which performs signals collection and analysis
- National Geospatial-Intelligence Agency (NGA), which performs imagery collection and analysis
- National Reconnaissance Office (NRO), which develops, acquires, and launches space systems for intelligence collection
- Other national reconnaissance programs

Departmental intelligence agencies:

- Defense Intelligence Agency (DIA) of the Department of Defense
- Intelligence entities of the Army, Navy, Air Force, and Marines
- Bureau of Intelligence and Research (INR) of the Department of State
- Office of Terrorism and Finance Intelligence of the Department of Treasury
- Office of Intelligence and the Counterterrorism and Counterintelligence Divisions of the Federal Bureau of Investigation of the Department of Justice
- Office of Intelligence of the Department of Energy
- Directorate of Information Analysis and Infrastructure Protection (IAIP) and Directorate of Coast Guard Intelligence of the Department of Homeland Security

The need to restructure the intelligence community grows out of six problems that have become apparent before and after 9/11:

- *Structural barriers to performing joint intelligence work.* National intelligence is still organized around the collection disciplines of the home agencies, not the joint mission. The importance of integrated, all-source analysis cannot be overstated. Without it, it is not possible to "connect the dots." No one component holds all the relevant information.

By contrast, in organizing national defense, the Goldwater-Nichols legislation of 1986 created joint commands for operations in the field, the Unified Command Plan. The services—the Army, Navy, Air Force, and Marine Corps—organize, train, and equip their people and units to perform their missions. Then they assign personnel and units to the joint combatant commander, like the commanding general of the Central Command (CENTCOM). The Goldwater-Nichols Act required officers to serve tours outside their service in order to win promotion. The culture of the Defense Department was transformed, its collective mind-set moved from service-specific to "joint," and its operations became more integrated.

- *Lack of common standards and practices across the foreign-domestic divide.* The leadership of the intelligence community should be able to pool information gathered overseas with information gathered in the United States, holding the work—wherever it is done—to a common standard of quality in how it is collected, processed (e.g., translated), reported, shared, and analyzed. A common set of personnel standards for intelligence can create a group of professionals better able to operate in joint activities, transcending their own service-specific mind-sets.

- *Divided management of national intelligence capabilities.* While the CIA was once "central" to our national intelligence capabilities, following the end of the Cold War it has been less able to influence the use of the nation's imagery and signals intelligence capabilities in three national agencies housed within the Department of Defense: the National Security Agency, the National Geospatial-Intelligence Agency, and the National Reconnaissance Office. One of the lessons learned from the 1991 Gulf War was the value of national intelligence systems (satellites in particular) in precision warfare. Since that war, the department has appropriately drawn these agencies into its transformation of the military. Helping to orchestrate this transformation is the under secretary of defense for intelligence, a position established by Congress after 9/11. An unintended consequence of these developments has been the far greater demand made by Defense on technical systems, leaving the DCI less able to influence how these technical resources are allocated and used.

- *Weak capacity to set priorities and move resources.* The agencies are mainly organized around what they collect or the way they collect it. But the priorities for collection are national. As the DCI makes hard choices about moving resources, he or she must have the power to reach across agencies and reallocate effort.

- *Too many jobs.* The DCI now has at least three jobs. He is expected to run a particular agency, the CIA. He is expected to manage the loose confederation of agencies that is the intelligence community. He is expected to be the analyst in chief for the government, sifting evidence and directly briefing the President as his principal intelligence adviser. No recent DCI has been able to do all three effectively. Usually what loses out is management of the intelligence community, a difficult task even in the best case because the DCI's current authorities are weak. With so much to do, the DCI often has not used even the authority he has.

- *Too complex and secret.* Over the decades, the agencies and the rules surrounding the intelligence community have accumulated to a depth that practically defies public comprehension. There are now 15 agencies or parts of agencies in the intelligence community. The community and the DCI's authorities have become arcane matters, understood only by initiates after long study. Even the most basic information about how much money is actually allocated to or within the intelligence community and most of its key components is shrouded from public view.

The current DCI is responsible for community performance but lacks the three authorities critical for any agency head or chief executive officer: (1) control over purse strings, (2) the ability to hire or fire senior managers, and (3) the ability to set standards for the information infrastructure and personnel.

The only budget power of the DCI over agencies other than the CIA lies in coordinating the budget requests of the various intelligence agencies into a single program for submission to Congress. The overall funding request of the 15 intelligence entities in this program is then presented to the president and Congress in 15 separate volumes.

When Congress passes an appropriations bill to allocate money to intelligence agencies, most of their funding is hidden in the Defense Department in order to keep intelligence spending secret. Therefore, although the House and Senate Intelligence committees are the authorizing committees for funding of the intelligence community, the final budget review is handled in the Defense Subcommittee of the Appropriations committees. Those committees have no subcommittees just for intelligence, and only a few members and staff review the requests.

The appropriations for the CIA and the national intelligence agencies—NSA, NGA, and NRO—are then given to the secretary of defense. The secretary transfers the CIA's money to the DCI but disburses the national agencies' money directly. Money for the FBI's national security components falls within the appropriations for Commerce, Justice, and State and goes to the attorney general.

In addition, the DCI lacks hire-and-fire authority over most of the intelligence community's senior managers. For the national intelligence agencies housed in the Defense Department, the secretary of defense must seek the DCI's concurrence regarding the nomination of these directors, who are presidentially appointed. But the secretary may submit recommendations to the president without receiving this concurrence. The DCI cannot fire these officials. The DCI has even less influence over the head of the FBI's national security component, who is appointed by the attorney general in consultation with the DCI.

### Combining Joint Work with Stronger Management

We have received recommendations on the topic of intelligence reform from many sources. Other commissions have been over this same ground. Thoughtful bills have been introduced, most recently a bill by the chairman of the House Intelligence Committee, Porter Goss (R-Fla.), and another by the ranking minority member, Jane Harman (D-Calif.). In the Senate, Senators Bob Graham (D-Fla.) and Dianne Feinstein (D-Calif.) have introduced reform proposals as well. Past efforts have foundered, because the president did not support them; because the DCI, the secretary of defense, or both opposed them; and because some proposals lacked merit. We have tried to take stock of these experiences, and borrow from strong elements in many of the ideas that have already been developed by others.

**Recommendation: The current position of Director of Central Intelligence should be replaced by a National Intelligence Director with two main areas of responsibility: (1) to oversee national intelligence centers on specific subjects of interest across the U.S. government and (2) to manage the national intelligence program and oversee the agencies that contribute to it.**

First, the National Intelligence Director should oversee *national intelligence centers* to provide all-source analysis and plan intelligence operations for the whole government on major problems.

- One such problem is counterterrorism. In this case, we believe that the center should be the intelligence entity (formerly TTIC) inside the National Counterterrorism Center we have proposed. It would sit there alongside the operations management unit we described earlier, with both making up the NCTC, in the Executive Office of the President. Other national intelligence centers—for instance, on counterproliferation, crime and narcotics, and China—would be housed in whatever department or agency is best suited for them.
- The National Intelligence Director would retain the present DCI's role as the principal intelligence adviser to the president. We hope the president will come to look directly to the directors of the national intelligence centers to provide all-source analysis in their areas of responsibility, balancing the advice of these intelligence chiefs against

the contrasting viewpoints that may be offered by department heads at State, Defense, Homeland Security, Justice, and other agencies.

Second, the National Intelligence Director should manage the national intelligence program and oversee the component agencies of the intelligence community. (See diagram [p. 236].)

- The National Intelligence Director would submit a unified budget for national intelligence that reflects priorities chosen by the National Security Council, an appropriate balance among the varieties of technical and human intelligence collection, and analysis. He or she would receive an appropriation for national intelligence and apportion the funds to the appropriate agencies, in line with that budget, and with authority to reprogram funds among the national intelligence agencies to meet any new priority (as counterterrorism was in the 1990s). The National Intelligence Director should approve and submit nominations to the president of the individuals who would lead the CIA, DIA, FBI Intelligence Office, NSA, NGA, NRO, Information Analysis and Infrastructure Protection Directorate of the Department of Homeland Security, and other national intelligence capabilities.
- The National Intelligence Director would manage this national effort with the help of three deputies, each of whom would also hold a key position in one of the component agencies.
  - foreign intelligence (the head of the CIA)
  - defense intelligence (the under secretary of defense for intelligence)
  - homeland intelligence (the FBI's executive assistant director for intelligence or the under secretary of homeland security for information analysis and infrastructure protection)

  Other agencies in the intelligence community would coordinate their work within each of these three areas, largely staying housed in the same departments or agencies that support them now.

  Returning to the analogy of the Defense Department's organization, these three deputies—like the leaders of the Army, Navy, Air Force, or Marines—would have the job of acquiring the systems, training the people, and executing the operations planned by the national intelligence centers.

  And, just as the combatant commanders also report to the secretary of defense, the directors of the national intelligence centers— e.g., for counterproliferation, crime and narcotics, and the rest—also would report to the National Intelligence Director.

- The Defense Department's military intelligence programs—the joint military intelligence program (JMIP) and the tactical intelligence and related activities program (TIARA)—would remain part of that department's responsibility.

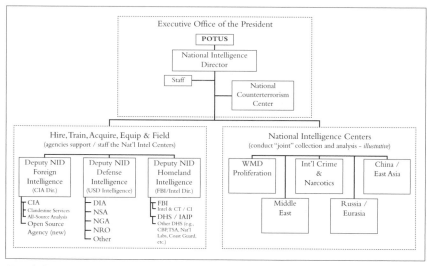

*Unity of Effort in Managing Intelligence*

- The National Intelligence Director would set personnel policies to establish standards for education and training and facilitate assignments at the national intelligence centers and across agency lines. The National Intelligence Director also would set information sharing and information technology policies to maximize data sharing, as well as policies to protect the security of information.
- Too many agencies now have an opportunity to say no to change. The National Intelligence Director should participate in an NSC executive committee that can resolve differences in priorities among the agencies and bring the major disputes to the president for decision.

The National Intelligence Director should be located in the Executive Office of the President. This official, who would be confirmed by the Senate and would testify before Congress, would have a relatively small staff of several hundred people, taking the place of the existing community management offices housed at the CIA.

In managing the whole community, the National Intelligence Director is still providing a service function. With the partial exception of his or her responsibilities for overseeing the NCTC, the National Intelligence Director should support the consumers of national intelligence—the president and policymaking advisers such as the secretaries of state, defense, and homeland security and the attorney general.

We are wary of too easily equating government management problems with those of the private sector. But we have noticed that some very large private firms rely on a powerful CEO who has significant control over how money is spent and can hire or fire leaders of the major divisions, assisted by a relatively modest staff, while leaving responsibility for execution in the operating divisions.

There are disadvantages to separating the position of National Intelligence Director from the job of heading the CIA. For example, the National Intelligence Director will not head a major agency of his or her own and may have a weaker base of support. But we believe that these disadvantages are outweighed by several other considerations:

- The National Intelligence Director must be able to directly oversee intelligence collection inside the United States. Yet law and custom has counseled against giving such a plain domestic role to the head of the CIA.
- The CIA will be one among several claimants for funds in setting national priorities. The National Intelligence Director should not be both one of the advocates and the judge of them all.
- Covert operations tend to be highly tactical, requiring close attention. The National Intelligence Director should rely on the relevant joint mission center to oversee these details, helping to coordinate closely with the White House. The CIA will be able to concentrate on building the capabilities to carry out such operations and on providing the personnel who will be directing and executing such operations in the field.
- Rebuilding the analytic and human intelligence collection capabilities of the CIA should be a full-time effort, and the director of the CIA should focus on extending its comparative advantages.

# 37

# "Pentagon Balking at Intel Reform Recommendations"

## JOE PAPPALARDO

Pentagon officials are publicly questioning some of the recommendations made by the National Commission on Terrorist Attacks Upon the United States.

Among their concerns are the blurring lines between civilian and military intelligence, a shifting of responsibility for paramilitary operations from the Central Intelligence Agency to the Special Operations Command and the specter of slowing the flow of crucial data to front-line commanders.

Pentagon officials and many members of Congress support the commission's proposals, including the creation of the National Intelligence Director (NID) position and a new counterterrorism center to replace the Terrorist Threat Integration Center, but other suggestions are being met with skepticism.

"If we allow a rush to judgment to be dictated by the need to simply get this done during an election cycle, then I think we're going to make ourselves more vulnerable and cause the nation more harm," said Duncan Hunter, R-Calif., chairman of the House Armed Services Committee (HASC).

Hunter and other critics are following the lead of senior Pentagon officials, who simultaneously say they welcome some reforms, such as joint intelligence sharing between agencies, but balk at much of the departmental restructuring.

Stephen A. Cambone, the Pentagon's undersecretary for intelligence, suggested, "We need to back up a little bit and reconsider" the proposed changes because the intelligence demands of the military and the civilian leadership are different.

The NID would oversee the entire U.S. intelligence community, including agencies currently under Pentagon control, such as the National Reconnaissance Office, National Security Agency, National Geospatial-Intelligence Agency and Defense Intelligence Agency.

Commission members are recommending the defense undersecretary for intelligence become a key deputy to the NID, charged with balancing "the needs of the war fighter and the national policy-maker," according to a joint statement given to the HASC by commission Chairman Thomas H. Kean and Vice Chairman Lee Hamilton.

The lines between intelligence and operations are being more than blurred, they are being consolidated, Army Maj. Gen. Raymond Odierno, former commander of the 4th Infantry Division which fought in Iraq, noted to lawmakers. "Today, strategic and tactical intelligence [are] interwoven. They are no longer separate like they used to be," he said.

Some experts do not agree. "I see some pretty important differences, in terms of the nature and timeliness of the information," said Michele Flournoy, a senior advisor at the Center for Strategic and International Studies. "Tactical information has a much more refined and detailed level of specificity . . . At the strategic level, you have to show there's a nuclear facility at Point X. On the tactical level, you'd want to know, how do I get into it?"

Anything that delays the relay of important information would be devastating to commanders. Commanders on the front lines need to know "what's on the other side of the hill" very quickly, and preferably from analysts who are judging the importance of data from the perspective of the combat zone, not Washington, D.C., Odierno said.

"One thing we learned in Iraq was that we need information immediately . . . Targets are fleeting," he said. "The value of [real-time intelligence] cannot be overestimated."

However, Hamilton, speaking at a congressional hearing, noted, "You cannot always assume that tactical intelligence takes priority."

The commission wants to integrate joint intelligence and operations planning in a National Counterterrorism Center, an institution the Bush administration has signaled it will create.

CSIS' Flournoy said that the commission's proposal to merge both kinds of operations under one roof made sense, if the differences in intelligence needs are taken into account. "There is value in knowing what each other is doing and thinking . . . I think there's some in the military who are worried this will tempt [civilians] into micromanaging. I think that can be handled, and depends on leadership."

The key, Flournoy said, is keeping "two teams working on two sides of the same coin" in the same way J-2s and J-3s work independently, but share information and goals, on the staff of the Joint Chiefs.

Another major recommended change that is meeting resistance at the Pentagon is an elevated role for the Special Operations Command in paramilitary operations.

The commission concluded that SOCOM is better qualified than the CIA to direct these combat operations, given the tactics and heavy weaponry often employed. The report also described directors of the CIA as being overwhelmed by the myriad responsibilities of their position, and unable to fulfill all the necessary functions.

But Army Gen. Bryan D. Brown, head of SOCOM, signaled he was not so sure. He told HASC members that the high-level planning involvement of "other government agencies" in operations was vital to the war fighter. "I just think we need more study on it," he said diplomatically, following the lead of other skeptical senior Pentagon officials.

The fear, Brown said, was that the restructuring might sever the ties and workarounds that operators have hashed out with their CIA counterparts during current overseas missions. Important information in the hands of the CIA might not make it to operators' planning tables, and vital intelligence updates would have to go a longer way to reach the front lines.

"I would not want any impediments," he said. "I want to make sure every piece of intelligence that's available is instantly available to my guy on the ground wherever he is, or my guy in the air or out in a boat."

SOCOM is undergoing a transformation already, a response to being put on the front lines of the war against global terrorism.

Thomas O'Connell, assistant secretary of defense for special operations, said in congressional testimony earlier this year that SOCOM will use the $2 billion increase of the $6.5 billion allocated to it in President Bush's fiscal 2005 budget request to modernize its equipment and training.

Special operations forces originally were conceived for "supporting or leveraging" conventional forces, or for use in limited strategic missions, he said. Fighting scattered cells nested across the globe has given SOCOM a "prominent, front-line, essential role," he added.

SOCOM has set several new priorities aimed at transforming its capabilities, including critical "low-density high-demand" aviation assets. Training operators in the culture, language and politics of a potential combat environment is essential, O'Connell said.

It's not all foot-dragging within the Pentagon, however. A commission idea to bring the intelligence sources from disparate military and civilian intelligence organizations into one central collection point is being better received.

"Increased jointness in intelligence is very attractive for the Department of Defense," Cambone said, adding that the structure should allow for surging and reprioritizing intelligence assets to meet changing situations.

An interactive and security-sensitive database maintained by the NID would inspire unfettered information exchanges, said Vice Adm. Lowell Jacoby, the director of the Defense Intelligence Agency. "Resistance to sharing would be swept away," he said.

Missouri Rep. Ike Skelton, the ranking Democrat on the committee, noted that military commanders resisted the same jointness of military operations extolled by the Pentagon today when it was introduced by the Goldwater-Nichols legislation of 1986. "At the end of the day, the military saluted and made it happen," Skelton said.

He also noted that the military was a major player in the intelligence game, and hinted that reforms that didn't involve them would be lacking depth. "Remember that the Defense Department is the greatest consumer and producer of intelligence," he said. "The time for change is now."

# 38

# "Worlds Apart"

## SIOBHAN GORMAN

Is the FBI from Mars, and the CIA from Venus? They've been immersed in a kind of White House-ordered couples' counseling for a while—since September 11, 2001, to be precise. And even though they both need their relationship to work, they have such different approaches to life that they remain worlds apart. In fact, they speak such different languages that they can barely even communicate.

Since the Central Intelligence Agency's birth in 1947, its relationship with the much-older Federal Bureau of Investigation has rarely, if ever, been close. For decades, the two agencies' interactions were hostile and sporadic. Since 9/11, though, their shared desire to prevent another terrorist attack on the United States has forced them to try to move beyond turf wars and talk to each other. But the organizations' institutional cultures are so different that real coordination will be very difficult to achieve.

FBI agents resemble the stereotypical men in John Gray's best-selling book, *Men Are from Mars, Women Are from Venus: A Practical Guide for Improving Communication and Getting What You Want in Your Relationships.* G-men speak and think about very concrete, quantifiable things, such as arrests and suspects, and they value individual achievement. CIA officers—like women from Venus—often operate in less-regimented, less-hierarchical ways and put a high value on sharing information and developing longtime relationships.

"It's not that [FBI agents and CIA officers] don't like each other, but they're really different people," said Jim Simon, a former CIA analyst. "They have a hard time communicating."

A CIA officer's best tip may come from splitting a bottle of scotch with an "asset"—someone the FBI would call an informer or a snitch—in a safe house halfway around the world. Meanwhile, the FBI's cops-and-robbers mission has been to put bad guys behind bars. The more cerebral CIA's raison d'etre has been to do virtually whatever it takes to keep policy makers—especially the president—well informed about foreign threats to U.S. national security. Those contrasting missions have attracted two very different kinds of people and produced two very different institutional cultures.

"There is, fortunately, a fundamental cultural chasm that divides the FBI from the CIA. That's the good news," says intelligence expert John Pike, director of GlobalSecurity.org. "The FBI enforces the law, and the CIA breaks the law."

While Mars and Venus functioned well, for the most part, when they worked independently of each other during the Cold War, they've been drawn to each other—willingly or not—by their post-9/11 presidential mandate to prevent another terrorist attack. That mandate gives the intelligence agencies a complicated new mission: Determine where the danger to the United States lies here, on American soil.

Having an organizational culture appropriate to carrying out the new mission is "absolutely fundamental," says Greg Treverton, a former vice chairman of the National Intelligence Council, which complies the national intelligence estimates for the director of central intelligence. What's unclear is whether the FBI and CIA can together create such a culture.

The July release of Congress's joint inquiry into the intelligence failures leading up to 9/11 has intensified the calls for overhauling the nation's intelligence apparatus. But in an age in which "connecting the dots" is all the rage as the way to avoid another surprise attack, institutional culture has been an underappreciated factor in understanding how a given intelligence agency operates and what it can reasonably be expected to do—without completely transforming itself and its worldview.

One senior administration official's reaction to a query about the FBI-CIA culture clash typifies the mind-set that an agency's ethos isn't worth worrying about because it's easy to change if need be: An agency's culture "is the sort of thing that can be corrected by leadership in the agencies. The [FBI and CIA] are led by people who are not captive of that culture, if there is one at all. I don't think it requires a different mind-set. I think it requires a different direction. They're professionals. They do what they're told by their leadership."

Often, outsiders dismiss the FBI-CIA culture clash as a mere turf battle that the organizations simply need to get over. But turf aside, FBI agents and CIA officers see the world—and their roles in it—very differently.

To be sure, for FBI-CIA cooperation to succeed, leadership is crucial. And removing legal barriers to communication and establishing better technological and bureaucratic links are necessary steps, too. But the agencies' vast cultural divide cannot be legislated away, cannot be rewired or redrawn out of existence. And many experts in both the law enforcement and intelligence worlds say that any effort to fulfill this new homeland-security mission by reengineering the FBI or CIA, or by creating a new agency, would ignore the agencies' cultures at its peril. Culture clashes are often at the root of multibillion-dollar failed corporate mergers. But in this governmental culture clash, the stakes are counted not in dollars but in lives.

Contrary to conventional wisdom, the FBI and CIA were on speaking terms before 9/11; they just weren't really hearing each other. In the mid-1990s, they established a kind of cultural exchange program in which CIA and FBI counterterrorism officials would serve temporary stints as deputies in the other side's counterterrorism division. And a group known as the Gang of Eight—four top officials from the CIA and four from the FBI—was formed to jump-start cooperative efforts. The results were encouraging: Each side learned that the folks on the other side didn't have horns.

In 1999, the FBI's top emissary to the Gang of Eight, then FBI Deputy Director Robert Bryant, left. The group didn't meet again until a few weeks after 9/11, when it concluded that relations were good and its work was done. The gang reached that conclusion even though outsiders were already beginning to say that the FBI and CIA were going to have to start working together more closely if they were going to prevent a recurrence of 9/11. But the meetings stopped. And each side's culture remained fundamentally unchanged.

"If we [had] kept up with this process of pushing people to move forward, I think we would have had an impact," says John MacGaffin, a Gang of Eight member who was the CIA's associate deputy director for operations. "In the end, the cultures defeated themselves."

This May, as investigations continued into the intelligence failures leading up to the 9/11 attacks, President Bush established the Terrorist Threat Integration Center, known as T-TIC, as the central repository of all terrorism-related information. Meanwhile, FBI Director Robert S. Mueller III has informally become the FBI's culture czar. His reorganization aims to reorient the FBI's mind-set—focusing agents on terrorism-prevention rather than solely on traditional crime-solving. But Mueller alone can't make it easy for the FBI and CIA to communicate effectively enough to prevent terrorist attacks.

Among analysts who study the intelligence agencies, a consensus seems to be forming that the United States needs some government body whose sole mission is determining where the danger of terrorism lies on the home front and whose institutional culture marries the best of the FBI and CIA. In the meantime, the current division of labor—with the FBI working mostly within U.S. borders and the CIA working abroad—gives Al Qaeda and its brethren a leg up on America, contends Ronald Marks, a 16-year CIA veteran. "I don't think the domestic Al Qaeda is worried about [how to coordinate with] the foreign Al Qaeda," he says. "I find the logic of Washington a bit mind-bending. These [terrorists] don't care. They're interested in killing us."

*The FBI Is From Mars*

The FBI's wins in the war on terrorism are easy to count. The bureau has charged 200 suspected terrorists around the country, including in Lackawanna, N.Y.; Detroit; Seattle; Oregon; and the Washington, D.C., area. For the FBI, success is measured one arrest at a time, one case at a time, one prosecution at a time. Individual agents are publicly identified by the cases they break and rewarded for those successes, and they work to hand ironclad cases to prosecutors. Those factors largely define what the FBI is and how its agents see information and the world—and make it the globe's preeminent law enforcement agency.

An FBI agent's professional world starts, and for the most part ends, in the field. The crowning glory of an agent's career is to become a special agent in charge of a field office. The agent's mission is to gather as many facts as legally possible. Evidence in a given case, regardless of where the information is discovered, is controlled by the field office responsible for the case because the prosecutor in that location is ultimately responsible for bringing it to court. "As a prosecutor, I would always say, 'This is my case; here's my file,'" says Steven Cash, a former state prosecutor who then went to work for the CIA and, later, for the Senate's intelligence panel and the House's Select Committee on Homeland Security.

FBI agents almost always speak in the first person because they or their witnesses need to testify to what they saw, heard, tasted, felt, or touched. The FBI's world is tangible.

Law enforcement work is linear and restrospective. Agents follow a lead's trail until they solve—or shelve—their case. Evidence that does not pertain to that particular case is considered a distraction. Certainty is a must, and complex relationships between people and places only make it more difficult to convince a judge or jury that a suspect should be thrown in prison.

And FBI cases are finite. Cash recalled wrapping each case he finished in red tape and stashing it in his file cabinet as finished business. "Facts were only relevant to a case, and each case was a new case," recalls Cash, who fashions himself a bit of a pop anthropologist. "The case ends, and that contributes not only to how you promote people but how you see yourself—where you get your psychic gratification. I loved the end of a case."

As the term "law enforcement" implies, force is an inherent part of the FBI agent's job. FBI agents arrest, they handcuff, they jail, they prosecute. FBI agents often find that threatening prosecution is the key to persuading people to divulge information. And informers are not FBI agents' buddies. "I never would have wanted anybody who I ran as a confidential informant to get anywhere near my family," Cash says.

Because of constitutional restrictions on the government's domestic use of force, FBI life is also a jungle gym of rules. Evidence is collected according to rules established to protect the rights of John Q. Public. And if the evidence isn't collected properly, it's useless in court. These rules maintain the reputation of the FBI, and law enforcement in general, as good cops deserving the public trust. "They are the last true Boy and Girl Scouts in America," says Glenn Kelly, executive director of the FBI Agents Association.

The bureau's natural emphasis on force and rules also shapes its recruitment efforts. The FBI draws largely from the top talent in state and local law-enforcement agencies, the military, and more recently, failed tech start-ups.

"The type of people that go into the CIA is completely different from the type of people who go into the FBI," says John Vincent, a 27-year veteran of the FBI who worked in counterterrorism until last year. "Most of the FBI people are pretty normal Joes off the street. The CIA guys— they're a different group of people. Most of the CIA guys I've met are very intelligent but wouldn't know how to put a nut on a bolt. They're nice guys—don't get me wrong—but they're a different breed. . . . [CIA talent scouts] recruit these intellectuals. They don't have a lot of practical knowledge." From the FBI's perspective, CIA officers are like girls who don't know how to change a tire but who raise their hands in class all the time.

*The CIA Is From Venus*

Dale Watson, then the No. 2 FBI official in the bureau's Kansas City, Mo., office, had just come off the Oklahoma City bombing case in December 1995, when he got a call from Bryant, his boss. "I've got a job for you," Bryant said as he explained a new exchange program that made an FBI official the CIA's No. 2 counterterrorism official and vice versa. "I've got a great job now," Watson shot back. He turned Bryant down twice. Finally, Bryant called again in late January in the middle of the night: "I put you out there, and I'll take you back anytime I want. Have a good evening." Two weeks later, Watson got "one of those funny envelopes" from the FBI. He reported for duty at the CIA in early 1997.

"It was a huge learning curve," Watson recalls of an experience he now says is "probably the best thing that could have happened to me professionally." Watson was often introduced as an FBI "officer," and he had to correct that. He discovered that the CIA has a strange way of telling time: 0700Z is 7 a.m. Zulu time, or Greenwich Mean Time. Watson mistook "L.A." for Los Angeles instead of Latin America. "Culturally, looking back on it, it was a wide divide of how you do business," says Watson, who spent years at the CIA and recently retired as the head of FBI counterterrorism. "The FBI is case-driven. And we operate under probable cause, not just suspicion." But suspicion fuels the work of CIA officers.

The CIA is focused less on individual facts than on connections between them, so officers approach information-gathering as creating a mosaic. They want to collect enough pieces for the agency to figure out the whole picture. While the FBI looks for fact patterns to lead them to whodunit, the CIA looks for patterns to determine what is "normal" so it can better see what is threateningly abnormal. The CIA officer's job is prospective and predictive. The value a CIA officer adds to an intelligence cable is in the connections drawn, conclusions reached, and decisions about what to include or exclude. So, a CIA officer's world is full of intangibles, and he's rewarded accordingly. CIA officers are known more for the skills they bring to a new operation than for past operations they've run.

To make connections between far-flung bits of information, a CIA officer is heavily dependent on headquarters. That reality affects how CIA officers think of and speak about themselves. They rarely discuss their work in the first person; "we" is more appropriate. They'll often refer to themselves in the third person. In their interdependent world, one connection begets another, so there is never a case to close. And because threat assessments are constantly changing based on information from different sources, the CIA is consensus-driven.

CIA officers are very protective of their sources, because they see an "asset" as a good person in an unfortunate situation who is giving them information to help American national security. Officers feel personally responsible for keeping their assets out of harm's way. And that leads to a certain insularity—officers love to share information from their sources among themselves but rarely want to let it outside the agency.

Watson remembers that when he arrived at the CIA, its lax attitude toward rules caught him by surprise. The CIA's world is bounded by few rules—chiefly, stay away from anyone who is inside the United States. "They operated overseas without worrying about collection of evidence. We [at the FBI] were always very concerned about collection of evidence," Watson says. "We only got one chance to do it [right] under our federal rules."

The CIA values judgment over rules. "You have a source who will tell you X. Your judgment of that source is based on the time you've spent with them. You're dealing in a pretty murky world," says former CIA officer Marks. "That's the world of judgment. You're dealing with different sources, and you're matching up a story."

The universe of people who exercise good judgment in murky national security matters isn't large. The CIA, which traditionally had a reputation for attracting Ivy Leaguers, increasingly seeks new recruits from elite ranks of a range of talent pools. Joining the CIA is often a new career for those who have already gained experience as, for example, microbiologists or international finance analysts, as well as for those with specialized language skills and a demonstrated understanding of international affairs. Still, says former CIA General Counsel Jeffrey Smith, "there is something to this image of the tweed-coated, pipe-smoking, thoughtful intelligence officer, who says, 'Hmmmm, what can we make of all that?' "

### Culture Clash

Deborah Tannen, a Georgetown University linguistics professor who has written several books about male-female communication problems, including *That's Not What I Meant!*, sees a very familiar pattern in the difficulty the FBI and CIA have in finding a common language. "It's amazing that it's so parallel," marvels Tannen. Miscommunication, she says, is "very hurtful in a personal relationship. It's very destructive in a professional relationship. When you think about FBI and CIA—the implications can be devastating."

The FBI-CIA culture clash reminds Tannen of her favorite—and also very typical—husband-wife miscommunication story. A couple is driving, and the wife asks her husband if he wants to stop and get something to drink. The husband says no and keeps driving. The wife gets frustrated because she wanted to get a drink. She didn't think she was asking a yes-or-no question but rather opening a topic for discussion.

Likewise, what FBI officials think they're saying and what CIA officials hear them saying can be quite different—and vice versa.

FBI officials, from special agents to Director Mueller himself, resort to case-counting to prove that they know much more about the threat Al Qaeda poses in the United States now than they did before 9/11, says former CIA Deputy Director MacGaffin. When asked, "How do you know?" the answer is invariably, "I'll tell you how we know. Before 9/11, we had only 17 cases open on Al Qaeda across the United States. Now we have more than 75," says MacGaffin, improvising the actual numbers.

In a breakfast interview, MacGaffin, who spent six years at the FBI as a senior adviser to the director and the assistant director, pauses and pounds on the table. "They're answering the wrong question. What does that have to do with anything?" he asks. "Seventeen to 75 doesn't help you understand where the danger lies. It means you've got more cases."

To Mueller, preventing terrorism means making sure any terrorism-related information that the FBI encounters in the course of an investigation makes its way to headquarters. MacGaffin's recipe is to determine where the danger lies in the United States. Mueller is trying to improve the process; MacGaffin is asking for a result—one that is virtually impossible to quantify. Mars, meet Venus.

In the case of homeland security, the CIA's traditional approach seems more likely to stop terrorists from blowing things up—as opposed to arresting and convicting them once they've struck. And the CIA, not the FBI, is the foundation of the new central repository for terrorism, T-TIC. "We looked around and said, 'Who has the greatest capability?' And there was no question that, for the purpose of analysis, it was the CIA," said a senior Bush administration official. "They had the greatest existing capability to do the intelligence analysis."

Yet, the American public is uncomfortable with having the CIA run the show domestically, so the plan has been to get the FBI—the good cops—to think more like their CIA counterparts. Transplanted CIA agents are doing much of the anti-terrorism training at the FBI. After his tour at the CIA, Watson found religion and could translate "CIA-speak and CIA-think" for FBI colleagues. Success in the war on terrorism, he says, "is not measured in the number of cases you solved. It's how do you really know what is going on in the United States?"

But while Watson and fellow alumni of the FBI-CIA exchange program have steeped themselves in the other side's culture, the vast majority of agents and officers haven't. And anyone who's tried to learn a foreign language—let alone a foreign culture—knows that classroom learning has its limits.

"A lot of [FBI] people thought that they were hired to chase bank robbers or do white-collar crime, when in fact, the priorities of the bureau had changed," Watson says. "It's hard to refocus. I think a lot of people struggled with that." The FBI has never been in the business of trying to figure out how many bank robberies are going to happen and where and why—or of being expected to prevent every one of them. But that's now essentially its anti-terrorism mission. A bank robbery is not considered an FBI failure; it's a new case. But a new terror attack would now very much be seen as an FBI failure.

Watson estimates that it will take at least five years—others say 10—to see real change in the FBI's mind set. And that slow transformation, he says, will come largely through retirements and recruiting.

Last week, in testimony before a Senate oversight panel, Mueller depicted his bureau as embracing change. He highlighted the FBI's intelligence-gathering efforts and praised the bureau's switch from "thinking about intelligence as a case" to "finding intelligence in the case."

But the in-the-case approach is still case-based and won't help the FBI determine the overall nature of the terrorist threat. MacGaffin scoffs at what he calls "intelligence by serendipity" because it relies on FBI agents bumping into critical information in the course of their investigations— and then passing it along. He likens Mueller's approach to playing defense and expecting to win the game on the assumption that the other team will fumble: "You're banking the nation's safety on a defense. It's foolish."

That's not to say the CIA's anti-terrorism record is stellar either. The joint congressional investigation pointed to numerous ways in which the CIA's post-Cold War counterterrorism effort was below par, including the agency's inadequate analytic resources, its insufficient human-intelligence efforts, and its failure to share key pieces of information with the FBI.

But if the FBI is going to be the de facto homeland-security intelligence agency because it has the authority to operate in U.S. territory, the bureau's methods require closer scrutiny. In the view of one outside analyst, the FBI's changes since 9/11 have amounted to "running faster and jumping higher," which "is better than running slower and jumping lower." But they don't amount to thinking differently.

The analyst adds that one major change that needs to occur is in how the FBI measures success. It should be counting such things as how many times it has penetrated Al Qaeda. The current tally is said to be zero.

If the FBI thought more like the CIA, that count might be at least one or two by now. Instead of successfully pursuing six guilty pleas in Lackawanna, the FBI could have tried to recruit one or more of the men to return to a Qaeda training camp, this time as an informer. The danger in doing so appears minimal. The "Lackawanna Six" weren't convicted of plotting an attack. Rather, they appeared to be on the jihadist fence—intrigued by the idea of it but not enough to endure even a sprained ankle in a terrorist training camp. Yet the FBI mind-set is to rack up guilty pleas, not turn someone into a spy for the United States. This week, Attorney General John D. Ashcroft, who oversees the FBI, awarded medals to the agents who collared the Lackawanna Six.

*A Homeland-Security Culture*

A bomb exploded on August 7, 1998, in Nairobi, Kenya, killing 258 people, and another went off in Tanzania. As wounded victims milled about in the shadow of the blood-spattered shell of the U.S. Embassy in Nairobi, FBI and CIA operatives flooded the scene. America had been attacked, and as FBI and CIA guys ate meals-ready-to-eat together every night, a personal trust rapidly evolved. "We quickly realized that no one was really out to upstage one another," Watson said. One U.S. government official, who was on the scene in Kenya, called it "a good first date" for the bureau and the agency.

The CIA and FBI have worked relatively well together when investigating an actual attack. It's in working together between bombings, to prevent another one, that the system breaks down.

The key to solving the culture problem, say a host of veterans of law enforcement and intelligence agencies, is having a single-minded mission to determine the terrorist threat in the United States. The mission will shape the culture. That culture, ideally, would recruit and reward the intellectual, analytic, linguistic, and international curiosity of a CIA officer as well as the discipline and focus of an FBI agent.

There are, however, two dangers in establishing a best-of-both-worlds culture—either it wouldn't work or it would work too well. The danger of the former is 9/11 redux. The danger of the latter is that a monstrous cross between the KGB and the Gestapo will suddenly be monitoring the American people: Imagine the CIA with a badge and a gun coming to a hometown near you. Erring on the side of the first danger, Bush's Plan A is to reform the FBI and establish T-TIC.

Even if the FBI is able to adopt a culture that focuses on the new preventive mission, some intelligence experts, such as University of California (Los Angeles) professor Amy Zegart, worry that the change will come at the expense of the bureau's traditional and important law enforcement responsibilities. "Not only are we running the risk the FBI will do a relatively poor job at fighting terrorism," she says, "but it may be doing a worse job at the things it's traditionally very good at."

So far, the T-TIC, instead of being a cultural blank slate, is a collection of 100 cultural ambassadors—most of them from the CIA. The T-TIC, says former CIA counsel Smith, is "necessary but not sufficient." He adds that while it's good to get FBI and CIA people into the same room, the primary homeland-security intelligence organization must be able to collect information—not just sift data and details that other organizations have dug up. And T-TIC is unlikely to remedy the FBI-CIA communications problems, says John Hamre, former deputy secretary of Defense. "At this stage, the T-TIC is really a liaison cell linking the two organizations," he said in an e-mail exchange with *National Journal*.

T-TIC already appears to be a stage for cultural and turf battles. There was a dispute over whether John O. Brennan, a 23-year veteran of the CIA who now heads T-TIC, should be writing the President's Daily Brief, the CIA's daily compilation of worldwide threats. CIA Director of Intelligence Jami Miscik, who's responsible for the document, protested the decision. The solution was that Brennan would produce a separate document called the President's Terrorism Threat Report. On the FBI side, when the bureau was filling its top T-TIC job, at the last minute it decided against a candidate who had a reputation for being a broad thinker and instead opted for James Bernazzani, who was then the FBI's representative at the CIA Counter-Terrorism Center and has a reputation for representing the official word.

If T-TIC, a.k.a. Plan A, doesn't work, what's Plan B? It's likely to be an entirely new agency with a single mission and a new culture to match.

Hamre, MacGaffin, and Smith were part of a group of six former FBI and intelligence officials who recently floated a plan to combine the effort to reform the FBI with a desire for a new organization and a new culture. The proposal, unveiled in *The Economist*, is modeled after the National Security Agency, which is independent but housed in the Defense Department. The new organization would be established within the FBI and would take on the bureau's counterterrorism and national security duties. But the new entity would be staffed by a largely new crop of agents with strong analytical skills and would have its own personnel and promotion system that would prize analytical expertise. The head of the new organization would be a presidential appointee from outside law enforcement and would report to the director of central intelligence.

There are many variations on this theme. The most popular and most drastic envisions something similar to Britain's MI-5 domestic intelligence agency that would have authority to spy on Americans but would be required to obtain warrants for surveillance and would have no police powers.

Yet, regardless of what entity is ultimately responsible for preventing another terrorist attack against the U.S. homeland, that organization will still need the FBI and CIA to do a better job of communicating and of understanding each other's aspirations and perspectives. And that means Mars and Venus can expect to need couples' counseling for a very long time.

## DISCUSSION QUESTIONS

1. Why is it so hard to change an organization's culture? Why can't a leader simply say, "This is how it's going to be" and force change?

2. After reading these three articles, have you changed your view (for or against) of the PATRIOT act? Does the act address the different organizational cultures of the various law-enforcement and intelligence agencies? Does it make them better? Worse?

3. Are there any disadvantages to sharing information (which in these areas will be extremely sensitive and considered top secret)? Are there any good reasons why the FBI, or CIA, or other agency would refuse to provide information to another government organization?

# CHAPTER 8

# The Federal Judiciary

## 39

## *The Federalist*, No. 78

### Alexander Hamilton

*The judiciary, Hamilton wrote in defending the proposed Constitution, "will always be the least dangerous to the political rights of the Constitution; because it will be least in a capacity to annoy or injure them." The lack of danger Hamilton spoke of stems from the Court's lack of enforcement or policy power, or as Hamilton more eloquently put it, the Court has "no influence over either the sword or the purse": it must rely on the executive branch and state governments to enforce its rulings, and depends on the legislature for its appropriations and rules governing its structure. Critics of "judicial activism" would likely disagree about the weakness of the Court relative to the other branches of government. But Hamilton saw an independent judiciary as an important check on the other branches' ability to assume too much power (the "bulwarks of a limited Constitution against legislative encroachments"). He also argued that the Court, as interpreter of the Constitution, would gain its power from the force of its judgments, which were rooted in the will of the people.*

**To the People of the State of New York:**

We proceed now to an examination of the judiciary department of the proposed government.

In unfolding the defects of the existing Confederation, the utility and necessity of a federal judicature have been clearly pointed out. It is the less necessary to recapitulate the considerations there urged, as the propriety of the institution in the abstract is not disputed; the only questions which have been raised being relative to the manner of constituting it, and to its extent. To these points, therefore, our observations shall be confined.

The manner of constituting it seems to embrace these several objects:

1ST. The mode of appointing the judges. 2D. The tenure by which they are to hold their places. 3D. The partition of the judiciary authority between different courts, and their relations to each other.

*First.* As to the mode of appointing the judges; this is the same with that of appointing the officers of the Union in general, and has been so fully discussed in the two last numbers, that nothing can be said here which would not be useless repetition.

*Second.* As to the tenure by which the judges are to hold their places: this chiefly concerns their duration in office; the provisions for their support; the precautions for their responsibility.

According to the plan of the convention, all judges who may be appointed by the United States are to hold their offices *during good behavior*; which is conformable to the most approved of the State constitutions, and among the rest, to that of this State. Its propriety having been drawn into question by the adversaries of that plan, is no light symptom of the rage for objection, which disorders their imaginations and judgments. The standard of good behavior for the continuance in office of the judicial magistracy is certainly one of the most valuable of the modern improvements in the practice of government. In a monarchy it is an excellent barrier to the despotism of the prince; in a republic it is a no less excellent barrier to the encroachments and oppressions of the representative body. And it is the best expedient which can be devised in any government to secure a steady, upright, and impartial administration of the laws.

Whoever attentively considers the different departments of power must perceive, that, in a government in which they are separated from each other, the judiciary, from the nature of its functions, will always be the least dangerous to the political rights of the Constitution; because it will be least in a capacity to annoy or injure them. The Executive not only dispenses the honors, but holds the sword of the community. The legislature not only commands the purse, but prescribes the rules by which the duties and rights of every citizen are to be regulated. The judiciary, on the contrary, has no influence over either the sword or the purse; no direction either of the strength or of the wealth of the society; and can take no active resolution whatever. It may truly be said to have neither FORCE nor WILL, but merely judgment; and must ultimately depend upon the aid of the executive arm even for the efficacy of its judgments.

This simple view of the matter suggests several important consequences. It proves incontestably that the judiciary is beyond comparison the weakest of the three departments of power that it can never attack with success either of the other two; and that all possible care is requisite to enable it to defend itself against their attacks. It equally proves that though individual oppression may now and then proceed from the courts of justice, the general liberty of the people can never be endangered from that quarter; I mean so long as the judiciary remains truly distinct from both the legislature and the Executive. For I agree, that "there is no liberty, if the power of judging be not separated from the legislative and executive powers." And it proves, in the last place, that as liberty can have nothing to fear from the judiciary alone, but would have every thing to fear from its union with either of the other departments; that as all the effects of such a union must ensue from a dependence of the former on the latter, notwithstanding a nominal and apparent separation; that as, from the natural feebleness of the judiciary it is in continual jeopardy of being overpowered, awed, or influenced by its coordinate branches; and that as nothing can contribute so much to its firmness and independence as permanency in office, this quality may therefore be justly regarded as an indispensable ingredient in its constitution, and, in a great measure, as the citadel of the public justice and the public security.

The complete independence of the courts of justice is peculiarly essential in a limited Constitution. By a limited Constitution, I understand one which contains certain specified exceptions to the legislative authority; such, for instance, as that it shall pass no bills of attainder, no *ex-post-facto* laws, and the like. Limitations of this kind can be preserved in practice no other way than through the medium of courts of justice, whose duty it must be to declare all acts contrary to the manifest tenor of the Constitution void. Without this, all the reservations of particular rights or privileges would amount to nothing.

Some perplexity respecting the rights of the courts to pronounce legislative acts void, because contrary to the constitution, has arisen from an imagination that the doctrine would imply a superiority of the judiciary to the legislative power. It is urged that the authority which can declare the acts of another void must necessarily be superior to the one whose acts may be declared void. As this doctrine is of great importance in all the American constitutions, a brief discussion of the ground on which it rests cannot be unacceptable.

There is no position which depends on clearer principles than that every act of a delegated authority, contrary to the tenor of the commission under which it is exercised, is void. No legislative act, therefore, contrary to the Constitution, can be valid. To deny this would be to affirm that the deputy is greater than his principal; that the servant is above his master; that the representatives of the people are superior to the people themselves; that men acting by virtue of powers may do not only what their powers do not authorize, but what they forbid.

If it be said that the legislative body are themselves the constitutional judges of their own powers, and that the construction they put upon them is conclusive upon the other departments, it may be answered that this cannot be the natural presumption where it is not to be collected from any particular provisions in the Constitution. It is not otherwise to be supposed that the Constitution could intend to enable the representatives of the people to substitute their *will* to that of their constituents. It is far more rational to suppose that the courts were designed to be an intermediate body between the people and the legislature, in order, among other things, to keep the latter within the limits assigned to their authority. The interpretation of the laws is the proper and peculiar province of the courts. A constitution is, in fact, and must be regarded by the judges, as a fundamental law. It therefore belongs to them to ascertain its meaning, as well as the meaning of any particular act proceeding from the legislative body. If there should happen to be an irreconcilable variance between the two, that which has the superior obligation and validity ought, of course, to be preferred; or, in other words, the Constitution ought to be preferred to the statute, the intention of the people to the intention of their agents.

Nor does this conclusion by any means suppose a superiority of the judicial to the legislative power. It only supposes that the power of the people is superior to both; and that where the will of the legislature, declared in its statutes, stands in opposition to that of the people, declared in the Constitution, the judges ought to be governed by the latter rather than the former. They ought to regulate their decisions by the fundamental laws, rather than by those which are not fundamental.

This exercise of judicial discretion, in determining between two contradictory laws, is exemplified in a familiar instance. It not uncommonly happens that there are two statutes existing at one time, clashing in whole or in part with each other, and neither of them containing any repealing clause or expression. In such a case, it is the province of the courts to liquidate and fix their meaning and operation. So far as they can, by any fair construction, be reconciled to each other, reason and law conspire to dictate that this should be done; where this is impracticable, it becomes a matter of necessity to give effect to one in exclusion of the other. The rule which has obtained in the courts for determining their relative validity is, that the last in order of time shall be preferred to the first. But this is a mere rule of construction, not derived from any positive law but from the nature and reason of the thing. It is a rule not enjoined upon the courts by legislative provision but adopted by themselves, as consonant to truth and propriety for the direction of their conduct as interpreters of the law. They thought it reasonable, that between the interfering acts of an *equal* authority, that which was the last indication of its will should have the preference.

But in regard to the interfering acts of a superior and subordinate authority, of an original and derivative power, the nature and reason of the thing indicate the converse of that rule as proper to be followed. They teach us that the prior act of a superior ought to be preferred to the subsequent act of an inferior and subordinate authority; and that accordingly, whenever a particular statute contravenes the Constitution, it will be the duty of the judicial tribunals to adhere to the latter and disregard the former.

It can be of no weight to say that the courts, on the pretence of a repugnancy, may substitute their own pleasure to the constitutional intentions of the legislature. This might as well happen in the case of two contradictory statutes; or it might as well happen in every adjudication upon any single statute. The courts must declare the sense of the law; and if they should be disposed to exercise WILL instead of JUDGMENT, the consequence would equally be the substitution of their pleasure to that of the legislative body. The observation, if it prove any thing, would prove that there ought to be no judges distinct from that body.

If, then, the courts of justice are to be considered as the bulwarks of a limited Constitution against legislative encroachments, this consideration will afford a strong argument for the permanent tenure of judicial offices, since nothing will contribute so much as this to that independent spirit in the judges which must be essential to the faithful performance of so arduous a duty.

This independence of the judges is equally requisite to guard the Constitution and the rights of individuals from the effects of those ill humors, which the arts of designing men or the influence of particular conjunctures sometimes disseminate among the people themselves; and which, though they speedily give place to better information and more deliberate reflection, have a tendency, in the meantime, to occasion dangerous innovations in the government, and serious oppressions of the minor party in the community. Though I trust the friends of the proposed Constitution will never concur with its enemies in questioning that fundamental principle of republican government, which admits the right of the people to alter or abolish the established Constitution whenever they find it inconsistent with their happiness; yet it is not to be inferred from this principle that the representatives of the people, whenever a momentary inclination happens to lay hold of a majority of their constituents, incompatible with the provisions in the existing Constitution, would, on that account, be justifiable in a violation of those provisions; or that the courts would be under a greater obligation to connive at infractions in this shape, than when they had proceeded wholly from the cabals of the representative body. Until the people have by some solemn and authoritative act annulled or changed the established form, it is binding upon themselves collectively, as well as individually; and no presumption, or even knowledge, of their sentiments, can warrant their representatives in a departure from it, prior to such an act. But it is easy to see that it would require an uncommon portion of fortitude in the judges to do their duty as faithful guardians of the Constitution, where legislative invasions of it had been instigated by the major voice of the community.

But it is not with a view to infractions of the Constitution only that the independence of the judges may be an essential safeguard against the effects of occasional ill humors in the society. These sometimes extend no farther than to the injury of the private rights of particular classes of citizens by unjust and partial laws. Here also the firmness of the judicial magistracy is of vast importance in mitigating the severity and confining the operation of such laws. It not only serves to moderate the immediate mischiefs of those which may have been passed, but it operates as a check upon the legislative body in passing them; who, perceiving that obstacles to the success of iniquitous intention are to be expected from the scruples of the courts, are in a manner compelled by the very motives of the injustice they meditate to qualify their attempts. This is a circumstance calculated to have more influence upon the character of our governments, than but few may be aware of. The benefits of the integrity and moderation of the judiciary have already been felt in more States than one; and though they may have displeased those whose sinister expectations they may have disappointed, they must have commanded the esteem and applause of all the virtuous and disinterested. Considerate men of every description ought to prize whatever will tend to beget or fortify that temper in the courts; as no man can be sure that he may not be tomorrow the victim of a spirit of injustice by which he may be a gainer today. And every man must now feel that the inevitable tendency of such a spirit is to sap the foundations of public and private confidence, and to introduce in its stead universal distrust and distress.

That inflexible and uniform adherence to the rights of the Constitution and of individuals, which we perceive to be indispensable in the courts of justice, can certainly not be expected from judges who hold their offices by a temporary commission. Periodical appointments, however regulated or by whomsoever made, would, in some way or other, be fatal to their necessary independence. If the power of making them was committed either to the Executive or legislature, there would be danger of an improper complaisance to the branch which possessed it; if to both, there would be an unwillingness to hazard the displeasure of either; if to the people or to persons chosen by them for the special purpose, there would be too great a disposition to consult popularity, to justify a reliance that nothing would be consulted but the Constitution and the laws.

There is yet a further and a weightier reason for the permanency of the judicial offices, which is deducible from the nature of the qualifications they require. It has been frequently remarked, with great propriety, that a voluminous code of laws is one of the inconveniences necessarily connected with the advantages of a free government. To avoid an arbitrary discretion in the courts, it is indispensable that they should be bound down by strict rules and precedents, which serve to define and point out their duty in every particular case that comes before them; and it will readily be conceived from the variety of controversies which grow out of the folly and wickedness of mankind, that the records of those precedents must unavoidably swell to a very considerable bulk, and must demand long and laborious study to acquire a competent knowledge of them. Hence it is, that there can be but few men in the society who will have sufficient skill in the laws to qualify them for the stations of judges. And making the proper deductions for the ordinary depravity of human nature, the number must be still smaller of those who unite the requisite integrity with the requisite knowledge. These considerations apprise us that the government can have no great option between fit character; and that a temporary duration in office, which would naturally discourage such characters from quitting a lucrative line of practice to accept a seat on the bench, would have a tendency to throw the administration of justice into hands less able, and less well qualified, to conduct it with utility and dignity. In the present circumstances of this country and in those in which it is likely to be for a long time to come, the disadvantages on this score would be greater than they may at first sight appear; but it must be confessed that they are far inferior to those which present themselves under the other aspects of the subject.

Upon the whole, there can be no room to doubt that the convention acted wisely in copying from the models of those constitutions which have established *good behavior* as the tenure of their judicial offices, in point of duration; and that so far from being blamable on this account, their plan would have been inexcusably defective if it had wanted this important feature of good government. The experience of Great Britain affords an illustrious comment on the excellence of the institution.

PUBLIUS

## Discussion Questions

1. Was Hamilton correct in arguing that the judiciary is the least dangerous branch of government?

2. Critics of the Court often charge that it takes control of issues that should be properly decided in the legislature, while supporters claim that the Court is often the last check against the tyranny of the majority. Who has the stronger case? Can both sides be correct?

3. Hamilton argues that the "power of the people is superior to both" the legislature and the Court, and that the Court upholds the power of the people when it supports the Constitution over a statute that runs counter to the Constitution. Can you think of instances in which Congress may have been a stronger supporter of the "people" than the Court? Is it legitimate to argue that the Court is supporting the will of the people, given that it is an unelected body?

# 40

# "The Court in American Life" from
## *Storm Center: The Supreme Court in American Politics*

### DAVID O'BRIEN

*The "textbook" view of the federal judiciary is one in which judges sit in dispassionate review of complex legal questions, render decisions based on a careful reading of constitutional or statutory language, and expect their rulings to be adhered to strictly; the law is the law. This selection shows how unrealistic that picture is: O'Brien notes that the Supreme Court is very much a political institution, whose members pay more attention to the political cycle and public opinion than one might expect. O'Brien reviews the decision-making process in the famous* Brown v. Board of Education of Topeka, Kansas, *in which the Court invalidated segregated public schools, as an example of how the Court fits itself into the political process. Throughout the case, Justices delayed their decision, consolidated cases from around the country, and refused to set a firm timetable for implementation, relying instead on the ambiguous standard "with all deliberate speed." Far from being a purely objective arbiter of legal questions, the Court must pay close attention to its own legitimacy, and by extension the likelihood of compliance: it does no good to issue decisions that will be ignored.*

W hy does the Supreme Court pass the school desegregation case?" asked one of Chief Justice Vinson's law clerks in 1952. *Brown v. Board of Education of Topeka, Kansas* had arrived on the Court's docket in 1951, but it was carried over for oral argument the next term and then consolidated with four other cases and reargued in December 1953. The landmark ruling did not come down until May 17, 1954. "Well," Justice Frankfurter explained, "we're holding it for the election"—1952 was a presidential election year. "You're holding it for the election?" The clerk persisted in disbelief. "I thought the Supreme Court was supposed to decide cases without regard to elections." "When you have a major social political issue of this magnitude," timing and public reactions are important considerations, and, Frankfurter continued, "we do not think this is the time to decide it." Similarly, Tom Clark recalled that the Court awaited, over Douglas's dissent, additional cases from the District of Columbia and other regions, so as "to get a national coverage, rather than a sectional one." Such political considerations are by no means unique. "We often delay adjudication. It's not a question of evading at all," Clark concluded. "It's just the practicalities of life—common sense."

Denied the power of the sword or the purse, the Court must cultivate its institutional prestige. The power of the Court lies in the persuasiveness of its rulings and ultimately rests with other political institutions and public opinion. As an independent force, the Court has no chance to resolve great issues of public policy. *Dred Scott v. Sandford* (1857) and *Brown v. Board of Education* (1954) illustrate the limitations of Supreme Court policy-making. The "great folly," as Senator Henry Cabot Lodge characterized *Dred Scott*, was not the Court's interpretation of the Constitution or the unpersuasive moral position that blacks were not persons under the Constitution. Rather, "the attempt of the Court to settle the slavery question by judicial decision was simple madness." As Lodge explained:

> Slavery involved not only the great moral issue of the right of one man to hold another in bondage and to buy and sell him but it involved also the foundations of a social fabric covering half the country and caused men to feel so deeply that it finally brought them beyond the question of nullification to a point where the life of the Union was at stake and a decision could only be reached by war.[1]

A hundred years later, political struggles within the country and, notably, presidential and congressional leadership in enforcing the Court's school desegregation ruling saved the moral appeal of *Brown* from becoming another "great folly."

Because the Court's decisions are not self-executing, public reactions inevitably weigh on the minds of the justices. Justice Stone, for one, was furious at Chief Justice Hughes's rush to hand down *Powell v. Alabama* (1932). Picketers protested the Scottsboro boys' conviction and death sentence. Stone attributed the Court's rush to judgment to Hughes's "wish to put a stop to the [public] demonstrations around the Court." Opposition to the school desegregation ruling in *Brown* led to bitter, sometimes violent confrontations. In Little Rock, Arkansas, Governor Orval Faubus encouraged disobedience by southern segregationists. The federal National Guard had to be called out to maintain order. The school board in Little Rock unsuccessfully pleaded, in *Cooper v. Aaron* (1958), for the Court's postponement of the implementation of *Brown's* mandate. In the midst of the controversy, Frankfurter worried that Chief Justice Warren's attitude had become "more like that of a fighting politician than that of a judicial statesman." In such confrontations between the Court and the country, "the transcending issue," Frankfurter reminded the brethren, remains that of preserving "the Supreme Court as the authoritative organ of what the Constitution requires." When the justices move too far or too fast in their interpretation of the Constitution, they threaten public acceptance of the Court's legitimacy.

* * *

When deciding major issues of public law and policy, justices must consider strategies for getting public acceptance of their rulings. When striking down the doctrine of "separate but equal" facilities in 1954 in *Brown v. Board of Education (Brown I)*, for instance, the Warren Court waited a year before issuing, in *Brown II*, its mandate for "all deliberate speed" in ending racial segregation in public education.

Resistance to the social policy announced in *Brown I* was expected. A rigid timetable for desegregation would only intensify opposition. During oral arguments on *Brown II*, devoted to the question of what kind of decree the Court should issue to enforce *Brown*, Warren confronted the hard fact of southern resistance. The attorney for South Carolina, S. Emory Rogers, pressed for an open-ended decree—one that would not specify when and how desegregation should take place. He boldly proclaimed:

> Mr. Chief Justice, to say we will conform depends on the decree handed down. I am frank to tell you, right now [in] our district I do not think that we will send—[that] the white people of the district will send their children to the Negro schools. It would be unfair to tell the Court that we are going to do that. I do not think it is. But I do think that something can be worked out. We hope so.

"It is not a question of attitude," Warren shot back, "it is a question of conforming to the decree." Their heated exchange continued as follows:

> CHIEF JUSTICE WARREN: But you are not willing to say here that there would be an honest attempt to conform to this decree, if we did leave it to the district court [to implement]?
> MR. ROGERS: No, I am not. Let us get the word "honest" out of there.
> CHIEF JUSTICE WARREN: No, leave it in.
> MR. ROGERS: No, because I would have to tell you that right now we would not conform—we would not send our white children to the Negro schools.[2]

The exchange reinforced Warren's view "that reasonable attempts to start the integration process is [sic] all the court can expect in view of the scope of the problem, and that an order to immediately admit all negroes in white schools would be an absurdity because impossible to obey in many areas. Thus, while total immediate integration might be a reasonable order for Kansas, it would be unreasonable for Virginia, and the district judge might decide that a grade a year or three grades a year is [sic] reasonable compliance in Virginia." Six law clerks were assigned to prepare a segregation research report. They summarized available studies, discussed how school districts in different regions could be desegregated, and projected the effects and reactions to various desegregation plans.

The Court's problem, as one of Reed's law clerks put it, was to frame a decree "so as to allow such divergent results without making it so broad that evasion is encouraged." The clerks agreed that there should be a simple decree but disagreed on whether there should be guidelines for its implementation. One clerk opposed any guidelines. The others thought that their absence "smacks of indecisiveness, and gives the extremists more time to operate." The problem was how precise a guideline should be established. What would constitute "good-faith" compliance? "Although we think a 12-year gradual desegregation plan permissible," they confessed, "we are not certain that the opinion should explicitly sanction it."

At conference, Warren repeated these concerns. Black and Minton thought that a simple decree, without an opinion, was enough. As Black explained, "the less we say the better off we are." The others disagreed. A short, simple opinion seemed advisable for reaffirming *Brown I* and providing guidance for dealing with the inevitable problems of compliance. Harlan wanted *Brown II* expressly to recognize that school desegregation was a local problem to be solved by local authorities. The others also insisted on making clear that school boards and lower courts had flexibility in ending segregation. In Burton's view, "neither this Court nor district courts should act as a school board or formulate the program" for desegregation.

Agreement emerged that the Court should issue a short opinion-decree. In a memorandum, Warren summarized the main points of agreement. The opinion should simply state that *Brown I* held racially segregated public schools to be unconstitutional. *Brown II* should acknowledge that the ruling created various administrative problems, but emphasize that "local school authorities have the primary responsibility for assessing and solving these problems; [and] the courts will have to consider these problems in determining whether the efforts of local school authorities" are in good-faith compliance. The cases, he concluded, should be remanded to the lower courts "for such proceedings and decree necessary and proper to carry out this Court's decision." The justices agreed, and along these lines Warren drafted the Court's short opinion-decree.

The phrase "all deliberate speed" was borrowed from Holmes's opinion in *Virginia v. West Virginia* (1911), a case dealing with how much of the state's public debt, and when, Virginia ought to receive at the time West Virginia broke off and became a state. It was inserted in the final opinion at the suggestion of Frankfurter. Forced integration might lead to a lowering of educational standards. Immediate, court-ordered desegregation, Frankfurter warned, "would make a mockery of the Constitutional adjudication designed to vindicate a claim to equal treatment to achieve 'integrated' but lower educational standards." The Court, he insisted, "does its duty if it gets effectively under way the righting of a wrong. When the wrong is deeply rooted state policy the court does its duty if it decrees measures that reverse the direction of the unconstitutional policy so as to uproot it `with all deliberate speed.'" As much an apology for not setting precise guidelines as a recognition of the limitations of judicial power, the phrase symbolized the Court's bold moral appeal to the country.

Ten years later, after school closings, massive resistance, and continuing litigation, Black complained. "There has been entirely too much deliberation and not enough speed" in complying with *Brown*. "The time for mere 'deliberate speed' has run out." *Brown*'s moral appeal amounted to little more than an invitation for delay.

*    *    *

Twenty years after *Brown*, some schools remained segregated. David Mathews, secretary of the Department of Health, Education, and Welfare, reported to President Ford the results of a survey of half of the nation's primary and secondary public schools, enrolling 91 percent of all students: of these, 42 percent had an "appreciable percentage" of minority students, 16 percent had undertaken desegregation plans, while 26 percent had not, and 7 percent of the school districts remained racially segregated.

For over three decades, problems of implementing and achieving compliance with *Brown* persisted. Litigation by civil rights groups forced change, but it was piecemeal, costly, and modest. The judiciary alone could not achieve desegregation. Evasion and resistance were encouraged by the reluctance of Presidents and Congress to enforce the mandate. Refusing publicly to endorse *Brown*, Eisenhower would not take steps to enforce the decision until violence erupted in Little Rock, Arkansas. He then did so "*not* to enforce integration but to prevent opposition by violence to orders of a court." Later the Kennedy and Johnson administrations lacked congressional authorization and resources to take major initiatives in enforcing school desegregation. Not until 1964, when Congress passed the Civil Rights Act, did the executive branch have such authorization.

Enforcement and implementation required the cooperation and coordination of all three branches. Little progress could be made, as Assistant Attorney General Stephen Pollock has explained, "where historically there had been slavery and a long tradition of discrimination [until] all three branches of the federal government [could] be lined up in support of a movement forward or a requirement for change." The election of Nixon in 1968 then brought changes both in the policies of the executive branch and in the composition of the Court. The simplicity and flexibility of *Brown*, moreover, invited evasion. It produced a continuing struggle over measures, such as gerrymandering school district lines and busing in the 1970s and 1980s, because the mandate itself had evolved from one of ending segregation to one of securing integration in public schools.

Republican and Democratic administrations in turn differed on the means and ends of their enforcement policies in promoting integration.

Almost forty years after *Brown*, over 500 school desegregation cases remained in the lower federal courts. At issue in most was whether schools had achieved integration and become free of the vestiges of past segregation. Although lower courts split over how much proof school boards had to show to demonstrate that present *de facto* racial isolation was unrelated to past *de jure* segregation, the Court declined to review major desegregation cases from the mid-1970s to the end of the 1980s. During that time the dynamics of segregation in the country changed, as did the composition and direction of the Court.

\*  \*  \*

"By itself," the political scientist Robert Dahl observed, "the Court is almost powerless to affect the course of national policy." Another political scientist, Gerald Rosenberg, goes much farther in claiming that "courts can *almost never* be effective producers of significant social reform." *Brown*'s failure to achieve immediate and widespread desegregation is instructive, Rosenberg contends, in developing a model of judicial policy-making on the basis of two opposing theories of judicial power. On the theory of a "Constrainted Court" three institutional factors limit judicial policy-making: "[t]he limited nature of constitutional rights;" "[t]he lack of judicial independence;" and "[t]he judiciary's lack of powers of implementation." On the other hand, a "Dynamic Court" theory emphasizes the judiciary's freedom "from electoral constraints and [other] institutional arrangements that stymie change," and thus enable the courts to take on issues that other political institutions might not or cannot. But neither theory is completely satisfactory, according to Rosenberg, because occasionally courts do bring about social change. The Court may do so when the three institutional restraints identified with the "Constrained Court" theory are absent and at least one of the following conditions exist to support judicial policy-making: when other political institutions and actors offer either (a) incentives or (b) costs to induce compliance; (c) "when judicial decisions can be implemented by the market;" or (d) when the Court's ruling serves as "a shield, cover, or excuse, for persons crucial to implementation who are *willing to act*." On the historical basis of resistance and forced compliance with *Brown*'s mandate, Rosenberg concludes that "*Brown* and its progeny stand for the proposition that courts are impotent to produce significant social reform."

*Brown*, nonetheless, dramatically and undeniably altered the course of American life in ways and for reasons that Rosenberg underestimates. Neither Congress nor President Eisenhower would have moved to end segregated schools in the 1950s, as their reluctance for a decade to enforce *Brown* underscores. The Court lent moral force and legitimacy to the civil rights movement and to the eventual move by Congress and President Johnson to enforce compliance with *Brown*. More importantly, to argue that the Court is impotent to bring about social change overstates the case. Neither Congress nor the President, any more than the Court, could have singlehandedly dismantled racially segregated public schools. As political scientist Richard Neustadt has argued, presidential power ultimately turns on a President's power of persuasion, the Court's power depends on the persuasiveness of its rulings and the magnitude of change in social behavior mandated. The Court raises the ante in its bid for compliance when it appeals for massive social change through a prescribed course of action, in contrast to when it simply says "no" when striking down a law. The unanimous but ambiguous ruling in *Brown* reflects the justices' awareness that their decisions are not self-enforcing, especially when they deal with highly controversial issues and their rulings depend heavily on other institutions for implementation. Moreover, the ambiguity of *Brown*'s remedial decree was the price of achieving unanimity. Unanimity appeared necessary if the Court was to preserve its institutional prestige while pursuing revolutionary change in social policy. The justices sacrificed their own policy preferences for more precise guidelines, while the Court tolerated lengthy delays in recognition of the costs of open defiance, building consensus, and gaining public acceptance. But in the ensuing decades *Brown*'s mandate was also transformed from that of a simple decree for putting an end to state-imposed segregation into the more vexing one of achieving integrated public schools. With that transformation of *Brown*'s mandate the political dynamics of the desegregation controversy evolved, along with a changing Court and country.

## Discussion Questions

1. In what ways does the Supreme Court take "politics" into account in making decisions? Is this appropriate? What would the alternative be?

2. How does the process of appointment to the Supreme Court shape Court decisions? Should presidents make nominations based on the political views of potential justices?

3. Does O'Brien's argument reflect Hamilton's observations about the power of the Court?

4. In two rulings, in November 2003 and February 2004, the Massachusetts Supreme Court ruled that bans on gay marriage were unconstitutional. This set off a national firestorm of protest, and arguably a backlash against gay marriage. Did the Massachusetts court's ruling damage the court's own public standing by ignoring the political context of its decision (a nation in which two-thirds of

the people are opposed to gay marriage), or did the court do the correct and courageous thing by supporting the basic rights of a minority group? Is there some way the court could have finessed the issue, the way the Supreme Court did in *Brown*?

## NOTES

1. Letter to Charles Warren, July 19, 1923, Charles Warren Papers, Box 2, Library of Congress, Manuscripts Division, Washington, D.C.
2. Transcript of Oral Argument, Stanley Reed Papers, Box 43, University of Kentucky, Special Collections Library, Lexington, Kentucky.

# 41

# "Overruling the Court"

## LEON FRIEDMAN

*This article develops another theme that was addressed in Alexander Hamilton's Federalist. Hamilton argued that the Supreme Court should be the final interpreter of the Constitution. If Congress passed a law that was clearly unconstitutional, the Court must strike it down. However, as Friedman points out, Congress often disagrees with Supreme Court decisions and will pass legislation that overrules specific decisions (even if the Court claims that it has the final say). These tussles between Congress and the Supreme Court may often go back and forth for several rounds before one of the branches backs down. In general, Congress should have the upper hand if the question concerns statutory interpretation (that is, what a law passed by Congress really means), while the Supreme Court gets the final word concerning Constitutional interpretation.*

*Friedman explores these issues in the context of civil rights legislation in the past twenty years. The Supreme Court has been trying to impose its more narrow conception of civil rights in a series of decisions going back to 1982. On several occasions Congress has passed new legislation to restore the original intention of the 1964 Civil Rights Act and other laws. Friedman argues that the time has come for additional corrective legislation. He outlines five Supreme Court decisions on age discrimination, disability discrimination, language discrimination, lawyers fees for civil rights cases, and remedies for violence against women that all restrict the scope of civil rights in the United States. Friedman also discusses the types of actions that Congress could take to overturn these decisions. Some changes would be relatively direct, in the case of statutory interpretation; others would be more indirect, when dealing with constitutional issues such as federalism.*

One of the myths of our political system is that the Supreme Court has the last word on the scope and meaning of federal law. But time and time again, Congress has shown its dissatisfaction with Supreme Court interpretations of laws it passes—by amending or re-enacting the legislation to clarify its original intent and overrule a contrary Court construction.

The Supreme Court often insists that Congress cannot really "overrule" its decisions on what a law means: The justices' interpretation has to be correct since the Constitution gives final say to the highest court in the land. But Congress certainly has the power to pass a new or revised law that "changes" or "reverses" the meaning or scope of the law as interpreted by the Court, and the legislative history of the new law usually states that it was intended to "overrule" a specific Court decision.

Often the reversal is in highly technical areas, such as the statute of limitations in securities-fraud cases, the jurisdiction of tribal courts on Indian reservations, or the power of state courts to order denaturalization of citizens. But in the last 20 years, a main target of congressional "overruling" has been the Supreme Court's decisions in the area of civil rights. In 1982, for example, Congress amended the Voting Rights Act of 1965 to overrule a narrow Supreme Court holding in *Mobile v. Bolden*, a 1980 decision that addressed whether intentional discrimination must be shown before the act could be invoked. In 1988, Congress overruled another Supreme Court decision (in the 1984 case *Grove City College v. Bell*) by passing the Civil Rights Restoration Act, which broadened the coverage of Title VI of the Civil Rights Act of 1964. The legislative history of that law specifically recited that "certain aspects of recent decisions and opinions of the Supreme Court have unduly narrowed or cast doubt upon" a number of federal civil rights statutes and that "legislative action is necessary to restore the prior consistent and long-standing executive branch interpretations" of those laws.

And in 1991, Congress passed a broad, new Civil Rights Act that specifically reversed no fewer than five Supreme Court cases decided in 1989—decisions that severely restricted and limited workers' rights under federal antidiscrimination laws. Led by Massachusetts Democrat Edward Kennedy in the Senate and New York Republican Hamilton Fish, Jr., in the House, Congress acted to undo those rulings, as well as make other changes to federal law that strengthened the weapons available to workers against discrimination. Despite partisan contention over the language of certain provisions (which led to last-minute-compromise language), President George Bush the elder supported the changes. The new law recited in its preamble that its purpose was "to respond to recent decisions of the Supreme Court by expanding the scope of relevant civil rights statutes in order to provide adequate protection to victims of discrimination."

Given the current Supreme Court's track record in civil rights cases, there can be no doubt that congressional remediation is again necessary. In a series of cases over the past two years, the Court has been giving narrow readings to various federal civil rights laws. And once again, an attentive Congress can and should overrule the Court's decisions if the legislators care about fairness in the operation of government and in the workplace.

The recent cases were decided by identical 5–4 votes: Three conservative justices (William Rehnquist, Antonin Scalia, and Clarence Thomas) were joined by two centrists (Sandra Day O'Connor and Anthony

Kennedy) to narrow the reach of the laws at issue. Four liberal justices (John Paul Stevens, David Souter, Ruth Bader Ginsburg, and Stephen Breyer) dissented in all of the cases, four of which are described below.

- Last year [2000], on the grounds of federalism, the Supreme Court held in *Kimel v. Florida Board of Regents* that persons working for state governments cannot sue in federal court under the Age Discrimination in Employment Act, which Congress adopted in 1967. Such suits, the high court said, were constitutionally barred by the 11th Amendment's prohibition of suits against states in federal court. This ruling removed 3.4 percent of the nation's total workforce from the federal law's protections against age bias—some 5 million state employees across the country.
- On the same basis as the age-discrimination case, the Court held in February of this year that state employees cannot sue in federal court under the Americans with Disabilities Act. In this ruling, *Board of Trustees of the University of Alabama v. Garrett*, state workers who alleged disabilities discrimination were relegated to seeking recourse through state courts, where the available remedies are often much weaker than those provided under federal law.
- In April of this year [2001], the Supreme Court narrowed the reach of Title VI, the 1964 provision that prohibits recipients of federal financial assistance from discriminating on the basis of race, color, or national origin. In *Alexander v. Sandoval*, the Court held that Title VI is violated only if a plaintiff proves that the funded party *intentionally* discriminated on the basis of race—an interpretation that runs contrary to the rule for other civil rights laws (such as Title VII), which require only a showing of a discriminatory impact to trigger enforcement. At the same time, the justices held that neither public nor private recipients of federal financial aid who violate the nation's antidiscrimination regulations can be sued in federal court. Thus the state of Alabama was not vulnerable to suit when it established an "English only" requirement for taking a driver's license exam, even though federal regulations prohibit such restrictions. The only remedy, the Court held, was termination of federal funding to the state entity that violated the regulations (a sanction that entails a complicated administrative process).
- On May 29, the Court decided that civil rights litigants who bring suit against the government or an employer cannot collect attorney fees if the defendant voluntarily ceases the practice complained of or settles the claim before going to trial (the case was *Buckhannon Board and Care Home, Inc., v. West Virginia Department of Health and Human Services*). In 1976, Congress passed the Civil Rights Attorneys Fees Award Act to encourage lawyers to take civil rights cases as "private attorney generals." Such cases "vindicate public policies of the highest order,"

Congress explained when it passed the law. The act specified that the legal fees of "prevailing parties" would be paid by the losing party—generally a government that violated the plaintiff's constitutional rights. As Justice Ginsburg pointed out in her dissent in the *Buckhannon* case, Congress enacted the law to "ensure that nonaffluent plaintiffs would have effective access to the Nation's courts to enforce . . . civil rights laws." The effect of the Buckhannon decision is that a government body can tenaciously litigate a case until the last minute, then throw in the towel and evade the requirement of paying attorney fees. Since lawyers can no longer be sure that they'll be paid if they file civil rights suits, this ruling will certainly discourage them from taking on such cases, even those that clearly have merit.

Two of these cases are quite easy to correct. Congress can reverse the Supreme Court's decision about attorney fees by simply amending the civil rights law to provide that a litigant is considered a prevailing party entitled to fees if the lawsuit "was a substantial factor" in remedial action taken by the government and the suit brought by the plaintiff had a "substantial basis in fact and law." That was the rule generally applied by the lower courts before the Supreme Court decision.

The *Sandoval* rule can also be corrected by legislation. Congress could amend Title VI to provide that "any person aggrieved by the violation of any regulation issued pursuant to this act may bring a civil action in an appropriate federal court. Such actions may include suits challenging any discriminatory practice or policy that would be deemed unlawful if it has a disparate impact upon persons protected by this title."

The *Kimel* and *Garrett* decisions are more difficult to attack. The Supreme Court held that the 11th Amendment to the Constitution protects states against suits in federal court for age or disabilities discrimination by their employees. Although Congress cannot overrule a constitutional determination made by the Court, it can condition federal financial assistance on state adherence to federal requirements. In 1987 the Supreme Court held in *South Dakota v. Dole* (a 7–2 decision written by Chief Justice Rehnquist, in which Justice Scalia joined) that Congress could insist that South Dakota increase the minimum drinking age to 21 as a condition of obtaining federal highway funds. In other words, while Congress cannot force states to do its bidding, it in effect may bribe them to follow federal requirements.

Thus Congress could condition federal grants under Medicaid, Medicare, or the Social Security Act on the states' surrendering their 11th Amendment immunity under the federal acts banning discrimination based on age and disability. If a state wished to obtain federal funds under various social-welfare provisions, it would have to accede to the U.S. antidiscrimination laws and waive its immunity from being sued by its employees in federal court. Indeed, the 1986 Civil Rights Remedies

Equalization Amendment specifically declared that Congress intended for states to waive their 11th Amendment immunity in order to receive federal financial assistance.

Congress could use the same device to overrule another recent Supreme Court decision: last year's 5–4 holding in *United States v. Morrison* that the civil-remedy provisions of the Violence Against Women Act of 1994 are unconstitutional. The majority held that the law exceeded congressional power under the Constitution's commerce clause—the first time a federal law had been invalidated on that basis since 1936. But Congress can counter the Court's action by ensuring that such civil remedies are available to victims of gender-motivated acts of violence through state courts. How? By making the federal funds that are available through Medicare or Social Security programs contingent on a state's provision of such remedies.

In 1991, Congress and the first President Bush acted courageously to overrule manifestly narrow decisions of the Supreme Court that violated a national consensus against discrimination by government or by employers. Now that the Democrats have control of the Senate, they should make similar corrective legislation one of their first objectives. And who knows? This President Bush might even follow the lead of his father and endorse the changes.

## DISCUSSION QUESTIONS

1. The issues discussed here return to some of the themes raised in the chapter on federalism (in terms of the Court playing a role in the institutional balance of power). To what extent should the Supreme Court shape policy in an area such as civil rights, and to what extent should policy be made by Congress or the states?

2. If you think that the Court should play a central role in policy- and lawmaking, how would you answer critics who say that laws should be made by popularly elected institutions and not by unelected judges? If you think that Congress should play a central role, how would you answer those who point to the mid-twentieth century and show that Congress was dominated by southern segregationists who killed civil rights legislation for decades? Do the answers to these questions depend, at least in part, on how you view the policy in question and which branch of government would be more sympathetic to your views?

DEBATING THE ISSUES: INTERPRETING THE CONSTITUTION:
ORIGINALISM OR A LIVING CONSTITUTION?

Debates over the federal judiciary's role in the political process often focus on the question of how judges should interpret the Constitution. Should judges apply the document's original meaning as stated by the Framers, or should they use a broader interpretive framework that incorporates a more flexible view? This debate intensified during Earl Warren's tenure as Chief Justice (1953–1969), because of Court decisions that expanded the scope of civil liberties and criminal rights far beyond what strict constructionists thought the Constitution's language authorized. The debate continues in the current Court as an activist, conservative majority has implemented its interpretation of the Constitution over a broad range of cases, in some instances overturning six decades of precedents. The two readings in this section offer contrasting viewpoints from two sitting Supreme Court Justices.

Antonin Scalia, the intellectual force behind the conservative wing of the Court, argues that Justices must be bound by the original meaning of the document, as this is the only neutral principle that allows the judiciary to function as a legal body instead of a political one. The alternative is to embrace an evolving or "Living Constitution," which Scalia criticizes as allowing judges to decide cases on the basis of what seems right at the moment. He says that this "evolutionary" approach does not have any overall guiding principle and therefore "is simply not a practicable constitutional philosophy." He provides several examples of how the Living Constitution approach had produced decisions that stray from the clear meaning of the Constitution in the areas of property rights, the right to bear arms, and the right to confront one's accuser. This last example is especially provocative, given that it concerned the right of an accused child molester to confront the child who accused him of the crime. Scalia also challenges the notion that the Living Constitution approach produces more individual freedoms. Instead, he says, this approach has led to a variety of new restrictions on practices that had previously been allowed in the political process.

Stephen Breyer argues for the Living Constitution approach, but Breyer places it within a broader constitutional and theoretical framework. He argues for a "consequentialist" approach that is rooted in basic constitutional purposes, the most important of which is "active liberty," which he defines as "an active and constant participation in collective power." Breyer applies this framework to a range of difficult constitutional issues, including freedom of speech in the context of campaign finance and privacy rights in the context of rapidly evolving technology. He shows that the plain language of the Constitution does not provide enough guidance to answer these difficult questions. He turns the tables on Scalia, arguing that it is the "literalist" or "originalist" position that will, ironically, lead Justices to rely too heavily on their own personal views while his consequentialist position is actually the view that is more likely to produce judicial restraint. Breyer goes on to criticize the originalist position as fraught with inconsistencies. It is inherently subjective, despite its attempt to emphasize the "objective" words of the Constitution. By relying on the consequentialist perspective, which emphasizes democratic participation and active liberty, Justices are more likely to reach limited conclusions that apply to the facts at hand, while maximizing the positive implications for democracy. Breyer is keenly aware of the Court's place within the political process and wants to use it as a positive tool to improve that process, within the limits of the Constitution.

One observer of the Supreme Court summarized the debate between Scalia and Breyer in these terms: "It is a debate over text versus context. For Justice Scalia, who focuses on text, language is supreme, and the court's job is to derive and apply rules from the words chosen by the Constitution's framers or a statute's drafters. For Justice Breyer, who looks to context, language is only a starting point to an inquiry in which a law's purpose and a decision's likely consequences are the more important elements."[1]

# 42

# "Common-Law Courts in a Civil-Law System: The Role of United States Federal Courts in Interpreting the Constitution and Laws"

## ANTONIN SCALIA

I want to say a few words about the distinctive problem of interpreting our Constitution. The problem is distinctive, not because special principles of interpretation apply, but because the usual principles are being applied to an unusual text. Chief Justice Marshall put the point as well as it can be put in *McCulloch v. Maryland*:

> A constitution, to contain an accurate detail of all the subdivisions of which its great powers will admit, and of all the means by which they may be carried into execution, would partake of the prolixity of a legal code, and could scarcely be embraced by the human mind. It would probably never be un-

derstood by the public. Its nature, therefore, requires, that only its great outlines should be marked, its important objects designated, and the minor
ingredients which compose the objects be deduced from the nature of the
objects themselves.

In textual interpretation, context is everything, and the context of the
Constitution tells us not to expect nit-picking detail, and to give words
and phrases an expansive rather than narrow interpretation—though
not, of course, an interpretation that the language will not bear.

Take, for example, the provision of the First Amendment that forbids
abridgment of "the freedom of speech, or of the press." That phrase does
not list the full range of communicative expression. Handwritten letters,
for example, are neither speech nor press. Yet surely there is no doubt
they cannot be censored. In this constitutional context, speech and press,
the two most common forms of communication, stand as a sort of syn-
ecdoche for the whole. That is not strict construction, but it is reasonable
construction.

It is curious that most of those who insist that the drafter's intent gives
meaning to a statute reject the drafter's intent as the criterion for interpretation of the Constitution. I reject it for both. I will consult the writings of some men who happened to be Framers—Hamilton's and
Madison's writings in the *Federalist*, for example. I do so, however, not
because they were Framers and therefore their intent is authoritative and
must be the law; but rather because their writings, like those of other
intelligent and informed people of the time, display how the text of the
Constitution was originally understood. Thus, I give equal weight to
Jay's pieces in the *Federalist*, and to Jefferson's writings, even though
neither of them was a Framer. What I look for in the Constitution is
precisely what I look for in a statute: the original meaning of the text,
not what the original draftsmen intended.

But the Great Divide with regard to constitutional interpretation is
not that between Framers' intent and objective meaning; but rather that
between *original* meaning (whether derived from Framers' intent or not)
and *current* meaning. The ascendant school of constitutional interpretation affirms the existence of what is called the "Living Constitution," a
body of law that (unlike normal statutes) grows and changes from age
to age, in order to meet the needs of a changing society. And it is the
judges who determine those needs and "find" that changing law. Seems
familiar, doesn't it? Yes, it is the common law returned, but infinitely
more powerful than what the old common law ever pretended to be, for
now it trumps even the statutes of democratic legislatures. Recall the
words I quoted earlier from the Fourth-of-July speech of the avid codifier
Robert Rantoul: "The judge makes law, by extorting from precedents
something which they do not contain. He extends his precedents, which
were themselves the extension of others, till, by this accommodating
principle, a whole system of law is built up without the authority or

interference of the legislator." Substitute the word "people" for "legis-lator," and it is a perfect description of what modern American courts have done with the Constitution.

If you go into a constitutional law class, or study a constitutional-law casebook, or read a brief filed in a constitutional-law case, you will rarely find the discussion addressed to the text of the constitutional provision that is at issue, or to the question of what was the originally understood or even the originally intended meaning of that text. Judges simply ask themselves (as a good common-law judge would) what *ought* the result to be, and then proceed to the task of distinguishing (or, if necessary, overruling) any prior Supreme Court cases that stand in the way. Should there be (to take one of the less controversial examples) a constitutional right to die? If so, there is. Should there be a constitutional right to reclaim a biological child put out for adoption by the other parent? Again, if so, there is. If it is good, it is so. Never mind the text that we are supposedly construing; we will smuggle these in, if all else fails, under the Due Process Clause (which, as I have described, is textually incapable of containing them). Moreover, what the Constitution meant yesterday it does not necessarily mean today. As our opinions say in the context of our Eighth Amendment jurisprudence (the Cruel and Unusual Punishments Clause), its meaning changes to reflect "the evolving standards of decency that mark the progress of a maturing society."[2]

This is preeminently a common-law way of making law, and not the way of construing a democratically adopted text. I mentioned earlier a famous English treatise on statutory construction called *Dwarris on Statutes*. The fourth of Dwarris's Maxims was as follows: "An act of Parliament cannot alter by reason of time; but the common law may, since *cessante ratione cessat lex*."[3] This remains (however much it may sometimes be evaded) the formally enunciated rule for statutory construction: statutes do not change. Proposals for "dynamic statutory construction," such as those of Judge Calabresi and Professor Eskridge that I discussed yesterday, are concededly avant-garde. The Constitution, however, even though a democratically adopted text, we formally treat like the common law. What, it is fair to ask, is our justification for doing so?

One would suppose that the rule that a text does not change would apply *a fortiori* to a constitution. If courts felt too much bound by the democratic process to tinker with statutes, when their tinkering could be adjusted by the legislature, how much more should they feel bound not to tinker with a constitution, when their tinkering is virtually irreparable. It surely cannot be said that a constitution naturally suggests changeability; to the contrary, its whole purpose is to prevent change—to embed certain rights in such a manner that future generations cannot take them away. A society that adopts a bill of rights is skeptical that "evolving standards of decency" always "mark progress," and that societies always "mature," as opposed to rot. Neither the text of such a document nor the intent of its framers (whichever you choose) can possibly lead to the conclusion that its only effect is to take the power of changing rights away from the legislature and give it to the courts.

The argument most frequently made in favor of the Living Constitution is a pragmatic one: Such an evolutionary approach is necessary in order to provide the "flexibility" that a changing society requires; the Constitution would have snapped, if it had not been permitted to bend and grow. This might be a persuasive argument if most of the "growing" that the proponents of this approach have brought upon us in the past, and are determined to bring upon us in the future, were the *elimination* of restrictions upon democratic government. But just the opposite is true. Historically, and particularly in the past thirty-five years, the "evolving" Constitution has imposed a vast array of new constraints— new inflexibilities—upon administrative, judicial, and legislative action. To mention only a few things that formerly could be done or not done, as the society desired, but now cannot be done:

> admitting in a state criminal trial evidence of guilt that was obtained by an unlawful search;
> permitting invocation of God at public-school graduations;
> electing one of the two houses of a state legislature the way the United States Senate is elected (i.e., on a basis that does not give all voters numerically equal representation);
> terminating welfare payments as soon as evidence of fraud is received, subject to restoration after hearing if the evidence is satisfactorily refuted;
> imposing property requirements as a condition of voting;
> prohibiting anonymous campaign literature;
> prohibiting pornography.

And the future agenda of constitutional evolutionists is mostly more of the same—the creation of *new* restrictions upon democratic government, rather than the elimination of old ones. *Less* flexibility in government, not *more*. As things now stand, the state and federal governments may either apply capital punishment or abolish it, permit suicide or forbid it—all as the changing times and the changing sentiments of society may demand. But when capital punishment is held to violate the Eighth Amendment, and suicide is held to be protected by the Fourteenth Amendment, all flexibility with regard to those matters will be gone. No, the reality of the matter is that, generally speaking, devotees of the Living Constitution do not seek to faciliate social change but to *prevent* it.

There are, I must admit, a few exceptions to that—a few instances in which, historically, greater flexibility *has been* the result of the process. But those exceptions only serve to refute another argument of the proponents of an evolving Constitution, that evolution will always be in the direction of greater personal liberty. (They consider that a great advantage, for reasons that I do not entirely understand. All government represents a balance between individual freedom and social order, and it is not true that every alteration of that balance in the direction of greater individual freedom is necessarily good.) But in any case, the record of history refutes the proposition that the evolving Constitution will invariably enlarge individual rights. The most obvious refutation is the modern Court's limitation of the constitutional protections afforded to property. The provision prohibiting impairment of the obligation of contracts, for example, has been gutted. I am sure that We the People agree with that development; we value property rights less than the Founders did. So also, we value the right to bear arms less than the Founders (who thought the right of self-defense to be absolutely fundamental), and there will be few tears shed if and when the Second Amendment is held to guarantee nothing more than the State National Guard. But this just shows that the Founders were right when they feared that some (in their view misguided) future generation might wish to abandon liberties that they considered essential, and so sought to protect those liberties in a Bill of Rights. We may *like* the abridgment of property rights, and *like* the elimination of the right to bear arms; but let us not pretend that these are not a *reduction* of *rights*.

Or if property rights are too cold to get your juices flowing, and the right to bear arms too dangerous, let me give another example: Several terms ago a case came before the Supreme Court involving a prosecution for sexual abuse of a young child. The trial court found that the child would be too frightened to testify in the presence of the (presumed) abuser, and so, pursuant to state law, she was permitted to testify with only the prosecutor and defense counsel present, the defendant, the judge, and the jury watching over closed-circuit television. A reasonable enough procedure, and it was held to be constitutional by my Court.[4] I dissented, because the Sixth Amendment provides that "[i]n *all* criminal prosecutions" (let me emphasize the word "all") "the accused shall enjoy the right . . . to be confronted with the witnesses against him." There is no doubt what confrontation meant—or indeed means today. It means face-to-face, not watching from another room. And there is no doubt what one of the major purposes of that provision was: to induce *precisely* that pressure upon the witness which the little girl found it difficult to endure. It is difficult to accuse someone to his face, particularly when you are lying. Now no extrinsic factors have changed since that provision was adopted in 1791. Sexual abuse existed then, as it does now; little children were more easily upset than adults, then as now; a means of placing the defendant out of sight of the witness existed then as now (a screen could easily have been erected that would enable the defendant to see the witness, but not the witness the defendant). But the Sixth Amendment nonetheless gave *all* criminal defendants the right to *confront* the witnesses against them, because that was thought to be an important protection. The only significant thing that *has* changed, I think, is the society's sensitivity to so-called psychic trauma (which is what we are told the child witness in such a situation suffers) and the society's assessment of where the proper balance ought to be struck between the two extremes of a procedure that assures convicting 100 percent of all child abusers, and a procedure that assures acquitting 100 percent of those who have been falsely accused of child abuse. I have no doubt that the society is, as a whole, happy and pleased with what my Court decided. But we should not pretend that the decision did not *eliminate* a liberty that previously existed.

My last remarks may have created the false impression that proponents of the Living Constitution follow the desires of the American people in determining how the Constitution should evolve. They follow nothing so precise; indeed, as a group they follow nothing at all. Perhaps the most glaring defect of Living Constitutionalism, next to its incompatibility with the whole anti-evolutionary purpose of a constitution, is that there is no agreement, and no chance of agreement, upon what is to be the guiding principle of the evolution. *Panta rhei* [all things are in constant flux] is not a sufficiently informative principle of constitutional interpretation. What is it that the judge must consult to determine when, and in what direction, evolution has occurred? Is it the will of the majority, discerned from newspapers, radio talk shows, public opinion polls, and chats at the country club? Is it the philosophy of Hume, or of John Rawls, or of John Stuart Mill, or of Aristotle? As soon as the discussion goes beyond the issue of whether the Constitution is static, the evolutionists divide into as many camps as there are individual views of the good, the true, and the beautiful. I think that is inevitably so, which means that evolutionism is simply not a practicable constitutional philosophy.

I do not suggest, mind you, that originalists always agree upon their answer. There is plenty of room for disagreement as to what original meaning was, and even more as to how that original meaning applies to the situation before the court. But the originalist at least knows what he is looking for: the original meaning of the text. Often, indeed I dare say usually, that is easy to discern and simple to apply. Sometimes (thought not very often) there will be disagreement regarding the original meaning; and sometimes there will be disagreement as to how that original meaning applies to new and unforeseen phenomena. How, for example, does the First Amendment guarantee of "the freedom of speech" apply to new technologies that did not exist when the guarantee was created—to sound trucks, or to government-licensed over-the-air television? In such new fields the Court must follow the trajectory of the First Amendment, so to speak, to determine what it requires—and assuredly that enterprise is not entirely cut-and-dried, but requires the exercise of judgment.

But the difficulties and uncertainties of determining original meaning and applying it to modern circumstances are negligible compared with the difficulties and uncertainties of the philosophy which says that the Constitution *changes*; that the very act which it once prohibited it now permits, and which it once permitted it now forbids; and that the key to that change is unknown and unknowable. The originalist, if he does not have all the answers, has many of them. The Confrontation Clause, for example, requires confrontation. For the evolutionist, however, every question is an open question, every day a new day. No fewer than three of the Justices with whom I have served have maintained that the death penalty is unconstitutional, *even though its use is explicitly contemplated in the Constitution*. The Due Process Clause of the Fifth and Fourteenth Amendments say that no person shall be deprived of life without due process of law; and the Grand Jury Clause of the Fifth Amendment says that no person shall be held to answer for a capital crime without grand jury indictment. No matter. Under the Living Constitution the death penalty may have *become* unconstitutional. And it is up to each Justice to decide for himself (under no standard I can discern) when that occurs.

In the last analysis, however, it probably does not matter what principle, among the innumerable possibilities, the evolutionist proposes to determine in what direction the Living Constitution will grow. For unless the evolutionary dogma is kept a closely held secret among us judges and law professors, it will lead to the result that the Constitution evolves the way the majority wishes. The people will be willing to leave interpretation of the Constitution to a committee of nine lawyers so long as the people believe that it is (like the interpretation of a statute) lawyers' work—requiring a close examination of text, history of the text, traditional understanding of the text, judicial precedent, etc. But if the people come to believe that the Constitution is *not* a text like other texts; if it means, not what it says or what it was understood to mean, but what it *should* mean, in light of the "evolving standards of decency that mark the progress of a maturing society," well then, they will look for qualifications other than impartiality, judgment, and lawyerly acumen in those whom they select to interpret it. More specifically, they will look for people who agree with *them* as to what those evolving standards have evolved to; who agree with *them* as to what the Constitution *ought* to be.

It seems to me that that is where we are heading, or perhaps even where we have arrived. Seventy-five years ago, we believed firmly enough in a rock-solid, unchanging Constitution that we felt it necessary to adopt the Nineteenth Amendment to give women the vote. The battle was not fought in the courts, and few thought that it could be, despite the constitutional guarantee of Equal Protection of the Laws; that provision* did not, when it was adopted, and hence did not in 1920, guarantee equal access to the ballot, but permitted distinctions on the

*[Scalia is referring to the "equal protection clause" of the Fourteenth Amendment, which states, "No state shall . . . deny to any person within its jurisdiction the equal protection of the laws."]

basis not only of age, but of property and of sex. Who can doubt that, if the issue had been deferred until today, the Constitution would be (formally) unamended, and the courts would be the chosen instrumentality of change? The American people have been converted to belief in the Living Constitution, a "morphing" document that means, from age to age, what it ought to mean. And with that conversion has inevitably come the new phenomenon of selecting and confirming federal judges, at all levels, on the basis of their views regarding a whole series of proposals for constitutional evolution. If the courts are free to write the Constitution anew, they will, by God, write it the way the majority wants; the appointment and confirmation process will see to that. This, of course, is the end of the Bill of Rights, whose meaning will be committed to the very body it was meant to protect against: the majority. By trying to make the Constitution do everything that needs doing from age to age, we shall have caused it to do nothing at all.

## NOTES

1. Linda Greenhouse, "The Nation: Judicial Intent; the Competing Visions of the Role of the Court." *New York Times*, July 7, 2002, sec. 4, p. 3.
2. *Trop v. Dulles*, 356 U.S. 86, 101 (1958) (plurality opinion).
3. *Rhodes v. Chapman*, 452 U.S. 337, 346 (1981), quoting from Fortunatus Dwarris, *A General Treatise on Statutes, with American Notes and Additions by Platt Potter* (1871), 122.
4. See *Maryland v. Craig*, 497 U.S. 836 (1990).

# 43

# "Our Democratic Constitution"

## STEPHEN BREYER

* * * *[Breyer begins with a brief discussion of "ancient" and "modern" liberty.]* * *
I shall focus upon several contemporary problems that call for governmental action and potential judicial reaction. In each instance I shall argue that, when judges interpret the Constitution, they should place greater emphasis upon the "ancient liberty," i.e., the people's right to "an active and constant participation in collective power." I believe that increased emphasis upon this active liberty will lead to better constitutional law, a law that will promote governmental solutions consistent with individual dignity and community need.

At the same time, my discussion will illustrate an approach to constitutional interpretation that places considerable weight upon consequences—consequences valued in terms of basic constitutional purposes. It disavows a contrary constitutional approach, a more "legalistic" approach that places too much weight upon language, history, tradition, and precedent alone while understating the importance of consequences. If the discussion helps to convince you that the more "consequential" approach has virtue, so much the better.

Three basic views underlie my discussion. First, the Constitution, considered as a whole, creates a framework for a certain kind of government. Its general objectives can be described abstractly as including (1) democratic self-government, (2) dispersion of power (avoiding concentration of too much power in too few hands), (3) individual dignity (through protection of individual liberties), (4) equality before the law (through equal protection of the law), and (5) the rule of law itself.[1]

The Constitution embodies these general objectives in particular provisions. In respect to self-government, for example, Article IV guarantees a "republican Form of Government;" Article I insists that Congress meet at least once a year, that elections take place every two (or six) years, that a census take place every decade; the Fifteenth, Nineteenth, Twenty-fourth, and Twenty-sixth Amendments secure a virtually universal adult suffrage. But a general constitutional objective such as self-government plays a constitutional role beyond the interpretation of an individual provision that refers to it directly. That is because constitutional courts must consider the relation of one phrase to another. They must consider the document as a whole.[2] And consequently the document's handful of general purposes will inform judicial interpretation of many individual provisions that do not refer directly to the general objective in question. My examples seek to show how that is so. And, as I have said, they will suggest a need for judges to pay greater attention to one of those general objectives, namely participatory democratic self-government.

Second, the Court, while always respecting language, tradition, and precedent, nonetheless has emphasized different general constitutional objectives at different periods in its history. Thus one can characterize the early nineteenth century as a period during which the Court helped to establish the authority of the federal government, including the federal judiciary.[3] During the late nineteenth and early twentieth centuries, the Court underemphasized the Constitution's efforts to secure participation by black citizens in representative government—efforts related to the participatory "active" liberty of the ancients.[4] At the same time, it overemphasized protection of property rights, such as an individual's freedom to contract without government interference,[5] to the point where President Franklin Roosevelt commented that the Court's Lochner-era decisions had created a legal "no-man's land" that neither state nor federal regulatory authority had the power to enter.[6]

The New Deal Court and the Warren Court in part reemphasized "active liberty." The former did so by dismantling various Lochner-era distinctions, thereby expanding the scope of democratic self-government.[7] The latter did so by interpreting the Civil War Amendments in light of their purposes and to mean what they say, thereby helping African-Americans become members of the nation's community of self-governing citizens—a community that the Court expanded further in its "one person, one vote" decisions.[8]

More recently, in my view, the Court has again underemphasized the importance of the citizen's active liberty. I will argue for a contemporary reemphasis that better combines "the liberty of the ancients" with that "freedom of governmental restraint" that Constant called "modern."

Third, the real-world consequences of a particular interpretive decision, valued in terms of basic constitutional purposes, play an important role in constitutional decision-making. To that extent, my approach differs from that of judges who would place nearly exclusive interpretive weight upon language, history, tradition and precedent. In truth, the difference is one of degree. Virtually all judges, when interpreting a constitution or a statute, refer at one time or another to language, to history, to tradition, to precedent, to purpose, and to consequences. Even those who take a more literal approach to constitutional interpretation sometimes find consequences and general purposes relevant. But the more "literalist" judge tends to ask those who cannot find an interpretive answer in language, history, tradition, and precedent alone to rethink the problem several times, before making consequences determinative. The more literal judges may hope to find in language, history, tradition, and precedent objective interpretive standards; they may seek to avoid an interpretive subjectivity that could confuse a judge's personal idea of what is good for that which the Constitution demands; and they may believe that these more "original" sources will more readily yield rules that can guide other institutions, including lower courts. These objectives are desirable, but I do not think the literal approach will achieve them, and, in any event, the constitutional price is too high. I hope that my examples will help to show you why that is so, as well as to persuade some of you why it is important to place greater weight upon constitutionally-valued consequences, my consequential focus in this lecture being the affect of a court's decisions upon active liberty.

To recall the fate of Socrates is to understand that the "liberty of the ancients" is not a sufficient condition for human liberty. Nor can (or should) we replicate today the ideal represented by the Athenian agora or the New England town meeting. Nonetheless, today's citizen does participate in democratic self-governing processes. And the "active" liberty to which I refer consists of the Constitution's efforts to secure the citizen's right to do so.

To focus upon that active liberty, to understand it as one of the Constitution's handful of general objectives, will lead judges to consider the constitutionality of statutes with a certain modesty. That modesty embodies an understanding of the judges' own expertise compared, for example, with that of a legislature. It reflects the concern that a judiciary too ready to "correct" legislative error may deprive "the people" of "the political experience and the moral education that come from . . . correcting their own errors."[9] It encompasses that doubt, caution, prudence, and concern—that state of not being "too sure" of oneself—that Learned Hand described as the "spirit of liberty."[10] In a word, it argues for traditional "judicial restraint."

But active liberty argues for more than that. I shall suggest that increased recognition of the Constitution's general democratic participatory objectives can help courts deal more effectively with a range of specific constitutional issues. To show this I shall use examples drawn from the areas of free speech, federalism, privacy, equal protection and statutory interpretation. In each instance, I shall refer to an important modern problem of government that calls for a democratic response. I shall then describe related constitutional implications. I want to draw a picture of some of the different ways that increased judicial focus upon the Constitution's participatory objectives can have a positive effect.

*   *   *

I begin with free speech and campaign finance reform. The campaign finance problem arises out of the recent explosion in campaign costs along with a vast disparity among potential givers. * * * [Breyer reviews the data on increasing campaign costs] * * * The upshot is a concern by some that the matter is out of hand—that too few individuals contribute too much money and that, even though money is not the only way to obtain influence, those who give large amounts of money do obtain, or appear to obtain, too much influence. The end result is a marked inequality of participation. That is one important reason why legislatures have sought to regulate the size of campaign contributions.

The basic constitutional question, as you all know, is not the desirability of reform legislation but whether, how, or the extent to which, the First Amendment permits the legislature to impose limitations or ceilings on the amounts individuals or organizations or parties can contribute to a campaign or the kinds of contributions they can make. * * *

One cannot (or, at least, I cannot) find an easy answer to the constitutional questions in language, history, or tradition. The First Amendment's language says that Congress shall not abridge "the freedom of speech." But it does not define "the freedom of speech" in any detail. The nation's founders did not speak directly about campaign contributions. Madison, who decried faction, thought that members of Congress would fairly represent all their constituents, in part because the "electors" would not be the "rich" any "more than the poor."[11] But this kind of statement, while modestly helpful to the campaign reform cause, is hardly determinative.

Neither can I find answers in purely conceptual arguments. Some argue, for example, that "money is speech;" others say "money is not speech." But neither contention helps much. Money is not speech, it is money. But the expenditure of money enables speech; and that expenditure is often necessary to communicate a message, particularly in a political context. A law that forbid the expenditure of money to convey a message could effectively suppress that communication.

Nor does it resolve the matter simply to point out that campaign contribution limits inhibit the political "speech opportunities" of those who wish to contribute more. Indeed, that is so. But the question is whether, in context, such a limitation abridges "the freedom of speech." And to announce that this kind of harm could never prove justified in a political context is simply to state an ultimate constitutional conclusion; it is not to explain the underlying reasons.

To refer to the Constitution's general participatory self-government objective, its protection of "active liberty" is far more helpful. That is because that constitutional goal indicates that the First Amendment's constitutional role is not simply one of protecting the individual's "negative" freedom from governmental restraint. The Amendment in context also forms a necessary part of a constitutional system designed to sustain that democratic self-government. The Amendment helps to sustain the democratic process both by encouraging the exchange of ideas needed to make sound electoral decisions and by encouraging an exchange of views among ordinary citizens necessary to encourage their informed participation in the electoral process. It thereby helps to maintain a form of government open to participation (in Constant's words "by all citizens without exception").

The relevance of this conceptual view lies in the fact that the campaign finance laws also seek to further the latter objective. They hope to democratize the influence that money can bring to bear upon the electoral process, thereby building public confidence in that process, broadening the base of a candidate's meaningful financial support, and encouraging greater public participation. They consequently seek to maintain the integrity of the political process—a process that itself translates political speech into governmental action. Seen in this way, campaign finance laws, despite the limits they impose, help to further the kind of open public political discussion that the First Amendment also seeks to encourage, not simply as an end, but also as a means to achieve a workable democracy.

For this reason, I have argued that a court should approach most campaign finance questions with the understanding that important First Amendment-related interests lie on both sides of the constitutional equation and that a First Amendment presumption hostile to government regulation, such as "strict scrutiny" is consequently out of place.[12] Rather, the Court considering the matter without benefit of presumptions, must look realistically at the legislation's impact, both its negative impact on the ability of some to engage in as much communication as they wish and the positive impact upon the public's confidence, and consequent ability to communicate through (and participate in) the electoral process.

The basic question the Court should ask is one of proportionality. Do the statutes strike a reasonable balance between their electoral speech-restricting and speech-enhancing consequences? Or do you instead impose restrictions on that speech that are disproportionate when measured against their corresponding electoral and speech-related benefits, taking into account the kind, the importance, and the extent of those benefits, as well as the need for the restrictions in order to secure them?

The judicial modesty discussed earlier suggests that, in answering these questions, courts should defer to the legislatures' own answers insofar as those answers reflect empirical matters about which the legislature is comparatively expert, for example, the extent of the campaign finance problem, a matter that directly concerns the realities of political life. But courts cannot defer when evaluating the risk that reform legislation will defeat the very objective of participatory self-government itself, for example, where laws would set limits so low that, by elevating the reputation-related or media-related advantages of incumbency to the point where they would insulate incumbents from effective challenge.

I am not saying that focus upon active liberty will automatically answer the constitutional question in particular campaign finance cases. I argue only that such focus will help courts find a proper route for arriving at an answer. The positive constitutional goal implies a systemic role for the First Amendment; and that role, in turn, suggests a legal framework, i.e., a more particular set of questions for the Court to ask. Modesty suggests where, and how, courts should defer to legislatures in doing so. The suggested inquiry is complex. But courts both here and abroad have engaged in similarly complex inquiries where the constitutionality of electoral laws is at issue. That complexity is demanded by a Constitution that provides for judicial review of the constitutionality of electoral rules while granting Congress the effective power to secure a fair electoral system.

* * * [*The omitted sections apply these same arguments to commercial speech and then discuss recent Supreme Court cases on federalism. The next two sections apply Breyer's argument to privacy and majority-minority districts.*] * * *

I next turn to a different kind of example. It focuses upon current threats to the protection of privacy, defined as "the power to control what others can come to know about you." It seeks to illustrate what

active liberty is like in modern America, when we seek to arrive democratically at solutions to important technologically-based problems. And
it suggests a need for judicial caution and humility when certain privacy
matters, such as the balance between free speech and privacy, are at
issue.

First, I must describe the "privacy" problem. That problem is unusually complex. It has clearly become even more so since the terrorist
attacks. For one thing, those who agree that privacy is important disagree
about why. Some emphasize the need to be left alone, not bothered by
others, or that privacy is important because it prevents people from being
judged out of context. Some emphasize the way in which relationships
of love and friendship depend upon trust, which implies a sharing of
information not available to all. Others find connections between privacy
and individualism, in that privacy encourages non-conformity. Still others find connections between privacy and equality, in that limitations
upon the availability of individualized information lead private businesses to treat all customers alike. For some, or all, of these reasons, legal
rules protecting privacy help to assure an individual's dignity.

For another thing, the law protects privacy only because of the way
in which technology interacts with different laws. Some laws, such as
trespass, wiretapping, eavesdropping, and search-and-seizure laws, protect particular places or sites, such as homes or telephones, from searches
and monitoring. Other laws protect not places, but kinds of information,
for example laws that forbid the publication of certain personal information even by a person who obtained that information legally. Taken
together these laws protect privacy to different degrees depending upon
place, individual status, kind of intrusion, and type of information.

Further, technological advances have changed the extent to which
present laws can protect privacy. Video cameras now can monitor shopping malls, schools, parks, office buildings, city streets, and other places
that present law left unprotected. Scanners and interceptors can overhear
virtually any electronic conversation. Thermal imaging devices can detect activities taking place within the home. Computers can record and
collate information obtained in any of these ways, or others. This technology means an ability to observe, collate and permanently record a
vast amount of information about individuals that the law previously
may have made available for collection but which, in practice, could not
easily have been recorded and collected. The nature of the current or
future privacy threat depends upon how this technological/legal fact
will affect differently situated individuals.

These circumstances mean that efforts to revise privacy law to take
account of the new technology will involve, in different areas of human
activity, the balancing of values in light of prediction about the technological future. If, for example, businesses obtain detailed consumer purchasing information, they may create individualized customer profiles.

Those profiles may invade the customer's privacy. But they may also help firms provide publicly desired products at lower cost. If, for example, medical records are placed online, patient privacy may be compromised. But the ready availability of those records may lower insurance costs or help a patient carried unconscious into an operating room. If, for example, all information about an individual's genetic make-up is completely confidential, that individual's privacy is protected, but suppose a close relative, a nephew or cousin, needs the information to assess his own cancer risk?

Nor does a "consent" requirement automatically answer the dilemmas suggested, for consent forms may be signed without understanding and, in any event, a decision by one individual to release or to deny information can affect others as well.

Legal solutions to these problems will be shaped by what is technologically possible. Should video cameras be programmed to turn off? Recorded images to self-destruct? Computers instructed to delete certain kinds of information? Should cell phones be encrypted? Should web technology, making use of an individual's privacy preferences, automatically negotiate privacy rules with distant web sites as a condition of access?

The complex nature of these problems calls for resolution through a form of participatory democracy. Ideally, that participatory process does not involve legislators, administrators, or judges imposing law from above. Rather, it involves law revision that bubbles up from below. Serious complex changes in law are often made in the context of a national conversation involving, among others, scientists, engineers, businessmen and -women, the media, along with legislators, judges, and many ordinary citizens whose lives the new technology will affect. That conversation takes place through many meetings, symposia, and discussions, through journal articles and media reports, through legislative hearings and court cases. Lawyers participate fully in this discussion, translating specialized knowledge into ordinary English, defining issues, creating consensus. Typically, administrators and legislators then make decisions, with courts later resolving any constitutional issues that those decisions raise. This "conversation" is the participatory democratic process itself.

The presence of this kind of problem and this kind of democratic process helps to explain, because it suggests a need for, judicial caution or modesty. That is why, for example, the Court's decisions so far have hesitated to preempt that process. In one recent case the Court considered a cell phone conversation that an unknown private individual had intercepted with a scanner and delivered to a radio station. A statute forbid the broadcast of that conversation, even though the radio station itself had not planned or participated in the intercept. The Court had to determine the scope of the station's First Amendment right to broadcast given the privacy interests that the statute sought to protect. The Court held that the First Amendment trumped the statute, permitting the radio station to broadcast the information. But the holding was narrow. It focused upon the particular circumstances present, explicitly leaving open broadcaster liability in other, less innocent, circumstances.

The narrowness of the holding itself serves a constitutional purpose. The privacy "conversation" is ongoing. Congress could well rewrite the statute, tailoring it more finely to current technological facts, such as the widespread availability of scanners and the possibility of protecting conversations through encryption. A broader constitutional rule might itself limit legislative options in ways now unforeseeable. And doing so is particularly dangerous where statutory protection of an important personal liberty is at issue.

By way of contrast, the Court held unconstitutional police efforts to use, without a warrant, a thermal imaging device placed on a public sidewalk.[13] The device permitted police to identify activities taking place within a private house. The case required the Court simply to ask whether the residents had a reasonable expectation that their activities within the house would not be disclosed to the public in this way—a well established Fourth Amendment principle. Hence the case asked the Court to pour new technological wine into old bottles; it did not suggest that doing so would significantly interfere with an ongoing democratic policy conversation.

The privacy example suggests more by way of caution. It warns against adopting an overly rigid method of interpreting the constitution—placing weight upon eighteenth-century details to the point where it becomes difficult for a twenty-first-century court to apply the document's underlying values. At a minimum it suggests that courts, in determining the breadth of a constitutional holding, should look to the effect of a holding on the ongoing policy process, distinguishing, as I have suggested, between the "eavesdropping" and the "thermal heat" types of cases. And it makes clear that judicial caution in such matters does not reflect the fact that judges are mitigating their legal concerns with practical considerations. Rather, the Constitution itself is a practical document—a document that authorizes the Court to proceed practically when it examines new laws in light of the Constitution's enduring, underlying values.

My fourth example concerns equal protection and voting rights, an area that has led to considerable constitutional controversy. Some believe that the Constitution prohibits virtually any legislative effort to use race as a basis for drawing electoral district boundaries—unless, for example, the effort seeks to undo earlier invidious race-based discrimination.[14] Others believe that the Constitution does not so severely limit the instances in which a legislature can use race to create majority-minority districts.[15] Without describing in detail the basic argument between the two positions, I wish to point out the relevance to that argument of the Constitution's democratic objective.

That objective suggests a simple, but potentially important, constitutional difference in the electoral area between invidious discrimination, penalizing members of a racial minority, and positive discrimination, assisting members of racial minorities. The Constitution's Fifteenth Amendment prohibits the former, not simply because it violates a basic Fourteenth Amendment principle, namely that the government must treat all citizens with equal respect, but also because it denies minority citizens the opportunity to participate in the self-governing democracy that the Constitution creates. By way of contrast, affirmative discrimination ordinarily seeks to enlarge minority participation in that self-governing democracy. To that extent it is consistent with, indeed furthers, the Constitution's basic democratic objective.[16] That consistency, along with its more benign purposes, helps to mitigate whatever lack of equal respect any such discrimination might show to any disadvantaged member of a majority group.

I am not saying that the mitigation will automatically render any particular discriminatory scheme constitutional. But the presence of this mitigating difference supports the view that courts should not apply the strong presumptions of unconstitutionality that are appropriate where invidious discrimination is at issue. My basic purpose, again, is to suggest that reference to the Constitution's "democratic" objective can help us apply a different basic objective, here that of equal protection. And in the electoral context, the reference suggests increased legislative authority to deal with multiracial issues.

* * * [This omitted section discusses statutory interpretation. The remainder of the essay draws out the broader implications of a jurisprudence based on broader democratic objectives rather than a more narrow, literalist approach.] * * *

The instances I have discussed encompass different areas of law—speech, federalism, privacy, equal protection, and statutory interpretation. In each instance, the discussion has focused upon a contemporary social problem—campaign finance, workplace regulation, environmental regulation, information-based technological change, race-based electoral districting, and legislative politics. In each instance, the discussion illustrates how increased focus upon the Constitution's basic democratic objective might make a difference—in refining doctrinal rules, in evaluating consequences, in applying practical cautionary principles, in interacting with other constitutional objectives, and in explicating statutory silences. In each instance, the discussion suggests how that increased focus might mean better law. And "better" in this context means both (a) better able to satisfy the Constitution's purposes and (b) better able to cope with contemporary problems. The discussion, while not proving its point purely through logic or empirical demonstration, uses example to create a pattern. The pattern suggests a need for increased judicial emphasis upon the Constitution's democratic objective.

My discussion emphasizes values underlying specific constitutional phrases, sees the Constitution itself as a single document with certain basic related objectives, and assumes that the latter can inform a judge's understanding of the former. Might that discussion persuade those who prefer to believe that the keys to constitutional interpretation instead lie in specific language, history, tradition, and precedent and who fear that a contrary approach would permit judges too often to act too subjectively?

Perhaps so, for several reasons. First, the area of interpretive disagreement is more limited than many believe. Judges can, and should, decide most cases, including constitutional cases, through the use of language, history, tradition, and precedent. Judges will often agree as to how these factors determine a provision's basic purpose and the result in a particular case. And where they differ, their differences are often differences of modest degree. Only a handful of constitutional issues— though an important handful—are as open in respect to language, history, and basic purpose as those that I have described. And even in respect to those issues, judges must find answers within the limits set by the Constitution's language. Moreover, history, tradition, and precedent remain helpful, even if not determinative.

Second, those more literalist judges who emphasize language, history, tradition, and precedent cannot justify their practices by claiming that is what the Framers wanted, for the Framers did not say specifically what factors judges should emphasize when seeking to interpret the Constitution's open language.[17] Nor is it plausible to believe that those who argued about the Bill of Rights, and made clear that it did not contain an exclusive detailed list, had agreed about what school of interpretive thought should prove dominant in the centuries to come. Indeed, the Constitution itself says that the "enumeration" in the Constitution of some rights "shall not be construed to deny or disparage others retained by the people." Professor Bailyn concludes that the Framers added this language to make clear that "rights, like law itself, should never be fixed, frozen, that new dangers and needs will emerge, and that to respond to these dangers and needs, rights must be newly specified to protect the individual's integrity and inherent dignity."[18] Instead, justification for the literalist's practice itself tends to rest upon consequences. Literalist arguments often seek to show that such an approach will have favorable results, for example, controlling judicial subjectivity.

Third, judges who reject a literalist approach deny that their decisions are subjective and point to important safeguards of objectivity. A decision that emphasizes values, no less than any other, is open to criticism based upon (1) the decision's relation to the other legal principles (precedents, rules, standards, practices, institutional understandings) that it modifies and (2) the decision's consequences, i.e., the way in which the entire bloc of decision-affected legal principles subsequently affects the world. The relevant values, by limiting interpretive possibilities and guiding interpretation, themselves constrain subjectivity, indeed the democratic values that I have emphasized themselves suggest the importance of judicial restraint. An individual constitutional judge's need for consistency over time also constrains subjectivity. That is why Justice O'Connor has explained that need in terms of a constitutional judge's initial decisions creating "footprints" that later decisions almost inevitably will follow.

Fourth, the literalist does not escape subjectivity, for his tools, language, history, and tradition, can provide little objective guidance in the comparatively small set of cases about which I have spoken. In such cases, the Constitution's language is almost always nonspecific. History and tradition are open to competing claims and rival interpretations.[19] Nor does an emphasis upon rules embodied in precedent necessarily produce clarity, particularly in borderline areas or where rules are stated abstractly. Indeed, an emphasis upon language, history, tradition, or prior rules in such cases may simply channel subjectivity into a choice about: Which history? Which tradition? Which rules? It will then produce a decision that is no less subjective but which is far less transparent than a decision that directly addresses consequences in constitutional terms.

Finally, my examples point to offsetting consequences—at least if "literalism" tends to produce the legal doctrines (related to the First Amendment, to federalism, to statutory interpretation, to equal protection) that I have criticized. Those doctrines lead to consequences at least as harmful, from a constitutional perspective, as any increased risk of subjectivity. In the ways that I have set out, they undermine the Constitution's efforts to create a framework for democratic government—a government that, while protecting basic individual liberties, permits individual citizens to govern themselves.

To reemphasize the constitutional importance of democratic self-government may carry with it a practical bonus. We are all aware of figures that show that the public knows ever less about, and is ever less interested in, the processes of government. Foundation reports criticize the lack of high school civics education.[20] Comedians claim that more students know the names of the Three Stooges than the three branches of government. Even law school graduates are ever less inclined to work for government—with the percentage of those entering government (or nongovernment public interest) work declining at one major law school from 12% to 3% over a generation. Indeed, polls show that, over that same period of time, the percentage of the public trusting the government declined at a similar rate.[21]

This trend, however, is not irreversible. Indeed, trust in government has shown a remarkable rebound in response to last month's terrible tragedy [September 11].[22] Courts cannot maintain this upward momentum by themselves. But courts, as highly trusted government institutions, can help some,[23] in part by explaining in terms the public can understand just what the Constitution is about. It is important that the public, trying to cope with the problems of nation, state, and local community, understand that the Constitution does not resolve, and was not intended to resolve, society's problems. Rather, the Constitution provides a framework for the creation of democratically determined solutions, which protect each individual's basic liberties and assures that individual equal respect by government, while securing a democratic form of government. We judges cannot insist that Americans participate in that government, but we can make clear that our Constitution depends upon it. Indeed, participation reinforces that "positive passion for the public good," that John Adams, like so many others, felt a necessary condition for "Republican Government" and any "real Liberty."[24]

That is the democratic ideal. It is as relevant today as it was 200 or 2000 years ago. Today it is embodied in our Constitution. Two thousand years ago, Thucydides, quoting Pericles, set forth a related ideal—relevant in his own time and, with some modifications, still appropriate to recall today. "We Athenians," said Pericles, "do not say that the man who fails to participate in politics is a man who minds his own business. We say that he is a man who has no business here."

## DISCUSSION QUESTIONS

1. Critics of the strict-construction, originalist perspective often point to ambiguities in the language of the Constitution. Justice Breyer outlines several of these in his speech. What are some other examples of ambiguous language in the Constitution (look at the Bill of Rights as a start), and what alternative interpretations can you develop?

2. Critics of the Living Constitution, such as Justice Scalia, often argue that judges substitute their own reading of what they think the law *should* be for what the law *is*. Justice Breyer replies that subjectivity is even more inherent in the originalist perspective. First, do you think it is possible for Justices to avoid having their own views shape their decisions? If it is impossible, which perspective, Scalia's or Breyer's, is more likely to produce such subjectivity?

3. Should judges take public opinion or changing societal standards into account when ruling on the constitutionality of a statute or practice? Apply your answer to the "confrontation doctrine" that Scalia talks about (the right to confront your accuser, even in the context of a child having to confront the person who sexually molested her or him).

4. Does Breyer's focus on political participation provide Justices with the type of guidance they need to make decisions? Do you think this focus would help restore the public's confidence in political institutions, as Breyer hopes?

5. Consider Scalia's list of activities that are no longer allowed by the Court (the list begins with using illegally obtained evidence in a criminal trial). How would Breyer's approach of active liberty decide these cases? Which do you think is the better outcome? Should this consequentialist approach be the basis for deciding cases before the Court?

6. After considering the arguments, do you find Breyer or Scalia more compelling? Which do you think you would be more likely to employ if you were a justice and why?

## NOTES

1. For an in-depth and nuanced discussion of the principles underlying the third and fourth objectives, see generally Ronald Dworkin, *Freedom's Law: The Moral Reading of the American Constitution* 15–35 (1996), and Ronald Dworkin, *Law's Empire* 176–265 (1986).
2. See Jack Rakove, *Original Meanings* 11–13 (1996).
3. See, e.g., *McCulloch* v. *Maryland*, 4 Wheat 316 (1819); *Marbury* v. *Madison*, 1 Cranch 137 (1803).
4. See, e.g., *Giles* v. *Harris*, 189 U.S. 475 (1903); *Civil Rights Cases*, 109 U.S. 3 (1883).
5. See, e.g., *Lochner* v. *New York*, 198 U.S. 45 (1905).
6. Leuchtenburg, *The Supreme Court Reborn* 103 (1995).
7. See, e.g., *Wickard* v. *Filburn*, 317 U.S. 111 (1942); *NLRB* v. *Jones & Laughlin Steel Corp.*, 301 U.S. 1 (1937); *West Coast Hotel Co.* v. *Parrish*, 300 U.S. 379 (1937).
8. See, e.g., *Baker* v. *Carr*, 369 U.S. 186 (1962); *Reynolds* v. *Sims*, 377 U.S. 533 (1964); *Gomillion* v. *Lightfoot*, 383 U.S. 663 (1966).
9. James Bradley Thayer, *John Marshall* 107 (1901).
10. Learned Hand, *The Spirit of Liberty* 190 (3d ed. 1960); cf. also id., at 109.
11. *The Federalist*, No. 57 (James Madison).
12. See, Nixon, supra n. 22 at 22.
13. *Kyllo* v. *United States*, 533 U.S. 27 (2001).
14. See, e.g., *Hunt* v. *Cromartie*, 526 U.S. 541 (1999).
15. See, e.g., *Shaw* v. *Reno*, 509 U.S. 630 (1993) (White, J., dissenting).
16. Cf. John Hart Ely, *Democracy and Distrust* (1980).
17. Rakove, supra n. 2 at 339-65.
18. Bernard Bailyn, *The Ideological Origins of the American Revolution* (1967).
19. See, e.g., *Alden* v. *Maine*, 527 U.S. 706 (1999).
20. See, e.g., U.S. Dept. of Educ., Office of Educ. Research and Improvement, Nat'l Ctr. for Educ. Stats., *The NAEP 1998 Civics Report Card* (1999).
21. Lydia Saad, "Americans' Faith in Government Shaken But Not Shattered by Watergate," available at http://www.gallup.com.
22. Tom Shoop, "Trust in Government Up Dramatically, Polls Show," *Government Executive Magazine*, Oct. 1, 2001.
23. See Saad, supra n. 21.
24. John Adams, Letter to Mercy Warren (1776), in *I The Founder's Constitution* 670.

# PART III

# Political Behavior: Participation

# CHAPTER 9

# Public Opinion and the Mass Media

## 44

## "Polling the Public" from *Public Opinion in a Democracy*

### George Gallup

*Assessing public opinion in a democracy of 300 million people is no easy task. George Gallup, who is largely responsible for the development of modern opinion polling, argued that public opinion polls enhanced the democratic process by providing elected officials with a picture of what Americans think about current events. Despite Gallup's vigorous defense of his polling techniques and the contribution of polling to democracy, the public opinion poll remains controversial. Some critics charge that public officials pay too much attention to polls, making decisions based on fluctuations in public opinion rather than on informed, independent judgment. Others say that by urging respondents to give an opinion, even if they initially respond that they have no opinion on a question, polls may exaggerate the amount of division in American society. And some critics worry that election-related polls may affect public behavior: if a potential voter hears that her candidate is trailing in the polls, perhaps she becomes demoralized, doesn't vote, and the poll becomes a self-fulfilling prophecy. In effect, rather than reporting on election news, the poll itself makes news.*

We have a national election every two years only. In a world which moves as rapidly as the modern world does, it is often desirable to know the people's will on basic policies at more frequent intervals. We cannot put issues off and say "let them be decided at the next election." World events do not wait on elections. We need to know the will of the people at all times.

If we know the collective will of the people at all times the efficiency of democracy can be increased, because we can substitute specific knowledge of public opinion for blind groping and guesswork. Statesmen who know the true state of public opinion can then formulate plans with a sure knowledge of what the voting public is thinking. They can know what degree of opposition to any proposed plan exists, and what efforts are necessary to gain public acceptance for it. The responsibility for initiating action should, as always, rest with the political leaders of the country. But the collective will or attitude of the people needs to be learned without delay.

### The Will of the People

How is the will of the people to be known at all times?

Before I offer an answer to this question, I would like to examine some of the principal channels by which, at the present time, public opinion is expressed.

The most important is of course a national election. An election is the only official and binding expression of the people's judgment. But, as viewed from a strictly objective point of view, elections are a confusing and imperfect way of registering national opinion. In the first place, they come only at infrequent intervals. In the second place, as [James] Bryce pointed out in *The American Commonwealth*, it is virtually impossible to separate issues from candidates. How can we tell whether the public is voting for the man or for his platform? How can we tell whether all the candidate's views are endorsed, or whether some are favored and others opposed by the voters? Because society grows more and more complex, the tendency is to have more and more issues in an election. Some may be discussed; others not. Suppose a candidate for office takes a position on a great many public issues during the campaign. If elected, he inevitably assumes that the public has endorsed all his planks, whereas this may actually not be the case.

\* \* \*

### The Role of the Elected Representative

A second method by which public opinion now expresses itself is through elected representatives. The legislator is, technically speaking, supposed to represent the interests of all voters in his constituency. But under the two-party system there is a strong temptation for him to represent, and be influenced by, only the voters of his own party. He is subject to the pressure of party discipline and of wishes of party leaders back home. His very continuance in office may depend on giving way to such pressure. Under these circumstances his behavior in Congress is likely to be governed not by what he thinks the voters of his State want, but by what he thinks the leaders of his own party in that State want.

\* \* \*

Even in the event that an elected representative does try to perform his duty of representing the whole people, he is confronted with the problem: What is the will of the people? Shall he judge their views by the letters they write him or the telegrams they send him? Too often such expressions of opinion come only from an articulate minority. Shall the congressman judge their views by the visitors or delegations that come to him from his home district?

*Pressure Groups and the Whole Nation*

Legislators are constantly subject to the influence of organized lobbies and pressure groups. Senator Tydings * * * pointed out recently that the United States is the most fertile soil on earth for the activity of pressure groups. The American people represent a conglomeration of races, all with different cultural backgrounds. Sections and groups struggle with one another to fix national and international policy. And frequently in such struggles, as Senator Tydings pointed out, "self-interest and sectionalism, rather than the promotion of national welfare, dominate the contest." Senator Tydings mentions some twenty important group interests. These include labor, agriculture, veterans, pension plan advocates, chambers of commerce, racial organizations, isolationists and internationalists, high-tariff and low-tariff groups, preparedness and disarmament groups, budget balancers and spending advocates, soft-money associations and hard-money associations, transportation groups and states righters and centralizationists.

The legislator obviously owes a duty to his home district to legislate in its best interests. But he also owes a duty to legislate in the best interests of the whole nation. In order, however, to carry out this second duty he must *know* what the nation thinks. Since he doesn't always know what the voters in his own district think, it is just that much more difficult for him to learn the views of the nation. Yet if he could know those views at all times he could legislate more often in the interest of the whole country.

\* \* \*

*The Cross-Section Survey*

This effort to discover public opinion has been largely responsible for the introduction of a new instrument for determining public opinion— the cross-section or sampling survey. By means of nationwide studies taken at frequent intervals, research workers are today attempting to measure and give voice to the sentiments of the whole people on vital issues of the day.

Where does this new technique fit into the scheme of things under our form of government? Is it a useful instrument of democracy? Will it prove to be vicious and harmful, or will it contribute to the efficiency of the democratic process?

The sampling referendum is simply a procedure for sounding the opinions of a relatively small number of persons, selected in such manner as to reflect with a high degree of accuracy the views of the whole voting population. In effect such surveys canvass the opinions of a miniature electorate.

Cross-section surveys do not place their chief reliance upon numbers. The technique is based on the fact that a few thousand voters correctly selected will faithfully reflect the views of an electorate of millions of voters. The key to success in this work is the cross section—the proper selection of voters included in the sample. Elaborate precautions must be taken to secure the views of members of all political parties—of rich and poor, old and young, of men and women, farmers and city dwellers, persons of all religious faiths—in short, voters of all types living in every State in the land. And all must be included in correct proportion.

\*   \*   \*

*Reliability of Opinion Surveys*

Whether opinion surveys will prove to be a useful contribution to democracy depends largely on their reliability in measuring opinion. During the last four years [1935–1939] the sampling procedure, as used in measuring public opinion, has been subjected to many tests. In general these tests indicate that present techniques can attain a high degree of accuracy, and it seems reasonable to assume that with the development of this infant science, the accuracy of its measurements will be constantly improved.

The most practical way at present to measure the accuracy of the sampling referendum is to compare forecasts of elections with election results. Such a test is by no means perfect, because a preelection survey must not only measure opinion in respect to candidates but must also predict just what groups of people will actually take the trouble to cast their ballots. Add to this the problem of measuring the effect of weather on turnout, also the activities of corrupt political machines, and it can easily be seen that election results are by no means a perfect test of the accuracy of this new technique.

\*   \*   \*

Many thoughtful students of government have asked: Why shouldn't the Government itself, rather than private organizations, conduct these sampling surveys? A few political scientists have even suggested the establishment of a permanent federal bureau for sounding public opinion, arguing that if this new technique is a contribution to democracy, the government has a duty to take it over.

The danger in this proposal, as I see it, lies in the temptation it would place in the way of the party in power to conduct surveys to prove itself right and to suppress those which proved it to be wrong. A private organization, on the other hand, must stand or fall not so much on what it reports or fails to report as on the accuracy of its results, and the impartiality of its interpretations. An important requirement in a democracy is complete and reliable news reports of the activities of all branches of the government and of the views of all leaders and parties. But few persons would argue that, for this reason, the government should take over the press, and all its news gathering associations.

\* \* \*

### Cloture on Debate?

It is sometimes argued that public opinion surveys impose a cloture on debate. When the advocates of one side of an issue are shown to be in the majority, so the argument runs, the other side will lose hope and abandon their cause believing that further efforts are futile.

Again let me say that there is little evidence to support this view. Every election necessarily produces a minority. In 1936 the Republicans polled less than 40 percent of the vote. Yet the fact that the Republicans were defeated badly wasn't enough to lead them to quit the battle. They continued to fight against the New Deal with as much vigor as before. An even better example is afforded by the Socialist Party. For years the Socialist candidate for President has received but a small fraction of the total popular vote, and could count on sure defeat. Yet the Socialist Party continues as a party, and continues to poll about the same number of votes.

Sampling surveys will never impose a cloture on debate so long as it is the nature of public opinion to change. The will of the people is dynamic; opinions are constantly changing. A year ago an overwhelming majority of voters were skeptical of the prospects of the Republican Party in 1940. Today, half the voters think the G.O.P. will win. If elections themselves do not impose cloture on debate, is it likely that opinion surveys will?

### Possible Effect on Representative Government

The form of government we live under is a representative form of government. What will be the effect on representative government if the will of the people is known at all times? Will legislators become mere rubber stamps, mere puppets, and the function of representation be lost?

Under a system of frequent opinion measurement, the function of representation is not lost, for two reasons. First, it is well understood that the people have not the time or the inclination to pass on all the problems that confront their leaders. They cannot be expected to express judgment on technical questions of administration and government. They can pass judgment only on basic general policies. As society grows more complex there is a greater and greater need for experts. Once the voters have indicated their approval of a general policy or plan of action, experts are required to carry it out.

Second, it is not the province of the people to initiate legislation, but to decide which of the programs offered they like best. National policies do not spring full-blown from the common people. Leaders, knowing the general will of the people, must take the initiative in forming policies that will carry out the general will and must put them into effect.

Before the advent of the sampling referendum, legislators were not isolated from their constituencies. They read the local newspapers; they toured their districts and talked with voters; they received letters from their home State; they entertained delegations who claimed to speak for large and important blocs of voters. The change that is brought about by sampling referenda is merely one which provides these legislators with a truer measure of opinion in their districts and in the nation.

*   *   *

*How Wise Are the Common People?*

The sampling surveys of recent years have provided much evidence concerning the wisdom of the common people. Anyone is free to examine this evidence. And I think that the person who does examine it will come away believing as I do that, collectively, the American people have a remarkably high degree of common sense. These people may not be brilliant or intellectual or particularly well read, but they possess a quality of good sense which is manifested time and again in their expressions of opinion on present-day issues.

*   *   *

It is not difficult to understand why the conception of the stupidity of the masses has so many adherents. Talk to the first hundred persons whom you happen to meet in the street about many important issues of the day, and the chances are great that you will be struck by their lack of accurate or complete knowledge on these issues. Few of them will likely have sufficient information in this particular field to express a well founded judgment.

But fortunately a democracy does not require that every voter be well informed on every issue. In fact a democracy does not depend so much on the enlightenment of each individual, as upon the quality of the collective judgment or intelligence of thousands of individuals.

\*   \*   \*

It would of course be foolish to argue that the collective views of the common people always represent the most intelligent and most accurate answer to any question. But results of sampling referenda on hundreds of issues do indicate, in my opinion, that we can place great faith in the collective judgment or intelligence of the people.

### The New England Town Meeting Restored

One of the earliest and purest forms of democracy in this country was the New England town meeting. The people gathered in one room to discuss and to vote on the questions of the community. There was a free exchange of opinions in the presence of all the members. The town meeting was a simple and effective way of articulating public opinion, and the decisions made by the meeting kept close to the public will. When a democracy thus operates on a small scale it is able to express itself swiftly and with certainty.

But as communities grew, the town meeting became unwieldy. As a result the common people became less articulate, less able to debate the vital issues in the manner of their New England forefathers. Interest in politics lagged. Opinion had to express itself by the slow and cumbersome method of election, no longer facilitated by the town meeting with its frequent give and take of ideas. The indifference and apathy of voters made it possible for vicious and corrupt political machines to take over the administration of government in many states and cities.

The New England town meeting was valuable because it provided a forum for the exchange of views among all citizens of the community and for a vote on these views. Today, the New England town meeting idea has, in a sense, been restored. The wide distribution of daily newspapers reporting the views of statesmen on issues of the day, the almost universal ownership of radios which bring the whole nation within the hearing of any voice, and now the advent of the sampling referendum which provides a means of determining quickly the response of the public to debate on issues of the day, have in effect created a town meeting on a national scale.

How nearly the goal has been achieved is indicated in the following data recently gathered by the American Institute of Public Opinion. Of the 45,000,000 persons who voted in the last presidential election [1936], approximately 40,000,000 read a daily newspaper, 40,000,000 have radios, and only 2,250,000 of the entire group of voters in the nation neither have a radio nor take a daily newspaper.

This means that the nation is literally in one great room. The newspapers and the radio conduct the debate on national issues, presenting both information and argument on both sides, just as the townsfolk did in person in the old town meeting. And finally, through the process of the sampling referendum, the people, having heard the debate on both sides of every issue, can express their will. After one hundred and fifty years we return to the town meeting. This time the whole nation is within the doors.

## DISCUSSION QUESTIONS

1. What are the advantages and disadvantages of modern public opinion polling?

2. How would our political system change if polls were banned?

3. All the major broadcast networks and news networks, the campaigns, some Web sites and blogs, and most reporters know who is ahead in a presidential election early on Election Day, because of "exit polling" of people who have just voted. In 2004, early exit polls seemed to indicate that a very good day was in store for Democratic presidential candidate John Kerry, but the day proved to be a disappointment for his campaign. Should early exit-poll results be kept secret by the networks or should they be broadcast?

# 45

# "Choice Words: If You Can't Understand Our Poll Questions, Then How Can We Understand Your Answers?"

### Richard Morin

*Although polls play a prominent role in contemporary politics, Richard Morin cautions that polls can be "risky." Morin, director of polling for the* Washington Post, *notes that minor differences in question wording can—and, during the impeachment of President Clinton,* did—*result in dramatically different polling results. Other problems arise because people will answer questions "even if they don't really have an opinion or understand the question that has been asked." Ultimately, argues Morin, pollsters and the politicians who rely upon them should be somewhat skeptical of the depth or significance of any individual response.*

If his current government job ends abruptly, President Clinton might think about becoming a pollster. Anyone who ponders the meaning of the word *is* has precisely the right turn of mind to track public opinion in these mindless, mindful times.

Never has polling been so risky—or so much in demand. Never have so many of the rules of polling been bent or broken so cleanly, or so often. Pollsters are sampling public reaction just hours—sometimes minutes—after events occur. Interviewing periods, which traditionally last several days to secure a solid sample, have sometimes shrunk to just a few hours on a single night. Pollsters have been asking questions that were taboo until this past year. Is oral sex really sex? (Yes, said 76 percent of those interviewed in a *Newsweek* poll conducted barely a week after the scandal broke back in January.)

"No living pollster has ever had to poll in a situation like this," said Michael Kagay, the editor of news surveys at the *New York Times*. "We're in uncharted territory." After all, Andrew Johnson had to deal with political enemies, but not pollsters. And Richard Nixon's resignation before impeachment meant that pollsters didn't have a chance to ask whether the Senate should give him the boot.

Clinton has it about right: Words do have different meanings for different people, and these differences matter. At the same time, some seemingly common words and phrases have no meaning at all to many Americans; even on the eve of the impeachment vote last month, nearly a third of the country, didn't know or didn't understand what *impeachment* meant.

Every pollster knows that questions with slightly different wording can produce different results. In the past year, survey researchers learned just how big and baffling those differences can be, particularly when words are used to capture public reaction to an arcane process that no living American—not even [ninety-something Senator] Strom Thurmond—has witnessed in its entirety.

Fear of getting it wrong—coupled with astonishment over the persistent support for Clinton revealed in poll after poll—spawned a flood of novel tests by pollsters to determine precisely the right words to use in our questions.

Last month, less than a week before Clinton was impeached by the House, *The Washington Post* and its polling partner ABC News asked half of a random sampling of Americans whether Clinton should resign if he were impeached or should "fight the charges in the Senate." The other half of the sample was asked a slightly different question: Should Clinton resign if impeached or should he "remain in office and face trial in the Senate?"

The questions are essentially the same. The results were not. Nearly six in 10—59 percent—said Clinton should quit rather than fight impeachment charges in the Senate. But well under half—43 percent—said he should resign when the alternative was to "remain in office and stand trial in the Senate." What gives?

The difference appears to be the word *fight*. America is a peaceable kingdom; we hate it when our parents squabble and are willing to accept just about any alternative—including Clinton's resignation—to spare the country a partisan fight. But when the alternative is less overtly combative—stand trial in the Senate—Americans are less likely to scurry to the resignation option.

Such a fuss over a few words. But it is just more proof that people do not share the same understanding of terms, and that a pollster who ignores this occupational hazard may wind up looking for a new job.

Think I'm exaggerating? Then let's do another test. A month ago, [December 1998], how would you have answered this question: "If the full House votes to send impeachment articles to the Senate for a trial, then do you think it would be better for the country if Bill Clinton resigned from office, or not?"

And how would you have answered this question: "If the full House votes to impeach Bill Clinton, then do you think it would be better for the country if Bill Clinton resigned from office, or not?"

The questions (asked in a *New York Times*/CBS News poll in mid-December) seem virtually identical. But the differences in results were stunning: Forty-three percent said the president should quit if the House sends "impeachment articles to the Senate" while 60 percent said he should quit if the House "votes to impeach."

What's going on here? Kagay says he doesn't know. Neither do I, but here's a guess: Perhaps "impeach" alone was taken as "found guilty" and the phrase "send impeachment articles to the Senate for a trial" suggests that the case isn't over. If only we could do another wording test. . . .

Language problems have challenged pollsters from the very start of the Monica Lewinsky scandal. Among the first: How to describe Monica herself? *The Washington Post*'s first survey questions referred to her as a "21-year-old intern at the White House," as did questions asked by other news organizations. But noting her age was potentially biasing. Highlighting her youthfulness conjured up visions of innocence and victimhood that appeared inconsistent with her apparently aggressive and explicitly amorous conduct with Clinton. In subsequent *Post* poll questions, she became a "former White House intern" of indeterminate age.

Then came the hard part: How to describe what she and Bill were accused of doing in a way that didn't offend, overly titillate or otherwise stampede people into one position or the other? In these early days, details about who did what to whom and where were sketchy but salacious. It clearly wasn't a classic adulterous love affair; love had apparently little to do with it, at least on Clinton's part. Nor was it a one-night stand. It seemed more like the overheated fantasy of a 16-year-old boy or the musings of the White House's favorite pornographer, *Penthouse* magazine publisher Larry Flynt. Piled on top of the sex were the more complex and less easily understood issues of perjury and obstruction of justice. After various iterations, we and other organizations settled on simply "the Lewinsky matter"—nice and neutral, leaving exactly what that meant to the imaginations (or memories) of survey respondents.

One thing is clear, at least in hindsight: Results of hypothetical questions—those that ask what if?—did not hold up in the past 12 months, said political scientist Michael Traugott of the University of Michigan. Last January, pollsters posed questions asking whether Clinton should resign or be impeached if he lied under oath about having an affair with Lewinsky. Clear majorities said he should quit or be impeached.

Fast forward to the eve of the impeachment vote. Nearly everybody believed Clinton had lied under oath about his relationship with Lewinsky, but now healthy majorities said he should not be impeached—a tribute, perhaps, to the White House strategy of drawing out (dare we say stonewalling?) the investigation to allow the public to get used to the idea that their president was a sleazy weasel.

Fortunately, pollsters had time to work out the kinks in question wording. Demand for polling produced a flood of questions of all shades and flavors, and good wording drove out the bad. At times, it seemed even to pollsters that there may be too many questions about the scandal, said Kathy Frankovic, director of surveys for CBS News. Through October [1998], more than 1,000 survey questions specifically mentioned Lewinsky's name—double the number of questions that have ever been asked about the Watergate scandal, Frankovic said.

Polling's new popularity has attracted a tonier class of critic. In the past, mostly assistant professors and aggrieved political operatives or their bosses trashed the public polls. Today, one of the fiercest critics of polling is syndicated columnist Arianna Huffington, the onetime Cambridge University debating champ, A-list socialite and New Age acolyte. A few weeks ago, Huffington revealed in her column that lots of people refuse to talk to pollsters, a problem that's not new (except, apparently, to Huffington).

Actually, I think Huffington has it backward. The real problem is that people are too willing to answer poll questions—dutifully responding to poll takers even if they don't really have an opinion or understand the question that has been asked.

A famous polling experiment illustrates the prevalence of pseudo-opinions: More than 20 years ago, a group of researchers at the University of Cincinnati asked a random sample of local residents whether the 1975 Public Affairs Act should be repealed. About half expressed a view one way or another.

Of course there never was a Public Affairs Act of 1975. Researchers made it up to see how willing people were to express opinions on things they knew absolutely nothing about.

I duplicated that experiment a few years ago in a national survey, and obtained about the same result: Forty-three percent expressed an opinion, with 24 percent saying it should be repealed and 19 percent saying it should not.

But enough about the problems. In hindsight, most experts say that the polls have held up remarkably well. Within a month of the first disclosure, the public moved quickly to this consensus, as captured by the polls: Clinton's a good president but a man of ghastly character who can stay in the White House—but stay away from my house, don't touch my daughter and don't pet the dog.

"It is so striking. The public figured this one out early on and stuck with it," said Thomas E. Mann, director of governmental studies at the Brookings Institution. "If anything, the only changes were these upward blips in support for Clinton in the face of some dramatic development that was certain to presage his collapse."

Mann and others argue that public opinion polls may never have played a more important role in American political life. "This last year illustrates the wisdom of George Gallup's optimism about the use of polls in democracy: to discipline the elites, to constrain the activists, to allow ordinary citizens to register sentiments on a matter of the greatest public importance," Mann said.

Well, hooray for us pollsters! Actually, there is evidence suggesting that all the attention in the past year may have improved the public's opinions of opinion polls and pollsters. And why shouldn't they? These polls have had something for everyone: While Democrats revel in Clinton's high job-approval ratings and otherwise bulletproof presidency, Republicans can point to the equally lopsided majority who think Clinton should be censured and formally reprimanded for his behavior.

A few weeks ago, as bombs fell in Baghdad and talk of impeachment roiled Washington, pollster Nancy Belden took a break from business to attend the annual holiday pageant at her 10-year-old son's school. As she left the auditorium, the steadfast Republican mother of one of her son's classmates approached Belden and clapped her on the shoulder. "Thank heavens for you pollsters," she said.

"I was stunned. I was delighted," Belden laughed. "I've spent many years being beat up on by people who complain that public opinion polling is somewhat thwarting the political process, as opposed to helping it. Suddenly, people are coming up to me at parties and saying thanks for doing what you do. What a relief!"

## DISCUSSION QUESTIONS

1. Morin presents striking differences in poll results when a word or a few words in a question are changed. Does this diminish the value of public opinion polls in the democratic process?

2. How might Morin respond to the arguments that George Gallup makes in "Polling the Public"?

3. Try to think of an example where subtly different wording might lead to very different polling results. Why do you think it would have that effect?

# 46

# "The Not-So-Swift Mainstream Media"

## Jonathan V. Last

*From the 1960s through the 1980s, when people thought of media and news, they thought of newspapers and, increasingly, the broadcast television networks. Cable news soon emerged to provide an alternative, but one that for the most part followed the same operating procedure as the big networks. Late in the 1980s, talk radio, which had been around for some time, boomed in popularity and hosts such as Rush Limbaugh became household words. Talk radio entertained, informed, and perhaps misinformed. Hosts gleefully tweaked the mainstream media and embraced a much more aggressive, hard-hitting style that was blatantly ideological and partisan. There was, in this new forum, no pretense to being objective but, talk-radio fans would argue, the mainstream media were also not objective—they just pretended to be. In the 1990s the Internet would provide more alternatives in the form of Web sites, chatrooms, and, in the early years of the twenty-first century, blogs. Jonathan Last contends that the new media have had a profound effect on the presentation of news in the United States. In particular, new media can force items onto the agenda of the old media. By hammering away at stories and insistently pursuing them, new-media outlets create enough of a buzz around a story that journalists in the traditional media feel obliged to pick up these stories themselves. What Last describes is a news world in which control over the agenda—over what gets defined as news and by whom—may be slipping out of the hands of the members of the traditional media.*

During the August 19 [2004] edition of PBS's *NewsHour*, Tom Oliphant unspooled. "The standard of clear and convincing evidence—and it's easy when you leave out the exculpatory stuff—is what keeps this story in the tabloids," the *Boston Globe* columnist sputtered, "because it does not meet basic standards." "This story" (shades of "that woman") is the story of the Swift boat veterans who have raised a number of troubling allegations against John Kerry. Sitting across from John O'Neill, co-author of *Unfit for Command* and John Kerry's successor as commander of PCF-94 in Vietnam, Oliphant did a fair imitation of Al Gore—sighing, harumphing, and exhaling loudly—whenever O'Neill spoke.

" 'Almost conclusive' doesn't cut it in the parts of journalism where I live," Oliphant lectured O'Neill, who graduated first in a class of 554 from the University of Texas Law School and clerked for U.S. Supreme

Court Justice William Rehnquist. "You haven't come within a country mile of meeting first-grade journalistic standards for accuracy." Watching the media's reaction to the Swift boat controversy, it's clear that many journalists agree with Oliphant.

Two days later, Adam Nagourney paused in the middle of a news story in the *New York Times* to worry about how campaigns should deal with attacks "in this era when so much unsubstantiated or even false information can reach the public through so many different forums, be it blogs or talk-show radio." In an article in *Editor & Publisher*, Alison Mitchell, the deputy national editor at the *Times*, admitted, "I'm not sure that in an era of no-cable television we would even have looked into [the Swift boat story]." James O'Shea, managing editor of the *Chicago Tribune*, went further: "There are too many places for people to get information. I don't think newspapers can be the gatekeepers anymore—to say this is wrong and we will ignore it. Now we have to say this is wrong and here is why."

There are many reasons why the mainstream media don't like the Swift boat story, but chief among them is that they've been strong-armed into covering it by the "new" media: talk-radio, cable television, and Internet blogs.

The Swift boat story first surfaced on May 4, when an op-ed by John O'Neill ran in the *Wall Street Journal*, in print and online, and the group Swift Boat Veterans for Truth, to which O'Neill belongs, held a press conference at the National Press Club in Washington, D.C. The event received scant notice by traditional media. CBS News mentioned it briefly and tried to tie the group to Bush. The *Washington Post* and *New York Times* had short items about it, as did the *Boston Globe*. The most in-depth coverage came from the Fox News Channel. On the May 4 edition of *Special Report*, Carl Cameron reported on the press conference, aired some of the Swifties' allegations, and then reported that certain of these veterans—Grant Hibbard and George Elliott—had previously supported John Kerry, immediately casting doubt on them.

The story went away for a while, but was always lurking in dark corners of the Internet, on websites like *KerryHaters.blogspot.com*. And clearly the big media weren't blind to it. "There are a few who served with him who dispute his record and question his leadership," Peter Jennings noted during an ABC News broadcast on July 29. "We'll hear from them in the weeks ahead," he continued, moving abruptly on to a pretaped package on Kerry's Vietnam heroism.

The next big break for the Swifties came on August 4, with the release of their first TV ad. Fox News covered the ad closely. The next night *Hannity & Colmes* featured members of the Swift boat group as well as veterans who supported Kerry.

That same day some print media outlets covered the ad buy, but not the substance of the ad's allegations. On television, only one broadcast network mentioned the spot: CBS spent two sentences on the "harsh" ad, in order to air John McCain's denunciation of it.

On August 6, NBC also reported on the "harsh" ad, but only as a way of segueing into a segment on "527 groups," independent political organizations funded with soft money. On MSNBC, Keith Olbermann mentioned O'Neill's forthcoming *Unfit for Command*. Since it's published by the conservative house Regnery, Olbermann reported, "you now bring in the whole mystical right-wing conspirary jazz." The night before, Olbermann had repeatedly referred to Swift Boat Veterans for Truth as "Swift Boat Veterans for Bush."

But the big news on August 6 was that Regnery allowed people to download the "Christmas in Cambodia" section of O'Neill's book. While Olbermann and others were worrying about mystical jazz, the new media swung into action. Hugh Hewitt, Glenn Reynolds, *Powerline*, and other bloggers immediately began investigating the book's allegations. The blog *JustOneMinute* was the first to find the 1986 "seared—seared" speech in which Kerry described his memory of being in Cambodia in December 1968. On August 8, Reynolds took his digital camera to the University of Tennessee law library and photographed the section of the Congressional Record with the Kerry speech, further verifying the chapter's central claim. That same weekend, Al Hunt talked about the Swift boat ad on CNN's *Capital Gang*, calling it "some of the sleaziest lies I've ever seen in politics."

Over the next 11 days, an interesting dynamic took hold: Talk-radio and the blog world covered the Cambodia story obsessively. They reported on border crossings during Vietnam and the differences between Swift boats and PBRs. They also found two other instances of Kerry's talking about his Christmas in Cambodia. Spurred on by the blogs, Fox led the August 9 *Special Report* with a Carl Cameron story on Kerry's Cambodia discrepancy.

All the while, traditional print and broadcast media tried hard to ignore the story—even as Kerry officially changed his position on his presence in Cambodia. Then on August 19, Kerry went public with his counter assault against Swift Boat Veterans for Truth, and suddenly the story was news. The numbers are fairly striking: Before August 19, the *New York Times* and *Washington Post* had each mentioned Swift Boat Veterans for Truth just 8 times; the *Los Angeles Times* 7 times; the *Boston Globe* 4 times. The broadcast networks did far less. According to the indefatigable Media Research Center, before Kerry went public, ABC, CBS, and NBC together had done a total of 9 stories on the Swifties. For comparison, as of August 19 these networks had done 75 stories on the accusation that Bush had been AWOL from the National Guard.

After Kerry, the deluge. On August 24, the *Washington Post* ran three op-eds and an editorial on the Swifties; other papers expanded their coverage as well. But, curiously, they didn't try to play catch-up with the new media in ascertaining the veracity of the Swifties' claims. Instead, they pursued (or rather, repeated) the charge Kerry made: that Bush was behind Swift Boat Veterans for Truth. It was a touch surreal—as it would have been if Democratic national chairman Terry McAuliffe's criticism of Bush's National Guard record had prompted the media to investigate Terry McAuliffe.

But even here, it seemed their hearts weren't in it. In *Time* magazine, Joe Klein called the whole affair "incendiary nonsense." As the *Los Angeles Times* observed in an editorial, "Whether the Bush campaign is tied to the Swift boat campaign in the technical, legal sense that triggers the wrath of the campaign-spending reform law is not a very interesting question." As last week wore on, the coverage continued to ignore the specifics of the allegations against Kerry and began to concentrate on the dangers of the new media. In the *New York Times*, Alessandra Stanley warned that in the seedy world of cable news, "facts, half-truths and passionately tendentious opinions get tumbled together on screen like laundry in an industrial dryer—without the softeners of fact-checking or reflection." It is perhaps impolite to note that it took the *Times* nearly four months to catch up with the reporting Carl Cameron did in the beginning of May.

Still, the baying of the *Times* and the rest of the old media is a sign of capitulation. Against their will, the best-funded and most prestigious journalists in America have been forced to cover a story they want no part of—or at the very least, they've been compelled to explain why they aren't covering it. How did this happen? Analyzing how the Swift boat veterans had injected their story into the mainstream media, Adam Nagourney blamed summer. The Swift boat ad buys, he wrote, had "become the subject of television news shows . . . because the advertisements and [*Unfit for Command*] were released in August, a slow month when news outlets are hungry for any kind of news."

But Nagourney has it exactly backwards: Even though it was August, network television and most cable news shows stayed away from the Swift boat story for as long as they possibly could.

Instead, James O'Shea is right. An informal network—the new media—has arisen that has the power to push stories into the old media. The combination of talk radio, a publishing house, blogs, and Fox News has given conservatives a voice independent of the old media.

It's unclear which of these was most critical for bringing the Swift boat story out into the open. Without *Unfit for Command*, the story would never have had a focal point with readily checkable facts. Talk radio kept the story alive on a daily basis. The blogs served as fact-checkers vetting the story, at least some aspects of it, for credibility and chewing it over enough so that producers and editors who read the blogs could approach it without worrying they were being snookered by black-helicopter nuts.

Despite all that, however, no other medium has the reach of television, which is still the only way to move a story from a relatively small audience of news-obsessives to the general public.

Yet the blogosphere has had a particular interest in taking credit for making the Swift boat story pop. Blogs from *Instapundit* to *The Belmont Club* to *Powerline* were reveling in the demise of the old media and heaping scorn upon professional journalists. "I have been both a lawyer/law professor for two decades and a television/radio/print journalist for 15 years of those 20," Hugh Hewitt blogged. "It takes a great deal more intelligence and discipline to be the former than to be the latter, which is why the former usually pays a lot more than the latter. It is no surprise to me, then, when lawyers/law professors like those at *Powerline* and *Instapundit* prove to be far more adept at exposing the 'Christmas-in-Cambodia' lie and other Kerry absurdities than old-school journalists."

John Hinderaker, one of the bloggers behind *Powerline*, summed up the mood of the blogosphere by comparing journalism with brain surgery: "A bunch of amateurs, no matter how smart and enthusiastic, could never outperform professional neurosurgeons, because they lack the specialized training and experience necessary for that field," he said. "But what qualifications, exactly, does it take to be a journalist? What can they do that we can't? Nothing."

## DISCUSSION QUESTIONS

1. As explained by Last, journalists in the traditional media complain that the new media operate without any strong standards of evidence, accuracy, or fair play. Do you agree with these journalists?

2. Do you believe that some part of the media should have the "gatekeeper" role identified by a managing editor in the article? What are the advantages and disadvantages for a democratic society if a part of the media plays that role?

3. Which part or parts of the news media—newspapers, television, Internet, blogs, radio—do you rely on most? Which would you say you trust the most?

## Debating the Issues: Is Objectivity in Media Desirable or Possible?

Although everyone has contact with the government nearly every day—attending a public school, driving on public roads, using government-regulated electricity, and so on—few citizens have direct contact with the policymaking process. Because of this distance between the public and policymakers, the behavior of intermediaries between the government and the governed is a significant issue in a democratic polity. The media, in particular the news media, are among the most significant of these intermediaries that tell the people what the government is doing and tell the government what the people want.

The central place of the media concerns political advocates from across the political spectrum. They believe that through priming (how the media define what is newsworthy) and framing (how the news is presented to us), the news media can significantly shape public opinion and, ultimately, public policy. To these observers, "media bias" is corrosive to American democracy. And, perhaps even of more immediate concern to these advocates, liberals worry that the media help conservative political causes while conservatives worry about the opposite.

These charges of bias in the media usually assume that something that can be considered "objective" journalism is possible. Is it? This debate provides three perspectives on that question. In his short article, Robert Bresler suggests that the media cannot be separated from the society in which it works. Contending that America is in the midst of a significant cultural division, he argues that it is inevitable that the media will reflect that split. Mainstream media was once centrist or conservative, he notes, but has now become liberal, and this has spawned the rise of alternative media outlets that tend to be conservative. To Brent Cunningham, the pursuit of objectivity has led to problems for the news media. In particular, he argues that the media often miss stories or allow misleading statements to be broadcast without challenge because of a desire to be seen as treating any statement as potentially valid and not choosing sides. Reporters become "passive recipients of news, rather than aggressive analyzers and explainers of it." Journalists have become so sensitive to charges of bias, he believes, that they follow notions of "balance" that can mean little more than allowing misleading statements on one side of an issue to be balanced with misleading statements on another side, without comment or qualification. Cunningham does believe the pursuit of objectivity has some benefits, but he sees many costs as well. He asserts that reporters and editors should be less concerned with whether a story "is tendentious, but whether it is true." Howard Myrick defines objectivity as "expressing or dealing with facts or conditions as perceived without distortion by personal feelings, prejudices, or interpretations." Myrick asks whether objectivity in news reporting is possible and, if so, whether we as news consumers should reasonably expect reporting to be objective. He notes that objectivity faces many challenges, including the nature of the human mind, the desire to support one's community, and the lure of financial or other gain. Despite this, Myrick posits that "the pursuit of objectivity—however elusive—[is] not only worthwhile, but indispensable . . . It is a goal well worth pursuing, for the good of the profession of journalism and, more importantly, the good of the nation."

# 47

# "Media Bias and the Culture Wars"

## Robert J. Bresler

It is hard to separate our understanding of the media from the larger culture. Just as the cultural landscape has been altered over the past several decades, so has the media—its quality and its politics. This cannot be otherwise. Is the media biased against conservatives and against the left (as opposed to mainstream liberals)? No doubt, but I would not overestimate its impact on public opinion or the direction of the country's politics.

From the 1930s to the 1960s, when liberalism was the dominant ideology and the Democratic Party ruled government, liberals did not have the influence on the media they have today. In those years, *Time* magazine was run by Henry Luce, a feisty conservative, although no reactionary. *Newsweek* was so bland and careful that its politics were hardly discernable. *U.S. News & World Report*, under the iron rule of conservative editor-publisher David Lawrence, was characterized by its easy-to-read economic reporting—complete with many charts and graphs that basically served the businessman who could not take the time to wade through the *Wall Street Journal*. The *New York Times* was the good gray lady, understated, bland, slightly right of center, and regarded as the paper of record for its accuracy and coverage. The *Los Angeles Times* was run by the Chandler Family and was chummy with the California Republican establishment. The *New York Herald Tribune* was just as chummy with the New York Republican establishment. The editors of the *Washington Post*, slightly more liberal than the other newspapers, were very close with the Kennedys. The *Chicago Tribune*, meanwhile, was the voice of irascible midwestern conservatism, excoriating the New Deal and the Roosevelts.

Routinely, most of the local newspaper editorial boards endorsed the Republican candidate for president, although voters paid little attention. The television news networks—with their 15-minute encapsulated news programs—seemed to lack any point of view. Edward R. Murrow's famous attack on Joe McCarthy in 1954 was a dramatic exception and harbinger of things to come. The major columnists—James Reston, Walter Lippmann, Arthur Krock, the Alsop Brothers, Marquis Childs, and Doris Fleeson—hovered around the center. The newspapers in the Scripps-Howard and Hearst chains certainly were conservative. Most reporters did not come out of elite colleges and liberal journalism schools. Communications hardly was a recognized major at most universities. Reporters, largely male, were known as a hard-drinking, cynical, tough, and not particularly ideological lot.

Most of the commentators in the days before talk radio—Alastair Cooke, Erwin E. Canham, Eric Sevareid, and Murrow—reflected a kind of centrism with their five–15 minute commentaries. There were Paul Harvey and Fulton Lewis on the right and Edward Morgan on the left, but they were the exceptions. The opinion programs on radio and television such as "American Forum of the Air" and "Author Meets the Critics" often were disputatious. Nonetheless, they were marked by a degree of civility.

The common consensus and culture that created this type of media long has disappeared. Many locally owned and operated newspapers have been bought out by large chains. The great conservative media moguls—Luce, McCormick, Hearst, and Lawrence—are gone; only Rupert Murdoch still fits that bill. The politics and the culture of *Time*, *Newsweek*, and *U.S. News* have changed dramatically. The *New York Times* is hardly the gray lady of the past; the *Washington Post*, *Philadelphia Inquirer*, and *L.A. Times* now are routinely liberal; most newspaper columnists are predictably liberal or conservative; and few bother with reportage, that combination of reporting and commentary. (Robert Novak is an exception.)

The line between news programs and entertainment on radio and television often is blurred beyond recognition as the sensational, lurid, and controversial push out any sustained focus on complex issues. Since Watergate, the Washington press corps, hunting for scandals and the sensational, has moved to a far more contentious attitude toward the White House and Congress. It is hard to believe that the public is starved for opinion. Cable television and talk radio seem to give us nothing but when we need thorough, disinterested reporting and analysis. Almost everybody in the media has chosen sides in these tiresome culture wars. If you look at the major magazines such as *Vanity Fair*, *New Yorker*, *Atlantic Monthly*, and *Harper's*, they all reflect a distinctive liberal perspective. If you add to that the liberal bias of many of the major foundations, college and university faculties, and most of the publishing houses, you have clear liberal domination of much of what we call elite media. Given this state of affairs, it should come as no surprise that conservative talk radio has filled a particular need. It has taken the place of old right-leaning newspaper dailies as an outlet for conservative opinion.

When you have such a profound cultural division in the country, it is hard to find those who are above the fray. Cultural differences are, in fact, far more profound than political differences. Whether one is culturally liberal or conservative defines the way you see the world, your basic values. People seem to choose up sides, especially those in the world of communications—be it media or academia. This is most unfortunate. For example, it is hard to find an intelligent columnist or commentator whose views or conclusions on a particular issue cannot be predicted. The public needs a calm, intelligent discussion of issues where the participants recognize the complexity of a topic and help listeners and readers work through it. Too often, the so-called experts on TV are paid political consultants or spokesmen for the various ideological think tanks that populate Washington, D.C.

Until we have a truce or respite in the cultural wars, the media is more likely to reflect this division and contention. Unfortunately for the citizenry, this does appear to be in the wind. The cleavage seems to get deeper. In a democracy, people often get the government they deserve; they also get the media they deserve.

## 48

# "The Search for Objectivity in Journalism"

## HOWARD A. MYRICK

The definition of the word "objectivity"—expressing or dealing with facts or conditions as perceived without distortion by personal feelings, prejudices, or interpretations—is so clear and uncomplicated that to begin this article with it would seem at first glance to be gratuitous or, worse, superfluous. On closer examination, objectivity is easier to define than it is to attain in practice. Were that not the case, there would not be the unending allegations of biased reporting leveled at the news media. As any newspaper editor or broadcast news director will attest—and a reading of letters to the editor will confirm—the news media, industry and its individual practitioners (i.e., journalists and television news anchors) are assailed constantly with complaints regarding distortion, bias, and lack of objectivity.

Complaints about the lack of objectivity in the electronic media are as frequent, if not more so, than in the print media. Comparisons between print and electronic media aside, the net result is a loss of confidence on the part of the news-consuming public in what is reported to them. Since the Sept. 11 terrorist attacks on the U.S., such concerns about objective reporting have taken on a new level of importance, both with regard to the assuaging of personal fears and about the implications the availability of reliable information can have on the participation of the nation's citizens in the formulation of important decisions facing the government. Public participation in the affairs of state at this juncture in the country's response to these cataclysmic events is becoming increasingly important as various people and organizations (including "political watch" groups, individual politicians, and Congress) question the effectiveness, appropriateness, and legality of some of the government's actions in the war against terrorism.

To avoid the easy temptation to engage in media bashing myself, and for the sake of objectivity, this article is begun without accepting at face value damning accusations against the news media. Moreover, the subject of objectivity in the news media deserves, itself, to be analyzed with as much objectivity as is humanly possible. Emphasis on the word "humanly" is deliberate and essential, for (returning to the definition of "objectivity") it is clear that it is the interposition of the human element in the business of perceiving, processing, and interpreting information through the prism of personal feelings and, yes, prejudices that determines objectivity.

A viable starting point is the posing of a pair of questions: Is the achievement of objectivity in news reporting even possible, and is the expectation of objectivity on the part of the news-consuming public a reasonable one? These are questions that must be asked if we accept that journalists' intervening prism of perception and, ultimately, reporting is the product of the sum total of all of their prior experiences, socialization, beliefs, and indoctrination—in brief, their culture, augmented by race, ethnicity, sex, and myriad other intervening variables.

In the words of communications scholar Ben Bagdikian (in his seminal book, *The Media Monopoly*), "News, like all human observations, is not truly objective. . . . Human scenes described by different individuals are seen with differences." The differences to which Bagdikian and other similarly disposed scholars refer are not only the variables cited above, but numerous others falling under the heading of psychosocial and behavioral factors conditioned by mankind's proclivity to receive, process, and respond to stimuli (and information) selectively and not in a one-to-one, immutable way from one person to another.

Walter Lippmann, the dean emeritus of every school of journalism, provided exceedingly incisive insight into the "asymmetrical relationship of fact and the presentation of fact" (to use the terminology of D. Steven Blum in his book, *Walter Lippmann, Cosmopolitanism in the Century of Total War*). Lippmann is credited with concluding that "the mechanism of human perception itself was a prime culprit in the distortion of information . . . Mechanisms of obfuscation operate within the mind as well as without, and perception was made as problematic by the tricks one's own mind played on itself as by the willful contrivance of others."

Lippmann's conclusion points out a kind of double bind that both the news provider and news consumer face. On one hand, journalists, irrespective of their commitment to the pursuit of objectivity, are likely to have their reportage attenuated or skewed by the inherent psychological function of their own minds and by the "willful contrivance of others" —e.g., editors, news directors, "spinmeisters," et al. Finally, news consumers, policymakers, and the electorate all fall prey to the consequences of distorted journalism.

The psychosocial phenomenon expostulated by Lippmann is exacerbated when the subject matter of the reportage is itself sensitive and/or emotionally charged. In America, for example, race is such a subject, even as the nation moves inexorably to the highest level of racial and ethnic diversity in history. As journalist, author, and media critic Ellis Cose observed in *The Media in Black and White*, "For reporters, race can be a treacherous subject, raising questions that go to the heart of the journalist's craft." Cose comments, "Is objectivity (or, even fairness) possible when dealing with people from different racial groups and cultural backgrounds?" After all, he continues, "perceptions vary radically as a function of the very different experiences members of various racial groups have endured."

Directing the attention of journalists to the fact of their inescapable susceptibility to the phenomenon of selective perception—and thus their chance of failing to meet the requisite standards of objectivity—is not a cause for self-flagellation or becoming paranoically defensive when confronted with evidence of their failure. In many instances, in fact, it would be sufficient, instructive, and healthy for them simply to imagine their interviewee or information source reciting the adage, "I know you believe you understand what you think I said, but I am not sure you realize that what you heard is not what I meant." The willingness on the part of the journalist or newscaster to accept the wisdom of this adage could prevent further errors of distortion, bias, and various other injuries to objectivity in their reporting.

I hasten to emphasize that to accord some degree of latitude to the journalist in this connection is not to condone transgressions. Also, it is not to engage in what philosopher C.P. Snow refers to as the "intricate defense of the status quo"—that is, to provide an excuse to practice sloppy and irresponsible journalism without regard for the critical need to rid the profession of the mounting number of egregious infractions committed in the name of press freedom and First Amendment rights. Rather, this is but the first of several recommendations I would offer to whomever is privileged to work in the profession of journalism, print and electronic.

To broadcast journalists, for example, who rely on the use of video clips from syndicated news services and/or their own electronic news gathering and field production units—a common and unavoidable practice in the fast-paced world of broadcast journalism—it would serve them well to be reminded that failure to analyze the "word" (the narrative) without paying close attention to the "picture" (the visual) can lead to some grievous distortions or misinterpretations. The picture (video) is an iconic code or stream of iconic codes exceedingly subject to variable interpretation, as has been found in research in culture and visual perception.

The term "iconic" in an audiovisual context refers to meaning embedded in the visual or pictographic component of an audiovisual communication or message. It includes, importantly, what can/may be vital nonverbal cues or messages. Facial expressions and other body language cues, for instance, can be highly communicative, often serving to clarify the depth of affective (feeling) components of a message or interview.

It may be argued that asking journalists to engage in such analysis invites them into the realm of even greater subjectivity. In responding to such arguments or fears, suffice it to say that the truly experienced journalists—those who are willing to go to the greatest lengths in pursuit of truth and objectivity—have worked at honing their skills (or have achieved facility) in polyphasic perception and analysis, to the ultimate benefit of the product of the practice of their craft.

## Post–Sept. 11 Reflection

At the time of this writing (coinciding almost to the day with the first-year anniversary of the terrorist attacks on the World Trade Center and Pentagon), reflection on the quality, importance, and role of the news media in society could not be more timely. The public's interest in this horrific story remains high, due to the cataclysmic nature of the events, in terms of the thousands of lives lost, the millions in property damages, and the sheer psychic shock suffered by a population that still has not come to terms with the catastrophe and what it portends for the future. Interest remains high as well because of the continued focus of the mass media, not at all surprising, given the convergence of Americans' appetite—indeed, manifested need—for information that might assuage their sense of disequilibrium and the media industry's insatiable need for content to fill their program schedules and the blank pages of newsprint paper that also carry, indispensably, the advertisements their profits depend on.

What is notable, if not surprising, about the media-sustained public interest is the fact that the media (especially television) have not only set the public's news-consuming agenda—that is, determining what subjects the public thinks about, but also, in large measure, how the public thinks about, for example, Muslims, Arabs, and even Arab-Americans. Indeed, until most recently, the news media industry has been a near-collaborator in fomenting a fundamental agreement between the public and the Federal government in determining what the nation's response to the threat of terrorism should be and who the perpetrators are.

An admittedly anecdotal, but telling, manifestation of the electronic media's unabashed expression of its sentiments on the government's war against terrorism is the wearing on camera of miniature American flags as lapel pins—a symbol of national pride, if not necessarily of support of national policies. Arguably, the wearing of a miniature flag should not be a cause for concern or be regarded as inappropriate in a society that espouses the virtues of free speech, especially in a time of national suffering and pain. There is the fact, though, especially since Pres. Bush's "Axis of Evil" speech and his apparent "go it alone" attitude concerning launching a preemptive military strike against Iraq, lively and important public debate and some serious anti-Administration criticism have surfaced involving different branches of the government and by influential and ordinary citizens. It would seem, therefore, that the cause of objectivity in the news is not well-served by this gesture on the part of some television journalists.

It would be a missed opportunity and, indeed, an error on my part if I failed to acknowledge my emotional reaction to the tenor of the times—i.e., the public's persisting anger over the events of Sept. 11, deployment of the nation's military forces in search of redress against the enemy and reclamation of national pride, and desire of no one to be guilty of harboring or displaying unpatriotic sentiments. These are all developments that have had a chilling effect on this author's willingness to attempt to be objective. The same feelings of restraint must influence more than a few journalists who would not like to find themselves in a widely discordant position with the prevailing sentiments of their viewers, listeners, and/ or readers. The implications of these considerations on objectivity in the news are obvious, for journalists, too, are citizens, members of communities and political parties, and connected with numerous other affiliations that can have influence on their beliefs and perceptions.

*Vagaries and Temptations*

Having dealt with the psychosocial and problematic nature of the mechanisms of the human mind and their impact on objectivity in reporting the news, the point must be made that there is no intent on my part to give short shrift to the "willful contrivances of others" or the willful contrivances of journalists themselves in distorting the news—or what passes as news. As with all humans, journalists are susceptible to the vagaries and temptations of the material world. There are editors and publishers to please if one is to keep one's job. Editors, publishers, news directors, station managers, and owners, in turn, are not impervious to the influence of politicians and business interests.

News organizations—print and electronic (though they often are one and the same in the current deregulated media industry)—are first and foremost businesses. The notion that such organizations exist to provide news and public service is one that still too frequently is espoused in classrooms in journalism schools. The abject and uncomfortable truth is that the profit incentive is the force that guides the daily activities of news organizations. The reality of the profit motive and its impact on the character, quality, and, especially, objectivity in the news is inescapable—and usually negative. As noted by Michael Schudson in *Discovering the News*, "Objectivity is a peculiar demand to make of institutions which, as businesses . . . are dedicated first of all to economic survival. It is a peculiar demand to make of institutions which, often by tradition or explicit credo, are political organs. It is a peculiar demand to make of editors and reporters who have none of the professional apparatus which for doctors or lawyers or scientists is supposed to guarantee objectivity."

As the nation—indeed, the world—watches the current implosion of the telecommunications industry, brought on in part by bigness, mergermania, and the volatility of the market forces unleashed by near-unbridled deregulation, the struggle for survival intensifies. What is becoming increasingly evident is the fact that, like all entities whose survival and profits are threatened, the media industries will do whatever it takes to stay afloat—although staying afloat in their milieu does not mean simply paying the rent and making a modest profit, but paying exorbitant wages to media "stars" granting astronomical salaries and stock options to executives, and engaging in business practices which often cross the line into the realm of criminal conduct.

The loser in this equation is the news media-dependent public and, by extension, the nation. Referring to the Jeffersonian vision of the role of the press in a free society, it is not outlandish to subscribe to the proposed remedy of Lawrence K. Grossman, former head of NBC News and president of PBS, who concludes in *The Electronic Republic: Reshaping Democracy in the Information Age* that the way to "discourage inaccuracies and encourage more responsible reporting is to make the press pay for its own mistakes that unfairly damage reputations, even if the victims are government officials or public figures." In Grossman's view, the rise of "utterly irresponsible, scandal-driven, sensationalist tabloid and television press" is totally unacceptable since, among other injuries, it inhibits

citizens' ability to "make sound and reasoned judgments," thus nega-
tively affecting the functioning of participatory government . . . in a government "of the people, by the people and for the people."

After consideration of all the obstacles which stand in the way of
achieving objectivity in the news, one's response might be like that of a
participant in a debate (actually, in response to my testimony in a legal
deposition involving alleged libel and defamation). The participant, the
deposing attorney, raised his arms in feigned despair and demanded ve-
hemently, "If this is the way journalists are to be criticized, why not just
shut down all the newspapers?" This was not just lawyer histrionics.
Rather, it was a case of one person strenuously suggesting that objectivity
is an unattainable goal. Therefore, why not forget about it?

Trying not to be dismissive, I set about trying to explain why the pursuit of objectivity—however elusive—was not only worthwhile, but indispensable. Conceding that often the case is not patently clear and that
journalists sometimes make honest mistakes, but, to the extent that they
move in a positive direction on the continuum from speculation, innu-
endo, yielding to extraneous pressures, and the sloppiness of depending
on press releases and staged press conferences which too frequently are
designed to manipulate public opinion rather than inform, to that extent
they will be regarded as responsible journalists. When they reach the
point on the continuum that is defined by accuracy, integrity, and honesty, to that extent the prerequisites of objectivity will be achieved. It is a
goal well worth pursuing, for the good of the profession of journalism
and, more importantly, the good of the nation.

# 49

# "Rethinking Objective Journalism"

## BRENT CUNNINGHAM

In his Mar. 6 press conference, in which he laid out his reasons for
the coming war, President Bush mentioned al Qaeda or the attacks of
Sept. 11 fourteen times in fifty-two minutes. No one challenged him on it,
despite the fact that the CIA had questioned the Iraq-al Qaeda connection, and that there has never been solid evidence marshaled to support
the idea that Iraq was involved in the attacks of 9/11.

When Bush proposed his $726 billion tax cut in January, his sales pitch
on the plan's centerpiece—undoing the "double-taxation" on dividend

earnings—was that "It's unfair to tax money twice." Over the next two months, the tax plan was picked over in hundreds of articles and broadcasts, yet a Nexis database search turned up few news stories (notably, one by Donald Barlett and James Steele in *Time* on Jan. 27, and another by Daniel Altman in the business section of *The New York Times* on Jan. 21) that explained in detail what was misleading about the president's pitch: in fact, there is plenty of income that is doubly, triply, or even quadruply taxed; and these other taxes affect many more people than the sliver who would benefit from the dividend tax cut.

Before the fighting started in Iraq, in the dozens of articles and broadcasts that addressed the potential aftermath of a war, much was written and said about the maneuverings of the Iraqi exile community, the shape of a postwar government, and the cost and duration and troop numbers. Important subjects all. But few of those stories, dating from late last summer, delved deeply into the numerous and plausible complications of the aftermath.

That all changed on Feb. 26, when President Bush spoke grandly of making Iraq a model for retooling the entire Middle East. After Bush's speech, "aftermath" articles began to flow like the waters of the Tigris—including cover stories in *Time* and *The New York Times Magazine*—culminating in *The Wall Street Journal*'s page-one story on Mar. 17, just days before the first cruise missiles rained down on Baghdad. The article revealed how the administration planned to hand the multibillion-dollar job of rebuilding Iraq to U.S. corporations. It was as if the subject of the war's aftermath was more or less off the table until the president put it there himself.

There is no single explanation for these holes in the coverage, but I would argue that our devotion to what we call "objectivity" played a role. It's true that the Bush administration is like a clenched fist with information, one that won't hesitate to hit back when pressed. And that reporting on the possible aftermath of a war before the war occurs, in particular, was a difficult and speculative story.

Yet these three examples—which happen to involve the current White House, although every White House spins stories—provide a window into a particular failure of the press: allowing the principle of objectivity to make us passive recipients of news, rather than aggressive analyzers and explainers of it. We all learned about objectivity in school or at our first job. Along with its twin sentries "fairness" and "balance," it defined journalistic standards.

Or did it? Ask ten journalists what objectivity means and you'll get ten different answers. Some, like the *Washington Post*'s editor, Leonard Downie, define it so strictly that they refuse to vote lest they be forced to take sides. My favorite definition was from Michael Bugeja, who teaches journalism at Iowa State: "Objectivity is seeing the world as it is, not how you wish it were." In 1996, the Society of Professional Journalists acknowledged this dilemma and dropped "objectivity" from its ethics code. It also changed "the truth" to simply "truth."

### Tripping Toward the Truth

As E. J. Dionne wrote in his 1996 book, *They Only Look Dead*, the press operates under a number of conflicting diktats: be neutral yet investigative; be disengaged but have an impact; be fair-minded but have an edge. Therein lies the nut of our tortured relationship with objectivity. Few would argue that complete objectivity is possible, yet we bristle when someone suggests we aren't being objective—or fair, or balanced—as if everyone agrees on what these words all mean.

Over the last dozen years a cottage industry of bias police has sprung up to exploit this fissure in the journalistic psyche, with talk radio leading the way followed by Shout TV and books like Ann Coulter's *Slander* and Bernard Goldberg's *Bias*. Now the left has begun firing back with Eric Alterman's book *What Liberal Media?* and a group of wealthy Democrats' plans for a liberal radio network. James Carey, a journalism scholar at Columbia, points out that we are entering a new age of partisanship.

One result is a hypersensitivity among the press to charges of bias, and it shows up everywhere: In Oct. 2001, with the war in Afghanistan under way, then CNN chairman Walter Isaacson sent a memo to his foreign correspondents telling them to "balance" reports of Afghan "casualties or hardship" with reminders to viewers that this was, after all, in response to the terrorist attacks of Sept. 11. More recently, a CJR intern, calling newspaper letters-page editors to learn whether reader letters were running for or against the looming war in Iraq, was told by the letters editor at *The Tennessean* that letters were running 70 percent against the war, but that the editors were trying to run as many prowar letters as possible lest they be accused of bias.

Objectivity has persisted for some valid reasons, the most important being that nothing better has replaced it. And plenty of good journalists believe in it, at least as a necessary goal. Objectivity, or the pursuit of it, separates us from the unbridled partisanship found in much of the European press. It helps us make decisions quickly—we are disinterested observers after all—and it protects us from the consequences of what we write. We'd like to think it buoys our embattled credibility, though the deafening silence of many victims of Jayson Blair's fabrications would argue otherwise. And as we descend into this new age of partisanship, our readers need, more than ever, reliable reporting that tells them what is true when that is knowable, and pushes as close to truth as possible when it is not.

But our pursuit of objectivity can trip us up on the way to "truth." Objectivity excuses lazy reporting. If you're on deadline and all you have is "both sides of the story," that's often good enough. It's not that such stories laying out the parameters of a debate have no value for readers, but too often, in our obsession with, as *The Washington Post*'s Bob Woodward puts it, "the latest," we fail to push the story, incrementally, toward a deeper understanding of what is true and what is false. Steven R. Weisman, the chief diplomatic correspondent for *The New York Times* and a believer in the goal of objectivity ("even though we fall short of the ideal every day"), concedes that he felt obliged to dig more when he was an editorial writer, and did not have to be objective. "If you have to decide who is right, then you must do more reporting," he says. "I pressed the reporting further because I didn't have the luxury of saying X says this and Y says this and you, dear reader, can decide who is right."

It exacerbates our tendency to rely on official sources, which is the easiest, quickest way to get both the "he said" and the "she said," and, thus, "balance." According to numbers from the media analyst Andrew Tyndall, of the 414 stories on Iraq broadcast on NBC, ABC, and CBS from last September to February, all but thirty-four originated at the White House, Pentagon, and State Department. So we end up with too much of the "official" truth.

More important, objectivity makes us wary of seeming to argue with the president—or the governor, or the CEO—and risk losing our access. Jonathan Weisman, an economics reporter for *The Washington Post*, says this about the fear of losing access: "If you are perceived as having a political bias, or a slant, you're screwed."

Finally, objectivity makes reporters hesitant to inject issues into the news that aren't already out there. "News is driven by the zeitgeist," says Jonathan Weisman, "and if an issue isn't part of the current zeitgeist then it will be a tough sell to editors." But who drives the zeitgeist, in Washington at least? The administration. In short, the press's awkward embrace of an impossible ideal limits its ability to help set the agenda.

This is not a call to scrap objectivity, but rather a search for a better way of thinking about it, a way that is less restrictive and more grounded in reality. As Eric Black, a reporter at the *Minneapolis Star Tribune*, says, "We need a way to both do our job and defend it."

*An Ideal's Troubled Past*

American journalism's honeymoon with objectivity has been brief. The press began to embrace objectivity in the middle of the nineteenth century, as society turned away from religion and toward science and empiricism to explain the world. But in his 1998 book, *Just the Facts*, a history of the origins of objectivity in U.S. journalism, David Mindich argues that by the turn of the twentieth century, the flaws of objective journalism were beginning to show. Mindich shows how "objective" coverage of lynching in the 1890s by the *New York Times* and other papers created a false balance on the issue and failed "to recognize a truth, that African-Americans were being terrorized across the nation."

After World War I, the rise of public relations and the legacy of wartime propaganda—in which journalists such as Walter Lippman had played key roles—began to undermine reporters' faith in facts. The war, the Depression, and Roosevelt's New Deal raised complex issues that defied journalism's attempt to distill them into simple truths. As a result, the use of bylines increased (an early nod to the fact that news is touched by human frailty), the political columnist crawled from the primordial soup, and the idea of "interpretive reporting" emerged. Still, as Michael Schudson argued in his 1978 book, *Discovering the News*, journalism clung to objectivity as the faithful cling to religion, for guidance in an uncertain world. He wrote: "From the beginning, then, criticism of the 'myth' of objectivity has accompanied its enunciation . . . Journalists came to believe in objectivity, to the extent that they did, because they wanted to, needed to, were forced by ordinary human aspiration to seek escape from their own deep convictions of doubt and drift."

By the 1960s, objectivity was again under fire, this time to more fundamental and lasting effect. Straight, "objective" coverage of McCarthyism a decade earlier had failed the public, leading Alan Barth, an editorial writer at *The Washington Post*, to tell a 1952 gathering of the Association for Education in Journalism: "There can be little doubt that the way [Senator Joseph McCarthy's charges] have been reported in most papers serves Senator McCarthy's partisan political purposes much more than it serves the purposes of the press, the interest of truth." Government lies about the U2 spy flights, the Cuban missile crisis, and the Vietnam War all cast doubt on the ability of "objective" journalism to get at anything close to the truth. The New Journalism of Tom Wolfe and Norman Mailer was in part a reaction to what many saw as the failings of mainstream reporting. In Vietnam, many of the beat reporters who arrived believing in objectivity eventually realized, if they stayed long enough, that such an approach wasn't sufficient. Says John Laurence, a former CBS News correspondent, about his years covering Vietnam: "Because the war went on for so long and so much evidence accumulated to suggest it was a losing cause, and that in the process we were destroying the Vietnamese and ourselves, I felt I had a moral obligation to report my views as much as the facts."

As a result of all these things, American journalism changed. "Vietnam and Watergate destroyed what I think was a genuine sense that our officials knew more than we did and acted in good faith," says Anthony Lewis, the former *New York Times* reporter and columnist. We became more sophisticated in our understanding of the limits of objectivity. And indeed, the parameters of modern journalistic objectivity allow reporters quite a bit of leeway to analyze, explain, and put news in context, thereby helping guide readers and viewers through the flood of information.

Still, nothing replaced objectivity as journalism's dominant professional norm. Some 75 percent of journalists and news executives in a 1999 Pew Research Center survey said it was possible to obtain a true, accurate, and widely agreed-upon account of an event. More than two-thirds thought it feasible to develop "a systematic method to cover events in a disinterested and fair way." The survey also offered another glimpse of the objectivity fissure: more than two-thirds of the print press in the Pew survey also said that "providing an interpretation of the news is a core principle," while less than half of those in television news agreed with that.

*The More Things Change*

If objectivity's philosophical hold on journalism has eased a bit since the 1960s, a number of other developments have bound us more tightly to the objective ideal and simultaneously exacerbated its shortcomings. Not only are journalists operating under conflicting orders, as E. J. Dionne argued, but their corporate owners don't exactly trumpet the need to rankle the status quo. It is perhaps important to note that one of the original forces behind the shift to objectivity in the nineteenth century was economic. To appeal to as broad an audience as possible, first the penny press and later the new wire services gradually stripped news of "partisan" context. Today's owners have squeezed the newshole, leaving less space for context and analysis.

If space is a problem, time is an even greater one. The nonstop news cycle leaves reporters less time to dig, and encourages reliance on official sources who can provide the information quickly and succinctly. "We are slaves to the incremental daily development," says one White House correspondent, "but you are perceived as having a bias if you don't cover it." This lack of time makes a simpleminded and lazy version of objectivity all the more tempting. In *The American Prospect* of Nov. 6, 2000, Chris Mooney wrote about how "e-spin," a relentless diet of canned attacks and counterattacks e-mailed from the Bush and Gore campaigns to reporters, was winding up, virtually unedited, in news stories. "Lazy reporters may be seduced by the ease of readily provided research," Mooney wrote. "That's not a new problem, except that the prevalence of electronic communication has made it easier to be lazy."

Meanwhile, the Internet and cable news's Shout TV, which drive the nonstop news cycle, have also elevated the appeal of "attitude" in the news, making the balanced, measured report seem anachronistic. In the January/February issue of CJR, young journalists asked to create their dream newspaper wanted more point-of-view writing in news columns. They got a heavy dose of it during the second gulf war, with news "anchors" like Fox's Neil Cavuto saying of those who opposed the war, "You were sickening then; you are sickening now."

Perhaps most ominous of all, public relations, whose birth early in the twentieth century rattled the world of objective journalism, has matured into a spin monster so ubiquitous that nearly every word a reporter hears from an official source has been shaped and polished to proper effect. Consider the memo from the Republican strategist Frank Luntz, as described in a Mar. 2 *New York Times* story, that urged the party—and President Bush—to soften their language on the environment to appeal to suburban voters. "Climate change" instead of "global warming," "conservationist" rather than "environmentalist." To the extent that the threat of being accused of bias inhibits reporters from cutting through this kind of manipulation, challenging it, and telling readers about it, then journalism's dominant professional norm needs a new set of instructions.

\* \* \*

*To Fill the Void*

\* \* \*

In November, James Fallows wrote a cover story for *The Atlantic Monthly* entitled "The Fifty-First State? The Inevitable Aftermath of Victory in Iraq." In it, with the help of regional experts, historians, and retired military officers, he gamed out just how difficult the aftermath could be. Among the scenarios he explored: the financial and logistical complications caused by the destruction of Baghdad's infrastructure; the possibility that Saddam Hussein would escape and join Osama bin Laden on the Most Wanted list; how the dearth of Arabic speakers in the U.S. government would hinder peacekeeping and other aftermath operations; how the need for the U.S., as the occupying power, to secure Iraq's borders would bring it face to face with Iran, another spoke in the "axis of evil"; the complications of working with the United Nations after it refused to support the war; what to do about the Iraqi debt from, among other things, UN-imposed reparations after the first gulf war, which some estimates put as high as $400 billion.

Much of this speculation has since come to pass and is bedeviling the U.S.'s attempt to stabilize—let alone democratize—Iraq. So are some other post-war realities that were either too speculative or too hypothetical to be given much air in the prewar debate. Looting, for instance, and general lawlessness. The fruitless (thus far) search for weapons of mass destruction. The inability to quickly restore power and clean water. A decimated health-care system. The difficulty of establishing an interim Iraqi government, and the confusion over who exactly should run things in the meantime. The understandably shallow reservoir of patience among the long-suffering Iraqis. The hidden clause in Halliburton's contract to repair Iraq's oil wells that also, by the way, granted it control of production and distribution, despite the administration's assurances that the Iraqis would run their own oil industry.

In the rush to war, how many Americans even heard about some of these possibilities? Of the 574 stories about Iraq that aired on NBC, ABC, and CBS evening news broadcasts between Sept. 12 (when Bush addressed the UN) and Mar. 7 (a week and a half before the war began), only twelve dealt primarily with the potential aftermath, according to Andrew Tyndall's numbers.

The Republicans were saying only what was convenient, thus the "he said." The Democratic leadership was saying little, so there was no "she said." "Journalists are never going to fill the vacuum left by a weak political opposition," says *The New York Times*'s Steven R. Weisman. But why not? If something important is being ignored, doesn't the press have an obligation to force our elected officials to address it? We have the ability, even on considerably less important matters than war and nation-building. Think of the dozens of articles *The New York Times* published between Jul. 10, 2002, and Mar. 31 about the Augusta National Country Club's exclusion of women members, including the one from Nov. 25 that carried the headline "CBS Staying Silent in Debate on Women Joining Augusta." Why couldn't there have been headlines last fall that read: "Bush Still Mum on Aftermath," or "Beyond Saddam: What Could Go Right, and What Could Go Wrong?" And while you're at it, consider the criticism the *Times*'s mini-crusade on Augusta engendered in the media world, as though an editor's passion for an issue never drives coverage.

This is not inconsequential nitpicking. *The New Yorker*'s editor, David Remnick, who has written in support of going to war with Iraq, wrote of the aftermath in the Mar. 31 issue: "An American presence in Baghdad will carry with it risks and responsibilities that will shape the future of the United States in the world." The press not only could have prepared the nation and its leadership for the aftermath we are now witnessing, but should have.

\*    \*    \*

*Toward a Better Definition of Objectivity*

In the last two years, Archbishop Desmond Tutu has been mentioned in more than 3,000 articles on the Nexis database, and at least 388 (11 percent) included in the same breath the fact that he was a Nobel Peace Prize winner. The same search criteria found that Yasser Arafat turned up in almost 96,000 articles, but only 177 (less than .2 percent) mentioned that he won the Nobel Prize. When we move beyond stenography, reporters make a million choices, each one subjective. When, for example, is it relevant to point out, in a story about Iraq's weapons of mass destruction, that the U.S. may have helped Saddam Hussein build those weapons in the 1980s? Every time? Never?

The rules of objectivity don't help us answer such questions. But there are some steps we can take to clarify what we do and help us move forward with confidence. A couple of modest proposals:

> Journalists (and journalism) must acknowledge, humbly and publicly, that what we do is far more subjective and far less detached than the aura of objectivity implies—and the public wants to believe. If we stop claiming to be mere objective observers, it will not end the charges of bias but will allow us to defend what we do from a more realistic, less hypocritical position.

> Secondly, we need to free (and encourage) reporters to develop expertise and to use it to sort through competing claims, identify and explain the underlying assumptions of those claims, and make judgments about what readers and viewers need to know to understand what is happening. In short, we need them to be more willing to "adjudicate factual disputes," as Kathleen Hall Jamieson and Paul Waldman argue in *The Press Effect*. Bill Marimow, the editor of the *Baltimore Sun*, talks of reporters "mastering" their beats. "We want our reporters to be analysts," he told a class at Columbia in March. "Becoming an expert, and mastering the whole range of truth about issues will give you the ability to make independent judgments."

\* \* \*

In a March 18 piece headlined "Bush Clings to Dubious Allegations About Iraq," the *Washington Post*'s Walter Pincus and Dana Milbank laid out all of Bush's "allegations" about Saddam Hussein "that have been challenged—and in some cases disproved—by the United Nations, European governments, and even U.S. intelligence." It was noteworthy for its bluntness, and for its lack of an "analysis" tag. In commenting on that story, Steven Weisman of the *New York Times* illustrates how conflicted journalism is over whether such a piece belongs in the news columns: "It's a very good piece, but it is very tendentious," he says. "It's interesting that the editors didn't put it on page one, because it would look like they are calling Bush a liar. Maybe we should do more pieces like it, but you must be careful not to be argumentative."

\* \* \*

The test, though, should not be whether it is tendentious, but whether it is true.

There are those who will argue that if you start fooling around with the standard of objectivity you open the door to partisanship. But mainstream reporters by and large are not ideological warriors. They are imperfect people performing a difficult job that is crucial to society. Letting them write what they know and encouraging them to dig toward some deeper understanding of things is not biased, it is essential. Reporters should feel free, as Daniel Bice says, to "call it as we see it, but not be committed to one side or the other." Their professional values make them * * * akin to reformers, and they should embrace that aspect of what they do, not hide it for fear of being slapped with a bias charge.

* * *

## DISCUSSION QUESTIONS

1. If objective journalism faces as many challenges as Myrick contends, is it just unrealistic to think it is a "goal well worth pursuing"? Why do you think he suggests it is a worthy goal for the good of the nation?

2. Bresler bemoans the influence of cultural divisions on the news media. Should that influence be applauded rather than feared? Would you prefer that news media outlets be explicitly ideological?

3. Do you agree with Cunningham that journalists should challenge the arguments and facts offered by the individuals they cover? Or should journalists simply present as many sides as possible, allowing each side to make a case, and leave it up to news consumers to determine which case is most convincing?

# CHAPTER 10

# Elections and Voting

## 50

## "The Voice of the People: An Echo" from *The Responsible Electorate*

### V. O. KEY, JR.

*The votes are cast, the tallies are in, the winning candidate claims victory and a mandate to govern—the people have spoken! But just what have the people said when they cast a plurality of the votes for one candidate? Political scientist V. O. Key, Jr., argued that the voice of the people was nothing more than an echo of the cacophony and hubbub of candidates and parties scrambling for popular support. "Even the most discriminating popular judgment," wrote Key, "can reflect only ambiguity, uncertainty, or even foolishness if those are the qualities of the input into the echo chamber."*

*So what was the logic of the voting decision? Key argued that the effort among social scientists to develop theories for understanding the voting decision was important because of the ways political candidates and political leaders would respond to them. If research demonstrated that voters are influenced by "images and cultivation of style," rather than the "substance of politics," then that is what candidates will offer the voters. And if the people receive only images and style as the input to the echo chamber, then eventually that is all they will come to expect. However, Key argues that contrary to the picture of voters held by many politicians and some academic research of his day, the "voters are not fools" who are easily manipulated by campaign tactics or who vote predictably according to the social groups they are in. Individual voters may behave oddly, he concedes, but "in the large, the electorate behaves about as rationally and responsibly as we should expect." His analysis of presidential elections convinced him that the electorate made decisions based upon a concern for public policy, the performance of government, and the personality of the candidates.*

In his reflective moments even the most experienced politician senses a nagging curiosity about why people vote as they do. His power and his position depend upon the outcome of the mysterious rites we perform as opposing candidates harangue the multitudes who finally march to the polls to prolong the rule of their champion, to thrust him, ungratefully, back into the void of private life, or to raise to eminence a new tribune of the people. What kinds of appeals enable a candidate to win the favor of the great god, The People? What circumstances move voters to shift their preferences in this direction or that? What clever propaganda tactic or slogan led to this result? What mannerism of oratory or style of rhetoric produced another outcome? What band of electors rallied to this candidate to save the day for him? What policy of state attracted the devotion of another bloc of voters? What action repelled a third sector of the electorate?

The victorious candidate may claim with assurance that he has the answers to all such questions. He may regard his success as vindication of his beliefs about why voters vote as they do. And he may regard the swing of the vote to him as indubitably a response to the campaign positions he took, as an indication of the acuteness of his intuitive estimates of the mood of the people, and as a ringing manifestation of the esteem in which he is held by a discriminating public. This narcissism assumes its most repulsive form among election winners who have championed intolerance, who have stirred the passions and hatreds of people, or who have advocated causes known by decent men to be outrageous or dangerous in their long-run consequences. No functionary is more repugnant or more arrogant than the unjust man who asserts, with a color of truth, that he speaks from a pedestal of popular approbation.

It thus can be a mischievous error to assume, because a candidate wins, that a majority of the electorate shares his views on public questions, approves his past actions, or has specific expectations about his future conduct. Nor does victory establish that the candidate's campaign strategy, his image, his television style, or his fearless stand against cancer and polio turned the trick. The election returns establish only that the winner attracted a majority of the votes—assuming the existence of a modicum of rectitude in election administration. They tell us precious little about why the plurality was his.

For a glaringly obvious reason, electoral victory cannot be regarded as necessarily a popular ratification of a candidate's outlook. The voice of the people is but an echo. The output of an echo chamber bears an inevitable and invariable relation to the input. As candidates and parties clamor for attention and vie for popular support, the people's verdict can be no more than a selective reflection from among the alternatives and outlooks presented to them. Even the most discriminating popular judgment can reflect only ambiguity, uncertainty, or even foolishness if those are the qualities of the input into the echo chamber. A candidate may win despite his tactics and appeals rather than because of them. If the people can choose only from among rascals, they are certain to choose a rascal.

Scholars, though they have less at stake than do politicians, also have an abiding curiosity about why voters act as they do. In the past quarter of a century [since the 1940s] they have vastly enlarged their capacity to check the hunches born of their curiosities. The invention of the sample survey—the most widely known example of which is the Gallup poll—enabled them to make fairly trustworthy estimates of the characteristics and behaviors of large human populations. This method of mass observation revolutionized the study of politics—as well as the management of political campaigns. The new technique permitted large-scale tests to check the validity of old psychological and sociological theories of human behavior. These tests led to new hunches and new theories about voting behavior, which could, in turn, be checked and which thereby contributed to the extraordinary ferment in the social sciences during recent decades.

The studies of electoral behavior by survey methods cumulate into an imposing body of knowledge which conveys a vivid impression of the variety and subtlety of factors that enter into individual voting decisions. In their first stages in the 1930s the new electoral studies chiefly lent precision and verification to the working maxims of practicing politicians and to some of the crude theories of political speculators. Thus, sample surveys established that people did, indeed, appear to vote their pocketbooks. Yet the demonstration created its embarrassments because it also established that exceptions to the rule were numerous. Not all factory workers, for example, voted alike. How was the behavior of the deviants from "group interest" to be explained? Refinement after refinement of theory and analysis added complexity to the original simple explanation. By introducing a bit of psychological theory it could be demonstrated that factory workers with optimistic expectations tended less to be governed by pocketbook considerations than did those whose outlook was gloomy. When a little social psychology was stirred into the analysis, it could be established that identifications formed early in life, such as attachments to political parties, also reinforced or resisted the pull of the interest of the moment. A sociologist, bringing to play the conceptual tools of his trade, then could show that those factory workers who associate intimately with like-minded persons on the average vote with greater solidarity than do social isolates. Inquiries conducted with great ingenuity along many such lines have enormously broadened our knowledge of the factors associated with the responses of people to the stimuli presented to them by political campaigns.

Yet, by and large, the picture of the voter that emerges from a combination of the folklore of practical politics and the findings of the new electoral studies is not a pretty one. It is not a portrait of citizens moving to considered decision as they play their solemn role of making and unmaking governments. The older tradition from practical politics may regard the voter as an erratic and irrational fellow susceptible to manipulation by skilled humbugs. One need not live through many campaigns to observe politicians, even successful politicians, who act as though they regarded the people as manageable fools. Nor does a heroic conception of the voter emerge from the new analyses of electoral behavior. They can be added up to a conception of voting not as a civic decision but as an almost purely deterministic act. Given knowledge of certain characteristics of a voter—his occupation, his residence, his religion, his national origin, and perhaps certain of his attitudes—one can predict with a high probability the direction of his vote. The actions of persons are made to appear to be only predictable and automatic responses to campaign stimuli.

*   *   *

Conceptions and theories of the way voters behave do not raise solely arcane problems to be disputed among the democratic and antidemocratic theorists or questions to be settled by the elegant techniques of the analysts of electoral behavior. Rather, they touch upon profound issues at the heart of the problem of the nature and workability of systems of popular government. Obviously the perceptions of the behavior of the electorate held by political leaders, agitators, and activists condition, if they do not fix, the types of appeals politicians employ as they seek popular support. These perceptions—or theories—affect the nature of the input to the echo chamber, if we may revert to our earlier figure, and thereby control its output. They may govern, too, the kinds of actions that governments take as they look forward to the next election. If politicians perceive the electorate as responsive to father images, they will give it father images. If they see voters as most certainly responsive to nonsense, they will give them nonsense. If they see voters as susceptible to delusion, they will delude them. If they see an electorate receptive to the cold, hard realities, they will give it the cold, hard realities.

In short, theories of how voters behave acquire importance not because of their effects on voters, who may proceed blithely unaware of them. They gain significance because of their effects, both potentially and in reality, on candidates and other political leaders. If leaders believe the route to victory is by projection of images and cultivation of styles rather than by advocacy of policies to cope with the problems of the country, they will project images and cultivate styles to the neglect of the substance of politics. They will abdicate their prime function in a democratic system, which amounts, in essence, to the assumption of the risk of trying to persuade us to lift ourselves by our bootstraps.

Among the literary experts on politics there are those who contend that, because of the development of tricks for the manipulation of the masses, practices of political leadership in the management of voters have moved far toward the conversion of election campaigns into obscene parodies of the models set up by democratic idealists. They point to the good old days when politicians were deep thinkers, eloquent orators, and farsighted statesmen. Such estimates of the course of change in social institutions must be regarded with reserve. They may be only manifestations of the inverted optimism of aged and melancholy men who, estopped from hope for the future, see in the past a satisfaction of their yearning for greatness in our political life.

Whatever the trends may have been, the perceptions that leadership elements of democracies hold of the modes of response of the electorate must always be a matter of fundamental significance. Those perceptions determine the nature of the voice of the people, for they determine the character of the input into the echo chamber. While the output may be governed by the nature of the input, over the longer run the properties of the echo chamber may themselves be altered. Fed a steady diet of buncombe [bunkum], the people may come to expect and to respond with highest predictability to buncombe. And those leaders most skilled in the propagation of buncombe may gain lasting advantage in the recurring struggles for popular favor.

The perverse and unorthodox argument of this little book is that voters are not fools. To be sure, many individual voters act in odd ways indeed; yet in the large the electorate behaves about as rationally and responsibly as we should expect, given the clarity of the alternatives presented to it and the character of the information available to it. In American presidential campaigns of recent decades the portrait of the American electorate that develops from the data is not one of an electorate straitjacketed by social determinants or moved by subconscious urges triggered by devilishly skillful propagandists. It is rather one of an electorate moved by concern about central and relevant questions of public policy, of governmental performance, and of executive personality. Propositions so uncompromisingly stated inevitably represent overstatements. Yet to the extent that they can be shown to resemble the reality, they are propositions of basic importance for both the theory and the practice of democracy.

To check the validity of this broad interpretation of the behavior of voters, attention will center on the movements of voters across party lines as they reacted to the issues, events, and candidates of presidential campaigns between 1936 and 1960. Some Democratic voters of one election turned Republican at the next; others stood pat. Some Republicans of one presidential season voted Democratic four years later; others remained loyal Republicans. What motivated these shifts, sometimes large and sometimes small, in voter affection? How did the standpatters differ from the switchers? What led them to stand firmly by their party preference of four years earlier? Were these actions governed by images, moods, and other irrelevancies; or were they expressions of judgments about the sorts of questions that, hopefully, voters will weigh as they responsibly cast their ballots? On these matters evidence is available that is impressive in volume, if not always so complete or so precisely relevant as hindsight would wish. If one perseveres through the analysis of this extensive body of information, the proposition that the voter is not so irrational a fellow after all may become credible.

## DISCUSSION QUESTIONS

1. When you go into the voting booth, how do you decide whom to vote for? Is your decision process affected by the nature of the political campaign that has just been completed?

2. Does the 2004 presidential election support Key's view of the electoral process?

# 51

# "Power to the Voters"

## Richard D. Parker

*We live in a republic, not a pure democracy. That is, rather than have citizens make direct choices on questions of public policy, we delegate that responsibility to elected officials. They make decisions on our behalf, and we exercise control over them through periodic elections. To its supporters, one advantage of a republic is that it can thwart popular ideas that might be built on passionate impulses and reactions rather than thoughtful responses to public problems. Critics of this type of system, though they do not challenge its fundamental legitimacy, argue for more direct public participation in the policy process. This might include allowing voters to indicate their preference for specific public policies on election day, as is allowed in many states via the initiative and referendum processes. Or it might mean a system where citizens, perhaps through the Internet, vote for public policies on an ongoing basis.*

*Richard Parker falls squarely into what we might call the populist camp. In his view, direct public participation has many public benefits: it emphasizes the equality of voters (rather than the distinction between the mass electorate and political elites); it transcends the traditional left-right orientation of most political debate; and has a positive impact on communities. Contemporary politics, in his view, focuses on minimizing direct participation by the public; elites view public participation as a good thing only under limited conditions. He calls for a "revitalization through democracy," i.e., using existing democratic processes and channels to reinvigorate participation. His solution calls for a dramatic effort to increase voting turnout: this is, in his view, the only way to create political equality. To accomplish this goal, Parker wants to encourage third parties, impose term limits, and support the ballot initiatives process. The latter two would require constitutional amendments, and the first might, depending on the remedy proposed.*

*A theme that runs through this article is one of skepticism about the idea of political professionalism. The political process, in Parker's view, should be less friendly to incumbents and public officials in general: "[N]ow is the time to start treating [officials] . . . with a somewhat exaggerated disrespect." On the other hand, Parker has great faith in the virtue of mass participation.*

I am, or try to be, a populist democrat. For decades, populism was largely invisible, barely a straw man, in the discourse of the law schools. Well-meaning ideologues of the governing class were accustomed to prescribe—for the people—policies and institutional processes based on an assumption that government of and by the people is—obviously and of course—not to be trusted. Now, that is changing. Populism, today, is a recognized position in legal academia. The ideal is now embraced, its possible implications explored, by a growing band.[1]

Its meaning is, to say the the least, contested. At a minimum, though, my premise is that populism should involve taking popular sovereignty more seriously than has been the practice in legal discourse. More particularly, it ought to involve a renewed emphasis on the value of political equality which—in negotiation with values of political freedom and political community—constitutes the democratic idea. From this it follows that populism ought to involve renewed respect for majority rule as generally the fairest practical guarantor of political equality among persons as well as the most practical way of approximating popular sovereignty over time.

If populism is imagined, above all, in terms of popular sovereignty and political equality, it may acquire a bite that cuts across and shakes up stultified left/right lines of "debate." By the same token, if notions of popular sovereignty and political equality are injected with a populist sensibility—an acceptance and, more, an embrace of ordinariness: ranging from our own ordinariness (and so our deep equality) to the ordinariness of "the people"[2]—these ideas may recover from their torpor of several long decades and acquire, at last, new critical vigor.

What such a re-orientation yields is a back-to-basics approach to the revitalization of democracy. Let me sketch, in three steps, a few fundamental features of this approach.

*Mass Political Participation: A Good in Itself*

The most potent rationalizations for "governance" of the masses by enlightened elites are, nowadays, packaged as paeans to democracy. Against a backdrop of perfectionist premises, they insist that participation by the mass of real people in the real world of politics has value *only* if other conditions are met—only if reality is radically transformed in one way or another. They deplore the inadequacy (even the "corruption") of democracy as we know it. And they conclude, regretfully of course, that the world is not yet safe for democracy. This line of argument must be rejected at the outset as a barrier, rather than a roadmap, to democratic revitalization.

The most transparently naked rationalization focuses on *outcomes* of political processes. The political empowerment of ordinary people is good, so the argument goes, only insofar as its likely outcomes are good. Today, the argument continues, the masses tend to have "bad values" or, at the very least, a mistaken understanding of their own interests. Hence, bad outcomes. There are, sad to say, some who would call themselves populists who take this line. The assumption of these rationalizers of political elitism is that they know better and, so, that they and their ilk should "lead"—be the "spokesmen" or "advocates" for—ordinary people. For them, political equality is but an "idealistic" fantasy—to be used, if at all, as a cynical smoke screen.

A somewhat more subtle version of the argument focuses on the *quality* of political processes. The participation of the masses in politics is good, it asserts, only so long as the political process is otherwise a good one. Today, it continues, our political process is utterly spoiled—poisoned by a few who, with clever thirty second spots, play on the ignorance, shortsightedness and emotions of the many. Thus, it concludes, the political influence of the many may have to be restricted. Again, there are self-styled populists who make this argument. The assumption is that ordinary people are incompetent dupes in need of enlightened cosseting. Again, political equality is imagined as an "ideal" too fine to flourish as a practice—much less motivate and enable a challenge, even if a messy one, to the few by the many—in the real world.

The most sophisticated version of the argument focuses on *preconditions* of democracy. Mass political participation is good, it claims, only after some level of social and economic empowerment, enlightenment and equality has first been achieved for everyone. Again, there are "populists" who take this line. But at bottom, despite the apparent sophistication, it repeats the other versions of the argument. For it assumes that ordinary people who suffer deprivation and inequality need help from their betters before acting politically on their own. It sees them as victims. It presupposes that they cannot or will not—if and as they choose—help themselves.

In place of these pseudo-democratic rationalizations of elite rule, movement toward a revitalization of democracy requires a different, more positive as well as more realistic, attitude toward mass participation, on a basis of political equality, in democratic rule. It requires an appreciation of such participation in politics as a good in itself. But how so?

The answer, I think, is not to invoke the inherent value of self-government, of autonomy. For in politics there are, after all, going to be winners and losers. The losers do not govern themselves in the same way the winners do. They are governed, instead, by the winners, at least for a time, to a degree and in some respects. The argument from self-government is, as we know, too easily turned by losers in the democratic arena into yet another claim for vindication—and, in the end, a claim for the government of everyone—by an elite of paternalistic protectors.

The answer, rather, lies in an old idea of personal and public hygiene. The idea is that active engagement in political life—win or lose—is good for you and for your community.[3] It is good in the same way that an experience of vitality—regularly summoning and expressing and disciplining your energy (successfully or not) toward a chosen end—is good for you. In an old-fashioned sense, it is good for your "constitution." It is an important way in which you constitute yourself. As participants in the mid-century civil rights movement understood (and as some "civil rights leaders" of the *fin de siècle* seem to have forgotten) political self-help is an indispensable (though not, of course, the exclusive) route to an achievement of respect as well as self-respect.

To be sure, politics can be boring, perverse, even depressing. But physical exercise, too, is often painful. And in a regime of competition among political—if not (yet) social and economic—equals, the gain resulting from the pain is likely all the greater.

Should it be surprising that the prescription for a revitalization of democracy is a promise of revitalization *through* democracy?

*The Apex of Political Equality: One Person, One Vote*

No one can say, nowadays, that cultural and political elites are uninterested in political equality. In fact, one huge sector of the establishment—the one that nods when it reads editorials in *The New York Times*—talks about no topic more passionately than it does about this one. The focus of its concern, however, is skewed.

The focus is, of course, on equality in the realm of political campaign speech. Indeed, campaign finance reform has surpassed even "minority" rights as *the* cause of the establishment sector I have in mind. But while I support many reform proposals—public financing of campaigns, free television time for candidates, an abolition of "soft money"—I believe we all should be skeptical of claims that such reform would go far toward a goal of political equality.

There is, first, the problem of political advertising "independent" of official campaign organizations.[4] If (as I am convinced) the Supreme Court will never allow a closing of this "loophole"—if wealthy people remain free to spend as much as they want "independently" of the candidate they promote—then it is fatuous to suppose that other reforms will produce anything like political equality in campaign speech. If, on the other hand, "independent" expenditures are somehow shut down—so that the political marketplace is left exclusively to limited spending by campaign organizations—the result would be political *in*equality of another kind. For, then, electoral discourse would be controlled by an even *more* concentrated group: the *coterie* of official campaign managers. Establishment advocates of campaign finance reform tend not to see this as a problem. For their goal is orderly equality among officials of campaign organizations—not among citizens.[5] Nevertheless, as a practical matter, the issue is whether campaign advertising will be dominated by a larger, more fluid and chaotic elite—or a smaller, more tightly organized one, as many reform advocates prefer.

Second, there is the matter of the "free press" exception for media corporations.[6] Plainly, the Court would not permit a limitation (much less a suppression) of speech about candidates by the owners and managers of print and electronic media. They are imagined as "independent" by definition. Indeed, many establishment advocates of campaign finance reform seem surprised that rich people who own newspapers might be regarded as rich people. Their horror at a mixing of "money and politics" tends to disappear abruptly when the money belongs to the owners of *The New York Times.* Nonetheless, so long as the wealthy are free to buy—and then, bluntly or subtly, to support candidates through—such media, participation in campaign debate before a mass audience will be anything but equal.

The problem with focusing our concern about political equality on campaign finance reform is not just the barrier posed by the Supreme Court. Nor is it just that reformers find themselves aspiring to little more than a rearrangement of the elite domination of campaign discourse. There are two deeper problems: On one hand, anything like real equality of *effective* participation in political debate is a chimera. Given the protean nature of "speech," the most that can be imagined (if not hoped for) is a very, very rough equality of opportunity. On the other hand, the assumption underlying the focus on the financing of political advertising is typically an assumption of political inequality—that the mass of ordinary people are passive and rather incompetent consumers (rather than actors), easily duped or swayed (rather than appropriately persuaded) by competing waves of thirty-second spots. If we want to vindicate political equality—as we should if we want to revitalize democracy—we ought to focus, instead, on something that does not, from the very outset, tend to compromise or contradict our goal.

We should focus on the vote. Taking the vote, rather than speech, as the key resource for participation in democratic politics—seeking to promote its use and the effect of using it—is the best way to take political equality seriously. For a focus on voting enables us to begin with a standard of equality that is both strong and established in law: one person, one vote. What's more, equal participation in voting is a practical goal. Not everyone can speak at once or as effectively as everyone else. But everyone can vote at once. And every vote counts as much as every other. Most important, the aspiration to enhance the value of the vote is grounded in a respect for ordinary people—as political actors, indeed as rulers—that is unambiguous.

Strangely, the vote seems now to be out of favor. Across the conventional political spectrum, many denigrate the value of voting and the one person, one vote standard. Some claim voting is irrational. Others purvey a narcissistic notion of "deliberative" democracy to eclipse what they imagine as the tawdry marking of a ballot. Still others claim that "communities"—rather than shifting collections or coalitions of individuals—should somehow express themselves in politics. On the surface, what unites them all is a tendency to idealize democracy and, so, to find its reality disappointing. But what accounts for this idealizing tendency? It is, I think, fear—fear of losing and of trying to win, fear of ordinary people and of their own ordinariness. To them, I would say: Get over it. Get into voting. It will be good for you. And for others as well.

### Rock the Vote

How, then, might democracy be revitalized by promoting the use and effect of the vote? The central scandal of American democracy, from my populist point of view, is that most people do not cast a ballot in most elections. To promote use of the vote, the obvious strategy is to promote its effect. If something really significant seems to be at stake, people are more likely to take part. Even if no one believes her own vote will make the difference, she will see value—as have so many, from soldiers to protestors—in doing her part. For the moment, all I can do is gesture toward a few ways of enhancing the effect—and so the value, and so the use—of the vote. With respect to each, I want to encourage not only law reform, but also political action.

First of all, in candidate elections the voters must be presented with a real contest. In 2000, only about 35 seats in the U.S. House of Representatives are said to be in play. In a great many districts, the incumbent faces no (or only nominal) opposition. In other districts—and in many other elections up to and including presidential elections—there frequently seems not much more than a dime's (or perhaps a dollar's) worth of difference between the candidates. Hardly a motivation to cast a ballot.

For this condition, the legal remedy need not go so far as instituting systems of proportional representation. (Such systems tend to funnel power to party elites and, so, should be rejected by populists.) But barriers to entry—from ballot qualification requirements to exclusions from debates[7]—facing "minor" party candidates surely must be lowered. Once a number of "minor" parties gain a foothold, run-off elections should be held. In the run-offs, the two highest vote-getters would be moved to address issues of concern to the others while, at the same time, the principle of popular majority rule would be vindicated. At the same time, the system for drawing legislative districts needs to be transformed. Districting should be taken from the hands of incumbent-friendly politicians and transferred to incumbent-unfriendly commissions. The commissions should be given one overriding instruction: draw and re-draw district lines so as to promote hotly contested elections in as many as possible.

In support of such legal remedies, a political one may now be underway. For the bulk of "alienated" non-voters may now be so huge as to have reached a critical mass. Politicians are more and more likely to take the opportunity to offer the "something different" these non-voters seem to want. In the last decade, candidates ranging from Ross Perot to Jesse Ventura to John McCain to Ralph Nader have done just that and, so, have begun to shake up political business-as-usual. The lesson for democratic populists is: When in doubt, support a maverick.

Second, the suffocating smugness of officialdom must be dispelled. In the last few decades, this pathological condition has become acute. Whether they be elected officials pompously touting "Burkean" notions of representation or civil servants claiming indispensable experience and expertise or judges relying on imagined wisdom and independence, these self-important middlemen—ensconced between voters and lawmaking—now are an incubus, cabining and repressing the political energy essential to popular sovereignty at the ballot box.

The primary legal remedy should be term limits. With respect to elected officials, term limits are an important supplement to the promotion of contested elections. But with respect to unelected officials, they are even more vital. If civil servants and judges (judges!) were limited to no more than fifteen years in office, government in all its nooks and crannies would, to a significant degree, be cracked open to the influence of the voters in periodic elections.

The political remedy, in this case, is largely attitudinal. We must stop acting as the enablers of the inflated arrogance of officialdom. For too long, we have treated officials with exaggerated respect. Now, it is time to start treating them—as they were treated in the early decades of our history—with a somewhat exaggerated disrespect. As reformers of bygone days knew well, regularly exposing the misdeeds, the incompetence, the hypocrisy of officials is not cynicism or nihilism; it is realism, the tonic of democratic lawmaking. (And that goes for lazy Justices and lying Presidents.)

The third and most important way of enhancing the effect, and so the use, of the vote is to eliminate the middlemen entirely. I am referring, of course, to direct democracy, lawmaking by initiative and referendum. What is at stake at the ballot box is, there, about as clear and immediate as can be. Popular support for direct democratic lawmaking, in states that allow it, is strong and consistent. So, however, is elite opposition to it.[8] Today, direct democracy is at a turning point.

The pressing legal challenge, right now, is to resist growing efforts to hem in and hobble the initiative and referendum. That will involve challenges to new infringements on the right to petition, new ballot qualification requirements, and new "interpretations" of arcane rules like the "single subject" standard. Eventually, it is likely also to involve defense against federal constitutional arguments, particularly the claim that direct democracy violates the "republican form of government" clause.[9] (In the 1950s and 1960s, it was exclusively conservatives who insisted that "America is a republic, not a democracy." Now, it is mostly progressives.) While turning back these anti-democratic thrusts, the time is ripe to go on the offensive as well—mending (rather than ending) processes by which proposals for popular lawmaking are drafted and summarized, then extending the initiative and referendum to all fifty states and even experimenting (at first) with "advisory" or "instructive" initiatives and referenda at the federal level.

Politically, beyond exposing elitist assumptions behind the wave of assault on direct democracy, I have one main suggestion: If there is an initiative or referendum proposal that you don't like, oppose it actively. And if it is passed, don't throw up your hands and go to the courts or the newspapers to pontificate about "republican" government. Instead, launch your own initiative campaign to repeal the popularly made law you don't like or to enact one you do like.

My bottom line is this: Democracy will be revitalized when more and more and then more of us give it a try.

## DISCUSSION QUESTIONS

1. Do you agree with Parker's argument that increased mass participation is, by definition, a good thing? Is it "elitist" to disagree with him?

2. Is Parker correct in arguing that third parties, term limits, referenda, and increased competitiveness in elections would spur more participation? What positive (and negative) consequences might arise under his proposals?

3. What might the Framers be likely to say about Parker's ideas? Does it matter?

## NOTES

1. *See, e.g.,* Akhil Reed Amar & Alan Hirsch, *For the People: What the Constitution Really Says About Your Rights* (1998); Richard D. Parker, *"Here, the People Rule": A Constitutional Populist Manifesto* (1994); Mark V. Tushnet, *Taking the Constitution away from the Courts* (1999); J. M. Balkin, "Populism and Progressivism as Constitutional Categories," 104 Yale L.J. 1935 (1995).
2. *See generally* James Agee & Walker Evans, *Let Us Now Praise Famous Men* (1941); Parker, *supra* note 1; *cf.* Lionel Trilling, *The Liberal Imagination: Essays on Literature and Society* 88 (1950) ("We who are liberal and progressive know that the poor are our equals in every sense except that of being equal to us.").
3. *See* Albert Camus, *The Plague* (1948); *cf.* Hannah Arendt, *The Human Condition*, 22–78 (1958).
4. *See* Buckley v. Valeo, 424 U.S. 1, 39–59 (1976).
5. *See* Richard D. Parker, "Taking Politics Personally," 12 Cardozo Stud. L. & Literature 103, 112 (2000).
6. *See* Austin v. Michigan State Chamber of Commerce, 494 U.S. 652, 668 (1990). The Court opined:

The media exception ensures that [a campaign finance law] does not hinder or prevent the institutional press from reporting on, and publishing editorials about, newsworthy events. A valid distinction thus exists between corporations that are part of the media industry and other corporations that are not involved in the regular business of imparting news to the public. Although the press' unique societal role may not entitle the press to greater protection under the Constitution, it does provide a compelling reason for the State to exempt media corporations from the scope of political expenditure limitations.

*Id.* (citations omitted).

7.  *See, e.g.,* Munro v. Socialist Workers Party, 479 U.S. 189 (1986) (upholding state statute requiring a minor party candidate to get at least 1% of the total votes cast in the primary to be placed on the general election ballot); Forbes v. Arkansas Educ. Television Communication Network Found, 22 F.3d 1423, 1426 (1994) (upholding the right of a public television station to exclude an independent candidate for Congress from participation in a debate even though "[h]e had obtained enough signatures to qualify for the ballot under state law").

8.  *See, e.g.,* David S. Broder, *Democracy Derailed: Initiative Campaigns and the Power of Money* (2000).

9.  *See, e.g.,* Hans A. Linde, "On Reconstituting 'Republican Government,'" 19 Okla. City U. L. Rev. 193, 199–201 (1994); Hans A. Linde, "When Initiative Lawmaking Is Not 'Republican Government': The Campaign Against Homosexuality," 72 Or. L. Rev. 19 (1993).

# 52

# "The Unpolitical Animal: How Political Science Understands Voters"

### Louis Menand

*How well do Americans measure up to the ideal of highly informed, engaged, attentive, involved citizens? V. O. Key argued that Americans, on the whole, do reasonably well in making sound collective judgments. Writing around the same time as Key, another political scientist, Philip Converse, reached a gloomier conclusion. Most Americans couldn't be "ideal" citizens because most had minimal and inconsistent political belief systems. To a large part, he concluded, Americans had a lot of top-of-the-head opinions that had no strong connection to a set of principles. Louis Menand revisits the question addressed by V. O. Key: Do elections represent the will of the people? Menand reviews Converse's conclusions and then discusses three theories that attempt to make some sense of Americans' failure to behave as ideal citizens. One theory declares that elections are more or less random events in which a large bloc of voters responds to "slogans, misinformation, 'fire alarms' (sensational news), 'October surprises' (last-minute sensational news), random personal associations, and 'gotchas.' " Another theory posits that voter decisions are not guided simply by random events and information, but by elite opinion. Elites do understand the issues and work within ideological frameworks, and they find ways to pitch ideas to voters so that they gain a governing majority. Elections are thus primarily about the interests and beliefs of rival elite factions. The third theory, in part, rescues the voter from these unflattering portraits. Here, voters use information shortcuts, especially but not only political party labels, to render verdicts that are substantively meaningful. "People use shortcuts—the social-scientific term is 'heuristics'—to reach judgments about political candidates, and, on the whole, these shortcuts are as good as the long and winding road of reading party platforms, listening to candidate debates, and all the other elements of civic duty." Menand concludes that voter decisions may be based on shortcuts that make sense to them—like which candidate is more optimistic—rather than the weighing and balancing of principles and policy positions that ideologues would prefer.*

In every Presidential-election year, there are news stories about undecided voters, people who say that they are perplexed about which candidate's positions make the most sense. They tell reporters things like "I'd like to know more about Bush's plan for education," or "I'm worried that Kerry's ideas about Social Security don't add up." They say that they are thinking about issues like "trust," and whether the candidate cares about people like them. To voters who identify strongly with a political party, the undecided voter is almost an alien life form. For them, a vote for Bush is a vote for a whole philosophy of governance and a vote for Kerry is a vote for a distinctly different philosophy. The difference is obvious to them, and they don't understand how others can't see it, or can decide whom to vote for on the basis of a candidate's personal traits or whether his or her position on a particular issue "makes sense." To an undecided voter, on the other hand, the person who always votes for the Democrat or the Republican, no matter what, must seem like a dangerous fanatic. Which voter is behaving more rationally and responsibly?

If you look to the political professionals, the people whose job it is to know what makes the fish bite, it is clear that, in their view, political philosophy is not the fattest worm. *Winning Elections: Political Campaign Management, Strategy & Tactics* (M. Evans; $49.95) is a collection of articles drawn from the pages of *Campaigns & Elections: The Magazine for People in Politics*. The advice to the political professionals is: Don't assume that your candidate's positions are going to make the difference. "In a competitive political climate," as one article explains, "informed citizens may vote for a candidate based on issues. However, uninformed or undecided voters will often choose the candidate whose name and packaging are most memorable. To make sure your candidate has that 'top-of-mind' voter awareness, a powerful logo is the best place to start." You want to present your candidate in language that voters will understand. They understand colors. "Blue is a positive color for men, signaling authority and control," another article advises. "But it's a negative color for women, who perceive it as distant, cold and aloof. Red is a warm, sentimental color for women—and a sign of danger or anger to men. If you use the wrong colors to the wrong audience, you're sending a mixed message."

It can't be the case, though, that electoral outcomes turn on things like the color of the buttons. Can it? When citizens stand in the privacy of the booth and contemplate the list of those who bid to serve, do they really think, That's the guy with the red logo. A lot of anger there. I'll take my chances with the other one? In Civics 101, the model voter is a citizen vested with the ability to understand the consequences of his or her choice; when these individual rational choices are added up, we know the will of the people. How accurate is this picture?

Skepticism about the competence of the masses to govern themselves is as old as mass self-government. Even so, when that competence began to be measured statistically, around the end of the Second World War, the numbers startled almost everyone. The data were interpreted most powerfully by the political scientist Philip Converse, in an article on "The Nature of Belief Systems in Mass Publics," published in 1964. Forty years later, Converse's conclusions are still the bones at which the science of voting behavior picks.

Converse claimed that only around ten per cent of the public has what can be called, even generously, a political belief system. He named these people "ideologues," by which he meant not that they are fanatics but that they have a reasonable grasp of "what goes with what"—of how a set of opinions adds up to a coherent political philosophy. Non-ideologues may use terms like "liberal" and "conservative," but Converse thought that they basically don't know what they're talking about, and that their beliefs are characterized by what he termed a lack of "constraint": they can't see how one opinion (that taxes should be lower, for example) logically ought to rule out other opinions (such as the belief that there should be more government programs). About forty-two per cent of voters, according to Converse's interpretation of surveys of the 1956 electorate, vote on the basis not of ideology but of perceived self-interest. The rest form political preferences either from their sense of whether times are good or bad (about twenty-five per cent) or from factors that have no discernible "issue content" whatever. Converse put twenty-two per cent of the electorate in this last category. In other words, about twice as many people have no political views as have a coherent political belief system.

Just because someone's opinions don't square with what a political scientist recognizes as a political ideology doesn't mean that those opinions aren't coherent by the lights of some more personal system of beliefs. But Converse found reason to doubt this possibility. When pollsters ask people for their opinion about an issue, people generally feel obliged to have one. Their answer is duly recorded, and it becomes a datum in a report on "public opinion." But, after analyzing the results of surveys conducted over time, in which people tended to give different and randomly inconsistent answers to the same questions, Converse concluded that "very substantial portions of the public" hold opinions that are essentially meaningless—off-the-top-of-the-head responses to questions they have never thought about, derived from no underlying set of principles. These people might as well base their political choices on the weather. And, in fact, many of them do.

Findings about the influence of the weather on voter behavior are among the many surveys and studies that confirm Converse's sense of the inattention of the American electorate. In election years from 1952 to 2000, when people were asked whether they cared who won the Presidential election, between twenty-two and forty-four per cent answered "don't care" or "don't know." In 2000, eighteen per cent said that they decided which Presidential candidate to vote for only in the last two weeks of the campaign; five per cent, enough to swing most elections, decided the day they voted.

Seventy per cent of Americans cannot name their senators or their congressman. Forty-nine per cent believe that the President has the power to suspend the Constitution. Only about thirty per cent name an issue when they explain why they voted the way they did, and only a fifth hold consistent opinions on issues over time. Rephrasing poll questions reveals that many people don't understand the issues that they have just offered an opinion on. According to polls conducted in 1987 and 1989, for example, between twenty and twenty-five per cent of the public thinks that too little is being spent on welfare, and between sixty-three and sixty-five per cent feels that too little is being spent on assistance to the poor. And voters apparently do punish politicians for acts of God. In a paper written in 2004, the Princeton political scientists Christopher Achen and Larry Bartels estimate that "2.8 million people voted against Al Gore in 2000 because their states were too dry or too wet" as a consequence of that year's weather patterns. Achen and Bartels think that these voters cost Gore seven states, any one of which would have given him the election.

All political systems make their claim to legitimacy by some theory, whether it's the divine right of kings or the iron law of history. Divine rights and iron laws are not subject to empirical confirmation, which is one reason that democracy's claims have always seemed superior. What polls and surveys suggest, though, is that the belief that elections express the true preferences of the people may be nearly as imaginary. When you move downward through what Converse called the public's "belief strata," candidates are quickly separated from ideology and issues, and they become attached, in voters' minds, to idiosyncratic clusters of ideas and attitudes. The most widely known fact about George H. W. Bush in the 1992 election was that he hated broccoli. Eighty-six per cent of likely voters in that election knew that the Bushes' dog's name was Millie; only fifteen per cent knew that Bush and Clinton both favored the death penalty. It's not that people know nothing. It's just that politics is not what they know.

In the face of this evidence, three theories have arisen. The first is that electoral outcomes, as far as "the will of the people" is concerned, are essentially arbitrary. The fraction of the electorate that responds to substantive political arguments is hugely outweighed by the fraction that responds to slogans, misinformation, "fire alarms" (sensational news), "October surprises" (last-minute sensational news), random personal associations, and "gotchas." Even when people think that they are thinking in political terms, even when they believe that they are analyzing candidates on the basis of their positions on issues, they are usually operating behind a veil of political ignorance. They simply don't understand, as a practical matter, what it means to be "fiscally conservative," or to have "faith in the private sector," or to pursue an "interventionist foreign policy." They can't hook up positions with policies. From the point of view of democratic theory, American political history is just a random walk through a series of electoral options. Some years, things turn up red; some years, they turn up blue.

A second theory is that although people may not be working with a full deck of information and beliefs, their preferences are dictated by something, and that something is elite opinion. Political campaigns, on this theory, are essentially struggles among the elite, the fraction of a fraction of voters who have the knowledge and the ideological chops to understand the substantive differences between the candidates and to argue their policy implications. These voters communicate their preferences to the rest of the electorate by various cues, low-content phrases and images (warm colors, for instance) to which voters can relate, and these cues determine the outcome of the race. Democracies are really oligarchies with a populist face.

The third theory of democratic politics is the theory that the cues to which most voters respond are, in fact, adequate bases on which to form political preferences. People use shortcuts—the social-scientific term is "heuristics"—to reach judgments about political candidates, and, on the whole, these shortcuts are as good as the long and winding road of reading party platforms, listening to candidate debates, and all the other elements of civic duty. Voters use what Samuel Popkin, one of the proponents of this third theory, calls "low-information rationality"—in other words, gut reasoning—to reach political decisions; and this intuitive form of judgment proves a good enough substitute for its high-information counterpart in reflecting what people want.

An analogy (though one that Popkin is careful to dissociate himself from) would be to buying an expensive item like a house or a stereo system. A tiny fraction of consumers has the knowledge to discriminate among the entire range of available stereo components, and to make an informed choice based on assessments of cost and performance. Most of us rely on the advice of two or three friends who have recently made serious stereo-system purchases, possibly some online screen shopping, and the pitch of the salesman at J&R Music World. We eyeball the product, associate idiosyncratically with the brand name, and choose from the gut. When we ask "experts" for their wisdom, mostly we are hoping for an "objective" ratification of our instinctive desire to buy the coolest-looking stuff. Usually, we're O.K. Our tacit calculation is that the marginal utility of more research is smaller than the benefit of immediate ownership.

On the theory of heuristics, it's roughly the same with candidates: voters don't have the time or the inclination to assess them in depth, so they rely on the advice of experts—television commentators, political activists, Uncle Charlie—combined with their own hunches, to reach a decision. Usually (they feel), they're O.K. If they had spent the time needed for a top-to-toe vetting, they would probably not have chosen differently.

Some voters might get it wrong in one direction, choosing the liberal candidate when they in fact preferred a conservative one, but their error is cancelled out by the voters who mistakenly choose the conservative. The will of the people may not be terribly articulate, but it comes out in the wash.

This theory is the most attractive of the three, since it does the most to salvage democratic values from the electoral wreckage Converse described. It gives the mass of voters credit for their decisions by suggesting not only that they can interpret the cues given by the campaigns and the elite opinion-makers but that the other heuristics they use—the candidate seems likable, times are not as good as they were—are actually defensible replacements for informed, logical reasoning. Popkin begins his well-regarded book on the subject, *The Reasoning Voter*, with an example from Gerald Ford's primary campaign against Ronald Reagan in 1976. Visiting a Mexican-American community in Texas, Ford (never a gaffe-free politician) made the mistake of trying to eat a tamale with the corn husk, in which it is traditionally served, still on it. This ethnic misprision made the papers, and when he was asked, after losing to Jimmy Carter in the general election, what the lesson of his defeat was, Ford answered, "Always shuck your tamales." Popkin argues that although familiarity with Mexican-American cuisine is not a prerequisite for favoring policies friendly to Mexican-Americans, Mexican-Americans were justified in concluding that a man who did not know how to eat a tamale was not a man predisposed to put their needs high on his list. The reasoning is illogical: Ford was not running for chef, and it was possible to extrapolate, from his positions, the real difference it would make for Mexican-Americans if he were President rather than Reagan or Carter. But Mexican-Americans, and their sympathizers, felt "in their gut" that Ford was not their man, and that was enough.

The principal shortcut that people use in deciding which candidates to vote for is, of course, the political party. The party is the ultimate Uncle Charlie in American politics. Even elite voters use it when they are confronted, in the voting booth, with candidates whose names they have never seen before. There is nothing in the Constitution requiring candidates to be listed on the ballot with their party affiliations, and, if you think about it, the custom of doing so is vaguely undemocratic. It makes elections a monopoly of the major parties, by giving their candidates an enormous advantage—the advantage of an endorsement right there on the ballot—over everyone else who runs. It is easy to imagine a constitutional challenge to the practice of identifying candidates by party, but it is also easy to imagine how wild the effects would be if voters were confronted by a simple list of names with no identifying tags. Every election would be like an election for student-body president: pure name recognition.

Any time information is lacking or uncertain, a shortcut is generally better than nothing. But the shortcut itself is not a faster way of doing the math; it's a way of skipping the math altogether. My hunch that the coolest-looking stereo component is the best value simply does not reflect an intuitive grasp of electronics. My interest in a stereo is best served if I choose the finest sound for the money, as my interest in an election is best served if I choose the candidate whose policies are most likely to benefit me or the people I care about. But almost no one calculates in so abstract a fashion. Even voters who supported Michael Dukakis in 1988 agreed that he looked ridiculous wearing a weird helmet when he went for a ride in a tank, and a lot of those people felt that, taken together with other evidence of his manner and style of self-expression, the image was not irrelevant to the substance of his campaign. George H. W. Bush underwent a similar moment in 1992, when he was caught showing astonishment at the existence of scanners at supermarket checkout counters. Ideologues opposed to Bush were pleased to propose this as what psychologists call a "fast and frugal" means of assessing the likely effects of his economic policies.

When political scientists interpret these seat-of-the-pants responses as signs that voters are choosing rationally, and that representative government therefore really does reflect the will of the people, they are, in effect, making a heuristic of heuristics. They are not doing the math. Doing the math would mean demonstrating that the voters' intuitive judgments are roughly what they would get if they analyzed the likely effects of candidates' policies, and this is a difficult calculation to perform. One shortcut that voters take, and that generally receives approval from the elite, is pocketbook voting. If they are feeling flush, they vote for the incumbent; if they are feeling strapped, they vote for a change. But, as Larry Bartels, the co-author of the paper on Gore and the weather, has pointed out, pocketbook voting would be rational only if it could be shown that replacing the incumbent did lead, on average, to better economic times. Without such a demonstration, a vote based on the condition of one's pocketbook is no more rational than a vote based on the condition of one's lawn. It's a hunch.

Bartels has also found that when people do focus on specific policies they are often unable to distinguish their own interests. His work, which he summed up in a recent article for *The American Prospect*, concerned public opinion about the estate tax. When people are asked whether they favor Bush's policy of repealing the estate tax, two-thirds say yes—even though the estate tax affects only the wealthiest one or two per cent of the population. Ninety-eight per cent of Americans do not leave estates large enough for the tax to kick in. But people have some notion—Bartels refers to it as "unenlightened self-interest"—that they will be better off if the tax is repealed. What is most remarkable about this opinion is that it is unconstrained by other beliefs. Repeal is supported by sixty-six per cent of people who believe that the income gap between the richest and the poorest Americans has increased in recent decades, and that this is a bad thing. And it's supported by sixty-eight per cent of people who say that the rich pay too little in taxes. Most Americans simply do not make a connection between tax policy and the overall economic condition of the country. Whatever heuristic they are using, it is definitely not doing the math for them. This helps make sense of the fact that the world's greatest democracy has an electorate that continually "chooses" to transfer more and more wealth to a smaller and smaller fraction of itself.

But who *ever* does the math? As Popkin points out, everybody uses heuristics, including the elite. Most of the debate among opinion-makers is conducted in shorthand, and even well-informed voters rely on endorsements and party affiliations to make their choices. The very essence of being an ideologue lies in trusting the label—liberal or conservative, Republican or Democrat. Those are "bundling" terms: they pull together a dozen positions on individual issues under a single handy rubric. They do the work of assessment for you.

It is widely assumed that the upcoming Presidential election will be decided by an electorate that is far more ideological than has historically been the case. Polls indicate much less volatility than usual, supporting the view that the public is divided into starkly antagonistic camps—the "red state-blue state" paradigm. If this is so, it suggests that we have at last moved past Converse's picture of an electoral iceberg, in which ninety per cent of the population is politically underwater. But Morris Fiorina, a political scientist at Stanford, thinks that it is not so, and that the polarized electorate is a product of elite opinion. "The simple truth is that there is no culture war in the United States—no battle for the soul of America rages, at least none that most Americans are aware of," he says in his short book *Culture War? The Myth of a Polarized America* (Longman; $14.95). Public-opinion polls, he argues, show that on most hot-button issues voters in so-called red states do not differ significantly from voters in so-called blue states. Most people identify themselves as moderates, and their responses to survey questions seem to substantiate this self-description. What has become polarized, Fiorina argues, is the elite. The chatter—among political activists, commentators, lobbyists, movie stars, and so on—has become highly ideological. It's a non-stop *Crossfire*, and this means that the candidates themselves come wrapped in more extreme ideological coloring. But Fiorina points out that the ideological position of a candidate is not identical to the position of the people who vote for him or her. He suggests that people generally vote for the candidate whose views strike them as closest to their own, and "closest" is a relative term. With any two candidates, no matter how far out, one will always be "closer" than the other.

Of course, if Converse is correct, and most voters really don't have meaningful political beliefs, even ideological "closeness" is an artifact of survey anxiety, of people's felt need, when they are asked for an opinion, to have one. This absence of "real opinions" is not from lack of brains; it's from lack of interest. "The typical citizen drops down to a lower level of mental performance as soon as he enters the political field," the economic theorist Joseph Schumpeter wrote, in 1942. "He argues and analyzes in a way which he would readily recognize as infantile within the sphere of his real interests. He becomes a primitive again. His thinking is associative and affective." And Fiorina quotes a passage from the political scientist Robert Putnam: "Most men are not political animals. The world of public affairs is not their world. It is alien to them—possibly benevolent, more probably threatening, but nearly always alien. Most men are not interested in politics. Most do not participate in politics."

Man may not be a political animal, but he is certainly a social animal. Voters do respond to the cues of commentators and campaigners, but only when they can match those cues up with the buzz of their own social group. Individual voters are not rational calculators of self-interest (nobody truly is), and may not be very consistent users of heuristic shortcuts, either. But they are not just random particles bouncing off the walls of the voting booth. Voters go into the booth carrying the imprint of the hopes and fears, the prejudices and assumptions of their family, their friends, and their neighbors. For most people, voting may be more meaningful and more understandable as a social act than as a political act.

That it is hard to persuade some people with ideological arguments does not mean that those people cannot be persuaded, but the things that help to convince them are likely to make ideologues sick—things like which candidate is more optimistic. For many liberals, it may have been dismaying to listen to John Kerry and John Edwards, in their speeches at the Democratic National Convention, utter impassioned bromides about how "the sun is rising" and "our best days are still to come." But that is what a very large number of voters want to hear. If they believe it, then Kerry and Edwards will get their votes. The ideas won't matter, and neither will the color of the buttons.

## Discussion Questions

1. What information shortcuts do you think it would be reasonable to use when making voting decisions?

2. Menand is concerned that voters' heuristics might not be reliable if voters actually "did the math." What heuristics do you think might be particularly unreliable guides to voting choices?

3. What, if any, risks are posed to the American political system by voters basing their decisions on information shortcuts? Which of the three theories discussed by Menand would be the most troubling for democracy, in your view?

## Debating the Issues: Voter Fraud or Voter Suppression?

The 2000 presidential election raised many concerns about the voting system and the standards for administering elections in the United States. Charges of impropriety in voting procedures and vote counting as well as complaints that certain voting technologies were systematically likely to produce more voter error or not record voter choices were legion. As the 2004 presidential campaign began to heat up, it became apparent that voter interest in the election was unusually large and that turnout might surge. Massive voter mobilization campaigns on both the political left and right registered millions of new voters. Huge sums were poured into campaign advertising, further stoking the interest of these newly registered voters and the public in general. In such a charged political environment, and with the presidential election widely expected to be close, concerns about the integrity of the process took on a particular urgency. The battle lines were drawn in the months leading up to the election. One argument, presented here by John Fund, was that voter fraud was the main area where reform was needed. This argument pointed to voters registered in multiple locations, voting more than once, illegally registered, voting or registering without identification, or paid an inducement to vote, as symptomatic of the lack of control over the voting process. The opposing argument, presented here by People for the American Way, contends that these complaints about fraud are part of a strategy to discourage or scare away potential voters. Proponents of this argument point to examples that they allege are clear attempts to suppress voter turnout by adding obstacles in the way of voting or interpreting statutes and regulations in the way that is least likely to allow someone's vote to be counted. The dispute centers around turnout: those complaining about vote suppression say we should err on the side of getting as many people voting as possible, while those complaining about voter fraud ask what the good is in increasing turnout if we cannot be sure that those who voted were indeed supposed to vote.

## 53

# "Run-up to Election Exposes Widespread Barriers to Voting"

### PEOPLE FOR THE AMERICAN WAY

On the eve of the November 2 election, news stories and reports from voting rights activists around the country indicate that the nation is poised for a repeat of widespread voter disenfranchisement on Election Day. Too many public and political Party officials are trying to discourage and prevent voters from exercising their right to vote, rather than devoting their energies to resolving the kinds of problems that disenfranchised millions of Americans nationwide in 2000. The failure to resolve those problems and the existence of ongoing organized voter suppression efforts represent a profound failure of leadership and pose a tremendous moral challenge to Americans and their elected representatives. Meanwhile, reports about dirty tricks campaigns designed to intimidate or discourage voters have escalated as Election Day approaches.

*Introduction*

\* \* \*

Over the past two months, news reports and voting rights organizations, including the nonpartisan Election Protection coalition, have identified additional activities that could suppress minority turnout, as well as a wide range of more broadly defined incidents and official actions—some based on partisan considerations—that will keep people from having the opportunity to have their vote counted on Election Day.

Some problems are the actions of individuals or local Party officials. Even more disturbing are those that involve public officials using the power of their office to restrict access to the ballot box. Among the examples of the latter is the decision by some state election officials—with the backing of the U.S. Department of Justice—to violate the spirit if not the letter of federal election reform law by adopting restrictive procedures regarding provisional ballots that will lead to thousands of voters unnecessarily having their votes disregarded.

Another appalling stand taken by some state election officials is to reject registration forms from voters who did not check a box indicating their U.S. citizenship, even though the same form includes an affirmation of citizenship signed by the voter. Both of these decisions indicate officials focused more on preventing rather than facilitating civic participation.

These official actions—along with systemic problems with registration procedures, voter identification, and equipment problems that persist a full four years after a traumatic, divisive, and tainted election—should engender a nationwide outcry that forces elected officials to muster the political will to establish and maintain standards and accountability safeguards that will protect all American voters in the months and years ahead.

This report summarizes some of the threats to voter rights that have emerged in recent weeks. It is illustrative and by no means comprehensive, as new incidents seem to come to light daily, others almost certainly have remained hidden from public scrutiny, and legal developments are changing hour to hour.

*Unprecedented Voter Challenges*

In the last two weeks leading up to the election, a clear pattern has emerged across the country. Republican Party officials in several states have launched twin initiatives. First, the Party mailed out hundreds of thousands, perhaps millions, of letters to new and existing voters, and is making last-minute challenges to voter eligibility before Election Day on the basis of returned mail. Second, the Party is placing extraordinary numbers of poll challengers at the polls to challenge individual voters on Election Day as they attempt to cast their ballots.

The first initiative is a strategy that has long been employed by the Party on the state and national level. These initiatives, undertaken in the name of "ballot security" or "ballot integrity," have resulted in three court decrees, in which the party has been forced to agree that it will no longer base its challenges of voters on race, a violation of the 1965 Voting Rights Act. In each of the past court cases, the decrees came long after the election, far too late to help voters who were disenfranchised. This year, the strategy has been reported in Ohio and Wisconsin, and may be underway in other states.

The second is an initiative that uses various state laws permitting vote challenges by partisan poll watchers stationed inside the polls, or by individual electors or voters. Huge numbers of such partisan poll watchers have been registered where prior registration is required, including Florida and Ohio.

With election officials across the country predicting huge voter turnout, these initiatives hold the potential for long lines, increasing voter frustration and disenfranchising voters who do not have the time or resources to wait in line for many hours on a weekday. Further, the experience of past years gives reason to suggest that many of these challenges might be racially targeted. However, only a thorough study of the patterns of the challenges could determine such targeting, which again could not take place until after Election Day.

### Voter Intimidation/Suppression

There are a discouraging number of incidents where actions taken by individuals, political party organizations, or elected officials are clearly intended to intimidate, misinform, confuse, hamper or otherwise discourage potential voters from casting a ballot.

- In **Lake County, Ohio,** a fake letter appearing to come from the Lake County Board of Elections was sent to newly registered voters. The letter said voter registrations gathered by the Kerry or Capri Cafaro campaigns or the NAACP are illegal and those voters will not be able to vote. The incident is being investigated by the Sheriff, who says, "It will be a federal offense because you have interfered with the constitutionally protected right to vote."

\* \* \*

- The week before the election, flyers were circulated in **Milwaukee** under the heading "Milwaukee Black Voters League" with some "warnings for election time." The false information on the flyer included warnings that anyone who had already voted this year cannot vote in the presidential election; that anyone convicted of any offense, however minor, is ineligible to vote; that any family member having been convicted of anything would disqualify a voter; and that any violation of these warnings would result in ten years in prison and a voter's children being taken away.

\* \* \*

- A flyer designed to look like an official announcement from McCandless Township in **Allegheny County, Pennsylvania,** was designed to misinform voters on a partisan basis. The flyer claimed that, "Due to the immense voter turnout that is expected on Tuesday, November 2 the state of Pennsylvania has requested an extended voting period." The flyer claims that voters will be able to vote on both November 2 and November 3 and says that, in "an attempt to limit voter conflict," Allegheny County is requesting that Republicans vote on November 2 and Democrats on November 3.

\* \* \*

- In **Florida,** the *St Petersburg Times* reported, "Across Florida, elections officials say voters are being approached by individuals misrepresenting themselves and offering misleading or inaccurate information about voting." The paper reported on incidents of people coming to voters' homes and telling them their vote could be recorded by the canvasser and they didn't have to vote, that people were asking voters at an early voting center whether they had been arrested or had outstanding parking tickets or any debt.

\* \* \*

- In **Arizona,** a Fox Network affiliate accused a student group of illegally registering voters. A women's studies group at the University of Arizona was conducting a voter registration drive on campus when a reporter and film crew showed up to film the event. The reporter accused the students of participating in felony voter fraud, claiming that Arizona law prohibits students from out of state from registering in Arizona. Though students attempted to explain that Arizona law requires only that those registering be residents of the state 29 days before the election, the reporter remained unconvinced. That evening's broadcast included an interview with an official from the County Registrar's office that echoed the reporter's charges.

\* \* \*

- In **New Mexico** in September 2004, Republican U.S. Attorney David Iglesias formed a task force—involving the U.S. Justice Department, the FBI, the New Mexico Department of Public Safety and the secretary of state's office—to investigate allegations of voter fraud in the run up to the election. The move came at the request of the co-chair of the Bush-Cheney campaign for Bernalillo County, who claims that thousands of voter registration forms from Democratic-leaning groups are suspect. Civil rights advocates argue that by starting the investigation mere weeks before the presidential election, Iglesias runs the risk of intimidating legitimate voters. These concerns are echoed by the Justice Department's own manual on election crime, which states that "Federal prosecutors and investigators should be extremely careful to not conduct overt investigations during the pre-election period" so as to avoid "chilling legitimate voting and campaign activities." Other battleground states, including **Ohio** and **West Virginia** have initiated similar criminal investigations into voter fraud as part U.S. Attorney General John Ashcroft's "Voting Access and Integrity Initiative."

- In Alamance County, North Carolina, the sheriff directed his deputies to single out Latino voters in a voter fraud investigation. Sheriff Terry Johnson sent a "sample list" of 125 Latino registered voters to the Bureau of Immigration and Customs Enforcement. He said that the agency could only confirm that 38 were in the country legally. He told county commissioners that illegal immigrants used false documents to obtain drivers licenses and, at the same time, registered to vote. The director of a local group serving the Latino community expressed concern: "The sheriff has asked for a list of those who have Hispanic last names and then he is assuming that group is committing fraud. If the people in that list are citizens and they are being investigated, that is worrisome."

\*　\*　\*

- In preparation for the November elections, Milwaukee Mayor Tom Barrett requested 938,000 ballots, arguing that extra were needed in case of spoiled ballots and noting that **Wisconsin** law allowing same-day voter registration makes turnout unpredictable. However, Milwaukee County Executive Scott Walker refused Barrett's request, voicing concerns of vote fraud and even going so far as to suggest that unruly voters might try to steal extra ballots from polling places. Walker offered Milwaukee 679,000 ballots, fewer than were distributed in either the 2000 presidential election or the 2002 gubernatorial race. Barrett and civil rights groups charged that Walker was attempting to suppress Milwaukee voters. The controversy was politically charged, as Walker is a state co-chair of President Bush's re-election campaign and Barrett is state co-chair of the John Kerry campaign.

\*　\*　\*

Ultimately, a compromise was reached. Milwaukee got all of the ballots originally requested, the cost of the additional ballots was split between the city and the county, and unused ballots will be returned to the County Election Commission to allay concerns of vote fraud.

\*　\*　\*

- Republican operatives in **Pennsylvania** working in support of President Bush failed in a last-minute bid to relocate 63 Philadelphia polling places, most of which are located in African-American neighborhoods. The Republicans argued that they had made the request in the interest of voter "comfort" and to make polls more accessible to disabled voters. However, some of the requests were clearly racially motivated. Matt Robb, the GOP leader in South Philadelphia's 48th ward, said that he pressed for changes because he felt uncomfortable going to a polling place in an African-American neighborhood. "It's predominantly, 100 percent black," said Robb, who is white. "I'm just not going in there to get a knife in my back." The voter registration administrator for Philadelphia's City Commission refused the GOP's request, arguing that it was designed to suppress voter turnout and that it had come too soon before the election to be considered by the Commission. However, a successful effort by Republicans resulted in the last-minute relocation of 21 polling places in Scranton, Pennsylvania.

The move is likely to confuse voters and suppress turnout in an area where citizens typically vote Democratic more that 60 percent of the time.

• In **Michigan,** newly registered voters in at least two Secretary of State offices were incorrectly informed that they would not be eligible to vote in November's elections, prompting accusations of voter suppression. The notices, which were placed in offices in Ann Arbor and Battle Creek prior to the general election registration deadline, read: "Registering today? Please be advised that you are not eligible to vote in the November 2, 2004 General Election." State Senator Mark Schauer (D-Battle Creek) said, "This flier is either intended to suppress voter turnout or is a serious mistake." Michigan's Secretary of State, Republican Terri Lynn Land, said that accusations of suppression were "absolutely ludicrous." While all newly registered voters in these locations will be notified by mail of the mistake, State Senator Liz Brater (D-Ann Arbor) worried that some potential voters, having seen the erroneous notice, chose not to register.

*   *   *

*Voter Registration*

Vigorous voter registration drives by both nonpartisan and partisan organizations have resulted in dramatic increases in the number of registered voters. Some efforts were plagued by individual employees' failure to follow procedures that prevented registrations from being turned in. Some have been marred by deceptive practices, for example, by groups portraying themselves as nonpartisan to gain access to public places, but registering voters on a partisan basis. Some efforts have met with active resistance from public officials, who have relied on suspect logic or interpretations of election law to disallow registrations. And there are indications that some election officials have not invested in sufficient equipment and staff to handle the additional registrations and ensure that election day runs smoothly enough to allow every eligible voter a chance to cast a ballot.

*   *   *

• Officials in Miami Beach, **Florida,** in conjunction with the Department of Homeland Security, blocked a voter registration drive for new citizens, citing crowd control and public safety issues. In August, John C. Shewairy, Chief of Staff to the District Director of Homeland Security, informed Mi Familia Vota (MFV), a nonpartisan voter registration project run by the Center for Immigrant Democracy in conjunction with People For the American Way Foundation, that they would no longer be allowed to conduct voter registration drives on the sidewalks just outside the Miami Beach Convention Center at the conclusion of naturalization ceremonies. Mi Familia Vota attempted to solve the issue without resorting to litigation, but when Mr. Shewairy refused to respond to their requests and Miami Beach officials denied MFV access to the public sidewalks in front of the convention center in September, the organization went to federal court seeking an injunction. The judge issued an injunction restraining DHS and Miami Beach officials from prohibiting MFV's registration drive.

\* \* \*

- In **Nevada,** a company hired by the Republican National Committee to register Republicans in the state has been accused of throwing away registration forms signed by Democrats. A consulting firm headed by Nathan Sproul, a former director of the Arizona Republican Party, was paid nearly $500,000 by the RNC to carry out the voter registration drive and began operating in Nevada under the name Voter Outreach for America. Former employees allege that they were ordered to register only Republicans and one alleges that his pay was docked for also registering Democrats. This same employee alleges that his supervisor then tore up the Democratic registration forms and tossed them in the trash. The Democratic Party filed a petition requesting that registration be re-opened for those voters who may have had their registration cards destroyed but a Nevada district judge denied the request.

    Similar allegations have arisen against Sproul-run registration operations in **Oregon, Pennsylvania** and **West Virginia.** In some cases, the group misrepresented itself as the nonpartisan America Votes organization in order to gain access to public libraries and other locations, but then registered voters in a highly partisan manner. In West Virginia, temporary workers were reportedly hired to pose as opinion pollsters and instructed to only offer registration forms to those indicating they supported President Bush. In Pennsylvania, registration workers were also told not to register Democrats and instructed to ask undecided voters if they were "pro-choice or pro-life." If they answered "pro-life," the canvassers were to offer to help them register. If they answered "pro-choice," the canvassers were instructed to walk away.

\* \* \*

- In **New Mexico,** officials at several Indian Health Service (IHS) hospitals and clinics stopped an on-site, nonpartisan voter registration program saying that even nonpartisan voter registration was prohibited on federal property. Clinic staff involved in the registration complained, noting that the federal government has encouraged registration on military bases. As criticism mounted, the Indian Health Service, a division of the Department of Health and Human Services, clarified its position saying that outside groups may register voters at IHS facilities but that "no IHS employee will be registering voters as part of his or her official duties." When asked for clarification, IHS officials would only say that employees are expected to follow the Hatch Act, the law restricting partisan activity by federal workers.

- Students at universities across the country are finding it difficult, if not impossible, to register to vote in the towns where they reside. In **Virginia,** two students at the College of William and Mary had their registrations rejected by the Williamsburg registrar, citing the fact that the dorms where they lived were temporary residences "like a hotel room or a time share." Williamsburg Registrar David Andrews claimed that he gave extra scrutiny to registration forms listing on-campus addresses and questioned those applicants regarding the address on their car registration and drivers licenses. Students in **New York** and **Michigan** face similar hurdles, with the latter being prohibited by state law from registering to vote unless the address on their drivers license matches the address on their voter registration card. The Michigan law also mandates that first-time voters must register in person if they intend to vote via an absentee ballot, often forcing students to travel to their home districts in order to register. In **New Hampshire,** the head of the Coalition of New Hampshire Taxpayers vowed to fight students' efforts to register in that state, arguing that he didn't want the state to be "stuck with a bunch of left-leaning whack jobs from the colleges."

*   *   *

*Voting Rights*

- Civil rights advocates charge that in 2000, a faulty list intended to purge felons from **Florida**'s voting rolls resulted in the disenfranchisement of possibly thousands of eligible voters, many of whom were African Americans. In May 2004, in a move eerily reminiscent of 2000, Florida's Department of State went ahead with plans to purge nearly 48,000 suspected felons from the voter rolls despite serious concerns regarding the accuracy of the purge list. According to an October 16th report in *The Sarasota Herald-Tribune*, prior to the release of the list, state election officials warned Governor Jeb Bush, the President's brother, that the list was so unreliable that it should be abandoned, but Bush rejected their advice. Governor Bush denies this account.

    Shortly after the list went into effect, CNN sued to have it made public. Although Florida Secretary of State Glenda Hood, who oversees Florida elections, spent more that $100,000 in legal fees in an attempt to keep the list secret, a judge released it to the public in July. Almost immediately, newspapers reported that thousands of people had been put on the list in error. In addition, voting rights groups noted that half of the people listed were black, and Democrats outnumbered Republicans by 3 to 1. Only 61 Hispanics, who tend to vote for Republicans in Florida, appeared on the list. In the wake of public outcry, Hood scrapped the list and asked her inspector general to determine how it became so riddled with errors. Meanwhile, People For the American Way Foundation has called on U.S. Attorney General Ashcroft to appoint a special counsel to investigate the incident.

*   *   *

*Early Voting*

Early voting has been adopted in a number of states. By allowing voters to cast ballots during a period before Election Day, early voting can reduce the Election Day pressure of enormous crowds and long lines that might discourage or prevent some people from voting. Early voting itself, however, is not immune to problems.

*   *   *

- **Florida's** early voting got off to a shaky start, with problems reported at polling places across the state.

*   *   *

Civil rights groups and Republicans legislators complained to election officials about the lack of early voting sites in minority districts. In Duval County, the Southern Christian Leadership Conference and others sued to force officials to open more early voting sites for the county's minority residents. Later that day, election officials agreed to open four more early voting sites in geographically diverse locations, but the group sought an emergency order from the court to provide an additional eight sites, claiming that the placement of the new locations discriminated against the African-American population. In Miami-Dade, two Republican congressmen complained that the lack of voting machines and early voting sites in the Hispanic community constituted a "pattern of discrimination." The Miami-Dade supervisors office agreed to provide more machines, but an elections supervisor claimed that Republicans in the state legislature had intentionally limited the number of early voting sites in order to prevent minority voters from voting. The lawyer for the state House committee in question flatly denied the charge.

*   *   *

- Nearly 100 voters in **Iowa**, many of whom were students from a local university, were prevented from voting early after a Republican county auditor instructed the polling places to close as scheduled despite the fact that many people were still waiting in line. State law requires that polling places remain open until all voters who arrived before the scheduled closing time have voted, but County Auditor Mary Mosiman insisted that each precinct only had a "finite number of hours to work with." Moisman also stated that, at the time the polls closed, poll workers only had four unused ballots left and wouldn't have had enough supplies to allow everyone on line to vote. Furthermore, she declared that she had no intention of changing her policy and that, in the future, she would work to make sure that people know that voting hours will not be extended, regardless of how many people are still in line.

*Absentee Ballots*

Allowing voters to cast absentee ballots is another way to relieve pressure on the election system on Election Day, as well as to accommodate voters who have difficulty traveling to a polling site or whose schedule will have them away from home on Election Day. Absentee ballots have also been the source of errors and disputes.

\*   \*   \*

- In **Pennsylvania**, a court challenge over whether candidate Ralph Nader's name would appear on the state's ballot caused problems with overseas mailing of absentee ballots. The shifting status of Nader's listing as a presidential candidate resulted in some ballots being sent with his name and some without. The U.S. Justice Department sought an emergency order seeking to force the state to send corrected ballots to overseas voters and extend the period for ballot returns by two weeks. A federal judge denied the request, saying it could do more harm than good.

  In Lancaster County, election officials defied state election officials and voted along party lines to mail thousands of absentee ballots including presidential candidate Ralph Nader, even though his appearance on the ballot was the subject of court challenge and a decision was imminent. A court threw Nader off the ballot the same day that county officials mailed ballots including his name.

\*   \*   \*

*Provisional Balloting*

Some have suggested that provisional ballots have the potential to become the "hanging chads" of the 2004 election. Provisional ballots were mandated by the Help America Vote Act of 2002 in response to the chaotic 2000 presidential election. The law requires that when voters who arrive at the polls are not listed on the rolls, they be given the option of voting provisionally. If their registration information is later confirmed, their votes will be counted. However, states differ over when the ballots should count. While some states count statewide and national votes for those who cast their ballots in the wrong locality, other states require that ballots be cast in the correct precinct to be counted. There is also a wide variation from state to state regarding how much time election officials have to tabulate provisional ballots. For example, while California officials have 28 days to count them, Florida, which was the location of so much electoral strife in 2000, gives officials a mere two days to reach a final tally. In several states, voting rights activists have filed suit in an effort to make the provisional balloting process more inclusive.

- In September, **Ohio** Secretary of State Kenneth Blackwell directed county election officials to only give provisional ballots to voters who report to the correct precinct. His ruling has the potential to be particularly problematic this election cycle because many polling places have changed since the last federal election, increasing the likelihood that voters will show up at the wrong precinct.

    Both the state Democratic Party and the Ohio Voter Protection Project, a voting-rights group, filed lawsuits contending that Blackwell's rules violate the Help America Vote Act of 2002. In mid-October, U.S. District Judge James Carr ruled that Ohio voters who go to the wrong polling place should still have their provisional ballots counted as long as they are in the county where they are registered. "Lessened participation at the polls diminishes the vitality of our democracy," said Carr. Still, Blackwell was defiant, filing an appeal to 6th U.S. Circuit Court of Appeals and vowing to take his case all the way to the U.S. Supreme Court if necessary. Promising that he would go to jail before allowing out-of-precinct voters to have their provisional ballots counted, Blackwell likened his stance to those of Gandhi and the Rev. Martin Luther King, Jr. Responded a spokesman for the Ohio Democratic Party's Voter Protection Program, "Many civil rights leaders went to jail to defend the right to vote. If this official wants to go to jail to thwart it, that would be unfortunate." A federal appeals court then reversed the lower court ruling, thereby preventing Ohio voters from casting their provisional ballots anywhere in the county.

\* \* \*

- Meanwhile, in **Michigan** in October, U.S. District Judge David Lawson took the opposite view, ruling that as long as voters go to the right city, township, or village, their votes for federal offices should count. The state is appealing the decision, which came about due to a suit filed by Michigan Democrats, the NAACP and voting rights groups. Lawson's ruling came in spite of protests raised by the U.S. Department of Justice. "Congress made an explicit decision not to disturb states' long-standing authority to determine how ballots are to be counted, and the United States believes that courts must respect that congressional decision," said Justice Department spokesman Mark Corallo. Justice's stance prompted a rebuke from Robert F. Bauer, national counsel for voter protection at the Democratic National Committee: "Here you have the Justice Department waiting until two weeks before the election and suddenly taking this position, which is the Republican Party's position." A federal appeals court issued a stay of the lower court's ruling and agree to hear an expedited appeal of the case.

*Voter ID*

Voter identification requirements are the frequent cause of confusion at polling places, where poorly trained poll workers often wrongly insist that voters provide photo IDs or neglect to inform voters without identification of alternatives, like signing an affidavit. Overly restrictive identification requirements have a disproportionate impact on minority voters, who are less likely to have photo identification.

- Two lawsuits pressed by Republican state representatives could have resulted in onerous identification requirements for 112,000 **New Mexico** voters. The suits contended that all first-time voters who do not register in person with their county clerk are required to produce identification at the polls on Election Day. According to the plaintiffs in these cases, new voters who register in person at other government offices or in voter registration drives would face the ID requirement. New Mexico's Secretary of State, a Democrat, disagreed, arguing that the ID requirement only applies to new voters who register by mail. The broader ID requirement could have been particularly burdensome for college students, rural voters, returning veterans, and minorities. After conflicting decisions from lower courts, the state Supreme Court ruled that only first-time voters who registered by mail were required to show ID on Election Day.

\* \* \*

- **Colorado's** new law requiring identification at the polls was challenged by Colorado Common Cause and three voters who were turned away from the polls in the August 2004 primary. In September, they filed a suit against Secretary of State Donetta Davidson, arguing that the rule amounted to a poll tax because most proof of identification costs money. Election officials claimed that voter identification was needed to prevent fraud. Republican Governor Bill Owens said he would appeal the decision if a judge overturns the identification requirement.

*Machines and Miscellaneous*

\*   \*   \*

• According to the *Columbus Dispatch*, voters in **Ohio's** predominantly black neighborhoods face the prospect of having their votes go uncounted at a rate nearly three times higher than those in the rest of the state because of the continued use of punch-card ballots. Based on an analysis conducted by the paper, in 2000, the percentage of votes cast in predominately black areas for which no presidential vote was counted was about 5 percent versus less than 2 percent for the rest of Ohio. A further analysis of the areas with the most uncounted votes revealed that the chances of a majority white district falling into that category was 2 in 33 versus 2 in 3 for majority black districts. Every one of those majority black precincts will be using punch-card ballots again in 2004.

\*   \*   \*

# 54

# "Make Way for Election Month: The Floridafication of Our Political Waters Continues Unabated"

### JOHN H. FUND

Forget Election Day. If the legal maneuverings by the Kerry and Bush campaigns are any measure, America may soon face an Election Month. "After Florida in 2000, Election Night is not necessarily the finish line anymore," says Doug Chapin, director of the nonpartisan Election Reform Information Project. "If you think of election problems as akin to forest fires, the woods are no drier than they were in 2000, but many more people have matches." In a country of 170,000 polling places, it's a given that at least some ballot boxes will be subject to mistakes or chicanery. About 25 percent of Americans will be using new controversial electronic voting machines sure to become a magnet for lawsuits. Many other voters will have to rely on the same punch-card voting machines that resulted in so much confusion in Florida's 2000 election.

The warring political camps have already sent out clear signs that they

intend to see each other in court. John Kerry has announced the creation
of a nationwide SWAT team of election lawyers who will take "tough
action" against the voter "intimidation and harassment" he claims
"stole" the votes of 57,000 African Americans in Florida in 2000. The fact
that his campaign has failed to identify any of these countless victims is a
sign that his new legal brigade may be more about bending the rules in
his favor than it is about righting any voting wrongs.

The 57,000 figure comes from the controversial U.S. Commission on
Civil Rights, which issued an election report sorely lacking in specifics or
detail. Florida Attorney General Bob Butterworth—a Democrat—testified
that of the 2,600 complaints he received on Election Day, only three were
about racial discrimination. The League of Women Voters testified it had
not received "any evidence of race-based problems." Republicans, meanwhile, are conducting training sessions to respond to complaints of absentee ballot fraud, duplicate registrations, and elderly residents in
nursing homes being overly "assisted" in marking their ballot. They also
fear Democratic lawyers will take advantage of a flood of provisional ballots cast by people who aren't on the voter registration rolls and demand
that all of them be counted. If the number of provisional ballots exceed
the margin of victory in any state, you can bet a lawyer will echo the
Florida 2000 argument that "every vote must count," regardless of eligibility. From now on, candidates will have to hope their vote totals are beyond the "margin of litigation."

But when it comes to the legal arms race this fall, Democrats have the
big guns. It doesn't hurt that John Edwards, a former trial lawyer, is now
on the Democratic ticket. Fred Baron, one-time president of the Association of Trial Lawyers of America (ATLA) and a leading asbestos plaintiffs' lawyer, is a top fundraiser for the Kerry-Edwards ticket. In 2002,
ATLA became the largest single contributor to federal candidates, almost
all of its money flowing to Democrats. E-mails have already gone out to
trial lawyers requesting they help prepare cookie-cutter lawsuits to be
filed before the election.

Voters should expect to see troops of attorneys from both parties monitoring the polls this fall. Some even plan to wear identifying signs
around their neck so that voters with a problem can procure legal representation on the spot.

This year, the lawsuits started early. Missouri Democrats sued to allow
St. Louis City, a Democratic stronghold, to be the only jurisdiction in the
state to allow early voting, in which citizens can cast their ballots weeks
in advance at government buildings. Since GOP counties would not be
holding early voting, such a move would clearly advantage Democrats.
A judge threw the case out, ruling that the state legislature had announced plans for early voting systems, but had not implemented any. In
New Mexico, which Al Gore carried by only 366 votes in 2000, Rebecca

Vigil-Giron, the Democratic secretary of state, ordered county clerks not to obey a new federally mandated law requiring that first-time voters who registered outside an election office must show a form of ID to vote.

Ms. Vigil-Giron, who stepped out of her official capacity as an election officer to make automated campaign phone calls on behalf of Al Gore in 2000, says the law shouldn't apply to the thousands of new voters signed up by political parties or liberal activist groups such as the Association of Community Organizations for Reform Now—also known as ACORN. The outcome is important because one out of nine registered voters in New Mexico has been signed up just in the last year, an astonishing 115,000 people. Since ACORN is paying workers a bounty if they register more than 24 people a day, there are natural concerns about fraud. At least 3,000 voter registrations in Albuquerque's Bernalillo County are suspect.

Last month, Bernalillo County Sheriff Darren White asked the local U.S. attorney to investigate reports that people were registering multiple times and that a 13-year-old boy along with his 15-year-old friend had been signed up to vote. New Mexico officials have been alerted to stories from neighboring Colorado, where the *Denver Post* reports that "ACORN has already admitted to Colorado law enforcement officials it may have turned in fraudulent voter registration cards in Denver." Glen Stout, the father of the 13-year-old boy, says his son Kevin never filled out a voter registration card. He has joined a suit to enforce the law the state legislature passed in January mandating that first-time voters show identification. "Every fraudulent vote cancels out the vote of an honest New Mexican," he says.

But Vigil-Giron says the law does not apply to first-time registrations that are filled out in the presence of a third party, such as an ACORN worker. Matthew Henderson, the head of the local ACORN drive, says that ID requirements are "no different than what was going on in the civil rights movement of the '60s. This is about a set of people trying to stop another set of people from voting." One of the plaintiffs demanding that Secretary of State Vigil-Giron obey the law is Toby Gutierrez, who responded to Henderson by saying, "I am Hispanic, a former Army Ranger and disgusted by the Democrats' fear tactics. Hispanics ought to be outraged at the Democratic Party's contention that we are so uninformed and so uneducated that we are incapable of showing the type of ID required to rent a movie."

Henderson has been largely silent since a court hearing on the case in early September before state Judge Robert L. Thompson. At that hearing, Henderson invoked his Fifth Amendment protections and refused to say whether his organization illegally copies voter registration cards. However, he had previously admitted to the practice when he told the *Albuquerque Tribune* that ACORN "made photocopies of all the cards it delivered to the county." Henderson also claimed in court that ACORN does not pay bounties or bonuses to its employees and that their only compensation is an $8-an-hour wage. But ACORN crew leaders told reporters that anyone who turned in more than 24 cards a day got a $50 bonus—a sum almost equal to their $64 pay for an 8-hour day.

While Judge Thompson ruled in early September that the state law, which was passed by a Democratic legislature, was "clear on its face," he ruled that requiring all new registrants to show ID would be disruptive so close to the election. The case is being appealed to the state supreme court, a solidly liberal body that is unlikely to overrule the judge.

The fear now is that impostors will find it easy to vote. Chaves County Clerk Dave Kunko called the judge's ruling to waive the ID requirement for newly registered voters "puzzling." Kunko, a Republican, added: "It would take our office no more than a few days to flag voters for identification. Does this mean if it's inconvenient to follow a law, we don't have to follow it?"

To his credit, David Iglesias, the local U.S. attorney, is forming a task force to probe charges of voter fraud. Without an ID requirement for first-time voters, his office may have a lot of work on its hands after Election Night.

The land of Enchantment isn't the only state that's been despoiled by ACORN's bad seeds. In Columbus, Ohio, ACORN was forced to fire two workers after several "blatantly false" voter registration forms were filed with election officials. In St. Louis, the local election board has discovered more than 1,000 suspicious new voter registrations from a pile of more than 5,000 turned in by a local ACORN chapter. The group sent in another batch of 500 voter-registration cards that also were suspect, Keena Carter, the election board's deputy director and a Democrat, told the *St. Louis Post-Dispatch*. Many were filled out by people who gave addresses in Illinois or elsewhere in Missouri. Nor is ACORN the only liberal group that appears to be engaged in a wholesale con of the election system. America Coming Together (ACT), an anti-Bush group funded by $5 million from financier George Soros, hired dozens of felons to go door-to-door to register voters in Florida, Missouri, and Ohio.

ACT's counteroffensive on the charges was swift and predictable. First, ACT claimed it hadn't employed violent felons. Then, when the AP reported that ACT employees included people convicted of assault and sex offenses, the group admitted it might also have hired felons in 14 other battleground states. It also promised to fire anyone guilty of "violent or other serious offenses." In some cases it won't have to; four felons it hired in Missouri have already gone back to prison, including one for endangering the welfare of a minor.

That's one reason the Missouri Department of Corrections banned ACT from its list of potential employers for parolees in halfway houses. Noting that the felons would have to handle driver's license information and telephone numbers as part of the voter-registration process, the department concluded that "from a public safety standpoint, we didn't want offenders to be in a situation where they would be handling that information."

ACT also denied that it is violating federal election laws which prohibit it from engaging in partisan activity on behalf of the Kerry campaign, even though its website says it is "laying the groundwork to defeat George W. Bush and elect Democrats." Its roster of staffers is chock-full of Democratic operatives with close ties to Sen. Kerry. Recently, ACT staffer Rodney Shelton left to join the Kerry campaign as its Arkansas state director. At the same time, former Kerry campaign manager Jim Jordan has joined ACT. Federal law forbids any coordination between ACT and the Kerry campaign, but the law is impossible to enforce.

Ellen Malcolm, ACT's president, says the attacks on her group represent an attempt "to distort and play politics with this situation, to attempt to disrupt ACT and our grassroots activities." But in light of the felon scandal, ACT's activities now merit closer scrutiny, because they may be making the problem of our sloppy voter rolls worse. The Federal Election Commission found in 2002 that 12 percent of all registered voters nationally were "inactive voters," and thus subject to possible misuse by having someone else vote in their name. In Missouri, a swing state George W. Bush narrowly won in 2000, ACT bought at least $40,000 worth of voter lists from the state's Democratic Party and then paid 75 canvassers between $8 and $12 an hour to go door-to-door to sign up new voters. Since January, they have signed up 12,000 new voter registrations in St. Louis alone.

The St. Louis Election Board reports that about three-quarters of ACT's registrations were valid, but trusting any numbers they report is a perilous exercise. St. Louis is one of several American cities in which registered voters outnumber residents of voting age. State Auditor Claire McCaskill, a Democrat, issued a scathing report on the Election Board's procedures in June. It found that nearly 10 percent, or 24,000, of the city's voters were "questionable." The report tabulated 4,405 dead people, 2,242 felons, 1,453 people voting from vacant lots and 15,963 also registered somewhere else in Missouri or Illinois. At least 935 of the felons, or some 40 percent, had apparently cast a ballot in a recent election.

"You have felons registering felons who then commit another felony by casting an illegal vote," says Missouri's Sen. Kit Bond, who coauthored the 2002 Help America Vote Act to start the process of cleaning up the nation's voter rolls. He was motivated by the chaotic Election Day of 2000 in which the Gore campaign sued to keep the polls open in St. Louis on the grounds people had been denied the right to vote. Its "plaintiff," Robert D. Odom, turned out to be dead. An aide to a Democratic congressman with the same last name was then substituted as the plaintiff, but it was discovered that he had successfully voted earlier that day.

A St. Louis judge nonetheless ordered the polls kept open, and they were for 45 minutes until a higher court overruled her. Ms. McCaskill, the state auditor, has concluded the St. Louis Election Board is beyond fixing. She says it needs "local control and direct accountability" and suggests control of it be transferred directly to the mayor. Gov. Bob Holden, a fellow Democrat, agrees.

Reform may finally be in the cards in St. Louis, but at least a dozen other major U.S. cities, ranging from Philadelphia to Miami, also need a complete house-cleaning. In 2001, the *Palm Beach Post* concluded that more than 5,600 people voted in Florida who appeared to perfectly match names on a list of suspected felons who were barred from voting. A smaller number of people were also mistakenly listed on voter rolls as being felons when they were not. But anyone who combats voter fraud or questions the accuracy of voter rolls is likely to come in for abuse. When the *Miami Herald* won a Pulitzer Prize for its reporting on the rampant absentee ballot fraud in that city's 1998 mayoral election, the Pulitzer jury noted it had been subject to "a public campaign accusing the paper of ethnic bias and attempted intimidation." Local officials in several states who've tried to purge voter rolls of felons and noncitizens have been hit with nuisance lawsuits alleging civil-rights abuse.

It's no surprise that many rolls remain clogged with voter deadwood. A generation ago, the existence of insidious poll taxes and other forms of voter intimidation represented a real threat to free and fair elections. But those problems have receded, only to be replaced by old-fashioned ballot rigging. We now send teams of election observers to countries such as Venezuela, Cambodia, and Albania, where fraud has been rampant. The mess in St. Louis and other cities should prompt us to consider having some election observers in our own backyard. Surely the right to vote includes an equal right not to have that ballot diluted by nonexistent or ineligible voters.

In 1998, the mayor of Miami was removed from office after it was learned 56 absentee-ballot "vote brokers" had forged ballots. It shouldn't surprise anyone then that in the 2002 election Miami election officials hired the Center for Democracy, which normally observes elections in places like Guatemala and Russia, to send 20 election monitors to south Florida.

Now that our elections are being scrutinized the way the U.S. looks at developing countries, who will monitor the lawyers as they turn American politics into another breeding ground for endless litigation? A new federal law is sending states money for better election systems and training, but at the state level we badly need clearer laws and better protections against fraud if we are to avoid the further Floridafication of our politics.

DISCUSSION QUESTIONS

1. If you were an election official, would you abide by a "letter of the law" approach when considering voter registration issues, or would you be flexible in order to maximize turnout? What are the advantages and disadvantages of each strategy?

2. Would you approve of a proposal that all voters had to show photo identification at polling places? Do you think that would decrease turnout? If so, is that a reasonable cost?

3. Based on the reports in these articles, identify and defend three reforms you would make to the voting process in the United States.

4. Do you have any concerns about voting conducted over the Internet? Are there benefits that outweigh these concerns?

# CHAPTER 11

# Political Parties

## 55

## "The Decline of Collective Responsibility in American Politics"

### MORRIS P. FIORINA

*For more than three decades, political scientists have studied the changing status of American political parties. Morris Fiorina, writing in the early 1980s, suggests that political parties provide many benefits for American democracy, in particular by clarifying policy alternatives and letting citizens know whom to hold accountable when they are dissatisfied with government performance. He sees decline in all the key areas of political-party involvement: the electorate, in government, and in party organizations. He argues that the decline eliminates the motivation for elected members of the parties to define broad policy objectives, leading to diminished political participation and a rise of alienation. Policies are aimed at serving the narrow interests of the various single-issue groups that dominate politics rather than the broad constituencies represented by parties. Without strong political parties to provide electoral accountability, American politics has suffered a "decline in collective responsibility" in Fiorina's view. In the effort to reform the often-corrupt political parties of the late 1800s—often referred to as "machines" led by "bosses"—Fiorina asks us to consider whether we have eliminated the best way to hold elected officials accountable at the ballot box.*

Though the Founding Fathers believed in the necessity of establishing a genuinely national government, they took great pains to design one that could not lightly do things *to* its citizens; what government might do *for* its citizens was to be limited to the functions of what we know now as the "watchman state."

\* \* \*

Given the historical record faced by the Founders, their emphasis on constraining government is understandable. But we face a later historical record, one that shows two hundred years of increasing demands for government to act positively. Moreover, developments unforeseen by the Founders increasingly raise the likelihood that the uncoordinated actions of individuals and groups will inflict serious damage on the nation as a whole. The by-products of the industrial and technological revolutions impose physical risks not only on us, but on future generations as well. Resource shortages and international cartels raise the spectre of economic ruin. And the simple proliferation of special interests with their intense, particularistic demands threatens to render us politically incapable of taking actions that might either advance the state of society or prevent foreseeable deteriorations in that state. None of this is to suggest that we should forget about what government can do *to* us—the contemporary concern with the proper scope and methods of government intervention in the social and economic orders is long overdue. But the modern age demands as well that we worry about our ability to make government work *for* us. The problem is that we are gradually losing that ability, and a principal reason for this loss is the steady erosion of *responsibility* in American politics.

*    *    *

Unfortunately, the importance of responsibility in a democracy is matched by the difficulty of attaining it. In an autocracy, individual responsibility suffices; the location of power in a single individual locates responsibility in that individual as well. But individual responsibility is insufficient whenever more than one person shares governmental authority. We can hold a particular congressman individually responsible for a personal transgression such as bribe-taking. We can even hold a president individually responsible for military moves where he presents Congress and the citizenry with a *fait accompli*. But on most national issues individual responsibility is difficult to assess. If one were to go to Washington, randomly accost a Democratic congressman, and berate him about a 20-percent rate of inflation, imagine the response. More than likely it would run, "Don't blame me. If 'they' had done what I've advocated for $x$ years, things would be fine today."

*    *    *

American institutional structure makes this kind of game-playing all too easy. In order to overcome it we must lay the credit or blame for national conditions on all those who had any hand in bringing them about: some form of *collective responsibility* is essential.

The only way collective responsibility has ever existed, and can exist given our institutions, is through the agency of the political party; in American politics, responsibility requires cohesive parties. This is an old claim to be sure, but its age does not detract from its present relevance. In fact, the continuing decline in public esteem for the parties and continuing efforts to "reform" them out of the political process suggest that old arguments for party responsibility have not been made often enough or, at least, convincingly enough, so I will make these arguments once again in this essay.

A strong political party can generate collective responsibility by creating incentive for leaders, followers, and popular supporters to think and act in collective terms. First, by providing party leaders with the capability (e.g., control of institutional patronage, nominations, and so on) to discipline party members, genuine leadership becomes possible. Legislative output is less likely to be a least common denominator—a residue of myriad conflicting proposals—and more likely to consist of a program actually intended to solve a problem or move the nation in a particular direction. Second, the subordination of individual officeholders to the party lessens their ability to separate themselves from party actions. Like it or not, their performance becomes identified with the performance of the collectivity to which they belong. Third, with individual candidate variation greatly reduced, voters have less incentive to support individuals and more incentive to support or oppose the party as a whole. And fourth, the circle closes as party-line voting in the electorate provides party leaders with the incentive to propose policies that will earn the support of a national majority, and party back-benchers* with the personal incentive to cooperate with leaders in the attempt to compile a good record for the party as a whole.

In the American context, strong parties have traditionally clarified politics in two ways. First, they allow citizens to assess responsibility easily, at least when the government is unified, which it more often was in earlier eras when party meant more than it does today. Citizens need only evaluate the social, economic, and international conditions they observe and make a simple decision for or against change. They do not need to decide whether the energy, inflation, urban, and defense policies advocated by their congressman would be superior to those advocated by [the president]—were any of them to be enacted!

The second way in which strong parties clarify American politics follows from the first. When citizens assess responsibility on the party as a whole, party members have personal incentives to see the party evaluated favorably. They have little to gain from gutting their president's program one day and attacking him for lack of leadership the next, since they share in the president's fate when voters do not differentiate within the party. Put simply, party responsibility provides party members with a personal stake in their collective performance.

---

* Back-benchers are junior members of the Parliament, who sit in the rear benches of the House of Commons. Here, the term refers to junior members of political parties.

Admittedly, party responsibility is a blunt instrument. The objection immediately arises that party responsibility condemns junior Democratic representatives to suffer electorally for an inflation they could do little to affect. An unhappy situation, true, but unless we accept it, Congress as a whole escapes electoral retribution for an inflation they *could* have done something to affect. Responsibility requires acceptance of both conditions. The choice is between a blunt instrument or none at all.

\* \* \*

In earlier times, when citizens voted for the party, not the person, parties had incentives to nominate good candidates, because poor ones could have harmful fallout on the ticket as a whole. In particular, the existence of presidential coattails (positive and negative) provided an inducement to avoid the nomination of narrowly based candidates, no matter how committed their supporters. And, once in office, the existence of party voting in the electorate provided party members with the incentive to compile a good *party* record. In particular, the tendency of national midterm elections to serve as referenda on the performance of the president provided a clear inducement for congressmen to do what they could to see that their president was perceived as a solid performer. By stimulating electoral phenomena such as coattail effects and mid-term referenda, party transformed some degree of personal ambition into concern with collective performance.

\* \* \*

*The Continuing Decline of Party in the United States*

### Party Organizations

In the United States, party organization has traditionally meant state and local party organization. The national party generally has been a loose confederacy of subnational units that swings into action for a brief period every four years. This characterization remains true today, despite the somewhat greater influence and augmented functions of the national organizations. Though such things are difficult to measure precisely, there is general agreement that the formal party organizations have undergone a secular decline since their peak at the end of the nineteenth century. The prototype of the old-style organization was the urban machine, a form approximated today only in Chicago.

\* \* \*

*[Fiorina discusses the reforms of the late nineteenth and early twentieth century.]*

In the 1970s two series of reforms further weakened the influence of organized parties in American national politics. The first was a series of legal changes deliberately intended to lessen organized party influence in the presidential nominating process. In the Democratic party, "New Politics" activists captured the national party apparatus and imposed a series of rules changes designed to "open up" the politics of presidential nominations. The Republican party—long more amateur and open than the Democratic party—adopted weaker versions of the Democratic rules changes. In addition, modifications of state electoral laws to conform to the Democratic rules changes (enforced by the federal courts) stimulated Republican rules changes as well.

*    *    *

A second series of 1970s reforms lessened the role of formal party organizations in the conduct of political campaigns. These are financing regulations growing out of the Federal Election Campaign Act of 1971 as amended in 1974 and 1976. In this case the reforms were aimed at cleaning up corruption in the financing of campaigns; their effects on the parties were a by-product, though many individuals accurately predicted its nature. Serious presidential candidates are now publicly financed. Though the law permits the national party to spend two cents per eligible voter on behalf of the nominee, it also obliges the candidate to set up a finance committee separate from the national party. Between this legally mandated separation and fear of violating spending limits or accounting regulations, for example, the law has the effect of encouraging the candidate to keep his party at arm's length.

*    *    *

The ultimate results of such reforms are easy to predict. A lesser party role in the nominating and financing of candidates encourages candidates to organize and conduct independent campaigns, which further weakens the role of parties. . . . [I]f parties do not grant nominations, fund their choices, and work for them, why should those choices feel any commitment to their party?

### Party in the Electorate

In the citizenry at large, party takes the form of a psychological attachment. The typical American traditionally has been likely to identify with one or the other of the two major parties. Such identifications are transmitted across generations to some degree, and within the individual they tend to be fairly stable. But there is mounting evidence that the basis of identification lies in the individual's experiences (direct and vicarious, through family and social groups) with the parties in the past. Our current party system, of course, is based on the dislocations of the Depression period and the New Deal attempts to alleviate them. Though only a small proportion of those who experienced the Depression directly are active voters today, the general outlines of citizen party identifications much resemble those established at that time.

Again, there is reason to believe that the extent of citizen attachments to parties has undergone a long-term decline from a nineteenth-century high. And again, the New Deal appears to have been a period during which the decline was arrested, even temporarily reversed. But again, the decline of party has reasserted itself in the 1970s.

\* \* \*

As the 1960s wore on, the heretofore stable distribution of citizen party identifications began to change in the general direction of weakened attachments to the parties. Between 1960 and 1976, independents, broadly defined, increased from less than a quarter to more than a third of the voting-age population. Strong identifiers declined from slightly more than a third to about a quarter of the population.

\* \* \*

Indisputably, party in the electorate has declined in recent years. Why? To some extent the electoral decline results from the organizational decline. Few party organizations any longer have the tangible incentives to turn out the faithful and assure their loyalty. Candidates run independent campaigns and deemphasize their partisan ties whenever they see any short-term electoral gain in doing so. If party is increasingly less important in the nomination and election of candidates, it is not surprising that such diminished importance is reflected in the attitudes and behavior of the voter.

Certain long-term sociological and technological trends also appear to work against party in the electorate. The population is younger, and younger citizens traditionally are less attached to the parties than their elders. The population is more highly educated; fewer voters need some means of simplifying the choices they face in the political arena, and party, of course, has been the principal means of simplification. And the media revolution has vastly expanded the amount of information easily available to the citizenry. Candidates would have little incentive to operate campaigns independent of the parties if there were no means to apprise the citizenry of their independence. The media provide the means.

Finally, our present party system is an old one. For increasing numbers of citizens, party attachments based on the Great Depression seem lacking in relevance to the problems of the late twentieth century. Beginning with the racial issue in the 1960s, proceeding to the social issue of the 1970s, and to the energy, environment, and inflation issues of today, the parties have been rent by internal dissension. Sometimes they failed to take stands, at other times they took the wrong ones from the standpoint of the rank and file, and at most times they have failed to solve the new problems in any genuine sense. Since 1965 the parties have done little or nothing to earn the loyalties of modern Americans.

## Party in Government

If the organizational capabilities of the parties have weakened, and their psychological ties to the voters have loosened, one would expect predictable consequences for the party in government. In particular, one would expect to see an increasing degree of split party control within and across the levels of American government. The evidence on this point is overwhelming.

\* \* \*

The increased fragmentation of the party in government makes it more difficult for government officeholders to work together than in times past (not that it has ever been terribly easy). Voters meanwhile have a more difficult time attributing responsibility for government performance, and this only further fragments party control. The result is lessened collective responsibility in the system.

What has taken up the slack left by the weakening of the traditional [party] determinants of congressional voting? It appears that a variety of personal and local influences now play a major role in citizen evaluations of their representatives. Along with the expansion of the federal presence in American life, the traditional role of the congressman as an all-purpose ombudsman has greatly expanded. Tens of millions of citizens now are directly affected by federal decisions. Myriad programs provide opportunities to profit from government largesse, and myriad regulations impose costs and/or constraints on citizen activities. And, whether seeking to gain profit or avoid costs, citizens seek the aid of their congressmen. When a court imposes a desegregation plan on an urban school board, the congressional offices immediately are contacted for aid in safeguarding existing sources of funding and in determining eligibility for new ones. When a major employer announces plans to quit an area, the congressional offices immediately are contacted to explore possibilities for using federal programs to persuade the employer to reconsider. Contractors appreciate a good congressional word with DOD [Department of Defense] procurement officers. Local artistic groups cannot survive without NEA [National Endowment for the Arts] funding. And, of course, there are the major individual programs such as social security and veterans' benefits that create a steady demand for congressional information and aid services. Such activities are nonpartisan, nonideological, and, most important, noncontroversial. Moreover, the contribution of the congressman in the realm of district service appears considerably greater than the impact of his or her single vote on major national issues. Constituents respond rationally to this modern state of affairs by weighing nonprogrammatic constituency service heavily when casting their congressional votes. And this emphasis on the part of constituents provides the means for incumbents to solidify their hold on the office. Even if elected by a narrow margin, diligent service activities enable a congressman to neutralize or even convert a portion of those who would otherwise oppose him on policy or ideological grounds. Emphasis on local, nonpartisan factors in congressional voting enables the modern congressman to withstand national swings, whereas yesteryear's uninsulated congressmen were more dependent on preventing the occurrence of the swings.

\*    \*    \*

*[The result is the insulation of the modern congressional member from national forces altogether.]*

The withering away of the party organizations and the weakening of party in the electorate have begun to show up as disarray in the party in government. As the electoral fates of congressmen and the president have diverged, their incentives to cooperate have diverged as well. Congressmen have little personal incentive to bear any risk in their president's behalf, since they no longer expect to gain much from his successes or suffer much from his failures. Only those who personally agree with the president's program and/or those who find that program well suited for their particular district support the president. And there are not enough of these to construct the coalitions necessary for action on the major issues now facing the country. By holding only the president responsible for national conditions, the electorate enables officialdom as a whole to escape responsibility. This situation lies at the root of many of the problems that now plague American public life.

### Some Consequences of the Decline of Collective Responsibility

The weakening of party has contributed directly to the severity of several of the important problems the nation faces. For some of these, such as the government's inability to deal with inflation and energy, the connections are obvious. But for other problems, such as the growing importance of single-issue politics and the growing alienation of the American citizenry, the connections are more subtle.

### Immobilism

As the electoral interdependence of the party in government declines, its ability to act also declines. If responsibility can be shifted to another level or to another officeholder, there is less incentive to stick one's neck out in an attempt to solve a given problem. Leadership becomes more difficult, the ever-present bias toward the short-term solution becomes more pronounced, and the possibility of solving any given problem lessens.

. . . [P]olitical inability to take actions that entail short-run costs ordinarily will result in much higher costs in the long run—we cannot continually depend on the technological fix. So the present American immobilism cannot be dismissed lightly. The sad thing is that the American people appear to understand the depth of our present problems and, at least in principle, appear prepared to sacrifice in furtherance of the long-run good. But they will not have an opportunity to choose between two or more such long-term plans. Although both parties promise tough, equitable policies, in the present state of our politics, neither can deliver.

### Single-Issue Politics

In recent years both political analysts and politicians have decried the increased importance of single-issue groups in American politics. Some in fact would claim that the present immobilism in our politics owes more to the rise of single-issue groups than to the decline of party. A little thought, however, should reveal that the two trends are connected. Is single-issue politics a recent phenomenon? The contention is doubtful; such groups have always been active participants in American politics. The gun lobby already was a classic example at the time of President Kennedy's assassination. And however impressive the antiabortionists appear today, remember the temperance movement, which succeeded in getting its constitutional amendment. American history contains numerous forerunners of today's groups, from anti-Masons to abolitionists to the Klan—singularity of purpose is by no means a modern phenomenon. Why, then, do we hear all the contemporary hoopla about single-issue groups? Probably because politicians fear them now more than before and thus allow them to play a larger role in our politics. Why should this be so? Simply because the parties are too weak to protect their members and thus to contain single-issue politics.

In earlier times single-issue groups were under greater pressures to reach accommodations with the parties. After all, the parties nominated candidates, financed candidates, worked for candidates, and, perhaps most important, party voting protected candidates. When a contemporary single-issue group threatens to "get" an officeholder, the threat must be taken seriously.

\* \* \*

Not only did the party organization have greater ability to resist single-issue pressures at the electoral level, but the party in government had greater ability to control the agenda, and thereby contain single-issue pressures at the policy-making level. Today we seem condemned to go through an annual agony over federal abortion funding. There is little doubt that politicians on both sides would prefer to reach some reasonable compromise at the committee level and settle the issue. But in today's decentralized Congress there is no way to put the lid on. In contrast, historians tell us that in the late nineteenth century a large portion of the Republican constituency was far less interested in the tariff and other questions of national economic development than in whether German immigrants should be permitted to teach their native language in their local schools, and whether Catholics and "liturgical Protestants" should be permitted to consume alcohol. Interestingly, however, the national agenda of the period is devoid of such issues. And when they do show up on the state level, the exceptions prove the rule; they produce party splits and striking defeats for the party that allowed them to surface.

In sum, a strong party that is held accountable for the government of a nation-state has both the ability and the incentive to contain particularistic pressures. It controls nominations, elections, and the agenda, and it collectively realizes that small minorities are small minorities no matter how intense they are. But as the parties decline they lose control over nominations and campaigns, they lose the loyalty of the voters, and they lose control of the agenda. Party officeholders cease to be held collectively accountable for party performance, but they become individually exposed to the political pressure of myriad interest groups. The decline of party permits interest groups to wield greater influence, their success encourages the formation of still more interest groups, politics becomes increasingly fragmented, and collective responsibility becomes still more elusive.

### Popular Alienation from Government

For at least a decade political analysts have pondered the significance of survey data indicative of a steady increase in the alienation of the American public from the political process. . . . The American public is in a nasty mood, a cynical, distrusting, and resentful mood. The question is, Why?

If the same national problems not only persist but worsen while ever-greater amounts of revenue are directed at them, why shouldn't the typical citizen conclude that most of the money must be wasted by incompetent officials? If narrowly based interest groups increasingly affect our politics, why shouldn't citizens increasingly conclude that the interests run the government? For fifteen years the citizenry has listened to a steady stream of promises but has seen very little in the way of follow-through. An increasing proportion of the electorate does not believe that elections make a difference, a fact that largely explains the much-discussed post-1960 decline in voting turnout.

Continued public disillusionment with the political process poses several real dangers. For one thing, disillusionment begets further disillusionment. Leadership becomes more difficult if citizens do not trust their leaders and will not give them the benefit of a doubt. Policy failure becomes more likely if citizens expect the policy to fail. Waste increases and government competence decreases as citizens disrespect for politics encourages a lesser breed of person to make careers in government. And "government by a few big interests" becomes more than a cliché if citizens increasingly decide the cliché is true and cease participating for that reason.

Finally, there is the real danger that continued disappointment with particular government officials ultimately metamorphoses into disillusionment with government per se. Increasing numbers of citizens believe that government is not simply overextended but perhaps incapable of any further bettering of the world. Yes, government is overextended, inefficiency is pervasive, and ineffectiveness is all too common. But government is one of the few instruments of collective action we have, and even those committed to selective pruning of government programs cannot blithely allow the concept of an activist government to fall into disrepute.

Of late, however, some political commentators have begun to wonder whether contemporary thought places sufficient emphasis on government *for* the people. In stressing participation have we lost sight of *accountability*? Surely, we should be as concerned with what government produces as with how many participate. What good is participation if the citizenry is unable to determine who merits their support?

Participation and responsibility are not logically incompatible, but there is a degree of tension between the two, and the quest for either may be carried to extremes. Participation maximizers find themselves involved with quotas and virtual representation schemes, while responsibility maximizers can find themselves with a closed shop under boss rule. Moreover, both qualities can weaken the democracy they supposedly underpin. Unfettered participation produces Hyde Amendments* and immobilism.

## DISCUSSION QUESTIONS

1. How do political parties provide "collective responsibility" and improve the quality of democracy? Do you believe the complaints raised by Fiorina nearly twenty-five years ago remain persuasive?

2. Are strong parties in the interest of individual politicians? What might be some reasons why members of Congress would agree to strong parties or would distance themselves from their party's leadership?

---

* The Hyde Amendment, passed in 1976 (three years after Roe v. Wade), prohibited using Medicaid funds for abortion.

# 56

# "Parliamentary Government in the United States?" from *The State of the Parties*

## Gerald M. Pomper

*Writing in the late 1990s, Gerald Pomper revisits the issues raised by Fiorina and reaches a somewhat more positive assessment of the state of American political parties. Like Fiorina, Pomper believes that political parties should have a strong, prominent place in American politics. Unlike him, he believes that parties have that place. Looking at developments since the 1980s, Pomper argues that parties are today doing nearly everything that political scientists seem to want from them—they are constructing meaningful, coherent policy programs at the congressional level and in the party platforms; they are implementing the promises they make in campaigns; they are strikingly unified in Congress; they present clear, competing visions of the role of government; they are aggressively involved in campaigning, especially through providing campaign funds; and successful presidential candidates are largely those backed by the party rather than outsiders or mavericks. Although the president is obviously still a major institution in American government, Pomper wonders whether the U.S. might be evolving toward its own form of parliamentary government, in which the leadership of government clearly rests in the congressional parties. Suggesting that the presidency is a diminished institution, he asserts that "it may well be time to end the fruitless quest for a presidential savior and instead turn our attention, and our support, to the continuing and emerging strengths of our political parties."*

In 1996, the important political decision for American political warriors was not the contest between Bill Clinton and Robert Dole. "For virtually all of the powerful groups behind the Republican Party their overriding goal of keeping control of the House stemmed from their view that that was where the real political power—near- and long-term—lay." Moreover, "Sitting in his office on the sixth floor of the AFL-CIO building on 16th Street, political director Steve Rosenthal said that labor, too, saw the House elections as the most important of 1996—more important than the contest for the Presidency."

These informed activists alert us to a major shift in the character of American politics. To baldly summarize my argument, I suggest that the United States is moving toward a system of parliamentary government, a fundamental change in our constitutional regime. This change is not a total revolution in our institutions, and it will remain incomplete, given the drag of historical tradition. Nevertheless, this trend can be seen if we look beyond the formal definition of parliamentary governments, the union of legislature and executive.

The parliamentary model is evident in both empirical and normative political science. Anthony Downs begins his classic work by defining a political party virtually as a parliamentary coalition, "a team of men seeking to control the governing apparatus by gaining office in a duly constituted election." Normatively, for decades, some political scientists have sought to create a "responsible party system," resembling such parliamentary features as binding party programs and legislative cohesion.

Significant developments toward parliamentary government can be seen in contemporary American politics. The evidence of these trends cannot be found in the formal institutions of the written (capital C) Constitution. Institutional stability, however, may disguise basic change. For example, in formal terms, the president is not chosen until the electoral college meets in December, although we know the outcome within hours of the closing of the polls in early November.

Let us go beyond "literary theory"[1] and compare the present reality of U.S. politics with more general characteristics attributed to parliamentary systems. In the ideal parliamentary model, elections are contests between competitive parties presenting alternative programs, under leaders chosen from and by the parties' legislators or activists. Electoral success is interpreted as a popular mandate in support of these platforms. Using their parliamentary powers, the leaders then enforce party discipline to implement the promised programs.

The United States increasingly evidences these characteristics of parliamentary government. This fundamental change is due to the development of stronger political parties. In particular, I will try to demonstrate transformations of American politics evident in the following six characteristics of the parties:

- The parties present meaningful programs;
- They bridge the institutional separations of national government;
- They reasonably fulfill their promises;
- They act cohesively under strong legislative leadership;
- They have assumed a major role in campaigning; and
- They provide the recruitment base for presidential candidates.

*Party Programs*

A parliamentary system provides the opportunity to enact party programs. By contrast, in the American system, observers often have doubted that there were party programs, and the multiple checks and balances of American government have made it difficult to enact any coherent policies. For evidence, I examine the major party platforms of 1992–1996, the 1994 Republican Contract with America, and the 1996 Democratic Families First Agenda.

In previous research, we argued that party platforms were meaningful statements and that they were good forecasts of government policy. We found, contrary to cynical belief, that platforms were composed of far more than hot air and empty promises. Rather, a majority of the platforms were relevant defenses and criticisms of the parties' past records and reasonably specific promises of future actions. Moreover, the parties delivered: close to 70 percent of their many specific pledges were actually fulfilled to some degree.

Furthermore, parties have differed in their programs. Examining party manifestos in the major industrial democracies over forty years, 1948–1988, Budge concludes, "American Democrats and Republicans . . . consistently differentiate themselves from each other on such matters as support for welfare, government intervention, foreign aid, and defense, individual initiative and freedom. . . . Indeed, they remain as far apart as many European parties on these points, and more so than many."

In recent years, we might expect platforms to be less important. National conventions have become television exercises rather than occasions for party decision making. The expansion of interest groups has made it more difficult to accomplish policy intentions. Candidate-centered campaigning reduces the incentives to achieve collective, party goals and appears to focus more on individual characteristics than on policy issues.

The party platforms of 1992 provide a test. An independent replication confirms our previous research on platform content. Perhaps surprisingly, this new work indicates that the most recent platforms, like those of previous years, provide significant political and policy statements. These manifestos meet one of the tests of a parliamentary system: meaningful party programs.

The 1992 platforms[2] can be divided into three categories: puff pieces of rhetoric and fact, approvals of one's own party policy record and candidates or disapproval of the opposition, and pledges for future action. The pledges, in turn, can be categorized as being simply rhetorical or general promises or more useful statements of future intentions, such as promises to continue existing policies, expressions of party goals, pledges of action, or quite detailed promises.[3]

Much in the platforms induces yawns and cynicism. The Democrats were fond of such rhetorical statements as "It is time to listen to the grassroots of America." (Actually a difficult task, since most plants are speechless.) The Republicans were prone to vague self-congratulation, as when they boasted, "Republicans recognize the importance of having fathers and mothers in the home." (Possibly even more so if these parents are unemployed, not distracted by jobs?)

Nevertheless, these documents—while hardly models of rational discussion—did provide useful guides to party positions. When the Democrats criticized "the Bush administration's efforts to bankrupt the public school system . . . through private school vouchers," and when the Republicans declared that "American families must be given choice in education," there was an implicit policy debate. Comparison was also facilitated by the similar distributions of platform statements across policy areas. Each party tended to devote about as much attention to particular or related policy areas as its opposition. The only important difference is that Democrats gave far more attention to issues involving women and abortion. Overall, about half of the platforms were potentially useful to the voters in locating the parties on a policy continuum.[4]

The 1994 Contract with America was even more specific. It consisted entirely of promises for the future, potentially focusing attention on public policy. Moreover, the large majority of its fifty-five sentences were reasonably specific promises. Pledges of definite action comprised 42 percent of the total document, and detailed pledges another 27 percent, while less than 4 percent consisted of only vague rhetoric. From the promise of a balanced budget amendment to advocacy of term limits, the Republicans foreshadowed major innovations in American institutions and law. This high degree of specificity can facilitate party accountability to the electorate.

### Party as Programmatic Bridge

The great obstacle to party responsibility in the United States has always been the separation of national institutions, the constitutional division between the executive and legislative branches. Party has sometimes been praised as a bridge across this separation, and party reformers have often sought to build stronger institutional ties, even seeking radical constitutional revision to further the goal. Despite these hopes and plans, however, the separation has remained. Presidential parties make promises, but Congress has no institutional responsibility to act on these pledges.

In a parliamentary system, the most current research argues—contrary to Downs—"that office is used as a basis for attaining policy goals, rather than that policy is subordinated to office." In the United States as well, party program rather than institutional discipline may provide the bridge between the legislature and its executive. In previous years, however, we lacked a ready means to compare presidential and congressional programs. Now we have authoritative statements from both institutionalized wings of the parties. The Republican Contract with America marks a major first step toward coherent, interinstitutional programs.

The 1994 contract was far more than a campaign gimmick or an aberrational invention of Newt Gingrich. It was actually a terse condensation of continuing Republican Party doctrine. A majority of these promises had already been anticipated in 1992 and the party endorsed five-sixths of its provisions in 1996.

For example, the 1992 national platform criticized the Democratic Congress for its refusal "to give the President a line-item veto to curb their self-serving porkbarrel projects" and promised adoption of the procedure in a Republican Congress. The 1994 contract repeated the pledge of a "line-item veto to restore fiscal responsibility to an out-of-control Congress," while the 1996 platform reiterated, "A Republican president will fight wasteful spending with the line-item veto which was finally enacted by congressional Republicans this year over bitter Democrat opposition."[5] Republicans built on traditional party doctrine, specified the current party program, and then affirmed accountability for their actions. Building on this achievement in party building, and their claims of legislative "success," the Republicans have already promised to present a new contract for the elections at the turn of the century.

The Democrats imitatively developed a congressional program, the Families First Agenda, for the 1996 election. Intended primarily as a campaign document by the minority party, it is less specific than the Republican contract. Still, 90 of its 204 statements were reasonably precise promises. The legislative Democrats also showed significant and increasing agreement with their presidential wing and platform. By 1996, three-fourths of the congressional agenda was also incorporated into the Clinton program, and the official platform specifically praised the congressional program. The agenda's three sections—"security," "opportunity," and "responsibility"—paralleled those of the national platform (which added "freedom," "peace," and "community"—values presumably shared by congressional Democrats), and many provisions are replicated from one document to another.

The Republican contract with America and the Democratic Families First agenda, then, can be seen as emblems of party responsibility and likely precedents for further development toward parliamentary practice in American politics. Party doctrine has become a bridge across the separation of institutions.

*Program Fulfillment*

Both Democrats and Republicans, as they held power, followed through on their election promises, as expected in a parliamentary model. Despite the clumsiness of the Clinton administration, and despite the Democrats' loss of their long-term control of Congress in their catastrophic election defeat in 1994, they actually fulfilled most of the 167 reasonably specific pledges in their 1992 manifest.

A few examples illustrate the point. The Democrats promised negative action, in opposing major change in the Clean Air Act—and they stood fast. In their 1993 economic program, the Democrats won action similar to their platform pledge to "make the rich pay their fair share in taxes." Through executive action, the Clinton administration redeemed its promise to reduce U.S. military forces in Europe. The Democrats achieved full action on their promise of "A reasonable waiting period to permit background checks for purchases of handguns."

To be sure, the Democrats have not become latter-day George Washingtons, unable to tell an untruth. There clearly has been no action on the pledge to "limit overall campaign spending and . . . the disproportionate and excessive role of PACs." In other cases, the Democrats did try but were defeated, most notably in their promise of "reform of the health-care system to control costs and make health care affordable." (It is obviously too early to judge fulfillment of 1996 Democratic pledges, made in either the presidential platform or the congressional party Families First Agenda.)

Most impressive are not the failures but the achievements. Altogether, Democrats did accomplish something on nearly 70 percent of their 1992 promises, in contrast to inaction on only 19 percent. In a completely independent analysis, another researcher came to remarkably similar conclusions, calculating Clinton's fulfillment of his campaign promises at the same level, 69 percent (Shaw 1996).[6] I do not believe this record is the result of the virtues of the Democratic Party, which I use for this analysis simply because it controlled the government, nor can this record be explained by Bill Clinton's personal qualities of steadfast commitment to principle. The explanation is that we now have a system in which parties, whatever their names or leaders, make and keep promises.

This conclusion is strengthened if we examine the Republicans. While the GOP of course did not hold the presidency, it did win control of Congress in 1994. In keeping with the model of parliamentary government, Republicans interpreted their impressive victory as an endorsement of the Contract with America, and then they attempted to implement the program. We must remember that the 1994 election cannot be seen as a popular mandate for the Republican manifesto: two-thirds of the public had not even heard of it in November, and only 19 percent expressed support. The contract expressed party ideology, not voter demands.

Despite its extravagant tone and ideological character, the Republicans delivered on their contract just as Democrats fulfilled much of their 1992 platform. Of the more specific pledges, 69 percent were accomplished in large measure[7] (coincidentally, perhaps, the same success rate as the Democrats). Even if we include the rhetorical and unspecific sentences in our test, more than one-half of this party program was accomplished.

Despite the heroics of vetoes and government shutdown, despite bicameralism and the vaunted autonomy of the Senate, and despite popular disapproval, the reality is that most of the Contract with America was implemented. The Republicans accomplished virtually all that they promised in regard to congressional reform, unfunded mandates and welfare, as well as substantial elements of their program in regard to crime, child support, defense, and the social security earnings limit. Defeated on major economic issues, they later achieved many of these goals, including a balanced budget agreement in place of a constitutional amendment, a children's tax credit, and a reduction in capital gains taxes. On these questions, as indeed on the general range of American government, they won the greatest victory of all: they set the agenda for the United States, and the Democratic president eventually followed their lead. Such initiative is what we would expect in a parliamentary system.

*  *  *

*Party Cohesion*

Program fulfillment results from party unity. The overall trend in Congress, as expected in a parliamentary system, is toward more party differentiation.[8] One indicator is the proportion of legislative votes in which a majority of one party is opposed to a majority of the other (i.e., "party unity" votes). Not too long ago, in 1969, such party conflict was evident on only about one-third of all roll calls. By 1995, nearly three-fourths of House votes and over two-thirds of Senate roll calls showed these clear party differences. There is another trend—the increasing commitment of representatives and senators to their parties. The average legislator showed party loyalty (expressed as a "party unity score") of less than 60 percent in 1970. In 1996, the degree of loyalty had climbed to 80 percent for Democrats and to an astounding 87 percent for Republicans. Cohesion was still greater on the thirty-three House roll calls in 1995 on final passage of items in the Contract with America. Republicans were unanimous on sixteen of these votes, and the *median* number of Republican dissents was but *one*. Neither the British House of Commons nor the erstwhile Supreme Soviet could rival this record of party unity.

The congressional parties now are ideologically cohesive bodies, even with the occasional but significant split among Democrats on such issues as trade and welfare reform. We need to revise our political language to take account of this ideological cohesion. There are no more "Dixiecrats" or southern conservative Democrats, and therefore there is no meaningful "conservative coalition" in Congress. Supportive evidence is found in the same roll call data: the average southern Democrat supported his or her party 71 percent of the time in 1996, and barely over a tenth of the roll calls found Dixie legislators in opposition to their own party and in alliance with a majority of Republicans. It also seems likely that "liberal Republican" will soon be an oxymoron restricted to that patronized minority holding a pro-choice attitude on abortion, confined to the back of the platform or, so to speak, to the back of the party bus.

Republicans have been acting like a parliamentary party beyond their ideological unity on a party program. The "central leaders efforts during the Contract period were attempts to *impose* a form of party government," which succeeded in winning cooperation from committee chairman and changed roll call behavior as "many Republicans modified their previous preferences in order to accommodate their party colleagues." Beyond programmatic goals, the Republicans have created strong party institutions in Congress, building on previous Democratic reforms.

Even after the Contract with America is completely passed or forgotten, these institutions will likely remain. In their first days in power, as they organized the House, the Republicans centralized power in the hands of the Speaker, abolished institutionalized caucuses of constituency interests, distributed chairmanships on the basis of loyalty to the party program and in disregard of seniority, and changed the ratios of party memberships on committees to foster passage of the party program. Instruments of discipline have become more prevalent and more exercised, including caucus resolutions, committee assignments, aid in securing campaign contributions, and disposition of individual members' bills.

The building of parliamentary party institutions continues. Some of the structural changes in the House have now been adopted by both the Senate and the Democrats, perhaps most significantly the rotation of committee chairmanships, curbing the antiparty influence of seniority. The Republicans have insisted that committees report party bills, even when opposed by the chair, as in the cases of term limits and telecommunications. The party record became the major issue in the 1996 congressional elections, with party leaders Newt Gingrich and Richard Armey doing their best to aid loyalists—but only loyalists—through fund-raising and strong-arming of ideological allies among political action committees.

The party differences and cohesion in Congress partially reflect the enhanced power of legislative leaders. The more fundamental reason for congressional party unity—as in parliamentary systems—is not discipline as much as agreement. Party members vote together because they think the same way. Republicans act as conservatives because they *are* conservatives; Democrats act like liberals or as they now prefer, progressives because they believe in these programs.

\*   \*   \*

The most recent nominating conventions provide further support for the ideological cohesion of the national parties. The CBS/*New York Times* Poll found massive differences between Republican and Democratic delegates on questions involving the scope of government, social issues, and international affairs. A majority of these partisans opposed each other on *all* of ten questions; they were remotely similar on only one issue—international trade—and were in essentially different political worlds (fifty or more percentage points apart) on issues of governmental regulation, the environment, abortion, assault weapons, civil rights, affirmative action, and immigration.

## Party Organization

Party unity has another source, related to the recruitment of individual candidates with a common ideology. Unity is also fostered by the development of strong national party organizations, precisely measured by the dollars of election finance. Amid all of the proper concern over the problems of campaign contributions and spending, we have neglected the increasing importance of the parties in providing money, "the mother's milk of politics."

There are two large sources of party money: the direct subsidies provided by the federal election law, and the "soft money" contributions provided for the parties' organizational work. Together, even in 1992, these funds totaled $213 million for the major candidates and their parties.[9] Underlining the impact of this party spending, the Republican and Democratic presidential campaigns in 1992 each spent twice as much money as did billionaire Ross Perot, whose candidacy is often seen as demonstrating the decline of the parties.

An enhanced party role was also evident in the other national elections of 1992. Beyond direct contributions and expenditures, the parties developed a variety of ingenious devices, such as bundling, coordinated spending, and agency agreements, to again become significant players in the election finance game. Overall, in 1992, the six national party committees spent $290 million. (For comparison, total spending in all House and Senate races was $678 million.)[10] The party role became even more evident in 1994, with the victory of a Republican majority originally recruited and financed by Newt Gingrich's GOPAC, a party body disguised as a political action committee.

The party role expanded hugely in 1996, bolstered by the Supreme Court, in its 1996 *Colorado* decision.[11] The Court approved unlimited "independent" spending by political parties on behalf of its candidates. Moreover, four justices explicitly indicated that they were prepared to approve even direct unlimited expenditures by parties, and three other justices are ready to rule on that issue in a future case.

The parties quickly took advantage of the Court's opening. Together, Republican and Democratic party groups spent close to a billion dollars, conservatively 35 percent of all election spending, without even counting the $160 million in federal campaign subsidies for the presidential race.[12]

Despite the commonplace emphasis on "candidate-centered" campaigns, the parties' expenditures were greater than that of all individual House and Senate candidates combined. In discussions of election finance, political action committees receive most of the attention, and condemnation, but the reality is that PACs are of decreasing importance. PACs' money has barely increased since 1988, and they were outspent 2 to 1 by the parties in 1996.[13] The parties now have the muscle to conduct campaigns and present their programs, to act as we would expect of parliamentary contestants.

## Party Leadership

Parties need leaders as much as money. In parliamentary governments, leaders achieve power through their party activity. That has always been the case even in America when we look at congressional leadership: a long apprenticeship in the House and Senate has usually been required before one achieves the positions of Speaker, majority and minority leader, and whip. A strong indication of the development of parliamentary politics in the United States is the unrecognized trend toward party recruitment for the presidency, the allegedly separated institution.

*   *   *

Contrary to the fears of many observers, the new presidential nominating system has developed along with new institutions of party cohesion. Front-runners have great advantages in this new system, but that means that prominent party figures—rather than obscure dark horses stabled in smoke-filled rooms—are most likely to win nomination. Contrary to fears of a personalistic presidency, the candidates chosen in the postreform period tackle tough issues, support their party's program, and agree with their congressional party's leaders on policy positions as much, or even more, than in the past.

Contemporary presidential nominations have become comparable—although not identical—to the choice of leadership in a hypothetical U.S. parliamentary system. Is the selection of Reagan in 1980 that different from the British Tories' choice of Margaret Thatcher to lead the party's turn toward ideological free market conservatism? In a parliamentary system, would not Bush and Dole, Reagan's successors, be the ideal analogues to Britain's John Major? Is the selection of Mondale as the liberal standard-bearer of the liberal Democratic Party that different from the lineage of left-wing leaders in the British Labour Party? Is the Democratic turn toward the electoral center with Clinton not analogous to Labour's replacement of Michael Foot by Neil Kinnock, John Smith, and Tony Blair?

To be sure, American political leadership is still quite open, the parties quite permeable. Presidential nominations do depend greatly on personal coalitions, and popular primaries are the decisive points of decision. Yet it is also true that leadership of the parties is still, and perhaps increasingly, related to prominence within the parties.

### Toward Parliamentary Government?

Do these changes amount to parliamentary government in the United States? Certainly not in the most basic definitional sense, since we will surely continue to have separated institutions, in which the president is elected differently from the legislature, and the Senate differently from the House. Unlike a formal parliamentary system, the president will hold his office for a fixed term, regardless of the "votes of confidence" he wins or loses in Congress. By using his veto and the bully pulpit of the White House, Bill Clinton has proven that the president is independent and still "relevant." It is also true that we will never have a system in which a single political party can both promise and deliver a complete and coherent ideological program. As Jones correctly maintains, American government remains a "separated system," in which "serious and continuous in-party and cross-party coalition building typifies policy making." These continuing features were strikingly evident in the adoption of welfare reform in the 104th Congress.

But parliaments also evidence coalition building, particularly in multiparty systems. British parliamentarians can be stalemated by factional and party differences on issues such as Northern Ireland just as the Democrats and Republicans were on health care in the 103d Congress. Achieving a consensual policy on the peace process in Israel's multiparty system is as difficult as achieving a consensual policy on abortion among America's two parties.

*   *   *

The party basis of parliamentary government will continue, because the ideological basis of intraparty coherence and interparty difference will continue and even be increased with the ongoing departure of moderate legislators of both parties. The need for strong party institutions in Congress will also be furthered by new policy problems, more rapid turnover of membership, and the continuation of split-party control of government.

Of course, the presidency will remain relevant, yet it may also come to be seen as almost superfluous. A principal argument on behalf of Bob Dole's candidacy was that he would sign the legislation passed by a Republican Congress—hardly a testament to presidential leadership. President Clinton fostered his reelection by removing himself from partisan leadership, "triangulating" the White House between congressional Democrats and Republicans, and following the model of patriotic chief of state created by George Washington and prescribed in *The Federalist*: "to guard the community against the effects of faction, precipitancy, or of any impulse unfriendly to the public good."

* * *

The absence of presidential initiative is more than a problem of the Clinton administration. Throughout American history, the president has persistently provided the energy of American government, the source of new "regimes" and policy initiatives. Perhaps the lassitude of contemporary politics is only the latest example of the recurrent cycle of presidential initiative, consolidation, and decline. Or, more profoundly, perhaps it marks the decline of the executive office itself as a source of creativity in the government of the United States.

America needs help. It may well be time to end the fruitless quest for a presidential savior and instead turn our attention, and our support, to the continuing and emerging strengths of our political parties. We are developing, almost unnoticed, institutions of semiparliamentary, semi-responsible government. To build a better bridge between the past and the future, perhaps this new form of American government is both inevitable and necessary.

## DISCUSSION QUESTIONS

1. Does Pomper address the concerns raised by Fiorina, or are there aspects of his argument that have not been resolved by the changes in political parties identified by Pomper?

2. If the U.S. is evolving toward a semi-parliamentary system, is this a good thing? Pomper suggests that the presidency is weakening. Are there advantages to a system like this compared to a system with a stronger presidency?

3. Pomper was writing before the presidency of George W. Bush. Has the evolution toward congressional-party leadership continued under the Bush presidency?

## NOTES

I gratefully acknowledge the help of Andrea Lubin, who performed the content analyses of party platforms included in this essay.

1. The phrase is from Walter Baghot's (1928: 1) classic analysis of the realities of British politics.

2. The texts are found in *The Vision Shared* (Washington, D.C.: Republican National Committee, 1992) and for the less loquacious Democrats, *Congressional Quarterly Weekly Report* 50 (July 18, 1992): 2107–13.

3. Each sentence, or distinct clause within these sentences, constituted the unit of analysis. Because of its great length, only alternate sentences in the Republican platform were included. No selection bias is evident or, given the repetitive char-

acter of the platforms, likely. In total, there are 426 units of analysis in the Democratic platform, 758 in the Republican. For further details on the techniques used, see Pomper and Lederman (1980: 235–48). To avoid contamination or wishful thinking on my part, Lubin did the analysis independently. My later revisions tended to classify the platform sentences as less specific and meaningful than hers, contrary to any optimistic predisposition.

4. The "useful" categories are policy approval and policy criticism, candidate approval and candidate criticism, and future policy promises classified as pledges of continuity, expressions of goals, pledges of action, and detailed pledges.

5. *The Vision Shared* (1992 Republican Platform), p. 46; "Contract with America," in Wilcox (1995: 70): *Restoring the American Dream* (1996 Republican Platform), p. 25.

6. Using the same content categories, Carolyn Shaw (1996), of the University of Texas, lists 150 presidential campaign promises of 1992 in the more specific categories. In regard to fulfillment, she employs the methods of Fishel (1985). With this method, she finds that there was "fully comparable" or "partially comparable" action on 69 percent of Clinton's proposals. This record is higher than that found by Fishel for any president from Kennedy through Reagan.

7. Even this figure underestimates the impact of the Contract with America. I have counted the failure to pass term limits as a defeat, although the Republicans actually promised no more than a floor vote, and I have not given the party credit for achievements in the following Congress.

8. These data are drawn from *Congressional Quarterly Weekly Report* 54 (December 21, 1996): 3461–67.

9. *Congressional Quarterly Weekly Report* 51 (May 15, 1993): 1197.

10. *Congressional Quarterly Weekly Report* 51 (March 20, 1993): 691: Federal Election Commission, *Record* 19 (May 1993): 22.

11. *Colorado Republican Federal Campaign Committee et al. v. Federal Election Commission* (No. 95-489. 1996 U.S. LEXIS 4258).

12. The parties spent $628 million directly, plus at least $263 million and up to $400 million in soft money. For detailed figures, see *Congressional Quarterly Weekly Report* 55 (April 5, 1997): 767–73.

13. For an excellent discussion of 1996 election spending, see Corrado (1997).

# 57

# "Needed: A Political Theory for the New Era of Coalition Government in the United States"

## James L. Sundquist

*Writing in the latter half of the 1980s, James L. Sundquist largely agrees with Morris Fiorina's early-1980s assessment that political parties are weaker than in the past. Sundquist highlights how divided government has become the norm in the United States, but that this was not always so. In the first half of the twentieth century, divided government was rare, but since then, government has been under divided party control more often than not. To Sundquist, this development has shattered much of what political scientists and other observers expected from government. But is this such a bad thing? Sundquist asks the question whether the divided control of government has had the dire effects that many political scientists might have expected. His answer is: yes. In the age of divided government, he charges, government cannot make policy coherently and cannot respond to public needs effectively. The incentive for both parties, according to Sundquist, is to block and obstruct, and to create an issue for the next campaign, rather than enact good public policy.*

On 8 November 1988, when the American voters decreed that Republican George Bush would succeed Ronald Reagan in the White House but the opposition Democratic Party would control both houses of the Congress, it was the sixth time in the last nine presidential elections that the electorate chose to split the government between the parties. As in 1988, so in the earlier elections of 1956, 1968, 1972, 1980, and 1984, the people placed their faith in Republican presidential leadership but voted to retain Democratic majorities in the House of Representatives and in the first three of those elections (as well as in 1988), Democratic majorities in the Senate also.

This is something new in American politics. When Dwight D. Eisenhower took his second oath of office in 1957, he was the first chief executive in seventy-two years—since Grover Cleveland in 1885—to confront on Inauguration Day a Congress of which even one house was controlled by the opposition party. Sometimes the opposition would win majorities in the House or the Senate, or both, at the midterm election, but even such occasions were relatively rare. In the fifty-eight years from 1897 through 1954, the country experienced divided government during only eight years—all in the last half of a presidential term—or 14 percent of the time. Yet in the thirty-six years from 1955 through 1990, the government will have been divided between the parties for twenty-four years—exactly two-thirds of that period.

A generation ago, then, the country passed from a long era of party government, when either the Republican or the Democratic Party controlled both the presidency and the Congress almost all of the time, to an era when the government was divided between the parties most of the time. Under these circumstances, the United States has its own unique version of coalition government—not a coalition voluntarily entered into by the parties but one forced upon them by the accidents of the electoral process.

It is the argument of this article that the advent of the new era has rendered obsolete much of the theory developed by political scientists, from the day of Woodrow Wilson to the 1950s, to explain how the United States government can and should work. That theory identified the political party as the indispensable instrument that brought cohesion and unity, and hence effectiveness, to the government as a whole by linking the executive and legislative branches in a bond of common interest. And, as a corollary, the party made it possible for the president to succeed in his indispensable role as leader and energizer of the governmental process; it accomplished that end because the congressional majorities, while they would not accept the president's leadership by virtue of his constitutional position as chief executive—institutional rivalry would bar that—would accept it in his alternate capacity as head of the political party to which the majorities adhered.

The generations of political scientists who expounded this theory paid little attention to how the government would and should function when the president and the Senate and House majorities were not all of the same party. They could in good conscience disregard that question because intervals of divided government in their experience had been infrequent and short-lived. Whenever the midterm election brought a division of the government, anyone concerned about that could take a deep breath and wait confidently for the next presidential election to put the system back into its proper alignment. As late as 1952 it had always done so in the memory of everybody writing on the subject. But since 1956, that has no longer been a certainty. It has not even been the probability. And that represents a momentous change in the American governmental system, for institutional processes and relationships are profoundly altered when the unifying bond of party disappears.

\*   \*   \*

*The Theory of Party Government and Presidential Leadership*

Madison did not expound a new theory to supplant the one that he had been so instrumental in embedding in the Constitution. But without benefit of much explicit doctrine, the nation's political leaders developed in practice the system of party government—as distinct from nonpartisan government—that settled into place in the Jacksonian era and prevailed throughout the next century and a quarter. In each presidential election two national parties sought exactly what the Madisonian theory written into the Constitution was supposed to forestall: the capture of all three of the policy-making elements of the government—the presidency, Senate and House—by the same faction or party, so that the party could carry out its program.

No major party has ever said, "We want only the presidency," or only the Senate or the House. They have always said, "give us *total* responsibility." Since early in the nineteenth century, they have presented their programs formally in official party platforms. Asking for total power in the two elected branches, they have been eager to accept the total responsibility and accountability that would accompany it.

That was the theory of party government; and not only the politicians, but the people accepted it. The parties lined up naturally on opposite sides of whatever were the great issues of the day—creating a national bank, opening the West with turnpikes and railroads and canals financed by the national government, prohibiting slavery in the western territories, raising or lowering tariffs, mobilizing the national government to help the victims of the Great Depression, and so on. The people listened to the arguments of the two parties and made their choices. And when they did, the party they elected had a full opportunity to carry out is mandate, because when the voters chose a president each four years they normally entrusted control of the Congress to the president's party, thus making it fully responsible. From Andrew Jackson's time until the second election of Dwight Eisenhower in 1956, only four presidents—Zachary Taylor elected in 1848, Rutherford B. Hayes in 1876, James A. Garfield in 1880, and Grover Cleveland in 1884—had to confront immediately upon inauguration either a House of Representatives or a Senate organized by the opposition. In the nineteenth century these results may have been largely an artifact of the election process itself. The parties printed separate ballots listing their slates, and the voter selected the ballot of the party he preferred, marked it, and dropped it in the box. Yet after the government-printed, secret ballot came into universal use early in this century, straight-ticket voting and the resultant single-party control of the government continued to prevail. The voters gave the Republican Party responsibility for the entire government in the 1900s, again in the 1920s, and finally in 1952; and they chose the Democratic Party in the 1910s, 1930s, and 1940s. No president in the first half of this century ever had to suffer divided government upon taking office, and few had the problem even after the normal setback to the president's party in the midterm election.

As soon as political science emerged as a scholarly discipline, its adherents began to pronounce and elaborate the theoretical foundation of the system of party government that was in being. Parties were not only natural, since people were bound to organize to advance their differing notions as to the goals and programs of government, but the scholars concluded that they were useful and necessary too. Among their uses was the one that is the concern of this paper: their utility in unifying a government of dispersed powers and thereby making it effective.

*   *   *

By the time the Committee on Political parties of the American Political Science Association made its landmark report in 1950, it could simply assert, without feeling obliged to argue the case, that political parties are "indispensable instruments of government," necessary "to furnish a general kind of direction over the government as a whole" and for "integration of all of the far-flung activities of modern government." It then offered a series of reforms that would make the parties better organized, more tightly disciplined, and hence "more responsible."[1]

*   *   *

Like the Committee on Political Parties, the later writers who saw political parties as the unifying instrument in the governmental system generally agreed that they often failed to perform that function satisfactorily. Decentralized and federal in their organization, without authoritative central institutions, and made up of diverse ideological and cultural elements, the parties lacked discipline. Yet even without the reforms recommended by the committee, the political party was seen as nonetheless succeeding to some degree in bridging the gaps between the separated branches of the government.

*   *   *

And how is that degree of party discipline and responsibility achieved? In the national government, political scientists proclaim with virtual unanimity that it is through presidential leadership. When the party serves its unifying function, it is because the members of the president's party in the Congress recognize the president as not merely the head of the executive branch but as the leader of the band of "brothers in the same political lodge." In enacting as well as in administering the laws, the government cannot move dynamically and prudently without a recognized and accepted prime mover, a leader. And that leader is logically and necessarily the man chosen by the whole national party to carry its standard, and who has done so successfully in the most recent presidential election. Besides, the president has the resources of the entire executive branch to help him to develop coordinated programs. "The President proposes and the Congress disposes" long ago became the catch phrase to describe the legislative process.

\*   \*   \*

By the 1960s, political science had developed a dominating theory as to how the American constitutional system should—and at its best, did —work. The political party was the institution that unified the separated branches of the government and brought coherence to the policymaking process. And because the president was the leader of his party, he was the chief policy maker of the entire government, presiding directly over the executive branch and indirectly working through and with his party's congressional leadership over the legislative branch as well.

### The Old Theory in a New Era

This established theory presupposed one essential condition: there would in fact be a majority party in control of both branches of government. Rereading the literature of the midcentury, one is struck with how easily this condition was taken for granted. The writers could well do so, for in the twentieth century until 1955, the government had been divided between the parties only for four periods of two years each, and in each case in the last half of a presidential term—those of Taft, Wilson, Hoover, and Truman. A scholar who happened to be writing during or immediately after one of these intervals (or who was commenting on state governmental systems) might observe in parenthetical style that divided government could sometimes obscure responsibility, impede leadership, and thus thwart the fulfillment of the party government ideal. But the aberration was passed over quickly, without interrupting the flow of the basic argument. In the normal state of affairs, one party would have control of the policy-making branches of government; the other would be in opposition.

\*   \*   \*

Divided government invalidates the entire theory of party government and presidential leadership, both elements of it. Divided government requires that the United States "construct a successful government out of antagonisms," which Wilson warned could not be done, and renders impossible the "close synthesis of active parts" that he found necessary. How can a party cast its web over the dispersed organs of government to bring a semblance of unity, in Key's phrase, if it controls but one of the branches? How can the majority party fulfill Burns's "vital function of integration," or rally the government's elements behind Penniman's "common purpose," or provide Rossiter's "bridges across the gaps," or Sorauf's "unifying force" if there is no majority party? How can the president lead the Congress if either or both houses are controlled by the party that fought to defeat him in the last election and has vowed to vanquish him, or his successor as his party's candidate, in the next one? But if the president cannot lead, Rossiter has told us, "weak and disorganized government" must follow. Our "toughest problems," Hyneman has admonished, will in that circumstance remain unsolved.[2]

The question at once arises: In our twenty-two years thus far of forced coalition government, have those gloomy forecasts been fulfilled? Eleven Congresses during the administrations of four presidents would appear to have given ample time for putting the established theory to the test. * * *

My own conclusion is that the predictions of the sages of the earlier generation have been borne out in this modern era of divided or coalition government. True, in the administrations of the four Republican presidents who had to make their peace with House Democratic majorities— and usually Democratic Senate majorities as well—there were significant accomplishments. President Dwight D. Eisenhower achieved a successful bipartisan foreign policy, and President Ronald Reagan managed to carry enough Democrats with him to enact for better or worse the essentials of his economic program in 1981. In subsequent Reagan years, the Congress and the administration collaborated across party lines to enact measures to bring illegal immigration under control, rescue social security, and reform the tax code. But Eisenhower and the Democratic Congress were stalemated on domestic measures throughout his six years of coalition government; the Nixon-Ford period was one of almost unbroken conflict and deadlock on both domestic and foreign issues; and the last seven years of Reagan found the government immobilized on some of the central issues of the day, unwilling to follow the leadership of the President or anyone else and deferring those issues in hope that somehow the 1988 election would resolve matters and render the government functional again.

By common consent, the most conspicuous among the urgent but unresolved problems has been, of course, the federal budget deficit, which has been running at between $150 billion and $200 billion a year since the great tax cut of 1981 took effect. The national debt now stands at well over $2 trillion, more than doubled in seven years of divided government. The United States has suffered the shock of falling from the status of a great creditor nation to the world's largest debtor nation, living on borrowing from abroad. The huge trade deficit, the shortfall in investment, and high interest rates are all blamed on the inability of the government to get the budget deficit under control. For all these reasons, virtually all of the country's responsible leaders—the president, the congressional leaders, and members of both parties in both houses—have for nearly over half a dozen years been proclaiming loudly and in unison that the nation simply cannot go on this way. The experts from outside —in the academic world, the Federal Reserve System, on Wall Street, in foreign countries—likewise agree that these deficits are economically perilous, whether or not they can be termed morally outrageous as well.

But during all that time that the country has seen a virtual consensus on the urgency of this problem, its governmental institutions have floundered in trying to cope with it. President Reagan sent the Congress his program, but the Congress flatly rejected it. The legislators in their turn floated suggestions, but the President killed them by promising a veto if they were passed. The congressional leaders and others pleaded for a summit meeting between the executive and legislative branches to hammer out a common policy. Finally, in November 1986, the meeting took place. But it is a measure of the national predicament that it took a half-trillion-dollar collapse in the stock market—a five-hundred-billion-dollar panic—before the two branches of the U.S. government would even sit down together. It was easier for Mikhail Gorbachev to get a summit meeting with the President of the United States than it was for the Speaker of the United States House of Representatives. And even the domestic summit that was finally held essentially papered over the problem rather than solved it.

Or we can draw examples of the failure of coalition government from international affairs. The country lost a war for the first time in history —in Vietnam—after another period of floundering in search of a policy, with the president pulling in one direction and the Congress in another. And the situation in Nicaragua was throughout the Reagan years almost a replica of Vietnam. The government could adopt no clear and effective policy at all; it could neither take measures strong enough to force the Sandinista government out of power, as the President and his administration wished to do, nor accept that government and make peace with it, as many in the Senate and the House would like. Then there is the Iran-contra debacle. President Reagan in his own summation of that episode spoke of the "failure" of his policy, of "a policy that went astray," of "the damage that's been done," and he blamed it all on mistrust between the executive and legislative branches.[3]

But, some will argue, even if these or other instances can indeed be considered governmental failures attributable to mistrust between the unwilling partners of a forced coalition, the performance of recent unified government has been no better. The Kennedy and Carter years cannot claim overwhelming success, they will maintain, and while Lyndon Johnson proved to be a spectacular presidential leader of the Congress in the enactment of his Great Society measures in 1964 and 1965, he also led the country into the quagmire of Vietnam that in turn launched a devastating spiral of inflation. That is the difficulty of arguing from cases, as I suggested earlier.

* * * For better or worse, the discussion of the relative merits of unified

over divided government has to be pursued in abstract terms, as it was for the most part in the political science literature cited earlier.

The essence of the theoretical argument in favor of the unified government has been and is: For coherent and timely policies to be adopted and carried out—in short, for government to work effectively, as the established theory held—the president, the Senate, and the House must come into agreement. When the same party controls all three of these power centers, the incentive to reach such agreement is powerful despite the inevitable institutional rivalries and jealousies. The party *does* serve as the bridge or the web, in the metaphors of political science. But in divided government, it is not merely the separated institutions of government that must overcome their built-in rivalries but the opposing parties themselves. And that is bound to be a difficult, arduous process, characterized by conflict, delay, and indecision, and leading frequently to deadlock, inadequate and ineffective policies, or no policies at all.

Competition is the very essence of democratic politics. It gives democracy its meaning, and its vitality. The parties are the instruments of that competition. They are and should be organized for combat, not for collaboration and compromise. They live to win elections in order to advance their philosophies and programs. Therefore, each party strives and must strive to defeat the opposing party. But in a divided government, this healthy competition is translated into an unhealthy, debilitating conflict between the institutions of government themselves. Then, the president and Congress are motivated to try to discredit and defeat each other. Yet these are the institutions that, for anything constructive to happen, simply have to get together.

The average citizen reacts by simply condemning all politicians as a class. "Why don't those people in Washington stop playing politics and just get together and do what's right?" But that is not in the nature of things. Political parties, as the textbooks have always told us, are organized because people have genuine, deep disagreements about the goals and the programs of their societies. If a coalition government is to work, the leaders of committed groups have to be willing to submerge or abandon the very philosophies that caused them to organize their parties in the first place. They have to set aside the principles that are their reason for seeking governmental power. And they will do that only under compulsion of clear and grave necessity—usually, in other words, after deadlock has deteriorated into crisis.

In the American form of coalition government, if the president sends a proposal to Capitol Hill or takes a foreign policy stand, the opposition-controlled House or houses of Congress—unless they are overwhelmed by the president's popularity and standing in the country—simply *must* reject it. Otherwise they are saying the president is a wise and prudent leader. That would only strengthen him and his party for the next election, and how can the men and women of the congressional majority do that, when their whole object is to defeat him when that time arrives? By the same token, if the opposition party in control of Congress initiates a measure, the president has to veto it—or he is saying of his opponents that they are sound and statesmanlike, and so is building them up for the next election.

So when President Reagan sent his budgets to the Congress, the Democrats who controlled both houses had to pronounce them "dead on arrival," as they did. And when they came up with their alternatives, the President had to condemn them and hurl them back. Eventually, when the stream of recrimination and vetoes ran dry each year, some kind of budget was necessarily adopted; but it did not reflect the views of either party, and in terms of the consensus objective of deficit reduction it was a pale and ineffective compromise. Neither party would take responsibility, neither could be held accountable, each could point the finger at the other when the things went wrong.

In such circumstances, the people in their one solemn, sovereign act of voting cannot render a clear verdict and thus set the course of government. Elections lose their purpose and their meaning. The President, all through 1988, was saying, "Don't blame me for the budget deficit. It's those Democrats in Congress." And the Democrats were replying, "Don't blame us. Blame that man in the White House for not giving us the proper leadership." In November, the voters were not able to hold anybody clearly responsible, because, in fact nobody had been.

Our struggles with coalition government have demonstrated also the truth of the established wisdom concerning presidential leadership: in the American system there is simply no substitute for it. The Congress has 535 voting members, organized in two houses and in innumerable committees and subcommittees; every member is in principle the equal of every other member, and nobody can give directions to anybody else and make them stick. Such a body is simply not well designed for making coherent, decisive, coordinated policy. As the old theory told us, the system works best when the president proposes and the Congress disposes, when the president sets the agenda and leads, as everyone expects him to.

But how can leaders lead if followers don't follow? In divided government, presidential leadership becomes all but impossible. The president is not the leader of the congressional majority. He is precisely the opposite—the leader of their opposition, the man they are most dedicated to discredit and defeat. With great fanfare and immense hope, the people elect a president each four years. But then, most of the time these days, they give him a Congress a majority of whose members tried their best to beat him in the last election and will do so again in the next. To lead in those circumstances would be beyond the capability of any mortal. No one should blame presidents when they fail in a time of coalition government. It is the system that is at fault.

Nobody planned it this way. The country in no way made a conscious decision thirty years ago to abandon the responsible-party system that had served it well for almost the whole life of the nation. It was simply an accident of the electoral system. Almost unique in the world, the United States has an electoral process that permits people to split their tickets—to vote one way for president and the other way for Congress, if they so choose. And that is what enough of them have done to produce a divided outcome most of the time of late.

\*   \*   \*

## DISCUSSION QUESTIONS

1. Sundquist emphasizes the problems caused by divided government. Can you identify some potential benefits of having control of government split between the parties?

2. If we grant that divided government is as problematic as Sundquist argues, what are we to do about it? What kinds of reforms might make divided government less likely, and would you favor such reforms? Should Americans be discouraged from splitting their tickets when voting?

3. By the end of 2006, the United States will have had unified government—control by a single party—in five of the previous six years. What can you point to that would suggest unified control of government will continue, and what could you point to that might suggest a return to divided government?

## NOTES

1. Committee on Political Parties, *Toward a More Responsible Two-Party System,* supplement to the *American Political Science Review* 44 (September 1950), also published by Rinehart & Co., 1950. Quotation from Rinehart ed., 15, 16.
2. Fortunately for believers in party government, the problem of intra-party cohesion and discipline that so preoccupied the writers of the midcentury has to a large extent been solved by the events. The realignment of the party system since they wrote has produced Democratic and Republican parties that are more homogeneous than at any time within the memory of anyone now living; the minority wings that were once strong enough to disrupt the internal unity of both parties have withered. First to fade were the liberal Republicans, who until a couple of decades ago were potent enough to seriously contest for the presidential nomination; they are now ineffectual remnants that did not even put forward a candidate in 1988. Their mirror-image counterparts, the conservative Democrats, have been vanishing as well, although more slowly. Since the New Deal era, their wing of the party has been virtually confined to the South, and for thirty years its base there has been steadily eroding as conservatives find their political home in the burgeoning Republican Party. New Democratic senators from the South are no longer the Byrds, Robertsons, Eastlands, Russells, Thurmonds, and Hollands, who automatically voted with the Republicans on

major issues and made life miserable for Democratic presidents, Senate majority leaders, and House speakers; for the most part they are people who fit quite comfortably into the moderate-to-liberal national party, such as Terry Sanford, Bob Graham, and Wyche Fowler. (Strom Thurmond himself became a Republican long ago, and the son of Democratic Senator A. Willis Robertson made his race for the presidency in the Republican, not the Democratic, caucuses and primaries.) The same transformation has taken place in the House.

So the Republicans have become a solidly right-of-center party, very much in Ronald Reagan's image. If Republicans ever were to capture the Congress, they would have a little trouble attaining the unity necessary for true party government. And the Democrats, if and when they elect a president, will demonstrate a cohesion that will astound those who recall the schismatic party of thirty or even twenty years ago. Moreover, the reforms of congressional organization and procedures, which have strengthened the position of party leaders, party policy committees, and party caucuses, make it far more likely now that the cohesive Democratic majorities in the Congress would be able to overcome any obstruction that the truncated conservative wing might still attempt.

3. Address to the nation, 12 August 1987, as reported in *New York Times*, 13 August 1987.

## DEBATING THE ISSUES: RED AMERICA, BLUE AMERICA: MYTH OR REALITY?

In 1992, Patrick Buchanan famously stated at the Republican national convention that the United States was in the midst of a culture war that posited traditional, conservative social values against liberal, secular values. Bill Clinton's defeat of President George H. W. Bush seemed to defuse that idea: Clinton was a southern Democrat who had pushed his party toward the ideological center and, although only garnering 43 percent of the vote, he won states in all regions of the country. His 1996 victory was broader, adding states he had lost in 1992. In the 2000 presidential election, however, a striking regional pattern emerged in the results. Al Gore, the Democratic candidate, did well on the coasts and in the upper Midwest, while George W. Bush, the Republican candidate, picked up the remaining states. Many analysts were struck by this "red state/blue state" pattern—named after the coloring of the states on post-election maps—and suggested that it told us something more fundamental about American politics. Indeed, these analysts argued, Patrick Buchanan was in large measure right: the American public was deeply divided and polarized and in many respects living in two different worlds culturally. This polarization showed up not only in voting, but in presidential approval ratings, with the partisan gap in evaluations of Bill Clinton and George W. Bush being larger than for any previous presidents. The 2004 presidential election proved to be a near carbon-copy of 2000: with a few exceptions, the red states stayed red and the blue states stayed blue. President Bush picked up the votes of 78 percent of white, born-again evangelical Christians, while John Kerry received the support of 56 percent of all other voters. Bush received 60 percent of the votes of those individuals attending religious services at least once weekly; Kerry picked up 57 percent of the votes of individuals who attended services a few times a year or not at all. Eighty-five percent of conservatives voted for Bush; the same percentage of liberals voted for Kerry; and moderates split 54-45 percent for Kerry. Among those who believe abortion should be illegal in most or all cases, Bush received 75 percent of the vote. Among those who believe abortion should be legal in most or all cases, Kerry received 66 percent. Is America deeply polarized along partisan lines? Is there a culture war? Is the red state/blue state split real? Is there division on certain highly charged issues but not on most others? Are the divisions just artifacts of the way that survey questions are worded? In this debate, Liz Marlantes argues that the cultural split is deep and is reflected in party competition and the fortunes of the two parties. Morris Fiorina counters that the idea of a cultural war is vastly exaggerated—there might be a skirmish, but there is no war.

# 58

# "Inside Red-and-Blue America"

## Liz Marlantes

Of all the forces governing this campaign, the greatest may not be the candidates themselves or the jolt of external events but something far more basic: The split personality of the U.S. electorate. The election is being played out on a political landscape more sharply—and evenly—divided than any other in generations.

The "red-blue divide," as it has come to be known, entered public consciousness in the 2000 election, when the nation split down the middle between George W. Bush and Al Gore. The color-coded electoral map told a blunt geographic tale: Mr. Bush's red swept across the South, the Great Plains, and most of the Rocky Mountain West, while Mr. Gore's blue covered almost all of New England, the Mid-Atlantic, and the West Coast. The dramatic results recast the United States as a bipolar, "50-50 nation," in which where one lived translated into differences in culture, values—and partisan allegiance.

Four years later, after the worst terrorist attack in American history, a protracted economic pause, and a controversial war, the nation's political divide has not only stuck but, if anything, seems to be intensifying.

Bush, the first president in 112 years to win the electoral but not the popular vote, now stands as one of the most polarizing presidents in history. Republicans grant him enthusiastic approval, while Democrats express an equally strong loathing. Although few observers expect this fall's election to come down to just 537 votes in Florida, Bush and Sen. John Kerry have been running virtually neck-and-neck from the beginning of the campaign. Some pollsters believe each candidate already has a lock on as much as 47 percent of the vote—leaving the outcome up to an unusually small number of swing voters in a small number of swing states.

The same dynamic holds true in Congress. Republicans now control both houses of Congress, but by narrow margins and with deepening partisan rifts that have kept both parties in a confrontational posture. At the state level, too, power hangs in the balance. Nearly half the states could easily see a branch of their legislatures change control this fall.

And in a broader sense, the national discourse seems unusually inflamed. Accusations of media bias are on the rise, even as left- and right-wing polemicists, from Michael Moore to Bill O'Reilly, enjoy growing success. Voters speak of being unable to discuss politics with members of the opposite party, and many are seeking out like-minded environ-ments—from news they watch to the neighborhoods where they live.

\* \* \*

Like most trends in politics, the red-blue divide has been oversim-plified and overstated. Skeptics note that a more accurate electoral map—taking margins of victory into account—would show the nation colored not red and blue but various hues of purple. And many Ameri-cans don't stand that far apart on the issues. While activists on both sides of the political spectrum may sharply disagree on everything from taxes to terrorism, polls show most voters see themselves as moderates.

But if voters often lean instinctively toward the middle, they are also sorting themselves into parties that are growing more ideologically pure, which is having a polarizing effect.

## Ideological Segregation

Significantly, the correlation between ideology and party has been grow-ing much stronger in recent years. Surveys show an uptick in people choosing to be Republicans or Democrats (rather than independent) and in straight-ticket voting. Self-identified conservatives are more and more likely to be Republicans, while self-identified liberals are now almost ex-clusively Democrats.

At the same time, experts see greater geographic segregation by party. Compared with 30 or 40 years ago, more states now tilt strongly toward one party or the other. Most notably, the biggest states—California, New York, and Texas—have all transformed in recent decades from electoral battlegrounds into partisan bastions.

## Migration and Realignment

The polarized electoral map can be traced in part to demographics, with migration and immigration changing the makeup of many states. But it's also the result of ideological realignment, as voters in traditionally con-servative states have gravitated toward the Republican Party and voters in liberal states toward the Democrats. "It's not that the voters in Texas have become more conservative," explains Alan Abramowitz, a political scientist at Emory University. "They were always pretty conservative. But now they're Republicans."

The region most dramatically transformed is the South. There, conser-vative whites have all but abandoned the Democrats, propelled initially by civil rights issues and later by the GOP's growing emphasis on conser-vative cultural values. Once known as the Democrats' "Solid South," it's now a Bush stronghold. It has helped Republicans go head-to-head with

Democrats nationally, after more than half a century of Democratic dominance.

But the South isn't the only region that's changed. There's been a smaller but significant counter-movement in other areas—particularly the Northeast—away from the GOP.

Analysts say the forces propelling this realignment are both top-down and bottom-up. Voters are clearly taking cues from party leaders, who, since the days of Ronald Reagan, have become more pointedly ideological. But, as Professor Abramowitz points out, "it's a mutually reinforcing process, because the leaders also respond to the voters—especially if you think about what a Republican or Democratic primary electorate looks like."

At the congressional level, so many districts are now gerrymandered to be safe for one party that the election is essentially determined by the primary contest. One result: candidates tailor their messages to primary voters, who tend to have stronger ideological views.

Technology, too, has played a key role. The parties have been assembling databases to target voters with ads that are ever more tightly honed. It's an effective way of motivating voters, perhaps, but limits voter exposure to a broader range of issues and debate.

The shift is also strategic. With fewer swing voters to compete over—and a lower turnout rate among those voters, anyway—winning elections is now increasingly about generating higher and higher turnout in each party's base. This has led the parties to emphasize more ideological wedge issues, inflaming activists on both sides but leaving many moderate voters feeling unhappy with their choices.

*The Passion Factor*

Today's red-blue phenomenon is hardly the most intense political division the nation has seen. The Republic's founding, for example, pitted Federalists against Anti-Federalists in a bitter rivalry that formed a backdrop for the tragic duel between Alexander Hamilton and Aaron Burr. The issue of slavery, of course, cleaved the nation into parties representing North and South.

"Americans have always divided along some lines," says Philip Klinkner, a political scientist at Hamilton College. Sometimes, you can plot the divisions on a map. At other times, splits run mainly along class or ideological lines.

In some ways, the red-blue division of today can be seen as simply the latest version of a fundamental—and age-old—philosophical clash over the role of government. In broad terms, red America is a land of freedom and entrepreneurship, where anyone can get ahead as long as the government doesn't hold them back. Blue America, by contrast, is a land where government should provide equal opportunity, and a safety net, for those who would otherwise be left behind. The differences have largely to do with emphasis, but they lead to diverging views on everything from taxes to privatizing Social Security.

A similarly longstanding tension has to do with foreign affairs and America's role in the world. In red America, patriotism means America has an exceptional role to play; in blue America, there's a stronger emphasis on the global community and international cooperation.

### The Values Divide

Yet what makes the current split more unusual are the layers of cultural and even moral attitudes that go with it, centering around questions of values. By this measure, red America is a land of right and wrong, where voters believe public and private spheres should be bound by a set of core, often religious, principles. In blue America, morality is more of personal matter, and voters put a stronger emphasis on tolerance. These differing attitudes have put the two parties on opposite sides of a range of highly charged social issues such as abortion, gay marriage, and prayer in schools.

Significantly, one of the biggest partisan gaps now centers on religion: White Americans who attend church regularly are much likelier to be Republicans, and white Americans who rarely or never attend church are much likelier to be Democrats.

Experts trace the roots of this values divide to the social and cultural revolutions of the 1960s and '70s, and the changes they instituted in family life. In 1970, for example, about two-thirds of Americans families consisted of a married couple. Today, with the rise in divorce and unmarried couples living together, it's less than one-third.

The rise of the religious right during the Reagan years—emphasizing traditional families and morals—put these cultural differences in partisan terms.

But it was during the 1990s, when Bill Clinton became the first baby boomer president, that the culture gap exploded. Hillary Clinton famously ignited controversy in the campaign when she remarked about not staying home and baking cookies. At the 1992 GOP convention, conservative Pat Buchanan declared the U.S. in the throes of a "culture war." That war hit a peak during the Monica Lewinsky scandal, which pushed debates over sex and privacy to the fore, and led to President Clinton's impeachment.

The 1990s also seemed to take the cultural divide beyond policy into the broader realm of lifestyle and taste. Today, pundits routinely boil down red vs. blue to things like: barbecue vs. sushi; pickups vs. hybrids; country vs. hip-hop; church vs. spirituality. As John White, a political scientist at Catholic University, puts it: "We live in two parallel universes."

These categories don't fit all voters. But they serve as code for demographic and class differences that increasingly translate to party affiliation: People who live in rural and exurban areas, married voters, and whites are more likely to be Republicans. People in urban (and increasingly suburban) areas, singles, and minorities tend to be Democrats. People with college degrees tilt toward the GOP. Those with graduate degrees are more likely to be Democrats, as are people whose schooling ended in high school.

Taken together, these layers of differences are fostering a partisan divide that increasingly seems to be about identity. Voters are aligning with the party they feel best projects the values they want to pass on to their children. Moreover, each side seems to feel their identity is under threat, a perception the campaigns are subtly encouraging. Kerry's slogan, "Let America be America Again," evokes a sense of lost national greatness, while Bush's "Steady Leadership in a Time of Change" reinforces the image of a president guarding the nation against dangerous and corrosive forces.

This dimension has generated a tribal, us-versus-them attitude that colors everything else, with partisan loyalties often shaping people's views on issues rather than the other way around. Some analysts wonder, for example, what the split on Iraq would look like if Clinton, rather than Bush, had led the country to war.

It has also engendered an overall "lack of respect," says Professor White, by bringing debates about issues and ideas down to a personal level. "Both sides of the divide believe the other side disses" their values and their way of life.

### Good or Bad for U.S. Politics?

Still, the resurgence of partisanship isn't necessarily a bad thing for democracy. For one thing, more people tend to vote when they see real differences between the parties—and feel a personal stake in the outcome of an election.

According to a recent Pew Research Center poll, public interest in this election is much higher than at a similar point four year ago: 58 percent of voters say they are giving "quite a lot" of thought to the election, versus 46 percent in 2000. And 63 percent say it "really matters" who wins, versus 45 percent in 2000.

During the 1960s and '70s, by contrast, political analysts worried that partisanship was in a dangerous decline. In 1968, George Wallace famously charged there wasn't a dime's worth of difference between the two parties—and many voters seemed to agree with him, as rates of participation steadily dropped.

Yet the current partisan divide also means the losing side is likelier to feel upset and angry. And it creates real challenges for the winning side when it comes to governing.

Many analysts also worry that polarization has a self-perpetuating quality to it. "As the electorate becomes more polarized, [so do leaders], and each part of that reinforces the other," says Abramowitz.

In the past, it has often taken an intervening event to bridge such a stalemate. The close partisan division at the beginning of the 20th century ended with the Great Depression and Franklin Roosevelt's New Deal, which gave Democrats an advantage for decades thereafter. Demographic changes might eventually break the deadlock, giving one party or the other a natural advantage. Or the parties may shift, as they fight over the allegiance of certain groups.

Because of the limits of the two-party system, strategists say both parties inevitably include members with conflicting ideologies, who could be lured to the other side.

A strong third-party candidate could also break the divide by peeling off support from one or both sides.

The current campaign could polarize the nation even further. Yet as a referendum on the incumbent, analysts say the election may not wind up as close as it appears, and could even prove a turning point that swings the advantage to one side or the other—for a time.

"You can always point to some rule or dynamic in American politics that people think is enduring," Klinkner says, "until it's not."

# 59

# *"What* Culture Wars? Debunking the Myth of a Polarized America"

## Morris P. Fiorina

> "There is a religious war going on in this country, a cultural war as critical to the kind of nation we shall be as the Cold War itself, for this war is for the soul of America."

With those ringing words insurgent candidate Pat Buchanan fired up his supporters at the 1992 Republican National Convention. To be sure, not all delegates cheered Buchanan's call to arms, which was at odds with the "kinder, gentler" image that George H.W. Bush had attempted to project. Election analysts later included Buchanan's fiery words among the factors contributing to the defeat of President Bush, albeit one of lesser importance than the slow economy and the repudiation of his "Read my lips, no new taxes" pledge.

In the years since Buchanan's declaration of cultural war, the idea of a clash of cultures has become a common theme in discussions of American politics. The culture war metaphor refers to a displacement of the classic economic conflicts that animated twentieth-century politics in the advanced democracies by newly emergent moral and cultural ones. The literature generally attributes Buchanan's inspiration to a 1991 book, *Culture Wars*, by sociologist James Davison Hunter, who divided Americans into the culturally "orthodox" and the culturally "progressive" and argued that increasing conflict was inevitable.

No one has embraced the concept of the culture war more enthusiastically than journalists, ever alert for subjects that have "news value." Conflict is high in news value. Disagreement, division, polarization, battles, and war make good copy. Agreement, consensus, moderation, compromise, and peace do not. Thus, the notion of a culture war fits well with the news sense of journalists who cover politics. Their reports tell us that contemporary voters are sharply divided on moral issues. As David Broder wrote in the *Washington Post* in November 2000, "The divide went deeper than politics. It reached into the nation's psyche. . . . It was the moral dimension that kept Bush in the race."

Additionally, it is said that close elections do not reflect indifferent or ambivalent voters; rather, such elections reflect evenly matched blocs of deeply committed partisans. According to a February 2002 report in *USA Today*, "When George W. Bush took office, half the country cheered and the other half seethed"; some months later the *Economist* wrote that "such political divisions cannot easily be shifted by any president, let alone in two years, because they reflect deep demographic divisions. . . . The 50-50 nation appears to be made up of two big, separate voting blocks, with only a small number of swing voters in the middle."

The 2000 election brought us the familiar pictorial representation of the culture war in the form of the "red" and "blue" map of the United States. Vast areas of the heartland appeared as Republican red, while coastal and Great Lakes states took on a Democratic blue hue. Pundits reified the colors on the map, treating them as prima facie evidence of deep cultural divisions: Thus "Bush knew that the landslide he had wished for in 2000 . . . had vanished into the values chasm separating the blue states from the red ones" (John Kenneth White, in *The Values Divide*). In the same vein, the *Boston Herald* reported Clinton adviser Paul Begala as saying, on November 18, 2000, that "tens of millions of good people in Middle America voted Republican. But if you look closely at that map you see a more complex picture. You see the state where James Byrd was lynched—dragged behind a pickup truck until his body came apart—it's red. You see the state where Matthew Shepard was crucified on a split-rail fence for the crime of being gay—it's red. You see the state where right-wing extremists blew up a federal office building and murdered scores of federal employees—it's red."

Claims of bitter national division were standard fare after the 2000 elections, and few commentators publicly challenged them. On the contrary, the belief in a fractured nation was expressed even by high-level political operatives. Republican pollster Bill McInturff commented to the *Economist* in January 2001 that "we have two massive colliding forces. One is rural, Christian, religiously conservative. [The other] is socially tolerant, pro-choice, secular, living in New England and the Pacific Coast." And Matthew Dowd, a Bush reelection strategist, explained to the *Los Angeles Times* why Bush has not tried to expand his electoral base: "You've got 80 to 90 percent of the country that look at each other like they are on separate planets."

The journalistic drumbeat continues unabated. A November 2003 report from the Pew Research Center led E. J. Dionne Jr. of the *Washington Post* to comment: "The red states get redder, the blue states get bluer, and the political map of the United States takes on the coloration of the Civil War."

And as the 2004 election approaches, commentators see a continuation, if not an intensification, of the culture war. *Newsweek*'s Howard Fineman wrote in October 2003, "The culture war between the Red and Blue Nations has erupted again—big time—and will last until Election Day next year. Front lines are all over, from the Senate to the Pentagon to Florida to the Virginia suburbs where, at the Bush-Cheney 2004 headquarters, they are blunt about the shape of the battle: 'The country's split 50-50 again,' a top aide told me, 'just as it was in 2000.' "

In sum, observers of contemporary American politics have apparently reached a new consensus around the proposition that old disagreements about economics now pale in comparison to new divisions based on sexuality, morality, and religion, divisions so deep and bitter as to justify talk of war in describing them.

Yet research indicates otherwise. Publicly available databases show that the culture war script embraced by journalists and politicos lies somewhere between simple exaggeration and sheer nonsense. There is no culture war in the United States; no battle for the soul of America rages, at least none that most Americans are aware of.

Certainly, one can find a few warriors who engage in noisy skirmishes. Many of the activists in the political parties and the various cause groups do hate each other and regard themselves as combatants in a war. But their hatreds and battles are not shared by the great mass of Americans—certainly nowhere near "80–90 percent of the country"—who are for the most part moderate in their views and tolerant in their manner. A case in point: To their embarrassment, some GOP senators recently learned that ordinary Americans view gay marriage in somewhat less apocalyptic terms than do the activists in the Republican base.

If swing voters have disappeared, how did the six blue states in which George Bush ran most poorly in 2000 all elect Republican governors in

2002 (and how did Arnold Schwarzenegger run away with the 2003 recall in blue California)? If almost all voters have already made up their minds about their 2004 votes, then why did John Kerry surge to a 14-point trial-heat lead when polls offered voters the prospect of a Kerry-McCain ticket? If voter partisanship has hardened into concrete, why do virtually identical majorities in both red and blue states favor divided control of the presidency and Congress, rather than unified control by their party? Finally, and ironically, if voter positions have become so uncompromising, why did a recent CBS story titled "Polarization in America" report that 76 percent of Republicans, 87 percent of Democrats, and 86 percent of Independents would like to see elected officials compromise more rather than stick to their principles?

Still, how does one account for reports that have almost 90 percent of Republicans planning to vote for Bush and similarly high numbers of Democrats planning to vote for Kerry? The answer is that while voter *positions* have not polarized, their *choices* have. There is no contradiction here; positions and choices are not the same thing. Voter choices are functions of their positions and the positions and actions of the candidates they choose between.

Republican and Democratic elites unquestionably have polarized. But it is a mistake to assume that such elite polarization is equally present in the broader public. It is not. However much they may claim that they are responding to the public, political elites do not take extreme positions because *voters* make them. Rather, by presenting them with polarizing alternatives, elites make voters appear polarized, but the reality shows through clearly when voters have a choice of more moderate alternatives—as with the aforementioned Republican governors.

Republican strategists have bet the Bush presidency on a high-risk gamble. Reports and observation indicate that they are attempting to win in 2004 by getting out the votes of a few million Republican-leaning evangelicals who did not vote in 2000, rather than by attracting some modest proportion of 95 million other non-voting Americans, most of them moderates, not to mention moderate Democratic voters who could have been persuaded to back a genuinely compassionate conservative. Such a strategy leaves no cushion against a negative turn of events and renders the administration vulnerable to a credible Democratic move toward the center. Whether the Democrats can capitalize on their opportunity remains to be seen.

## DISCUSSION QUESTIONS

1. According to Marlantes, what are the chief factors contributing to polarization and cultural division in the United States? Are these factors likely to change anytime soon?

2. Based on the articles and other information you might have, do you think Fiorina is right that the American public is not deeply split on a range of issues? Do you think the two parties represent very different ways of thinking about society and values?

3. If you were an adviser for one of the two major parties, how would you advise them to address the issue of polarization or culture war? Should they emphasize issues where broader consensus might be possible? Or is it the job of political parties to emphasize precisely those issues that might be the most divisive?

4. Party strategists often talk about changing the party's public image. In your view, what would a party have to do to change its public image significantly? That is, what would convince you that a party had changed?

# CHAPTER 12

# Groups and Interests

## 60

## "Political Association in the United States" from *Democracy in America*

### ALEXIS DE TOCQUEVILLE

*The right of political association has long been a cornerstone of American democracy. Alexis de Tocqueville, a French citizen who studied early-nineteenth-century American society, argued that the right to associate provides an important check on a majority's power to suppress a political minority. Tocqueville pointed out that allowing citizens to associate in a variety of groups with a variety of crosscutting interests provides a political outlet for all types of political interests, and enables compromises to be reached as each interest group attempts to build support among shifting coalitions. "There is a place for individual independence," Tocqueville argued, in the American system of government. "[A]s in society, all the members are advancing at the same time toward the same goal, but they are not obliged to follow exactly the same path."*

Better use has been made of association and this powerful instrument of action has been applied to more varied aims in America than anywhere else in the world.

\* \* \*

The inhabitant of the United States learns from birth that he must rely on himself to combat the ills and trials of life; he is restless and defiant in his outlook toward the authority of society and appeals to its power only when he cannot do without it. The beginnings of this attitude first appear at school, where the children, even in their games, submit to rules settled by themselves and punish offenses which they have defined themselves. The same attitude turns up again in all the affairs of social life. If some obstacle blocks the public road halting the circulation of traffic, the neighbors at once form a deliberative body; this improvised assembly produces an executive authority which remedies the trouble before anyone has thought of the possibility of some previously constituted authority beyond that of those concerned. Where enjoyment is concerned, people associate to make festivities grander and more orderly. Finally, associations are formed to combat exclusively moral troubles: intemperance is fought in common. Public security, trade and industry, and morals and religion all provide the aims for associations in the United States. There is no end which the human will despairs of attaining by the free action of the collective power of individuals.

*   *   *

The right of association being recognized, citizens can use it in different ways. An association simply consists in the public and formal support of specific doctrines by a certain number of individuals who have undertaken to cooperate in a stated way in order to make these doctrines prevail. Thus the right of association can almost be identified with freedom to write, but already associations are more powerful than the press. When some view is represented by an association, it must take clearer and more precise shape. It counts its supporters and involves them in its cause; these supporters get to know one another, and numbers increase zeal. An association unites the energies of divergent minds and vigorously directs them toward a clearly indicated goal.

Freedom of assembly marks the second stage in the use made of the right of association. When a political association is allowed to form centers of action at certain important places in the country, its activity becomes greater and its influence more widespread. There men meet, active measures are planned, and opinions are expressed with that strength and warmth which the written word can never attain.

But the final stage is the use of association in the sphere of politics. The supporters of an agreed view may meet in electoral colleges and appoint mandatories to represent them in a central assembly. That is, properly speaking, the application of the representative system to one party.

*   *   *

In our own day freedom of association has become a necessary guarantee against the tyranny of the majority. In the United States, once a party has become predominant, all public power passes into its hands; its close supporters occupy all offices and have control of all organized forces. The most distinguished men of the opposite party, unable to cross the barrier keeping them from power, must be able to establish themselves outside it; the minority must use the whole of its moral authority to oppose the physical power oppressing it. Thus the one danger has to be balanced against a more formidable one.

The omnipotence of the majority seems to me such a danger to the American republics that the dangerous expedient used to curb it is actually something good.

Here I would repeat something which I have put in other words when speaking of municipal freedom: no countries need associations more— to prevent either despotism of parties or the arbitrary rule of a prince —than those with a democratic social state. In aristocratic nations secondary bodies form natural associations which hold abuses of power in check. In countries where such associations do not exist, if private people did not artificially and temporarily create something like them, I see no other dike to hold back tyranny of whatever sort, and a great nation might with impunity be oppressed by some tiny faction or by a single man.

* * *

In America the citizens who form the minority associate in the first place to show their numbers and to lessen the moral authority of the majority, and secondly, by stimulating competition, to discover the arguments most likely to make an impression on the majority, for they always hope to draw the majority over to their side and then to exercise power in its name.

Political associations in the United States are therefore peaceful in their objects and legal in the means used; and when they say that they only wish to prevail legally, in general they are telling the truth.

* * *

The Americans * * * have provided a form of government within their associations, but it is, if I may put it so, a civil government. There is a place for individual independence there; as in society, all the members are advancing at the same time toward the same goal, but they are not obliged to follow exactly the same path. There has been no sacrifice of will or of reason, but rather will and reason are applied to bring success to a common enterprise.

## DISCUSSION QUESTIONS

1. Tocqueville argues that "freedom of association has become a necessary guarantee against the tyranny of the majority." Although freedom of association is clearly a central part of any free society, are there features of contemporary American politics that would suggest a rethinking of this benign view?

2. Placing restrictions on interest-group activities is difficult because of the constitutional protections afforded to these groups. The Constitution guarantees the people the right to assemble and to petition government regarding their grievances, and it also guarantees

freedom of speech. All these are the essence of interest-group activity. Nonetheless, many Americans are uneasy with the influence wielded by organized interest groups. What, if any, restrictions on interest groups would you be comfortable with? Can you think of any instances where the influence of groups should be limited (for example, political extremists like the various militia groups, or large political-action committees in electoral campaigns)?

# 61

# "The Logic of Collective Action" from *The Rise and Decline of Nations*

### Mancur Olson

*Americans organize at a tremendous rate to pursue common interests in the political arena. Yet not all groups are created equal, and some types of political organizations are much more common than others. In particular, it is far easier to organize groups around narrow economic interests than it is to organize around broad "public goods" interests. Why do some groups organize while others do not?*

*The nature of collective goods, according to economist Mancur Olson, explains this phenomenon. When a collective good is provided to a group, no member of the group can be denied the benefits of the good. For example, if Congress passes a law that offers subsidies for a new telecommunications technology, any company that produces that technology will benefit from the subsidy. The catch is, any company will benefit* even if *they did not participate in the collective effort to win the subsidy. Olson argues that "the larger the number of individuals or firms that would benefit from a collective good, the smaller the share of the gains . . . that will accrue to the individual or firm"; hence, the less likely any one member of the group will contribute to the collective effort to secure the collective benefit. For smaller groups, any one member's share of the collective good is larger and more meaningful, so the more likely any one member of the group will be willing to make an individual sacrifice to provide a benefit shared by the entire group. An additional distinction is that in a large group, there is often a tendency to assume that someone else will take care of the problem—this is known as the "free rider" problem, or, as Olson puts it, "let George do it." This is less likely to happen in smaller groups.*

*The logic helps to explain the greater difficulty "public interest groups" have in organizing and staying organized to provide such collective goods as clean air, consumer product safety, and banking regulations aimed at promoting inner-city investments by banks. These goods benefit very large numbers of people, but the benefit to any one person, Olson would argue, is not sufficient for them to sacrifice time or money for the effort to succeed, especially if the individual believes that he or she will benefit from the collective good even if they do not contribute. Olson identifies "selective incentives" as one way in which these larger groups are able to overcome the incentive to free ride.*

*The Logic*

The argument of this book begins with a paradox in the behavior of groups. It has often been taken for granted that if everyone in a group of individuals or firms had some interest in common, then there would be a tendency for the group to seek to further this interest. Thus many students of politics in the United States for a long time supposed that citizens with a common political interest would organize and lobby to serve that interest. Each individual in the population would be in one or more groups and the vector of pressures of these competing groups explained the outcomes of the political process. Similarly, it was often supposed that if workers, farmers, or consumers faced monopolies harmful to their interests, they would eventually attain countervailing power through organizations such as labor unions or farm organizations that obtained market power and protective government action. On a larger scale, huge social classes are often expected to act in the interest of their members; the unalloyed form of this belief is, of course, the Marxian contention that in capitalist societies the bourgeois class runs the government to serve its own interests, and that once the exploitation of the proletariat goes far enough and "false consciousness" has disappeared, the working class will in its own interest revolt and establish a dictatorship of the proletariat. In general, if the individuals in some category or class had a sufficient degree of self-interest and if they all agreed on some common interest, then the group would to some extent also act in a self-interested or group-interested manner.

If we ponder the logic of the familiar assumption described in the preceding paragraph, we can see that it is fundamentally and indisputably faulty. Consider those consumers who agree that they pay higher prices for a product because of some objectionable monopoly or tariff, or those workers who agree that their skill deserves a higher wage. Let us now ask what would be the expedient course of action for an individual consumer who would like to see a boycott to combat a monopoly or a lobby to repeal the tariff, or for an individual worker who would like a strike threat or a minimum wage law that could bring higher wages. If the consumer or worker contributes a few days and a few dollars to organize a boycott or a union or to lobby for favorable legislation, he or she will have sacrificed time and money. What will this sacrifice obtain? The individual will at best succeed in advancing the cause to a small (often imperceptible) degree. In any case he will get only a minute share of the gain from his action. The very fact that the objective or interest is common to or shared by the group entails that the gain from any sacrifice an individual makes to serve this common purpose is shared with everyone in the group. The successful boycott or strike or lobbying action will bring the better price or wage for everyone in the relevant category, so the individual in any large group with a common interest will reap only a minute share of the gains from whatever sacrifices the individual makes to achieve this common interest. Since any gain goes to everyone in the group, those who contribute nothing to the effort will get just as much as those who made a contribution. It pays to "let George do it," but George has little or no incentive to do anything in the group interest either, so (in the absence of factors that are completely left out of the conceptions mentioned in the first paragraph) there will be little, if any, group action. The paradox, then, is that (in the absence of special arrangements or circumstances to which we shall turn later) large groups, at least if they are composed of rational individuals, will *not* act in their group interest.

This paradox is elaborated and set out in a way that lets the reader check every step of the logic in a book I wrote entitled *The Logic of Collective Action*.

\* \* \*

Organizations that provide collective goods to their client groups through political or market action \* \* \* are \* \* \* not supported because of the collective goods they provide, but rather because they have been fortunate enough to find what I have called *selective incentives*. A selective incentive is one that applies selectively to the individuals depending on whether they do or do not contribute to the provision of the collective good.

A selective incentive can be either negative or positive; it can, for example, be a loss or punishment imposed only on those who do *not* help provide the collective good. Tax payments are, of course, obtained with the help of negative selective incentives, since those who are found not to have paid their taxes must then suffer both taxes and penalties. The best-known type of organized interest group in modern democratic societies, the labor union, is also usually supported, in part, through negative selective incentives. Most of the dues in strong unions are obtained through union shop, closed shop, or agency shop arrangements which make dues paying more or less compulsory and automatic. There are often also informal arrangements with the same effect; David McDonald, former president of the United Steel Workers of America, describes one of these arrangements used in the early history of that union. It was, he writes, a technique

> which we called . . . visual education, which was a high-sounding label for a practice much more accurately described as dues picketing. It worked very simply. A group of dues-paying members, selected by the district director (usually more for their size than their tact) would stand at the plant gate with pick handles or baseball bats in hand and confront each worker as he arrived for his shift.[1]

As McDonald's "dues picketing" analogy suggests, picketing during strikes is another negative selective incentive that unions sometimes need; although picketing in industries with established and stable unions is usually peaceful, this is because the union's capacity to close down an enterprise against which it has called a strike is clear to all; the early phase of unionization often involves a great deal of violence on the part of both unions and anti-union employers and scabs.

\* \* \*

Positive selective incentives, although easily overlooked, are also commonplace, as diverse examples in *The Logic* demonstrate. American farm organizations offer prototypical examples. Many of the members of the stronger American farm organizations are members because their dues payments are automatically deducted from the "patronage dividends" of farm cooperatives or are included in the insurance premiums paid to mutual insurance companies associated with the farm organizations. Any number of organizations with urban clients also provide similar positive selective incentives in the form of insurance policies, publications, group air fares, and other private goods made available only to members. The grievance procedures of labor unions usually also offer selective incentives, since the grievances of active members often get most of the attention. The symbiosis between the political power of a lobbying organization and the business institutions associated with it often yields tax or other advantages for the business institution, and the publicity and other information flowing out of the political arm of a movement often generates patterns of preference or trust that make the business activities of the movement more remunerative. The surpluses obtained in such ways in turn provide positive selective incentives that recruit participants for the lobbying efforts.

Small groups, or occasionally large "federal" groups that are made up of many small groups of socially interactive members, have an additional source of both negative and positive selective incentives. Clearly most people value the companionship and respect of those with whom they interact. In modern societies solitary confinement is, apart from the rare death penalty, the harshest legal punishment. The censure or even ostracism of those who fail to bear a share of the burdens of collective action can sometimes be an important selective incentive. An extreme example of this occurs when British unionists refuse to speak to uncooperative colleagues, that is, "send them to Coventry." Similarly, those in a socially interactive group seeking a collective good can give special respect or honor to those who distinguish themselves by their sacrifices in the interest of the group and thereby offer them a positive selective incentive. Since most people apparently prefer relatively like-minded or agreeable and respectable company, and often prefer to associate with those whom they especially admire, they may find it costless to shun those who shirk the collective action and to favor those who over-subscribe.

Social selective incentives can be powerful and inexpensive, but they are available only in certain situations. As I have already indicated, they have little applicability to large groups, except in those cases in which the large groups can be federations of small groups that are capable of social interaction. It also is not possible to organize most large groups in need of a collective good into small, socially interactive subgroups, since most individuals do not have the time needed to maintain a huge number of friends and acquaintances.

The availability of social selective incentives is also limited by the social heterogeneity of some of the groups or categories that would benefit from a collective good. Everyday observation reveals that most socially interactive groups are fairly homogeneous and that many people resist extensive social interaction with those they deem to have lower status or greatly different tastes. Even Bohemian or other nonconformist groups often are made up of individuals who are similar to one another, however much they differ from the rest of society. Since some of the categories of individuals who would benefit from a collective good are socially heterogeneous, the social interaction needed for selective incentives sometimes cannot be arranged even when the number of individuals involved is small.

\* \* \*

In short, the political entrepreneurs who attempt to organize collective action will accordingly be more likely to succeed if they strive to organize relatively homogeneous groups. The political managers whose task it is to maintain organized or collusive action similarly will be motivated to use indoctrination and selective recruitment to increase the homogeneity of their client groups. This is true in part because social selective incentives are more likely to be available to the more nearly homogeneous groups, and in part because homogeneity will help achieve consensus.

Information and calculation about a collective good is often itself a collective good. Consider a typical member of a large organization who is deciding how much time to devote to studying the policies or leadership of the organization. The more time the member devotes to this matter, the greater the likelihood that his or her voting and advocacy will favor effective policies and leadership for the organization. This typical member will, however, get only a small share of the gain from the more effective policies and leadership: in the aggregate, the other members will get almost all the gains, so that the individual member does not have an incentive to devote nearly as much time to fact-finding and thinking about the organization as would be in the group interest. Each of the members of the group would be better off if they all could be coerced into spending more time finding out how to vote to make the organization best further their interests. This is dramatically evident in the case of the typical voter in a national election in a large country. The gain to such a voter from studying issues and candidates until it is clear what vote is truly in his or her interest is given by the difference in the value to the individual of the "right" election outcome as compared with the "wrong" outcome, *multiplied by the probability a change in the individual's vote will alter the outcome of the election*. Since the probability that a typical voter will change the outcome of the election is vanishingly small, the typical citizen is usually "rationally ignorant" about public affairs. Often, information about public affairs is so interesting or entertaining that it pays to acquire it for these reasons alone—this appears to be the single most important source of exceptions to the generalization that *typical* citizens are rationally ignorant about public affairs.

Individuals in a few special vocations can receive considerable rewards in private goods if they acquire exceptional knowledge of public goods. Politicians, lobbyists, journalists, and social scientists, for example, may earn more money, power, or prestige from knowledge of this or that public business. Occasionally, exceptional knowledge of public policy can generate exceptional profits in stock exchanges or other markets. Withal, the typical citizen will find that his or her income and life chances will not be improved by zealous study of public affairs, or even of any single collective good.

The limited knowledge of public affairs is in turn necessary to explain the effectiveness of lobbying. If all citizens had obtained and digested all pertinent information, they could not then be swayed by advertising or other persuasion. With perfectly informed citizens, elected officials would not be subject to the blandishments of lobbyists, since the constituents would then know if their interests were betrayed and defeat the unfaithful representative at the next election. Just as lobbies provide collective goods to special-interest groups, so their effectiveness is explained by the imperfect knowledge of citizens, and this in turn is due mainly to the fact that information and calculation about collective goods is also a collective good.

*    *    *

The fact that the typical individual does not have an incentive to spend much time studying many of his choices concerning collective goods also helps to explain some otherwise inexplicable individual contributions toward the provision of collective goods. The logic of collective action that has been described in this chapter is not immediately apparent to those who have never studied it; if it were, there would be nothing paradoxical in the argument with which this chapter opened, and students to whom the argument is explained would not react with initial skepticism. No doubt the practical implications of this logic for the individual's own choices were often discerned before the logic was ever set out in print, but this does not mean that they were always understood even at the intuitive and practical level. In particular, when the costs of individual contributions to collective action are very small, the individual has little incentive to investigate whether or not to make a contribution or even to exercise intuition. If the individual knows the costs of a contribution to collective action in the interest of a group of which he is a part are trivially small, he may rationally not take the trouble to consider whether the gains are smaller still. This is particularly the case since the size of these gains and the policies that would maximize them are matters about which it is usually not rational for him to investigate.

This consideration of the costs and benefits of calculation about public goods leads to the testable prediction that voluntary contributions toward the provision of collective goods for large groups without selective incentives will often occur when the costs of the individual contributions are negligible, but that they will *not* often occur when the costs of the individual contributions are considerable. In other words, when the costs of individual action to help to obtain a desired collective good are small enough, the result is indeterminate and sometimes goes one way and sometimes the other, but when the costs get larger this indeterminacy disappears. We should accordingly find that more than a few people are willing to take the moment of time needed to sign petitions for causes they support, or to express their opinions in the course of discussion, or to vote for the candidate or party they prefer. Similarly, if the argument here is correct, we should not find many instances where individuals voluntarily contribute substantial sums of resources year after year for the purpose of obtaining some collective good for some large group of which they are a part. Before parting with a large amount of money or time, and particularly before doing so repeatedly, the rational individual will reflect on what this considerable sacrifice will accomplish. If the individual is a typical individual in a large group that would benefit from a collective good, his contribution will not make a perceptible difference in the amount that is provided. The theory here predicts that such contributions become less likely the larger the contribution at issue.

Even when contributions are costly enough to elicit rational calculation, there is still one set of circumstances in which collective action can occur without selective incentives. This set of circumstances becomes evident the moment we think of situations in which there are only a few individuals or firms that would benefit from collective action. Suppose there are two firms of equal size in an industry and no other firms can enter the industry. It still will be the case that a higher price for the industry's product will benefit both firms and that legislation favorable to the industry will help both firms. The higher price and the favorable legislation are then collective goods to this "oligopolistic" industry, even though there are only two in the group that benefit from the collective goods.

Obviously, each of the oligopolists is in a situation in which if it restricts output to raise the industry price, or lobbies for favorable legislation for the industry, it will tend to get half of the benefit. And the cost-benefit ratio of action in the common interest easily could be so favorable that, even though a firm bears the whole cost of its action and gets only half the benefit of this action, it could still profit from acting in the common interest. Thus if the group that would benefit from collective action is sufficiently small and the cost-benefit ratio of collective action for the group sufficiently favorable, there may well be calculated action in the collective interest even without selective incentives.

*   *   *

Untypical as my example of equal-sized firms may be, it makes the general point intuitively obvious: other things being equal, *the larger the number of individuals or firms that would benefit from a collective good, the smaller the share of the gains from action in the group interest that will accrue to the individual or firm that undertakes the action. Thus, in the absence of selective incentives, the incentive for group action diminishes as group size increases, so that large groups are less able to act in their common interest than small ones.* If an additional individual or firm that would value the collective good enters the scene, then the share of the gains from group-oriented action that anyone already in the group might take must diminish. This holds true whatever the relative sizes or valuations of the collective good in the group.

*   *   *

The significance of the logic that has just been set out can best be seen by comparing groups that would have the same net gain from collective action, if they could engage in it, but that vary in size. Suppose there are a million individuals who would gain a thousand dollars each, or a billion in the aggregate, if they were to organize effectively and engage in collective action that had a total cost of a hundred million. If the logic set out above is right, they could not organize or engage in effective collective action without selective incentives. Now suppose that, although the total gain of a billion dollars from collective action and the aggregate cost of a hundred million remain the same, the group is composed instead of five big corporations or five organized municipalities, each of which would gain two hundred million. Collective action is not an absolute certainty even in this case, since each of the five could conceivably expect others to put up the hundred million and hope to gain the collective good worth two hundred million at no cost at all. Yet collective action, perhaps after some delays due to bargaining, seems very likely indeed. In this case any one of the five would gain a hundred million from providing the collective good even if it had to pay the whole cost itself; and the costs of bargaining among five would not be great, so they would sooner or later probably work out an agreement providing for the collective action. The numbers in this example are arbitrary, but roughly similar situations occur often in reality, and the contrast between "small" and "large" groups could be illustrated with an infinite number of diverse examples.

The significance of this argument shows up in a second way if one compares the operations of lobbies or cartels within jurisdictions of vastly different scale, such as a modest municipality on the one hand and a big country on the other. Within the town, the mayor or city council may be influenced by, say, a score of petitioners or a lobbying budget of a thousand dollars. A particular line of business may be in the hands of only a few firms, and if the town is distant enough from other markets only these few would need to agree to create a cartel. In a big country, the resources needed to influence the national government are likely to be much more substantial, and unless the firms are (as they sometimes are) gigantic, many of them would have to cooperate to create an effective cartel. Now suppose that the million individuals in our large group in the previous paragraph were spread out over a hundred thousand towns or jurisdictions, so that each jurisdiction had ten of them, along with the same proportion of citizens in other categories as before. Suppose also that the cost-benefit ratios remained the same, so that there was still a billion dollars to gain across all jurisdictions or ten thousand in each, and that it would still cost a hundred million dollars across all jurisdictions or a thousand in each. It no longer seems out of the question that in many jurisdictions the groups of ten, or subsets of them, would put up the thousand-dollar total needed to get the thousand for each individual. Thus we see that, if all else were equal, small jurisdictions would have more collective action per capita than large ones.

Differences in intensities of preference generate a third type of illustration of the logic at issue. A small number of zealots anxious for a particular collective good are more likely to act collectively to obtain that good than a larger number with the same aggregate willingness to pay. Suppose there are twenty-five individuals, each of whom finds a given collective good worth a thousand dollars in one case, whereas in another there are five thousand, each of whom finds the collective good worth five dollars. Obviously, the argument indicates that there would be a greater likelihood of collective action in the former case than in the latter, even though the aggregate demand for the collective good is the same in both. The great historical significance of small groups of fanatics no doubt owes something to this consideration.

The argument in this chapter predicts that those groups that have access to selective incentives will be more likely to act collectively to obtain collective goods than those that do not, and that smaller groups will have a greater likelihood of engaging in collective action than larger ones. The empirical portions of *The Logic* show that this prediction has been correct for the United States.

\*   \*   \*

## DISCUSSION QUESTIONS

1. Besides the size of a group, what other considerations do you think would play a role in people's decisions to join a collective endeavor? Are you convinced that the size of a group is as important as Olson argues?

2. Think of your own decisions to join or not to join a group. Have you ever been a "free rider"? For example, have there been protests against tuition increases at your school that you supported but did not participate in? If so, what would it have taken to get you to join?

3. If Olson is right, would Tocqueville's view about the role of groups in overcoming the potential tyranny of majority need to be modified?

## NOTE

1. David J. McDonald, *Union Man* (New York: Dutton, 1969), p. 121.

62

# "Associations Without Members"

## Theda Skocpol

*One of the hot topics in social science research since the mid-1990s has been the idea of "social capital." Put simply, social capital suggests that involvement in group and social activities generates side benefits that promote the health of the political system. Involvement in these groups tends to contribute to trust, efficacy, and a broader interest and involvement in public affairs. The idea emerged as scholars noted that several measures of public participation in politics—voting turnout, for example—had declined markedly since the early 1960s. At the same time, measures of public disaffection, mistrust, and alienation from politics were growing. Analysts, such as the political scientist Robert Putnam, noted that, in fact, not only were measures like voting turnout on the downswing, but many indicators of social involvement were also drooping. As Putnam famously pointed out, it seemed that even bowling-league memberships were dropping and that Americans were increasingly "bowling alone." If in fact involvement, broadly speaking, was on the decline, then the positive effects of involvement ("social capital") would also be on the decline, with significant impacts on social and political life.*

*These ideas generated a mountain of research, ranging from studies questioning the thesis of participatory decline, to those trying to explain the decline, to those evaluating the effects of the decline. Theda Skocpol steps into this debate by offering an analysis of how Americans have changed not so much the quantity, but the quality, of their participation. Once, Americans were group members who participated in group activities and group decision making. These associations, in many senses, reflected America's democratic political system, both in terms of their decision making and in terms of their often federal structure. Increasingly, however, the civic world is filled with "associations without members" centered not in communities but in Washington, D.C., led not by ordinary members, but by elite professionals. "Membership" in these organizations usually means little more than writing a check that entitles the check-writer to receive a monthly publication. Meetings and local involvement are absent. Of course, not all associations operate this way, but Skocpol suggests that this is increasingly becoming the norm and that it has had deleterious effects for the political system. She identifies a range of reasons for this transformation, including "racial and gender change; shifts in the political opportunity structure; new techniques and models for building organizations; and recent transformations in U.S. class relations."*

In just a third of a century, Americans have dramatically changed their style of civic and political association. A civic world once centered in locally rooted and nationally active membership associations is a relic. Today, Americans volunteer for causes and projects, but only rarely as ongoing members. They send checks to service and advocacy groups run by professionals, often funded by foundations or professional fundraisers. Prime-time airways echo with debates among their spokespersons: the National Abortion Rights Action League debates the National Right to Life Committee; the Concord Coalition takes on the American Association of Retired Persons; and the Environmental Defense Fund counters business groups. Entertained or bemused, disengaged viewers watch as polarized advocates debate.

The largest membership groups of the 1950s were old-line and well-established, with founding dates ranging from 1733 for the Masons to 1939 for the Woman's Division of Christian Service (a Methodist women's association formed from "missionary" societies with nineteenth-century roots). Like most large membership associations throughout American history, most 1950s associations recruited members across class lines. They held regular local meetings and convened periodic assemblies of elected leaders and delegates at the state, regional, or national levels. Engaged in multiple rather than narrowly specialized pursuits, many associations combined social or ritual activities with community service, mutual aid, and involvement in national affairs. Patriotism was a leitmotif; during and after World War II, a passionate and victorious national endeavor, these associations sharply expanded their memberships and renewed the vigor of their local and national activities.

To be sure, very large associations were not the only membership federations that mattered in postwar America. Also prominent were somewhat smaller, elite-dominated civic groups—including male service groups like Rotary, Lions, and Kiwanis, and longstanding female groups like the American Association of University Women and the League of Women Voters. Dozens of ethnically based fraternal and cultural associations flourished, as did African-American fraternal groups like the Prince Hall Masons and the Improved Benevolent and Protective Order of Elks of the World.

For many membership federations, this was a golden era of national as well as community impact. Popularly rooted membership federations rivaled professional and business associations for influence in policy debates. The AFL-CIO was in the thick of struggles about economic and social policies; the American Legion and the Veterans of Foreign Wars advanced veterans' programs; the American Farm Bureau Federation (AFBF) joined other farmers' associations to influence national and state agricultural policies; and the National Congress of Parents and Teachers (PTA) and the General Federation of Women's Clubs were influential on educational, health, and family issues. The results could be decisive, as exemplified by the pivotal role of the American Legion in drafting and lobbying for the GI Bill of 1944.

Then, suddenly, old-line membership federations seemed passé. Upheavals shook America during "the long 1960s," stretching from the mid-1950s through the mid-1970s. The southern Civil Rights movement challenged white racial domination and spurred legislation to enforce legal equality and voting rights for African Americans. Inspired by Civil Rights achievements, additional "rights" movements exploded, promoting equality for women, dignity for homosexuals, the unionization of farm workers, and the mobilization of other nonwhite ethnic minorities. Movements arose to oppose U.S. involvement in the war in Vietnam, champion a new environmentalism, and further other public causes. At the forefront of these groundswells were younger Americans, especially from the growing ranks of college students and university graduates.

The great social movements of the long 1960s were propelled by combinations of grassroots protest, activist radicalism, and professionally led efforts to lobby government and educate the public. Some older membership associations ended up participating and expanding their bases of support, yet the groups that sparked movements were more agile and flexibly structured than pre-existing membership federations.

The upheavals of the 1960s could have left behind a reconfigured civic world, in which some old-line membership associations had declined but others had reoriented and reenergized themselves. Within each great social movement, memberships could have consolidated and groups coalesced into new omnibus federations able to link the grass roots to state, regional, and national leaderships, allowing longstanding American civic traditions to continue in new ways.

But this is not what happened. Instead, the 1960s, 1970s, and 1980s brought extraordinary organizational proliferation and professionalization. At the national level alone, the *Encyclopedia of Associations* listed approximately 6,500 associations in 1958. This total grew by 1990 to almost 23,000. Within the expanding group universe, moreover, new kinds of associations came to the fore: relatively centralized and professionally led organizations focused on policy lobbying and public education.

Another wave of the advocacy explosion involved "public interest" or "citizens" groups seeking to shape public opinion and influence legislation. Citizens' advocacy groups espouse "causes" ranging from environmental protection (for example, the Sierra Club and the Environmental Defense Fund), to the well-being of poor children (the Children's Defense Fund), to reforming politics (Common Cause) and cutting public entitlements (the Concord Coalition).

*The Fortunes of Membership Associations*

As the associational explosions of 1960 to 1990 took off, America's once large and confident membership federations were not only bypassed in national politics; they also dwindled as locally rooted participant groups. To be sure, some membership associations have been founded or expanded in recent decades. By far the largest is the American Association of Retired Persons (AARP), which now boasts more than 33 million adherents, about one-half of all Americans aged 50 or older. But AARP is not a democratically controlled organization. Launched in 1958 with backing from a teachers' retirement group and an insurance company, the AARP grew rapidly in the 1970s and 1980s by offering commercial discounts to members and establishing a Washington headquarters to monitor and lobby about federal legislation affecting seniors. The AARP has a legislative and policy staff of 165 people, 28 registered lobbyists, and more than 1,200 staff members in the field. After recent efforts to expand its regional and local infrastructure, the AARP involves about 5 to 10 percent of its members in (undemocratic) membership chapters. But for the most part, the AARP national office—covering an entire city block with its own zip code—deals with masses of individual adherents through the mail.

Four additional recently expanded membership associations use modern mass recruitment methods, yet are also rooted in local and state units. Interestingly, these groups are heavily involved in partisan electoral politics. Two recently launched groups are the National Right to Life Committee (founded in 1973) and the Christian Coalition (founded in 1989). They bridge from church congregations, through which they recruit members and activists, to the conservative wing of the Republican Party, through which they exercise political influence. Two old-line membership federations—the National Education Association (founded in 1857) and the National Rifle Association (founded in 1871)—experienced explosive growth after reorienting themselves to take part in partisan politics. The NRA expanded in the 1970s, when right-wing activists opposed to gun control changed what had traditionally been a network of marksmen's clubs into a conservative, Republican-leaning advocacy group fiercely opposed to gun control legislation. During the same period, the NEA burgeoned from a relatively elitist association of public educators into a quasi-union for public school teachers and a stalwart in local, state, and national Democratic Party politics.

Although they fall short of enrolling 1 percent of the adult population, some additional chapter-based membership associations were fueled by the social movements of the 1960s and 1970s. From 1960 to 1990, the Sierra Club (originally created in 1892) ballooned from some 15,000 members to 565,000 members meeting in 378 "local groups." And the National Audubon Society (founded in 1905) went from 30,000 members and 330 chapters in 1958 to about 600,000 members and more than 500 chapters in the 1990s. The National Organization for Women (NOW) reached 1,122 members and 14 chapters within a year of its founding in 1966, and spread across all 50 states with some 125,000 members meeting in 700 chapters by 1978. But notice that these "1960s" movement associations do not match the organizational scope of old-line membership federations. At its post—World War II high point in 1955, for example, the General Federation of Women's Clubs boasted more than 826,000 members meeting in 15,168 local clubs, themselves divided into representative networks within each of the 50 states plus the District of Columbia. By contrast, at its high point in 1993, NOW reported some 280,000 members and 800 chapters, with no intermediate tier of representative governance between the national center and local chapters. These membership associations certainly matter, but mainly as counter-examples to dominant associational trends—of organizations without members.

After nearly a century of civic life rooted in nation-spanning membership federations, why was America's associational universe so transformed? A variety of factors have contributed, including racial and gender change; shifts in the political opportunity structure; new techniques and models for building organizations; and recent transformations in U.S. class relations. Taken together, I suggest, these account for civic America's abrupt and momentous transition from membership to advocacy.

*Society Decompartmentalized*

Until recent times, most American membership associations enrolled business and professional people together with white-collar folks, farmers, and craft or industrial workers. There was a degree of fellowship across class lines—yet at the price of other kinds of exclusions. With only a few exceptions, old-line associations enrolled either men or women, not both together (although male-only fraternal and veterans' groups often had ties to ladies' auxiliaries). Racial separation was also the rule. Although African Americans did manage to create and greatly expand fraternal associations of their own, they unquestionably resented exclusion by the parallel white fraternals.

Given the pervasiveness of gender and racial separation in classic civic America, established voluntary associations were bound to be shaken after the 1950s. Moreover, changing gender roles and identities blended with other changing values to undercut not just membership appeals but long-standing routes to associational leadership. For example, values of patriotism, brotherhood, and sacrifice had been celebrated by all fraternal groups. During and after each war, the Masons, Knights of Pythias, Elks, Knights of Columbus, Moose, Eagles, and scores of other fraternal groups celebrated and memorialized the contributions of their soldier-members. So did women's auxiliaries, not to mention men's service clubs and trade union "brotherhoods." But "manly" ideals of military service faded after the early 1960s as America's bitter experiences during the war in Vietnam disrupted the intergenerational continuity of male identification with martial brotherliness.

In the past third of a century, female civic leadership has changed as much or more than male leadership. Historically, U.S. women's associations—ranging from female auxiliaries of male groups to independent groups like the General Federation of Women's Clubs, the PTA, and church-connected associations—benefited from the activism of educated wives and mothers. Although a tiny fraction of all U.S. females, higher-educated women were a surprisingly substantial and widespread presence—because the United States was a pioneer in the schooling of girls and the higher education of women. By 1880, some 40,000 American women constituted a third of all students in U.S. institutions of higher learning; women's share rose to nearly half at the early twentieth-century peak in 1920, when some 283,000 women were enrolled in institutions of higher learning. Many higher-educated women of the late 1800s and early 1900s married immediately and stayed out of the paid labor force. Others taught for a time in primary and secondary schools, then got married and stopped teaching (either voluntarily or because school systems would not employ married women). Former teachers accumulated in every community. With skills to make connections within and across communities—and some time on their hands as their children grew older—former teachers and other educated women became mainstays of classic U.S. voluntary life.

Of course, more American women than ever before are now college-educated. But contemporary educated women face new opportunities and constraints. Paid work and family responsibilities are no longer separate spheres, and the occupational structure is less sex-segregated at all levels. Today, even married women with children are very likely to be employed, at least part-time. Despite new time pressures, educated and employed women have certainly not dropped out of civic life. Women employed part-time are more likely to be members of groups or volunteers than housewives; and fully employed women are often drawn into associations or civic projects through work. Yet styles of civic involvement have changed—much to the disadvantage of broad-gauged associations trying to hold regular meetings.

### The Lure of Washington, D.C.

The centralization of political change in Washington, D.C. also affected the associational universe. Consider the odyssey of civil rights lawyer Marian Wright Edelman. Fresh from grassroots struggles in Mississippi, she arrived in Washington, D.C. in the late 1960s to lobby for Mississippi's Head Start program. She soon realized that arguing on behalf of children might be the best way to influence legislation and sway public sympathy in favor of the poor, including African Americans. So between 1968 and 1973 Edelman obtained funding from major foundations and developed a new advocacy and policy research association, the Children's Defense Fund (CDF). With a skillful staff, a small national network of individual supporters, ties to social service agencies and foundations, and excellent relationships with the national media, the CDF has been a determined proponent of federal antipoverty programs ever since. The CDF has also worked with Democrats and other liberal advocacy groups to expand such efforts; and during periods of conservative Republican ascendancy, the CDF has been a fierce (if not always successful) defender of federal social programs.

Activists, in short, have gone where the action is. In this same period, congressional committees and their staffs subdivided and multiplied. During the later 1970s and 1980s, the process of group formation became self-reinforcing—not only because groups arose to counter other groups, but also because groups begot more groups. Because businesses and citizens use advocacy groups to influence government outside of parties and between elections, it is not surprising that the contemporary group explosion coincides with waning voter loyalty to the two major political parties. As late as the 1950s, U.S. political parties were networks of local and state organizations through which party officials often brokered nominations, cooperated with locally rooted membership associations, and sometimes directly mobilized voters. The party structure and the associational structure were mutually reinforcing.

Then, demographic shifts, reapportionment struggles, and the social upheavals of the 1960s disrupted old party organizations; and changes in party rules led to nomination elections that favored activists and candidate-centered efforts over backroom brokering by party insiders. Such "reforms" were meant to enhance grassroots participation, but in practice have furthered oligarchical ways of running elections. No longer the preserve of party organizations, U.S. campaigns are now managed by coteries of media consultants, pollsters, direct mail specialists, and—above all—fundraisers. In this revamped electoral arena, advocacy groups have much to offer, hoping to get access to elected officials in return for helping candidates. In low-turnout battles to win party nominations, even groups with modest mail memberships may be able to field enough (paid or unpaid) activists to make a difference. At all stages of the electoral process, advocacy groups with or without members can provide endorsements that may be useful in media or direct mail efforts. And PACs pushing business interests or public interests causes can help candidates raise the huge amounts of money they need to compete.

*A New Model of Association-Building*

Classic American association-builders took it for granted that the best way to gain national influence, moral or political, was to knit together national, state, and local groups that met regularly and engaged in a degree of representative governance. Leaders who desired to speak on behalf of masses of Americans found it natural to proceed by recruiting self-renewing mass memberships and spreading a network of interactive groups. After the start-up phase, associational budgets usually depended heavily on membership dues and on sales of newsletters or supplies to members and local groups. Supporters had to be continuously recruited through social networks and person-to-person contacts. And if leverage over government was desired, an association had to be able influence legislators, citizens, and newspapers across many districts. For all of these reasons, classic civic entrepreneurs with national ambitions moved quickly to recruit activists and members in every state and across as many towns and cities as possible within each state.

Today, nationally ambitious civic entrepreneurs proceed in quite different ways. When Marian Wright Edelman launched a new advocacy and research group to lobby for the needs of children and the poor, she turned to private foundations for funding and then recruited an expert staff of researchers and lobbyists. In the early 1970s, when John Gardner launched Common Cause as a "national citizens lobby" demanding governmental reforms, he arranged for start-up contributions from several wealthy friends, contacted reporters in the national media, and purchased mailing lists to solicit masses of members giving modest monetary contributions. Patron grants, direct mail techniques, and the capacity to convey images and messages through the mass media have changed the realities of organization building and maintenance.

The very model of civic effectiveness has been up-ended since the 1960s. No longer do civic entrepreneurs think of constructing vast federations and recruiting interactive citizen-members. When a new cause (or tactic) arises, activists envisage opening a national office and managing association-building as well as national projects from the center. Even a group aiming to speak for large numbers of Americans does not absolutely need members. And if mass adherents are recruited through the mail, why hold meetings? From a managerial point of view, interactions with groups of members may be downright inefficient. In the old-time membership federations, annual elections of leaders and a modicum of representative governance went hand in hand with membership dues and interactive meetings. But for the professional executives of today's advocacy organizations, direct mail members can be more appealing because, as Kenneth Godwin and Robert Cameron Mitchell explain, "they contribute without 'meddling'" and "do not take part in leadership selection or policy discussions." This does not mean the new advocacy groups are malevolent; they are just responding rationally to the environment in which they find themselves.

## Associational Change and Democracy

This brings us, finally, to what may be the most civically consequential change in late-twentieth-century America: the rise of a very large, highly educated upper middle class in which "expert" professionals are prominent along with businesspeople and managers. When U.S. professionals were a tiny, geographically dispersed stratum, they understood themselves as "trustees of community," in the terminology of Stephen Brint. Working closely with and for nonprofessional fellow citizens in thousands of towns and cities, lawyers, doctors, ministers, and teachers once found it quite natural to join—and eventually help to lead—locally rooted, cross-class voluntary associations. But today's professionals are more likely to see themselves as expert individuals who can best contribute to national well-being by working with other specialists to tackle complex technical or social problems.

Cause-oriented advocacy groups offer busy, privileged Americans a rich menu of opportunities to, in effect, hire other professionals and managers to represent their values and interests in public life. Why should highly trained and economically well-off elites spend years working their way up the leadership ladders of traditional membership federations when they can take leading staff roles at the top, or express their preferences by writing a check?

If America has experienced a great civic transformation from membership to advocacy—so what? Most traditional associations were racially exclusive and gender segregated; and their policy efforts were not always broad-minded. More than a few observers suggest that recent civic reorganizations may be for the best. American public life has been rejuvenated, say the optimists, by social movements and advocacy groups fighting for social rights and an enlarged understanding of the public good.

Local community organizations, neighborhood groups, and grassroots protest movements nowadays tap popular energies and involve people otherwise left out of organized politics. And social interchanges live on in small support groups and occasional volunteering. According to the research of Robert Wuthnow, about 75 million men and women, a remarkable 40 percent of the adult population, report taking part in "a small group that meets regularly and provides caring and support for those who participate in it." Wuthnow estimates that there may be some 3 million such groups, including Bible study groups, 12-step self-help groups, book discussion clubs, singles groups, hobby groups, and disease support groups. Individuals find community, spiritual connection, introspection, and personal gratification in small support groups. Meanwhile, people reach out through volunteering. As many as half of all Americans give time to the community this way, their efforts often coordinated by paid social service professionals. Contemporary volunteering can be intermittent and flexibly structured, an intense one-shot effort or spending "an evening a week on an activity for a few months as time permits, rather than having to make a long-term commitment to an organization."

In the optimistic view, the good civic things Americans once did are still being done—in new ways and in new settings. But if we look at U.S. democracy in its entirety and bring issues of power and social leverage to the fore, then optimists are surely overlooking the downsides of our recently reorganized civic life. Too many valuable aspects of the old civic America are not being reproduced or reinvented in the new public world of memberless organizations.

Despite the multiplicity of voices raised within it, America's new civic universe is remarkably oligarchical. Because today's advocacy groups are staff-heavy and focused on lobbying, research, and media projects, they are managed from the top with few opportunities for member leverage from below. Even when they have hundreds of thousands of adherents, contemporary associations are heavily tilted toward upper-middle-class constituencies. Whether we are talking about memberless advocacy groups, advocacy groups with some chapters, mailing-list associations, or nonprofit institutions, it is hard to escape the conclusion that the wealthiest and best-educated Americans are much more privileged in the new civic world than their (less numerous) counterparts were in the pre-1960s civic world of cross-class membership federations.

Mostly, they involve people in "doing for" others—feeding the needy at a church soup kitchen; tutoring children at an after-school clinic; or guiding visitors at a museum exhibit—rather than in "doing with" fellow citizens. Important as such volunteering may be, it cannot substitute for the central citizenship functions that membership federations performed.

A top-heavy civic world not only encourages "doing for" rather than "doing with." It also distorts national politics and public policymaking. Imagine for a moment what might have happened if the GI Bill of 1944 had been debated and legislated in a civic world configured more like the one that prevailed during the 1993–1994 debates over the national health insurance proposal put forward by the first administration of President Bill Clinton. This is not an entirely fanciful comparison, because goals supported by the vast majority of Americans were at issue in both periods: in the 1940s, care and opportunity for millions of military veterans returning from World War II; in the 1990s, access for all Americans to a modicum of health insurance coverage. Back in the 1940s, moreover, there were elite actors—university presidents, liberal intellectuals, and conservative congressmen—who could have condemned the GI Bill to the same fate as the 1990s health security plan. University presidents and liberal New Dealers initially favored versions of the GI Bill that would have been bureaucratically complicated, niggardly with public expenditures, and extraordinarily limited in veterans' access to subsidized higher education.

But in the actual civic circumstances of the 1940s, elites did not retain control of public debates or legislative initiatives. Instead, a vast voluntary membership federation, the American Legion, stepped in and drafted a bill to guarantee every one of the returning veterans up to four years of post-high school education, along with family and employment benefits, business loans, and home mortgages. Not only did the Legion draft one of the most generous pieces of social legislation in American history, thousands of local Legion posts and dozens of state organizations mounted a massive public education and lobbying campaign to ensure that even conservative congressional representatives would vote for the new legislation.

Half a century later, the 1990s health security episode played out in a transformed civic universe dominated by advocacy groups, pollsters, and big-money media campaigns. Top-heavy advocacy groups did not mobilize mass support for a sensible reform plan. Hundreds of business and professional groups influenced the Clinton administration's complex policy schemes, and then used a combination of congressional lobbying and media campaigns to block new legislation. Both the artificial polarization and the elitism of today's organized civic universe may help to explain why increasing numbers of Americans are turned off by and pulling back from public life. Large majorities say that wealthy "special interests" dominate the federal government, and many Americans express cynicism about the chances for regular people to make a difference. People may be entertained by advocacy clashes on television, but they are also ignoring many public debates and withdrawing into privatism. Voting less and less, American citizens increasingly act—and claim to feel—like mere spectators in a polity where all the significant action seems to go on above their heads, with their views ignored by pundits and clashing partisans.

From the nineteenth through the mid-twentieth century, American democracy flourished within a unique matrix of state and society. Not only was America the world's first manhood democracy and the first nation in the world to establish mass public education. It also had a uniquely balanced civic life, in which markets expanded but could not subsume civil society, in which governments at multiple levels deliberately and indirectly encouraged federated voluntary associations. National elites had to pay attention to the values and interests of millions of ordinary Americans.

Over the past third of a century, the old civic America has been bypassed and shoved to the side by a gaggle of professionally dominated advocacy groups and nonprofit institutions rarely attached to memberships worthy of the name. Ideals of shared citizenship and possibilities for democratic leverage have been compromised in the process. Since the 1960s, many good things have happened in America. New voices are now heard, and there have been invaluable gains in equality and liberty. But vital links in the nation's associational life have frayed, and we may need to find creative ways to repair those links if America is to avoid becoming a country of detached spectators. There is no going back to the civic world we have lost. But we Americans can and should look for ways to recreate the best of our civic past in new forms suited to a renewed democratic future.

## DISCUSSION QUESTIONS

1. What does Skocpol mean by "shifts in the political opportunity structure"?

2. Skocpol is obviously alarmed by the shift in organizational style over the latter half of the twentieth century. What are her concerns? Do you share her concerns? Can you see any advantages to the new model over the old?

3. Do you belong to any national associations that have local group meetings? If so, do you agree that this involvement might generate social capital? What about campus groups? Do you think your involvement in these groups has any "spillover" effect that makes you more likely to be involved elsewhere or increases your sense that your involvement makes a difference?

## Debating the Issues: Was Madison Right?

In his famous essay, *The Federalist,* No. 10, future president James Madison expressed concern about the "mischief of factions." It was natural, he argued, for people to organize around a principle or interest they held in common, and the most common motivation for organizing such factions was property—those who had it versus those who did not, creditors versus lenders. The danger in such efforts, however, was that a majority faction might usurp the rights of a minority. In a small direct democracy, where a majority of the people could share a "common passion," the threat was very real. Expand the geographic size of the country, however, and replace direct democracy with a system of elected representatives, separation of powers, and checks and balances, and the threat diminished. The likelihood of any one faction appealing to a majority of citizens in a large republic governed by representatives from diverse geographic regions was remote. To Madison, factions were a natural outgrowth of the differences between people, and the only way to eliminate factions would be to eliminate liberty. Eliminating factions might not be possible or desirable, but the mischief of factions could be controlled with a system of representation based upon varied constituencies that embraced multiple, diverse interests. From the competition of diverse interests would arise compromise and balanced public policy.

Madison's concerns about interests, and particularly organized interests, have resonated throughout American history. At various times in the United States, the public has seemed to become especially concerned with the power of interests in politics. One political scientist refers to this as the "ideals vs. institutions" gap—there are times when "what is" is so different from what Americans believe "should be," that pressure mounts to reform lobbying laws, campaign regulations, business practices, and so on. Positions on these issues do not always neatly sort out into the typical liberal and conservative categories. For example, a Democratic senator (Russ Feingold) and Republican senator (John McCain) joined forces to lead the effort for campaign finance reform, but liberal and conservative interest groups joined forces in 2003 to, unsuccessfully, challenge the constitutionality of some of the new law's limits on interest-group campaign advertising.

Was Madison right about the benefits that would emerge from the competition of interests? In the following excerpt from "The Group Basis of Politics," Earl Latham answers with an emphatic "yes!" Despite the popular criticism of "special" interests that seem to taint the political process with their dominant influence, Latham argues that such groups have been a common and inevitable feature of American government. Groups form to give individuals a means of self-expression and to help individuals find security in an uncertain world. In fact, the uncertainty of the social environment, and the resulting threat to one's interests, is a chief motivation for groups to form and "taming" this environment is a central concern for group members. Rather than leading to a system ruled by a few dominant powers, Latham suggests the reality is much more fluid. Although it is true that groups that are highly organized are likely to be more powerful, Latham argues that "organization begets counterorganization." The ascendancy of one group will prompt other groups to form to advance their cause. Defeated groups can always try again: "Today's losers may be tomorrow's winners." Groups that lose in the legislature may have more luck with a bureaucratic agency or in a courtroom. There are, in short, multiple avenues of influence and many roads to political success for organized groups, and there are no permanent winners or losers.

Jonathan Rauch disagrees. He views with pessimism the ever-expanding number of interest groups in the political process. Whether groups claim to represent narrow economic interests or a broader public interest, Rauch does not see balance and compromise as the result of their competition in the political arena. Rather, he sees a nation suffering from "hyperpluralism," or the explosion of groups making claims on government power and resources. When elected officials attempt to reduce budget deficits or to establish new priorities and refocus expenditures, they are overwhelmed by the pressures of a wide range of groups. As a result, government programs are never terminated or restructured; tough budget cuts or tax changes are rarely made; and a very rich democratic country and its government become immobile. Rather than the dynamic system of change and compromise envisioned by Latham, Rauch sees a system characterized primarily by inertia because of the power of groups to prevent government action.

# 63

# *The Federalist*, No. 10

## James Madison

*To the People of the State of New York:*

Among the numerous advantages promised by a well-constructed Union, none deserves to be more accurately developed than its tendency to break and control the violence of faction. The friend of popular governments never finds himself so much alarmed for their character and fate, as when he contemplates their propensity to this dangerous vice. He will not fail, therefore, to set a due value on any plan which, without violating the principles to which he is attached, provides a proper cure for it. The instability, injustice, and confusion introduced into the public councils, have, in truth, been the mortal diseases under which popular governments have everywhere perished; as they continue to be the favorite and fruitful topics from which the adversaries to liberty derive their most specious declamations. The valuable improvements made by the American constitutions on the popular models, both ancient and modern, cannot certainly be too much admired; but it would be an unwarrantable partiality, to contend that they have as effectually obviated the danger on this side, as was wished and expected. Complaints are everywhere heard from our most considerate and virtuous citizens, equally the friends of public and private faith, and of public and personal liberty, that our governments are too unstable; that the public good is disregarded in the conflicts of rival parties; and that measures are too often decided, not according to the rules of justice and the rights of the minor party, but by the superior force of an interested and overbearing majority. However anxiously we may wish that these complaints had no foundation, the evidence of known facts will not permit us to deny that they are in some degree true. It will be found, indeed, on a candid review of our situation, that some of the distresses under which we labor have been erroneously charged on the operation of our governments; but it will be found, at the same time, that other causes will not alone account for many of our heaviest misfortunes; and, particularly, for that prevailing and increasing distrust of public engagements, and alarm for private rights, which are echoed from one end of the continent to the other. These must be chiefly, if not wholly, effects of the unsteadiness and injustice with which a factious spirit has tainted our public administrations.

By a faction, I understand a number of citizens, whether amounting to a majority or minority of the whole, who are united and actuated by some common impulse of passion, or of interest, adverse to the rights of other citizens, or to the permanent and aggregate interests of the community.

There are two methods of curing the mischiefs of faction: the one, by removing its causes; the other, by controlling its effects.

There are again two methods of removing the causes of faction: the one, by destroying the liberty which is essential to its existence; the other, by giving to every citizen the same opinions, the same passions, and the same interests.

It could never be more truly said than of the first remedy, that it is worse than the disease. Liberty is to faction what air is to fire, an aliment without which it instantly expires. But it could not be less folly to abolish liberty, which is essential to political life, because it nourishes faction, than it would be to wish the annihilation of air, which is essential to animal life, because it imparts to fire its destructive agency.

The second expedient is as impracticable as the first would be unwise. As long as the reason of man continues fallible, and he is at liberty to exercise it, different opinions will be formed. As long as the connection subsits between his reason and his self-love, his opinions and his passions will have a reciprocal influence on each other; and the former will be objects to which the latter will attach themselves. The diversity in the faculties of men, from which the rights of property originate, is not less an insuperable obstacle to a uniformity of interests. The protection of these faculties is the first object of government. From the protection of different and unequal faculties of acquiring property, the possession of different degrees and kinds of property immediately results; and from the influence of these on the sentiments and views of the respective proprietors, ensues a division of the society into different interests and parties.

The latent causes of faction are thus sown in the nature of man; and we see them everywhere brought into different degrees of activity, according to the different circumstances of civil society. A zeal for different opinions concerning religion, concerning government, and many other points, as well of speculation as of practice; an attachment to different leaders ambitiously contending for pre-eminence and power; or to persons of other descriptions whose fortunes have been interesting to the human passions, have, in turn, divided mankind into parties, inflamed them with mutual animosity, and rendered them much more disposed to vex and oppress each other than to co-operate for their common good. So strong is this propensity of mankind to fall into mutual animosities, that where no substantial occasion presents itself, the most frivolous and fanciful distinctions have been sufficient to kindle their unfriendly passions and excite their most violent conflicts. But the most common and durable source of factions has been the various and unequal distribution of property. Those who hold and those who are without property have ever formed distinct interests in society. Those who are creditors, and those who are debtors, fall under a like discrimination. A landed interest, a manufacturing interest, a mercantile interest, a moneyed interest, with many lesser interests, grow up of necessity in civilized nations, and divide them into different classes, actuated by different sentiments and views. The regulation of these various and interfering interests forms the principal task of modern legislation, and involves the spirit of party and faction in the necessary and ordinary operations of the government.

No man is allowed to be a judge in his own cause, because his interest would certainly bias his judgment, and, not improbably, corrupt his integrity. With equal, nay with greater reason, a body of men are unfit to be both judges and parties at the same time; yet what are many of the most important acts of legislation, but so many judicial determinations, not indeed concerning the rights of single persons, but concerning the rights of large bodies of citizens? and what are the different classes of legislators but advocates and parties to the causes which they determine? Is a law proposed concerning private debts? It is a question to which the creditors are parties on one side and the debtors on the other. Justice ought to hold the balance between them. Yet the parties are, and must be, themselves the judges; and the most numerous party, or, in other words, the most powerful faction must be expected to prevail. Shall domestic manufactures be encouraged, and in what degree, by restrictions on foreign manufactures? are questions which would be differently decided by the landed and the manufacturing classes, and probably by neither with a sole regard to justice and the public good. The apportionment of taxes on the various descriptions of property is an act which seems to require the most exact impartiality; yet there is, perhaps, no legislative act in which greater opportunity and temptation are given to a predominant party to trample on the rules of justice. Every shilling with which they overburden the inferior number is a shilling saved to their own pockets.

It is in vain to say that enlightened statesmen will be able to adjust these clashing interests and render them all subservient to the public good. Enlightened statesmen will not always be at the helm. Nor, in many cases, can such an adjustment be made at all without taking into view indirect and remote considerations, which will rarely prevail over the immediate interest which one party may find in disregarding the rights of another or the good of the whole.

The inference to which we are brought is, that the *causes* of faction cannot be removed, and that relief is only to be sought in the means of controlling its *effects*.

If a faction consists of less than a majority, relief is supplied by the republican principle, which enables the majority to defeat its sinister views by regular vote. It may clog the administration, it may convulse the society; but it will be unable to execute and mask its violence under the forms of the Constitution. When a majority is included in a faction, the form of popular government, on the other hand, enables it to sacrifice to its ruling passion or interest both the public good and the rights of other citizens. To secure the public good and private rights against the danger of such a faction, and at the same time to preserve the spirit and the form of popular government, is then the great object to which our inquiries are directed. Let me add that it is the great desideratum [desire] by which this form of government can be rescued from the opprobrium under which it has so long labored, and be recommended to the esteem and adoption of mankind.

By what means is this object attainable? Evidently by one of two only. Either the existence of the same passion or interest in a majority at the same time must be prevented, or the majority, having such coexistent passion or interest, must be rendered by their number and local situation unable to concert and carry into effect schemes of oppression. If the impulse and the opportunity be suffered to coincide, we well know that neither moral nor religious motives can be relied on as an adequate control. They are not found to be such on the injustice and violence of individuals, and lose their efficacy in proportion to the number combined together, that is, in proportion as their efficacy becomes needful.

From this view of the subject it may be concluded that a pure democracy, by which I mean a society consisting of a small number of citizens, who assemble and administer the government in person, can admit of no cure for the mischiefs of faction. A common passion or interest will, in almost every case, be felt by a majority of the whole; a communication and concert result from the form of government itself; and there is nothing to check the inducements to sacrifice the weaker party or an obnoxious individual. Hence it is that such democracies have ever been spectacles of turbulence and contention; have ever been found incompatible with personal security or the rights of property; and have in general been as short in their lives as they have been violent in their deaths. Theoretic politicians, who have patronized this species of government, have erroneously supposed that by reducing mankind to a perfect equality in their political rights, they would, at the same time, be perfectly equalized and assimilated in their possessions, their opinions, and their passions.

A republic, by which I mean a government in which the scheme of representation takes place, opens a different prospect, and promises the cure for which we are seeking. Let us examine the points in which it varies from pure democracy, and we shall comprehend both the nature of the cure and the efficacy which it must derive from the Union.

The two great points of difference between a democracy and a republic are: first, the delegation of the government in the latter to a small number of citizens elected by the rest; secondly, the greater number of citizens and greater sphere of country over which the latter may be extended.

The effect of the first difference is, on the one hand, to refine and enlarge the public views, by passing them through the medium of a chosen body of citizens, whose wisdom may best discern the true interest of their country, and whose patriotism and love of justice will be least likely to sacrifice it to temporary or partial considerations. Under such a regulation, it may well happen that the public voice, pronounced by the representatives of the people, will be more consonant to the public good than if pronounced by the people themselves, convened for the purpose. On the other hand, the effect may be inverted. Men of factious tempers, of local prejudices, or of sinister designs, may by intrigue, by corruption, or by other means, first obtain the suffrages, and then betray the interests of the people. The question resulting is, whether small or extensive republics are more favorable to the election of proper guardians of the public weal; and it is clearly decided in favor of the latter by two obvious considerations.

In the first place, it is to be remarked that, however small the republic may be, the representatives must be raised to a certain number in order to guard against the cabals of a few; and that, however large it may be, they must be limited to a certain number in order to guard against the confusion of a multitude. Hence, the number of representatives in the two cases not being in proportion to that of the two constituents, and being proportionally greater in the small republic, it follows that, if the proportion of fit characters be not less in the large than in the small republic, the former will present a greater option and consequently a greater probability of a fit choice.

In the next place, as each representative will be chosen by a greater number of citizens in the large than in the small republic, it will be more difficult for unworthy candidates to practise with success the vicious arts by which elections are too often carried; and the suffrages of the people being more free, will be more likely to centre in men who possess the most attractive merit and the most diffusive and established characters.

It must be confessed that in this, as in most other cases, there is a mean, on both sides of which inconveniences will be found to lie. By enlarging too much the number of electors, you render the representative too little acquainted with all their local circumstances and lesser interests: as by reducing it too much, you render him unduly attached to these, and too little fit to comprehend and pursue great and national objects. The federal Constitution forms a happy combination in this respect; the great and aggregate interests being referred to the national, the local and particular to the State legislatures.

The other point of difference is, the greater number of citizens and extent of territory which may be brought within the compass of republican than of democratic government; and it is this circumstance principally which renders factious combinations less to be dreaded in the former than in the latter. The smaller the society, the fewer probably will be the distinct parties and interests composing it; the fewer the distinct parties and interests, the more frequently will a majority be found of the same party; and the smaller the number of individuals composing a majority, and the smaller the compass within which they are placed, the more easily will they concert and execute their plans of oppression. Extend the sphere, and you take in a greater variety of parties and interests; you make it less probable that a majority of the whole will have a common motive to invade the rights of other citizens; or if such a common motive exists, it will be more difficult for all who feel it to discover their own strength and to act in unison with each other. Besides other impediments, it may be remarked that, where there is a consciousness of unjust or dishonorable purposes, communication is always checked by distrust in proportion to the number whose concurrence is necessary.

Hence, it clearly appears that the same advantage which a republic has over a democracy in controlling the effects of faction is enjoyed by a large over a small republic,—is enjoyed by the Union over the States composing it. Does the advantage consist in the substitution of representatives whose enlightened views and virtuous sentiments render them superior to local prejudices and to schemes of injustice? It will not be denied that the representation of the Union will be most likely to possess these requisite endowments. Does it consist in the greater security afforded by a greater variety of parties, against the event of any one party being able to outnumber and oppress the rest? In an equal degree does the increased variety of parties comprised within the Union, increase this security. Does it, in fine, consist in the greater obstacles opposed to the concert and accomplishment of the secret wishes of an unjust and interested majority? Here, again, the extent of the Union gives it the most palpable advantage.

The influence of factious leaders may kindle a flame within their particular States, but will be unable to spread a general conflagration through the other States. A religious sect may degenerate into a political faction in a part of the Confederacy; but the variety of sects dispersed over the entire face of it must secure the national councils against any danger from that source. A rage for paper money, for an abolition of debts, for an equal division of property, or for any other improper or wicked project, will be less apt to pervade the whole body of the Union than a particular member of it; in the same proportion as such a malady is more likely to taint a particular county or district, than an entire State.

In the extent and proper structure of the Union, therefore, we behold a republican remedy for the diseases most incident to republican government. And according to the degree of pleasure and pride we feel in being republicans, ought to be our zeal in cherishing the spirit and supporting the character of Federalists.

PUBLIUS

# 64

# "The Group Basis of Politics: Notes for a Theory"

## Earl Latham

The chief social values cherished by individuals in modern society are realized through groups. These groupings may be simple in structure, unicellular, so to speak, like a juvenile gang. Or they may be intricate meshes of associated, federated, combined, consolidated, merged, or amalgamated units and sub-units of organization, fitted together to perform the divided and assigned parts of a common purpose to which the components are dedicated. They may operate out of the direct public gaze like religious organizations, which tend to have a low degree of visibility. Or they may, like Congress and many other official groups, occupy the front pages for weeks at a time. National organizations are usually conspicuous; indeed, so much is this so at times that they tend to divert the eye from the great number of groups which stand at the elbow of the citizen of every small town. Everywhere groups abound, and they may be examined at close range and from afar.

So far, we have been concerned with the nature of the structure of society and its principal communities, and with the composition and classification of the group forms which are basic to both. They have been held still, so to speak, while they were being viewed. But they do not in fact hold still; they are in a state of constant motion, and it is through this motion and its interactions that these groups generate the rules by which public policy is formulated and the community is to be governed. It is necessary now to consider the impulses which animate the group motion and produce these penetrating and far-reaching results.

To consider further a point which has been made, groups organize for the self-expression and security of the members which comprise them. Even when the group is a benevolent, philanthropic association devoted to the improvement of the material and spiritual fortunes of people outside its membership—a temperance or a missionary organization, for example—the work towards this goal, the activity of the organization, is a means through which the members express themselves. Satisfaction in the fulfillment of the received purposes of the group is an important element in keeping groups intact, as Barnard has shown. Indeed, if these satisfactions are not fulfilled, the group suffers loss of morale, energy, and dedication. It is for this reason that military organizations and the civil authorities to which they are responsible seek to inculcate in the soldier some sense of the general purposes for which force by arms is being employed, in an attempt to identify the soldier's personal purpose with that of the community he serves. The soldier then can fulfill his own purposes in combat, as well as those of various groups in the country whose uniform he bears.

At the same time, security is an object of every group organization if security is understood only in its elemental sense of the survival of the group itself in order to carry forward its mission. At the very least, the interest of security means the maintenance of the existence of the group. In different groups one or the other of these impulses—self-expression or security—will predominate.

Self-expression and security are sought by the group members through control of the physical and social environment which surrounds each group and in the midst of which it dwells. It is an elemental fact that environments are potentially dangerous to every group, even as homes are potentially dangerous to the members of the household, as the statistics of accidents in the home will attest. The military battalion runs the risk of being shot up. The church, new or old, runs the risk of losing its members to other and competing claims of interest and devotion. The businessman runs the risk of losing his profit or his customer to his rival. The philanthropic organization devoted to good works often regards other agencies in the same field with a venomous eye. Councils of social agencies in large cities are sometimes notorious for the rancor with which the struggle for prestige and recognition (i.e., self-expression and security) is conducted among them. Every group, large and small, must come to terms with its environment if it is to endure and to prosper.

There are three modes by which this is done. First, the environment may be made safe and predictable by putting restraints upon it. Jurisdictional fights between unions may be explained in this way. Jurisdictional fights are battles in which each claimant union seeks to make an environment for itself in the area of dispute, but to exclude its rival from this environment. On the employer side, the Mohawk Valley Formula was a pattern of actions in a planned sequence by which employers, if they followed it, could break union movements. The objective of this formula was to discredit each union and its leadership and to enlist the support of the townspeople on the side of the plant; it thus was a concerted plan to make an environment unfavorable to the success of unions. One overcomes the hostility in the environment most directly by destroying the influence which creates the hostility.

Second, the environment may be made safe and predictable by neutralizing it. In the propaganda war of giant world powers, the effort is ceaseless to neutralize the effects of propaganda with counterpropaganda so as to render the international environment favorable, or at least not hostile—that is, neutral. The Atlantic and Pacific Tea Company similarly bought a great deal of advertising space in newspapers all over the country to counteract the expectedly unfavorable impressions created by a Department of Justice action against it under the anti-trust laws. The object, among other purposes, was to make the customer-inhabited environment of the business enterprise favorable if possible, neutral at the least, concerning the merits of the charges against it.

Third, the environment may be made safe and predictable, and therefore secure, by conciliating it and making it friendly. Even where there is no manifest hostile influence, a credit of good will may be accumulated by deeds and words which reflect favorably upon the doer. It is true that concessions to a potential hostile force may work sometimes, and again they may not. In the struggle of free nations with the dictatorships, appeasement did not succeed in producing that conciliation which was hoped for it. Nonetheless, politicians are constantly at work making friends and increasing votes by performing favors of one kind or another. Friendliness towards soap is generated on the radio by endless broadcasts of simple tales of never-ending strife and frustration. And during the Second World War advertising by business enterprises was a means of cultivating and keeping good will for the products advertised, even though there was no market for them because of the wartime restrictions on production.

All of these are methods by which the environment in which groups dwell is made safe and predictable to them, and therefore secure. And because the relations of people are myriad and shifting, subject to cycles of deterioration and decay, because the environment itself changes with each passing hour, there is a ceaseless struggle on the part of groups to dominate, neutralize, or conciliate that part of their environment that presses in upon them most closely. In this struggle, there is an observable balance of influence in favor of organized groups in their dealings with the unorganized, and in favor of the best and most efficiently organized in their dealings with the less efficiently organized. Strong nations tend to take advantage of the weak, and imperial powers to take advantage of their colonies. Or, to put it another way, organization represents concentrated power, and concentrated power can exercise a dominating influence when it encounters power which is diffuse and not concentrated, and therefore weaker.

The classic struggle of farmers against business enterprise is a case in point, the latter at first being more efficiently organized, and able (before the farmer became "class conscious") to gain advantages which the farmers thought exorbitant, under conditions which the farmers found offensive. But organization begets counterorganization. The farmer organizes in the American Farm Bureau Federation or the National Grange, and uses his influence with the legislatures to write rules to his advantage. In some states of the Middle West, for example, legislation even prescribes the terms of contracts for the sale of farm equipment. But the organized farmer pays little attention to the tenant and the share-cropper, and they in turn experience an impulse to organize for their own advantage. The history of the development of farmers' organizations is instructive; the whole program of farm subsidies which has evolved in the last twenty years may be seen as an effort on the part of the farmer (organized for the purpose) to make himself independent of the vicissitudes of the business economy, that is, to take himself out of the environment which he can control only imperfectly, and to insulate himself against economic adversity.

In the constant struggle of groups to come to terms with their environments, one other phenomenon of group politics may be noted. Simple groups tend to become more complex. And the more complex they become, the greater is the tendency to centralize their control. The structure of the business community in 1950 is different from that of 1860 precisely in that relatively simple forms of business organization have become complex—have gone through federations, combinations, reorganizations, mergers, amalgamations, and consolidations in a growing tendency to rationalize the complexity and to integrate the elements in comprehensive structures. Monopolies, combinations, cartels, giant integrated enterprises are characteristic of a mature phase of the evolution of group forms. Furthermore, the history of federal administration amply shows that the tendency of simple forms of organization to become complex by combination and to develop centralized bureaucracies to cope with this complexity is to be observed among official groups as well as among the groups, like the CIO and the American Legion, which dwell outside the domain of public government.

\* \* \*

The struggle of groups to survive in their environments and to carry forward the aims and interests of their members, if entirely uninhibited, would produce violence and war. Social disapproval of most of the forms of direct action, however, reduces this struggle to an effort to write the rules by which groups live with each other and according to which they compete for existence and advantage. Thus, in the development of mature institutions of collective bargaining from the raw material of unorganized workers, the time comes when violence, disorder, and force are put to one side as the normal aspect of labor relations and the conduct of negotiations occupies the energies of the leaders. In the relations of nations to each other, there has been a persistent effort to substitute diplomacy and the rule of law for war as the arbiter of the differences among national groups. As groups come to put away gross forms of coercion in their dealings with each other, by equal degree the area widens within which the behavior of each is subject to codification by rules. The struggle for advantage, for benefits to the group, for the self-expression and security of its members, tend then to concentrate upon the writing of the rules. Among the forms which the rules may take are statutes, administrative orders and decrees, rules and interpretations, and court judgments.

* * *

The legislature referees the group struggle, ratifies the victories of the successful coalitions, and records the terms of the surrenders, compromises, and conquests in the form of statutes. Every statute tends to represent compromise because the very process of accommodating conflicts of group interest is one of deliberation and consent. The legislative vote on any issue thus tends to represent the composition of strength, i.e., the balance of power among the contending groups at the moment of voting. What may be called public policy is actually the equilibrium reached in the group struggle at any given moment, and it represents a balance which the contending factions of groups constantly strive to weight in their favor. In this process, it is clear that blocks of groups can be defeated. In fact, they can be routed. Defeated groups do not possess a veto on the proposals and acts that affect them. But what they do possess is the right to make new combinations of strength if they are able to do so—combinations that will support a new effort to rewrite the rules in their favor. This process of regrouping is fully in accord with the American culture pattern, which rates high in the characteristics of optimism, risk, experimentalism, change, aggressiveness, acquisitiveness, and colossal faith in man's ability to subdue and bend nature to his desire. The entire process is dynamic, not static; fluid, not fixed. Today's losers may be tomorrow's winners.

In these adjustments of group interest, the legislature does not play the part of inert cash register, ringing up the additions and withdrawals of strength; it is not a mindless balance pointing and marking the weight and distribution of power among the contending groups. * * * Legislators have to be approached with a certain amount of deference and tact; they may be pressured, but some forms of pressure will be regarded as too gross. The Congressman, like men everywhere, comes to his position bearing in his head a cargo of ideas, principles, prejudices, programs, precepts, beliefs, slogans, and preachments. These represent his adjustment to the dominant group combination among his constituents. * * *

The function of the bureaucrat in the group struggle is somewhat different from that of the legislator. Administrative agencies of the regulatory kind are established to carry out the terms of the treaties that the legislators have negotiated and ratified. They are like armies of occupation left in the field to police the rule won by the victorious coalition. * * * The defeated coalition of groups, however, does not cease striving to wring interpretations favorable to it from the treaties that verbalize its defeats. Expensive legal talent is employed to squeeze every advantage which wit and verbal magic can twist from the cold prose of official papers; and the regulatory agencies are constantly besought and importuned to interpret their authorities in favor of the very groups for the regulation of which they were originally granted. This campaign against unfavorable rules which losing coalitions of groups address to the bureaucrats appointed to administer them is, of course, in addition to their constant effort to rewrite the rules in their favor through compliant legislators. Where the balance of power is precarious, the law will remain unsettled until the balance is made stable. * * *

# 65

# "The Hyperpluralism Trap"

## Jonathan Rauch

A nyone who believes Washington needs to get closer to the people ought to spend a little time with Senator Richard Lugar, the Indiana Republican. "Take a look at the people coming into my office on a normal Tuesday and Wednesday," Lugar said in a speech not long ago. "Almost every organization in our society has a national conference. The typical way of handling this is to come in on a Monday, rev up the troops, give them the bill number and send them up to the Hill. If they can't get in on Tuesday, strike again on Wednesday. I regularly have on Tuesday as many as fifteen constituent groups from Indiana, all of whom have been revved up by some skillful person to cite bills that they don't understand, have never heard of prior to that time, but with a score sheet to report back to headquarters whether I am for or against. It is so routine, it is so fierce, that at some point you [can't be] immune to it."

This is the reality of modern government. The rhetoric of modern politics, alas, is a little different. Take today's standard-issue political stem-winder, which goes something like this: "I think perhaps the most important thing that we understand here in the heartland . . . is the need to reform the political system, to reduce the influence of special interests and give more influence back to the kind of people that are in this crowd tonight by the tens of thousands." That stream of boilerplate is from Bill Clinton (from his election-night speech), but it could have come from almost any politician. It's pitched in a dominant key of political rhetoric today: *standard populism*—that is, someone has taken over the government and "we" must take it back, restore government to the people, etc. But who, exactly, are those thousands of citizens who troop weekly through Senator Lugar's suite, clutching briefing packets and waving scorecards? Standard populism says they are the "special interests," those boils on the skin of democracy, forever interposing themselves between the American people and the people's servants in Washington.

Well, fifty years ago that analysis may have been useful, but not anymore. In America today, the special interests and "the people" have become objectively indistinguishable. Groups are us. As a result, the populist impulse to blame special interests, big corporations and political careerists for our problems—once a tonic—has become Americans' leading political narcotic. Worse, it actually abets the lobbying it so righteously denounces.

Begin with one of the best known yet most underappreciated facts of our time: over the past three or four decades we have busily organized ourselves into interest groups—lobbies, loosely speaking—at an astonishing rate. Interest groups were still fairly sparse in America until about the time of World War II. Then they started proliferating, and in the 1960s the pace of organizing picked up dramatically.

Consider, for instance, the numbers of groups listed in Gale Research's *Encyclopedia of Associations*. The listings have grown from fewer than 5,000 in 1956 to well over 20,000 today. They represent, of course, only a small fraction of America's universe of interest groups. Environmental organizations alone number an estimated 7,000, once you count local clean-up groups and the like; the Washington *Blade*'s resource directory lists more than 400 gay groups, up from 300 at the end of 1990. Between 1961 and 1982 the number of corporate offices in Washington increased tenfold. Even more dramatic was the explosion in the number of public-interest organizations and grass-roots groups. These barely existed at all before the 1960s; today they number in the tens of thousands and collect more than $4 billion per year from 40 million individuals, according to political scientist Ronald Shaiko of American University.

Well, so what? Groups do many good things—provide companionship for the like-minded, collect and disseminate information, sponsor contests, keep the catering industry solvent. Indeed, conventional political theory for much of the postwar period was dominated by a strain known as pluralism, which holds that more groups equals more representation equals better democracy. Yet pluralism missed something. It assumed that the group-forming process was self-balancing and stable, as opposed to self-feeding and unstable. Which is to say, it failed to grasp the danger of what American University political scientist James Thurber aptly calls hyperpluralism.

In economics, inflation is a gradual increase in the price level. Up to a point, if the inflation rate is stable, people can plan around it. But if the rate starts to speed up, people start expecting more inflation. They hoard goods and dump cash, driving the inflation still faster. Eventually, an invisible threshold is crossed: the inflation now feeds on its own growth and undermines the stability of the whole economic system.

What the pluralists missed is that something analogous can happen with interest groups. People see that it pays to organize into groups and angle for benefits, so they do it. But as more groups make more demands, and as even more hungry groups form to compete with all the other groups, the process begins to feed on itself and pick up momentum. At some point there might be so many groups that they choke the political system, sow contention and conflict, even erode society's governability. That's hyperpluralism. And if it is less destabilizing than hyperinflation, it may be more insidious.

The pattern is most visible in smaller social units, such as local school districts, where groups colonize the curriculum—sex education for liberals, values instruction for conservatives, recycling lessons for environmentalists, voluntary silent prayer for Christians. But even among the general population the same forces are at work. Fifty years ago the phrase "the elderly" denoted a demographic category; today, thanks largely to federal pension programs and the American Association of Retired Persons (AARP), it denotes a giant and voracious lobby. In the 1930s the government set up farm-subsidy programs, one per commodity; inevitably, lobbies sprang up to defend each program, so that today American agriculture is fundamentally a collection of interest groups. With the help of group organizers and race-based benefits, loose ethnic distinctions coalesce into hard ethnic lobbies. And so on.

Even more depressing, any attempt to fight back against the proliferating mass of subdivision is foiled by the rhetoric of standard populism and its useful stooge: the special interest. The concept of a "special interest" is at the very core of standard populism—the "them" without which there can be no "us." So widely accepted is this notion, and so useful is it in casual political speech, that most of us talk routinely about special interests without a second thought. We all feel we know a special interest when we see one, if only because it is a group of which we are not a member. Yet buried in the special interest idea is an assumption that is no longer true.

The concept of the special interest is not based on nothing. It is, rather, out of date, an increasingly empty relic of the time of machine politics and political bosses, when special interests were, quite literally, special. Simply because of who they were, they enjoyed access that was available to no one else. But the process of everyone's organizing into more and more groups can go only so far before the very idea of a special interest loses any clear meaning. At some point one must throw up one's hands and concede that the hoary dichotomy between special interests and "us" has become merely rhetoric.

According to a 1990 survey conducted for the American Society of

Association Executives, seven out of ten Americans belong to at least one association, and one in four Americans belongs to four or more. Practically everyone who reads these words is a member of an interest group, probably several. Moreover, formal membership tallies omit many people whom we ordinarily think of as being represented by lobbies. For example, the powerful veterans' lobbies enroll only perhaps one-seventh of American veterans, yet the groups lobby on behalf of veterans as a class, and all 27 million veterans share in the benefits. Thus the old era of lobbying by special interests—by a well-connected, plutocratic few —is as dead now as slavery and Prohibition. We Americans have achieved the full democratization of lobbying: influence-peddling for the masses.

The appeal of standard populism today comes precisely from the phony reassurance afforded by its real message: "Other people's groups are the special interests. Less for them—more for you!" Spread that sweet manure around and the natural outgrowth is today's tendency, so evident in the Clinton style, to pander to interest groups frantically while denouncing them furiously. It is the public's style, too: sending ever more checks to the AARP and the National Rifle Association and the National Federation of Independent Business and the National Wildlife Federation and a million others, while railing against special interests. Join and join, blame and blame.

So hyperpluralism makes a hash of the usual sort of standard populist prescription, which calls for "the people" to be given more access to the system, at the expense of powerful Beltway figures who are alleged to have grown arrogant or corrupt or out of touch. Activists and reformers who think the answer to democracy's problems is more access for more of the people need to wake up. Uncontrolled access only breeds more lobbies. It is axiomatic that "the people" (whatever that now means) do not organize to seek government benefits; lobbies do. Every new door to the federal treasury is an opportunity for new groups to queue up for more goodies.

Populists resolutely refuse to confront this truth. Last year, for example, Republicans and the editors of *The Wall Street Journal* campaigned fiercely—and successfully—for new congressional rules making it easier for legislators and groups to demand that bottled-up bills be discharged from committee. The idea was to bring Congress closer to "the people" by weakening the supposedly high-handed barons who rule the Hill. But burying the Free Christmas Tree for Every American Act (or whatever) in committee—while letting members of Congress say they *would* have voted for it—was one of the few remaining ways to hold the door against hungry lobbies clamoring for gifts.

A second brand of populism, *left-populism*, is even more clueless than the standard brand, if that's possible. Many liberals believe the problem is that the wrong groups—the rich, the elites, the giant corporations, etc.—have managed to out-organize the good guys and take control of the system. One version of this model was elaborated by William Greider in his book *Who Will Tell the People*. The New Deal legacy, he writes, "rests upon an idea of interest group bargaining that has gradually been transformed into the random deal-making and permissiveness of the present. The alterations in the system are decisive and . . . the ultimate effects are anti-democratic. People with limited resources, with no real representation in the higher levels of politics, are bound to lose in this environment." So elaborate is the Washington machine of lobbyists, consultants, P.R. experts, political action committees and for-hire think tanks, says Greider, that "powerful economic interests," notably corporations and private wealth, inevitably dominate.

What's appealing about this view is the truism from which it springs: the wealthy enjoy a natural advantage in lobbying, as in almost everything else. Thus many lobbies—even liberal lobbies—are dominated by the comfortable and the wealthy. Consider the case of environmental groups. Anyone who doubts they are major players in Washington today need only look at the massive 1990 Clean Air Act, a piece of legislation that business gladly would have done without. Yet these groups are hardly battalions of the disfranchised. "Readers of *Sierra*, the magazine of the Sierra Club, have household incomes twice that of the average American," notes Senior Economist Terry L. Anderson of the Political Economy Research Center. And *The Economist* notes that "in 1993 the Nature Conservancy, with $915 million in assets, drew 73 percent of its income from rich individuals." When such groups push for emissions controls or pesticide rules, they may be reflecting the priorities of people who buy BMWs and brie more than the priorities of people who buy used Chevies and hamburger. So left-populism's claim to speak for "the people" is often suspect, to say the least.

The larger problem with left-populism, however, is its refusal to see that it is feeding the very problem it decries. Left-populism was supposed to fix the wealth-buys-power problem by organizing the politically disadvantaged into groups: unions, consumer groups, rainbow coalitions and so on. But the strategy has failed. As the left (the unions, the environmentalists) has organized ever more groups, the right (the bosses, the polluters) has followed suit. The group-forming has simply spiralled. This makes a joke of the left-populist prescription, which is to form more "citizens' groups" on the Naderite model, supposedly reinvigorating representative democracy and giving voice to the weak and the silenced. Greider proposes giving people subsidies to spend on political activism: "Giving individual citizens the capacity to deploy political money would inevitably shift power from existing structures and disperse it among the ordinary millions who now feel excluded."

Inevitably, it would do no such thing. Subsidies for activism would perforce go straight into the waiting coffers of (what else?) interest groups, new and old. That just makes matters worse, for if one side organizes more groups, the other side simply redoubles its own mobilization ad infinitum. That escalating cycle is the story of the last three decades. The only winner is the lobbying class. Curiously, then, left-populism has come to serve the very lobbying elites—the Washington lawyers and lobby shops and P.R. pros and interest group execs—whom leftists ought, by rights, to loathe.

The realization that the lobbying class is, to a large extent, both entrepreneurial and in business for itself has fed the third brand of populism, *right-populism*. In the right-populist model, self-serving political careerists have hijacked government and learned to manipulate it for profit. In refreshing contrast to the other two brands of populism, however, this one is in touch with reality. Washington *is* in business for itself, though not only for itself. Legislators and lobbies have an interest in using the tax code to please their constituents, but they also have an interest in churning the tax code to generate campaign contributions and lobbying fees. Luckily for them, those two imperatives generally coincide: the more everyone hunts for tax breaks, the more lobbying jobs there are. Right-populism has tumbled to the fact that so-called public interest and citizens' groups are no more immune to this self-serving logic of lobbying—create conflict, reap rewards—than is any other sort of professional lobby.

Yet right-populism fails to see to the bottom of the problem. It looks into the abyss but flinches. This is not to say that term limits and other procedural fine-tunes may not help; such reforms are no doubt worth trying. But even if noodling with procedures succeeded in diluting the culture of political careerism, it would help (or hurt) mainly at the margins. No, tinkering with the process isn't the answer. What we must do is go straight at the beast itself. We must attack and weaken the lobbies— that is, the *people*'s lobbies.

It sounds so simple: weaken the lobbies! Shove them aside, reclaim the government! "It's just that simple," twinkles Ross Perot. But it's not that simple. Lobbies in Washington have clout because the people who scream when "special interests" are attacked are Medicare recipients defending benefits, farmers defending price supports, small businesses defending subsidized loans, racial groups defending set-asides and so on. Inherently, challenging these groups is no one's idea of fun, which is why politicians so rarely propose to do it. The solution is to strip away lobbies' protections and let competition hammer them. In practice, that means:

*Balance the federal budget.* It is a hackneyed prescription, but it is the very first thing we should do to curtail the lobbies' ability to rob the future. Deficits empower lobbies by allowing them to raid the nation's scarce reserves of investment capital. Deprived of that ability, they will be forced to compete more fiercely for money, and they'll be unable to steal from the future.

*Cut the lobbies' lifelines.* Eliminate subsidies and programs, including tax loopholes, by the hundreds. Killing a program here or there is a loser's game; it creates a political uproar without actually making a noticeable difference. The model, rather, should be the 1986 tax reform measure, which proved that a wholesale housecleaning really is possible. Back then, tax loopholes were cleared away by the truckload. The trick was—and is—to do the job with a big package of reforms that politicians can tout back home as real change. That means ditching whole Cabinet departments and abolishing virtually all industry-specific subsidies. Then go after subsidies for the non-needy—wholesale, not retail.

*Promote domestic perestroika.\** Lobbies live to lock benefits in and competition out, so government restraints on competition should be removed—not indiscriminately, but determinedly. President Carter's deregulation of transportation industries and interest rates, though imperfectly executed, were good examples. Air travel, trucking and rail shipping are cheaper *and* safer. The affected industries have been more turbulent, but that's exactly the point. Domestic competition shakes up interest groups that settle cozily into Washington.

*Encourage foreign competition.* This is most important of all. The forces that breed interest groups never abate, and so fighting them requires a constant counterforce. Foreign competition is such a counterforce. Protection invariably benefits the industries and groups with the sharpest lobbyists and the fattest political action committees; stripping away protection forces them to focus more on modernizing and less on lobbying.

No good deed, they say, goes unpunished. We sought to solve pressing social problems, so we gave government vast power to reassign resources. We also sought to look out for ourselves and bring voices to all of our many natures and needs, so we built countless new groups to seek government's resources. What we did not create was a way to control the chain reaction we set off. Swarming interest groups excited government to perpetual activism, and government activism drew new groups to Washington by the thousands. Before we knew it, society itself was turning into a collection of ravenous lobbies.

Why was this not always a problem? Because there used to be control rods containing the chain reaction. Smoke-filled rooms, they were called. On Capitol Hill or in Tammany Hall, you needed to see one of about six people to have any hope of getting what you wanted, and those six people dispensed (and conserved) favors with parsimonious finesse. Seen from today's vantage, smoke-filled rooms and political machines did a creditable job of keeping a lid on the interest group frenzy—they just didn't do it particularly fairly. That's why we opened up access to anyone who wants to organize and lobby, and opened up power to sub-

* [1980s Soviet Union program of political and economic reform].

committee chairs and caucus heads and even junior legislators. In doing so, we abolished the venal gatekeepers. But that was only the good news. The bad news was that we also abolished the gate.

No, we shouldn't go back to smoke-filled rooms. But the way forward is harder than it ever was before. The maladies that now afflict government are ones in which the public is wholly, enthusiastically implicated. Still, there are sprigs and shoots of encouragement all around. There was the surprisingly strong presidential bid of former Senator Paul Tsongas, which built something of a constituency for straight talk. There's the rise of a school of Democrats in Congress— among them Senator Bob Kerrey and retiring Representative Tim Penny—who are willing to drag the White House toward sterner fiscal measures. There was the Clinton-led triumph of NAFTA [North American Free Trade Agreement] last year. Those developments show promise of a political movement that is counterpopulist yet also popular. Maybe—is it too much to hope?—they point beyond the desert of populism.

## DISCUSSION QUESTIONS

1. Why was Madison concerned about factions? What solutions to the "mischiefs of faction" did he suggest?

2. Can you think of any examples, perhaps from your hometown, your high school, or from campus, in which "organization begets counterorganization?" Did the emergence of new organizations appear to have a significant impact on the resolution of an issue? Can you think of instances in which, counter to Latham, a new organization did not emerge, leaving a group perhaps unrepresented?

3. Rauch complains that interest groups slow down the policymaking process, but isn't this what the Framers of the Constitution intended? Is the interest-group system as portrayed by Rauch a danger to democracy, or is it in fact implementing the principles implicit in the Constitution?

4. Among the many forms of interest-group activity, campaign contributions seem to provoke some of the harshest criticisms. Is this reasonable? Is there any reason to be more concerned about campaign contributions than about lobbying, lawsuits, funding research, or any other activities groups employ to pursue their cause?

# PART IV

# Public Policy

# CHAPTER 13

# Politics and Policy

## 66

## "The Science of Muddling Through"

### CHARLES E. LINDBLOM

*Today's national government plays a role in virtually every aspect of our lives. It provides health insurance for the elderly and the poor, welfare assistance, veterans' benefits, student loans, and a tax break for home owners paying a mortgage. It regulates the activities of the stock markets, polluting industries, worker safety and worker rights, the quality of our food, and air traffic. These programs and regulatory policies are all designed and implemented by the government to achieve particular goals—such as an expanding economy, healthy citizens, college education, and home ownership. It is important that we know just how the government goes about formulating and implementing public policy, and the consequences of those efforts. Who plays a role in the making of public policy besides elected officials, and what motivates their decision making? Who are the beneficiaries of various public policies, and is the "public interest" being served?*

*In the article below, the economist and political scientist Charles Lindblom argues that the efforts of scholars to study and improve upon the policy process were flawed because they were based on the assumption that public policy could be made in a "rational" manner. The problem, according to Lindblom, is that decision making for public policy normally proceeds incrementally: policymakers are incapable of defining and developing alternatives that encompass all possible means of achieving explicitly defined goals. Rather, decision makers start with what already exists, goals defined in part by what is known to work and by the interests that are the most vocal and powerful, and changes are made at the margin to achieve these various ends. Further, the way we evaluate any given policy is heavily dependent upon our values and beliefs about what government ought to do and how it ought to be achieved. There is rarely, according to Lindblom, a clear objective standard of a "good" policy that all policymakers and analysts can agree upon. Lindblom's article, originally printed in 1959, was groundbreaking in that it challenged conventional wisdom among analysts that rational comprehensive analysis was possible for purposes of formulating public policy.*

Suppose an administrator is given responsibility for formulating policy with respect to inflation. He might start by trying to list all related values in order of importance, e.g., full employment, reasonable business profit, protection of small savings, prevention of a stock market crash. Then all possible policy outcomes could be rated as more or less efficient in attaining a maximum of these values. This would of course require a prodigious inquiry into values held by members of society and an equally prodigious set of calculations on how much each value is equal to how much of each other value. He could then proceed to outline all possible policy alternatives. In a third step, he could undertake systematic comparison of his multitude of alternatives to determine which attains the greatest amount of values.

In comparing policies, he would take advantage of any theory available that generalized about classes of policies. In considering inflation, for example, he would compare all policies in the light of the theory of prices. Since no alternatives are beyond his investigation, he would consider strict central control and the abolition of all prices and markets on the one hand and elimination of all public controls with reliance completely on the free market on the other, both in the light of whatever theoretical generalizations he could find on such hypothetical economies.

Finally, he would try to make the choice that would in fact maximize his values.

An alternative line of attack would be to set as his principal objective, either explicitly or without conscious thought, the relatively simple goal of keeping prices level. This objective might be compromised or complicated by only a few other goals, such as full employment. He would in fact disregard most other social values as beyond his present interest, and he would for the moment not even attempt to rank the few values that he regarded as immediately relevant. Were he pressed, he would quickly admit that he was ignoring many related values and many possible important consequences of his policies.

As a second step, he would outline those relatively few policy alternatives that occurred to him. He would then compare them. In comparing his limited number of alternatives, most of them familiar from past controversies, he would not ordinarily find a body of theory precise enough to carry him through a comparison of their respective consequences. Instead he would rely heavily on the record of past experience with small policy steps to predict the consequences of similar steps extended into the future.

Moreover, he would find that the policy alternatives combined objectives or values in different ways. For example, one policy might offer price level stability at the cost of some risk of unemployment; another might offer less price stability but also less risk of unemployment. Hence, the next step in his approach—the final selection—would combine into one the choice among values and the choice among instruments for reaching values. It would not, as in the first method of policy-making, approximate a more mechanical process of choosing the means that best satisfied goals that were previously clarified and ranked. Because practitioners of the second approach expect to achieve their goals only partially, they would expect to repeat endlessly the sequence just described, as conditions and aspirations changed and as accuracy of prediction improved.

## By Root or by Branch

For complex problems, the first of these two approaches is of course impossible. Although such an approach can be described, it cannot be practiced except for relatively simple problems and even then only in a somewhat modified form. It assumes intellectual capacities and sources of information that men simply do not possess, and it is even more absurd as an approach to policy when the time and money that can be allocated to a policy problem is limited, as is always the case. Of particular importance to public administrators is the fact that public agencies are in effect usually instructed not to practice the first method. That is to say, their prescribed functions and constraints—the politically or legally possible—restrict their attention to relatively few values and relatively few alternative policies among the countless alternatives that might be imagined. It is the second method that is practiced.

Curiously, however, the literatures of decision-making, policy formulation, planning, and public administration formalize the first approach rather than the second, leaving public administrators who handle complex decisions in the position of practicing what few preach. For emphasis I run some risk of overstatement. True enough, the literature is well aware of limits on man's capacities and of the inevitability that policies will be approached in some such style as the second. But attempts to formalize rational policy formulation—to lay out explicitly the necessary steps in the process—usually describe the first approach and not the second.

The common tendency to describe policy formulation even for complex problems as though it followed the first approach has been strengthened by the attention given to, and success enjoyed by, operations research,* statistical decision theory,† and systems analysis.‡ The hallmarks of these procedures, typical of the first approach, are clarity of

---

* [*Operations research:* type of analysis, based on mathematical models, used to determine the most efficient use of resources for a set of goals.]
† [*Statistical decision theory:* theory that allows one to make choices between alternatives by objectifying problems and analyzing them quantitatively. Also called Bayesian decision theory after Thomas Bayes (1702–1761), who developed the mathematical foundation of inference, the method of using information on a sample to infer characteristics about a population.]
‡ [*Systems analysis:* analysis of systemic data by means of advanced quantitative techniques to aid in selecting the most appropriate course of action among a series of alternatives.]

objective, explicitness of evaluation, a high degree of comprehensiveness of overview, and, wherever possible, quantification of values for mathematical analysis. But these advanced procedures remain largely the appropriate techniques of relatively small-scale problem-solving where the total number of variables to be considered is small and value problems restricted. Charles Hitch, head of the Economics Division of RAND Corporation, one of the leading centers for application of these techniques, has written:

> I would make the empirical generalization from my experience at RAND and elsewhere that operations research is the art of sub-optimizing, i.e., of solving some lower-level problems, and that difficulties increase and our special competence diminishes by an order of magnitude with every level of decision making we attempt to ascend. The sort of simple explicit model which operations researchers are so proficient in using can certainly reflect most of the significant factors influencing traffic control on the George Washington Bridge, but the proportion of the relevant reality which we can represent by any such model or models in studying, say, a major foreign-policy decision, appears to be almost trivial.[1]

Accordingly, I propose in this paper to clarify and formalize the second method, much neglected in the literature. This might be described as the method of *successive limited comparisons*. I will contrast it with the first approach, which might be called the rational-comprehensive method. More impressionistically and briefly—and therefore generally used in this article—they could be characterized as the branch method and root method, the former continually building out from the current situation, step-by-step and by small degrees; the latter starting from fundamentals anew each time, building on the past only as experience is embodied in a theory, and always prepared to start completely from the ground up.

Let us put the characteristics of the two methods side by side in simplest terms.

### Rational-Comprehensive (Root)

1a. Clarification of values or objectives distinct from and usually prerequisite to empirical analysis of alternative policies.
2a. Policy-formulation is therefore approached through means-end analysis: First the ends are isolated, then the means to achieve them are sought.
3a. The test of a "good" policy is that it can be shown to be the most appropriate means to desired ends.
4a. Analysis is comprehensive; every important relevant factor is taken into account.
5a. Theory is often heavily relied upon.

Assuming that the root method is familiar and understandable, we proceed directly to clarification of its alternative by contrast. In explaining the second, we shall be describing how most administrators do in fact approach complex questions, for the root method, the "best" way as a blueprint or model, is in fact not workable for complex policy questions, and administrators are forced to use the method of successive limited comparisons.

## Intertwining Evaluation and Empirical Analysis (1B)

The quickest way to understand how values are handled in the method of successive limited comparisons is to see how the root method often breaks down in *its* handling of values or objectives. The idea that values should be clarified, and in advance of the examination of alternative policies, is appealing. But what happens when we attempt it for complex social problems? The first difficulty is that on many critical values or objectives, citizens disagree, congressmen disagree, and public administrators disagree. Even where a fairly specific objective is prescribed for the administrator, there remains considerable room for disagreement on sub-objectives. Consider, for example, the conflict with respect to locating public housing, described in Meyerson and Banfield's study of the Chicago Housing Authority—disagreement which occurred despite the clear objective of providing a certain number of public housing units in the city. Similarly conflicting are objectives in highway location, traffic control, minimum wage administration, development of tourist facilities in national parks, or insect control.

### Successive Limited Comparisons (Branch)

1b. Selection of value goals and empirical analysis of the needed action are not distinct from one another but are closely intertwined.
2b. Since means and ends are not distinct, means-end analysis is often inappropriate or limited.
3b. The test of a "good" policy is typically that various analysts find themselves directly agreeing on a policy (without their agreeing that it is the most appropriate means to an agreed objective).
4b. Analysis is drastically limited: i) Important possible outcomes are neglected. ii) Important alternative potential policies are neglected. iii) Important affected values are neglected.
5b. A succession of comparisons greatly reduces or eliminates reliance on theory.

Administrators cannot escape these conflicts by ascertaining the majority's preference, for preferences have not been registered on most issues; indeed, there often *are* no preferences in the absence of public discussion sufficient to bring an issue to the attention of the electorate. Furthermore, there is a question of whether intensity of feeling should be considered as well as the number of persons preferring each alternative. By the impossibility of doing otherwise, administrators often are reduced to deciding policy without clarifying objectives first.

Even when an administrator resolves to follow his own values as a criterion for decisions, he often will not know how to rank them when they conflict with one another, as they usually do. Suppose, for example, that an administrator must relocate tenants living in tenements scheduled for destruction. One objective is to empty the buildings fairly promptly, another is to find suitable accommodation for persons displaced, another is to avoid friction with residents in other areas in which a large influx would be unwelcome, another is to deal with all concerned through persuasion if possible, and so on.

How does one state even to himself the relative importance of these partially conflicting values? A simple ranking of them is not enough; one needs ideally to know how much of one value is worth sacrificing for some of another value. The answer is that typically the administrator chooses—and must choose—directly among policies in which these values are combined in different ways. He cannot first clarify his values and then choose among policies.

A more subtle third point underlies both the first two. Social objectives do not always have the same relative values. One objective may be highly prized in one circumstance, another in another circumstance. If, for example, an administrator values highly both the dispatch with which his agency can carry through its projects *and* good public relations, it matters little which of the two possibly conflicting values he favors in some abstract or general sense. Policy questions arise in forms which put to administrators such a question as: Given the degree to which we are or are not already achieving the values of dispatch and the values of good public relations, is it worth sacrificing a little speed for a happier clientele, or is it better to risk offending the clientele so that we can get on with our work? The answer to such a question varies with circumstances.

The value problem is, as the example shows, always a problem of adjustments at a margin. But there is no practicable way to state marginal objectives or values except in terms of particular policies. That one value is preferred to another in one decision situation does not mean that it will be preferred in another decision situation in which it can be had only at great sacrifice of another value. Attempts to rank or order values in general and abstract terms so that they do not shift from decision to decision end up by ignoring the relevant marginal preferences. The significance of this third point thus goes very far. Even if all administrators had at hand an agreed set of values, objectives, and constraints, and an agreed ranking of these values, objectives, and constraints, their marginal values in actual choice situations would be impossible to formulate.

Unable consequently to formulate the relevant values first and then choose among policies to achieve them, administrators must choose directly among alternative policies that offer different marginal combinations of values. Somewhat paradoxically, the only practicable way to disclose one's relevant marginal values even to oneself is to describe the policy one chooses to achieve them. Except roughly and vaguely, I know of no way to describe—or even to understand—what my relative evaluations are for, say, freedom and security, speed and accuracy in governmental decisions, or low taxes and better schools than to describe my preferences among specific policy choices that might be made between the alternatives in each of the pairs.

In summary, two aspects of the process by which values are actually handled can be distinguished. The first is clear: evaluation and empirical analysis are intertwined; that is, one chooses among values and among policies at one and the same time. Put a little more elaborately, one simultaneously chooses a policy to attain certain objectives and chooses the objectives themselves. The second aspect is related but distinct: the administrator focuses his attention on marginal or incremental values. Whether he is aware of it or not, he does not find general formulations of objectives very helpful and in fact makes specific marginal or incremental comparisons. Two policies, X and Y, confront him. Both promise the same degree of attainment of objectives $a$, $b$, $c$, $d$, and $e$. But X promises him somewhat more of $f$ than does Y, while Y promises him somewhat more of $g$ than does X. In choosing between them, he is in fact offered the alternative of a marginal or incremental amount of $f$ at the expense of a marginal or incremental amount of $g$. The only values that are relevant to his choice are these increments by which the two policies differ; and, when he finally chooses between the two marginal values, he does so by making a choice between policies.

As to whether the attempt to clarify objectives in advance of policy selection is more or less rational than the close intertwining of marginal evaluation and empirical analysis, the principal difference established is that for complex problems the first is impossible and irrelevant, and the second is both possible and relevant. The second is possible because the administrator need not try to analyze any values except the values by which alternative policies differ and need not be concerned with them except as they differ marginally. His need for information on values or objectives is drastically reduced as compared with the root method; and his capacity for grasping, comprehending, and relating values to one another is not strained beyond the breaking point.

\* \* \*

*Successive Comparison as a System*

Successive limited comparisons is, then, indeed a method or system; it is not a failure of method for which administrators ought to apologize. None the less, its imperfections, which have not been explored in this paper, are many. For example, the method is without a built-in safeguard for all relevant values, and it also may lead the decision-maker to overlook excellent policies for no other reason than that they are not suggested by the chain of successive policy steps leading up to the present. Hence, it ought to be said that under this method, as well as under some of the most sophisticated variants of the root method—operations research, for example—policies will continue to be as foolish as they are wise.

Why then bother to describe the method in all the above detail? Because it is in fact a common method of policy formulation, and is, for complex problems, the principal reliance of administrators as well as of other policy analysts. And because it will be superior to any other decision-making method available for complex problems in many circumstances, certainly superior to a futile attempt at superhuman comprehensiveness. The reaction of the public administrator to the exposition of method doubtless will be less a discovery of a new method than a better acquaintance with an old. But by becoming more conscious of their practice of this method, administrators might practice it with more skill and know when to extend or constrict its use. (That they sometimes practice it effectively and sometimes not may explain the extremes of opinion on "muddling through," which is both praised as a highly sophisticated form of problem-solving and denounced as no method at all. For I suspect that in so far as there is a system in what is known as "muddling through," this method is it).

One of the noteworthy incidental consequences of clarification of the method is the light it throws on the suspicion an administrator sometimes entertains that a consultant or adviser is not speaking relevantly and responsibly when in fact by all ordinary objective evidence he is. The trouble lies in the fact that most of us approach policy problems within a framework given by our view of a chain of successive policy choices made up to the present. One's thinking about appropriate policies with respect, say, to urban traffic control is greatly influenced by one's knowledge of the incremental steps taken up the present. An administrator enjoys an intimate knowledge of his past sequences that "outsiders" do not share, and his thinking and that of the "outsider" will consequently be different in ways that may puzzle both. Both may appear to be talking intelligently, yet each may find the other unsatisfactory. The relevance of the policy chain of succession is even more clear when an American tries to discuss, say, antitrust policy with a Swiss, for the chains of policy in the two countries are strikingly different and the two individuals consequently have organized their knowledge in quite different ways.

If this phenomenon is a barrier to communication, an understanding of it promises an enrichment of intellectual interaction in policy formulation. Once the source of difference is understood, it will sometimes be stimulating for an administrator to seek out a policy analyst whose recent experience is with a policy chain different from his own.

This raises again a question only briefly discussed above on the merits of like-mindedness among government administrators. While much of organization theory argues the virtues of common values and agreed organizational objectives, for complex problems in which the root method is inapplicable, agencies will want among their own personnel two types of diversification: administrators whose thinking is organized by reference to policy chains other than those familiar to most members of the organization and, even more commonly, administrators whose professional or personal values or interests create diversity of view (perhaps coming from different specialties, social classes, geographical areas) so that, even within a single agency, decision-making can be fragmented and parts of the agency can serve as watchdogs for other parts.

## DISCUSSION QUESTIONS

1. When you decide which pair of pants or type of shirt you will buy, do you use the "root" or "branch" method of decision making? How about when you decided which college you would go to or which career you might choose?

2. Do you see any problems with incremental decision making? What types of decisions does it tend to favor? Is this a good or a bad thing?

3. Is the comprehensive method of decision making possible, or is it too taxing for the human brain, as Lindblom suggests?

## NOTE

1. "Operations Research and National Planning—A Dissent," *Operations Research* 5 (October 1957), p. 718.

*67*

# "American Business, Public Policy, Case Studies, and Political Theory"

## Theodore J. Lowi

*Before Lowi's article appeared in 1964, many social scientists analyzed public policy through case studies that focused on one particular policy and its implementation. Lowi argued that what the social sciences lacked was a means to cumulate, compare, and contrast the diverse findings of these studies. We needed, in other words, a typology of policymaking. In the article below, Lowi argues that different types of public policies produce different patterns of participation. Public policies can be classified as distributive, regulatory, or redistributive, each with its own distinctive "arena of power." For example, public policies that provide benefits to a single congressional district, group, or company can be classified as distributive. In the distributive arena of power, policy beneficiaries are active in seeking to expand or extend their benefits, but there is no real opposition. Rather, legislators build coalitions premised upon "mutual non-interference" interests, and their representatives seek particular benefits, such as a research and development contract, a new highway, or a farm subsidy, but they do not oppose the similar requests of others.*

*The regulatory and redistributive policy arenas also display distinctive dynamics and roles that participants in the process play. Lowi's work was important not only for providing a classification scheme by which social scientists could think more systematically about different public policies, but for proposing that we study "politics" as a consequence of different types of public policy. Traditionally, social scientists have studied politics to see what kinds of policies are produced.*

. . . What is needed is a basis for cumulating, comparing, and contrasting diverse findings. Such a framework or interpretative scheme would bring the diverse cases and findings into a more consistent relation to each other and would begin to suggest generalizations sufficiently close to the data to be relevant and sufficiently abstract to be subject to more broadly theoretical treatment.

\*   \*   \*

The scheme is based upon the following argument: (1) The types of relationships to be found among people are determined by their expectations—by what they hope to achieve or get from relating to others. (2) In politics, expectations are determined by governmental outputs or policies. (3) Therefore, a political relationship is determined by the type of policy at stake, so that for every type of policy there is likely to be a distinctive type of political relationship. If power is defined as a share in the making of policy, or authoritative allocations, then the political relationship in question is a power relationship or, over time, a power structure.

*　*　*

There are three major categories of public policies in the scheme: distribution, regulation, and redistribution. These types are historically as well as functionally distinct, distribution being almost the exclusive type of national domestic policy from 1789 until virtually 1890. Agitation for regulatory and redistributive policies began at about the same time, but regulation had become an established fact before any headway at all was made in redistribution.

These categories are not mere contrivances for purposes of simplification. They are meant to correspond to real phenomena—so much so that the major hypotheses of the scheme follow directly from the categories and their definitions. Thus, *these areas of policy or government activity constitute real arenas of power.* Each arena tends to develop its own characteristic political structure, political process, elites, and group relations. What remains is to identify these arenas, to formulate hypotheses about the attributes of each, and to test the scheme by how many empirical relationships it can anticipate and explain.

### Areas of Policy Defined

(1) In the long run, all governmental policies may be considered redistributive, because in the long run some people pay in taxes more than they receive in services. Or, all may be thought regulatory because, in the long run, a governmental decision on the use of resources can only displace a private decision about the same resource or at least reduce private alternatives about the resource. But politics works in the short run, and in the short run certain kinds of government decisions can be made without regard to limited resources. Policies of this kind are called "distributive," a term first coined for nineteenth-century land policies, but easily extended to include most contemporary public land and resource policies; rivers and harbors ("pork barrel") programs; defense procurement and R & D [research and development]; labor, business, and agricultural "clientele" services; and the traditional tariff. Distributive policies are characterized by the ease with which they can be disaggregated and dispensed unit by small unit, each unit more or less in isolation from other units and from any general rule. "Patronage" in the fullest meaning of the word can be taken as a synonym for "distribu-

tive." These are policies that are virtually not policies at all but are highly individualized decisions that only by accumulation can be called a policy. They are policies in which the indulged and the deprived, the loser and the recipient, need never come into direct confrontation. Indeed, in many instances of distributive policy, the deprived cannot as a class be identified, because the most influential among them can be accommodated by further disaggregation of the stakes.

(2) Regulatory policies are also specific and individual in their impact, but they are not capable of the almost infinite amount of disaggregation typical of distributive policies. Although the laws are stated in general terms ("Arrange the transportation system artistically." "Thou shalt not show favoritism in pricing."), the impact of regulatory decisions is clearly one of directly raising costs and/or reducing or expanding the alternatives of private individuals ("Get off the grass!" "Produce kosher if you advertise kosher!"). Regulatory policies are distinguishable from distributive in that in the short run the regulatory decision involves a direct choice as to who will be indulged and who deprived. Not all applicants for a single television channel or an overseas air route can be propitiated. Enforcement of an unfair labor practice on the part of management weakens management in its dealings with labor. So, while implementation is firm-by-firm and case-by-case, policies cannot be disaggregated to the level of the individual or the single firm (as in distribution), because individual decisions must be made by application of a general rule and therefore become interrelated within the broader standards of law. Decisions cumulate among all individuals affected by the law in roughly the same way. Since the most stable lines of perceived common impact are the basic sectors of the economy, regulatory decisions are cumulative largely along sectoral lines; regulatory policies are usually disaggregable only down to the sector level.

(3) Redistributive policies are like regulatory policies in the sense that relations among broad categories of private individuals are involved and, hence, individual decisions must be interrelated. But on all other counts there are great differences in the nature of impact. The categories of impact are much broader, approaching social classes. They are, crudely speaking, haves and have-nots, bigness and smallness, bourgeoisie and proletariat. The aim involved is not use of property but property itself, not equal treatment but equal possession, not behavior but being. The fact that our income tax is in reality only mildly redistributive does not alter the fact of the aims and the stakes involved in income tax policies. The same goes for our various "welfare state" programs, which are redistributive only for those who entered retirement or unemployment rolls without having contributed at all. The nature of a redistributive issue is not determined by the outcome of a battle over how redistributive a policy is going to be. Expectations about what it *can* be, what it threatens to be, are determinative.

*Arenas of Power*

Once one posits the general tendency of these areas of policy or govern-mental activity to develop characteristic political structures, a number of hypotheses become compelling. And when the various hypotheses are accumulated, the general contours of each of the three arenas begin quickly to resemble, respectively, the three "general" theories of political process identified earlier. The arena that develops around distributive policies is best characterized in the terms of [E. E.] Schattschneider's findings. The regulatory arena corresponds to the pluralist school, and the school's general notions are found to be limited pretty much to this one arena. The redistributive arena most closely approximates, with some adaptation, an elitist view of the political process.

(1) The distributive arena can be identified in considerable detail from Schattschneider's case-study alone. What he and his pluralist successors did not see was that the traditional structure of tariff politics is also in largest part the structure of politics of all those diverse policies identified earlier as distributive. The arena is "pluralistic" only in the sense that a large number of small, intensely organized interests are operating. In fact, there is even greater multiplicity of participants here than the pressure-group model can account for, because essentially it is a politics of every man for himself. The single person and the single firm are the major activists.

\* \* \*

When a billion-dollar issue can be disaggregated into many millions of nickel-dime items and each item can be dealt with without regard to the others, multiplication of interests and of access is inevitable, and so is reduction of conflict. All of this has the greatest of bearing on the relations among participants and, therefore, the "power structure." In-deed, coalitions must be built to pass legislation and "make policy," but what of the nature and basis of the coalitions? In the distributive arena, political relationships approximate what Schattschneider called "mutual non-interference"—"a mutuality under which it is proper for each to seek duties [indulgences] for himself but improper and unfair to oppose duties [indulgences] sought by others."[1] In the area of rivers and harbors, references are made to "pork barrel" and "log-rolling," but these collo-quialisms have not been taken sufficiently seriously. A log-rolling co-alition is not one forged of conflict, compromise, and tangential interest but, on the contrary, one composed of members who have absolutely nothing in common; and this is possible because the "pork barrel" is a container for unrelated items. This is the typical form of relationship in the distributive arena.

The structure of these log-rolling relationships leads typically, though not always, to Congress; and the structure is relatively stable because all who have access of any sort usually support whoever are the leaders. And there tend to be "elites" of a peculiar sort in the Congressional committees whose jurisdictions include the subject-matter in question. Until recently, for instance, on tariff matters the House Ways and Means Committee was virtually the government. Much the same can be said for Public Works on rivers and harbors. It is a broker leadership, but "policy" is best understood as cooptation rather than conflict and compromise.

\*   \*   \*

(2) The regulatory arena could hardly be better identified than in the thousands of pages written for the whole polity by the pluralists. But, unfortunately, some translation is necessary to accommodate pluralism to its more limited universe. The regulatory arena appears to be composed of a multiplicity of groups organized around tangential relations. . . . Within this narrower context of regulatory decisions, one can even go so far as to accept the most extreme pluralist statement that policy tends to be a residue of the interplay of group conflict. This statement can be severely criticized only by use of examples drawn from non-regulatory decisions.

As I argued before, there is no way for regulatory policies to be disaggregated into very large numbers of unrelated items. Because individual regulatory decisions involve direct confrontations of indulged and deprived, the typical political coalition is born of conflict and compromise among tangential interests that usually involve a total sector of the economy. Thus, while the typical basis for coalition in distributive politics is uncommon interests (log-rolling), an entirely different basis is typical in regulatory politics. The pluralist went wrong only in assuming the regulatory type of coalition is *the* coalition.

\*   \*   \*

What this suggests is that the typical power structure in regulatory politics is far less stable than that in the distributive arena. Since coalitions form around shared interests, the coalitions will shift as the interests change or as conflicts of interest emerge. With such group-based and shifting patterns of conflict built into every regulatory issue, it is in most cases impossible for a Congressional committee, an administrative agency, a peak association governing board, or a social elite to contain all the participants long enough to establish a stable power elite. Policy outcomes seem inevitably to be the residue remaining after all the reductions of demands by all participants have been made in order to extend support to majority size. But a majority-sized coalition of shared interests on one issue could not possibly be entirely appropriate for some other issue. In regulatory decision-making, relationships among group leadership elements and between them on any one or more points of governmental access are too unstable to form a single policy-making elite. As a consequence, decision-making tends to pass from administrative agencies and Congressional committees to Congress, the place where uncertainties in the policy process have always been settled. Congress as an institution is the last resort for breakdowns in bargaining over policy, just as in the case of parties the primary is a last resort for breakdowns in bargaining over nominations. No one leadership group can contain the conflict by an almost infinite subdivision and distribution of the stakes. In the regulatory political process, Congress and the "balance of power" seem to play the classic role attributed to them by the pluralists.

\*   \*   \*

(3) Issues that involve redistribution cut closer than any others along class lines and activate interests in what are roughly class terms. If there is ever any cohesion within the peak associations, it occurs on redistributive issues, and their rhetoric suggests that they occupy themselves most of the time with these. In a ten-year period just before and after, but not including, the war years [World War II], the Manufacturers' Association of Connecticut, for example, expressed itself overwhelmingly more often on redistributive than on any other types of issues.

\*   \*   \*

Where the peak associations, led by elements of Mr. Mills's power elite,\* have reality, their resources and access are bound to affect power relations. Owing to their stability and the impasse (or equilibrium) in relations among broad classes of the entire society, the political structure of the redistributive arena seems to be highly stabilized, virtually institutionalized. Its stability, unlike that of the distributive arena, derives from shared interests. But in contrast to the regulatory arena, these shared interests are sufficiently stable and clear and consistent to provide the foundation for ideologies.

\*   \*   \*

. . . Finally, just as the nature of redistributive policies influences politics towards the centralization and stabilization of conflict, so does it further influence the removal of decision-making from Congress. A decentralized and bargaining Congress can cumulate but it cannot balance, and redistributive policies require complex balancing on a very large scale. What [William] Riker has said of budget-making applies here: ". . . legislative governments cannot endure a budget. Its finances must be totted up by party leaders in the legislature itself. In a complex fiscal system, however, haphazard legislative judgments cannot bring revenue

---

\* [According to C. Wright Mills, a small network of individuals, which he called the "power elite," controls the economy, the political system, and the military.]

into even rough alignment with supply. So budgeting is introduced—which transfers financial control to the budget maker. . . ."[2] Congress can provide exceptions to principles and it can implement those principles with elaborate standards of implementation as a condition for the concessions that money-providers will make. But the makers of principles of redistribution seem to be the holders of the "command posts."

None of this suggests a power elite such as Mills would have had us believe existed, but it does suggest a type of stable and continual conflict that can only be understood in class terms. The foundation upon which the social-stratification and power-elite school rested, especially when dealing with national power, was so conceptually weak and empirically unsupported that its critics were led to err in the opposite direction by denying the direct relevance of social and institutional positions and the probability of stable decision-making elites. But the relevance of that approach becomes stronger as the scope of its application is reduced and as the standards for identifying the scope are clarified. But this is equally true of the pluralist school and of those approaches based on a "politics of this-or-that policy."

*   *   *

## DISCUSSION QUESTIONS

1. Provide examples of each type of policy that Lowi discusses (distributive, regulatory, and redistributive).

2. If you were a member of Congress, which type of policy would you try to emphasize if your main interest was in getting reelected?

3. Are there any types of policies that do not seem to fit Lowi's framework? Are there some policies that are in more than one category?

## NOTES

1. E. E. Schattschneider, *Politics, Pressure and the Tariff* (New York: 1935), pp. 135–6.
2. William Riker, *Democracy in the United States* (New York: 1953), p. 216.

# 68

# "The Human Factor: Should the Government Put a Price on Your Life?"

## Jim Holt

*At the core of cost-benefit analysis is the ability to put a dollar value—a price—on the different results and burdens of any government action or policy. Obviously, there are limits to what we are willing to spend to save or preserve life: to argue otherwise requires you to support the expenditure of infinite resources to save even a single life. But if we are not willing to make infinite expenditures, we must then decide how much we will spend. That requires us to put a value on human life, as otherwise we will never know how much is enough, or what risks are worth taking. Even if money is not the issue, we still face trade-offs: drugs that can treat life-threatening diseases can themselves have fatal side effects, for example, and we must balance lives saved against the risk that some might also be lost.*

*How much is enough? As Holt notes, this is an "idiotic question." Most of us would give everything we have to save our own life, or the life of someone close to us. And even an infinite amount of money does us no good personally if we're dead. But we return to the problem that we are often forced to decide how much a life is worth when we are considering the effectiveness of policy choices. The federal government uses different methods to determine the monetary value of a life in its cost-benefit models, producing estimates in the $3–4 million range.*

How much is your life worth to you? On the face of it, that's an idiotic question. No amount of money could compensate you for the loss of your life, for the simple reason that the money would be no good to you if you were dead. And you might feel, for different reasons, that the dollar value of the lives of your spouse or children—or even a stranger living on the other side of the country—is also infinite. No one should be knowingly sacrificed for a sum of money: that's what we mean when we say that human life is priceless.

But the government set a price for it four years ago: $6.1 million. That's the figure the Environmental Protection Agency came up with when it was trying to decide how far to go in removing arsenic from drinking water. Arsenic can cause diseases, like bladder cancer, that will predictably kill a certain number of people. But reducing the arsenic in water gets more and more expensive as the poison levels approach zero.

How many dollars should be spent to save one "statistical life"? The answer, reasoned the people at the E.P.A., depends on how much that life is worth. And they're not the only ones doing such calculations. The Department of Transportation also puts a price tag on a human life when deciding which road improvements are worth making, although it's the rather more modest one of $3 million.

Presumably, losing your life in a highway smashup is less unpleasant than slowly dying of bladder cancer.

The advantage of this kind of cost-benefit analysis, its proponents declare, is that it promises to make our public policies more rational. But critics find the idea of putting a dollar value on human life preposterous. Part of their case is ethical: it is simply wrong, they say, to count death as a "cost"; no public action that involves lost lives should be evaluated in monetary terms. But they also object to the ways in which the price of life is calculated.

How, exactly, did the E.P.A. arrive at its figure of $6.1 million?

Economists looked at the salaries paid to workers in riskier jobs like mining. They figured out that such workers received, on average, an additional $61 a year for facing an extra 1-in-100,000 risk of accidental death. Evidently, these workers valued their own lives at 100,000 times $61, or $6.1 million. (In 2002, the E.P.A. revised the price of a life downward, to $3.7 million—or if you're older than 70, $2.3 million.)

Ingeniously simple, no? But on closer inspection, you begin to have misgivings about this methodology. In the first place, it is not at all obvious that workers really understand the risks they face in the workplace. Women seem to be much less willing to accept such risks than men. Does that mean their lives should be priced higher? Blacks and nonunionized workers demand little or no risk premium for taking dangerous jobs. Does that mean their lives should be priced lower? Poorer people, for whom an extra dollar is highly valuable, will take less compensation for facing danger. Thus, cost-benefit analysis tells us it is more efficient to locate toxic waste dumps near poorer neighborhoods.

Perhaps the strangest thing about the life-pricing business is the way the lives of future generations become discounted—quite literally. Regulators begin with the assumption that it's better to have $200 in your pocket today—when you can earn interest on it—than a promise of $200 in the future. Equating money with human life, they conclude that a life saved today should count twice as much, in dollar terms, as a life saved 10 years from now; a life saved a century from now scarcely counts at all. That is why cost-benefit analysis might sanction, say, nuclear reactors that provide you and me with cheap energy at the expense of lives lost to cancer decades down the road. But as Frank Ackerman and Lisa Heinzerling point out in their recent book, "Priceless: On Knowing the Price of Everything and the Value of Nothing," it is hardly clear why the same logic should apply to the value of our great-grandchildren. (On the other hand, those future generations may well have developed a cure for cancer, so perhaps we are justified in worrying about them less.)

Champions of cost-benefit analysis—from the controversial Bush administration regulatory guru John D. Graham to the more circumspect liberal law professor Cass Sunstein—maintain that the government is always valuing human life implicitly anyway, so we might as well be forthright about it. Only then, they say, will we be able to stop spending excessively large sums to protect against small risks and vice versa. Most of us, after all, are deficient in rationality: we are excessively fearful of unlikely hazards when those hazards are shockingly unfamiliar or disturbingly involuntary (like dying in a terrorist attack or from something in the drinking water). And we are far too cavalier about much more immediate risks like dying on the highway (which we do at a rate of 117 fatalities per day).

But are ordinary people really being irrational when they seem to "price" their lives differently at different times? Some people even put a *negative* price on their lives—when, for instance, they pay money to engage in a risky activity like mountain climbing. The economist E.J. Mishan, an early authority on cost-benefit analysis, has argued that the value of a human life has no meaning apart from the nature of the risk that is being measured. To say that a human life is "priceless" does not necessarily mean that it is worth more than any amount of money. It may just mean that money is the wrong yardstick to use when our decisions involve the loss of life. Even the most ardent cost-benefit analyst would spend more money to rescue a single actual child than to save 10 "statistical lives."

## Discussion Questions:

1. Not even Holt really answers the question of how much a life is worth. What factors should go into this kind of evaluation? Age? Income? Future-earnings capacity? What are the implications of concluding that some lives might be "worth" more than others?

2. Is it really correct to say that we're not willing to spend an infinite amount to save a life? In an actual life-threatening emergency—a child trapped in a well, people on a sinking ship, a collapsed building, coal miners trapped underground—we probably *would* spend without limit, until we either completed the rescue or knew that the victims were dead. Why aren't we willing to do this in the case of saving *potential* lives?

3. We could come close to eliminating forty thousand automotive fatalities each year by imposing a nationwide twenty-miles-per-hour speed limit. But such a step is inconceivable. Does this mean we are willing to trade lives for time and convenience? What are the implications of this decision?

DEBATING THE ISSUES: REGULATING RISK: GOVERNMENT
INTRUSION OR PROTECTING SOCIETY?

Government regulation is everywhere. From the time you wake up in
the morning to the time you go to sleep again, government regulations
are, usually invisibly, influencing what you do and affecting your
quality of life. The dorm room, apartment, or house you live in is governed by scores of regulations, particularly safety-oriented regulations.
The school you attend abides by a lengthy list of regulations concerning gender equity, access to buildings for disabled people, the confidentiality of student transcripts, and the dispensing of student
financial aid, among many others. Your transportation to and from
campus is affected by government regulations of the auto, mass transit, and road construction industries. The water you drink, the food
you eat, the medicines you take, the air you breathe—all are subject to
reams of government regulations.

Is it all too much? Have Americans gotten too used to government
coddling them and protecting them from their own actions? Roger
Scruton clearly believes the answer is yes. Scruton argues that
"Nanny" has gone too far in controlling individuals' lives and that, by
the same token, individuals have too willingly given away their freedoms to government bureaucrats. While many conservative arguments against government regulations focus on their ineffectiveness or
their cost, Scruton takes a more philosophical approach, arguing that
as spiritual beings, individuals must accept some risk. Scruton also
suggests that the regulatory structure is rampant with hypocrisy. That
is, the content of regulations favor the political values and agendas of
certain elites. These regulations are not designed to produce the best
social outcome but to satisfy the ideological viewpoints of particular
groups. Scruton suggests that many traditional or conventional behaviors in terms of marriage, heterosexual orientation, and religious belief, among others, have been shown to have significant health, life,
and safety benefits, but fear of making moral choices keeps government elites from acting. If government really wanted to maximize
health and safety, Scruton asks, why not push for regulations that encourage these behaviors?

Nurith Aizenman offers a very different perspective. Detailing
some alarming conduct by the nation's railroad and trucking industries, Aizenman suggests these industries are treating public safety
with contempt and that public regulators are doing very little about it.
Focusing on the transportation of hazardous materials, he discusses
several cases in which public safety was imperiled and identifies some
of the causes that contribute to these safety incidents. Increasingly,
these industries are being allowed to self-regulate as government
seeks a more "cooperative" business-government partnership. To

Aizenman, the central problem is that regulation has been delegit-imized; even liberals, he writes, are afraid to stand up and defend reg-ulation.

*69*

# "What Is Acceptable Risk?"

ROGER SCRUTON

The state of Massachusetts has passed a law against sushi—that is to say, you will be allowed to eat sushi only if it has first been either cooked or frozen, so ceasing, in effect, to be sushi. Why? A minuscule risk exists that sushi, in its normal condition, will make you sick. And this is a risk that the citizens of Massachusetts are no longer allowed to take.

Manufacturers of children's playgrounds now predict that swings in public playgrounds will become a thing of the past, since safety regu-lations require prohibitively expensive padding beneath them. Indeed, the regulations surrounding children's toys, clothes, and activities are now so strict that it is hard to have an adventurous childhood. In En-gland it is even against the law to allow your child to walk down a coun-try lane to school, since there is a one in a billion chance that he will be abducted.

In the past, the law made a distinction between those risks to health and safety that citizens might voluntarily assume and those from which the state should protect them. Since every act of protection by the state involves a loss of freedom, lawmakers assumed that only in very special cases should the state expropriate our risk taking. In matters of public hygiene, where the risks taken by one person also fall upon others, it seemed legitimate for the state to intervene: for example, the state could compel people to maintain standards of cleanliness in public places or to undergo vaccinations against contagious diseases. But it should not forbid a person to consume a certain product, merely because there is a tiny risk to his own physical well-being. For the state to extend its juris-diction so far involves a serious invasion of privacy. In matters that affect the citizen alone and that have no adverse consequences on others, the citizen should be free to choose. The state can inform him of the risk, but it should not forbid the choice.

Such, at any rate, was the orthodox position, as defended by John Stuart Mill and the "classical" liberals. But it is not the position adopted by our modern legislators, who do their best to remove both the risk and the freedom to run it. My neighbors are farmers who produce dairy products, livestock, and poultry. Within a few yards of my door is an abundance of milk, eggs, chicken, duck, bacon, beef, and cheese. But I must travel six miles if I am to buy any of these things, and what I buy will have traveled a further 1,000 miles, on average, before reaching me. This is because the state has forbidden me to take the risk of eating my neighbors' products, until they have been processed, packaged and purified, released into the endless stream of global produce, and entirely purged of their local identity and taste. Although the risk of eating the food that grows next door is solely mine, I am not allowed to take it.

The social, environmental, and political costs of such regulation far outweigh any narrow benefit in terms of health. This is especially apparent to someone who lives among farmers and who observes the decline of their industry, the ruination of the landscape, and the dereliction of the farms that has ensued as a result of the criminalization of their traditional economy. However, all protests against over-regulation fall on deaf ears. Governments now regard risk management as their preserve and their priority, and they are prepared to destroy the country's ability to feed itself in an emergency, rather than tolerate one "unnecessary" case of salmonella.

As soon as you look more closely at the matter, however, you discover that modern governments are very selective in the risks that they forbid, and that a law forbidding one risk will often coincide with a law permitting another. Several European governments are currently proposing to outlaw smoking in public places at the same time as legalizing marijuana. Our own government is destroying the local slaughterhouses on which our meat farmers depend on the grounds of wholly invented and unproven risks, while lowering the age of consent for homosexual intercourse and censuring as "homophobic" those who would alert us to the known medical consequences.

In fact, you will quickly discover that Nanny is not concerned with health so much as life-style. She is eager to protect young people from smoking and cites the health risk as her argument. But she does not wish to protect them from homosexual adventures and therefore forbids all discussion of the risk, far greater though it is than the risk attached to cigarettes. Health legislation is being used not to improve the state of the nation's health but to undermine its old, family-based values and to replace them with the antinomian morality of the urban elite.

This is why our government is indifferent to the effect of its legislative zeal on the lives of small farmers. The family farm is the quintessence of old English society, embodying all those virtues of continuity, tradition, patriotism, and local attachment that our ancestors embraced and defended in two world wars.

The farmer is probably the most politically incorrect of Englishmen, and the one most at odds with the media culture that surrounds our government. Hence his way of life can be sacrificed without compunction, and his protests go unheard.

The use of health and safety codes to penalize politically incorrect lifestyles was beautifully exemplified here in rural Wiltshire this last year. Nothing makes Nanny more angry than foxhunting—an offense against the manners, dress code, and morality of the urban elite that has the added taint of being a centuries-old tradition. Nanny is trying hard to make foxhunting illegal. In the meantime, self-appointed policemen patrol the hunts with cameras, looking for evidence of some criminal design. Last year, they photographed the kennel man of the Beaufort Hunt as he left the carcasses of chickens by an earth where some fox cubs lived. This outrageous act caused a national scandal: feeding foxes! Nurturing animals in order to hunt them! The fact that the cubs were orphans, abandoned when their mother was run over by a car, was of no account. Nanny had discovered that people who hunt encourage their quarry to live, sadistically preserving it for a gruesome death. The problem was that no rule in the statute book seemed to condemn it.

At last, after several months of delving, a bureaucrat discovered a piece of European legislation saying that you cannot freely dispose of animal waste without following official guidelines and undergoing official inspections. By leaving out uninspected meat in an uninspected place, the kennel man had committed a crime: the very crime that we all commit when putting out suet for birds. Of course, we bird lovers won't be prosecuted—not yet. So far as I can discover, the case of the Beaufort Hunt was the first and indeed the only time that this particular law has been invoked.

The emphasis on life-style also explains the extraordinary war now being waged against tobacco. Smoking belongs with those old and settled habits—like calling women "ladies," getting drunk on Friday nights with your mates, staying married nevertheless, and having babies in wedlock—that reflect the values of a society shaped by the clear division of sexual roles. It is a symbol of the old order, as portrayed by Hollywood and Ealing Studios in the post-war years, and its very innocence, when set beside cocaine or heroin, gives it the aspect of discarded and parental things.

Furthermore, tobacco advertising has specialized in evoking old ideas of male prowess and female seductiveness: even now, cigarette ads dramatize decidedly un-hip fantasies that stand opposed to the elite culture—after all, the target consumer is the ordinary person, whose fantasies these are. Nor should we forget that tobacco is big business, from which giant corporations make vast profits by the hour. In almost every way, tobacco offends against political correctness, and precisely because it seems to put older people at their ease and enable them to deal confidently with others, it raises the hackles of those who have never achieved that precious condition and whose discomfort is only increased by the sight of others so harmlessly and sociably enjoying themselves.

This is not to deny that tobacco is a risk to health: of course it is. Moreover, it is just about the only product on the market that relentlessly says so. But the health risk does not really explain the vehemence of the attacks on it or the extraordinary attempts by the Environmental Protection Agency and other bureaucracies to portray cigarette smoke as the single most important threat to our children's well-being. For the risk tobacco poses, when compared with those associated with marijuana, automobiles, fatty food, alcohol, or sedentary ways of life, is not actually very serious. Robert A. Levy and Rosalind B. Marimot have shown that smoking reduces the life expectancy of an American 20-year-old by 4.3 years. In an age when people manifestly live too long, why should Nanny be so worried? And why doesn't she turn her attention instead to those products that risk not the physical but the mental and moral health of the consumer: television, for example, or pornography?

It is difficult to avoid the conclusion that what offends about tobacco is not its medical guilt but its moral innocence. It is precisely because it is so harmless, from every point of view other than the medical one, that smoking gets on Nanny's nerves. People don't commit crimes under the influence of smoking, as they do under the influence of drink or drugs. People who smoke have a ready way of putting themselves at ease, of standing back from the world of troubles and taking benign stock of it. Their characters are not distorted or corrupted by their habit, nor is their moral sense betrayed. The smoker is a normal, responsible member of the community, and he can be relied upon, when asked, to put out his [cigarette]. He is not led by his habit into transgressing the established order or the old moral code; on the contrary, his habit has been entirely domesticated by the old sexual morality and recruited to the task of glamorizing it.

Contrast the vehement attacks on tobacco with the pussyfooting over AIDS. The fact that the promiscuous habits of many male homosexuals have greatly advanced this disease has done nothing to make Nanny warn against homosexuality or against exposing young people, even children, to its allure. Indeed, the medical facts about homosexuality are now more or less unmentionable in official circles. They are certainly unmentioned by the British government—in this as in most things a touchstone of political correctness—which has stepped up its campaign not merely to lower the age of consent for homosexual intercourse but also to introduce propaganda into junior schools that will legitimize the "gay" alternative. The medical consequences are brushed aside with advice about condoms and lubricants. Doctors who protest are sneered at, and even in writing this paragraph in *City Journal* I am conscious that I am doing my career as a commentator no good and probably ruling out any prospect of a return to a British university.

For all the fuss over the health and safety effects of various substances, it's interesting to see how little the authorities attend to the health and safety of different life-styles. Statistics show that people live longer, happier, and healthier lives if they are in a stable marriage, if they have the support of a religion, and if they adhere to the traditional sexual code. (Maybe you don't have to be a Darwinian to believe that this is no accident.) But where are the health campaigners and the bureaucrats who are drawing the legislative consequences? Who is agitating for the laws that will privilege these old-fashioned, not to say reactionary, ways of life or for the propaganda campaigns in schools and colleges that will communicate their benefits?

If an article were to appear in a newspaper describing a drug that prolonged life by so much as a year, the medicine would be hailed as a miracle cure. The real miracle cure—religious belief—seems to have a seven-year advantage over atheism, yet it goes unrecognized by Nanny. Indeed, the health consequences of the libertine life-style are, when compared with the consequences of smoking, truly disastrous. Add atheism, relativism, promiscuity, homosexuality, easy divorce, and unstable relationships together, and you probably knock ten years off your life expectancy. But Nanny will never tell you this and will go on reproaching you for your naughty habit of smoking in corners, even if it is the only way, with such a demanding life-style, to obtain in a moment's quiet relief.

Once we see that health legislation is less concerned with physical health than with life-style and the underlying values that life-styles express, we can understand the modern approach to drugs. From the medical point of view, marijuana is at least as dangerous as tobacco, with carcinogenic and cardiological effects comparable with those of ordinary cigarettes and an added danger of brain damage. Moreover, marijuana seems seriously to affect the character and moral responsiveness of those who become addicted to it, and it has a proven association with hard drugs like cocaine and heroin. The connection of all three drugs with crime is well documented by experts and well known to ordinary people. Ask parents what most concerns them among the dangers confronting their children, and you will surely find smoking very low down the list; far higher, and probably nearer the top, will be drugs and the culture that glamorizes them. Hard drugs like heroin kill the user, usually at a young age. But before doing so they rob him of his faculties, his peace of mind, his conscience and consideration for others, his ability to love and be loved. Then they send the body to extinction, already deprived of the soul. And they threaten the lives and the happiness of others— whether parents, lovers, or friends. They present as clear a case as a "classical" liberal could wish for substances whose use should be a crime.

But this is not the message Nanny relays. Drugs are associated with the life-style of which Nanny approves: transgressive, pleasure seeking, contemptuous of stable relationships and objective moral codes. Nanny approves of this life-style because it is subversive of those institutions— marriage, family, local societies, and other "little platoons"—that compete with the state for our loyalties. Where transgression rules, so does the state. Hence in the eyes of the state, the addict is at worst an object of compassion, at best a heroic defender of a valid way of life. His habit is an escape from the intolerable conventions of bourgeois society, and if he lives in a dream world of his own, isn't that his right, in a society that provides no better, or more real, alternative?

Such is the message that is gathering strength among the members of the British political establishment and that corresponds to the emerging reality of our schools. Relentless propaganda against smoking tobacco goes hand in hand with an easy toleration of those who smoke pot, even when they smoke it on the playground. Tobacco users are seeking initiation into the old sexual roles and are therefore subjects of obloquy; marijuana users are preparing themselves for the new, vague, omnisexual life-style, in which real relationships dissolve in a cloud of easy and promiscuous affection. Hence their habit has gained acceptance as no one's business but their own. As far as the health campaigners are concerned, there is no problem. They have averted their eyes, just as they have averted their eyes from the damage done by other habits associated with the youth culture: rock music, for example, which causes widespread deafness; or strobe lights, which cause disorientation of the brain and even epileptic fits.

All this would matter less if the habit of legislation did not encourage a false sense of security. By constantly intervening to save the citizen from self-imposed risk, the legislature creates the impression that everything else is harmless. The citizen need take no care over what he does, so long as he respects the surgeon general's warning and buys in the official market. The state is there to guarantee a risk-free life, and if a risk is not acknowledged by the state, then it doesn't exist. If Nanny sees no harm in pornography or 12-hour doses of television each day or promiscuous but protected sex, then there is no harm in them. Gradually the impression grows that the only risks facing the ordinary citizen are those associated with the old-fashioned life-style glamorized in the Marlboro ads.

Hence the state, by taking charge of risk, massively exposes us to it. The real risks are not those that the state forbids but those that it fosters through its ethos of political correctness. These permitted risks are permitted because it is forbidden to forbid them. To condemn them would be to "marginalize" some valid "alternative" and therefore to interfere with some newly invented or discovered "right." Hence the risks of promiscuity, drug taking, and other habits that short-circuit the rite of passage into adult life are not openly discussed. These practices belong to a culture that has grown under state protection and that is at war with traditional values.

In this way, by being over-protective of the individual, the state undermines society. Almost the entire energy of the health campaigners is devoted to forbidding habits that pose no conceivable social threat, while permitting others that promise social fragmentation. School notice boards now forbid virtually nothing that the young would like to do, save smoking. Their messages about sex, precisely because they are framed exclusively in the language of hygiene, are read as permissions, and their warnings about drugs are noticeably more muted than those relating to tobacco. I am reminded of the scene in *Catch-22* when the hero, going aft to the tail gunner and finding him slumped and bleeding, congratulates himself on the perfect dressing that he applies to the visible wound, only to see a moment later the gunner's guts sliding out from elsewhere.

Of course, a responsible parent would try to prevent his children from smoking. But when the parent takes responsibility, he sees health as part of a larger goal: the long-term fulfillment of his child. This is why it is better, not merely for society but for the individual, too, if education in the taking of risks is left to parents and not appropriated by the state. Wise parents know that their children must grow up and take their place in the community. The child will need nothing so much as the love and trust of others, and these benefits can't be won without a long process of character building and moral education. No sensible parents believe that the future well-being of their child depends entirely on the chemicals that he ingests, or that they can guarantee his happiness merely by ensuring that his bodily functions conform to the surgeon general's requirements.

By attending to the moral and spiritual health of their offspring mothers and fathers provide a far better guarantee of longevity than Nanny can offer. As a parent, it seems to me far more important to keep my children away from television than from "environmental tobacco smoke" and far more important to take them to church than to show them the use of a condom. This makes me a misfit, from the point of view of our official culture. But it is part of what makes me fit into the real culture that surrounds me, the culture that Nanny is trying to kill.

Moreover, those risks against which Nanny warns us are also, in a measure, good for us. It is good that children are surrounded by activities that are permitted but disapproved. For they have to learn to make choices and to know that something may be permitted by the law, and even encouraged by the state, despite being morally wrong. Smoking presents us with an easy apprenticeship in interdiction: a way of showing to a child that something that is not a crime nevertheless ought to be avoided. It belongs, with junk food, pop music, and television, to the world of daily temptations, which is the practice-ground for self-control.

Furthermore there are other risks that a child ought to be encouraged to take, despite the fact that Nanny doesn't like them. Children should not be officiously protected from every kind of danger. Just as their immune systems benefit from contact with hostile bacteria, so do their characters benefit from physical risk. In England, it is now almost impossible for a teacher to lead his class on an expedition, to camp out with his pupils on the moors, or to take them to sea in a boat. All such things occur in the gray area between enterprise and crime, where it is foolhardy for a teacher to trespass. In the world that Nanny is now creating, children encounter danger only on the TV screen, where it is the object of unhealthy and sadistic fantasies, rather than the occasion for cool-headed thinking and resourceful courage.

But this brings us to the crux. Underlying Nanny's attempts to police our way of life is an obsession with the body and its destiny and a refusal to acknowledge that human life is lived, when properly lived, on another plane. You must not smoke, because it harms your body, Nanny asserts (though smoking still leaves the soul in charge and the moral sense undamaged); whereas the harm drugs cause is less important, since drug taking liberates the body. The ecstasy of drugs is a kind of displacement of the soul—a rising up of the body, aided by a physical substance, to usurp the soul's dominion. Similarly, the damage done in the name of sex is done at the body's behest, and by way of overcoming the domain of moral scruples; it is damage done on the body's behalf and in the name of liberation. In all these ways, Nanny promotes the demoralization of the human being and his reconstitution as a purely physical, purely animal thing. Hence Nanny is unable by her very nature to notice that health is promoted far more effectively by a sober, righteous, and godly life than by a fat-free, smoke-free regimen.

But what, in a secular age, should we oppose to Nanny's demoralized vision? It is because people are at a loss for an answer to this question that they capitulate so readily before laws that forbid them to eat sushi, to smoke in public, or to bring up their children as their conscience suggests. In an age when the highest authority is the doctor, and when the state borrows the doctor's white coat, people find themselves insensibly drawn into the vision of themselves as farmyard animals, herded together for their own good.

The answer, it seems to me, is not to deny that we are animals but to recognize that we are animals of a special kind—animals that make themselves by their cooperative efforts into free and spiritual beings. We live by telling our own story, and that story can either ennoble us or demean us. We are ennobled when we learn to coexist with the body on terms, when we subordinate the body's needs to our true loves and loyalties, when we expose it to whatever risks are required by life among friends and neighbors, and when we prevent it from darkening or eclipsing our emotions. No other life is worth living, even if Nanny recommends it. And it is part of the good life that we should not "strive officiously to stay alive," but should recognize the grace of timely death—a death that does not come so late that no one regrets it.

# 70

# "The Case for More Regulation"

## NURITH C. AIZENMAN

In March of 1996, all 1,700 residents of Weyauwega, Wisconsin skipped town for three weeks—involuntarily. The reason for their impromptu spring break: an 81-car train carrying propane and sodium hydroxide derailed and exploded just outside the city center, creating a toxic fire so dangerous the entire community had to be evacuated while authorities struggled to contain it. But the Weyauwegans should consider themselves lucky. In Chicago this past August [1997], 19 people were treated for chemical exposure at area hospitals after the hose on a truck pumping sulfur trioxide into a holding tank broke and released a 50-foot-high lethal cloud. And in California several years earlier, 700 people fell ill after a tanker-car full of metam sodium plunged into the Sacramento River, killing all water life within 40 miles and contaminating California's largest reservoir.

These events point to a disturbing trend: serious accidents involving the transport of hazardous materials, or "hazmats," on trucks and trains have become an almost daily occurrence. In 1995 alone, there were 12,712 incidents involving hazardous materials released from trucks and 1,330 from rail cars. But what's really remarkable about these cases is that they were not more disastrous. Considering the recent massive increase in the volume of hazardous materials streaming across our nation's highways and railroads, combined with the industry's cavalier attitude towards safety and the government's cross-your-fingers-and-hope-for-the-best approach to regulation, it's a wonder we haven't witnessed a truly devastating catastrophe. Environmentalists warn it's only a matter of time before we're treated to a tragedy on the scale of the 1984 accident in Bhopal, India—where 3,500 people were suffocated in their sleep by a 20-ton cloud of methyl isocyanate seeping from a Union Carbide plant.

That's not to say there haven't been lots of close calls. Last December, the Department of Transportation's Federal Railroad Administration (FRA) discovered that despite the fact that military bombs being carried aboard a Union Pacific train had broken through their containers and were protruding onto the floor of a flat car, the company had allowed the train to travel from Oklahoma to California through several major terminals without taking any corrective action. As one FRA official noted in an internal memo: "[Union Pacific] needs a big time wake up call. . . . The way we see it, if they can't take care of class A explosives, makes you wonder what they are doing with other HM [hazardous materials]."

And there are plenty of other hazardous materials to wonder about. Between 1990 and 1995, hazmat transport by rail increased 27 percent to almost 1.8 million cars a year, each one carrying a payload that makes the lethal cargo aboard ValuJet flight 592 look like a shipment of fire-retardant blankets. Pick your poison: there are toxic-by-inhalation chemicals like chlorine and hydrogen fluoride, which can roll across miles of countryside in ground-hugging clouds that burn your body tissue, fill your lungs with fluid and cause you to literally drown in your own juices. There are explosives like ammonium nitrate—mix that with a little fuel and it's Oklahoma City time. Then, of course, there are your run-of-the-mill flammables, like liquefied petroleum gas, or propane, which comprises the bulk of the roughly four billion tons of hazardous materials hauled across our highways every year, and which, when released, vaporizes into a volatile gas that can ignite into a jet flame if so much as a spark comes near. And finally, there's the mother of all hazmats, nuclear waste, which could become a lot more familiar if the government goes ahead with plans to open a temporary nuclear materials repository in Nevada. By as early as 1999, up to 100,000 shipments of highly radioactive spent fuel from reactors across the country could begin the long journey to the storage site by rail and truck—in containers whose crash worthiness has been tested almost exclusively through computer simulations. With all these goodies making their way from sea to shining sea, perhaps it's not surprising that even some chemical company executives are reaching for their gas masks. "It scares the living daylights out of me," confides one former DuPont official.

*Dying for a Job*

The ugly reality of our industrial advances and booming economy is that we need—or at least want—more products made from dangerous substances. Unless we drastically change our consumption habits, one way or another these hazardous materials are going to have to be lugged around the country. But surely our government and industries have taken steps to ensure that the vehicles hauling these toxins are piloted by specially trained experts—crack professionals, alert and ready for the worst, right? Try zombified novices, bleary-eyed and poorly prepared.

To start with, hazardous material transporters are dangerously over-worked. At the railroads, the rise in hazardous shipments has been accompanied by large scale downsizing According to a study by an environmental group called The Good Neighbor Project, between 1985 and 1995, Union Pacific, by far the nation's largest hazmat rail carrier, doubled the ratio of its car shipments to workers from 85:1 to 170:1. Freight trains once served by teams of 5 or 6 people are now left in the hands of one engineer and a conductor. This duo is expected to work for up to 12 hours, take 8 hours off (for eating, sleeping, bill paying, etc.), then come back for more. The length of their shifts is bad enough: It's hard to imagine staying focused on your favorite TV show for 12 hours straight, let alone an endless stretch of railroad track—especially as viewed from an overheated, deafeningly loud engine cabin. But to make matters worse, rail workers are generally scheduled without regard to the basic requirements of a normal sleep cycle. Thus an engineer who is happily tucked in bed at 3 A.M. on one morning, is just as likely to find himself at the head of a 70-car train at 3 A.M. on the next—having received no more than two hours advance notice. "I've been forced to go out when I was so exhausted I hallucinated," recalls one Norfolk Southern engineer; "I've seen things that weren't there, almost gone past signals I thought were one color when they were another."

Maybe that's what happened to the engineer of a Union Pacific train who was killed in July after he sped past a rail stop sign near Rossville, Kansas, and collided with an oncoming train. Hazardous materials aboard his train were burned in the crash, and Rossville's residents had to be evacuated. The collision was one of three fatal Union Pacific accidents since June that finally prompted the Federal Railroad Administration to launch an 80-man inspection of the rail company—the most extensive investigation in the agency's history. After a week of probing, the FRA declared itself shocked, shocked, to discover that everyone from dispatchers, to engineers, to yard workers, were being "worked to the bone." Yet for years rail workers' unions have complained about such problems; last spring the Brotherhood of Locomotive Engineers even tried to shut Union Pacific down with a strike over safety, but they were halted by a court order. Still, according to the FRA's spokesman Jim Gower, the FRA "wasn't really aware of the vastness of the problem."

But this was only the tip of the iceberg. The FRA also found that Union Pacific routinely violates the already onerous 12-hour work limit —often keeping workers on duty for up to 17 hours at a stretch. Topping it all off, the agency determined that the training many workers receive is grossly inadequate and in some cases nonexistent—with some employees ordered to operate sophisticated equipment they've never been taught to use.

Among the things a good training program might emphasize would be the importance of watching for smaller problems that could be the harbinger of bigger ones. But even if they were taught to do so, rail workers might be disinclined to report any trouble they find. Many rail companies reward managers with a cash bonus tied [to] the safety record of the track under the manager's jurisdiction. CSX Transportation, for instance, has awarded a total of $4.5 million in company stock since 1995 under its "Take Stock in Safety" program. Sounds like a great incentive system, but the result, according to United Transportation Union's legislative director, J.M. Brunkenhoefer, is that many middle managers strongly discourage the rail workers they supervise from reporting accidents—threatening potential whistle blowers with either layoffs or "investigations" into the whistle blower's responsibility.

Of course, the railroads sometimes run into pesky FRA rules requiring that certain types of accidents be reported, for instance those in which a rail worker is injured seriously. No problem—the companies simply send workers to the doctor with a special note, like one from CSX that asks that "whenever possible, use of equally prudent NON-REPORTABLE treatment is encouraged in order to minimize reporting of less significant minor injuries to the Federal Railroad Administration" Among the "reportable" treatments doctors are urged to avoid: "issuing a prescription, injections, closing a wound with sutures, butterfly, staple or steristrip, application of immobilizing cast, sling or splint, . . . [and] restriction of employee's work activity" To be sure, the letter assures doctors that "appropriate treatment should be based upon your professional medical judgment;" but the message from CSX management to the doctor and, more importantly, to its employees couldn't be more blunt: Don't Rock the Boat.

That message was apparently heard loud and dear by the team aboard a CSX train that sideswiped an Amtrak passenger car and caused a derailment near Arlington, Va., this past July. Twice during the train's two-hour journey, crews on passing trains radioed the CSX crew with the warning that one of its flatcars was leaning precariously. Nonetheless, the crew ignored the warning and continued forward because a CSX supervisor had already inspected the car and insisted there was no danger.

*Highway to Hell*

But intimidated, badly trained and dog-tired as they may be, rail workers are still the envy of truckers. That's because while truckers can only be legally required to drive a mere 10 hours a day, trucking companies routinely—and knowingly—put them on schedules that make a mockery of the law. Consider the timetable of 23-year-old Peter Conway, the driver of a semitrailer loaded with 9,200 gallons of propane headed east on I-287 through New York state in July of 1994. Some time earlier, Conway's truck had been side-lined by a breakdown for 10 hours. Like most truckers, he was being paid by the mile as opposed to the hour, so after his rig was fixed, Conway faced a Hobson's choice: make up the lost time or take a financial hit. He opted to press on. On July 27, Conway's truck drifted off the left shoulder of the highway near White Plains and struck the column of an overpass. The propane leaking from his truck's damaged tank ignited—propelling the container 300 feet through the air onto a nearby house, which was quickly engulfed in flames. Conway was killed, and 23 others were injured. Although Conway had falsified the log book in which he was legally required to enter his work time, federal investigators were able to determine that he had been driving almost continuously for over 35 hours. Their unsurprising conclusion: Conway had dozed off at the wheel.

He's certainly not the first, nor the last, to have done so. A recent government study found that up to 40 percent of truck crashes were probably caused by fatigue. Another study determined that at least 58 percent of truckers had violated hours-of-service rules. In fact, log books are so routinely doctored that truckers have taken to calling them "comic books."

But even if he's awake, there's no guarantee the driver of that monster hazmat truck roaring up behind you on the highway is even marginally competent—or that his rig is remotely safe. Take the case of Willis Curry, a Washington D.C. trucker who, since 1988, has managed to amass 31 citations for such traffic violations as speeding, carrying overweight loads, disobeying red lights and ignoring railroad cross warnings. Back in January, the Department of Transportation's Federal Highway Administration (FHWA) informed Curry's employer of his record and he was promptly fired. But the FHWA waited until April to alert D.C. authorities that his license should be revoked. Two months later Curry, still the proud bearer of a D.C. license and now a driver for a local dump truck company, collided with the car of a young mother and her one-year-old son.

Police determined that the brakes on Curry's dump had failed. This should not have come as a surprise. Curry's vehicle gave a whole new meaning to the term "dump" truck. It had been cited for 28 mechanical safety violations in two random inspections last year. And during the first inspection the truck's wiring was so defective that when the brake pedal was pushed the windshield wipers starting going. On both occasions the truck had been ordered off the road for repairs.

But the story doesn't end there. After Curry's accident, no action was taken to investigate the dump's owner, or to revoke Curry's license. It wasn't until ten days later, when Curry made a routine request for a duplicate license, that a city clerk happened to notice his record and confiscated his license. And Curry quickly managed to win it back, with the proviso that he only drive between 4 A.M. and noon on weekdays. At 2 P.M. the very next week, Curry was once again behind the wheel when the brakes on his dump failed a second time, causing the 30-ton truck to veer out of control and roll over onto a car driven by a teenage honor student. The boy was killed instantly. It is small consolation that

Curry's truck wasn't carrying anything more dangerous than sand. Next time we may not be so lucky.

It's hard to say which was the greater menace to society, Curry or his truck. And that's not unusual. On the rare occasions when the Department of Transportation does random roadside inspections, nearly one out of every three rigs they pull over is found to be either unsafe, driven by an unsafe trucker, or both.

### Danger Zone

Defective equipment is a problem with which rail workers are also all too familiar. A 1995 surprise inspection of a Union Pacific rail yard in Fort Worth, Texas, found that 37 percent of the rail cars there were faulty—over a third of them with brake problems. And according to Union Pacific itself, 12 percent of the 8,000 plus chemical tank cars it inspected last year turned up "exceptions" like poor positioning of the tops on the cars, or mislabeling of their contents. That wasn't news to rail employees; they say it's not uncommon to work on a train with up to eight "sleeper cars" whose contents, hazardous or otherwise, are unknown to them.

\* \* \*

Just as frightening as the trains themselves are the tracks on which they travel. About 85 percent of rail transport occurs over "dark" areas where there is no automated signaling. Instead, engineers must rely on dispatchers to talk them through their journey. Yet, as the FRA recently "discovered," dispatchers are often unfamiliar with the tracks through which they are expected to guide a train—in many cases they haven't even traveled the route once. So perhaps it's not surprising that a June FRA inspection of Union Pacific found that 80 percent of dispatcher orders contained at least one error.

\* \* \*

### A Free Ride

But how does the industry get away with it? Where are all those government regulators conservatives are so fond of disparaging? Turns out they're not nearly as meddlesome as the GOP would have you think. A July study by the General Accounting Office (GAO)—which monitors federal agencies for Congress—found that in just one year, the number of safety inspections conducted by the FRA decreased by 23 percent. And between 1992 and 1995 the percentage of railroads inspected for hazardous materials safety by the FRA fell from 34 percent to 21 percent.

\* \* \*

But the FRA maintains there's no cause for alarm; it's all part of a new "cooperative" way of doing business that began under the Clinton administration. The idea is to move away from using violations and civil penalties as the primary means of obtaining compliance with the regulations. Instead, the agency relies on "partnerships" with the railroad companies. If you're wondering what that means, take a look at the way the FRA has responded to the results of its—admittedly laudable—massive investigation of Union Pacific. You might expect that the agency's discovery that rail employees are being dangerously overworked would prompt it to change the rules governing their schedule. How retro! "New regulations are not the answer," the FRA's Gower patiently explains. Instead, the FRA will simply ask Union Pacific to mend its ways: "After all, it's in their own interest." Union Pacific officials agree—pointing out that they're hiring an additional 2,600 employees this year. But just how much relief will those new hires be able to provide for the company's exhausted 54,000-strong work force? Officials like Barry Sweedler at the National Transportation Safety Board (NTSB)—the independent agency responsible for investigating accidents and making recommendations to transportation regulators—think the FRA is being naive. "What you have today is an industry that's willing to accept a certain number of collisions every year," observes Sweedler.

\* \* \*

Many of the FRA-mandated innovations that are actually in use were required by the FRA only after fatal foot-dragging. That was the case with a backup braking system called a "two-way end-of-train device" that allows an engineer to use a radio signal to apply brakes from the back of his train if his locomotive brakes fail. The FRA did not mandate use of the devices on all trains traveling through mountainous terrain until February of 1996—seven years after the NTSB first recommended them, and only after a runaway train had derailed at the bottom of the steep Cajon Pass in California not once, but twice. Similarly, while the FRA has (after over a decade of urging by the NTSB) finally conceded the considerable potential of using satellite-based proximity warning systems to alert engineers, and even apply the brakes, when one train is speeding or about to collide with another, the agency is now merely helping the rail companies run pilot projects—rather than insisting that they install it on a timetable.

\* \* \*

The Department of Transportation's record on hazmat trucking is just as deplorable. As you may have gathered from the case of dump truck driver Willis Curry, enforcement of the law by the Department's Federal Highway Administration is laughable. A March study by the Department's Inspector General—a sort of in-house independent watchdog—

found that in 1995, only 2.5 percent of trucking companies were reviewed by the Federal Highway Administration (FHWA) to see if they complied with safety rules. What's more, about two-thirds of the nation's interstate carriers have never been rated for safety. Most alarming, the Inspector General determined that 22 percent of trucking companies with high rates of on-the-road violations and accidents had never been rated for safety, and 42 percent had not been rated in the past two years.

\*    \*    \*

When the FHWA bothers to conduct inspections, it tends to favor the velvet-fist-in-the-velvet-glove approach. According to the Inspector General, FHWA inspectors consistently underreport violations, and low-ball fines. For instance, the penalties for 81 carriers surveyed did not include over half of the major violations found during their inspection. But the FHWA had a ready explanation for this dismal performance: "we're a regulatory agency, not an enforcement agency."

The trucking companies clearly share that impression. To get a sense of how little they fear the FHWA, you need only consider that in the Inspector General's survey, over a third of the companies deemed unsatisfactory by FHWA inspectors had to be inspected and scolded two more times before they cleaned up their act. Moreover—and this is the clincher—most of these delinquent companies were allowed to keep their trucks on the road even while they continued to fail one inspection after another. To cite just one example, a Missouri hazardous materials carrier continued to operate without interruption despite the fact that it had failed two general inspections—and despite the fact that one out of every two of its trucks had to be pulled out of service when stopped for random inspections along the road. It's enough to drive long-time highway safety advocate Gerald Donaldson to distraction. "Words fail me on the extent of the FHWA's ineptness," he sighs.

\*    \*    \*

Among the other possible improvements that could make hazardous materials trucks safer that the Department of Transportation has chosen to ignore: anti-lock brakes, a better internal compartment system to prevent the liquid in tankers from violently sloshing around and causing the truck to roll over, technology to keep the top and bottom ports of tankers from springing a leak when such rollovers do occur; and steel head shields like those used to such great effect on train tank cars. Many of these changes have long been advocated by the National Transportation Safety Board (NTSB) based on its investigation of serious accidents. But, once again, the Department of Transportation simply buries its head in the sand.

*Regulation Redeemed*

\* \* \*

\* \* \* It's time to re-think the conventional wisdom that regulation is a bad word. In recent years, conservatives have largely succeeded in convincing us that regulators are our number one enemy, strangling businesses with yards of expensive and impractical red tape. And the conservative cause has actually been helped by many liberals—who are quick to defend whatever regulation exists, without bothering to check how well it's working. Meanwhile, the Department of Transportation has all too readily absorbed the mood in Washington, speaking proudly of its new "partnership" with trucking and rail companies, as if having good relations with those industries were the primary goal. It's not. The government's duty is to protect the public—and it is falling seriously short.

Of course, it's not hard to understand why the regulators have lost sight of their mission: Like most of us, they don't enjoy hearing complaints from the people they work with, and no one howls louder than the industries being regulated. But both the government and the public need to start greeting those protests with a hefty grain of salt. From the dangerous overworking of employees, to the appalling condition of their vehicles, to the lack of inspections and penalties for safety violations, to the failure to install new life-saving technologies, the troubles plaguing the transport of hazardous materials by train and truck provide a dramatic illustration of how the real problem can be not too much government regulation, but far too little. If you think this lesson only applies to trucks and trains, just consider what smarter and tougher regulation could have done for the folks aboard ValuJet flight 592 [Improper labeling and packing of oxygen canisters led to the death of all 110 passengers and crew members on this 1996 flight.] And by the way, how do you feel about that hamburger in your freezer?

## DISCUSSION QUESTIONS

1. Do you agree with Scruton that government tries to insulate individuals too much from risk? Can you think of some examples?

2. Is Scruton right to argue that if government is to have regulation, it should have a broader moral content? He suggests that government chooses to regulate certain things (e.g., tobacco use) because it assuages the moral perspective of those implementing the regulations, but government won't consider regulating other behavior that may have even more serious health consequences? How would you draw the line between what government should and shouldn't be able to regulate?

3. One argument against excessive regulations is that they are a costly way of protecting people against miniscule risk—for example, the remote chance that we might contract cancer from food additives—while ignoring much larger risks, such as reckless driving, suicide, and prescription-drug interactions. What determines the sorts of risk that the public will accept? What determines the risks that we demand protection from?

CHAPTER 14

# Government and the Economy

## 71

## "Call for Federal Responsibility"

### FRANKLIN D. ROOSEVELT

*The national government has always played a role in the economy. Since the late 1700s, the government has provided property for private development, enforced contracts and prohibited the theft of private property, provided subsidies to encourage the growth of particular industries, developed the infrastructure of the growing country, and regulated trade. The question that commands the attention of political leaders and citizens alike today is what the limits of government involvement in the economy ought to be. To what extent should the free market make most economic decisions to maximize efficiency and productivity, or should the government regulate markets in the pursuit of other goals, such as equality, and to address market failures such as monopolies and public goods that are underprovided by the market (such as education and environmental protection)?*

*This debate reached a peak during the Great Depression, as the nation struggled to define the government's role in reviving the economy, and played a critical role in the 1932 presidential election between the Democratic candidate, Franklin D. Roosevelt, and the Republican president, Herbert Hoover. In the Roosevelt campaign speech printed here, FDR argued that the federal government should play a role in unemployment insurance, housing for the poor, and public works programs to compensate for the hardship of the Great Depression. Hoover, on the other hand, was very much opposed to altering the relationship between government and the private sector, which was "builded up by 150 years of toil of our fathers." It was the extension of freedom and the exercise of individual initiative, Hoover claimed, which made the American economic system strong and which would gradually bring about economic recovery, Hoover argued. Roosevelt prevailed, and the resulting New Deal changed the face of government. While the federal government adopted a much more active role in regulating the economy and providing social safety, the central issues discussed by Roosevelt and Hoover are still being debated today.*

The first principle I would lay down is that the primary duty rests on the community, through local government and private agencies, to take care of the relief of unemployment. But we then come to a situation where there are so many people out of work that local funds are insufficient.

It seems clear to me that the organized society known as the State comes into the picture at this point. In other words, the obligation of government is extended to the next higher unit.

I [practice] what I preach. In 1930 the state of New York greatly increased its employment service and kept in close touch with the ability of localities to take care of their own unemployed. But by the summer of 1931 it became apparent to me that actual state funds and a state-supervised system were imperative.

I called a special session of the legislature, and they appropriated a fund of $20 million for unemployment relief, this fund to be reimbursed to the state through the doubling of our income taxes. Thus the state of New York became the first among all the states to accept the definite obligation of supplementing local funds where these local funds were insufficient.

The administration of this great work has become a model for the rest of the country. Without setting up any complex machinery or any large overhead, the state of New York is working successfully through local agencies, and, in spite of the fact that over a million people are out of work and in need of aid in this one state alone, we have so far met at least the bare necessities of the case.

This past spring the legislature appropriated another $5 million, and on November 8 the voters will pass on a $30 million bond issue to tide us over this winter and at least up to next summer.

\*   \*   \*

I am very certain that the obligation extends beyond the states and to the federal government itself, if and when it becomes apparent that states and communities are unable to take care of the necessary relief work.

It may interest you to have me read a short quotation from my message to the legislature in 1931:

> What is the State? It is the duly constituted representative of an organized society of human beings, created by them for their mutual protection and well-being. One of the duties of the State is that of caring for those of its citizens who find themselves the victims of such adverse circumstances as make them unable to obtain even the necessities of mere existence without the aid of others.
>
> In broad terms, I assert that modern society, acting through its government, owes the definite obligation to prevent the starvation or the dire want of any of its fellowmen and women who try to maintain themselves but cannot. To these unfortunate citizens aid must be extended by the government, not as a matter of charity but as a matter of social duty.

That principle which I laid down in 1931, I reaffirm. I not only reaffirm it, I go a step further and say that where the State itself is unable successfully to fulfill this obligation which lies upon it, it then becomes the positive duty of the federal government to step in to help.

In the words of our Democratic national platform, the federal government has a "continuous responsibility for human welfare, especially for the protection of children." That duty and responsibility the federal government should carry out promptly, fearlessly, and generously.

It took the present Republican administration in Washington almost three years to recognize this principle. I have recounted to you in other speeches, and it is a matter of general information, that for at least two years after the crash, the only efforts made by the national administration to cope with the distress of unemployment were to deny its existence.

When, finally, this year, after attempts at concealment and minimizing had failed, it was at last forced to recognize the fact of suffering among millions of unemployed, appropriations of federal funds for assistance to states were finally made.

I think it is fair to point out that a complete program of unemployment relief was on my recommendation actually under way in the state of New York over a year ago; and that in Washington relief funds in any large volume were not provided until this summer, and at that they were pushed through at the demand of Congress rather than through the leadership of the President of the United States.

At the same time, I have constantly reiterated my conviction that the expenditures of cities, states, and the federal government must be reduced in the interest of the nation as a whole. I believe that there are many ways in which such reduction of expenditures can take place, but I am utterly unwilling that economy should be practised at the expense of starving people.

We must economize in other ways, but it shall never be said that the American people have refused to provide the necessities of life for those who, through no fault of their own, are unable to feed, clothe, and house themselves. The first obligation of government is the protection of the welfare and well-being, indeed the very existence, of its citizens.

*  *  *

The next question asks my attitude toward appropriations for public works as an aid to unemployment. I am perfectly clear as to the principles involved in this case also.

From the long-range point of view it would be advisable for governments of all kinds to set up in times of prosperity what might be called a nest egg to be used for public works in times of depression. That is a policy which we should initiate when we get back to good times.

But there is the immediate possibility of helping the emergency through appropriations for public works. One question, however, must be answered first because of the simple fact that these public works cost money.

We all know that government treasuries, whether local or state or federal, are hard put to it to keep their budgets balanced; and, in the case of the federal Treasury, thoroughly unsound financial policies have made its situation not exactly desperate but at least threatening to future stability if the policies of the present administration are continued.

All public works, including federal, must be considered from the point of view of the ability of the government Treasury to pay for them. There are two ways of paying for public works. One is by the sale of bonds. In principle, such bonds should be issued only to pay for self-sustaining projects or for structures which will without question have a useful life over a long period of years. The other method of payment is from current revenues, which in these days means in most cases added taxes. We all know that there is a very definite limit to the increase of taxes above the present level.

From this point, therefore, I can go on and say that, if funds can be properly provided by the federal government for increased appropriations for public works, we must examine the character of these public works. I have already spoken of that type which is self-sustaining. These should be greatly encouraged. The other type is that of public works which are honestly essential to the community. Each case must rest on its own merits.

It is impossible, for example, to say that all parks or all playgrounds are essential. One may be and another may not be. If a school, for instance, has no playground, it is obvious that the furnishing of a playground is a necessity to the community. But if the school already has a playground and some people seek merely to enlarge it, there may be a very definite question as to how necessary that enlargement is.

Let me cite another example. I am much interested in providing better housing accommodations for the poor in our great cities. If a slum area can be torn down and new modern buildings put up, I should call that almost a human necessity; but, on the other hand, the mere erection of new buildings in some other part of the city while allowing the slums to remain raises at once a question of necessity. I am confident that the federal government working in cooperation with states and cities can do much to carry on increased public works and along lines which are sound from the economic and financial point of view.

Now I come to another question. I am asked whether I favor a system of unemployment insurance reserves made compulsory by the states, supplemented by a system of federally coordinated state employment offices to facilitate the reemployment of jobless workers.

The first part of the question is directly answered by the Democratic platform which advocates unemployment insurance under state laws.

This is no new policy for me. I have advocated unemployment insurance in my own state for some time, and, indeed, last year six Eastern governors were my guests at a conference which resulted in the drawing up of what might be called an idea plan of unemployment insurance.

This type of insurance is not a cure-all but it provides at least a cushion to mitigate unemployment in times of depression. It is sound if, after starting it, we stick to the principle of sound insurance financing. It is only where governments, as in some European countries, have failed to live up to these sound principles that unemployment insurance has been an economic failure.

As to the coordinated employment offices, I can only tell you that I was for the bills sponsored by Senator Wagner of my own state and passed by the Congress. They created a nationally coordinated system of employment offices operated by the individual states with the advisory cooperation of joint boards of employers and employees.

To my very great regret this measure was vetoed by the President of the United States. I am certain that the federal government can, by furnishing leadership, stimulate the various states to set up and coordinate practical, useful systems.

# 72

# "Against the Proposed New Deal"

## Herbert Hoover

This campaign is more than a contest between two men. It is more than a contest between two parties. It is a contest between two philosophies of government.

We are told by the opposition that we must have a change, that we must have a new deal. It is not the change that comes from normal development of national life to which I object but the proposal to alter the whole foundations of our national life which have been built through generations of testing and struggle, and of the principles upon which we have builded the nation. The expressions our opponents use must refer to important changes in our economic and social system and our system of government, otherwise they are nothing but vacuous words. And I realize that in this time of distress many of our people are asking whether our social and economic system is incapable of that great primary function of providing security and comfort of life to all of the firesides of our 25 million homes in America, whether our social system provides for the fundamental development and progress of our people, whether our form of government is capable of originating and sustaining that security and progress.

This question is the basis upon which our opponents are appealing to the people in their fears and distress. They are proposing changes and so-called new deals which would destroy the very foundations of our American system.

Our people should consider the primary facts before they come to the judgment—not merely through political agitation, the glitter of promise, and the discouragement of temporary hardships—whether they will support changes which radically affect the whole system which has been builded up by 150 years of the toil of our fathers. They should not approach the question in the despair with which our opponents would clothe it.

Our economic system has received abnormal shocks during the past three years, which temporarily dislocated its normal functioning. These shocks have in a large sense come from without our borders, but I say to you that our system of government has enabled us to take such strong action as to prevent the disaster which would otherwise have come to our nation. It has enabled us further to develop measures and programs which are now demonstrating their ability to bring about restoration and progress.

We must go deeper than platitudes and emotional appeals of the public platform in the campaign if we will penetrate to the full significance of the changes which our opponents are attempting to float upon the wave of distress and discontent from the difficulties we are passing through. We can find what our opponents would do after searching the record of their appeals to discontent, group and sectional interest. We must search for them in the legislative acts which they sponsored and passed in the Democratic-controlled House of Representatives in the last session of Congress. We must look into measures for which they voted and which were defeated. We must inquire whether or not the presidential and vice-presidential candidates have disavowed these acts. If they have not, we must conclude that they form a portion and are a substantial indication of the profound changes proposed.

And we must look still further than this as to what revolutionary changes have been proposed by the candidates themselves.

We must look into the type of leaders who are campaigning for the Democratic ticket, whose philosophies have been well known all their lives, whose demands for a change in the American system are frank and forceful. I can respect the sincerity of these men in their desire to change our form of government and our social and economic system, though I shall do my best tonight to prove they are wrong. I refer particularly to Senator Norris, Senator La Follette, Senator Cutting, Senator Huey Long, Senator Wheeler, William R. Hearst and other exponents of a social philosophy different from the traditional American one. Unless these men feel assurance of support to their ideas, they certainly would not be supporting these candidates and the Democratic Party. The seal of these men indicates that they have sure confidence that they will have voice in the administration of our government.

I may say at once that the changes proposed from all these Democratic principals and allies are of the most profound and penetrating character. If they are brought about, this will not be the America which we have known in the past.

Let us pause for a moment and examine the American system of government, of social and economic life, which it is now proposed that we should alter. Our system is the product of our race and of our experience in building a nation to heights unparalleled in the whole history of the world. It is a system peculiar to the American people. It differs essentially from all others in the world. It is an American system.

It is founded on the conception that only through ordered liberty, through freedom to the individual, and equal opportunity to the individual will his initiative and enterprise be summoned to spur the march of progress.

It is by the maintenance of equality of opportunity and therefore of a

society absolutely fluid in freedom of the movement of its human particles that our individualism departs from the individualism of Europe.
We resent class distinction because there can be no rise for the individual
through the frozen strata of classes, and no stratification of classes can
take place in a mass livened by the free rise of its particles. Thus in our
ideals the able and ambitious are able to rise constantly from the bottom
to leadership in the community.

This freedom of the individual creates of itself the necessity and the
cheerful willingness of men to act cooperatively in a thousand ways and
for every purpose as occasion arises; and it permits such voluntary co-
operations to be dissolved as soon as they have served their purpose, to
be replaced by new voluntary associations for new purposes.

There has thus grown within us, to gigantic importance, a new conception. That is, this voluntary cooperation within the community. Cooperation to perfect the social organization; cooperation for the care of
those in distress; cooperation for the advancement of knowledge, of scientific research, of education; for cooperative action in the advancement
of many phases of economic life. This is self-government by the people
outside of government; it is the most powerful development of individual freedom and equal opportunity that has taken place in the century
and a half since our fundamental institutions were founded.

It is in the further development of this cooperation and a sense of its
responsibility that we should find solution for many of our complex
problems, and not by the extension of government into our economic
and social life. The greatest function of government is to build up that
cooperation, and its most resolute action should be to deny the extension
of bureaucracy. We have developed great agencies of cooperation by the
assistance of the government which promote and protect the interests of
individuals and the smaller units of business. The Federal Reserve System, in its strengthening and support of the smaller banks; the Farm
Board, in its strengthening and support of the farm cooperatives; the
Home Loan Banks, in the mobilizing of building and loan associations
and savings banks; the Federal Land Banks, in giving independence and
strength to land mortgage associations; the great mobilization of relief
to distress, the mobilization of business and industry in measures of
recovery, and a score of other activities are not socialism—they are the
essence of protection to the development of free men.

The primary conception of this whole American system is not the
regimentation of men but the cooperation of free men. It is founded upon
the conception of responsibility of the individual to the community, of
the responsibility of local government to the state, of the state to the
national government.

It is founded on a peculiar conception of self-government designed to
maintain this equal opportunity to the individual, and through decentralization it brings about and maintains these responsibilities. The

centralization of government will undermine responsibilities and will destroy the system.

Our government differs from all previous conceptions, not only in this decentralization but also in the separation of functions between the legislative, executive, and judicial arms of government, in which the independence of the judicial arm is the keystone of the whole structure.

It is founded on a conception that in times of emergency, when forces are running beyond control of individuals or other cooperative action, beyond the control of local communities and of states, then the great reserve powers of the federal government shall be brought into action to protect the community. But when these forces have ceased, there must be a return of state, local, and individual responsibility.

The implacable march of scientific discovery with its train of new inventions presents every year new problems to government and new problems to the social order. Questions often arise whether, in the face of the growth of these new and gigantic tools, democracy can remain master in its own house, can preserve the fundamentals of our American system. I contend that it can; and I contend that this American system of ours has demonstrated its validity and superiority over any other system yet invented by human mind.

It has demonstrated it in the face of the greatest test of our history— that is the emergency which we have faced in the past three years.

When the political and economic weakness of many nations of Europe, the result of the World War and its aftermath, finally culminated in collapse of their institutions, the delicate adjustment of our economic and social life received a shock unparalleled in our history. No one knows that better than you of New York. No one knows its causes better than you. That the crisis was so great that many of the leading banks sought directly or indirectly to convert their assets into gold or its equivalent with the result that they practically ceased to function as credit institutions; that many of our citizens sought flight for their capital to other countries; that many of them attempted to hoard gold in large amounts. These were but indications of the flight of confidence and of the belief that our government could not overcome these forces.

Yet these forces were overcome—perhaps by narrow margins—and this action demonstrates what the courage of a nation can accomplish under the resolute leadership in the Republican Party. And I say the Republican Party, because our opponents before and during the crisis, proposed no constructive program; though some of their members patriotically supported ours. Later on the Democratic House of Representatives did develop the real thought and ideas of the Democratic Party, but it was so destructive that it had to be defeated, for it would have destroyed, not healed.

In spite of all these obstructions, we did succeed. Our form of government did prove itself equal to the task. We saved this nation from a quarter of a century of chaos and degeneration, and we preserved the savings, the insurance policies, gave a fighting chance to men to hold their homes. We saved the integrity of our government and the honesty of the American dollar. And we installed measures which today are bringing back recovery. Employment, agriculture, business—all of these show the steady, if slow, healing of our enormous wound.

I therefore contend that the problem of today is to continue these measures and policies to restore this American system to its normal functioning, to repair the wounds it has received, to correct the weaknesses and evils which would defeat that system. To enter upon a series of deep changes, to embark upon this inchoate new deal which has been propounded in this campaign, would be to undermine and destroy our American system.

## DISCUSSION QUESTIONS

1. State governments have always played a role in regulating the economy, from consumer protection to using tax breaks as a way to attract business investment within a state's borders. What kind of economic activities are best regulated at the state level? When should the federal government play a role?

2. Which of the activities that the government performs do you consider essential? Why?

# 73

# "The GDP Myth: Why 'Growth' Isn't Always a Good Thing"

### Jonathan Rowe and Judith Silverstein

*"Gross Domestic Product," or GDP, is a familiar economic term: It is a standard measure of overall economic activity, or, as Jonathan Rowe and Judith Silverstein write, the amount of money that is spent during a particular period of time. Politicians are quick to take credit when the GDP grows, for it is a sign of economic expansion. And when communities are concerned about the environmental or quality-of-life impact of a new development or industrial site, community and business leaders reassure them by pointing to the economic growth that will result. But is all growth good growth? Rowe and Silverstein argue that GDP is an inaccurate measure of overall economic well-being. Higher GDP does not necessarily mean we are better off, since it includes all types of spending—even spending that results from waste (gasoline burned by people sitting in Los Angeles traffic jams), unhealthy activities (consumption of cholesterol-laden foods, and the cardiologists' bills that often result), or pollution (and the efforts to clean up toxic waste). The impact of this "growth" on the public differs from the perceptions of economists and political leaders, who always portray economic growth as a positive. Rowe and Silverstein urge journalists to stop accepting language such as "economic growth" at face value and force politicians, in particular, to be clear about what has grown in the economy, or what will grow.*

George Orwell really did see it coming. "As soon as certain topics are raised," he wrote, "the concrete melts into the abstract." Nowhere does it melt more quickly than in economics. Public discussion of the economy is a hothouse of evasive abstraction. Opinionators and politicians rarely name what they are talking about. Instead they waft into generalities they learned in Economics 101.

The President's [1999] State of the Union Address was a case in point. The President boasted of the "longest peacetime expansion of our history." That's how pols always talk. It sounds like truly wonderful news. But what actually has been expanding? A lot of things can grow, and do. Waistlines grow. Medical bills grow. Traffic, debt, and stress all grow. We can't know whether an "expansion" is good or not unless we know what it includes. Yet the President didn't tell, and the media hordes didn't ask, which was typical too.

A human economy is supposed to advance well-being. That is elementary. Yet politicians and pundits rarely talk about it in those terms. Instead they revert to the language of "expansion," "growth," and the like, which mean something very different. Cut through the boosterism and hysterics, and growth means simply "spending more money." It makes no difference where the money goes, and why. As long as the people spend more of it, the economy is said to "grow."

The technical term for this is "Gross Domestic Product" or GDP, which gives the proceedings an atmosphere of authority and expertise. But it doesn't take a genius to smell the fish. Spending more money doesn't always mean life is getting better. Often it means things are getting worse. This is exceedingly hard for most commentators to grasp. It simply does not fit with the story line we learned in the economics texts. A number of writers have argued, for example, that things are much better than Americans realize, and that only a jaundiced and elitist media obscures this fact. Yes, there is a Cassandra* industry of issue groups on both Left and Right that raise money on dire warnings. Yes, the media gets more attention with bad news than with good. But that doesn't mean Americans are wrong when they tell pollsters that they are concerned about the direction of the nation, even though their own economic fortunes are pretty good. When one looks at what is actually growing in America today, that view makes a lot of sense. Consider a few examples.

*The Flab Factor*

To put this delicately, Americans are becoming quite ample. Over half of us are overweight. The portion of middle-aged Americans who are clinically obese has doubled since the 1960s; it is now one out of three. The number that is grossly overweight—that is, can't fit into an airline seat—has ballooned 350 percent over the past thirty years.

That's a lot of girth, and a prodigious source of growth. Food is roughly a $700 billion industry in the United States, counting agriculture, supermarkets, restaurants and the rest. Unfortunately, a good deal of that industry ends up inside us Americans. The result is flab, and a diet and weight loss industry of some $32 billion nationwide and—yes—growing. Richard Armey, the House majority leader and an economist, has opined that "the market is rational and the government is dumb." Here's a bit of rationality for him. The food industry spends some $21 billion a year on advertising to goad us to eat more. Then we spend that and half again trying to rid ourselves of the inevitable effects.

When diets and treadmills don't work, which is often, there's always

---

* [This refers to the legendary phophetess Cassandra; in this context, it means one who predicts misfortune.]

the vacuum pump or knife. Cosmetic surgery is another booming sector, and much of it aims to detach unwanted pounds. There were roughly 110,000 liposuctions in the nation last year, at a cost of some $2,000 or more apiece. At five pounds per, that's 275 tons of flab up the tube. Pack it in, vac it off; it's pretty rational, especially if you are in the packing or the vacking business—or if, as in Armey's case, you get campaign contributions from those quarters.

Girth is one growth sector with a bright future. With Channel One and billboards filling schools with junk food ads, and with computers joining TV as a sedentary claim on time, kids are becoming broad of beam like their folks. The Surgeon General says childhood obesity is "epidemic," which is bad for kids but good for growth. Clothing lines for the "husky" child are expanding, as are summer camps for over-weight youngsters. Type II diabetes, the kind associated with weight, has quadrupled among kids since 1982, which is a boost for the pharmaco-medical establishment.

Meanwhile, eating disorders such as bulimia have become a growth sector unto themselves. Bulimia may be the trademark affliction of the growth era. It is a disease of literal obedience to the schizoid messages that barrage young girls: indulge yourself wantonly but also be taut and svelte. The teen magazines make the economy grow, and then the treat-ment for bulimia makes it grow more.

*Medical Costs*

If Clinton's clunky medical insurance proposal did nothing else, it at least put the medical insurance industry on good behavior for a while. Those days appear to be over. The Health Care Financing Administration says that nationwide, outlays for medical treatment are likely to double over the next decade. Many small employers already are getting hit with hikes of 20 percent or more.

That means more than a sixth of the economy as conventionally mea-sured will be devoted to treating disease. Not only is that major GDP; it's also a product of GDP. C. Everett Koop, the Surgeon General in the Reagan Administration, has said that some 70 percent of the nation's medical bill stems from preventable illnesses—that is, ones that are mainly lifestyle induced. We eat too much, drink too much, smoke too much, watch too much TV, absorb too much stress, and dump too many toxic substances into our air and water.

We are literally growing ourselves sick, and the resulting medical bills make the economy grow more. A study by the American Public Health Association a few years ago found that the United States could cut its medical costs by $17 billion a year if we all cut our daily intake of fat by just 8 grams, the amount in half a cup of premium ice cream.

"One way to reduce health costs is to get people to use the health care system less frequently," Dr. Koop said sensibly—but not rationally by Armey's standard. If people watched less TV, drove less, ate less but more healthfully, there would be less growth. So instead we resort to high-tech—and expensive—drugs and treatments to undo what we have done.

*Such Service*

When politicians crow about an expanding economy they make a big assumption—that people actually get something for the money they spend. That's life in the economics textbooks but not in the world we inhabit. W. Steven Albrecht, an accounting professor at Brigham Young University, estimates that white-collar fraud costs us some $200 billion a year. (The yearly take of burglars and robbers is more like $4 billion.) That estimate is probably low. Americans lose at least $40 billion a year to telemarketing fraud alone.

In an era of deregulation and belief in benign "market forces," the toll gets steadily worse. Phone bills and the like have become horrendously complex, for example. The Federal Communications Commission received 10,000 calls a month in the first five months of last year from people who couldn't understand their bills. The complexity has spawned a practice called "cramming" in which third parties slip phony charges for dating services, psychic help lines and the like into a generic category in the bill. Then there are the no-armed bandits that operate on practically every street corner under the alias "ATM machines." When banks began to install these in the late 1970s they promised lower costs and therefore lower fees. Today we literally have to pay for access to our own money, and increasingly we pay twice. The average bank customer in the United States pays over $150 a year in ATM fees, according to a study by the U.S. Public Interest Research Group. In California alone, ATM users pay over $1.5 billion a year, or as much as people making between $30,000 and $50,000 pay in state income taxes.

In their unfailing instinct for euphemism, economists call this a "service" industry. Banks pay us 1 to 2 percent for our deposits, loan the money to someone else at up to 18 percent, and then they tax us when we take our own money back. Good service. Next time the pols start touting "tax cuts," let's hope our alert media friends think to ask them about the privatized tax systems like this that take those cuts away.

*Pluck the Price-Payer*

How do they get away with it? Wise investing doesn't hurt. Banking interests put some $17 million into the last federal elections, not counting in-kind payments, loans and "soft money" contributions to political parties and the like. It doesn't take a cynic to suspect a connection between such outlays and the ability of the banks to impose their money-access tax upon the rest of us. When politicians hail the nation's "robust growth," they are talking in part about the robust flow of money to themselves. In California, campaign spending reached half a billion dollars this year, a new record. It is growing faster than major league baseball salaries. In national politics the cost of congressional campaigns has grown four times faster than the economy as a whole; and again, that's not counting "soft money." Few Americans would say that politics has gotten four times better over that time.

It is easy to forget that economically, the campaign finance system works much like the ATM machines: It gets us coming and going. First we provide the money that interest groups pass along to politicians. (The American Bankers Association doesn't pick its money from trees, but rather from us.) Next the pols support policies that enable such interest groups to extract still more from us. The pols get a cut of that extraction in the next round of campaign contributions, and the wheel turns again.

*Debt*

Americans have a new role in the world. No longer are we the arsenal of democracy, the sturdy producers of Depression-era murals. We are now consumers, the insatiable maws whose buying keeps the world economy afloat. "Amid the turmoil [in Asia]" *The Wall Street Journal* reports, "the U.S. consumer is emerging as a savior of sorts." Jim Hoagland of *The Washington Post* called this consumer "a truly heroic figure."

World salvation is serious business, and the United States fulfills this global obligation the way it has fought its wars—with borrowed money. Consumer debt has burgeoned in the United States. It has grown 73 percent since 1993 and is now some $1.5 trillion, which is about the size of the economy of France. (That doesn't even count home mortgages, which add about $3.8 trillion more.) The average American household has 11 credit cards and owes some $7,000 on them at any given time, plus the car loan and the mortgage.

If Americans feel apprehensive about the future, it just might be in part because they have burdened that future with debt. Yet debt is the Viagra of a growth economy in middle age. It provides an appearance of robust function when in reality we are borrowing ourselves into a financial hole. First the buying itself makes the GDP go up. About half of retail sales today—some $1.4 trillion—are done with debt. Then there's the interest on consumer debt, which comes to over $150 billion a year and growing. Buy a car on time and you can end up paying more for the money than you do for the car. The GDP adds the two together and calls it growth. If Americans paid their bills on time, the money they saved on interest would amount to a 100 percent federal income tax cut for everyone making between $20,000 to $50,000 a year.

But less debt would mean less GDP. It also would mean less business for the satellite industries that have grown up around debt. According to the Small Business Administration, the fastest growing small business in the country over the next decade will be debt collection. Employment there will increase at twice the rate of small business as a whole. Curb debt and you reduce the need for people to collect the debt, which is bad for growth. You also reduce the need for debt counselors and bankruptcy lawyers. Bankruptcies have doubled over this decade, with more to come. "We're going to be happy next year, but nobody else is," said the president of the Bankruptcy Institute, a lawyer's organization.

Consumer debt is another growth sector with a big future. Banks send out over 800 million credit card solicitations every three months, which will come as no surprise to most Americans who receive mail. Today some 28 percent of households making under $10,000 a year have cards, and over half of college students. Students get free T-shirts and Frisbees in college registration lines if they sign up for cards. Of course, many of these students are already in debt for tens of thousands of dollars because of student loans.

In the eyes of the opinion class there is nothing wrong with this. To the contrary, in the words of the *Post*'s Hoagland, it means that we "consumers" will continue to shoulder the world's burdens "by continuing to borrow, spend and consume with impressive single-mindedness." The only danger is that we might become less debt prone, but our banks are on the job. They are starting to punish customers who pay their bills on time. These conscientious citizens are now "freeloaders" who must bear extra fees, shortened grace periods, even cancellation of their cards.

*Growing Nowhere*

Clichés become that for a reason. When people associate growth with traffic, it's because that's how they experience it in their lives. Traffic is a plague; but it's both a result of growth and also a big source of it. In the strange abstracted world of economics, a plague is good so long as it makes us spend more money.

In California, pace-setter in traffic as in other things, drivers are experts on this subject. Los Angeles has been the most car-congested city in the country for 14 years running, and the rest of the state is not far behind. It's a lot of annoyance, but also a lot of gas. Angelenos alone burn over $800 million a year in gas while they sit in traffic and fume, and Americans generally spend over $4 billion more. That's GDP and the economic future toward which much of urban America is headed.

Cars fume too, of course, which means bad air and respiratory diseases. LA leads the nation, if that's the word, in hospital admissions due to asthma, bronchitis, and other breathing problems, which adds to the state's staggering medical bill. More traffic also means more car crashes. There's a collision almost every minute on California's crowded roads, which helps make car wrecks a $130 billion a year industry in the United States.

Call it the multiplier effect of misery. Yet as the roads become more clogged, the auto makers are pushing sports utility vehicles that burn more gas, take up more space, and do more damage when they crash. But they cost a fortune and that adds to growth. Meanwhile, the traffic takes a heavy toll on the roads themselves. Maintaining them costs some $800 million a year in California, and $20 billion in the nation; California drivers spend some $1.2 billion a year on extra car repairs because the roads are in such bad shape.

That's all GDP. So too is at least part of the $35–$40 billion the nation spends defending the foreign oil supplies that fuel all this misery and havoc.

*Stress*

Prosperity is supposed to bring satisfaction and peace. But today's version has led the other way. As the GDP has risen and the economy expands, Americans have felt more harried and under siege. Stress is a factor in over 70 percent of all doctor visits, according to the National Institute of Mental Health. "Nearly every patient I see leads a life influenced in some way by inordinate levels of stress," writes Dr. Richard Swenson of the University of Wisconsin Medical School in his book *Margin*. Stress is in large measure a product of the economy. It comes from the barrage of stimuli, the prolixity of choices, the pressures to perform and the multiplying claims upon our attention and time, which drive a rising GDP. Stress also is a producer of growth, in the form of an enlarging treatment industry of counselors, relaxation tapes, seminars, and spas. Sedatives and mood-enhancers of various kinds are roughly a $6 billion industry. Over 28 million Americans now use Prozac and kindred drugs. (Technically, Prozac is for depression. But the lines between depression and stress are blurry at best.) Even kids are taking these drugs; at last count, some one-half million and rising. Whether that's good for kids is questionable; that it's good for growth is not. "Antidepressant makers need a new market as growth slows in the adult segment," *The Wall Street Journal* explained. A Bay Area teenager told what happens when a society redefines a whole generation as a drug market "segment." "Close to half of the 15- to 18-year-olds I know are on Prozac," she wrote in *YO! Magazine*. "Their parents will do anything to get their kids to achieve, behave, clean their rooms—whatever—including supplying them with the latest in personality-altering drugs."

*A Simple Question*

The more closely one looks the more one understands the feelings of ambiguity in the land. We are glad for jobs and a buoyant stock market. But we are uneasy about the world we are creating in the process. Is growth an unalloyed good when the fastest growing industry of the '90s is gambling? Not entirely coincidentally, the prison business is another booming sector. Since 1980 it has grown five times over. Inmate pay-phone calls alone yield over a billion dollars a year.

Even the mundane and once-innocuous elements of growth can give one pause today. Are we really happy about the aggressive marketing that makes kids obsessed with brand names? Clothing sales go up, but parents have to pay, and others too, sometimes dearly. In January, in Prince George's County, a Washington suburb, three teen-agers were shot within a single 20-minute period. In each case the object of the assault was an Eddie Bauer jacket. Police refer to such incidents as "fashion crime."

It's little wonder that politicians and pundits resort instinctively to the abstract when they talk about the economy. The particulars are turning into a somewhat murky soup. They keep telling us they can solve the nation's problems with more "growth." Yet increasingly problems are what the GDP consists of. This syndrome has become an unacknowledged subtext in much of the daily news. The AP reported recently on a part of eastern Oregon that is the fastest growing in the state. The source of this prosperity? A state prison and a nerve gas incinerator, along with a Wal-Mart distribution center and a railroad maintenance yard. Similarly, there is a pesticide plant in Richmond, California that is owned by the Zeneca Group, an $8 billion corporation that also makes the breast cancer drug tamoxifen. Many researchers believe that pesticides, and the toxins created in the production of them, play a role in breast cancer.

"It's a pretty good deal," a local physician told the *East Bay Express*, a local weekly. "First you cause the cancer, then you profit from curing it." She was overstating of course, but the fact remains: both alleged cause and cure make the GDP go up.

Some economists would dismiss this as wrong headed. If people didn't spend their money on such things as cancer treatments and gas to stand still in traffic, they say, they'd spend it on something else. Growth would be the same or even more. In other words, we shouldn't worry about exactly what is growing because hypothetically it could be something else. The argument approaches professional self-parody. It is fine for those who have the luxury of dealing with the economy through computer models. But for the rest of us who have to deal with the economy in concrete terms, the question of what exactly is expanding matters a great deal.

This doesn't mean the end of growth. Rather, it means the end of the assumption that anything called "growth" is automatically good. It means a need to stop using a euphemistic language that has that assumption built in. Republicans argue, for example, that the government should use the budget surplus for tax cuts because individual Americans will use the money more "rationally" than the awful government would.

Maybe so. But to look at where the money actually goes these days gives one pause. Is it really more "rational" to feed traffic jams as opposed to investing more in other forms of transit? Does the high-growth industry of gambling really do more for the country than the lower growth industry (at least in the short term) of building new inner-city schools with bathrooms that work? Would more Eddie Bauer jackets really do more for the country than better teachers?

We won't even get to these questions unless we start talking about the economy as it is, rather than the way economists tend to think about it. The job is going to fall first to journalists, who frame the first draft of reality for the public mind. They've got to start to articulate the economy as Americans experience it; and to do this, reporters have got to cleanse their minds of the vocabulary and assumptions of economic doctrine and explore the economic dimension of our lives with uncluttered eyes. That's a big assignment, but it starts with a very simple question. The next time a Jack Kemp, say, promises to double the rate of growth, as he did in the vice presidential debate in '96, don't call Brookings or Heritage [political analysis institutes] to find out if it is possible in macroeconomic terms. Reporters must insist on details, as they would with any other story. Exactly what is going to double? Traffic? Consumer debt? Jet skis? The use of mood-altering pharmaceuticals? The next time the Commerce Department releases the GDP figures, don't just call a Wall Street "analyst" for comment. Insist on knowing what those flows of money are leaving in their wake—that is, exactly what is growing and the effects. If official Washington doesn't have this data then find out why not.

People don't experience "growth." They experience the things that growth consists of; and that's where good reporting begins. Until reporters start to look at these issues from the standpoint of those who experience the economy rather than those who pontificate about it, they are going to remain where many readers think they are—in another world.

## DISCUSSION QUESTIONS

1. If all growth (increases in spending) is not necessarily good growth, how can we distinguish between "good" growth and "bad" growth? What social factors might we consider? Would it be possible to have agreement on which factors to include? In other words, this may be an interesting theoretical discussion, but would it be politically possible to implement?

2. In public policy debates, analysts often distinguish "economic" indicators—inflation, unemployment, consumer spending—from "social" indicators, such as crime, divorce, school dropout rates, and teen pregnancies. In light of Rowe and Silverstein's argument, is this separation appropriate? Why or why not?

## DEBATING THE ISSUES: HOW TO REDUCE THE FEDERAL BUDGET DEFICIT

In the second edition of this book, we had a "Debating the Issues" section on "What to do with the Budget Surplus?" How times change! After running budget surpluses from 1998 through 2001, averaging about $140 billion per year, deficits shot up to more than $500 billion a year in 2004, with red ink projected to continue as far as projections are made. In November 2004, Congress raised the debt limit to $8.18 *trillion* dollars, which is nearly $28,000 of debt for every man, woman, and child in the United States. Under the White House's current projections, the accumulated federal debt between 2001 and 2011 will be as large as the total debt built up between 1789 and 2000!

The practice of deficit spending by the national government has been the subject of intense debate for many years. When the government spends more than it gathers in taxes and borrows to cover the deficit each year, is it an immoral and irresponsible act that will burden future generations, or is deficit spending and borrowing a practical investment in the future for building a national infrastructure and educating our children? In general, the answer to these questions are, "It depends." However, with deficits that are so large and debt that is accumulating at such an alarming rate, nearly all economists and most politicians agree that something has to be done to reduce (or some say, eliminate) the deficits. The difficult question, of course, is how to do that. In the most basic terms, the only way to reduce the deficit is to cut spending or increase taxes. The authors of this debate put forward several alternative scenarios.

Alice Rivlin and Isabel Sawhill, of the left-of-center think tank the Brookings Institution, begin by explaining why budget deficits are a problem. They also show that as bad as the numbers look right now, they are only going to get worse as the baby boomers start to retire. Right now Medicare, Medicaid, and Social Security take up 42 percent of the budget, but that percentage will grow dramatically over the next several decades. Economic growth will not take care of the problem, and they argue that "neither political party currently has a workable plan for reducing the long-term deficit." They propose three alternatives, each of which requires both spending cuts and tax increases. They label their plans as the "small government, large government, and better government" options. They do not state a strong preference for one plan over the others, but say that the "better government" plan is "likely to be more politically feasible than the other two over the next few years." One of their most forcefully stated conclusions is that any plan to balance the budget is going to have to raise taxes.

Brian M. Riedl couldn't disagree more. While he would agree with Rivlin and Sawhill's conclusion that budget deficits are "out of control and could do serious damage to the economy in the coming decades," Riedl sees the culprit as excessive spending. He rejects the calls for higher taxes and says that restraining spending will do the trick; however, he recognizes that it won't be easy. He begins by explaining why previous attempts at restraining spending have not worked (including the PAYGO provision of the budgeting process endorsed by Rivlin and Sawhill). Arguing that lawmakers will "exploit every possible weakness in spending constraints," the only possible solution is a "taxpayers' bill of rights" (or TABOR). Just as state governments led the way on welfare reform, Riedl says that Congress should pay attention to the success of a similar plan in Colorado. The idea is to limit the growth of spending to population growth and inflation (about 3.3% when the article was written). If some part of the budget is growing faster than others, such as Social Security and Medicare, then other parts of the budget will have to be cut to make up for it. Riedl concludes that TABOR is needed to "protect the family budget from the federal budget."

# 74

# "How to Balance the Budget"

## Alice M. Rivlin and Isabel V. Sawhill

The federal government is spending about $500 billion a year more than it is raising in taxes. If nothing is done, that gap will widen to around $700 billion annually by 2014 and accelerate rapidly thereafter, as baby boomers begin to retire.

Persistent deficits of this magnitude are likely to lower standards of living, make us dangerously dependent on the rest of the world, and pass on large fiscal burdens to future generations. Balancing the budget, while politically difficult, must be a priority. In an effort to stimulate debate over a compromise that would appeal to different groups, we present three ways to achieve balance over the next ten years. One option emphasizes spending cuts and leads to a smaller government. A second relies on tax increases and leads to bigger government. The third maintains government's current size, but makes it more effective, and contains a mix of spending reductions and tax increases, sufficient to achieve balance in ten years while preserving room for some high-priority new initiatives.

We conclude that neither political party currently has a workable plan for reducing the long-term deficit, that both spending cuts and tax increases will be needed, and that stronger budget process rules would help members of Congress be more fiscally responsible.

*An Overview of the Federal Budget*

In 2003, the federal government spent $2.2 trillion. Over two-fifths of this spending was for just three large programs: Social Security, Medicare, and Medicaid. About a third of current spending is for other (primarily) domestic programs—everything from unemployment insurance and farm subsidies to national parks, education, and programs for the poor. Many of these programs are funded through the annual appropriations process and, as a result, are referred to as "discretionary" since the funding for them is less automatic than spending on "mandatory" programs, such as Social Security or unemployment insurance. A significant chunk of the budget goes for defense (19 percent) and for interest on the debt (7 percent).

## Why Sustained Deficits are Harmful

Not all budget deficits are bad—indeed, recent deficits accelerated recovery from the recession that began in 2001. But longer-term deficits of the current magnitude are harmful for five reasons:

They slow economic growth. By 2014, the average family's income will be an estimated $1,800 lower because of the slower income growth that results when government competes with the private sector for a limited pool of savings or borrows more from other countries.

They increase household borrowing costs. A family with a $250,000, thirty-year mortgage, for example, will pay an additional $2,000 a year in interest.

They increase indebtedness to foreigners, which is both expensive and risky. The United States is the largest net debtor in the world. The income of Americans will ultimately be reduced by the interest, dividends, and profits paid to foreigners who have invested in the United States. Moreover, if foreigners lose confidence in the American economy—or begin to worry that the United States is not managing its fiscal affairs responsibly—they may reduce their investment. This can decrease the value of the dollar and raise the prices we have to pay for imported goods. If the dollar's fall were precipitous, it could cause rapid increases in interest rates, recession, or even a serious financial crisis.

They require that a growing proportion of federal revenues be devoted to paying interest on the national debt, which is estimated to increase by more than $5 trillion over the next decade. By 2014, this increase in government borrowing will cost the average household $3,000 in added interest on the debt alone. One out of every five tax dollars will need to be set aside for this purpose.

They impose enormous burdens on future generations. Today's children and young adults and their descendants will have to pay more because this generation has been fiscally irresponsible. At the same time, deficits and rising interest costs are likely to put downward pressure on spending for education, nutrition, and health care that could make today's children more productive and thus better able to pay these future obligations.

*The Budget Outlook*

Less than three years ago, in fiscal year 2001, the federal budget, was running a surplus of $127 billion. But a weak economy, tax cuts, spending increases, and a lack of concern for fiscal discipline turned the surplus into a deficit predicted to be over $500 billion in 2004. This shift in federal finances from deficit to surplus would not be a serious concern if it were temporary. Unfortunately, however, the current deficits are projected to continue for the next decade, rising to around $700 billion in 2014. Indeed, if the temporary surpluses in Social Security, Medicare, and federal retirement programs were not masking the size of the deficits in the rest of the budget, the deficit estimate for 2014 would exceed $1 trillion. These projections are based on those of the Congressional Budget Office (CBO), but they assume that the tax cuts enacted in recent years are made permanent, as the president has proposed, and that Congress will amend the alternative minimum tax (AMT) to prevent an increase in the number of taxpayers subject to the AMT. They also assume discretionary spending increases in line with population growth as well as with inflation—that is, real discretionary spending per person is held constant—and include the cost of the prescription drug benefit and other changes in Medicare enacted at the end of the first session of the 108th Congress.

*Deficits Beyond 2014*

A major additional reason for concern about continuous large deficits is that pressures on the budget are certain to escalate rapidly as the baby boom generation retires and longevity continues to increase. The CBO projects that even if medical care costs rise only 1 percent faster than per capita GDP—an optimistic assumption in view of recent increases— expenditures for providing existing benefits under Social Security, Medicare, and Medicaid would rise from 9.0 percent of GDP in 2010 to 14.3 percent in 2030 and to 17.7 percent in 2050. These exploding future costs highlight the need to address the challenge of reforming these entitlement programs as soon as possible. They also make clear the importance of fiscal policy that contributes to future economic growth by enhancing national saving—not reducing both growth and saving by running continuous deficits over the coming decade.

## Can Growth Solve the Problem?

Deficits are very sensitive to the rate of economic growth. Should the economy grow faster than the 3 percent rate, in real terms, assumed by the CBO and most private forecasters, deficits will be smaller. If the economy grows more slowly than this, they will be still larger. Some believe that recent changes in tax law will lead to higher rates of economic growth. But as long as these tax cuts are deficit financed, the weight of professional opinion suggests that they will not lead to higher growth.

### The Administration's Plan

In the administration's fiscal year 2005 budget, released in February of this year, the president proposes to reduce the deficit, as a share of GDP, by half over the next five years. If the recovery continues and the economy performs well, the deficit should decline for this reason alone. However, many analysts are skeptical that it will decline as much as the administration predicts. The full costs of the wars in Afghanistan and Iraq are not included. The AMT that will hit millions of middle class families with higher tax bills over the next five years is not fixed. And the assumptions about the government's ability to restrain domestic discretionary spending are very optimistic.

But even if some combination of policy actions and a strong economy reduces deficits over the next few years, they are almost certain to balloon again after that; and the administration has no long-term plan for restoring fiscal balance. The president's budget proposal for fiscal year 2005 recognized the importance of deficit reduction by announcing a goal of cutting the deficit in half (as a percent of GDP) in five years. However, after the five-year period, the red ink would flow even faster if the administration's plans were adopted. In addition to proposing to make the recently enacted tax cuts permanent (assumed in our own estimates of future deficits), the president's budget advocated new tax-preferred savings accounts and a Social Security plan that, if adopted, would increase deficit spending far beyond the projections in this study.

### Three Different Ways of Getting to Balance

In our book, *Restoring Fiscal Sanity*, we propose three alternative plans for balancing the budget over the next ten years. They differ in the mix of spending cuts and revenue increases used to achieve balance. All three plans start from our adjusted baseline projections, which indicate that in the absence of policy change, the deficit in 2014 will be about $687 billion. (This estimate and others in the table are based on the Congressional

Budget Office's August 2003 report, adjusted in the ways described above. CBO revised their forecast in December 2003 but these revisions, do not materially affect our analysis in any important way.)

Balancing the unified budget by 2014 will produce interest savings of around $153 billion, leaving a deficit of $534 billion to be eliminated by spending reductions or revenue increases in that year. If we chose the more stringent criterion of balancing the budget excluding the federal retirement programs, it would be necessary to reduce the deficit by another $316 billion. Although achieving the larger goal would be desirable, the plans amply illustrate that even meeting the less ambitious target requires tough choices that are sure to be unpopular.

*The Smaller Government Plan*

The smaller government plan would reduce total spending as a share of GDP from 20.2 percent in 2003 to 18.3 percent in 2014. It balances the budget primarily by cutting $400 billion from projected domestic spending in 2014.

These cuts are achieved by reducing government subsidies to commercial activities ($138 billion); returning responsibility for education, housing, training, environmental, and law enforcement programs to the states ($123 billion); slowing the growth of other nondefense discretionary spending ($58 billion); cutting entitlements such as Medicaid, Social Security, and Medicare ($74 billion); and eliminating some wasteful spending in these entitlement programs ($7 billion).

Revenue increases of $134 billion are added to the package, primarily by raising the gas tax, lowering but not repealing the estate tax, and improving enforcement of existing tax laws. Although tax increases are unpopular with those who favor smaller government, no one has suggested how to achieve balance without them. Moreover, the revenue measures included in this plan are relatively modest, they are focused on compliance with existing laws, and they avoid changes in the tax rates or brackets enacted in 2001 and 2003.

*The Larger Government Plan*

A larger government plan would increase total spending as a share of GDP from 20.2 percent in 2003 to 20.9 percent in 2014. The increase occurs partly because some existing programs are slated to grow rapidly over the coming decade, as the population ages and the costs of health care rise, and partly because the plan includes additional spending for health care, education, and some other priorities that are only partially offset by savings in existing programs. Paying for this new spending and balancing the budget requires that taxes be raised substantially. Revenue measures that would accomplish this objective include scaling back the 2001 tax cuts that benefited the affluent, eliminating the Social Security earnings ceiling so that all earnings would be taxable, and creating a new value-added tax that would affect almost everyone.

*The Better Government Plan*

The better government plan is based on the assumption that government has a positive role to play in improving people's lives but could perform this function far more effectively than it does now. What distinguishes the better government plan from the other two is that instead of changing the size of government, it reallocates spending in ways designed to improve government performance. The plan is likely to be more politically feasible than the other two over the next few years, no matter what the outcome of the 2004 presidential election. The next president will face a huge fiscal hole that cannot realistically be filled by spending cuts or revenue increases alone, and so a very substantial amount of both will be needed.

## National Security

Brookings experts Lael Brainard and Michael O'Hanlon, who wrote the portion of our budget report that addresses national security, argue that the United States can use the tools of hard power (military force), soft power (diplomacy and foreign assistance), and domestic counterterrorism (homeland security). These tools are complementary and the national security budget is best viewed as a unified whole. The better government plan calls for cuts in defense spending, but these are only possible because it is assumed that the reconstruction of Iraq will have been completed by 2014. The world is likely still to be a dangerous place in 2014, defense costs per uniformed member of the armed forces have generally risen by 2 to 3 percent a year, major weapons systems are aging and need to be modernized, and health care costs for military personnel are rising rapidly. Thus containment of defense spending to the levels assumed in this plan will only be possible if weapons modernization is very selective, if privatization of military support operations is more cost effective than it has been in the past, and if it proves feasible to share more of the defense burden with our allies.

While some cuts in defense spending are possible under this scenario, the plan calls for more spending on homeland security and foreign assistance. In the wake of the September 11 terrorist attacks, air travel is safer, more intelligence is being shared, and ports and public infrastructure are better protected, but additional steps are needed in these areas as well as in some others, such as protecting private infrastructure (chemical plants and trucking, for example). Finally, U.S. foreign assistance is arguably as important as military power in making the world a safer place. This assistance should be increased, but it could be allocated and organized far more effectively than at present, including combating global poverty.

## Domestic Programs

In the domestic arena, it is possible to trim spending on existing domestic programs sufficiently to both fund some new initiatives and contribute savings toward the goal of balancing the budget. The plan proposes modest additional outlays in a number of areas, including restructuring the safety net to encourage and reward work, improving preschool opportunities for disadvantaged children, extending health care coverage to lower-income families, and helping states fund the costs of the extensive testing and teacher training required by the No Child Left Behind Act of 2001. These kinds of public investments, if appropriately structured, can increase productivity and growth as much or more than private investments in new technologies, facilities, and equipment, while simultaneously creating opportunities for everyone to participate more fully in a stronger economy. There must also be more attention given to energy efficiency and a clean environment, but this need not increase budgetary costs. The best way to achieve these goals is to use taxes or a system of auctioned and tradable emissions permits to align the price of energy use with its social costs. The added revenue can then be used to help close the fiscal gap.

To fund the new initiatives and contribute savings toward balancing the budget, our proposal contains a menu of spending cuts that is far more selective than that of the smaller government plan. But like the smaller government plan, it attempts to identify programs, like farm subsidies, that provide unwarranted assistance to commercial activities or to state and local governments (for example, construction grants for wastewater and drinking water). It also includes cuts to programs—such as manned space flight—that have not produced benefits commensurate with their costs and to programs—such as student loans—that could be administered more efficiently.

## Entitlement Programs

Social Security, Medicare, and Medicaid are badly in need of long-term reforms, which will be less disruptive if they are made soon. But because significant cuts in benefits for retirees or people who are already close to retirement age are not desirable, such reforms will produce few budgetary savings over the next decade. Nonetheless, some savings are identified, primarily from accelerating (to 2012) implementation of the already enacted increase in the retirement age under Social Security, from more accurate inflation adjustments to Social Security benefits, and from increased premiums for Medicare.

Revenue Increases

Despite its reliance on a number of very controversial spending cuts, the better government plan necessarily depends heavily on revenue increases to achieve balance in 2014. Revenues as a share of GDP fell from 20.8 percent to 16.6 percent between 2000 and 2003, so all three plans—including the smaller government plan—must use revenue increases to fill at least some of the fiscal gap. The better government plan relies on revenue increases to fill 75 percent of this gap. The biggest increases in revenue come from returning the top four income tax rates to 2000 levels, raising the Social Security earnings ceiling so that 90 percent of earnings are taxable, repealing the 2003 capital gains and dividend tax reductions, and retaining the estate tax with a higher exemption. We refer to these changes as tax increases, but many are only increases relative to our adjusted baseline. Compared with the official tax code, which assumes that the tax cuts enacted in 2001, 2002, and 2003 will expire in 2010 or before, for most people the changes will still result in a tax reduction.

*Improving the Budget Process*

Reform of the budget process is essential to restoring fiscal discipline, and should involve at least three elements:

- Caps on discretionary spending that extend for ten years;
- "Pay-as-you-go" rules requiring that any tax cut or increase in mandatory spending be fully "paid for" by offsetting spending or tax changes over a ten-year period, and that these changes normally not be assumed to sunset;
- A stricter definition of "emergency spending."

While process reform alone will not restore fiscal responsibility, it can strengthen the resolve of politicians to do the right thing as well as provide political cover for resisting deficit-increasing actions.

*Conclusion*

America's fiscal situation is out of control and could do serious damage to the economy in the coming decades. It could sap U.S. economic strength—making it much more difficult to respond to unforeseen contingencies—and pass an unfair burden to future generations. However, no one in a political position to do something about the problem has thus far crafted an adequate solution. Unless policymakers move quickly to find a compromise and enact reforms, the budget problem will only get worse.

# 75

# "Restrain Runaway Spending with a Federal Taxpayers' Bill of Rights"

## Brian M. Riedl

Federal spending has leaped 25 percent since 2001, exceeding $20,000 per household. Frustrated taxpayers are seeking ways to protect their family budgets from the federal budget. These taxpayers should look to Colorado.

In 1992, Colorado citizens revolted against their free-spending lawmakers by petitioning for a referendum to limit the growth of state government to the inflation rate plus the population growth rate. Voters quickly approved the Taxpayers' Bill of Rights (TABOR), ushering in a new era of fiscal responsibility and economic growth. Over the next decade, spending was reined in, taxes plummeted, and the Colorado economy became the envy of the nation.

Just as Congress followed the states' lead on welfare reform in the 1990s, it should follow the states' lead on spending limits. A federal Taxpayers' Bill of Rights would succeed where other budget reforms have failed. It would protect taxpayers' paychecks by forcing lawmakers to live under constraints—just like families, business, and state and local governments do. This paper explains how such a policy could work.

*The Failure of Other Options*

During the past decade, reforming the budget process has been an exercise in futility. Lawmakers who focus obsessively on a single $100,000 pork project pay scant attention to the overall budgetary framework used to allocate $2.3 trillion in federal spending. When budget process reform is finally debated, lawmakers focus more on protecting their committees' turfs than on fixing the budget problems. The rare (and overly arcane) reforms that are enacted are first watered down to irrelevance and then riddled with loopholes. All four reforms of the budget process that have been tried in the past decade have failed.

Pay-As-You-Go (PAYGO) Rules and Discretionary Spending Caps.

PAYGO rules, in place from 1990 through 2002, mandated that any new law cutting taxes or expanding entitlements be balanced by equal tax increases or entitlement cuts. It was an abysmal failure: Mandatory spending actually grew faster *after* PAYGO was enacted. It failed because it limited only the creation of new entitlements, while allowing current programs—such as Social Security Medicare, Medicaid, and farm subsidies—to expand rapidly. Additionally, PAYGO placed barriers on tax relief, and Congress easily dismissed PAYGO rules when they became inconvenient.

Discretionary spending caps, written every three to five years, were more successful. Yet, even caps were too easily disregarded by lawmakers, who could exempt any program simply by labeling it an "emergency." In the House of Representatives, caps could be waived with a simple majority vote. Recently, Members of the House strongly rejected a measure that would have restored discretionary spending caps—effectively refusing to accept any statutory limit on their ability to spend tax dollars.

### The Family Budget Protection Act.

Proposed by several conservatives and moderates in the House, the Family Budget Protection Act (FBPA) contained over one dozen important procedural reforms.[1] These included converting the concurrent budget resolution into a joint budget resolution (which would have the force of law), entitlement caps, point-of-order reform, enhanced rescission, and rules making it easier to save money in appropriations bills. Instead of a bias toward bigger government and higher taxes, the budget process would finally protect taxpayers. Regrettably, these reforms were overwhelmingly defeated in the House.

The FBPA was rejected, in part, because it was too arcane to be understood outside the Beltway. Lawmakers are typically interested in protecting their committees' turf and retaining their ability to distribute government benefits. Only a popular outcry from the voters back home will persuade most lawmakers to overcome their own bias and vote for fiscal responsibility. Because the FBPA was too complex to be understood by most voters, there was no popular push for it, and lawmakers were free to reject it without serious political consequences.

### Balanced Budget Amendment.

Unlike the FBPA, the balanced budget amendment is widely understood by the American people (which is why it receives broader support from lawmakers, despite being a more radical reform). The movement for a balanced budget amendment has stalled as well, not only because the budget reached surplus between 1998 and 2001, but also because constitutional amendments are extremely difficult to enact.

Additionally, a balanced budget amendment focuses on the wrong issue. The budget deficit is merely a symptom; runaway spending is the disease. The United States could balance the budget tomorrow by raising taxes to levels that would devastate families, businesses, and the economy. Instead of seeing deficit reduction as end in itself, lawmakers should focus on the runaway spending that creates the deficits and high taxes in the first place.

## Trust Lawmakers to Cut Spending.

Lawmakers continue to work within a budget framework designed 30 years ago to maximize federal spending. Many Members of Congress claim that they can cut spending on their own and do not need any budget process reforms or spending limits to enforce what they plan to do anyway. This viewpoint represents the triumph of hope over experience. These lawmakers are absolutely correct that people, not process, are ultimately to blame for runaway spending. However, persistent runaway spending provides ample evidence that lawmakers are unable to control spending on their own without outside constraints.

According to public choice theory, lawmakers have incentives to continually expand government. This is exactly what is happening. The current federal budget process requires no priority setting, no trade offs, and no difficult decisions. Families operate under external budget constraints, as does virtually every state government. It is naïve and ahistorical to believe that Members of Congress will resist the budget process prospending bias and reduce spending on their own.

### Five Lessons

Five lessons can be drawn from these failures:

1. Members of Congress will not make difficult spending trade-offs unless required by law.
2. Although a constitutional amendment would be the most enforceable means of reform, it is too difficult to enact.
3. A successful proposal for reforming the budget process must be understood and strongly supported by voters in order to overcome the turf-protection and pro-spending bias in Congress.
4. Spending constraints should put all spending on the table—mandatory and discretionary, current and proposed. All programs should have to compete with each other for the limited federal funds.
5. Members of Congress will exploit every possible weakness in spending constraints.

### The Promise of a Taxpayers' Bill of Rights

A Taxpayers' Bill of Rights presents a simple, yet effective way to curb runaway spending. TABOR would limit the growth of federal spending to the inflation rate plus population growth. Rather than growing 6.4 percent annually (the average during the past five years), federal spending would typically increase by approximately 3.3 percent annually. Although this slower growth rate may not seem like a significant change, it would save taxpayers more than $4 trillion over the next 10 years.

Limiting annual federal spending growth to approximately 3.3 percent is not too much to ask of Congress, especially considering that the federal budget has expanded by 30 percent in the past five years and contains hundreds of billions of dollars worth of wasteful and obsolete programs. The current $2.3 trillion federal budget would still be large enough to fund all current programs, and these programs could continue growing at the inflation rate plus the population growth rate. Programs that expand at faster rates would need to be offset by reductions in the growth rates of other programs.

## Six Principles of a Federal TABOR

A federal Taxpayers' Bill of Rights should follow six basic principles:

### Principle 1: A TABOR Should Restrict Spending Growth, Not Revenues.

High tax rates devastate economies. Yet a law simply requiring low tax revenues without any spending controls is not sustainable because unrestrained spending would likely create unallowably large budget deficits until taxes would need to be raised. The simple truth is that federal spending determines the required level of taxes. Therefore, a law limiting federal spending is the most effective way to guarantee long-term tax relief.

Furthermore, lawmakers cannot exercise much control over tax revenues. Economic trends create short-run revenue fluctuations that make it nearly impossible to target a specified revenue level. A TABOR would be more effective by focusing on spending, which lawmakers can directly control.

TABOR spending restrictions can easily avoid two predictable problems: First, in order to prevent forecasting games, the TABOR inflation and population growth allowances should be a rolling average of the previous three years' rates. Second, TABOR should apply to outlays (actual expenditures) rather than budget authority (the credit limit Congress provides to an agency to spend down). Over the past few years, Congress has manipulated budget authority amounts to the point that they have become meaningless. Outlays are what matter because they are actual expenditures of taxpayer money.

Principle 2: TABOR Spending Limits Should Be Enforced by a
Two-thirds Supermajority and by Sequestration.

TABOR spending limits would be enforced during the budget resolution vote, as well as the vote on any discretionary appropriations bill or entitlement reform that would put total spending above the TABOR cap. (A projection of total mandatory outlays would need to be combined with the discretionary spending bills to arrive at the spending total.) Legislation violating TABOR would require a two-thirds super-majority.[2]

The two-thirds supermajority requirement recognizes that there will be rare emergencies (e.g., war) when Congress may need to spend more than TABOR allows. Setting the bar at two-thirds is low enough to clear during a national emergency or war, but high enough to prevent abuse. This policy would require Rules Committee reforms (or at least cooperation from the Rules Committee) to prevent the altering of this two-thirds requirement during key votes.[3]

If Congress exceeds TABOR spending without getting the two-thirds vote necessary to enact the spending override (for example, entitlement programs that spend more than projected), Congress could come back and cut spending elsewhere to remain in line with TABOR's limits. Otherwise, the Office of Management and Budget would sequester funds using preset sequestration formulas, which were used under discretionary spending caps and PAYGO.[4]

Principle 3: Congress Should Be Required to Budget for Emergencies.

No spending restraint is legislatively foolproof, so there must remain a political stigma attached to bypassing the spending limits. However, if two-thirds of Congress had to override TABOR every time there was a small emergency somewhere in America, these overrides would become routine and less controversial. Requiring Congress to reserve room in the budget for the predictable emergencies would keep all but the most catastrophic emergencies from requiring TABOR overrides.

Principle 4: States Should Be Protected from New Unfunded Mandates.

In a budget-cutting environment, lawmakers may be tempted to find savings by passing new unfunded mandates onto states. This is counter to TABOR's goal of reducing the cost of government. If Congress passes a new unfunded mandate, the TABOR cap should be reduced by the amount of federal money saved, as determined by the Congressional Budget Office.

Principle 5: Budget Surpluses Should Be Split Between Tax Rebates
and Debt Reduction.

The 1998–2001 budget surpluses induced a massive spending spree because these surpluses were portrayed as "free money" sitting in a pile waiting to be used. If TABOR successfully restrains spending and creates budget surpluses, lawmakers will surely be tempted to override TABOR and spend more on popular programs.

What if budget surpluses were automatically split between tax rebates and debt relief? Instead of spending "free money," lawmakers would be cutting the tax rebates to taxpayers as well as raiding a debt relief fund designed to reduce the debt burden passed onto future generations.[5]

Principle 6: TABOR Should Be a Statute, Not a
Constitutional Amendment.

While Colorado's TABOR is an amendment (and therefore well enforced), attempting to amend the U.S. Constitution would probably be a futile quest, which leaves reform by statute as the best option.

*What About Medicare and Social Security?*

The most predictable objection to a Taxpayers' Bill of Rights is that the exploding costs of Medicare and Social Security will make restraining federal spending nearly impossible. These programs are projected to grow 6 percent annually, which would seem to bar lawmakers from capping total federal spending at an annual growth rate of about 3.3 percent.

However, this is exactly why the nation needs a TABOR law. If Social Security and Medicare are allowed to grow at the current rate, they will bankrupt the federal budget. Within a few decades, taxes will have to increase by the current equivalent of $10,000 *per household* just to pay for Social Security and Medicare—unless these programs are reformed.

Furthermore, excluding Social Security and Medicare from TABOR would deny the fundamental reality that budgets are about setting priorities and making trade-offs. These programs do not exist in a vacuum and cannot be considered separately from the rest of the federal budget. If lawmakers choose to let these programs grow at their projected rates, they will be forced to either eliminate every other federal program or raise taxes to economically devastating levels. Exempting these programs from TABOR will not avoid this mathematical reality. It will merely delay the painful but inevitable trade-offs.

This does not mean that lawmakers would immediately have to reform Social Security and Medicare before the nation has developed a consensus on these issues. These programs are currently growing approximately $20 billion per year faster than they would if they grew at a 3.3 percent rate that would be consistent with a typical TABOR allowance. Over the next few years, Congress could easily offset the $20 billion increases by eliminating the hundreds of billions of dollars of wasteful and obsolete spending in the federal budget.[6] Those offsets would buy Congress at least five years to reform Social Security and Medicare before their costs begin to overwhelm TABOR spending levels.

*Conclusion*

The current federal spending spree is unsustainable; yet, Congress has rejected recent attempts to bring sanity to the budget process and encourage fiscal responsibility. A federal Taxpayers' Bill of Rights provides a simple, effective, proven model for spending reform. A TABOR would force lawmakers to live under spending restraints in the same manner that families, businesses, and state and local governments do. It would force lawmakers to set priorities, make trade-offs, and reduce wasteful spending. Colorado has proved that TABOR can restrain spending, reduce taxes, and facilitate economic growth. More than ever, a Taxpayers' Bill of Rights is needed to protect the family budget from the federal budget.

## DISCUSSION QUESTIONS

1. Why does Reidl think that TABOR is preferable to a balanced budget amendment to the Constitution? Do you agree with his assessment? Which approach (TABOR or the amendment) do you think is a more radical step to solve the problem of out-of-control budget deficits?

2. Do you think it is possible to significantly reduce deficits without raising taxes? If so, which government programs would you be in favor of cutting or eliminating?

3. How do the various plans deal with the explosion in entitlement spending that will come with the retirement of the baby boom generation? Which way of dealing with the "explosion" do you think is the most feasible?

## NOTES

1. H.R. 3800. For a summary of the bill, see Brian M. Riedl, "Better Budget Reform: A Guide to the Family Budget Protection Act," Heritage Foundation *Backgrounder* No. 1758, May 17, 2004, at *www.heritage.org/Research/Budget/BG1758.cfm*.
2. Colorado requires a voter referendum to exceed the spending limits, which is more effective but less feasible at a federal level.
3. Of course, a congressional majority could circumvent TABOR by simply writing a new law altering TABOR and adjusting the cap. (This was done with discretionary caps and PAYGO.) In the absence of a constitutional amendment, such chicanery cannot be completely prevented. One of the most feasible ways to pre-

vent such games is through political pressure to respect TABOR caps and restrict overrule votes to catastrophic emergencies.

4. Given that PAYGO exempted the vast majority of mandatory spending from sequestration, Congress should revisit sequestration formulas in order to guarantee sufficient room for these required spending cuts.

5. Lawmakers would not have to wait until the end of the year to cut taxes. They could reduce taxes any time in order to prevent a budget surplus from occurring in the first place.

6. For example, the federal government cannot account for $24.5 billion spent in 2003. This and other examples of government waste are detailed in Brian M. Riedl, "How to Get Federal Spending Under Control," Heritage Foundation *Backgrounder* No. 1733, March 10, 2004, at www.heritage.org/Research/Budget/bg1733.cfm.

# CHAPTER 15

# Government and Society

## 76

## "Growing American Inequality: Sources and Remedies"

### Gary Burtless

*How much, if anything, should the federal government do to promote greater income equality among its citizens? Ignoring the increasing income gap between the richest and poorest Americans, argues Gary Burtless, is a mistake. When more and more Americans see themselves as falling behind, they will show less confidence in political leaders and in government. In addition, income inequalities threaten public health, with larger gaps between rich and poor associated with higher mortality rates and higher incidence of disease. Burtless dismisses the argument that income inequality provides an incentive for the poorest Americans to work harder and earn more, citing evidence that the income of poor Americans has declined in recent years. Public policies that target the working poor—such as the 1986 Tax Reform Act, which eliminated taxes for many low-income Americans and increased the Earned Income Tax Credit—have elevated income levels. But there has been no comparable political support for the "non-working" poor, and critics charge that the EITC program is riddled with fraud. The 1996 welfare reform, moreover, has been particularly harsh, in Burtless's view. To begin the process of bridging the wage gap, he proposes efforts to bring the nonworking poor into the workforce, and publicly subsidized health care to ease the difficulties of poverty and provide the means for individual families to work their way out of poverty.*

O ver the past two decades the United States has experienced a startling increase in inequality. The incomes of poor Americans shrank and those of the middle class stagnated while the incomes of the richest families continued to grow. The well-being of families up and down the income scale has increased over the past five years, but the average income of the poorest Americans remains well below where it was at the end of the 1970s.

From the end of World War II until the 1970s, the percentage difference in average cash income between well-to-do and middle-class American families generally declined. In the 1980s, the gap began to widen noticeably. Better measurement of rich families' incomes accounts for some of the apparent jump in the early 1990s, but the gap between middle- and high-income families almost certainly increased after 1992. The cash income difference between middle-income and poor families followed a similar trend. After narrowing for several decades after World War II, largely because of increased wages and improved Social Security and welfare benefits for the poor, the gap began widening in the early 1970s. * * * [T]he trend in inequality has not been driven solely by worsening poverty among the poor or by spectacular income gains among the wealthy. It has been produced by growing disparities between Americans at every level of the income ladder.

Soaring inequality has not been confined to the United States. Rich nations around the world have seen inequality grow since the late 1970s. But the jump in income inequality has been particularly rapid in the United States—and it came on top of a higher initial level of inequality.

*Should We Care?*

Many Americans are not terribly concerned about income inequality or about the need for public policies to temper inequality. Although public opinion polls find that large majorities of residents in five European countries and Japan believe the government should guarantee each citizen a minimum standard of living, only about a quarter of Americans agree. By and large, Americans tend to believe that people bear primary responsibility for supporting themselves. U.S. citizens are also more likely to believe their society offers an equal opportunity for people who work hard to get ahead. Given these views, why should Americans be concerned about mounting inequality?

One reason for concern is that growing income disparities may undermine Americans' sense of social cohesion. Even if they are indifferent about the abstract principle of economic equality, most Americans probably believe in the ideals of political and legal equality. But greater inequality has almost certainly produced wider discrepancies in political influence and legal bargaining power. In 1979 the income of an American at the 95th percentile of the income distribution was three times the median income and thirteen times the income of an American at the 5th percentile. By 1996 an American at the 95th percentile had an income almost four times the median income and twenty-three times the income of the person at the 5th percentile. The growing income gap between rich, middle-class, and poor and its consequences for the distribution of political influence may contribute to Americans' dwindling confidence that their elected officials care very much about the views of ordinary citizens. According to polling experts Karlyn Bowman and Everett Ladd, in 1960 only a quarter of U.S. respondents agreed with the statement, "I don't think public officials care much about what people like me think." By 1996, the share who agreed had climbed to 60 percent.

Inequality may also affect public health. Demographers and public health researchers have found mounting though controversial evidence that greater inequality can boost mortality rates and contribute to poor health. Countries and communities with above-average inequality have higher mortality rates than countries or communities with comparable incomes and poverty rates but lower inequality. According to one public health researcher, low-income Americans have death rates comparable to those in Bangladesh, one of the world's poorest countries, even though absolute incomes, average consumption, and health care spending are much higher among America's poor than they are in Bangladesh. The possible link between public health and inequality may help explain why the United States, one of the world's wealthiest countries, does not have the longest average life span or the lowest infant mortality rate. If the benefits of U.S. income growth after 1979 had been more equally shared, the average health and life spans of Americans, especially poor Americans, might have improved faster than they did.

Defenders of American economic and political institutions correctly point out that inequality plays a crucial role in creating incentives for people to improve their situations through saving, hard work, and additional schooling. They argue that wage and income disparities must sometimes widen to send correct signals to people to save more, work harder, change jobs, or get a better education. In the long run, poor people might enjoy higher absolute incomes in a society where income disparities are permitted to widen than one where law and social convention keep income differentials small. According to this argument, widening inequality is in the best long-term interest of the poor themselves.

For poor people in the United States, however, the theoretical advantages of greater inequality have proved elusive over the past two decades. Their absolute incomes have not improved; they have declined. Their absolute incomes do not exceed those of low-income residents in countries with less inequality; typically they are lower than those of people in a comparable position in other rich countries. The efficiency advantages, if any, of growing U.S. inequality have not been enjoyed by the poor, at least so far. They have flowed to people much further up the income scale.

*Why Has Inequality Increased?*

Researchers on income inequality agree on two key facts. Greater family income inequality is closely connected to wider disparities in worker pay—disparities that in turn are associated with rising pay premiums for education, job experience, and occupational skills. In addition, shifts in family composition, specifically the continuing growth of single-parent families and the shrinking fraction of married-couple families, have reinforced the effects of widening wage inequality.

How much of the increase in family income inequality is attributable to rising wage disparities? Both male and female workers saw hourly pay disparities increase over the past two decades, though on average men saw their real earnings fall, while women got a raise. The hourly wage of workers at the 10th percentile fell 16 percent between 1979 and 1997. At the upper end of the pay ladder, wages at the 90th percentile rose 2 percent for men and 24 percent for women. Changes in annual earnings mirrored this pattern. Workers at the bottom of the pay scale saw their yearly labor incomes sink while workers at the top saw their annual pay increase. The gains were especially large among highly paid women.

One way to assess the impact of rising wage disparities on overall income inequality is to calculate how much overall inequality would have changed if wage disparities had remained unchanged. My calculation, using a standard statistical measure of income inequality known as the Gini coefficient, suggests that if male annual earnings disparities had remained unchanged between 1979 and 1996, personal income inequality would have increased about 72 percent of the actual jump. This means that the increase in men's earnings inequality explains about 28 percent of the overall increase in inequality. A similar calculation implies that despite the large increase in pay disparities among women, only about 5 percent of the increase in income inequality can be explained by growing earnings disparities among women. We can combine these two calculations to see what would have happened if male and female earnings inequality had both remained constant after 1979. This third set of calculations suggests that two-thirds of the increase in personal income inequality would have occurred, even without a change in pay disparities. An implication of this finding is that just one-third of the increase in personal income inequality was due to the growth of male and female earnings disparities. Most of the growth was due to some other set of factors.

One factor was the changing American household. In 1979, 74 percent of adults and children lived in married-couple households. By 1996, this share had fallen to 65 percent. Inequality and the incidence of poverty are much lower in married-couple households than in single-adult households. If the percentage of Americans living in married-couple families had remained unchanged after 1979, about one-fifth of the 1979–96 jump in inequality would have been avoided.

Another trend has pushed up income disparities. Women who are married to high-income husbands are increasingly likely to hold year-round jobs and earn high incomes themselves. The increased correlation between husbands' and wives' earnings has widened the income gap between affluent dual-earner families and the rest of the population. If the husband-wife earnings correlation had remained unchanged, about one-eighth of the rise in overall inequality since 1979 would have been avoided. In other words, roughly 13 percent of the increase in income inequality can be traced to the growing correlation between husbands' and wives' earned income.

*Policy Response*

Though critics of U.S. social policy often overlook the fact, policymakers have not stood still in the face of momentous changes in the income distribution. The direction of policy has shifted noticeably since the early 1980s.

The shift began under President Reagan, who attempted to scale back and reorient welfare programs targeted on the working-age poor. His goal was to make the programs less attractive to potential applicants by cutting benefits or making benefits harder to get. One important policy change, later reversed, was to scale back payments to poor families with a working adult. Reagan thought welfare benefits should be focused on the nonworking poor. He expected working adults to support themselves.

The steep decline in hourly wages of low-skill workers made this view increasingly untenable. Measured in inflation-adjusted dollars, the minimum wage fell more than 30 percent over the 1980s, and wages paid to unskilled young men fell almost as fast. Few breadwinners can support families on wages of $5 or $6 an hour.

Congress and the president responded by reforming tax policy toward low-income families and broadening eligibility for publicly financed health benefits. The Tax Reform Act of 1986 removed millions of low-income Americans from the income tax rolls and boosted the tax rebates low-income workers receive under the Earned Income Tax Credit. The EITC was further liberalized in 1990 and 1993, greatly increasing the credits flowing to low-income breadwinners and their children. Spending on the credit increased elevenfold in the decade after 1986, reaching more than $21 billion by 1996. The credit, payable to breadwinners even if they owe no federal income taxes, has raised the incomes of millions of families with extremely low earnings.

The EITC is the most distinctive American policy innovation on behalf of the working poor, and several European countries may eventually adopt a variant of it. While most cash assistance goes to people who do not work, the EITC goes only to low-income people who do work. In 1997 the credit provided as much as $3,656 to a breadwinner with two or more dependents. For a parent working full time in a minimum-wage job, the EITC can increase net earnings nearly 40 percent.

The idea behind the credit is to encourage work by increasing the incomes available to low-wage breadwinners who have dependent children. Instead of shrinking as a recipient's earnings grow, the credit rises, at least up to a limit. At low earnings levels the credit increases by 34¢ or 40¢ for each extra dollar earned. Most labor economists who have examined the credit conclude that it has contributed to the sudden and sizable increase in job holding among unmarried mothers.

Congress has also liberalized the eligibility requirements for Medicaid health insurance to include a broad population of low-income children with working parents. Until the late 1980s, working-age families with children were usually eligible for health protection only if the families were collecting public assistance. Children typically lost their eligibility for free health insurance when the family breadwinner returned to work. The Medicaid liberalizations of the late 1980s and early 1990s meant that many children were enrolled in the program even if their parents had modest earnings and were not collecting public assistance.

Some state governments have established new programs to provide subsidized health insurance to members of working-poor families, including the adult breadwinners. Congress passed legislation in 1997 offering states generous federal subsidies to establish or enlarge health insurance programs for the working poor and near-poor.

As U.S. policy has expanded tax and health benefits for the working poor, state and federal policymakers have slashed cash assistance to the nonworking poor. General assistance, which provides cash aid to childless adults, has been scaled back or eliminated in several states. Aid to Families with Dependent Children was eliminated in 1996 and replaced with Temporary Assistance to Needy Families (TANF). The new federal program pressures all states to curtail cash benefits to poor parents who are capable of working. The head of each family on welfare is required to work within two years after assistance payments begin. Work-hour requirements are stringent, and states face increasingly harsh penalties for failing to meet them. The law stipulates that the great majority of families may receive benefits for no longer than five years and permits states to impose even shorter time limits. Over a dozen states have already done so.

The new welfare law—and the new state welfare policies that preceded it—helped produce an unprecedented drop in the nation's child welfare rolls. Since peaking in 1994, the number of families collecting public assistance for children has dropped more than 2 million, or 40 percent.

In sum, U.S. policy has become much less generous to the nonworking (but working-age) poor, while it has become much more generous to working-poor adults with children. For many low-wage breadwinners with children, the recent policy changes—the increased generosity of the EITC, Medicaid, state-supported health plans, and child care subsidies—have offset the loss of potential earnings due to shrinking hourly wages.

The reforms are having other economic effects. Poor breadwinners with children have been induced to enter the work force—and stay there. Their entry contributes to the downward pressure on the wages of the least skilled. In effect, public subsidies to the working poor and cuts in welfare benefits to the nonworking poor have helped keep employers' costs low and thus helped fuel employers' creation of poorly paid jobs.

*Future Directions*

U.S. policies toward low-income, working-age families are not so callous that struggling families have been left wholly on their own to cope with declining wages. But they are not so generous that poor, working-age Americans have shared equally in the prosperity of the past two decades.

Different policies, such as those adopted in Western Europe, would have yielded different results. Some differences, including lower poverty rates and higher wages, make Western Europe a more pleasant place to live, especially for the poor. But others, including high unemployment, are unwelcome. It is not obvious that most Americans, even liberals, would prefer the European approach or approve the policies needed to achieve it.

While the current U.S. policy mix broadly reflects the preferences of U.S. voters, it is haphazard and fails to reach some of those who most need help. Two new policies could aid working-age people who have suffered the worst cuts in hourly pay. The first would assure some of the long-term unemployed a job at a modest wage. The second would make work subsidies more uniformly available and would provide them in a form that most voters approve.

Because public assistance to the nonworking but able-bodied poor is being drastically curtailed, it makes sense to assure at least some poor adults that they will be able to find jobs at a modest wage, however bad the local job market. In some cases this may involve creating publicly subsidized jobs that pay a little less than the minimum wage. It seems particularly important to extend this offer to parents who face the loss of cash public assistance. If voters and policymakers want unskilled parents to begin supporting themselves through jobs, they should assure these parents that some jobs will be available, at least eventually, even when unemployment is high.

For poorly paid breadwinners, it is essential to improve the rewards from working. One possibility is to make a basic package of subsidized health insurance available to all children and young adults. Many Americans regard health insurance for children as a fair and acceptable way to help those in need.

Most health insurance for children is either publicly subsidized through Medicaid or privately provided through employer health plans. When insurance is financed by employers, most of the cost to employers shows up as lower money wages paid to workers. By publicly assuming some or all of the cost of paying for a basic health package for children, we could push employers to boost the wages they pay to insured workers who have child dependents. Such a move would have a greater impact on the pay of low-wage workers, for whom health insurance represents a big fraction of compensation, than on the pay of high-wage workers.

About 15 percent of all children (and nearly a quarter of poor children) have no health insurance. For these children and their working parents, publicly subsidized child health insurance would directly improve well-being and reduce out-of-pocket spending on medical care. It would also greatly increase the reward to work. Parents who do not work qualify for free medical insurance for themselves and for their children under Medicaid. Some lose this insurance when they accept a job that pays modest but above-poverty-level wages. A public health insurance package for all children would reduce or eliminate this penalty for accepting a job.

American economic progress over the past two decades has been quite uneven. Families and workers at the top of the economic ladder have enjoyed rising incomes. Families in the middle have made much smaller income gains. Workers at the bottom have suffered a sharp erosion in their relative income position. For some low-income workers, new public policies have helped offset the loss of wages with larger earnings supplements and better health insurance. But many low-wage workers have not benefited from these policies. Humane public policy should try to assure that the most vulnerable Americans share at least modestly in the nation's prosperity.

## DISCUSSION QUESTIONS

1. According to the AFL-CIO, the average pay of working Americans grew by 68 percent between 1980 and 1998. The pay of an average major-company CEO, by contrast, grew by 1,600 percent during the same period, and is now 419 times higher than the wage of an average worker. These statistics seem to confirm Burtless's assessment that any "efficiency advantages . . . of growing U.S. inequality . . . have flowed to people much further up the income scale." Are

these differences in income the sign of a highly competitive free-market economy? Should government be concerned with these differentials? If so, what kind of government policy might address the concern?

2. To some, "reducing wage inequalities" is simply another way of saying "income redistribution." How would a policy geared toward reducing wage inequalities affect the economic incentives faced by individuals?

# 77

# "Objections to These Unions"

## Jonathan Rauch

*One of the most controversial and politically significant issues in the past few years is gay marriage. Many commentators attributed George W. Bush's victory in the 2004 presidential election to the presence of anti-gay-marriage initiatives on the ballot in eleven states, including several battleground states (Ohio, the pivotal state in the election, was among them). The anti-gay-marriage initiatives, which were resoundingly defeated in all eleven states, attracted conservative Christians to the polls who were much more likely to vote for Bush than John Kerry. Some have argued that gay rights supporters pushed too far, too fast, and the 2004 election was a backlash against some of the gains that they had made (most importantly, the 2003 Massachusetts Supreme Court ruling that legalized gay marriage).*

*Jonathan Rauch is less interested in the political impact of gay marriage than in trying to understand why people are opposed to gay marriage. He suggests two reasons: the simple anti-gay position and the not-so-simple view based on tradition. The latter is rooted in the gut-level feeling that marriage between two men or two women is simply wrong because marriage has always been between a man and a woman: no law can change this basic institution because it has roots that are deeper and older than any government or law. Rauch situates this argument within the political thought of F. A. Hayek, one of the great conservative thinkers of the twentieth century. Hayek warns that changing traditions and customs may lead to social chaos. This is precisely one of the arguments made against gay marriage: it will undermine the institution of marriage. Rauch replies that other changes have had a far greater impact on undermining the institution of marriage, such as allowing women to own property, the abolition of arranged marriages, legalized contraception, and "no-fault" divorce law. While recognizing the legitimacy of the concerns about gay marriage, Rauch concludes that the fears of its negative impact are overstated and the benefits of gay marriage for gay people outweigh the costs for non-gay people.*

There are only two objections to same-sex marriage that are intellectually honest and internally consistent. One is the simple anti-gay position: "It is the law's job to stigmatize and disadvantage homosexuals, and the marriage ban is a means to that end." The other is the argument from tradition—which turns out, on inspection, not to be so simple.

Many Americans may agree that there are plausible, even compelling, reasons to allow same-sex marriage, and that many of the objections to such unions are overwrought, unfair, or misguided. And yet they draw back. They have reservations that are hard to pin down but that seem not a whit less powerful for that. They may cite religion or culture, but the roots of their misgivings go even deeper. Press them, and they might say something like this:

"I understand how hard it must be to live a marriageless life, or at least I try to understand. I see that some of the objections to same-sex marriage are more about excluding gays than about defending marriage. Believe me, I am no homophobe; I want gay people to have joy and comfort. I respect their relationships and their love, even if they are not what I would want for myself.

"But look. No matter how I come at this question, I keep bumping into the same wall. For the entire history of civilization, marriage has been between men and women. In every religion, every culture, every society—maybe with some minor and rare exceptions, none of them part of our own heritage—marriage has been reserved for the union of male and female. All the words in the world cannot change that. Same-sex marriage would not be an incremental tweak but a radical reform, a break with all of Western history.

"I'm sorry. I am not prepared to take that step, not when we are talking about civilization's bedrock institution. I don't know that I can even give you good reasons. It is just that what you are asking for is too much."

Perhaps it doesn't matter what marriage is for, or perhaps we can't know exactly what marriage is for. Perhaps it is enough simply to say that marriage is as it is, and you can't just make it something else. I call this the Hayekian argument, for Friedrich August von Hayek, one of the 20th century's great economists and philosophers.

### Hayek the Conservative?

Hayek—Austrian by birth, British by adoption, winner of the 1974 Nobel Memorial Prize in Economic Sciences—is generally known as one of the leading theoreticians of free market economics and, more broadly, of libertarian (he always said "liberal") social thought. He was eloquent in his defense of the dynamic change that markets bring, but many people are less aware of a deeply traditionalist, conservative strand in his thinking, a strand that traces its lineage back at least to Edmund Burke, the 18th-century English philosopher and politician. Burke famously poured scorn on the French Revolution and its claims to be inventing a new and enlightened social order. The attempt to reinvent society on abstract principles would result not in Utopia, he contended, but in tyranny. For

Burke, the existing order might be flawed, even in some respects evil, but it had an organic sense to it; throwing the whole system out the window would bring greater flaws and larger evils.

Outside Britain and America, few people listened. The French Revolution inspired generations of reformers to propose their own Utopian social experiments. Communism was one such, fascism another; today, radical Islamism (the political philosophy, not the religion) is yet one more. "The attempt to make heaven on earth invariably produces hell," wrote Karl Popper, another great Austrian-British philosopher, in 1945, when the totalitarian night looked darkest. He and Hayek came of age in the same intellectual climate, when not only Marxists and fascists but many mainstream Western intellectuals took for granted that a handful of smart people could make better social decisions than could chaotic markets, blind traditions, or crude majorities.

It was in opposition to this "fatal conceit," as he called it, that Hayek organized much of his career. He vigorously argued the case for the dynamism and "spontaneous order" of free markets, but he asserted just as vigorously that the dynamism and freedom of constant change were possible only within a restraining framework of rules and customs and institutions that, for the most part, do not change, or change at a speed they themselves set. No expert or political leader can possibly have enough knowledge to get up every morning and order the world from scratch; decide whether to wear clothing, which side of the street to drive on, what counts as mine and what as yours. "Every man growing up in a given culture will find in himself rules, or may discover that he acts in accordance with rules and will similarly recognize the actions of others as conforming or not conforming to various rules," Hayek wrote in *Law, Legislation, and Liberty*. The rules, he added, are not necessarily innate or unchangeable, but "they are part of a cultural heritage which is likely to be fairly constant, especially so long as they are not articulated in words and therefore also are not discussed or consciously examined."

### Tradition Over Reason

Hayek the economist is famous for the insight that, in a market system, the prices generated by impersonal forces may not make sense from any one person's point of view, but they encode far more economic information than even the cleverest person or the most powerful computer could ever hope to organize. In a similar fashion, Hayek the social philosopher wrote that human societies' complicated web of culture, traditions, and institutions embodies far more cultural knowledge than anyone person could master. Like prices, the customs generated by societies over time may seem irrational or arbitrary. But the very fact that these customs have evolved and survived to come down to us implies that a practical logic may be embedded in them that might not be apparent from even a sophisticated analysis. And the web of custom cannot be torn apart and reordered at will, because once its internal logic is violated it may fall apart.

It was on this point that Hayek was particularly outspoken: Intellectuals and visionaries who seek to deconstruct and rationally rebuild social traditions will produce not a better order but chaos. In his 1952 book *The Counter-Revolution of Science: Studies in the Abuse of Reason*, Hayek made a statement that demands to be quoted in full and read at least twice:

> It may indeed prove to be far the most difficult and not the least important task for human reason rationally to comprehend its own limitations. It is essential for the growth of reason that as individuals we should bow to forces and obey principles which we cannot hope fully to understand, yet on which the advance and even the preservation of civilization depends. Historically this has been achieved by the influence of the various religious creeds and by traditions and superstitions which made man submit to those forces by an appeal to his emotions rather than to his reason. The most dangerous stage in the growth of civilization may well be that in which man has come to regard all these beliefs as superstitions and refuses to accept or to submit to anything which he does not rationally understand. The rationalist whose reason is not sufficient to teach him those limitations of the powers of conscious reason, and who despises all the institutions and customs which have not been consciously designed, would thus become the destroyer of the civilization built upon them. This may well prove a hurdle which man will repeatedly reach, only to be thrown back into barbarism.

For secular intellectuals who are unhappy with the evolved framework of marriage and who are excluded from it—in other words, for people like me—the Hayekian argument is very challenging. The age-old stigmas attached to illegitimacy and out-of-wedlock pregnancy were crude and unfair to women and children. On the male side, shotgun marriages were coercive and intrusive and often made poor matches. The shame associated with divorce seemed to make no sense at all. But when modern societies abolished the stigmas on illegitimacy, divorce, and all the rest, whole portions of the social structure just caved in.

Not long ago I had dinner with a friend who is a devout Christian. He has a heart of gold, knows and likes gay people, and has warmed to the idea of civil unions. But when I asked him about gay marriage, he replied with a firm no. I asked if he imagined there was anything I could say that might budge him. He thought for a moment and then said no again. Why? Because, he said, male-female marriage is a sacrament from God. It predates the Constitution and every other law of man. We could not, in that sense, change it even if we wanted to. I asked if it might alter his conclusion to reflect that legal marriage is a secular institution, that the separation of church and state requires us to distinguish God's law from civil law, and that we must refrain from using law to impose one group's religious precepts on the rest of society. He shook his head. No, he said. This is bigger than that.

I felt he had not answered my argument. His God is not mine, and in a secular country, law can and should be influenced by religious teachings but must not enforce them. Yet in a deeper way, it was I who had not answered his argument. No doubt the government has the right to set the law of marriage without kowtowing to, say the Vatican. But that does not make it wise for the government to disregard the centuries of tradition—of accumulated social knowledge—that the teachings of the world's great religions embody. None of those religions sanctions same-sex marriage.

My friend understood the church-state distinction perfectly well. He was saying there are traditions and traditions. Male-female marriage is one of the most hallowed. Whether you call it a sacrament from God or part of Western civilization's cultural DNA, you are saying essentially the same thing: that for many people a same-sex union, whatever else it may be, can never be a marriage, and that no judge or legislature can change this fact.

Here the advocates of same-sex marriage face peril coming from two directions. On the one side, the Hayekian argument warns of unintended and perhaps grave social consequences if, thinking we're smarter than our customs, we decide to rearrange the core elements of marriage. The current rules for marriage may not be the best ones, and they may even be unfair. But they are all we have, and you cannot reengineer the formula without causing unforeseen results, possibly including the implosion of the institution itself. On the other side, political realism warns that we could do serious damage to the legitimacy of marital law if we rewrote it with disregard for what a large share of Americans recognize as marriage.

If some state passed a law allowing you to marry a Volkswagen, the result would be to make a joke of the law. Certainly legal gay marriage would not seem so silly, but people who found it offensive or illegitimate might just ignore it or, in effect, boycott it. Civil and social marriage would fall out of step. That might not be the end of the world—the vast majority of marriages would be just as they were before—but it could not do marriage, or the law any good either. In such an environment, same-sex marriage would offer little beyond legal arrangements that could be provided just as well through civil unions, and it would come at a price in diminished respect for the law.

Call those, then, the problem of unintended consequences and the problem of legitimacy. They are the toughest problems same-sex marriage has to contend with. But they are not intractable.

## The Decoy of Traditional Marriage

The Hayekian position really comes in two quite different versions, one much more sweeping than the other. In its strong version, the Hayekian argument implies that no reforms of longstanding institutions or customs should ever be undertaken, because any legal or political meddling would interfere with the natural evolution of social mores. One would thus have had to say, a century and a half ago, that slavery should not be abolished, because it was customary in almost all human societies. More recently, one would have had to say that the federal government was wrong to step in and end racial segregation instead of letting it evolve at its own pace.

Obviously, neither Hayek nor any reputable follower of his would defend every cultural practice simply on the grounds that it must exist for a reason. Hayekians would point out that slavery violated a fundamental tenet of justice and was intolerably cruel. In calling for slavery's abolition, they would do what they must do to be human: They would establish a moral standpoint from which to judge social rules and reforms. They thus would acknowledge that sometimes society must make changes in the name of fairness or decency, even if there are bound to be hidden costs.

If the ban on same-sex marriage were only mildly unfair or if the costs of lifting it were certain to be catastrophic, then the ban could stand on Hayekian grounds. But if there is any social policy today that has a claim to being scaldingly inhumane, it is the ban on gay marriage. Marriage, after all, is the most fundamental institution of society and, for most people, an indispensable element of the pursuit of happiness. For the same reason that tinkering with marriage should not be undertaken lightly (marriage is important to personal and social well-being), barring a whole class of people from marrying imposes an extraordinary deprivation. Not so long ago, it was illegal in certain parts of the United States for blacks to marry whites; no one would call this a trivial disfranchisement. For many years, the champions of women's suffrage were patted on the head and told, "Your rallies and petitions are all very charming, but you don't really need to vote, do you?" It didn't wash. The strong Hayekian argument has traction only against a weak moral claim.

To rule out a moral and emotional claim as powerful as the right to marry for love, saying that bad things might happen is not enough. Bad things always might happen. People predicted that bad things would happen if contraception became legal and widespread, and indeed bad things did happen, but that did not make legalizing contraception the wrong thing to do; and, in any case, good things happened too. Unintended consequences can also be positive, after all.

Besides, by now the traditional understanding of marriage, however you define it, has been tampered with in all kinds of ways, some of them more consequential than gay marriage is likely to be. No-fault divorce dealt a severe blow to, "till death do us part," which was certainly an essential element of the traditional meaning of marriage.

It is hard to think of a bigger affront to tradition than allowing married women to own property independently of their husbands. In *What Is*

*Marriage For?*, her history of marriage, the journalist E. J. Graff quotes a 19th-century New York legislator as saying that allowing wives to own property would affront both God and nature, "degrading the holy bonds of matrimony [and] striking at the root of those divinely ordained principles upon which is built the superstructure of our society." In 1844 a New York legislative committee said that permitting married women to control their own property would lead to "infidelity in the marriage bed, a high rate of divorce, and increased female criminality" and would turn marriage "from its high and holy purpose" into something arranged for "convenience and sensuality." A British parliamentarian denounced the proposal as "contrary not only to the law of England but to the law of God."

Graff assembles other quotations in the same vein, and goes on to add, wryly, "The funny thing, of course, is that those jeremiads were right." Allowing married women to control their economic destinies did indeed open the door to today's high divorce rates; but it also transformed marriage into something less like servitude for women and more in keeping with liberal principles of equality in personhood and citizenship.

An off-the-cuff list of fundamental changes to marriage would include not only divorce and property reform but also the abolition of polygamy, the fading of dowries, the abolition of childhood betrothals, the elimination of parents' right to choose mates for their children or to veto their children's choices, the legalization of interracial marriage, the legalization of contraception, the criminalization of marital rape (an offense that wasn't even recognized until recently), and of course the very concept of civil marriage. Surely it is unfair to say that marriage may be reformed for the sake of anyone and everyone except homosexuals, who must respect the dictates of tradition.

Some people will argue that permitting same-sex marriage would be a more fundamental change than any of the earlier ones. Perhaps so; but equally possible is that we forget today just how unnatural and destabilizing and contrary to the meaning of marriage it once seemed, for example, to put the wife on a par, legally, with the husband. Anyway, even if it is true that gay marriage constitutes a more radical definitional change than earlier innovations, in an important respect it stands out as one of the narrowest of reforms. All the earlier alterations directly affected many or all married couples, whereas same-sex marriage would directly pertain to only a small minority. It isn't certain that allowing same-sex couples to marry would have any noticeable effect on heterosexual marriage at all.

True, you never know what might happen when you tinker with tradition. A catastrophe cannot be ruled out. It is worth bearing in mind, though, that predictions of disaster if open homosexuals are integrated into traditionally straight institutions have a perfect track record: They are always wrong. When openly gay couples began making homes together in suburban neighborhoods, the result was not Sodom on every street corner; when openly gay executives began turning up in corporate jobs, stud collars did not replace neckties. I vividly remember, when I lived in London in 1995, the forecasts of morale and unit cohesion crumbling if open homosexuals were allowed to serve in the British armed forces. But when integration came (under court order), the whole thing turned out to be a nonevent. Again and again, the homosexual threat turns out to be imaginary; straights have far less to fear from gay inclusion than gays do from exclusion.

### Jeopardizing Marriage's Universality

So the extreme Hayekian position—never reform anything—is untenable. And that point was made resoundingly by no less an authority than F. A. Hayek himself. In a 1960 essay called "Why I Am Not a Conservative," he took pains to argue that his position was as far from that of reactionary traditionalists as from that of utopian rationalists. "Though there is a need for a 'brake on the vehicle of progress,' " he said, "I personally cannot be content with simply helping to apply the brake." Classical liberalism, he writes, "has never been a backward-looking doctrine." To the contrary, it recognizes, as reactionary conservatism often fails to, that change is a constant and the world cannot be stopped in its tracks.

His own liberalism, Hayek wrote, "shares with conservatism a distrust of reason to the extent that the liberal is very much aware that we do not know all the answers," but the liberal, unlike the reactionary conservative, does not imagine that simply clinging to the past or "claiming the authority of supernatural sources of knowledge" is any kind of answer. We must move ahead, but humbly and with respect for our own fallibility.

And there are times, Hayek said (in *Law, Legislation, and Liberty*), when what he called "grown law" requires correction by legislation. "It may be due simply to the recognition that some past development was based on error or that it produced consequences later recognized as unjust," he wrote. "But the most frequent cause is probably that the development of the law has lain in the hands of members of a particular class whose traditional views made them regard as just what could not meet the more general requirements of justice . . . Such occasions when it is recognized that some hereto accepted rules are unjust in the light of more general principles of justice may well require the revision not only of single rules but of whole sections of the established system of case law."

That passage, I think, could have been written with gay marriage in mind. The old view that homosexuals were heterosexuals who needed punishment or prayer or treatment has been exposed as an error. What homosexuals need is the love of another homosexual. The ban on same-sex marriage, hallowed though it is, no longer accords with liberal justice or the meaning of marriage as it is practiced today. Something has to give. Standing still is not an option.

Hayek himself, then, was a partisan of the milder version of Hayekianism. This version is not so much a prescription as an attitude. Respect tradition. Reject utopianism. Plan for mistakes rather than for perfection. If reform is needed, look for paths that follow the terrain of custom, if possible. If someone promises to remake society on rational or supernatural or theological principles, run in the opposite direction. In sum: Move ahead, but be careful.

Good advice. But not advice, particularly, against gay marriage. Remember Hayek's admonition against dogmatic conservatism. In a shifting current, holding your course can be just as dangerous as oversteering. Conservatives, in their panic to stop same-sex marriage, jeopardize marriage's universality and ultimately its legitimacy. They are taking risks, and big ones, and unnecessary ones. The liberal tradition and the *Declaration of Independence* are not currents you want to set marriage against.

It is worth recalling that Burke, the patron saint of social conservatism and the scourge of the French Revolution, supported the American Revolution. He distinguished between a revolt that aimed to overthrow established rights and principles and a revolt that aimed to restore them. Many of the American founders, incidentally, made exactly the same distinction. Whatever else they may have been, they were not Utopian social engineers. Whether a modern-day Burke or Jefferson would support gay marriage, I cannot begin to say; but I am confident they would, at least, have understood and carefully weighed the possibility that to preserve the liberal foundation of civil marriage, we may find it necessary to adjust its boundaries.

## DISCUSSION QUESTIONS

1. Do you think that gay marriage would undermine the institution of marriage? If so, how?

2. If you are opposed to gay marriage, were you convinced by Rauch's arguments that it should be allowed?

3. If you are a supporter of gay marriage, what do you think is the best method for getting the practice established (working through the courts, Congress, state legislatures, etc.)? Given strong public opposition to gay marriage, as shown in the 2004 state referendums, do supporters of gay marriage need to slow down or change tactics?

# 78

# "Providing Social Security Benefits in the Future: A Review of the Social Security System and Plans to Reform It"

## David C. John

*There is wide agreement that Social Security requires major reforms if it is to continue to provide economic security to retirees. The baby boom generation will be retiring soon and the amount of money paid in benefits will exceed payroll taxes that are used to fund the system by 2017. The program has been running a surplus for the past two decades, but the government has been spending this money and giving the Social Security trust fund special treasury bonds that will be repaid with general revenue between 2017 and 2042, when the bonds will be gone. By 2030 there will be only 2.2 workers for every retiree, which means that this "pay as you go" program will be facing a series of increasingly difficult choices about how to meet its obligations.*

*At the heart of the debate are two contrasting perspectives of what the Social Security system should accomplish, both deeply rooted in American political culture: Should we view Social Security as a national guarantee of basic income for all individuals in their retirement, no matter what? Or should Social Security be an individualistic program that permits people to succeed—or fail—based on the choices that they make? To put it another way, is Social Security a social welfare program or an investment program?*

*David John weighs into this debate by outlining some principles for Social Security reform, providing an overview of the five main plans for reform, and then discussing the central characteristics of the Social Security program that are necessary for understanding the debate over reform. None of the plans reviewed here argue for the complete privatization of Social Security. Four of the five plans call for some type of Personal Retirement Account or PRA (the Heritage Foundation supports free market solutions to most social problems), but most of them are centrally managed, which allays some of the concerns of critics who are concerned that income inequality would be increased in retirement because many people are not adept at buying and selling stocks. John is a strong supporter of PRAs, saying, "Allowing workers to invest a portion of their Social Security taxes is the only alternative to raising Social Security taxes or reducing Social Security benefits."*

*However, as John notes, none of these plans address the "transition problem."*

*That is, because Social Security is a "pay as you go" program—today's workers pay for the Social Security benefits of today's retirees—if today's workers are allowed to take a portion of their Social Security taxes and put them in a PRA, this means that there will be even less money to pay for the current obligations to retirees than under the current system, at least for the next several decades. John says, "Neither the current system nor any of the proposed reform plans comes close to closing the gap" [between the costs of funding the PRAs and current obligations and the payroll taxes and trust fund bonds available]. This is the basic problem of President Bush's plan to allow 2 percent of the payroll tax to go into a PRA. The transition costs are huge, ranging from 5.8 to 16.4 trillion dollars. All of the plans (and John as well) also ignore the problem that between 2017 and 2042 the trust fund bonds, totalling about $2.4 trillion, will have to be repaid from general revenue (which means either raising taxes or increasing borrowing). So at precisely the same time transition costs will have to be funded the current obligations of the trust fund will have to be paid off. While the costs of reform appear to be daunting, the costs of doing nothing are even higher.*

Social Security is the best-loved American government program, but how it works and is financed is almost completely unknown. Most Americans have a vague idea that they pay taxes for their benefits and that their benefits are linked somehow to their earnings. Many also know that the program is in trouble and needs to be "fixed" sometime soon to deal with the retirement of the baby boomers. Beyond this, their knowledge of the facts is severely limited and often colored by rumors and stories.

Most politicians exploit this lack of knowledge and limit their statements on Social Security to platitudes and vague promises. To make matters worse, reformers tend either to be content with similar platitudes or to speak in such detail that few outside the policy world can understand what they are saying. The simple fact is that today's Social Security is extremely complex, and any reform plan that is more than fine words will be similarly complex.

This paper attempts to simplify the reform debate by comparing various plans (including the current system) side by side. Each of the six sections of this paper compares how the current system and the reform plans handle a specific subject. Only reform plans that have been scored by Social Security's Office of the Chief Actuary are included in this comparison, using numbers contained in the 2003 Report of the Social Security Trustees. * * *

While looking at just one or two sections of special interest may be tempting, this approach would probably be misleading. For the best effect, each section should be considered together with the other sections in order to form a complete picture of the plan. Using simply one section by itself to judge an entire plan will not yield an accurate result.

*Seven Important Rules for Real Social Security Reform*

Information in this side-by-side comparison is based on Social Security's scoring memos for each plan and conclusions that can be drawn from information contained in those memos. While there are many good points in the reform plans examined in this analysis, this is not an endorsement of any proposal by the author or The Heritage Foundation. Instead, this comparison provides details of specific plans. However, it would be wise for reformers to follow a set of general principles to ensure that any Social Security reform both resolves Social Security's problems and provides workers with greater retirement security. Those principles are listed below.

This comparison of plans makes no effort to examine whether the Social Security reform plans included in it meet or violate any or all of the principles.

Principles for Social Security Reform:

- **The benefits of current retirees and those close to retirement must not be reduced.** The government has a moral contract with those who currently receive Social Security retirement benefits, as well as with those who are so close to retirement, that they have no other options for building a retirement nest egg. If the benefits of younger workers cannot be maintained given the need to curb the burgeoning cost of the program, then they should have the opportunity to make up the difference by investing a portion of their Social Security taxes in a personal retirement account.
- **The rate of return on a worker's Social Security taxes must be improved.** Today's workers receive very poor returns on their Social Security payroll taxes. As a general rule, the younger a worker is or the lower his or her income, the lower his or her rate of return will be. Reform must provide a better retirement income to future retirees without increasing Social Security taxes. The best way to do this is to allow workers to divert a portion of their existing Social Security taxes into a personal retirement account that can earn significantly more than Social Security can pay.
- **Americans must be able to use Social Security to build a nest egg for the future.** A well-designed retirement system includes three elements: regular monthly retirement income, dependent's insurance, and the ability to save for retirement. Today's Social Security system provides a stable level of retirement income and does provide benefits for dependents. But it does not allow workers to accumulate cash savings to fulfill their own retirement goals or to pass on to their heirs. Workers should be able to use Social Security to build a cash nest egg that can be used to increase their retirement income or to build a better eco-

nomic future for their families. The best way to do this is to establish, within the framework of Social Security, a system of personal retirement accounts.

- **Personal retirement accounts must guarantee an adequate minimum income.** Seniors must be able to count on a reasonable and predictable minimum level of monthly income, regardless of what happens in the investment markets.
- **Workers should be allowed to fund their Social Security personal retirement accounts by allocating some of their existing payroll tax dollars to them.** Workers should not be required to pay twice for their benefits—once through existing payroll taxes and again through additional income taxes or contributions used to fund a personal retirement account. Moreover, many working Americans can save little after paying existing payroll taxes and so cannot be expected to make additional contributions to a personal account. Thus Congress should allow Americans to divert a portion of the taxes that they currently pay for Social Security retirement benefits into personal retirement accounts.
- **For currently employed workers, participation in the new accounts must be voluntary.** No one should be forced into a system of personal retirement accounts. Instead, currently employed workers must be allowed to choose between today's Social Security and one that offers personal retirement accounts.
- **Any Social Security reform plan must be realistic, cost-effective and reduce the unfunded liabilities of the current system.** True Social Security reform will provide an improved total retirement benefit. But it should also reduce Social Security's huge unfunded liabilities by a greater level than the "transition" cost needed to finance benefits for retirees during the reform. Like paying points to obtain a better mortgage, Social Security reform should lead to a net reduction in liabilities.

*The Social Security System and Plans for Reform*

The Current System.

Social Security currently pays an inflation-indexed monthly retirement and survivors' benefit, based on a worker's highest 35 years of earnings. Past earnings are indexed for average wage growth in the economy before calculating the benefit. The benefit formula is progressive, meaning that lower-income workers receive a benefit equal to a higher proportion of their average income than upper-income workers receive. The program is expected to continue to collect more in payroll taxes than it pays out in benefits until about 2018.

Unused payroll taxes are borrowed by the federal government and replaced by special-issue Treasury bonds. After the system begins to pay out more than it receives, the federal government will cover the resulting cash flow deficits by repaying the special-issue Treasury bonds out of general revenues. When the bonds run out in about 2042, Social Security benefits will automatically be reduced to a level equal to incoming revenue. This is projected to require a 27 percent reduction in 2042, with greater reductions after that.

### The DeMint Plan.

Representative Jim DeMint (R-SC) has introduced a voluntary personal retirement account (PRA) plan that would establish progressively funded voluntary individual accounts for workers under age 55 on January 1, 2005. The amount that goes into each worker's account would vary according to income, with lower-income workers able to save a higher percentage. For average-income workers, the account would equal about 5.1 percent of income.

The government would pay the difference between the monthly benefit that can be financed from an annuity paid for by using all or some of the PRA and the amount that the current system promises. The sum of the annuity and the government-paid portion of Social Security would be guaranteed at least to equal benefits promised under the current system, and 35 percent of PRA assets would be invested in government bonds to help pay for any Social Security cash flow deficits. This proportion would be reduced gradually in the future. General revenue money would be used to pay for additional cash flow deficits.

### The Graham Plan.

Senator Lindsay Graham (R-SC) has proposed a plan that would give workers under age 55 (in 2004) three options. (Workers above the age of 55 would be required to remain in the current system and would receive full benefits.)

Under *Option 1*, workers would establish PRAs funded with part of their existing payroll taxes, equal to 4 percent of pay up to a maximum of $1,300 per year. Workers' benefits would be reduced by changing the benefit indexing formula from the current wage growth index to one based on consumer prices. Over time, this change would reduce benefits for workers at all income levels, but the effect on lower-income workers would be eased by a mandated minimum benefit of at least 120 percent of the poverty level for workers with a 35-year work history. The government-paid monthly benefit would be further reduced to reflect the value of the PRA. This reduction would be calculated using the average earnings of government bonds so that, if the PRA earned more than government bonds, the total monthly benefit would be higher. Option 1 also raises survivor benefits to 75 percent of the couple's benefit for many survivors.

*Option 2* is essentially the same as Option 1, but without PRAs. The government would pay all benefits for workers who choose this option. Option 2 includes both the basic benefit reduction and the minimum benefit requirement.

*Option 3* pays the same level of benefits promised under current law, but workers who select this option would pay higher payroll taxes in return. Initially, the payroll tax rate for retirement and survivors benefits would increase from 12.4 percent of income to 14.4 percent of income (counting both the worker's and the employer's shares of the tax). In subsequent years, the tax rate would continue to climb in 0.25 percent increments.

### The Smith Plan.

Representative Nick Smith (R–MI) has proposed a voluntary PRA plan that would create personal retirement savings accounts funded with an amount equal to 2.5 percent of income, paid out of existing payroll taxes. This would increase to 2.75 percent of income in 2025 and could become larger after 2038 if Social Security has surplus cash flows. Retirement and survivors' benefits would be reduced by an amount equal to the value of lifetime account contributions plus a specified interest rate.

The Smith plan would also make many changes in Social Security's benefit formula, mainly affecting middle-income and upper-income workers. These changes would eventually result in most workers receiving a flat monthly benefit of about $550 in 2004 dollars. It would also gradually increase the retirement age for full benefits and require that all newly hired local and state workers be covered by Social Security. The Smith plan transfers $866 billion from general revenues to Social Security between 2007 and 2013 to help cover cash flow deficits and allows additional general revenue transfers when needed after that.

### The Ferrara Plan.

Peter Ferrara, Director of the International Center for Law and Economics, has proposed a plan that would create voluntary PRAs that would be funded according to a progressive formula that allows lower-income workers to save a higher proportion of their payroll taxes than upper-income workers. Average-income workers could save about 6.4 percent of their income. Workers would be guaranteed that the total of their PRA-generated benefits and government-paid monthly benefits would at least equal the benefits promised under the current system.

Any Social Security cash flow deficits that remain would be financed through general revenue transfers equal to a 1 percent reduction in the growth rate of all government spending for eight years, the corporate income taxes deemed to result from the investment of personal account contributions, and issuing about $1.4 trillion in "off-budget" bonds.

Under the Ferrara plan, these bonds would be considered a replacement for the existing system's unfunded liability and thus would not increase the federal debt.

### The Orszag-Diamond Plan.

Peter Orszag, Senior Fellow at the Brookings Institution, and Peter Diamond, Institute Professor of Economics at the Massachusetts Institute of Technology, have developed a plan that does not include any form of PRA or government investment of Social Security trust fund money in private markets. Instead, it gradually changes the benefit formula to reduce benefits for moderate-income and upper-income workers and requires that all state and local government workers come under Social Security. It would also gradually reduce benefits by raising the age at which workers could receive full benefits. Workers could still retire earlier, but at lower benefits. Benefits would increase for lower-income workers, widows, and the disabled.

In addition, the plan would gradually increase the payroll tax for all workers from the current 12.4 percent of income to 15.36 percent of income in 2078. It would also raise the earnings threshold on Social Security taxes—thus requiring higher-income workers to pay additional payroll taxes—and impose a new 3 percent tax on income above the earnings threshold. Workers would not receive any credit toward benefits for income covered by this new tax.

*    *    *

### 1. Personal Retirement Accounts

### What Is This, and Why Is It Important?

Allowing workers to invest a portion of their Social Security taxes is the only alternative to raising Social Security taxes or reducing Social Security benefits. However, personal retirement accounts are not all equal. The money that goes into the PRAs could come from diverting a portion of existing Social Security taxes or from some other source.

Similarly, the size of the accounts (usually expressed as a percentage of the worker's pay) is important. While larger accounts would temporarily increase the amount of additional funds required to pay benefits to retirees, they would also accumulate a pool of money faster than smaller accounts and finance a greater portion of benefits in future years. This can reduce the amount of additional tax dollars needed in future decades.

Finally, how the PRAs are invested is important. Even though they show steady growth over time stocks and commercial bonds are generally more volatile than government bonds. Investing a portion of the

PRAs in government bonds makes the accounts slightly less volatile while providing some of the additional dollars needed to pay benefits to current retirees.

## 2. Retirement and Survivors Benefits

### What Is This, and Why Is It Important?

Other than creating personal retirement accounts that allow workers to self-fund all or a portion of their Social Security retirement benefits, most reform plans deal with the program's coming deficits by either changing the level of retirement benefits promised or finding ways to increase program revenues. This section examines how various reform plans treat promised retirement benefits.

Social Security uses a complex formula to calculate an individual worker's retirement benefits. Subtle changes in this formula can cause a large change in benefits over time. For instance, changing how past income is indexed to a constant purchasing power will have only a minor impact for the first several years. However, the effect is cumulative and after several decades will result in major changes in benefits.

Similarly, seemingly minor changes in "bend points"[1] or other aspects of the benefit formula can, over the long term, cause major changes in benefits for upper-income and/or moderate-income workers. It is even possible to use the benefit formula to approximate an increase in the full retirement age without actually raising it. Thus, a plan could still allow workers to quality for "full retirement benefits" at 65, 66, or 67 but award them full retirement benefits (as defined under the current system) only if they wait to retire until a later age.

The first question that any plan must answer is whether it would pay the full level of benefits promised under the current system. If so, it must deal with how to pay the cost, since the current system cannot afford to pay for all of the promised benefits. Other important questions include whether the plan proposes benefit changes (usually reductions) if workers do not choose to have a personal retirement account, protects lower-income workers (who more often have an interrupted work history) by instituting some sort of minimum benefit level, and/or addresses the low benefits for certain lower-income, widowed, and disabled workers under the current system.

## 3. Payroll Taxes

### What Is This, and Why Is It Important?

Increasing Social Security payroll taxes would be one way to pay projected cash flow deficits. This method is closer to the self-funding that has characterized the system so far, but raising payroll taxes has significant drawbacks. Alternatives to payroll tax increases include instituting some form of personal retirement account to increase the return on taxes, reducing benefits, and using significant amounts of general revenue money to cover Social Security's cash flow deficits.

Currently, all workers pay 5.3 percent of their income to pay for Social Security retirement and survivors benefits. In 2004, this tax will be paid on the first $87,700 of an employee's income.[2] Employers match this tax for a total of 10.6 percent of each worker's income. In addition, both employer and employee pay an additional 0.9 percent of the worker's income (1.8 percent total) for Social Security disability benefits. Thus, the employer and employee pay a total Social Security payroll tax of 12.4 percent.[3]

Additional payroll taxes could be collected in three ways:

- The overall tax rate could be increased. However, this imposes higher taxes on all income groups and could reduce employment in the economy by making it more expensive to hire additional workers.
- The tax could be imposed on income levels above the threshold, currently at $87,700. In the short run, this would increase revenues, but since retirement benefits are paid on all income taxed for Social Security, it would also eventually increase the amount of benefits the system would have to pay each year and offset the amount raised through the higher taxes.
- Payroll taxes could be disconnected from the benefit formula. This could take the form of a new tax paid on income above the current $87,700 earnings threshold, collecting taxes on income up to the $87,700 level but counting only income up to $60,000 or some other level toward benefits, or some combination of the two. In either case, this type of tax would break the link between taxes and income that has existed since Social Security began in 1935. To date, neither the right nor the left has been willing to break this link for fear that it would be the first step toward turning Social Security into a welfare system. Both sides have worried that such a move—or even the perception of such a move—would undermine the program's widespread support among the American people.

*4. Social Security's Unfunded Liability*

## What Is This, and Why Is It Important?

Both the current Social Security system and every plan to reform it will require significant amounts of general revenue money in addition to the amount collected through payroll taxes. This additional money is necessary to reduce the difference between what Social Security currently owes and what it will be able to pay.

In the reform plans, the transition cost represents a major reduction from the unfunded liability of the current program. Even though the reform plans are expensive, all of them would require less additional money than the current system. However, both the amount and the timing of this additional money would vary depending on the plan.

The amount of additional money that is needed can be measured according to two different systems. Both measurements give valuable information.

*Present value* reflects the idea that a dollar today has more value to a person than that same dollar has sometime in the future. It gives an idea of when the additional money is needed by giving greater weight to money needed in the near future than to an equal amount needed further in the future. In addition to showing the amount of money needed, a higher present value number indicates that money is needed sooner rather than later. [The present value of the unfunded liability ranges from $929 billion in the Orszag-Diamond plan to $7.6 trillion in the Ferrara plan.]

The *sum of the deficits* indicates the total amount of additional money that will be needed. This measure gives $100 needed today the same weight as $100 needed in 15 years. This measure adds up only the future cash flow deficits; it does not include cash flow surpluses because the government does not have any way to save or invest that money for future use. Using both of these measurements gives a better picture of the situation than using just one. [The sum of the deficits of the unfunded liability ranges from $7.1 trillion in the Graham plan to $16.4 trillion in the Ferrara plan.]

Paying for the current system or any of the reform plans will require Congress to balance Social Security's needs against those of the rest of the economy. In general, as more additional dollars are needed for the current system or a reform plan, less money will be available for other government programs and the private sector.

As this burden on the general federal budget increases and persists, Congress would find it increasingly more difficult to come up with that money, and it would become increasingly less likely that such a plan would really be paid for on schedule. This is especially true for the current system, which will incur the massive deficits to pay all of the promised benefits.

*    *    *

## 5. Paying for Social Security's Unfunded Liability

### What Is This, and Why Is It Important?

Both the current Social Security program and all of the proposed reform plans will require large amounts of general revenue money to cover the annual cash flow deficits. Exactly when that money is first needed, how many years it will be needed, and the total amount that will be needed varies from plan to plan. Avoiding use of general revenue money would require either reducing Social Security benefits enough to eliminate the annual deficits or imposing new taxes to generate sufficient revenue. Neither the current system nor any of the proposed reform plans comes close to closing the gap.

Some plans do specify sources for the needed general revenues, but these are handicapped by the fact that no Congress can bind the hands of a future Congress. Thus, even if Congress did pass a plan that specified the source of the needed general revenues, a future Congress could change the plan by a majority vote. The only way to avoid this uncertainty would be for Congress to pass and the states to ratify the plan as a constitutional amendment—which would be prohibitively difficult.

In short, both the current system and all known reform plans would have to find the necessary general revenues from some combination of four sources: borrowing additional money collecting more taxes than needed to fund the rest of the government, reducing other government spending, or reducing Social Security benefits more than is called for under either current law or any of the reform plans.

The most important thing to remember is that the existing Social Security system and the reform plans all face this problem. This is not a weakness that is limited to PRA plans or any other reform plan. The only question is when the cash flow deficits begin and how large they will be.

### Current Law.

Current law makes no provision for funding Social Security's unfunded liability. The program has no credit line with the U.S. Treasury, and when its trust fund promises are exhausted, current law will require it to reduce benefits.

### The DeMint Plan.

While some press releases connected with Representative DeMint's plan suggest that some of its general revenue needs could be generated by reducing the growth of federal spending, no language specifying where the general revenues would come from is included in his legislation.

### The Graham Plan.

Senator Graham's plan includes a commission that would recommend reductions in corporate welfare and redirect the savings to reduce his plans unfunded liability. At best, a reduction in corporate welfare would generate only part of the needed general revenue. The commission would produce a legislative proposal that would then be considered by Congress.

Because the commission would be created by the same legislation that implements Graham's Social Security reforms, its recommendations could not even be considered until after the plan is enacted. As a result, passage of the Graham plan does not guarantee that these revenues would be available. Regardless of what the commission recommended, a future Congress could reject the proposed cuts in corporate welfare. In that case, Congress would have to come up with another method to raise the needed revenue.

### The Smith Plan.

Other than the proposed benefit changes that would partially reduce Social Security's unfunded liability, the Smith plan does not specify how it would pay cash flow deficits.

### The Ferrara Plan.

The Ferrara plan includes three mechanisms designed to create the needed general revenues.

*First*, it would mandate a 1 percent reduction in the growth of all federal spending (including entitlements such as Social Security) for at least 8 years and redirect that revenue to Social Security. Since Congress cannot legally force a subsequent Congress to follow a set course of action, the only enforcement mechanism available is a constitutional amendment. As a result, the Ferrara plan simply appropriates to Social Security the amount of revenue that would result if Congress were to reduce spending growth. In practice, a future Congress could choose not to reduce spending growth and, instead, just let the deficit grow larger or generate the necessary revenue in some other way.

*Second*, the Ferrara plan would transfer to Social Security the amount of corporate income taxes that could potentially result from the investment of personal accounts in corporate stocks and bonds. This is not a new or higher tax. This transfer is intended to reflect the taxes that would be paid at the current 35 percent corporate tax rate. Since SSA does not conduct dynamic scoring, this transfer is based on the static assumption that two-thirds of the stocks and bonds held through personal accounts reflect domestic corporate investment.

*Third*, the Ferrara plan would borrow about $1.4 trillion in special off-budget bonds. However, there is no practical way to create off-budget bonds that would not count against the federal debt. Even if there were, such a move would reduce the amount of transparency in the federal budget.

The Orszag-Diamond Plan.

While the Orszag Diamond plan includes both some benefit reductions and benefit increases for widows, the disabled, and low-income workers, the two elements of the plan are roughly equal. It reduces Social Security's unfunded liability using tax increases contained in the plan, including an increase in the payroll tax rate, a gradual increase in the amount of income subject to Social Security taxes, and a new 3 percent tax on any salary income not subject to Social Security taxes.

*6. Making Social Security a Better Deal for Workers*

### What Is This, and Why Is It Important?

In the long run, a reform plan should do more than just preserve the current Social Security system with its many flaws. While a key requirement of any reform plan is to provide a stable, guaranteed, and adequate level of benefits at an affordable cost, it should do more.

The current system fails to allow workers to build any form of nest egg for the future. Instead, it is the highest single tax for about 80 percent of workers. In return, each worker receives a life annuity that ends with the death(s) of the worker, the surviving spouse (if there is one), or young children (if any). In today's world, where two-earner families are increasingly the norm, the current system even limits survivor benefits to the higher of either the deceased spouses benefits or the surviving spouses benefits. Whichever account is lower, no matter how long that spouse worked, is marked paid in full and extinguished.

At a minimum, a reform plan should allow workers to pass on some of what they earned and paid in Social Security taxes to improve their spouse's retirement benefits. It should also allow workers the flexibility to use their entire account for retirement benefits or take a smaller retirement benefit and use the balance to pay for a grandchild's college education, start a small business, or pass on money to a later generation.

In judging whether each proposed reform would be better for America's workers, readers may differ sharply. However, while most summaries and studies examine Social Security reform from the viewpoint of federal budget impact, tax rates, and the survivability of the system, few consider the overall impact of reform on the workers it was designed to benefit in the first place. Social Security should not be reformed or "saved" for its own sake, but only if it more effectively provides the benefits workers need at a price they can afford.

## DISCUSSION QUESTIONS

1. The only plan that did not include partial privatization was the Orszag-Diamond plan. This could be called the "tough medicine"

plan because the solvency of Social Security is accomplished through benefit reductions and tax increases. It is the only one of the plans that is funded through cuts and tax increases. Is the tough medicine worth it, or do you agree with John that PRAs must be part of the overall reform?

2. One alternative to partial privatization that is not mentioned here is to have the federal government invest the Social Security surplus in the stock market or corporate bonds (as every state retirement system in the country does). This would, in theory, provide a high investment return, but critics claim it would also give the government too much leverage (as a large shareholder) over the activities of private corporations. Would this be a legitimate role for the government to play in the economy? Can you think of other ways in which the existing system could be reformed, other than turning portions of the fund over to individuals?

3. Are the broad objectives initially established for Social Security—income security for old age, income redistribution, and risk sharing across the population and across generations—still appropriate today? Are individuals more able to plan for and manage their retirement income today than in the 1930s or even the 1980s? Why or why not? What do you see as the major advantages and disadvantages of the current Social Security system and the plan for partial privatization?

## NOTES

1. The benefit formula used by the current Social Security system develops an "average indexed monthly earnings" for each worker by indexing his or her highest 35 years' earnings covered by Social Security taxes according to the growth in wages that has occurred between the date they were earned and the date that the benefit calculation is being made. In the next step, the actual retirement benefit is calculated. In 2003, the formula paid benefits equal to 90 percent of the first $606 of a worker's average indexed monthly earnings, 32 percent of the amount between $606 and $3,653, and 15 percent of any indexed earnings above $3,653. The divisions between the 90 percent, 32 percent, and 15 percent levels are called bend points.
2. This threshold is indexed and changes each year.
3. Although the federal government considers the employer's matching share as a separate item, most employers add their portions of the Social Security tax to a worker's salary when calculating the true cost of an employee.

## DEBATING THE ISSUES: HEALTH CARE REFORM

The health care system in the United States presents an important paradox: it provides the best health care in the world to the people who have insurance, but for the 40 to 45 million Americans who do not have insurance, health care can be a nightmare. Millions of people use the emergency room as their family doctor, which is not a very efficient way to provide health care. Millions more postpone receiving needed medical attention because they have no way of paying for it. Consequently, our nation spends twice as much on health care (as a percentage of GDP) as many other industrialized countries, while the overall health of Americans lags behind most of those nations that spend less than we do.

Despite the size of the problem, attempts to move in the direction of universal health care have always been met with stiff resistance. President Clinton's ill-fated health care plan in 1993–1994 (which Hillary Clinton refers to in her article, saying, "Been there. Didn't do that!") was the most recent and most spectacular failure. There have been successful incremental steps toward improving access to health care, such as the State Children's Health Insurance Program, which provides insurance to 3.3 million children. However, Hillary Clinton argues that the crisis in health care cannot be addressed through these incremental changes. The old problems with our health care system persist: health care costs are again rising faster than inflation, after several years of slower growth. Given the current budget crunches in many states and the rising costs of health care, states are trimming their spending on health care programs, which exacerbates the health care crunch. Administrative costs are high and much of what is spent on high-tech care is wasted. In addition, many new problems posed by medical advances and globalization make reforming health care even more complex. Clinton suggests that we need to change how we deliver care: creating a "personal health record" that would be securely linked to each persona, having better access to medical information, more of a focus on public health and prevention, and expanded health care coverage, with the ultimate goal of universal coverage. Clinton rejects the market-based approach that is supported by the other two authors in this section, saying, "But instead of putting consumers in the driver's seat, it actually leaves consumers at the mercy of a broken market. This system shifts the costs, the risks and the burdens of disease onto the individuals who have the misfortune of being sick."

Nina Owcharenko disagrees. She discusses three of the most popular incremental reforms that are currently being discussed in Congress: changes in flexible spending accounts to make them more useful for paying for health care costs, medical malpractice relief, and Associated Health Plans that would allow small businesses to pool together to get some of the health benefits that are currently only available to large employers. Owcharenko says that these proposals would all do some good, but she argues for more systematic changes in the federal income-tax law to provide tax credits for health care expenses to low-income people and tax deductions for health insurance for small businesses. She also would like to see the states become more active in developing "consumer friendly" health insurance markets.

Robert Gervais proposes even more radical surgery for the health care system. He says that the only way to have excellent health care at affordable prices is to introduce market forces. Without real market prices for health care, resources will be misallocated—that is, we will spend more on health care than we should. The core of the problem is that the consumers of health care services are not sensitive to prices and have come to expect health care as a free good. Without the restraining force of the market, prices spiral out of control and services are provided that are not needed. The answer, Gervais says, is only to use insurance for "costly, unpredictable medical interventions" after deductibles are applied. Everything else would be paid for out of pocket.

# 79

# "The Necessity of Free-Market Prices for Medical Care"

## ROBERT P. GERVAIS, M.D.

*How American Medical Payment Arrangements Differ from a Free Market*

A free market may be defined as the sum of those voluntary exchanges that furnish mutual benefit to participating individuals. Virtually innumerable positive-sum games occur in a genuinely free market: i.e. both parties are better off as a result of a trade, as of money for medical care. In such a market, neither medical services or medical insurance could be "too costly" because free-market prices spontaneously and rationally allocate available resources while constraining market participants to live within their means. Inflation, correctly defined, does not occur in the absence of fiat money.

Government intervention in the form of price controls and the creation of fiat money (the U.S. dollar) works to inhibit or preclude mutually beneficial exchanges.

The interposition of an insurer between patient and physician also interferes with the mutual benefit of a direct free-market transaction. A situation in which physicians feel that they are forced to contract with third parties rather than patients cannot be a free market. If contracts between physicians and third parties were mutually beneficial, both parties would gain from treating the sick. This is obviously not the case. The insurer always experiences a loss when a claim is submitted; it benefits only from payment of premiums, not from receiving a medical service. Thus, contracts between physicians or facilities and third parties are anomalous by nature. Such an arrangement gives third parties the incentive to pressure medical professionals to curtail medical interventions regardless of the best interest of the patients.

### How Should Limited Resources Be Allocated?

Economics is a science that studies that aspect of human action dealing with the problem of scarcity, a universal human condition. Because of scarcity, choices and trade-offs are necessary. The question is how to allocate scarce resources most efficiently.

For the sake of simplicity, it is useful to contrast two systems, pure capitalism and pure central planning. These two competing theories can best be grasped by determining how each one generates prices.

One theory maintains that functional knowledge transmitting prices can be discovered if resources are publicly controlled. This control can be either de jure or de facto. An example of de jure control is the U.S. Postal Service. An example of de facto government control is a physician's office. The other competing economic theory favors legally protected resources controlled by individuals (i.e. private property rights that are scrupulously respected by all economic actors including government). In other words, both economic paradigms maintain that prices are necessary to deal with the problem of scarcity but differ as to the mechanism whereby prices are generated.

The public property theory based on central planning asserts that "experts" in government can gain the vast knowledge required to dictate those prices that will efficiently allocate goods, including medical products and services. This theory, which presupposes virtual omniscience in a select few, stands in stark contrast to the modest free-market theory, which posits that knowledge about resources is radically dispersed amongst billions of individuals.

The consequence of the free-market theory is that all these individuals should be empowered to use their unique knowledge in order to discover the most valued use of resources. This is accomplished by consensual trades to generate prices. These real knowledge-transmitting prices are then utilized to guide the choices individual economic actors must make when communicating their preferences about resource allocation each time they make an economic transaction.

The free-market haggling process, which can instantly generate changes in prices (for example, the price of stocks changes quickly, reflecting new knowledge), is the only way to convey the rapid informational changes characterizing dynamic, free economies.

Those who espouse free markets readily admit that they do not possess the knowledge required to dictate what percentage of a country's wealth should be allocated to medical care, education, transportation, leisure, etc. But, they do confer a presumption of competence to individuals to employ their unique knowledge of local conditions and their own needs and values when choosing which trade-offs to make.

The alternative is to have government officials set priorities for resource use by asking it to pull nugatory prices out of a hat. Let us assume for the sake of argument that government could obtain the required dynamic knowledge to set functional prices. It would still be faced with another insurmountable problem, namely, the politics of theft. Under government central planning each and every one of us is spurred to plead with government to fix prices for our benefit, at the expense of others. This pleading or lobbying triggers a war of all against all in which everyone ultimately loses because lobbying circumvents mutually beneficial exchanges (in which everybody wins) and engenders the deadweight costs associated with unproductive government intervention.

Vast amounts of resources are wasted in the lobbying process itself, then by the overhead of regulatory agencies, and also by professionals such as accountants and lawyers retained by citizens and industry to avoid and resist the takings. The wealth squandered in attempts to influence central planning to advantage some at the expense of others or to avoid being disadvantaged could, in a genuine free market, be channeled to consumption, wealth creation, and charity.

Thus, there are two types of prices: genuine market prices determined by billions of individual decisions, or government-set pseudo-prices. The latter result in misallocation of resources and effort, and promote corruption at all levels.

### The Effect of Abolishing Prices

Government pseudo-prices have created havoc for the suppliers of medical care at the macro and micro level. The problem is compounded when demanders (patients) are not directly affected by prices at all. Third parties including government have duped patients into believing that medical care is a free good. The predictable result is that patients, in concert with doctors, have adopted consumption behaviors that allocate inordinate amounts of resources to medical care at the expense of future generations, education, food, defense, and all other needs.

This resource misallocation cannot be sustained. Something must be done, but what?

It is politically impossible for government to accept the blame for the economic chaos it created with legislation decreeing that a scarce good, limitlessly demanded, would be limitlessly supplied. Instead, government brazenly demonizes the suppliers of the "free" good, doctors, hospitals, drug manufacturers, and others, in order to justify regimentation ("regulation").

Needless to say, the demanders (i.e. patients), whose votes are needed to perpetuate the hoax, can neither be blamed nor directly regimented. As a practical matter, government has no other option but to limit supply by rescinding the liberty of the suppliers. Physicians are ignominiously reminded of that fact by managed care, which places them at financial risk for supplying medical care (the antithesis of free markets), by incomprehensible coding and documentation directives, by limited fees that do not cover costs, by the deadweight costs of bureaucratese, and increasingly numerous other hassle factors. But that is not enough. Government has discovered that bureaucratic requirements do not adequately curtail supply. Its next predictable step is to criminalize the medical profession in order to further limit the supply of medical care.

Unjust laws provide incentives to aggressive prosecutors to incarcerate doctors for picayune, undecipherable bureaucratic rules. Jailing physicians guarantees an absolute diminution in the supply of medical care; moreover, it impels their peers to assiduously obey government edicts prior to treating the sick. Obeisance supersedes patient care. Or to paraphrase Trotsky, one must obey before one is permitted to eat.

Government-created negative incentives not only discourage the supply of known medical cures but also curb future medical miracles brought to us by entrepreneurs. Arguably, these inimical government interventions are the most effective way to limit the supply of innovative medical care.

*How Free-Market Prices Work*

The salutary, harmonizing function of real prices is neatly summarized by the phrase coined by Randy Barnett in the context of criminal law: "to compensate for a reduced rate of capture."

A genuine pricing system not only fosters harmonious competition for scarce resources, but also serves to capture, to monitor, and to stop uneconomic trades (i.e. trades which are not mutually beneficial). The use of prices to stop patently uneconomic trades is easily understood: no competent person pays $1,000 for a $10 good. But the use of prices to reveal genuine consumer preferences and rationally allocate resources requires further comment.

Let us assume that patients carry real insurance that only pays for costly, unpredictable medical interventions after deductibles are met. (Such insurance is rare in the U.S. today.) How many patients would elect to undergo cataract or joint replacement surgery for borderline indications, instead of spending that deductible on other scarce goods such as travel? Absent real prices, there is no way to know. Patients will often choose both goods if one of them (i.e. surgery) is perceived to be free. But consuming scarce goods as if they are free causes economic chaos. Because government has eliminated the monitoring function of prices, it must compensate by setting up a substitute system in an attempt to control profligate consumption. This surrogate monitoring system is known to all doctors as managed care, coding, audits for "fraud and abuse" (including the provision of "medically unnecessary" services), and most ominously, as the criminalization of medicine.

The cost of abrogating free-market prices includes preventing one of the most educated segments of society from fully using its knowledge to improve the lives of patients.

*Regression from Wealth to Poverty: An Example from History*

Because a purely theoretical exposition of the benefits of a free market may not be convincing, a brief digression into history is offered.

In 960 A.D. the Chinese emperor Sung Taizu instituted a dynasty that embraced many free-market principles. These free-market provisions included the rule of law, free speech, tradable property rights, and a stable monetary system. Sung's policies produced dramatic results: a free market in land; free movement of goods and labor; and impressive growth of agriculture, trade, and manufacturing. For example, in 1078 China produced 125,000 tons of cast iron, an accomplishment not surpassed until England did it in the 1790s.

Additionally, China made a whole range of technological breakthroughs: type printing, paddle-wheel ships, the magnetic compass, and seaworthy vessels carrying up to 600 tons manned by 1,200 sailors.

But during the next millennium, the Chinese regressed to third-world status. A crisis occurred and was seized upon by a new dynasty as a pretext to implement government central planning. Under the Sung dynasty, China was invaded and largely destroyed by the Mongols (1268 to 1279). The Chinese regained control of their territory in 1371 under the Ming Dynasty, which blamed the Sung laissez-faire policies for China's defeat. In response, the Ming reintroduced central planning, with loss of private property in land, forced repopulation of Northern China, cessation of foreign trade, and destruction of technologies (all ship building became illegal). The predictable, unfortunate result is known to all. Over the course of the next 1,000 years China regressed from the most successful society on the planet to an impoverished status from which it has yet to recover.

*Conclusions*

The lesson to be learnt is always the same. Societies that reject the principle of liberty, which requires legal protection of private property and its use in exchange to generate prices, risk stagnation or regression. The implications for medicine are obvious. If the central planning policies hobbling medical care are not reversed, it may succumb to the Chinese scourge.

No one except the individual patient and physician should profess to know the value of a medical service or a physician's skills. Nor should anyone presume to know how much of a country's wealth should be allocated to medical care. To assist the government in implementing central planning and price controls only helps to perpetuate and enhance the credibility of these destructive interventions.

# 80

# "Bringing True Competitiveness to Health Care"

## Nina Owcharenko

The House of Representatives will soon consider a menu of proposals to address some of the problems facing America's health care system. While these proposals are well-intentioned, they only make minor structural modifications to the *status quo* and fail to address the root problem in the system: the continued absence of personal choice and control of health care options. Congress should instead consider a more aggressive and comprehensive approach to reforming America's troubled health care system, including the adoption of a generous system of health care tax credits.

The piecemeal approach to health care reform, often portrayed as eminently practical, is in reality often bereft of long-term goals or vision. Unquestionably, the three policy initiatives before the House of Representatives would offer some relief for individuals and families, but they fall short of the necessary structural reforms that would change what many American families have today into a robust system of consumer choice and free-market competition.

## Changes in Flexible Spending Accounts (FSAs)

The most promising of the three House proposals would change Flexible Spending Accounts. The proposed modifications in the "use-it-or-lose-it" restrictions would offer individuals the ability to carry over up to $500 in their FSAs each year. These tax-advantaged account options, offered through an employer, allow employees to set aside pre-tax dollars through salary reduction. The funds in these accounts can be used for medical and dental expense that are not covered by insurance.

However, current regulatory restrictions require that any funds left over at the end of the year must be forfeited to the employer. The forfeiture requirement wrongly implies that these set-aside funds are not the employee's. In addition, the "use-it-or-lose-it" rules create a disincentive for individuals to save for future health care expenses.

While, ideally, employees should be able to carry over *all* unused funds and/or be allowed to withdraw and pay taxes on the funds, the FSA policy changes in the House proposal are long overdue and would offer greater personal control over health care spending. In this sense, the FSA changes are a welcome injection of the free-market principle of consumer choice and consumer decision-making into the existing structure of employer-sponsored health care coverage.

## Medical Malpractice Relief

Medical malpractice is a major and multifaceted problem. The proposed changes in existing medical malpractice laws are well-intentioned and highlight the very serious problems facing doctors and patients in many states. Skyrocketing medical malpractice premiums are contributing to the rising cost of health care and forcing many physicians either to give up treating patients or to exit practice altogether, thus limiting patient access to medical treatment.

The lawsuit crisis in many states has little or nothing to do with increases in bad medical practices but instead results from exotic theories of legal liability, runaway juries, and absurd state tort rulings. Congressional efforts pose legitimate constitutional concerns with malpractice reform efforts that would impose uniform federal solutions to large areas of state tort law. Moreover, efforts by Congress to assert congressional power to overrule bad state tort laws allow that power (at a later date) to overrule good state tort reform laws.

Since the problems of medical malpractice are problems of state law, solutions must rest ultimately in changes in state law. The states remain the best laboratories for tort reform, particularly for medical malpractice claims that involve parties only from within a given state. Congress should strongly encourage states to reform their destructive medical malpractice system in ways that are consistent with the constitutional principle of federalism.

*Association Health Plans (AHPs)*

The creation of Association Health Plans is designed to expand coverage options for small businesses by allowing them to pool themselves together and to be regulated by the same federal laws as large employers. This, too, is a well-intentioned proposal that attempts to address a major shortcoming of the existing health insurance market. Small businesses are struggling to provide affordable health care coverage options to their employees, if they do so at all. Administrative costs, as well as the over-regulated and mandated state insurance laws, have forced many small businesses to reconsider health insurance altogether.

However, building on the very weaknesses of the *status quo* only perpetuates the limitations and shortfalls of the current system, in particular the reliance on place of employment or work status as the condition for access to affordable health care coverage. In many cases, locking employees into a system of company-based health insurance denies individuals and families real choices of health plans, benefits, and providers. Moreover, under the current system of employment-based health insurance, persons are deprived of true portability of coverage and individual ownership of their health care policies.

A far better policy for Congress is to focus on enabling small businesses to provide a fixed amount for each employee for individual and family coverage, directly assisting employees in purchasing their own health care coverage. This "defined contribution" approach is a better way to enhance choice. Policymakers could also encourage states to reduce unnecessary mandates and regulations while designing a reliable and consumer-friendly marketplace based on consumer choice and free-market competition.

*A Vision for Comprehensive Change*

Faced with the burgeoning numbers of uninsured, policymakers must recognize that the current health care system often fails individuals and families, particularly those who work for small businesses and are without insurance. Patchwork proposals based on the *status quo* offer only marginal assistance.

Instead, policymakers should consider a more fundamental reform of the health care system by fixing the inequitable and inefficient tax treatment of health insurance and encouraging states to design consumer-friendly marketplaces that incorporate a variety of health care options.

1. **Fix the tax treatment of health care.** The current federal tax code provides unlimited tax relief for the purchase of health insurance, but only through the place of work. As it turns out, lower-wage workers, particularly those who work in small firms, who need help the most, get less tax relief than high-wage workers. Moreover,

if workers in small firms go outside of the place of work to buy a health plan, they must do so with after-tax dollars, which often makes the cost of a plan prohibitive.

In the short term, offering low-income individuals and families a refundable, advanceable tax credit, as proposed by the President and several Members of Congress from both parties, would enable individuals to obtain their own health care coverage and further promote the efforts to allow businesses, especially small businesses, to provide financial assistance through a defined contribution approach.

In the long term, replacing the employer-based tax exclusion with a national system of refundable health care tax credits, with more help going to individuals and families with higher health care costs and/or lower income, is the better policy option. It would be more effective way to allocate scarce federal resources and undertake fundamental reform the health care system.

2. **Encourage the states to adopt consumer-friendly health insurance markets.** Policymakers should also consider ways to encourage states to design a consumer-friendly marketplace. Since states currently regulate the individual and small group insurance market, it is a practical option for states to establish these markets where consumers can shop for coverage that best suits their needs.

*Conclusion*

Members of the House of Representatives are putting forth a proactive health-related agenda. But while these efforts are praiseworthy, they do not go far enough, either in making substantive changes in the health care system or in offering a clear vision for future health care reform.

Policymakers must recognize that patchwork policies do little to achieve the fundamental restructuring of America's current health care system that is so badly needed. Major changes in the system should not be based on the *status quo*, but should represent real changes based on personal freedom and free markets. In practice, that means promoting individual choice, true portability of health insurance coverage, and personal ownership of health insurance policies.

# 81

# "Now Can We Talk About Health Care? The Crisis That Never Went Away Has Become Only More Complicated"

## Hillary Rodham Clinton

I know what you're thinking. Hillary Clinton and health care? Been there. Didn't do that!

No, it's not 1994; it's 2004. And believe it or not, we have more problems today than we had back then. Issues like soaring health costs and millions of uninsured have yet to fix themselves. And now we are confronting a new set of challenges associated with the arrival of the information age, the technological revolution and modern life.

Think for a moment about recent advances in genetic testing. Knowing you are prone to cancer or heart disease or Lou Gehrig's disease may give you a fighting chance. But just try, with that information in hand, to get health insurance in a system without strong protections against discrimination for pre-existing or genetic conditions. Each vaunted scientific breakthrough brings with it new challenges to our health system. But it's not only medicine that is changing. So, too, are the economy, our personal behaviors and our environment. Unless Americans across the political spectrum come together to change our health care system, that system, already buckling under the pressures of today, will collapse with the problems of tomorrow.

Twenty-first-century problems, like genetic mapping, an aging population and globalization, are combining with old problems like skyrocketing costs and skyrocketing numbers of uninsured, to overwhelm the 20th-century system we have inherited.

The way we finance care is so seriously flawed that if we fail to fix it, we face a fiscal disaster that will not only deny quality health care to the uninsured and underinsured but also undermine the capacity of the system to care for even the well insured. For example, if a hospital's trauma center is closed or so crowded that it cannot take any more patients, your insurance card won't help much if you're the one in the freeway accident.

Let's face it—if we were to start from scratch, none of us, from dyed-in-the-wool liberals to rock-solid conservatives, would fashion the kind of health care system America has inherited. So why should we carry the problems of this system into the future?

*21st-Century Problems*

At the dawn of the last century, America was coping with the effects of the industrial revolution—crowded living conditions, dangerous workplaces, inadequate sanitation and infrastructure in cities and pollution and infectious diseases like typhoid fever and cholera that exacted a huge toll on the oldest and youngest in society.

Since then, a century's worth of advances yielded remarkable results. Antibiotics were developed. Anesthesia was improved. Public health programs like mosquito control and childhood immunizations succeeded in reducing or even eradicating diseases like malaria and polio in this country. Congress passed legislation regulating the quality of food and drugs and assuring that safety and science guided medical developments. Workplace and product-safety standards resulted in fewer deaths and injuries from accidents. Effective campaigns cut tobacco use and alcohol abuse. Employers began providing some workers with health care coverage, primarily for hospitalization costs. And to aid some of those left out, President Lyndon B. Johnson persuaded Congress to establish Medicare and Medicaid to address the poorest, sickest, oldest and highest-risk patients in our society. As a result of these accumulated gains, life expectancy grew from 47 years in 1900 to 77 years for those born in 2000.

As astounding as those changes were, we are likely to see even more revolutionary changes in the next 100 years. Advances in medicine coincide with advances in computers and communications. The American workplace is changing in response to global pressures. But even positive advances may come with a negative underside. Our affluence contributes to an increasingly sedentary lifestyle that, combined with a diet filled with sugar and fat-rich foods, undermines our ability to fend off chronic diseases like diabetes. And research is proving that the pollutants and contaminants in our environment cause disease and mortality.

It is overwhelming just thinking about the problems, never mind dealing with them. But we have to begin applying American ingenuity and resolve or watch the best health care system in the world deteriorate.

*Medical Advances*

The pace of scientific development in medicine is so rapid that the next hundred years is likely to be called the Century of the Life Sciences. We have mapped the human genome and seen the birth of the burgeoning field of genomics, offering the opportunity to pinpoint and modify the genes responsible for a whole host of conditions. Scientists are exploring whether nanotechnology can target drugs to diseased tissues or implant sensors to detect disease in its earliest forms. We can look forward to "designer drugs" tailored to individual genetic profiles. But the advances we herald carry challenges and costs.

Think about the potential for inequities in drug research. Today, pharmaceutical and biotech companies have little incentive to research and develop treatments for individuals with rare diseases. Never heard of progeria? That's the point. This fatal syndrome, also called premature-aging disease, affects one in four million newborns a year. It's rare enough that there is no profit in developing a cure. This is known as the "orphan drug" problem. Genetic profiles and individualized therapies have the potential to increase the problem of orphaned drugs by further fragmenting the market. Even manufacturers of drugs for conditions like high blood pressure might focus their efforts on people with common genetic profiles. Depending on your genes, you could be out of luck.

The increasing understanding and use of genomics may also undermine the insurance system. Health insurance, like other insurance, exists to protect against unpredictable, costly events. It is based on risk. As genetic information allows us to predict illness with greater certainty, it threatens to turn the most susceptible patients into the most vulnerable. Many of us will become uninsurable, like the two young sisters with a congenital disease I met in Cleveland. Their father went from insurance company to insurance company trying to get coverage, until one insurance agent looked at him and said, "We don't insure burning houses."

Many have worked to get laws on the books to protect people from genetic discrimination, but we have yet to pass legislation that addresses job security and health coverage. The challenges do not stop there. Health insurance will have to change fundamentally to cope with predictable, knowable risks. Will health insurance companies offer coverage tailored to a person's future health prospects? Right now, if you have asthma, or even just allergies, insurers in the individual market can exclude your respiratory system from your health insurance policy. Will all health plans stop offering benefits that relate to genetic diseases?

The ability to predict illness may overwhelm more than just the insurance system; it may overwhelm the patient and the provider. Studies in The Journal of the American Medical Association found that nearly 6 out of 10 patients at risk for breast and ovarian cancer declined a genetic test, and a similar fraction of those at risk for colon cancer also declined testing. Why? One reason is probably to avoid higher insurance premiums. But the decision to undergo genetic testing is a complex one that involves many issues. Positive test results often indicate increased risk but no certainty that a disease will occur. Negative results also come without guarantees. The development of genetic profiles and individual therapies will exponentially increase the amount of information a physician is expected to manage. Instead of remembering one or two drugs for any condition, a physician will have to analyze all the different genetic, demographic and behavioral variables to generate optimal treatment for a patient.

Medical advances have the potential to overwhelm the health care system top to bottom. At the very least, the pace of technological progress is so rapid that our antiquated health care system is ill equipped to deliver the fruits of that progress. But these advances are not occurring in isolation from other factors affecting both how we finance health care and how much care we need and expect.

*Globalization*

The globalization of our economy has changed everything from how we work as individuals to what we produce as a nation to how quickly diseases can spread. American companies—and workers—compete not only with one another but all over the world. It is called competitive advantage, but it can put American businesses and workers at a disadvantage.

The United States' closest economic rivals have mandatory national health care systems rather than the voluntary employer-based model we have. Automakers in the United States and Canada pay taxes to help finance public health care. But in the United States, automakers also pay about $1,300 per midsize car produced for private employee health insurance. Automakers in Canada come out ahead, according to recent news reports, even after paying higher taxes.

At the same time, American companies are outsourcing jobs to countries where the price of labor does not include health coverage, which costs Americans jobs and puts pressure on employers who continue to cover their employees at home.

And many new jobs, especially those in the service sector and part-time jobs, don't include comprehensive health benefits. More uninsured and underinsured workers impose major strains on a health system that relies on employer-based insurance. In addition, the failure of government to help contain health costs for employers has led to a fraying of the implicit social contract in which a good job came with affordable coverage.

Gone are the days when a young person would start in the mail room and stay with the company until retirement. Employee mobility is now the rule rather than the exception. Those who pay for health care—insurance companies and employers—increasingly deal with employees who change jobs every few years. This has the effect of not only increasing the numbers of uninsured but also of decreasing the incentive for employers to underwrite access to preventive care.

At the same time, war, poverty, environmental degradation and increased world travel for business and pleasure mean greater migration of people across borders. And with people go diseases. The likes of SARS can travel quickly from Hong Kong to Toronto, and news of a strange flu in Asia worries us in New York. Welcome to the world without borders.

The Pulitzer Prize–winning science writer Laurie Garrett has described it as "payback for decades of shunning the desperate health needs of the poor world." No matter the blame, the need to act now to address issues of global health is no longer just a moral imperative; it is self-interest.

### Lifestyle and Demographic Changes

One hundred years ago, who could have predicted that living longer would be a problem?

In three decades, the number of Medicare beneficiaries will double. By the year 2050, one in five Americans will be 65 or older. We will have to find a way to finance the growing demand not only for health care but also for long-term care, which is now largely left out of Medicare.

Our society's affluence is only half of the story. Widening disparities in wealth and in health care too often cleave along ethnic lines. Today, a Hispanic child with asthma is far less likely than a non-Hispanic white child to get needed medication. African-Americans are systematically less likely to get state-of-the-art cardiac care. As our country becomes more and more diverse, these disparities become more obvious and more intolerable.

Our changing lifestyles also contribute to behavior-induced health problems. We can shop online, order in fast food, drive to our errands. Entertainment—movies, TV, video games and music—is one click away. The physical activity required to get through the day has decreased, while the pace and stress of daily life has quickened, affecting mental health. Persistent poverty, risky behaviors like substance abuse and un-protected sex and pollution from cars and power plants all add to the country's health problems. As Judith Stern of the University of California at Davis so aptly put it, genetics may load the gun, but environment pulls the trigger.

### Old Problems Persist

If all we had to do was face these tremendous changes, that would be daunting enough. But many of the systemic problems we have struggled with for decades—like high costs and the uninsured—are simply getting worse.

In 1993, the critics predicted that if the Clinton administration's universal health care coverage plan became law, costs would go through the roof. "Hospitals will have to close," they said, "Families will lose their choice of doctors. Bureaucrats will deny medically necessary care."

They were half-right. All that has happened. They were just wrong about the reason.

In 1993, there were 37 million uninsured Americans. In the late 90's, the situation improved slightly, largely because of the improved economy and the passage of the Children's Health Insurance Program. But now some 43.6 million Americans are uninsured, and the vast majority of them are in working families.

While employer-sponsored insurance remains a major source of coverage for workers, it is becoming less accessible and affordable for spouses, dependents and retirees. In 1993, 46 percent of companies with 500 or more employees offered some type of retiree health benefit. That declined to 29 percent in 2001. When you think about the new economy and worker mobility, it's no wonder employers are dropping retiree health benefits. You can only wonder how many yet-to-retire workers are next.

Even those Americans not among the ranks of the uninsured increasingly find themselves underinsured. In 2003, two-thirds of companies with 200 or more employees dealt with increasing costs by increasing the share that their employees had to pay and dropping coverage for particular services. With rising deductibles and co-pays, even if you have insurance, you may not be able to afford the care you need, and some benefits, like mental health services, may not be covered at all.

The problem of the uninsured and underinsured affects everyone. A recent Institute of Medicine study estimates that 18,000 25- to 64-year-old adults die every year as a result of lack of coverage. But even if you are insured, if you have a heart attack, and the ambulance that picks you up has to go three hospitals away because the nearby emergency rooms are full, you will have suffered from our inadequate system of coverage.

If, as a nation, we were saving money by denying insurance to some people, you could at least say there's some logic to it—no matter how cruel. But that's not the case. Despite the lack of universal coverage in our country, we still spend much more than countries that provide health care to all their citizens. We are No. 1 in the world in health care spending. On a per capita basis, health spending in the United States is 50 percent higher than the second-highest-spending country: Switzerland. Our health costs now constitute 14.9 percent of our gross domestic product and are growing at an alarming rate: by 2013, per capita health care spending is projected to increase to 18.4 percent of G.D.P.

What drives skyrocketing spending? The cost of prescription drugs rose almost twice as fast as spending on all health services, 40 percent in just the last few years.

Hospital costs have been rising as well, in large measure because more than one in four health care dollars go to administration. In 1999, that meant $300 billion per year went to pay for administrative bureaucracy: accountants and bookkeepers, who collect bills, negotiate with insurance companies and squeeze every possible reimbursement out of public programs like Medicare and Medicaid. Asthma and other pulmonary disorders linked to pollution contribute significantly to these costs, according to the health economist Ken Thorpe. Diabetes, high blood pressure and mental illness are also among the conditions that keep these costs rising.

If we spend so much, even after administrative costs, why does the United States rank behind 47 other countries in life expectancy and 42nd in infant mortality?

A lot of the money Americans spend is wasted on care that doesn't improve health. A recent study by Dartmouth researchers argues that close to a third of the $1.6 trillion we now spend on health care goes to care that is duplicative, fails to improve patient health or may even make it worse. A study in Santa Barbara, Calif., found that one out of every five lab tests and X-rays were conducted solely because previous test results were unavailable. A recent study found that for two-thirds of the patients who received a $15,000 surgery to prevent stroke, there was no compelling evidence that the surgery worked.

In situations in which the benefits of intervention are clear, many patients are not receiving that care. For example, few hospitalized patients at risk for bacterial pneumonia get the vaccine against it during their hospital stays. A recent study in The New England Journal of Medicine by Elizabeth McGlynn found that, overall, Americans are getting the care they should only 55 percent of the time.

As a whole, our ailing health care system is plagued with underuse, overuse and misuse. In a fundamental way, we pay for more for less than citizens in other advanced economies get.

*How We Deliver Care*

There is no "one size fits all" solution to our health care problems, but there are commonsense solutions that call for aggressive, creative and effective strategies as bold in their approach as they are practical in their effect.

First, the way we deliver health care must change. For too long our model of health care delivery has been based on the provider, the payer, anyone but the patient. Think about the fact that our medical records are still owned by a physician or a hospital, in bits and pieces, with no reasonable way to connect the dots of our conditions and our care over the years.

If we as individuals are responsible for keeping our own passports, 401(k) and tax files, educational histories and virtually every other document of our lives, then surely we can be responsible for keeping, or at least sharing custody of, our medical records. Studies have shown that when patients have a greater stake in their own care, they make better choices.

We should adopt the model of a "personal health record" controlled by the patient, who could use it not only to access the latest reliable health information on the Internet but also to record weight and blood sugar and to receive daily reminders to take asthma or cholesterol medication. Moreover, our current system revolves around "cases" rather than patients. Reimbursements are based on "episodes of treatment" rather than on a broader consideration of a patient's well-being. Thus it rewards the treatment of discrete diseases and injuries rather than keeping the patient alive and healthy. While we assure adequate privacy protections, we need care to focus on the patient.

Our system rewards clinicians for providing more services but not for keeping patients healthier. The structure of the health care system should shift toward rewarding doctors and health plans that treat patients with their long-term health needs in mind and rewarding patients who make sensible decisions about maintaining their own health.

*Harnessing Modernization*

As paradoxical as it is that advances in medical technology could potentially break our antiquated system, advances in other technologies may hold the answer to saving it. Using a 20th-century health care system to deal with 21st-century problems is nowhere more true than in the failure to use information technology.

Ten years ago, the Internet was used primarily by academics and the military. Now it is possible to imagine all of a person's health files stored securely on a computer file—test results, lab records, X-rays—accessible from any doctor's office. It is easy to imagine, yet our medical system is not there.

The average emergency-room doctor or nurse has minutes to gather information on a patient, from past records and from interviewing the patient or relatives. In the age of P.D.A.'s, why are these professionals forced to rely on a patient's memory?

Information technology can also be used to disseminate research. A government study recently documented that it takes 17 years from the time of a new medical discovery to the time clinicians actually incorporate that discovery into their practice at the bedside. Why not 17 seconds?

Why rely solely on the doctor's brain to store that information? Computers could crunch the variables on a particular patient's medical history, constantly update the algorithms with the latest scientific evidence and put that information at the clinician's fingertips at the point of care.

Americans may not be getting the care they should 45 percent of the time, but the tools exist to narrow that gap. Research shows that when physicians receive computerized reminders, statistics improve exponentially. Reminders can take the form of an alert in the electronic health record that the hospitalized patient has not had a pneumonia vaccine or as computerized questions to remind a doctor of the conditions that must be fulfilled before surgery is considered appropriate.

Newt Gingrich and I have disagreed on many issues, including health care, but I agree with some of the proposals he outlines in his book "Saving Lives and Saving Money," which support taking advantage of technological changes to create a more modern and efficient health care system. I have introduced legislation that promotes the use of information technology to update our health care system and organize it around the best interests of patients. Improvements in technology will end the paper chase, limit errors and reduce the number of malpractice suits.

I strongly believe that savings from information technology should not just be diffused throughout the system, never to be recaptured, but should be used to make substantial progress toward real universal coverage. By better using technology, we can lower health care costs throughout the system and thereby lower the exorbitant premiums that are placing a financial squeeze on businesses, individuals and the government. At the same time, some of those savings should be used to make substantial progress toward real universal coverage. (I may have just lost Newt Gingrich.)

*Taking the Broader View: Public Health And Prevention*

While we focus on empowering the individual through technology, we also have to recognize the larger factors that affect our health—from the environment to public health.

If asthma and other pulmonary disorders are the main drivers of increased health spending, that argues strongly that we should rethink how social and environmental factors impact our collective health. Consider that over the last century we have extended life expectancy by 30 years but that only 8 of those years can be credited to medical intervention. The rest of our gains stem from the construction of water and sewer systems, draining mosquito-infested swamps and addressing spoilage, quality and nutrition in our food supply. Yet we continue to underinvest in these important systematic measures—resulting in expensive health consequences like the explosion of asthma among children living in New York City or the harmful levels of lead found among children drinking water from the District of Columbia water system.

Our neglect of public health also contributes to spiraling health costs. We tend to address health care—as a nation and as individuals—after the sickness has taken hold, rather than addressing the cause through public health. Public health programs can help stop preventable disease and control dangerous behaviors. Take obesity, for example. Individuals should understand that they put their lives at risk with unhealthy behavior. But let's face it—we live in a fast-food nation, and we need to take steps, like restoring physical-education programs in schools, that support the individual's ability to master his or her own health. Studies conducted by the Centers for Disease Control and Prevention have identified "Programs That Work," which should be financed. It comes down to individual responsibility reinforced by national policy.

The public health system also needs to be brought up to date. The current public health tools were developed when the major threats to health were infectious diseases like malaria and tuberculosis. But now chronic diseases are the No. 1 killer in our country. We need to be concerned not just about pathogens but also about carcinogens.

Over the last three years, I have introduced legislation to increase investment in tracking and correlating environmental and health conditions. I have met with people from Long Island to Fallon, Nev., who want answers about cancer clusters in their communities. The data we have seen about lead and mercury contamination in our food and water suggest that the effects they have on the fetus and children may have contributed to the increasing number of children in special education with attention and learning disorders. We need more research to determine once and for all if increasing pollution in our communities and increasing rates of learning-related disabilities are cause and effect.

We should also be looking at sprawl—talking about the way we design our neighborhoods and schools and about our shrinking supply of safe, usable outdoor space—and how that contributes to asthma, stress and obesity. We should follow the example of the European Union and start testing the chemicals we use every day and not wait until we have a rash of birth defects or cancers on our hands before taking action. And we should look at factors in our society that lead to youth violence, substance abuse, depression and suicide and ultimately require insurance and treatment for mental health.

After Sept. 11, mental health was a significant factor in the health toll on our nation's first responders. And yet our mental health delivery system is underfinanced and unprepared.

Finally, as a society, we need greater emphasis on preventive care, an investment in people and their health that saves us money, because when families can't get preventive care, they often end up in the emergency room—getting the most expensive care possible.

*Expanding Coverage*

All that we have learned in the last decade confirms that our goal should continue to be what every other industrialized nation has achieved—health care that's always there for every citizen.

For the first time, this year a nonpartisan group dedicated to improving the nation's health, the Institute of Medicine, recommended that by 2010 everyone in the United States should have health insurance. Such a system would promote better overall health for individuals, families, communities and our nation by providing financial access for everyone to necessary, appropriate and effective health services.

It will, as I have been known to say, take the whole village to finance an affordable and accountable health system. Employers and individuals would share in its financing, and individuals would have to assume more responsibility for improving their own health and lifestyles. Private insurers and public programs would work together, playing complementary roles in ensuring that all Americans have the health care they need. Our society is already spending $35 billion a year to treat people who have no health insurance, and our economy loses $65 billion to $130 billion in productivity and other costs. We are already spending what it would cost if we reallocated those resources and required responsibility.

In the post 9/11 world, there is one more reason for universal coverage. The anthrax and ricin episodes, and the continuing threat posed by biological, chemical and radiological weapons, should make us painfully aware of the shortcomings of our fragmented system of health care. Can you imagine the aftermath of a bioterrorism attack, with thousands of people flooding emergency rooms and bureaucrats demanding proof of insurance coverage from each and every one? Those without coverage might not see a doctor until after they had infected others.

Insurance should be about sharing risk and responsibility—pooling resources and risk to protect ourselves from the devastating cost of illness or injury. It should not be about further dividing us. Competition should reward health plans for quality and cost savings, not for how many bad risks they can exclude—especially as we enter the genomic age, when all of us could have uninsurable risks written into our genes.

So achieving comprehensive health care reform is no simple feat, as I learned a decade ago. None of these ideas mean anything if the political will to ensure that they happen doesn't exist.

Some people believe that the only solution to our present cost explosion is to shift the cost and risk onto individuals in what is called "consumer driven" health care. Each consumer would have an individual health care account and would monitor his or her own spending. But instead of putting consumers in the driver's seat, it actually leaves consumers at the mercy of a broken market. This system shifts the costs, the risks and the burdens of disease onto the individuals who have the misfortune of being sick. Think about the times you have been sick or injured—were you able under those circumstances to negotiate for the best price or shop for the best care? And instead of giving individuals, providers and payers incentives for better care, this cost-shifting approach actually causes individuals to delay or skip needed services, resulting in worse health and more expensive health needs later on.

Meanwhile, proposals like those for individual health insurance tax credits, without reforms for the individual insurance market, leave individuals in the lurch as well. We know that asthmatics can have their entire respiratory systems excluded from coverage. Individual insurance companies can increase your premium or limit coverage for factors like age, previous medical history or even flat feet. Those in the individual market cannot pool their risk with colleagues or other members of the group. The coverage you can get and the price you pay for it will reflect individual risk, and you simply don't receive many of the benefits of what we consider traditional insurance when people pool risks. So the proposal to give individuals tax credits to buy coverage in the individual market, without any rules of fair play, won't provide much help for Americans who need health care. In the same way, the recent Medicare bill, which seeks to privatize Medicare benefits, long a government guarantee, threatens to leave the "bad risks" without any affordable coverage. With the new genetic information at our disposal, that could mean any one of us could one day be denied health insurance.

When many of those who opposed the Health Security Act look back, they are still proud of their achievement in blocking our reform plan. The focus of that proposal was to cover everybody by enabling the healthier to pool the "risk" with others. The plan was to redirect what we currently pay for uninsured care into expanding health coverage.

We could make cosmetic changes to the system we currently have, but that would simply take what is already a Rube Goldberg contraption and make it larger and even more unwieldy. We could go the route many have advocated, putting the burden almost entirely on individuals, thereby creating a veritable nationwide health care casino in which you win or lose should illness strike you or someone in your family. Or we could decide to develop a new social contract for a new century premised on joint responsibility to prevent disease and provide those who need care access to it. This would not let us as individuals off the hook. In fact, joint responsibility demands accountability from patients, employers, payers and society as a whole.

What will we say about ourselves 10 years from today? If we finally act to reform what we know needs to change, we may take credit in building a health care system that covers everyone and improves the quality of all our lives. But if we continue to dither and disagree, divided by ideology and frozen into inaction by competing special interests, then we will share in the blame for the collapse of health care in America, where rising costs break the back of our economy and leave too many people without the medical attention they need.

The nexus of globalization, the revolution in medical technology and the seismic pressures imposed by the contradictions in our current health care system will force radical changes whether we choose them or not. We can do nothing, we can take incremental steps—or we can implement wide-ranging reform.

To me, the case for action is clear. And as we work to develop long-term solutions, we can take steps now to help address the immediate problems we face. As Senator John Kerry has proposed, we should cover everyone living in poverty, and all children; allow people to buy into the federal employee health benefits program; and also help employers by reinsuring high-cost claims while assuming more of the costs from hard-pressed state and local governments.

We can pass real privacy legislation that will ensure that Americans continue to feel secure in the trust they place in others for their most intimate medical information. And we can realize the promise of savings through information technology and disease management by passing quality health legislation now.

If we do not fix the problems of the present, we are doomed to live with the consequences in the future. As someone who tried to promote comprehensive health care reform a decade ago and decided to push for incremental changes in the years since, I still believe America needs sensible, wide-ranging reform that, leads to quality health care coverage available to all Americans at an affordable cost.

The present system is unsustainable. The only question is whether we will master the change or it will master us.

## DISCUSSION QUESTIONS

1. One of the problems of passing comprehensive health care is rooted in the paradox presented in the introduction to this debate. If 80 percent of Americans are happy with their health care and 20 percent are not, the political impetus behind change will be absent unless those who have health insurance are willing to speak up on behalf of those who do not. This problem becomes worse if the situation is viewed as a zero-sum game (that is, under comprehensive health care, the quality of care for the 80 percent may not be quite as good as it is now). Are there any solutions to this problem? How do you view the issue? Would you be willing to have higher co-pays or a more narrow range of coverage to make sure that everyone has insurance?

2. One of the strongest arguments against comprehensive health care is that the government should not be involved in providing health care. What positive role can the government play in the provision of health care, and which parts of health care are better left to the market? Would you favor Gervais's radical surgery of having a true free market for health care? If this approach is taken, how would health care be provided for those who cannot afford it?

3. Of all the policy proposals outlined by the authors, which ones should be adopted as soon as possible and which ones are good long-term goals? Alternatively, which proposals are non-starters?

# CHAPTER 16

# Foreign Policy and World Politics

## 82

## "The Age of Open Society"

### GEORGE SOROS

*"Globalization" refers, generally speaking, to the diffusion of interests and ide-
ologies across national borders. Proponents of globalization point to the hope
that it will encourage global economic development, and foster universal human
rights that are not dependent on where someone happens to live. Critics fall
into two camps. One consists of those who fear that globalization will undermine national sovereignty and lead to a "one world" government that leaves
everyone at the mercy of distant bureaucrats and officials. The other camp consists of those who see globalization as a smokescreen for corporate hegemony,
where multinational corporations exploit workers in countries with low wages,
few job protections, and lax environmental regulation, all in the name of higher
profits.*

*Soros believes that economic globalization and political globalization are
out of sync: although capital and markets move freely across national boundaries, political institutions do not. A global "open society" would, in his view,
insure that the political and social needs of all countries are met (not simply the
needs of industrialized nations, whose interests tend to dominate international
markets), and would foster the development of stable political and financial institutions. This would require a broad international organization, either as part
of the United Nations or as an independent institution. It would have to be
based on the idea that there are interests that transcend questions of national
sovereignty.*

Global politics and global economics are dangerously out of sync.
Although we live in a global economy characterized by free trade
and the free movement of capital, our politics are still based on the sovereignty of the state. International institutions exist, but their powers are
limited by how much authority states are willing to confer on them. At

the same time, the powers of the state are limited by the freedom of capital to escape taxation and regulation by moving elsewhere. This is particularly true of the countries at the periphery of the global capitalist system, whose economic destiny depends on what happens at the center.

This state of affairs would be sustainable if the market mechanism could be trusted to satisfy social needs. But that is not the case.

We need to find international political arrangements that can meet the requirements of an increasingly interdependent world. These arrangements ought to be built on the principles of open society. A perfect society is beyond our reach. We must content ourselves with the next best thing: a society that holds itself open to improvement. We need institutions that allow people of different views, interests, and backgrounds to live together in peace. These institutions should assure the greatest degree of freedom compatible with the common interest. Many mature democracies come close to qualifying as open societies. But they refuse to accept openness as a universal principle.

How could this principle of openness be translated into practice? By the open societies of the world forming an alliance for this purpose. The alliance would have two distinct but interrelated goals: to foster the development of open society within individual countries; and to establish international laws, rules of conduct, and institutions to implement these norms.

It is contrary to the principles of open society to dictate from the outside how a society should govern itself. Yet the matter cannot be left entirely to the state, either. The state can be an instrument of oppression. To the extent possible, outside help should take the form of incentives; the evolution of open society requires aid for economic and institutional development. Punitive measures, though sometimes unavoidable, tend to be counterproductive.

Unfortunately, positive intervention is out of favor because of an excessive faith in the magic of the marketplace. There is an alliance of democratic countries, NATO, capable of military intervention, but there is no similar alliance to engage in constructive intervention. This open-society alliance ought to have a much broader membership than NATO, and it must include nongovernmental members as well as heads of state. As former U.S. Secretary of State Henry Kissinger points out, states have interests but no principles; we cannot rely on them to implement the principle of openness.

Democratic governments are, however, responsive to the wishes of their electorates. Therefore, the impulse for the alliance has to come from the people, not from their leaders. Citizens living in open societies must recognize a global open society as something worth sacrifice. This responsibility rests in particular with the United States, the sole surviving superpower and the dominant force in the global capitalist system. There can be no global open society without its leadership. But the United

States has become carried away by its success and fails to see why it should subordinate its self-interest to some nebulous common principle. The United States jealously guards its sovereignty and behaves as if it ought to be the sole arbiter of right and wrong. Washington will have to undergo a significant change of heart before it is ready to lead an open-society alliance.

The alliance, if it comes to pass, must not lose sight of its own fallibity. Foreign aid, though very valuable, is notoriously inefficient. Rule-based incentives are more promising. The international financial architecture needs to be redesigned to help give underdeveloped countries a leg up. Incentives would be conditional on each country's success in establishing open political and financial institutions.

The alliance could act within the United Nations, or it could go it alone. But a commitment to such an alliance would offer an opportunity to reform the United Nations. The noble intentions annunciated in the preamble of the U.N. Charter can never be attained as long as the United Nations remains a rigid association of sovereign states. But there is ample room for improvement, and an open-society alliance would be a start. Perhaps one day, then, historians will look back at these years to come as the Age of Open Society.

## Discussion Questions

1. Is Soros's suggestion about an open society practical? Do you think there are circumstances under which nations would agree to such a proposal?

2. How, if at all, will globalization change notions about national identity? Do you think that, twenty-five or fifty years from now, being a U.S. citizen—or a citizen of any other country—will have the same meaning as it does now?

# 83

# "Reality Check"

## PETER D. SUTHERLAND

*Sutherland confronts the arguments against globalization. Over the past few years, protesters have disrupted meetings of international economic organizations (especially the World Trade Organization, an institution created to foster global free trade). Susan George, a critic of the World Trade Organization, gave the flavor of the arguments against globalization in a recent article in the journal* The Nation: *" 'Free trade' as managed by the World Trade Organization and reinvigorated at the recent negotiations in Doha is largely the freedom of the fox in the henhouse. Despite the advance on generic drugs for pandemics like AIDS, tuberculosis and malaria, the South's needs are shelved and the transnationals continue to run the show according to their own preferred rules."*

*Sutherland has little patience with such protests, and believes that protesters are motivated by a simplistic and inaccurate view of what globalization is about: "The notion that globalization is an international conspiracy on the part of industrial-country governments and large firms to marginalize the poorest nations, to exploit low wages and social costs wherever they may be found . . . and even to undermine human rights and cut away democratic processes that stand in the way of ever more open markets is, of course, utter nonsense." He disagrees that international trade organizations ignore the needs of poor countries, and argues that increased global trade is (and has been) the most effective mechanism of economic development. At the same time, he offers some suggestions on how to insure that existing institutions are strengthened.*

The Seattle Ministerial Conference of the World Trade Organization (WTO) demonstrated with disturbing force the huge confusions that haunt the public mind and much of global politics about the nature of trade and the process now known as globalization. The notion that globalization is an international conspiracy on the part of industrial-country governments and large firms to marginalize the poorest nations, to exploit low wages and social costs wherever they may be found, to diminish cultures in the interests of an Anglo-Saxon model of lifestyle and language, and even to undermine human rights and cut away democratic processes that stand in the way of ever more open markets is, of course, utter nonsense. Yet the Seattle demonstrations vividly exhibited the worrying tendency to equate these concerns and others to the existence and potential development of the World Trade Organization, the institutional and legal face of the world trade system.

This outpouring of misconceived, ill-understood propaganda against a system that has brought vast gains to most nations over the past few decades is extraordinarily dangerous. It is a threat to the prospects of a better life for many millions, perhaps billions, of people at the start of the new millennium. If left unquestioned and unchallenged in the interests of political correctness or political advantage, this sentiment could set the cause of economic and social development back 20 years. This threat is made all the more serious by the difficult new challenges facing governments today. Still, Seattle showed more clearly some of the institutional difficulties of managing effective decision-making processes, with over 100 countries truly interested and involved in managing the geopolitical realities of the 21st century.

## The Biggest Straw Man

In order to understand the dangers implied by attacks on the WTO, one must first distinguish between "globalization" and the World Trade Organization. Neither as a body of international law nor as a governmental institution can the WTO be regarded as synonymous with globalization. The WTO, like its predecessor the General Agreement on Tariffs and Trade (GATT), is a collection of rules and undertakings voluntarily entered into and implemented by governments on the basis of consensus among those governments to provide a predictable, stable, and secure environment in which all types of firms can trade and invest. A small transfer of national sovereignty (insofar as any purely intergovernmental structure can affect sovereignty) in the interest of internationally enforceable disciplines brings economic gains for all and prevents economic muscle from being the sole arbiter of commercial advantage. It is easy to argue that in a period when business is as likely to be conducted at the global level as at the national, the WTO recovers a degree of sovereignty for governments that otherwise find themselves no longer able to influence significant aspects of their economic future.

Of course, open and secure markets have encouraged global trade and investment. They have provided jobs, consumer choice, and rising personal wealth in large parts of the world, including many developing countries. Governments everywhere want to see their firms able to trade, and they actively seek inward investment by foreign firms. But that is not the whole story of globalization. The WTO has had only a marginal effect on other significant elements, most of which relate to the mobility of people, information, culture, technology and capital. Air transport, telecommunications, the media, and now the internet are four of the most crucial drivers of globalization. While they are not without their dangers or inadequacies, few would seriously argue that they have not brought widespread benefits. These innovations represent the positive face of the global economy.

Are the more troublesome aspects of globalization really a reflection of the trading system, or do they represent quite different policy failures, including poor education and training, misplaced and inefficient government intervention in industry, corruption in both the public and private sectors, poor governance, crime, lack of transparency in regulatory systems, inadequate or inappropriate social security and pensions systems, and so on? Admittedly, the trading system has not always provided the right results; for instance, it ought to be able to deliver more for the least-developed countries, even if it cannot solve all their problems. However, equating the WTO with the difficulties of the global economy risks damaging a system which has given much and still has more to offer. Such thinking also neglects the importance of the WTO's fundamental role in simply facilitating trade and investment. The tendency to turn to the trade rules to resolve every challenge facing mankind—the environment, human rights, and labor standards—is almost as dangerous as the desire to dismantle the system in order to halt a process of globalization that is beyond the realm of any institution.

*Fruits of the Uruguay Round*

The first thing governments need to do in the current atmosphere of sometimes dubiously motivated protest and fear is to stop apologizing for the WTO and start defending it. The GATT helped create three decades of remarkably healthy economic growth. It succeeded in a low-profile manner because, in the 1950s and 1960s, high customs duties could be brought down steadily without attracting much political controversy. By the time the Uruguay Round was launched in 1986, the world was left with the hard cases of international trade. Negotiators finally had to face up to protectionism in the most sensitive industries of the developed countries, particularly in textiles, clothing, footwear, agriculture, steel, and automobiles. They also came to realize that the next stages of reducing protection and opening markets, and thus re-establishing the kind of trade growth spurred by the GATT, would mean moving some of the focus of negotiation from conditions at the border (such as tariffs and quota restrictions) to the heart of domestic regulation and sectoral support.

Immense political effort was required at the highest levels of government, but the Uruguay Round succeeded and established the WTO in the process. The advances made on all fronts cannot be underestimated. Policies in agriculture underwent a revolution: all market-access restrictions were translated into transparent tariffs, and the process of winding back the most distorting features of domestic support and export subsidies was initiated. A higher level of practical liberalization for farm goods might have been preferred, but the fundamental policy changes are irreversible and provide the basis to go further next time. Similarly, in textiles and clothing all the countries maintaining heavy quantitative controls on imports are committed to phasing them out. It will take nearly ten years, but the agreement at Uruguay marked a fundamental change of heart and direction.

Many other trade rules were amended, clarified, or added to the system. The practice of "negotiating" so-called "voluntary export restraints" affecting automobiles, steel, cutlery, and many other products for which consumers were forced to pay far more than was reasonable was outlawed. Some of the most damaging features of anti-dumping practices were cut back. Modern rules on technical barriers to trade and health and safety regulation were also put in place.

An agreement requiring intellectual property rights to be available and enforceable in all WTO countries was concluded for the first time, despite doubts and difficulties in some industrial and developing countries. There were two final jewels in the crown. First, an agreement on trade in services brought GATT-like disciplines and concessions in sectors as diverse as banking, telecommunications, professional services, travel, tourism, and the audio-visual industry. Financial services and telecommunications were the subject of additional valuable packages of concessions in the past three years, and the new negotiations, beginning this year, will take the process of progressive liberalization in the services sector much further. Second, the entire body of WTO disciplines and concessions was made enforceable through a tough dispute-settlement procedure that has now been used in nearly 200 cases.

It has become almost an article of faith that while all of these developments were good for the industrialized countries and some of the more advanced developing countries, many poorer countries lost out. Some critics suggest that these countries did not benefit from the results of the round, and that they were, in fact, further marginalized and impoverished. According to these critics, such marginalization is not surprising because developing countries had little or no voice in the negotiations that culminated in agreement at the end of 1993.

Such a position is an insult to the abilities of the many developing country trade negotiators who participated fully in the Uruguay Round. Although I took responsibility at a comparatively late stage, I can attest to the effectiveness and strength of purpose of these officials and ministers from poorer nations. They had considerable influence on the original development of the Uruguay Round agenda; worked assiduously through the eight-year process of examination and elucidation of issues, and negotiation of texts; and were in the foreground during the tough final months of bargaining. Certainly the United States, the European Union, and Japan were more influential, and many of the Uruguay Round texts pay particular attention to their interests. But the developing countries succeeded for the first time in any trade round in melding an influence on the final outcome quite disproportionate to their share of world trade. The WTO is very much their institution and the rules of world trade are as much their rules as those of the industrial countries.

## Myths and Realities

So, if it is untrue that developing countries were ignored in the establishment of the WTO, is it at least true that they saw few practical benefits in terms of trade and investment? Again, the answer is no. A few measures demonstrating the longterm trends rather than the shortterm aberrations bolster the point. Are developing countries benefiting from more open industrial-country markets? The answer is yes; despite the fall in trade during 1997 because of the drop in commodity prices and the Asian financial crisis, the share of developing countries and the transition economies in the imports of developed countries increased to 25 percent in 1998 from 22.8 percent in 1994. Has the developing countries' share in world trade grown? Again, yes. Despite the setbacks of 1997–1998, the latest WTO figures show that the share of developing countries in world exports of manufactures in 1998 was one percent higher than in 1994, and 6.4 percent higher than in 1990. The same overall growth trend can be observed for merchandise exports generally as well as agricultural products.

What about investment? Have developing countries seen an inward flow of productive investment, as they should if they offer more open markets with stable trade regimes based upon WTO disciplines? As with trade, the picture is mixed, with considerable variations in performance. However, figures from the UN Conference on Trade and Development show that overall inward foreign direct investment (FDI) flows to the developing world rose steadily and consistently from an average of US$35 billion a year in the period 1987–92 to US$166 billion in 1998. Taken as a percentage of gross fixed capital formation, FDI inflows to developing countries rose from an average of 3.9 percent in the period 1987–92 to 10.3 percent in 1998.

There is nothing fundamentally wrong with the system that calls for a wholesale rethinking on behalf of the developing countries. It is accepted that some developing countries have had difficulty in implementing some Uruguay Round commitments. Political and conceptual difficulties have hampered the implementation of certain intellectual property commitments in countries like India. In some of the poorest economies, the absence of solid institutional and technological infrastructure has made the implementation of agreements such as those on customs valuation and health and safety standards difficult. But patience and the right kind of technical assistance can resolve such problems over time. They are not evidence of a systemic failure in the WTO.

Indeed, many developing countries are successfully integrating themselves into the global economy through their commitment to WTO obligations. The failure of the Seattle meeting effectively blocked the continuation of that process or, at the very least, reduced opportunities for further progress. Essentially all that remains is the potential for negotiations on trade in services and agriculture that were mandated in the Uruguay Round agreements. This is not a small agenda, and any successful conclusion in the near future remains in question.

What has been lost or suspended is a larger and, in some respects more urgent, agenda. Developing countries have clearly been denied much that they rightly expected in the implementation of Uruguay Round commitments. They had reasonable demands that industrial countries implement in better faith the agreement to phase out textiles and clothing quotas. The agricultural agreement should have brought them more commercial advantage than has been the case. Antidumping legislation has continued to operate too stringently to the disadvantage of poorer countries. On the other hand, these countries have sometimes had difficulties in meeting their own obligations. That is hardly surprising since they have been required to go much further, much faster than was ever expected of industrial countries. In most cases, additional time needed for implementation of commitments should willingly be provided along with generous technical assistance efforts and the necessary funding for institutional capacity-building.

The least developed countries have been denied the duty-free treatment in market access that has long been promised and discussed in the context of a new round. The entire world has lost the commercial opportunities that would have sprung from global tariff and non-tariff-barrier negotiations covering industrial products. It is estimated that a 50 percent reduction in industrial tariffs would raise some US$270 billion in global income per year, and that developing countries could benefit from as much as 95 percent of the gains from liberalizing trade in manufactures.

### Before the Next Round

Perhaps those opportunities will re-emerge, but the immediate priority is not to rush to launch a new round. Governments need to learn the lessons of the Seattle meeting and prepare the ground for the multilateral trading system to move forward on the basis of willing consensus among governments. I would propose four major areas as needing profound reconsideration.

First, coherence in trade policymaking is needed. Until now, this has tended to mean cooperation between the secretariats of the WTO and other major international institutions like the World Bank and the International Monetary Fund. Coherence should now take on a different meaning. It should ensure that the stances of WTO member governments in trade negotiations reflect a domestic consensus. Government departments must coordinate effectively among themselves so that, for instance, environmental, public health, or development concerns are factored into trade-policy decision-making early on. Governments must listen to and work with many different constituencies in an open and transparent manner. Only then can the WTO be clear of the foolish charge that it is some form of government-business conspiracy.

Second, negotiations and decision-making within the WTO itself need to become more coherent and effective. This may require a high level management structure in Geneva, perhaps based upon a restricted constituency-based management or advisory board. Senior policymakers should come to Geneva regularly to set the body's business in the fullest context, including financial development, environmental concerns, and other considerations. Moreover, both the preparatory process and the Seattle ministerial meeting demonstrated that while full transparency is vital—and the institution will have to steel itself to become yet more open—efficient and effective decision-making is necessary if continued paralysis is to be avoided. Of course, negotiating positions may often be so far apart that compromise is simply not possible. Recent history suggests, however, that the techniques of negotiating in a multilateral environment are either inoperable or have been forgotten.

Third, careful consideration must now be given to the speed and intensity with which a new round or any other effort to extend the trading system is pursued. There can be little doubt that the Seattle meeting was both premature and over-burdened with proposals that were poorly thought-out, unnecessary, or premature. Is there really an urgent need to launch a broad-based new trade round in the immediate future? If one believes that neither agriculture nor services negotiations can progress outside such a round, then perhaps the answer is a qualified "yes." But, if the reality is such that an early start would be unlikely to move forward with any conviction, then perhaps governments should take a deep breath and await a more propitious time. Nothing would damage the WTO's image further than another failed attempt to initiate a round.

Fourth, regardless of a new round, governments must now live up to their responsibilities and start energetically defending the principles on which the WTO is based. A "human face" for the trading system is appropriate if it does not serve to undermine the foundations of the system and the huge gains it has provided humanity over the past 50 years. It is perfectly possible to understand and respond to the concerns of those who doubt the value of the system without holding it hostage to local politics. The critics must understand that however justified their causes, the world would not be a better place without the WTO and without continued efforts to make it still more effective for all its members.

This is a turning point for the global trading system. How governments respond to the challenges raised by the Seattle Ministerial Conference could have an overwhelming influence on the contribution that the institution can have on the creation of a better society in the future. Globalization remains a fact and an opportunity. The WTO is one of the most effective instruments at our disposal for translating the opportunity into the reality of improved welfare for billions of citizens. There is no question that it could be a better instrument. But it is the best that we have at our disposal and are likely to have in the future. Governments must learn to use it wisely, change it carefully, and support it convincingly.

## DISCUSSION QUESTIONS

1. Many critics of globalization argue that allowing goods and capital to move freely across borders only serves to move jobs to countries with the cheapest (and most exploitable) labor force. Supporters argue that these jobs, even though they might not pay much by Western standards, still provide much better opportunities than would otherwise be available. Who do you think has the better case?

2. Does your campus have organizations active in "anti-sweatshop" organizations (these groups, among other things, have encouraged universities to insure that clothing and other gear with university symbols are not made by child labor or in dangerous factories)? What impact have these organizations had on student opinion?

3. What is the alternative to globalization? What costs are associated with, for example, protecting domestic jobs from being exported? What are the benefits of such protection?

## DEBATING THE ISSUES: FOREIGN POLICY: THE WAR IN IRAQ

The United States is at war, and will likely be involved in reconstructing Iraq for decades. The war, which began in March 2003, is the focal point of both support and opposition to the Bush Administration. Bush's supporters argue that removing Saddam Hussein was a crucial step in the long-term war on terror, as it resulted in the elimination of a despot who clearly wanted weapons of mass destruction and was intent on fomenting global instability. Opponents of the war claimed that Bush flatly misrepresented the nature of the threat, relying on flawed intelligence, and fostered—without explicitly saying so—the inaccurate impression that Iraq was involved in the 9/11 attacks.

The recriminations continue into the second year of reconstruction. Critics, like Naomi Klein, argue that the entire effort was part of a neocon (neo-conservative) ideological fantasy to create an ideal free-market utopia that would prove their low-tax, no-regulation, privatization theories. The steps taken after the war were designed not to create stability, but reflected a radical agenda designed to shock Iraqis into submission and turn the entire country over to private corporate interests. "Year Zero" refers to the desire to simply erase existing Iraqi civil society and replace it with a pure capitalist vision. Operating from this premise, Klein maintains, led U.S. authorities to decimate the public sector by dismissing hundreds of thousands of civil servants and sell off public assets. This, she concludes, has fed the insurgency that still occupies the military more than two years later.

Lowry also notes that much has gone wrong in the post-war environment, but he disputes the common charge that it is the result of a lack of planning. There was plenty of planning, he says, but decision makers simply could not predict everything that might happen. The infrastructure turned out to be in far worse shape than anyone anticipated, and the looting was much quicker and more extensive than anyone would have believed would happen. Decision makers (as well as critics of the war) expected a huge humanitarian catastrophe that did not materialize. Bremer's "De-Baathification" policy—in which he removed all members of Hussein's Baath Party from public positions—and his decision to dissolve the Iraqi Army, were mistakes, according to Lowery, but the alternatives were just as unappealing. However, the difficulties, he concludes, do not mean that the war was not worth fighting.

David Gelernter, a Yale University computer scientist, criticizes opponents of the war for refusing to recognize the horror of the Hussein regime. Even if there were no weapons of mass destruction, deposing a dictator responsible for hundreds of thousands of deaths, mass graves, and unspeakable violence, has great value in itself. He likens the world's indifference to Hussein's brutality to the world's indifference to Hitler in the 1930s, what he calls "the Holocaust Shrug."

## 84

# "The Holocaust Shrug: Why Is There So Much Indifference to the Liberation of Iraq?"

### DAVID GELERNTER

I hear and read all the time about Democratic fury; evidently, enraged Democrats are prepared to do whatever it takes to rid the country of George W. Bush's foul presence. Somehow Republican rage doesn't seem quite as newsworthy (and when it does show up, the storyline is usually "Republicans Angry at Bush"). To be fair, Republicans do control the presidency and both houses of Congress, and ought to be far gone in euphoria. But they are not. There are lots of unhappy and quite a few furious ones out there, and they are not all mad at the president. Some reporters will find this hard to believe, but quite a lot of them are actually mad at the Democrats.

Consider Iraq. By overthrowing Saddam, we stopped a loathsome bloody massacre—a hell-on-earth that would have been all too easily dismissed as fantastic propaganda if we hadn't seen and heard the victims and watched the torturers on videotape. Now: There is all sorts of latitude for legitimate attack on the Bush administration and Iraq. A Bush critic could allege that our preparation was lousy, our strategy wrong, our postwar administration a failure, and so on ad inimitum . . . so long as he stays in ground contact with the basic truth: This war was an unmitigated triumph for humanity. Everything we have learned since the end of full-scale fighting has only made it seem more of a triumph.

But Democratic talk about Iraq is dominated not by the hell and horror we abolished or the pride and joy of what we achieved. Many Democrats mention Saddam's crimes only grudgingly. What they really want to discuss is how the administration "lied" about WMDs (one of the more infantile accusations in modern political history), how (thanks to Iraq) our allies can't stand us anymore, how (on account of Iraq) we are shortchanging the war on terror. But don't you understand, a listener wants to scream, that Saddam's government was ripping human flesh to shreds?

Was consuming whole populations by greedy mouthfuls, masticating them, drooling blood? Committing crimes that are painful even to describe? Don't you understand what we achieved by liberating Iraq, what mankind achieved? When we hear about Saddam and his two sons, how can we help but think of the three-faced Lucifer at the bottom of Dante's hell?—"with six eyes he was weeping and over three chins dripped tears and bloody foam," *Con sel occhi plangea, e per tre menti / gocciava 'l pianto e sanguinosa bava,* as he crushes human life between his teeth.

I could understand the Democrats' insisting that this was no Republican operation; "we were in favor of it too, we voted for it too, and then voted more money to fund it; we want some credit!" Those would be reasonable political claims. But if you talk as if this war were one big, stupid blunder that we are stuck with and have to make the best of—you are nowhere near shouting distance of reality; people would suspect your sanity if you were not a politician already. Instead of insisting that the war belongs to them, too, Democrats are running top speed in the other direction. Howard Dean led the way on this flight from duty, honor, and truth, but it didn't take long for most of the nation's prominent Democrats (with a few honorable exceptions) to jump aboard the Dean express—which is now, absent Dean, a runaway train.

People ask, why this big deal about Saddam? "Isn't X evil too, and what about Y, and how can you possibly ignore Z?" But we aren't automata; we are able to make distinctions. Some evil is beyond our power to stop. That doesn't absolve us from stopping what we can. All cruelty is bad. Yet some cruel and evil men are worse than others. By any standard we did right by overthrowing Saddam and do wrong by denying or belittling that fact.

The Democrats' refusal to acknowledge the moral importance of the Coalition's Iraq victory felt, at first, like the Clinton treatment—more relativistic, warped-earth moral geometry in which the truth gradually approaches infinite malleability. Overthrowing vicious dictatorships and stopping crimes against humanity were no longer that big a deal once Republicans were running the show. It seemed like the same old hypocrisy, sadly familiar. (I will even concede, for what it's worth, that Republicans can be inconsistent and hypocritical too.)

But as we learned more about Saddam's crimes, and Democrats grew less convinced that the war was right and was necessary . . . their response took on a far more sinister color. It started to resemble the Holocaust Shrug.

I suggest only diffidently that the world's indifference to the Coalition's achievement resembles its long-running, well-established lack of interest in Hitler's crimes. I don't claim that Saddam resembles Hitler; I do claim that the world's indifference to Saddam resembles its indifference to Hitler.

The Holocaust was unique—"fundamentally different," the German philosopher Karl Jaspers wrote, "from all crimes that have existed in the past." Hitler's mission was to convert Germany and eventually all Europe into an engine of annihilating Jew-hatred. He tore the heart out of the Jewish nation. There is nothing "universal" or "paradigmatic" about the Holocaust, and next to Hitler, Saddam is a mere child with a boyish love of torture and mass murder.

Yet Saddam, like Hitler, murdered people sadistically and systematically for the crime of being born. Saddam, like Hitler, believed that mass murder should be efficient, with minimal fuss and bother; it is no accident that both were big believers in poison gas. Saddam's program, like Hitler's, attracted all sorts of sadists; many of Saddam's and Hitler's crimes were not quite as no-fuss, no-muss as the Big Boss preferred. Evidently Saddam, like Hitler, did not personally torture his prisoners, but Saddam (like Hitler) allowed and condoned torture that will stand as a black mark against mankind forever.

Hitler was in a profoundly, fundamentally different league. And yet the distinction is unlikely to have mattered much to a Kurd mother watching her child choke to death on poison gas, or a Shiite about to be diced to bloody pulp. The colossal scale and the routine, systematic nature of torture and murder under Saddam puts him in a special category too. Saddam was small compared with Hitler, yet he was like Hitler not only in what he wanted but in what he did. When we marched into Iraq, we halted a small-scale holocaust.

I could understand people disagreeing with this claim, arguing that Saddam was evil but not that kind of evil, not evil enough to deserve being discussed in those terms. But the opposition I hear doesn't dwell on the nature of Saddam's crimes. It dwells on the nature of America's—our mistakes, our malfeasance, our "lies." It sounds loonier and farther from reality all the time, more and more like the Holocaust Shrug.

Turning away is not evil; it is merely human. And that's bad enough. For years I myself found it easy to ignore or shrug off Saddam's reported crimes. I had no love for Iraq or Iraqis. Before and during the war I wrote pieces suggesting that Americans not romanticize Iraqis; that we understand postwar Iraq more in terms of occupied Germany than liberated France. But during and after the war it gradually became impossible to ignore the staggering enormity of what Saddam had committed against his own people. And when we saw those mass graveyards and torture chambers, heard more and more victims speak, watched those videotapes, the conclusion became inescapable: This war was screamingly, shriekingly necessary.

But instead of exulting in our victory, too many of us shrug and turn away and change the subject.

Young people might be misled about the world's response to the Holocaust by the current academic taste for "Holocaust studies" and related projects. It wasn't always this way.

In the years right after the war, there was Holocaust horror all over the world. The appearance of such books as Eli Wiesel's *Night* and Anne Frank's diary kept people thinking. But after that, silence set in. In 1981 Lucy Dawidowicz, most distinguished of all Holocaust historians, wrote of "this historiographical mystery of why the Holocaust was belittled or overlooked in the history books." I remember the 1960s (when I was a child growing up) as years during which the Holocaust was old stuff. On the whole, neither Jews nor gentiles wanted to think about it much. I remember the time and mood acutely on account of travels with my grandfather.

He was a rabbi and a loving but not a happy man. His synagogue was in Brooklyn, at the heart of an area that was full of resettled Holocaust survivors. He would visit them often, especially ones who had lost their families and not remarried. Naturally they were the loneliest. But what they suffered from most was not loneliness but the pressure of not telling. Pressure against their skulls from the inside, hard to bear. They needed to speak, but no one needed to listen.

Old or middle-aged men with gray faces and narrow wrists where the camp number was tattooed forever in dirty turquoise, living alone in small apartments: They would go on for an hour or more, mumbling with down-cast eyes as if they were embarrassed—but they were not embarrassed; they were merely trying to keep emotion at bay so they could finish. Not to be cut down by emotion was the thing; they wanted to make it through to the end. So they would mumble quickly as if they were making a run for it, in Yiddish or sometimes Hebrew or, occasionally, heavily accented English. My Hebrew was inadequate and my Yiddish was worse, but I could get the gist, and my grandfather would fill me in afterward. Once an old man wanted to tell us how one man in a barracks of 40 had stolen a piece of bread (or something like that), and in retaliation the whole group was forced at gunpoint to duck-walk in the snow for hours. He didn't know the right word, so he got down on the floor to show us—an old man; but he had to tell us what had happened.

Steven Vincent went to Iraq after the war and reported in Commentary about Maha Fattah Karah, an old woman, sobbing. "I look to America. I ask America to help me. I ask America not to forget me." Saddam murdered her husband and son. That story takes me back.

My grandfather was driven. He spent years at one point translating a rabbi's memoir from Hebrew, then more years trying to find a publisher—any publisher; but no one wanted it. Holocaust memoirs were a dime a dozen, and (truth to tell) had rarely been hot literary properties in any case. Then he shopped the "private publishers" who would bring out a book for a fee. He tried hard to raise the money. He was a good money-raiser for many fine causes. But this time he failed. No one wanted to underwrite a Holocaust memoir. The book never did appear.

The Holocaust Shrug: To turn away is a natural human reaction. In

1999 (Steven Vincent reports) the Shiite cleric Sadeq al Sadr offended Saddam, whose operatives raped Sadeq's sister in front of him and then killed him by driving nails into his skull. Who can grasp it? In any case, today's sophisticates cultivate shallowness. They deal in cynicism, irony, casual bitterness; not in anguish or horror or joy.

Lucy Dawidowicz discussed the unique enormity of the Holocaust. It destroyed the creative center of world Jewry and transferred premeditated, systematic genocide from "unthinkable" to "thinkable, therefore doable." Mankind has crouched ever since beneath a black cloud of sin and shame.

Nothing will erase the Holocaust, but it is clear what kind of gesture would counterbalance it and maybe lift the cloud: If some army went selflessly to war (a major war, not a rescue operation) merely to stop mass murder.

That is not quite what the Coalition did in Iraq. We knew we could beat Saddam (although many people forecast a long, bloody battle); more important, we had plenty of good practical reasons to fight. Nonetheless: There were many steps on the way to the Holocaust, and we can speak of a step towards the act of selfless national goodness that might fix the broken moral balance of the cosmos. The Iraq war might be the largest step mankind has ever taken in this direction. It is a small step even so—but cause for rejoicing. Our combat troops did it. It is our privilege and our duty to make the most of it. To belittle it is a sad and sorry disgrace.

# 85

# "What Went Wrong?
# The Miscalculations and Missteps That Led
# to the Current Situation in Iraq"

## RICHARD LOWRY

By now, anyone who can't recite the standard critique of what has gone wrong in the Iraq war just hasn't been paying attention.

It goes something like this: There was no post-war planning. What little planning took place was spearheaded by the State Department, and then maliciously ignored by the ideologues at the Pentagon, who didn't want to hear a discouraging word about managing a liberated Iraq. Consumed by Rumsfeld's fixation on light forces, the Pentagon skimped on troop levels and ignored the advice of its commanders. Anyone who said anything inconvenient about the war was systematically punished. In this narrative, "Pentagon civilian" becomes a dirty phrase.

Almost every particular of this indictment is wrong. It has been created by liberal journalists such as James Fallows and David Rieff (with the help of disgruntled State Department leakers), entered the slipstream of conventional wisdom, and been repeated endlessly by John Kerry in the presidential campaign. These critics start from the premise that if a sparrow falls somewhere in Iraq, it must be the Pentagon's fault.

In fact, if one is playing a 20/20 second-guessing game over Iraq, the pure Defense Department pre-war vision that wasn't implemented would have avoided one of the pitfalls of what transpired: an occupation that alienated Iraqis and gave the U.S. sole control and responsibility over events in Iraq. The Pentagon favored the creation of an Iraqi government even before the invasion. And it pushed from the very beginning for a serious effort to train indigenous Iraqi forces, which would have given us a head start on what is now the consensus solution to Iraq's woes: that very training, so that Iraqis can carry on the fight for their country themselves.

Obviously, mistakes have been made in Iraq, including by the Pentagon. The story of the Iraq post-war is, in part, a tale of gross intelligence failures, debilitating intramural battles, miscommunications, unintended consequences, and counterproductive half-measures. Some of these missteps were the result of the inevitable uncertainties and surprises of warfare, others of incompetence, and many of something in between. What follows is drawn from interviews with current and former officials from across the U.S. government: from Defense, State, the National Security Council, the Coalition Provisional Authority, and the U.S. Central Command (CENTCOM). (Because of the sensitivity of the matters discussed, most everyone insisted on anonymity.)

If the picture portrayed here of Iraq operations is distressing, it isn't because these sources were, or are, doubters about the Iraq war. They all supported it, and continue to do so. Many conservative defenders of the Bush administration have taken to shrugging in reaction to the course of events in Iraq, "Things always go wrong in warfare." They do, but failing to examine the specific ways they went wrong is a cop-out. A look at the record in Iraq means confronting this hard fact: The Bush administration didn't know what it was getting into in Iraq, and then found itself stumbling into exactly the sort of heavy-handed occupation many American officials had wanted to avoid.

## "A Quick Collapse Saves Lives"

The level of troops in Iraq has been a constant source of contention, and a constant point of criticism of the Pentagon. Left and Right alike have argued that in invading with 150,000 troops, the administration didn't have adequate numbers to do the job. But every strategic choice has its benefits and drawbacks. If more troops would have enhanced security in the aftermath of the war (a debatable proposition, as we will see), the lighter and more mobile force had significant advantages in the prosecution of it. "The decision was made to collapse the regime as quickly and violently as possible," says a senior administration official. The most important advantage of this approach, he says, was simple: "A quick collapse saves American lives and Iraqi lives."

It served other objectives as well. It made it possible to take the oilfields—crucial to Iraq's rebuilding—mostly intact before Saddam had time to destroy them. And there was the political consideration. It was thought important to avoid a drawn-out war, and the destabilizing effect it might have on the region. "You don't want an American army slogging its way to an Arab capital," is how one official puts it. Another official familiar with the planning explains. "We identified a large number of risks, many of which quite obviously would have been made worse—graver, more likely to happen—if the war were prolonged, and if we could not achieve tactical surprise."

Amazingly enough, the U.S. did achieve such surprise. "Tommy Franks had 200,000 troops on the border of a country and still achieved tactical surprise when he invaded," a former defense official says. "When has that ever happened before?" We gained that advantage by suffering a significant diplomatic setback. We had wanted to send the 4th Infantry Division through Turkey to northern Iraq. Turkey refused—so the war began with the 4th Infantry Division still sitting in the Mediterranean.

"Saddam knew we were coming," says one official. "But he didn't know when. It appears that Saddam thought that we weren't going to start the war without the 4th Infantry Division. There were spools of wire and explosive material for bridges and for oil facilities that had been deployed to the area but were not yet hooked up. This showed the intention—but also that they thought they had time. That's pretty powerful evidence of surprise."

The theory of the war itself was borne out close to exactly. "We thought the regime was fairly brittle," an official explains. "If we got past the major Iraqi forces in the south and along [Saddam's] lines of communication closer to Baghdad, we could fracture the regime and not meet head-on his heaviest forces. Saddam would not be able to command and control those formations. That's what happened."

## "Probably Too Gracious in Our Victory"

And that's when things began to go wrong. The brilliant and successful war plan had unintended consequences. "You collapse the regime so quickly that the army, the security apparatus, ends up reconstituting because you didn't defeat it," an official says. The inadvertent Turkey gambit had its cost, too. Joint Chiefs of Staff chairman Gen. Richard Myers has said publicly that coming through Turkey to drive into the Sunni Triangle in force "would have helped somewhat with the current situation." Privately, officials are more categorical. One says, "I think we are paying for that to this day."

Bush critics would never put it this way, but a failing of the invasion plan turned out to be its excess of humanitarianism. "We wanted this to be as humane as a combat operation—as war—can be," General Myers told the Senate Armed Services Committee in June. "[The idea was] to let regular Iraqi divisions [go], while destroying equipment and some of their people. If they melted away, then let them melt away, because they were conscripts, after all. So if there is a blame here, it was making some assumptions on how the Iraqi people would react to that, and I would submit we were probably too gracious in our victory in hindsight."

This is a recurring theme. Over and over again in Iraq, the administration would demonstrate a lack of the necessary toughness to succeed: in how it conducted the initial war, how it handled the post-war looting, and how it approached the problem of restive cities such as Fallujah. Even in the post-war planning, it was the soft side of the enterprise, the potential humanitarian crisis, that was given priority. In Iraq, the conciliatory gesture, the half-measure, took priority over the work of smashing the enemy and establishing order. In this sense, the number of troops mattered less than what they were told to do, or not do.

But the most widely circulated criticism of the war is still simply that the U.S. didn't have enough troops. In the most stilted and politicized version of this critique, the administration is said to have ignored the express wishes of its commanders. This line of attack is dependent on the mythology surrounding Army chief of staff Gen. Eric Shinseki. He told a congressional committee prior to the war that it would take "several hundred thousand" troops to pacify Iraq. Critics claim that he was forced out for making this inconvenient estimate. But Shinseki had already been on the outs with Rumsfeld for his resistance to the defense secretary's transformation plans. He retired on schedule, which it had been clear he would do well before his statement about troop levels. Even if the U.S. did need more troops in Iraq, the Shinseki number of several hundred thousand—is that 300,000? more?—was clearly absurd.

Immediately after the war, widespread looting occurred. This is taken as a sign not just that there weren't enough troops, but that there was inadequate post-war planning. "Not preventing the looting was a huge mistake," says former CPA official Michael Rubin (an occasional contributor to NR and National Review Online), "but the problem wasn't a lack of planning on the part of DoD civilians or the State Department." CENTCOM divides a war, from pre-deployment to the post-war, into four phases. There was plenty of planning for Phase 3, the decisive operations of the war, and Phase 4, post-war stability operations. But the transition between the two was fumbled. "We can do all the planning we like," says Rubin, "but someone needs to make the call as to when Phase 3 ends."

CENTCOM basically said that the fall of Baghdad did not bring the end of Phase 3 because there wasn't security yet. Jay Garner, who was charged with leading the post-war as head of the Office of Reconstruction and Humanitarian Assistance (ORHA), said there wasn't security yet because Phase 4 operations that would reassure and win over the population hadn't started. "This is a very hazy, fog-of-war transition to make," says a senior administration official. "It was clearly a stumbling block." It was an area that could have used Rumsfeld's attention, and that of national security adviser Condoleezza Rice, whose job it is to impose coherence on U.S. national security policy.

At least some policy staff from State and Defense wanted commanders on the ground to guard buildings and shoot the looters, according to one official involved. But commanders were reluctant to put their men at risk for what they thought were just political objectives after they had already won the war. "People below Rumsfeld," says the official, "were saying, 'You have to shoot the looters,' but he didn't want to overrule his commanders."

Tommy Franks and his team didn't give the impression that they were eager to undertake stability operations. "Franks was supposed to plan for what CENTCOM called Phase 4, the period after major combat operations," says an official. "He knows that he has a responsibility for safety and stability in the country. He obviously concluded—I'm inferring—that he would have the resources available to fulfill this mission as the military occupier after major combat operations." But this official adds, "He was a Phase 3 kind of general." Another official says, "One of the unanswered questions is, 'What was Tommy Franks doing?' "

"Did we need more MPs [military police]?" Franks deputy Gen. Mike DeLong asks. "Yes. But we were funneling all our people through Kuwait and we couldn't get the MPs through there fast enough." Just prior to the war, Saddam had emptied the jails. "We were still fighting the war," says DeLong, "with all those criminals loose. We can't get our MPs in fast enough, but we don't want to pull out our front-line troops to guard buildings because they're still fighting Saddam's forces in other parts of the country." They guarded buildings they thought would be targeted, such as the key ministries, but other buildings were left defenseless.

The war ended on May 1. On May 22, the retirement of Tommy Franks was announced, a pretty stark statement of his lack of interest in Phase 4. "I was stunned by that, stunned," says one senior administration official. DeLong explains, "We had been fighting since the [attack on the USS] Cole, three years without a day off. There was a time we had to go. We didn't have any more blood to give."

Even if the commanders had been enthusiastic about Phase 4, stopping the looting wouldn't have been easy. "You couldn't put a soldier on every street corner in a city the size of Los Angeles and expect to stop everything," says an administration official. More important, it was hard psychologically for officials who believed they were liberating a country to turn around and crack down on civilians. "It's like sending troops into Warsaw Square to arrest people for being too unruly in 1989," says a former defense official. A former CPA official says, "There was a real sense of euphoria right after the fall of the statue. You would have stamped out any goodwill right at the start." An administration official explains, "It's very hard to say what would have been the right thing to do, when American forces were told in the lead-up to the war that we didn't want to impose ourselves as occupiers, that they have a police force, that they understand the rule of law; and have a civic infrastructure that will provide for stability."

### "Our Intelligence Was Very Limited"

All that proved wrong. Even though everyone knew that the military had to provide for stability and that there was a risk of public disturbances, the breadth and ferocity of the looting came as a shock. "We had no idea people would run into the bathrooms of public buildings and run off with the toilets and the sinks," says one official. "It's not something we contemplated as a possibility. We could not believe that the population would, in a revenge-like manner, strip away all the vestiges of Saddam's government and that government's infrastructure." He adds, "None of the estimates I saw anticipated that kind of looting."

It was a blow to the Iraqis' confidence in the U.S. It led to a conspiracy theory about how we wanted to punish the Iraqis through disorder, and it meant that people were sent home from work because their office equipment had been stolen. "It created a general atmosphere of lawlessness from which we didn't recover," says a former occupation official. Larry Diamond, another former official, argues, "That sent the signal of a lack of control that gave a lot of ideas to the jihadists and insurgents."

Missing the possibility of such wide-spread looting was just one way in which the intelligence was flawed. "Our intelligence about Iraq was very limited," says a senior administration official. "The intelligence community got a lot of things wrong, not simply the WMD. They did not understand the exact role of Iraqi police. They thought the police would be usable. We had no other basis for knowing that, to the contrary, police were viewed as political and an instrument of oppression." And "that was the basis of ORHA, of the CPA," says another official. "We based the plan on standing up the Iraqi police. It turned out that the corruption went so deep into the ranks that the police were useless. It meant a major recalibration of our plan that is going on to this day. It was an intelligence failure of the first magnitude."

Then there was the state of the infrastructure. One official involved in post-war planning recalls seeing the state of the infrastructure, which the U.S. had gone out of its way to avoid bombing during the war, on his first post-war visit to Iraq: "We were shocked." He explains, "Saddam had skimmed the money off the Oil for Food program and spent it on his palaces and basically nothing else. That was never picked up on. The infrastructure was so dilapidated. It added billions and billions to the reconstruction job."

Combine the rottenness of the infrastructure with the looting, and we were left to start almost from scratch. "When that violence, that looting, petered out," says an official, "we were left with an essential-services infrastructure [water, sewer, electricity] that was archaic to start with and now almost destroyed, and a governmental infrastructure [police, the ministries] that had abandoned its posts." The food-distribution network was so backward and irrational, it was almost incomprehensible. As one official puts it, "It was a process which a First World person from, say, USAID, would look at and say, 'I don't even know how a person would work through these problems.' " This was how Iraqis did things, he notes, "despite being touted as one of the most educated populaces in the Middle East."

That all this went wrong has created the idea that there was no post-war planning, or that all of it was based on a willfully rosy scenario. "We did a lot of thinking about what could go wrong in Iraq," says one official. "The standard line in the fever swamps is, 'We had one source of information in Iraq—Ahmad Chalabi [founder and leader of the main exile group, the Iraqi National Congress]. He told us everything was going to be a cakewalk.' As if we are complete idiots."

### "Dozens and Dozens of Briefings"

Before the war, Rumsfeld had been willing to look at the worst case. He prepared a memo for the president that listed everything defense officials could think of that might go wrong. "Literally, for two or three pages," says an official familiar with the memo, "with an item per line, he went through all the things that could go wrong with a war in Iraq: mass starvation, large numbers of international refugees, the blowing up of oil facilities, Scud-missile attacks on Israel, the overthrow of governments throughout the region, terrorist attacks in the U.S. and elsewhere, and on and on. He produced maybe 50, 60 of these hair-raising possibilities."

In late summer 2002, the NSC created the Executive Steering Group (ESG), a high-level body tasked with preparing for the post-war. "There were dozens and dozens of briefings, for vetting and approval, regarding the post-war," says an administration official. Interagency planning groups—the Iraq Pol-Mil Planning Cell, the Coalition Working Group, the Humanitarian Reconstruction Group, and the Energy Infrastructure Working Group—fed into the ESG. As did the work of other planners at State, Treasury, Commerce, CIA, OMB, and USAID. The ESG's work, in turn, went up the chain from the deputies to the principals to the president. "It was the standard NSC flow," says an official.

In January 2003, Bush signed NSPD-24, which led to the creation of the Office of Reconstruction and Humanitarian Assistance, charged with implementing the planning on the ground in Iraq and to be run by Garner. In addition, the military had its own planning group, the so-called JTF-4 that produced a 300-page op-order for Phase 4, the post-war operation.

Bush critics pretend that there was no planning besides that which took place through the State Department's Future of Iraq Project. It is alleged that the Pentagon ignored all the important planning done under this project for ideological and turf reasons. But the sprawling project was uneven, sometimes had an academic air, and didn't create an action plan, certainly not to deal with the dire problems that would face the coalition in Baghdad. The portions of its work that were considered relevant weren't ignored. They were briefed up to the higher levels of the administration, and used.

"Because it was the State Department, the project had a lot to do with justice and human rights," says an official, "not so much with looking at basic services." Bush critics have portrayed it as a panacea, but "it was not the answer to Phase 4. If we had taken the Future of Iraq Project and given it to ORHA and said, 'You can't deviate from this,' we still would have had a lot of the problems we encountered."

Some of the post-war planning turned out just fine-for instance, how to avoid a catastrophic collapse in the Iraqi currency, the dinar. "If we go in there and do it wrong," says one official, "we could destroy the value of billions of dollars of currency." But the planning overall was poorly coordinated. "Everyone thought they were doing all the planning," says one official of the disparate efforts. And a lot of it turned out to be for the wrong thing. The administration was prepared for an epic humanitarian disaster. "We were ready to take in Iraqi displaced persons," says one official, "because we thought that was the most likely scenario." Instead, public disorder was the biggest challenge. "They were prepared for a worst-case scenario on the humanitarian front and not on the political front and the security front," says Larry Diamond.

The level of the security challenge rendered a lot of the planning moot. According to one official, "The planning was so advanced that we were planning for the future bases of U.S. forces, where they would stay during Phase 4. We were laying out training ranges, making sure the soldiers would be able to continue their training while they would be in stability operations and humanitarian and civil-affairs work, helping the Iraqis stand back up their government. But we didn't know we would have to provide as much security as we would have to provide."

*"What Armitage Does for a Living"*

And so, Jay Garner, the retired three-star general heading ORHA, was thrown into an Iraq that had, against expectations, been looted bare, where the police had disappeared, and where infrastructure was decrepit or destroyed. There were still other surprises for Garner. "Another thing that the intelligence community told us was that there would be whole units of the Iraqi armed forces to come over to our side," says an official. "Jay Garner went there with an expectation that we were going to be able to use the Iraqi military for reconstruction."

Garner handled a bad situation badly. Rumsfeld had tapped him because of his work on Operation Provide Comfort, relieving the Kurds after the first Iraq war. But the humanitarian crisis he might have been suited to handle hadn't materialized. Instead he had a huge political and security problem on his hands.

He talked, absurdly, of convening a constitutional convention, writing a constitution, and holding an election all by August. He had a political tin ear, and the U.S. military didn't take him seriously. General DeLong says, "Initially we didn't get a powerful person into Iraq. Garner didn't have the muscle" to officiate between the military services and the State Department. "Here was a retired three-star general in there and not all the other generals thought he was that person"—the powerful person necessary.

Garner had expected to stay for 90 days, but was ushered out more quickly. If he was a failure, he wasn't a Pentagon failure. He surrounded himself with State Department and USAID officials. State not only waged turf battles (as did the Pentagon), but often won them. One official explains, "This is what [Colin Powell deputy Dick] Armitage does for a living: 'I want my guys in Baghdad.' That was out of control, and the DoD was just as guilty of that, but Armitage was winning these fights hand over fist."

State Department official Ryan Crocker, head of the Near East bureau, led Garner's political team. "That's the bureau that produced the Future of Iraq Project," says a different official. "There wasn't even an OSD [Office of Secretary of Defense] person doing political advice with Garner. If the people who did the Future of Iraq project think that their stuff was not picked up as it should have been, then what they're saying is that it wasn't picked up by the head of their own bureau in the State Department."

Garner was replaced by former ambassador Jerry Bremer, who was more a creature of the White House than the Pentagon, but ended up being something of an independent operator. With his arrival, the U.S. lurched into a full-fledged military occupation of a country in much worse shape than it had imagined. This represented a total defeat of the Pentagon's vision, which had been to avoid, or minimize, a U.S. occupation, by creating an Iraqi provisional government before the invasion or immediately after it. This was one of the many clashes between the State Department and Defense. State had wanted a Baghdad conference six or seven weeks after the occupation of Baghdad. The Department of Defense had wanted to set up an immediate government.

"We wanted to build on the theme of liberation, rather than occupation, and hand over more authority sooner. We would not have had an occupation government. That idea did not prevail. There was a lot of opposition throughout the government," says a defense official.

This would not necessarily have meant installing Ahmad Chalabi in power. The original conception was for a group of seven exiles, with a slot for a governor from each province as it became liberated. This approach was approved by consensus at a conference of the Iraqi opposition in February 2003 at Salahuddin in Iraqi Kurdistan. This meeting would have given the process—had it not been tossed aside—an Iraqi imprimatur. Such a government could have created the same situation as when sovereignty was handed over on June 28, 2004, only much sooner. Instead the compromise forged by the NSC had the U.S. picking a governing council after it was already occupying Iraq and running it according to the international law of occupation, thanks to the first post-war U.N. resolution (the British had insisted on the law-of-occupation language).

"The philosophy Rumsfeld had was that the goal should be from the very beginning to empower the Iraqis," says a former defense official. "If there is a legitimate criticism, it's the CPA being so heavy-handed for as long as it was. It was a violation of Rumsfeld's own principle that Iraq was for the Iraqis." Says another official: "That we would have a Jerry Bremer figure, that got people thinking of an occupation in Iraq. That was the fundamental error."

Bremer planned on a U.S. occupation that would last 18–24 months, much too long in the minds of many Pentagon officials. "We wanted it as short as possible," says one of them. "We eventually got it turned around." In the fall of 2003, Bremer was called back to Washington and the plan that eventually turned sovereignty back over to the Iraqis was adopted.

## "They Took the Urinals Out of the Barracks"

The problem was that Bremer was taking ownership of a failed society, and the occupation would inevitably be tarred with its failures. As the spring of last year turned into the summer, the mood began to sour, with the security situation worsening, with reconstruction therefore slowing, and with the sheer reality of the situation sinking in. A senior administration official explains, "An Iraqi sees that the sewage isn't any better, that there isn't 24/7 electricity and gas isn't available at a quarter a liter, and he says, 'I thought this would turn out differently.' He looks at raw sewage running down the middle of his street and says, 'This hasn't met my expectations.' "

This is by no means to say that Bremer per se was the problem. "The situation was nothing like we expected. There was much more resistance, much more violence, and much less control," says Larry Diamond. "We just weren't prepared." Bremer inherited an impossible situation—he was thrown into Iraq literally ten days after getting the assignment from the White House—and his powerful persona was needed to fill the post-Garner vacuum. "The good thing was," says an official, "you needed an assertion of authority. You needed somebody with a strong hand."

Everyone credits Bremer with great personal bravery, an ability to make tough decisions, and extraordinary organizational skills. His vision of the country's future was dogged and correct: a unified, democratic, and federal post-Saddam Iraq. Two of his biggest decisions have been widely panned, but were probably the right ones, even if they inevitably had drawbacks as well as benefits.

Bremer officially disbanded the Iraqi army, which the conventional wisdom says created disaffection that helped feed the insurgency. But the army had really disbanded itself. It was, in its essence, an instrument of repression. Shia conscripts weren't going to serve another day under the lash of Sunni officers. "They took the urinals out of the barracks," is how one official puts it, "and went home." Michael Rubin breaks it down this way: "The Shia conscripts left; the officers with skills went out and started their own businesses; the corrupt and incompetent officers stayed." The U.S. got a little taste of how trying to maintain Saddam's army would have worked in its April 2004 deal with former Baathist officers in Fallujah, who promised to police the city and promptly faded away or joined the other side.

The other Bremer decision generally considered a mistake is his de-Baathification order. It deprived the country of experienced governing talent, and the order eventually would, probably rightly, be moderated in its implementation. But given the realities of Iraq, something along the lines of Bremer's order was necessary. The future of the new Iraq could not be in the minority Sunnis attached to the benefits of Baathism, but had to be in the majority Shia and in the Kurds. These groups would have been justifiably alarmed at any attempt to reestablish the old order. "The decision was fundamentally correct," says one official. "Eighty percent of the country is Shia and Kurd. If we had looked like we were reconstituting the regime, we would have had a massive explosion in the rest of the country."

Former Bremer aide Dan Senor says of both decisions, on the army and de-Baathification, "The reason that the Shia let their guard down, the reason that the Kurds let their guard down, was that they saw we were taking serious steps to keep the Baathists from reemerging. If we hadn't done that, there may have been severe retribution against the Sunnis. And the Shia and Kurds might not have cooperated with us. Those symbolic steps were very important early on."

There would have been resistance in the Sunni heartland whatever Bremer did, since it appears that fading into the Sunni triangle was the strategy of the Saddamists from the beginning. Here was yet another unanticipated event that upset the administration's plans and expectations. "If there was any mistake we made, we thought that they would surrender, and we were wrong," says an administration official. The enemy had never been defeated, a rather large failing. This was one of the crucial differences between Japan and Germany on one hand and Iraq on the other—Japan and Germany had been crushed by the U.S., and so were ready to be compliant with their occupiers. Iraq never had this psychology of defeat.

### "Somebody Panicked"

The Baathists lived to fight another day, in an insurgency that was yet another surprise. The *New York Times* recently reported on an intelligence document that allegedly warned of an insurgency. But that warning was in the final sentence of a 38-page report. It was not one of the report's key findings. "As far as I know," says an official familiar with the pre-war information, "I don't recall anyone at State or the CIA talking about this kind of insurgency."

The insurgency prompted yet more calls for more troops. But the insurgency was mainly an intelligence and political problem not susceptible to solution by sheer numbers. "You hear it all the time, but it's true," says a former CPA official. "The generals weren't asking for more troops. I was in plenty of meetings with them, and they weren't asking for more troops."

Initially, the U.S. didn't take the insurgency seriously enough. Then it tried to crush it on its own, failing to appreciate that it had begun to take on a nationalist character (partly fueled by the occupation) and that having Iraqi forces to deal with it was politically essential. The initial efforts to train Iraqi forces were proved inadequate by the Najaf and Fallujah revolts this April. Iraq wasn't originally thought to need a proper army, so the emphasis was on training police to handle street crime. When the insurgency began to intensify, the police were incapable of handling it. Now there is much more intensive training, but the U.S. is behind the curve on a task everyone agrees is fundamental.

Given how long training has taken, it would have made sense to have a head-start prior to the war. Again, this was the Pentagon's idea. It had plans to train up to 10,000 Iraqis out of the country, creating a major asset in the form of people who knew the language and knew the society—who were Iraqis. "Rumsfeld from the very beginning was focused on training Iraqi forces," says a former defense official. But military commanders considered them only a potential nuisance underfoot and resisted. The State Department worried that training Iraqi forces, as a harbinger of the coming conflict, would undermine diplomacy at the U.N., and questioned what would be done with them if there were no war. In the end, the U.S. trained a mere 71 Iraqis.

Iraqi forces were what was needed to deal with nettlesome problems like Fallujah. There had been some sort of major security incident in Fallujah almost every month from the end of 2003 until April 2004, when things came to a head with the murder and mutilation of four U.S. contractors. The story of how the Marines started to take Fallujah, and then stopped, is murky. Even senior administration officials are confused about how things came to pass. "Somebody panicked," says one official, "and it was a mistake."

The Marines were reluctant to go in, but did so on the basis of a plan they had told the civilian leadership wouldn't create massive civilian casualties. When the Marines attacked, reports of such casualties began to filter back to the CPA. These reports created a political firestorm, with Sunnis threatening to withdraw from the political process, which was then focused on creating a new interim government. Bremer called off the assault, which may have been just days from achieving its objective.

The reason for stopping was understandable, but in retrospect it was disastrously shortsighted. It led to an increase in car bombings around the country as the insurgents worked from their safe haven. The terror attacks have eaten away at the credibility of the Iraqi government and the U.S., while radicals have worked to replicate the success of Fallujah elsewhere in the Sunni Triangle. The Fallujah Brigade, charged with policing Fallujah, proved a fiasco. The top U.S. commanders in Iraq, Generals Abizaid and Sanchez, hadn't known the Marines were creating the brigade of former Baathists, and neither had Bremer.

Fallujah is one of Prime Minister Allawi's major challenges to this day. But Allawi himself is a bright spot in the U.S. experience in Iraq. The fact that he was an exile demonstrates that one of the arguments wielded against the Pentagon—"Exiles can never govern Iraq"—was false. A lot of the dispute, of course, had to do with one exile in particular, Chalabi. "The folks that were deemed to be acceptable leaders by the Department of Defense were not deemed to be acceptable by the State Department, and when those folks were brought in [to Iraq] in the middle of April [2003], we found out that they did not have the kind of support that might have been anticipated," says a senior administration official.

Chalabi probably wasn't the man to run Iraq, and if the Pentagon didn't insist on anointing him—as officials now maintain—he was certainly high on their list. He didn't have political support on the ground. "He had no street credibility," says a former CPA official. "If you ask people about him, you would hear one of three things, or maybe all three:

1) He's a crook; 2) he's not one of us; 3) he's a stooge of the U.S." In any case, he lost all support from the U.S. government when he was quoted in the *Daily Telegraph* saying any erroneous information that members of his group might have given the U.S. about WMD prior to the war was fine, that they were "heroes in error."

Ideally, State and Defense could have compromised around an initial Iraqi government headed by someone other than Chalabi. But the compromise forged by the National Security Council produced Garner, and then Bremer, who ended up running Iraq. Again, that wasn't necessarily Bremer's fault. He couldn't give more authority to the Iraqi Governing Council that was formed after the war because its leadership proved so dysfunctional. It wasn't until the process that selected Allawi to head the interim government that some legitimate and responsible Iraqi politics began to take hold. CPA officials felt it wouldn't have been responsible to hand over the country to someone right after the war, because Iraqis weren't ready. But the alternative—the occupation—was no bargain.

*"A Miasma"*

That captures the way the U.S. experience in Iraq has been, in part, a tragedy—a series of choices that could never be entirely right. The initial invasion proved brilliant, confounding the critics who predicted months of heavy fighting and thousands of casualties? Well, at least some of the American lives it saved upfront may have been lost later on, confronting the Baathists who got away. Disbanding the army alienated the Sunnis? Well, keeping it would have likely alienated the Shias, who could have mounted a revolt that would have chased the U.S. from the country. Every decision had its tradeoffs.

But that is not to say that things couldn't have been handled better. Intelligence will never be perfect, and making that the standard is a formula for inaction. But the doctrine of preemption is folly without a first-rate covert service and a CIA that is better and more aggressive than it is today. The U.S. military has to take a more lively interest in post-combat stability operations, if the problems of the first year and a half in Iraq are to be avoided elsewhere. And the U.S. government must cohere in a way Bush's National Security Council has often failed to make it cohere in Iraq. "It has been a mess out of which no coherent policy has been made," says a distressed official. "It has been a miasma that no one has been in charge of. You can either say that the president wasn't in control, or you can say that the number-two person wasn't in control, and that's Condi."

For all that, the administration still hasn't lost Iraq, and, if it stays the course, it may well prevail. That it has not lost is testament to the skill and courage of the American soldier and to the Iraqis' desire—despite everything—to create something better. In this way, President Bush's vision for the country has been vindicated. Prime Minister Allawi has exercised responsible leadership, not only abiding, but working closely with the Americans. "The most powerful force getting us closer to a policy has been Allawi," says a U.S. official. The major religious figure in the country, Ayatollah Sistani, has been determined in favor of a democratic Iraq, and the performance of properly trained Iraqi forces, in places like Najaf and Samarra, has provided encouraging signs that they may yet be ready to step up to the plate.

There is no taking away the accomplishment of toppling Saddam Hussein. The Bush administration has been resolute in the face of all the difficulties, including, yes, its own missteps. If Iraq yet proves a success—creating a decent government in that strategically central country—the mistakes of the war's aftermath will be seen as speed bumps, inevitable mistakes and readjustments inherent in any grand enterprise.

Bush's critics, meanwhile, have had the luxury of irresponsibility that comes with being out of office, and have taken full advantage of it. They have indulged paranoid fantasies about the administration's "neocons," failed to offer constructive criticism, waged demagogic attacks based on Halliburton and all manner of other nonsense, fudged their answer to the all-important question of whether they would have invaded, and pounced on every hint of realistic analysis out of the administration (e.g., Rumsfeld's recent obvious statement that the Iraqi elections might not be perfect). Nothing in their performance during the Iraq episode marks them as deserving of power.

That Bush is the best thing going on national security makes it all the more imperative that he get better. "Every indication I have is that Bush is extremely unhappy with how this has gone for obvious reasons," says one official. "I think there is going to be vigorous retooling in a second term." He should get at it as soon as possible, assuming he has the opportunity. There's a war to be won, after all.

## 86

# "Baghdad Year Zero: Pillaging Iraq in Pursuit of a Neocon Utopia"

### NAOMI KLEIN

It was only after I had been in Baghdad for a month that I found what I was looking for. I had traveled to Iraq a year after the war began, at the height of what should have been a construction boom, but after weeks of searching I had not seen a single piece of heavy machinery apart from tanks and humvees. Then I saw it: a construction crane. It was big and yellow and impressive, and when I caught a glimpse of it around a corner in a busy shopping district I thought that I was finally about to witness some of the reconstruction I had heard so much about. But as I got closer I noticed that the crane was not actually rebuilding anything—not one of the bombed-out government buildings that still lay in rubble all over the city, nor one of the many power lines that remained in twisted heaps even as the heat of summer was starting to bear down. No, the crane was hoisting a giant billboard to the top of a three-story building. SUNBULAH: HONEY 100% NATURAL, made in Saudi Arabia.

Seeing the sign, I couldn't help but think about something Senator John McCain had said back in October. Iraq, he said, is "a huge pot of honey that's attracting a lot of flies." The flies McCain was referring to were the Halliburtons and Bechtels, as well as the venture capitalists who flocked to Iraq in the path cleared by Bradley Fighting Vehicles and laser-guided bombs. The honey that drew them was not just no-bid contracts and Iraq's famed oil wealth but the myriad investment opportunities offered by a country that had just been cracked wide open after decades of being sealed off, first by the nationalist economic policies of Saddam Hussein, then by asphyxiating United Nations sanctions.

Looking at the honey billboard, I was also reminded of the most common explanation for what has gone wrong in Iraq, a complaint echoed by everyone from John Kerry to Pat Buchanan; Iraq is mired in blood and deprivation because George W. Bush didn't have "a postwar plan." The only problem with this theory is that it isn't true. The Bush Administration did have a plan for what it would do after the war; put simply, it was to lay out as much honey as possible, then sit back and wait for the flies.

The honey theory of Iraqi reconstruction stems from the most cherished belief of the war's ideological architects: that greed is good. Not good just for them and their friends but good for humanity, and certainly good for Iraqis. Greed creates profit, which creates growth, which creates jobs and products and services and everything else anyone could possibly need or want. The role of good government, then, is to create the optimal conditions for corporations to pursue their bottomless greed, so that they in turn can meet the needs of the society. The problem is that governments, even neoconservative governments, rarely get the chance to prove their sacred theory right: despite their enormous ideological advances, even George Bush's Republicans are, in their own minds, perennially sabotaged by meddling Democrats, intractable unions, and alarmist environmentalists.

Iraq was going to change all that. In one place on Earth, the theory would finally be put into practice in its most perfect and uncompromised form. A country of 25 million would not be rebuilt as it was before the war; it would be erased, disappeared. In its place would spring forth a gleaming showroom for laissezfaire economics, a Utopia such as the world had never seen. Every policy that liberates multinational corporations to pursue their quest for profit would be put into place: a shrunken state, a flexible workforce, open borders, minimal taxes, no tariffs, no ownership restrictions. The people of Iraq would, of course, have to endure some short-term pain: assets, previously owned by the state, would have to be given up to create new opportunities for growth and investment. Jobs would have to be lost and, as foreign products flooded across the border, local businesses and family farms would, unfortunately, be unable to compete. But to the authors of this plan, these would be small prices to pay for the economic boom that would surely explode once the proper conditions were in place, a boom so powerful the country would practically rebuild itself.

The fact that the boom never came and Iraq continues to tremble under explosions of a very different sort should never be blamed on the absence of a plan. Rather, the blame rests with the plan itself, and the extraordinarily violent ideology upon which it is based.

\* \* \*

At first, the shock-therapy theory seemed to hold: Iraqis, reeling from violence both military and economic, were far too busy staying alive to mount a political response to Bremer's campaign. Worrying about the privatization of the sewage system was an unimaginable luxury with half the population lacking access to clean drinking water; the debate over the flat tax would have to wait until the lights were back on. Even in the international press, Bremer's new laws, though radical, were easily upstaged by more dramatic news of political chaos and rising crime.

Some people were paying attention, of course. That autumn was awash in "rebuilding Iraq" trade shows, in Washington, London, Madrid, and Amman. The *Economist* described Iraq under Bremer as "a capitalist dream," and a flurry of new consulting firms were launched promising to help companies get access to the Iraqi market, their boards of directors stacked with well-connected Republicans. The most prominent was New Bridge Strategies, started by Joe Allbaugh, former Bush-Cheney campaign manager. "Getting the rights to distribute Procter & Gamble products can be a gold mine," one of the company's partners enthused. "One well-stocked 7-Eleven could knock out thirty Iraqi stores; a WalMart could take over the country."

Soon there were rumors that a McDonald's would be opening up in downtown Baghdad, funding was almost in place for a Starwood luxury hotel, and General Motors was planning to build an auto plant. On the financial side, HSBC would have branches all over the country, Citigroup was preparing to offer substantial loans guaranteed against future sales of Iraqi oil, and the bell was going to ring on a New York-style stock exchange in Baghdad any day.

In only a few months, the postwar plan to turn Iraq into a laboratory for the neocons had been realized. Leo Strauss may have provided the intellectual framework for invading Iraq preemptively, but it was that other University of Chicago professor, Milton Friedman, author of the antigovernment manifesto Capitalism and Freedom, who supplied the manual for what to do once the country was safely in America's hands. This represented an enormous victory for the most ideological wing of the Bush Administration. But it was also something more: the culmination of two interlinked power struggles, one among Iraqi exiles advising the White House on its postwar strategy, the other within the White House itself.

As the British historian Dilip Hiro has shown, in *Secrets and Lies: Operation Iraqi Freedom and After*, the Iraqi exiles pushing for the invasion were divided, broadly, into two camps. On one side were "the pragmatists," who favored getting rid of Saddam and his immediate entourage, securing access to oil, and slowly introducing free-market reforms. Many of these exiles were part of the State Department's Future of Iraq Project, which generated a thirteen-volume report on how to restore basic services and transition to democracy after the war. On the other side was the "Year Zero" camp, those who believed that Iraq was so contaminated that it needed to be rubbed out and remade from scratch. The prime advocate of the pragmatic approach was Iyad Allawi, a former high-level Baathist who fell out with Saddam and started working for the CIA. The prime advocate of the Year Zero approach was Ahmad Chalabi, whose hatred of the Iraqi state for expropriating his family's assets during the 1958 revolution ran so deep he longed to see the entire country burned to the ground—everything, that is, but the oil Ministry, which would be the nucleus of the new Iraq, the cluster of cells from which an entire nation would grow. He called this process "de-Baathification."

A parallel battle between pragmatists and true believers was being waged within the Bush Administration. The pragmatists were men like Secretary of State Colin Powell and General Jay Garner, the first U.S. envoy to postwar Iraq. General Garner's plan was straightforward enough: fix the infrastructure, hold quick and dirty elections, leave the shock therapy to the International Monetary Fund, and concentrate on securing U.S. military bases on the model of the Philippines. "I think we should look right now at Iraq as our coaling station in the Middle East," he told the BBC. He also paraphrased T. E. Lawrence, saying, "It's better for them to do it imperfectly than for us to do it for them perfectly." On the other side was the usual cast of neoconservatives: Vice President Dick Cheney, Secretary of Defense Donald Rumsfeld (who lauded Bremer's "sweeping reforms" as "some of the most enlightened and inviting tax and investment laws in the free world"), Deputy Secretary of Defense Paul Wolfowitz, and, perhaps most centrally, Undersecretary of Defense Douglas Feith. Whereas the State Department had its Future of Iraq report, the neocons had USAID's contract with Bearing Point to remake

Iraq's economy: in 108 pages, "privatization" was mentioned no fewer than fifty-one times. To the true believers in the White House, General Garner's plans for postwar Iraq seemed hopelessly unambitious. Why settle for a mere coaling station when you can have a model free market? Why settle for the Philippines when you can have a beacon unto the world?

The Iraqi Year Zeroists made natural allies for the White House neo-conservatives: Chalabi's seething hatred of the Baathist state fit nicely with the neocons' hatred of the state in general, and the two agendas effortlessly merged. Together, they came to imagine the invasion of Iraq as a kind of Rapture: where the rest of the world saw death, they saw birth—a country redeemed through violence, cleansed by fire. Iraq wasn't being destroyed by cruise missiles, cluster bombs, chaos, and looting; it was being born again. April 9, 2003, the day Baghdad fell, was Day One of Year Zero.

*   *   *

I had been following the economic front of the war for almost a year before I decided to go to Iraq. I attended the "Rebuilding Iraq" trade shows, studied Bremer's tax and investment laws, met with contractors at their home offices in the United States, interviewed the government officials in Washington who are making the policies. But as I prepared to travel to Iraq in March to see this experiment in free-market utopianism up close, it was becoming increasingly clear that all was not going according to plan. Bremer had been working on the theory that if you build a corporate Utopia the corporations will come—but where were they? American multinationals were happy to accept U.S. taxpayer dollars to reconstruct the phone or electricity systems, but they weren't sinking their own money into Iraq. There was, as yet, no McDonald's or Wal-Mart in Baghdad, and even the sales of state factories, announced so confidently nine months earlier, had not materialized.

Some of the holdup had to do with the physical risks of doing business in Iraq. But there were other more significant risks as well. When Paul Bremer shredded Iraq's Baathist constitution and replaced it with what the *Economist* greeted approvingly as "the wish list of foreign investors," there was one small detail he failed to mention: It was all completely illegal. The CPA derived its legal authority from United Nations security Council Resolution 1483, passed in May 2003, which recognized the United States and Britain as Iraq's legitimate occupiers. It was this resolution that empowered Bremer to unilaterally make laws in Iraq. But the resolution also stated that the U.S. and Britain must "comply fully with their obligations under international law including in particular the Geneva Conventions of 1949 and the Hague Regulations of 1907." Both conventions were born as an attempt to curtail the unfortunate historical tendency among occupying powers to rewrite the rules so that they can economically strip the nations they control. With this in mind, the conventions stipulate that an occupier must abide by a country's existing laws unless "absolutely prevented" from doing so. They also state that an occupier does not own the "public buildings, real estate, forests and agricultural assets" of the country it is occupying but is rather their "administrator" and custodian, keeping them secure until sovereignty is reestablished. This was the true threat to the Year Zero plan: since America didn't own Iraq's assets, it could not legally sell them, which meant that after the occupation ended, an Iraqi government could come to power and decide that it wanted to keep the state companies in public hands, or, as is the norm in the Gulf region, to bar foreign firms from owning 100 percent of national assets. If that happened, investments made under Bremer's rules could be expropriated, leaving firms with no recourse because their investments had violated international law from the outset.

By November, trade lawyers started to advise their corporate clients not to go into Iraq just yet, that it would be better to wait until after the transition. Insurance companies were so spooked that not a single one of the big firms would insure investors for "political risk," that high-stakes area of insurance law that protects companies against foreign governments turning nationalist or socialist and expropriating their investments.

Even the U.S.-appointed Iraqi politicians, up to now so obedient, were getting nervous about their own political futures if they went along with the privatization plans. Communications Minister Haider al-Abadi told me about his first meeting with Bremer. "I said, 'Look, we don't have the mandate to sell any of this. Privatization is a big thing. We have to wait until there is an Iraqi government.' " Minister of Industry Mohamad Tofiq was even more direct: "I am not going to do something that is not legal, so that's it."

Both al-Abadi and Tofiq told me about a meeting—never reported in the press—that took place in late October 2003. At that gathering the twenty-five members of Iraq's Governing Council as well as the twenty-five interim ministers decided unanimously that they would not participate in the privatization of Iraq's state-owned companies or of its publicly owned infrastructure.

But Bremer didn't give up. International law prohibits occupiers from selling state assets themselves, but it doesn't say anything about the puppet governments they appoint. Originally, Bremer had pledged to hand over power to a directly elected Iraqi government, but in early November he went to Washington for a private meeting with President Bush and came back with a Plan B. On June 30 the occupation would officially end—but not really. It would be replaced by an appointed government chosen by Washington. This government would not be bound by the international laws preventing occupiers from selling off state assets, but it would be bound by an "interim constitution," a document that would protect Bremer's investment and privatization laws.

The plan was risky. Bremer's June 30 deadline was awfully close, and it was chosen for a less than ideal reason: so that President Bush could trumpet the end of Iraq's occupation on the campaign trail. If everything went according to plan, Bremer would succeed in forcing a "sovereign" Iraqi government to carry out his illegal reforms. But if something went wrong, he would have to go ahead with the June 30 handover anyway because by then Karl Rove, and not Dick Cheney or Donald Rumsfeld, would be calling the shots. And if it came down to a choice between ideology in Iraq and the electability of George W. Bush, everyone knew which would win.

At first, Plan B seemed to be right on track. Bremer persuaded the Iraqi Governing Council to agree to everything: the new timetable, the interim government, and the interim constitution. He even managed to slip into the constitution a completely overlooked clause, Article 26. It stated that for the duration of the interim government. "The laws, regulations, orders and directives issued by the Coalition Provisional Authority . . . shall remain in force" and could only be changed after general elections are held.

Bremer had found his legal loophole: There would be a window—seven months—when the occupation was officially over but before general elections were scheduled to take place. Within this window, the Hague and Geneva Conventions' bans on privatization would no longer apply, but Bremer's own laws, thanks to Article 26, would stand. During these seven months, foreign investors could come to Iraq and sign forty-year contracts to buy up Iraqi assets. If a future elected Iraqi government decided to change the rules, investors could sue for compensation.

But Bremer had a formidable opponent: Grand Ayatollah Ali al Sistani, the most senior Shia cleric in Iraq. Al Sistani tried to block Bremer's plan at every turn, calling for immediate direct elections and for the constitution to be written after those elections, not before. Both demands, if met, would have closed Bremer's privatization window. Then, on March 2, with the Shia members of the Governing Council refusing to sign the interim constitution, five bombs exploded in front of mosques in Karbala and Baghdad, killing close to 200 worshipers. General John Abizaid, the top U.S. commander in Iraq, warned that the country was on the verge of civil war. Frightened by this prospect, al Sistani backed down and the Shia politicians signed the interim constitution. It was a familiar story: the shock of a violent attack paved the way for more shock therapy.

When I arrived in Iraq a week later, the economic project seemed to be back on track. All that remained for Bremer was to get his interim constitution ratified by a Security Council resolution, then the nervous lawyers and insurance brokers could relax and the sell-off of Iraq could finally begin. The CPA, meanwhile, had launched a major new P.R. offensive designed to reassure investors that Iraq was still a safe and exciting place to do business. The centerpiece of the campaign was Destination Baghdad Exposition, a massive trade show for potential investors to be held in early April at the Baghdad International Fairgrounds. It was the first such event inside Iraq, and the organizers had branded the trade fair "DBX," as if it were some sort of Mountain Dew-sponsored dirtbike race. In keeping with the extreme sports theme, Thomas Foley traveled to Washington to tell a gathering of executives that the risks in Iraq are akin "to skydiving or riding a motorcycle, which are, to many, very acceptable risks."

But three hours after my arrival in Baghdad, I was finding these reassurances extremely hard to believe. I had not yet unpacked when my hotel room was filled with debris and the windows in the lobby were shattered. Down the street, the Mount Lebanon hotel had just been bombed, at that point the largest attack of its kind since the official end of the war. The next day, another hotel was bombed in Basra, then two Finnish businessmen were murdered on their way to a meeting in Baghdad. Brigadier General Mark Kimmitt finally admitted that there was a pattern at work: "the extremists have started shifting away from the hard targets . . . [and] are now going out of their way to specifically target softer targets." The next day, the State Department updated its travel advisory: U.S. citizens were "strongly warned against travel to Iraq."

The physical risks of doing business in Iraq seemed to be spiraling out of control. This, once again, was not part of the original plan. When Bremer first arrived in Baghdad, the armed resistance was so low that he was able to walk the streets with a minimal security entourage. During his first four months on the job, 109 U.S. soldiers were killed and 570 were wounded. In the following four months, when Bremer's shock therapy had taken effect, the number of U.S. casualties almost doubled, with 195 soldiers killed and 1,633 wounded. There are many in Iraq who argue that these events are connected—that Bremer's reforms were the single largest factor leading to the rise of armed resistance.

Take, for instance, Bremer's first casualties. The soldiers and workers he laid off without pensions or severance pay didn't all disappear quietly. Many of them went straight into the mujahedeen, forming the backbone of the armed resistance. "Half a million people are now worse off, and there you have the water tap that keeps the insurgency going. It's alternative employment," says Hussain Kubba, head of the prominent Iraqi business group Kubba Consulting. Some of Bremer's other economic casualties also have failed to go quietly. It turns out that many of the businessmen whose companies are threatened by Bremer's investment laws have decided to make investments of their own—in the resistance. It is partly their money that keeps fighters in Kalashnikovs and RPGs.

These developments present a challenge to the basic logic of shock therapy: the neocons were convinced that if they brought in their reforms quickly and ruthlessly, Iraqis would be too stunned to resist. But the shock appears to have had the opposite effect; rather than the predicted paralysis, it jolted many Iraqis into action, much of it extreme. Haider al-Abadi, Iraq's minister of communication, puts it this way: "We know that there are terrorists in the country, but previously they were not successful, they were isolated. Now because the whole country is unhappy, and a lot of people don't have jobs . . . these terrorists are finding listening ears."

Bremer was now at odds not only with the Iraqis who opposed his plans but with U.S. military commanders charged with putting down the insurgency his policies were feeding. Heretical questions began to be raised: instead of laying people off, what if the CPA actually created jobs for Iraqis? And instead of rushing to sell off Iraq's 200 state-owned firms, how about putting them back to work?

From the start, the neocons running Iraq had shown nothing but disdain for Iraq's state-owned companies. In keeping with their Year Zero-apocalyptic glee, when looters descended on the factories during the war, U.S. forces did nothing. Sabah Asaad, managing director of a refrigerator factory outside Baghdad, told me that while the looting was going on, he went to a nearby U.S. Army base and begged for help. "I asked one of the officers to send two soldiers and a vehicle to help me kick out the looters. I was crying. The officer said, 'Sorry, we can't do anything, we need an order from President Bush.' " Back in Washington, Donald Rumsfeld shrugged. "Free people are free to make mistakes and commit crimes and do bad things."

\*    \*    \*

The day I left Baghdad was the worst yet. Fallujah was under siege and Brig. Gen. Kimmitt was threatening to "destroy the al-Mahdi Army." By the end, roughly 2,000 Iraqis were killed in these twin campaigns. I was dropped off at a security checkpoint several miles from the airport, then loaded onto a bus jammed with contractors lugging hastily packed bags. Although no one was calling it one, this was an evacuation: over the next week 1,500 contractors left Iraq, and some governments began airlifting their citizens out of the country. On the bus no one spoke; we all just listened to the mortar fire, craning our necks to see the red glow. A guy carrying a KPMG briefcase decided to lighten things up. "So is there business class on this flight?" he asked the silent bus. From the back, somebody called out, "Not yet."

Indeed, it may be quite a while before business class truly arrives in Iraq. When we landed in Amman, we learned that we had gotten out just in time. That morning three Japanese civilians were kidnapped and their captors were threatening to burn them alive. Two days later Nicholas Berg went missing and was not seen again until the snuff film surfaced of his beheading, an even more terrifying message for U.S. contractors than the charred bodies in Fallujah. These were the start of a wave of kidnappings and killings of foreigners, most of them businesspeople, from a rainbow of nations: South Korea, Italy, China, Nepal, Pakistan, the Philippines, Turkey. By the end of June more than ninety contractors were reported dead in Iraq. When seven Turkish contractors were kidnapped in June, their captors asked the "company to cancel all contracts and pull out employees from Iraq." Many insurance companies stopped selling life insurance to contractors, and others began to charge premiums as high as $10,000 a week for a single Western executive—the same price some insurgents reportedly pay for a dead American.

For their part, the organizers of DBX, the historic Baghdad trade fair, decided to relocate to the lovely tourist city of Diyarbakir in Turkey, "just 250 km from the Iraqi border." An Iraqi landscape, only without those frightening Iraqis. Three weeks later just fifteen people showed up for a Commerce Department conference in Lansing, Michigan, on investing in Iraq. Its host, Republican Congressman Mike Rogers, tried to reassure his skeptical audience by saying that Iraq is "like a rough neighborhood anywhere in America." The foreign investors, the ones who were offered every imaginable free-market enticement, are clearly not convinced; there is still no sign of them. Keith Crane, a senior economist at the Rand Corporation who has worked for the CPA, put it bluntly: "I don't believe the board of a multinational company could approve a major investment in this environment. If people are shooting at each other, it's just difficult to do business." Hamid Jassim Khamis, the manager of the largest soft-drink bottling plant in the region, told me he can't find any investors, even though he landed the exclusive rights to produce Pepsi in central Iraq. "A lot of people have approached us to invest in the factory, but people are really hesitating now." Khamis said he couldn't blame them; in five months he has survived an attempted assassination, a carjacking, two bombs planted at the entrance of his factory, and the kidnapping of his son.

Despite having been granted the first license for a foreign bank to operate in Iraq in forty years, HSBC still hasn't opened any branches, a decision that may mean losing the coveted license altogether. Procter & Gamble has put its joint venture on hold, and so has General Motors. The U.S. financial backers of the Starwood luxury hotel and multiplex have gotten cold feet, and Siemens AG has pulled most staff from Iraq. The bell hasn't rung yet at the Baghdad Stock Exchange—in fact you can't even use credit cards in Iraq's cash-only economy. New Bridge Strategies, the company that had gushed back in October about how "a Wal-Mart could take over the country," is sounding distinctly humbled. "McDonald's is not opening anytime soon," company partner Ed Rogers told the *Washington Post*. Neither is Wal-Mart. The *Financial Times* has declared Iraq "the most dangerous place in the world in which to do business." It's quite an accomplishment: in trying to design the best place in the world to do business, the neocons have managed to create the worst, the most eloquent indictment yet of the guiding logic behind deregulated free markets.

The violence has not just kept investors out; it also forced Bremer, before he left, to abandon many of his central economic policies. Privatization of the state companies is off the table; instead, several of the state companies have been offered up for lease, but only if the investor agrees not to lay off a single employee. Thousands of the state workers that Bremer fired have been rehired, and significant raises have been handed out in the public sector as a whole. Plans to do away with the food-ration program have also been scrapped—it just doesn't seem like a good time to deny millions of Iraqis the only nutrition on which they can depend.

\*   \*   \*

The great historical irony of the catastrophe unfolding in Iraq is that the shock-therapy reforms that were supposed to create an economic boom that would rebuild the country have instead fueled a resistance that ultimately made reconstruction impossible. Bremer's reforms unleashed forces that the neocons neither predicted nor could hope to control, from armed insurrections inside factories to tens of thousands of unemployed young men arming themselves. These forces have transformed Year Zero in Iraq into the mirror opposite of what the neocons envisioned: not a corporate Utopia but a ghoulish dystopia, where going to a simple business meeting can get you lynched, burned alive, or beheaded. These dangers are so great that in Iraq global capitalism has retreated, at least for now. For the neocons, this must be a shocking development: their ideological belief in greed turns out to be stronger than greed itself.

Iraq was to the neocons what Afghanistan was to the Taliban: the one place on Earth where they could force everyone to live by the most literal, unyielding interpretation of their sacred texts. One would think that the bloody results of this experiment would inspire a crisis of faith: in the country where they had absolute free reign, where there was no local government to blame, where economic reforms were introduced at their most shocking and most perfect, they created, instead of a model free market, a failed state no right-thinking investor would touch. And yet the Green Zone neocons and their masters in Washington are no more likely to reexamine their core beliefs than the Taliban mullahs were inclined to search their souls when their Islamic state slid into a debauched Hades of opium and sex slavery. When facts threaten true believers, they simply close their eyes and pray harder.

Which is precisely what Thomas Foley has been doing. The former head of "private sector development" has left Iraq, a country he had described as "the mother of all turnarounds," and has accepted another turnaround job, as co-chair of George Bush's reelection committee in Connecticut. On April 30 in Washington he addressed a crowd of entrepreneurs about business prospects in Baghdad. It was a tough day to be giving an upbeat speech: that morning the first photographs had appeared out of Abu Ghraib, including one of a hooded prisoner with electrical wires attached to his hands. This was another kind of shock therapy, far more literal than the one Foley had helped to administer, but not entirely unconnected. "Whatever you're seeing, it's not as bad as it appears," Foley told the crowd. "You just need to accept that on faith."

## DISCUSSION QUESTIONS

1. Are the humanitarian benefits Gelernter discusses worth the cost in lives? What standards do you use in balancing the two?

2. Are you persuaded by the argument that we should not congratulate ourselves on removing Hussein when there are other equally tyrannical governments—North Korea, Syria, Iran—still in place? Or is this argument merely a justification for not doing anything, unless you can do everything?

3. Both Brooks and Klein agree that the reconstruction of Iraq has not gone as planned, although they attribute this to very different factors—Klein to ideological fantasy, Lowry to the inherent imperfections in human planning. Who do you think has the stronger case?

# Appendix

## *Marbury v. Madison* (1803)

*The power of judicial review—the authority of the federal courts to determine the constitutionality of state and federal legislative acts—was established early in the nation's history in the case of* Marbury v. Madison *(1803). While the doctrine of judicial review is now firmly entrenched in the American judicial process, the outcome of* Marbury *was by no means a sure thing. The doctrine had been outlined in* The Federalist, *No. 78, and had been relied upon implicitly in earlier, lower federal court cases, but there were certainly sentiments among some of the Founders to suggest that only Congress ought to be able to judge the constitutionality of its acts.*

*The facts leading up to the decision in* Marbury v. Madison *tell an intensely political story. Efforts to reform the federal judiciary had been ongoing with the Federalist administration of President Adams. Following the defeat of the Federalist party in 1800, and the election of Thomas Jefferson as president, the Federalist Congress passed an act reforming the judiciary. The act gave outgoing President Adams authority to appoint several Federalist justices of the peace before Jefferson's term as president began. This would have enabled the Federalist party to retain a large measure of power.*

*Marbury was appointed to be a justice of the peace by President Adams, but his commission, signed by the president and sealed by the secretary of state, without which he could not assume office, was not delivered to him before President Jefferson took office March 4, 1803. Jefferson refused to order James Madison, his secretary of state, to deliver the commission. Marbury, in turn, filed an action in the U.S. Supreme Court seeking an order—called a writ of mandamus—directing the secretary of state to compel the delivery of the commission.*

*The Constitution grants the Supreme Court original jurisdiction in only a limited number of cases—those involving ambassadors, public ministers, and those in which a state is a party; in the remaining cases, the Court has authority only as an appellate court. When it acts according to its original jurisdiction, the Court exercises initial authority over a controversy, just like a trial court, as distinguished from the more limited authority it exercises when a case is presented as an appeal from a lower court's decision.*

*In 1789, Congress passed legislation setting up the federal courts, called the Judiciary Act of 1789. That legislation gave the Supreme Court the original authority to "issue writs of mandamus in cases warranted by the principles and usage of law. . . ." Thus, the ultimate question in* Marbury v. Madison *was whether Congress could, by statute, enlarge the original jurisdiction of the Court.*

*The Court first considered whether Marbury's appointment was complete— and therefore irrevocable—before Jefferson took office. Under the law, the appointment was deemed complete when the president signed the commission and the secretary of state sealed it; the appointment was a completed fact at that time, and was not dependent upon delivery. Therefore, the Court found that Marbury was entitled to his commission. The Court then decided that by withholding the commission, Secretary of State Madison was violating Marbury's legal rights. The remaining question was whether the Supreme Court could issue an order compelling the delivery of the commission.*

CHIEF JUSTICE MARSHALL delivered the opinion of the Court.

. . . It is, then, the opinion of the Court,

1st. That by signing the commission of Mr. Marbury, the President of the United States appointed him a justice of peace for the county of Washington, in the District of Columbia; and that the seal of the United States, affixed thereto by the Secretary of State, is conclusive testimony of the verity of the signature, and of the completion of the appointment, and that the appointment conferred on him a legal right to the office for the space of five years.

2d. That, having this legal title to the office, he has a consequent right to the commission; a refusal to deliver which is a plain violation of that right, for which the laws of his country afford him a remedy.

It remains to be inquired whether,

3d. He is entitled to the remedy for which he applies. This depends on,

1st. The nature of the writ applied for; and,

2d. The power of this court.

\* \* \*

This . . . is a plain case for a mandamus, either to deliver the commission, or a copy of it from the record; and it only remains to be inquired,

Whether it can issue from this court.

The act to establish the judicial courts of the United States authorizes the Supreme Court "to issue writs of mandamus in cases warranted by the principles and usages of law, to any courts appointed, or persons holding office, under the authority of the United States."

The Secretary of State, being a person holding an office under the authority of the United States, is precisely within the letter of the description, and if this court is not authorized to issue a writ of mandamus to such an officer, it must be because the law is unconstitutional, and therefore absolutely incapable of conferring the authority, and assigning the duties which its words purport to confer and assign.

The constitution vests the whole judicial power of the United States in one Supreme Court, and such inferior courts as congress shall, from time to time, ordain and establish. This power is expressly extended to all cases arising under the laws of the United States; and, consequently, in some form, may be exercised over the present case; because the right claimed is given by a law of the United States.

In the distribution of this power it is declared that "the Supreme Court shall have original jurisdiction in all cases affecting ambassadors, other public ministers and consuls, and those in which a state shall be a party. In all other cases, the Supreme Court shall have appellate jurisdiction."

\*   \*   \*

To enable this court, then, to issue a mandamus, it must be shown to be an exercise of appellate jurisdiction, or to be necessary to enable them to exercise appellate jurisdiction.

\*   \*   \*

It is the essential criterion of appellate jurisdiction, that it revises and corrects the proceedings in a cause already instituted, and does not create that cause. . . . [Y]et to issue such a writ to an officer for the delivery of a paper, is in effect the same as to sustain an original action for that paper, and, therefore, seems not to belong to appellate, but to original jurisdiction.

The authority, therefore, given to the Supreme Court, by the act establishing the judicial courts of the United States, to issue writs of mandamus to public officers, appears not to be warranted by the constitution; and it becomes necessary to inquire whether a jurisdiction so conferred can be exercised.

The question, whether an act, repugnant to the constitution, can become the law of the land, is a question deeply interesting to the United States; but, happily, not of an intricacy proportioned to its interest. It seems only necessary to recognize certain principles, supposed to have been long and well established, to decide it.

That the people have an original right to establish, for their future government, such principles, as, in their opinion, shall most conduce to their own happiness is the basis on which the whole American fabric has been erected. The exercise of this original right is a very great exertion; nor can it, nor ought it, to be frequently repeated. The principles, therefore, so established, are deemed fundamental. And as the authority from which they proceed is supreme, and can seldom act, they are designed to be permanent.

This original and supreme will organizes the government, and assigns to different departments their respective powers. It may either stop here, or establish certain limits not to be transcended by those departments.

The government of the United States is of the latter description. The powers of the legislature are defined and limited; and that those limits may not be mistaken, or forgotten, the constitution is written. To what purpose are powers limited, and to what purpose is that limitation committed to writing, if these limits may, at any time, be passed by those intended to be restrained? The distinction between a government with limited and unlimited powers is abolished, if those limits do not confine the persons on whom they are imposed, and if acts prohibited and acts allowed, are of equal obligation. It is a proposition too plain to be contested, that the constitution controls any legislative act repugnant to it; or, that the legislature may alter the constitution by an ordinary act.

Between these alternatives there is no middle ground. The constitution is either a superior paramount law, unchangeable by ordinary means, or it is on a level with ordinary legislative acts, and, like other acts, is alterable when the legislature shall please to alter it.

If the former part of the alternative be true, then a legislative act contrary to the constitution is not law: if the latter part be true, then written constitutions are absurd attempts, on the part of the people, to limit a power in its own nature illimitable.

Certainly all those who have framed written constitutions contemplate them as forming the fundamental and paramount law of the nation, and, consequently, the theory of every such government must be, that an act of the legislature, repugnant to the constitution, is void.

This theory is essentially attached to a written constitution, and, is consequently, to be considered, by this court, as one of the fundamental principles of our society. It is not therefore to be lost sight of in the further consideration of this subject.

If an act of the legislature, repugnant to the constitution, is void, does it, notwithstanding its invalidity, bind the courts, and oblige them to give it effect? Or, in other words, though it be not law, does it constitute a rule as operative as if it was a law? This would be to overthrow in fact what was established in theory; and would seem, at first view, an absurdity too gross to be insisted on.

\*   \*   \*

It is emphatically the province and duty of the judicial department to say what the law is. Those who apply the rule to particular cases, must of necessity expound and interpret that rule. If two laws conflict with each other, the courts must decide on the operation of each.

So if a law be in opposition to the constitution; if both the law and the constitution apply to a particular case, so that the court must either decide that case conformably to the law, disregarding the constitution; or conformably to the constitution, disregarding the law; the court must determine which of these conflicting rules governs the case. This is of the very essence of judicial duty.

If, then, the courts are to regard the constitution, and the constitution is superior to any ordinary act of the legislature, the constitution, and not such ordinary act, must govern the case to which they both apply.

Those, then, who controvert the principle that the constitution is to be considered, in court, as a paramount law, are reduced to the necessity of maintaining that courts must close their eyes on the constitution, and see only the law.

This doctrine would subvert the very foundation of all written constitutions. It would declare that an act which, according to the principles and theory of our government, is entirely void, is yet, in practice, completely obligatory. It would declare that if the legislature shall do what is expressly forbidden, such act, notwithstanding the express prohibition, is in reality effectual. It would be giving to the legislature a practical and real omnipotence, with the same breath which professes to restrict their powers within narrow limits. It is prescribing limits, and declaring that those limits may be passed at pleasure.

That it thus reduces to nothing what we have deemed the greatest improvement on political institutions, a written constitution, would of itself be sufficient, in America, where written constitutions have been viewed with so much reverence, for rejecting the construction. But the peculiar expressions of the constitution of the United States furnish additional arguments in favour of its rejection.

The judicial power of the United States is extended to all cases arising under the constitution.

Could it be the intention of those who gave this power, to say that in using it the constitution should not be looked into? That a case arising under the constitution should be decided without examining the instrument under which it arises?

This is too extravagant to be maintained.

In some cases, then, the constitution must be looked into by the judges.

. . . [I]t is apparent, that the framers of the constitution contemplated that instrument as a rule for the government of courts, as well as of the legislature.

Why otherwise does it direct the judges to take an oath to support it? This oath certainly applies in an especial manner, to their conduct in their official character. How immoral to impose it on them, if they were to be used as the instruments, and the knowing instruments, for violating what they swear to support!

The oath of office, too, imposed by the legislature, is completely demonstrative of the legislative opinion on this subject.

\* \* \*

Why does a judge swear to discharge his duties agreeably to the constitution of the United States, if that constitution forms no rule for his government? If it is closed upon him, and cannot be inspected by him?

If such be the real state of things, this is worse than solemn mockery. To prescribe, or to take this oath, becomes equally a crime.

It is also not entirely unworthy of observation, that in declaring what shall be the supreme law of the land, the constitution itself is first mentioned; and not the laws of the United States generally, but those only which shall be made in pursuance of the constitution, have that rank.

Thus, the particular phraseology of the constitution of the United States confirms and strengthens the principle, supposed to be essential to all written constitutions, that a law repugnant to the constitution is void; and that courts, as well as other departments, are bound by that instrument.

# *McCulloch v. Maryland* (1819)

*Early in the nation's history, the United States Supreme Court interpreted the powers of the national government expansively. The first Supreme Court case to directly address the scope of federal authority under the Constitution was* McCulloch v. Maryland *(1819). The facts were straightforward: Congress created the Bank of the United States—to the dismay of many states who viewed the creation of a national bank as a threat to the operation of banks within their own state borders. As a result, when a branch of the Bank of the United States was opened in Maryland, that state attempted to limit the bank's ability to do business under a law that imposed taxes on all banks not chartered by the state.*

*In an opinion authored by Chief Justice Marshall, the Court considered two questions: whether Congress had the authority to create a national bank; and whether Maryland could in turn tax it. Marshall's answer to these two questions defends an expansive theory of implied powers for the national government and propounds the principle of national supremacy with an eloquence rarely found in judicial decisions.*

CHIEF JUSTICE JOHN MARSHALL delivered the opinion of the Court.

The first question made in the cause is, has Congress power to incorporate a bank? The power now contested was exercised by the first Congress elected under the present constitution. The bill for incorporating the Bank of the United States did not steal upon an unsuspecting legislature, and pass unobserved. Its principle was completely understood, and was opposed with equal zeal and ability. . . . In discussing this question, the counsel for the state of Maryland have deemed it of some importance, in the construction of the constitution, to consider that instrument not as emanating from the people, but as the act of sovereign and independent states. The powers of the general government, it has been said, are delegated by the states, who alone are truly sovereign; and must be exercised in subordination to the states, who alone possess supreme dominion. . . . No political dreamer was ever wild enough to think of breaking down the lines which separate the states, and of compounding the American people into one common mass. Of consequence, when they act, they act in their states. But the measures they adopt do not, on that account, cease to be the measures of the people themselves, or become the measures of the state governments.

From these conventions the constitution derives its whole authority. The government proceeds directly from the people; is "ordained and established" in the name of the people; and is declared to be ordained, "in order to form a more perfect union, establish justice, insure domestic tranquility, and secure the blessings of liberty to themselves and to their posterity." The assent of the states, in their sovereign capacity, is implied in calling a convention, and thus submitting that instrument to the people. But the people were at perfect liberty to accept or reject it; and their act was final. It required not the affirmance, and could not be negatived, by the state governments. The constitution, when thus adopted, was of complete obligation, and bound the state sovereignties.

The government of the Union, then (whatever may be the influence of this fact on the case), is, emphatically, and truly, a government of the people. In form and in substance it emanates from them. Its powers are granted by them, and are to be exercised directly on them, and for their benefit.

This government is acknowledged by all to be one of enumerated powers. The principle, that it can exercise only the powers granted to it, is now universally admitted. But the question respecting the extent of the powers actually granted, is perpetually arising, and will probably continue to arise, as long as our system shall exist. The government of the United States though limited in its powers, is supreme; and its laws, when made in pursuance of the constitution, form the supreme law of the land, "anything in the constitution or laws of any state to the contrary notwithstanding."

\*   \*   \*

A constitution, to contain an accurate detail of all the subdivisions of which its great powers will admit, and of all the means by which they may be carried into execution, would partake of the prolixity of a legal code, and could scarcely be embraced by the human mind. It would probably never be understood by the public. Its nature, therefore, requires, that only its great outlines should be marked, its important objects designated, and the minor ingredients which compose those objects be deduced from the nature of the objects themselves. . . . in considering this question, then, we must never forget, that it is a constitution we are expounding.

Although, among the enumerated powers of government, we do not find the word "bank" or "incorporation," we find the great powers to lay and collect taxes; to borrow money; to regulate commerce; to declare and conduct a war; and to raise and support armies and navies. The sword and the purse, all the external relations, and no inconsiderable portion of the industry of the nation, are entrusted to its government. . . . [I]t may with great reason be contended, that a government, entrusted with such ample powers, on the due execution of which the happiness and prosperity of the nation so vitally depends, must also be entrusted with ample means for their execution. The power being given, it is the interest of the nation to facilitate its execution. It can never be their interest, and cannot be presumed to have been their intention, to clog and embarrass its execution by withholding the most appropriate means. . . . It is, then, the subject of fair inquiry, how far such means may be employed.

The government which has a right to do an act, and has imposed on it the duty of performing that act, must, according to the dictates of reason, be allowed to select the means.

\* \* \*

But the constitution of the United States has not left the right of Congress to employ the necessary means, for the execution of the powers conferred on the government, to general reasoning. To its enumeration of powers is added that of making "all laws which shall be necessary and proper, for carrying into execution the foregoing powers, and all other powers vested by this constitution, in the government of the United States, or in any department [or officer] thereof."

The counsel for the state of Maryland have urged various arguments, to prove that this clause . . . is really restrictive of the general right, which might otherwise be implied, of selecting means for executing the enumerated powers.

. . . [Maryland argues that] Congress is not empowered by it to make all laws, which may have relation to the powers conferred on the government, but such only as may be "necessary and proper" for carrying them into execution. The word "necessary" is considered as controlling the whole sentence, and as limiting the right to pass laws for the execution of the granted powers, to such as are indispensable, and without which the power would be nugatory. That it excludes the choice of means, and leaves to Congress, in each case, that only which is most direct and simple.

Is it true, that this is the sense in which the word "necessary" is always used? . . . We think it does not. If reference be had to its use, in the common affairs of the world, or in approved authors, we find that it frequently imports no more than that one thing is convenient, or useful, or essential to another. To employ the means necessary to an end, is generally understood as employing any means calculated to produce the end, and not as being confined to those single means, without which the end would be entirely unattainable.

Let this be done in the case under consideration. The subject is the execution of those great powers on which the welfare of a nation essentially depends. It must have been the intention of those who gave these powers, to insure, as far as human prudence could insure, their beneficial execution. This could not be done by confiding the choice of means to such narrow limits as not to leave it in the power of Congress to adopt any which might be appropriate, and which were conducive to the end. This provision is made in a constitution intended to endure for ages to come, and consequently, to be adapted to the various crises of human affairs. To have prescribed the means by which government should, in all future time, execute its powers, would have been to change, entirely, the character of the instrument, and give it the properties of a legal code. It would have been an unwise attempt to provide, by immutable rules, for exigencies which, if foreseen at all, must have been seen dimly, and which can be best provided for as they occur. To have declared that the best means shall not be used, but those alone without which the power given would be nugatory, would have been to deprive the legislature of the capacity to avail itself of experience, to exercise its reason, and to accommodate its legislation to circumstances. If we apply this principle of construction to any of the powers of the government, we shall find it so pernicious in its operation that we shall be compelled to discard it.

\*   \*   \*

We admit, as all must admit, that the powers of the government are limited, and that its limits are not to be transcended. But we think the sound construction of the constitution must allow to the national legislature that discretion, with respect to the means by which the powers it confers are to be carried into execution, which will enable that body to perform the high duties assigned to it, in the manner most beneficial to the people. Let the end be legitimate, let it be within the scope of the constitution, and all means which are appropriate, which are plainly adapted to that end, which are not prohibited, but consist with the letter and spirit of the constitution, are constitutional.

\*   \*   \*

It being the opinion of the court that the act incorporating the bank is constitutional, and that the power of establishing a branch in the state of Maryland might be properly exercised by the bank itself, we proceed to inquire: Whether the state of Maryland may, without violating the constitution, tax that branch?

That the power of taxation is one of vital importance; that it is retained by the states; that it is not abridged by the grant of a similar power to the government of the Union; that it is to be concurrently exercised by the two governments; are truths which have never been denied. But, such is the paramount character of the constitution that its capacity to withdraw any subject from the action of even this power, is admitted. . . . [T]he paramount character [of the Constitution] would seem to restrain, as it certainly may restrain, a state from such other exercise of this power as is in its nature incompatible with, and repugnant to, the constitutional laws of the Union. A law, absolutely repugnant to another, as entirely repeals that other as if express terms of repeal were used.

\* \* \*

This great principle is, that the constitution and the laws made in pursuance thereof are supreme; that they control the constitution and laws of the respective states, and cannot be controlled by them. From this, which may be almost termed an axiom, other propositions are adduced as corollaries, on the truth or error of which, and on their application to this case, the cause has been supposed to depend. These are, 1st. That a power to create implies a power to preserve. 2d. That a power to destroy, if wielded by a different hand, is hostile to, and incompatible with, these powers to create and to preserve. 3d. That where this repugnance exists, that authority which is supreme must control, not yield to that over which it is supreme.

. . . [T]axation is said to be an absolute power, which acknowledges no other limits than those expressly prescribed in the constitution, and like sovereign powers of every other description, is trusted to the discretion of those who use it. But the very terms of this argument admit that the sovereignty of the state, in the article of taxation itself, is subordinate to, and may be controlled by the constitution of the United States. How far it has been controlled by that instrument must be a question of construction. In making this construction, no principle not declared can be admissible, which would defeat the legitimate operations of a supreme government.

\* \* \*

All subjects over which the sovereign power of a state extends, are objects of taxation; but those over which it does not extend, are, upon the soundest principles, exempt from taxation. . . . The sovereignty of a state extends to everything which exists by its own authority, or is introduced by its permission; but does it extend to those means which are employed by Congress to carry into execution—powers conferred on that body by the people of the United States? We think it demonstrable that it does not. Those powers are not given by the people of a single state. They are given by the people of the United States, to a government whose laws, made in pursuance of the constitution, are declared to be supreme. Consequently, the people of a single state cannot confer a sovereignty which will extend over them.

If we apply the principle for which the state of Maryland contends, to the constitution generally, we shall find it capable of changing totally the character of that instrument. We shall find it capable of arresting all the measures of the government, and of prostrating it at the foot of the states. The American people have declared their constitution, and the laws made in pursuance thereof, to be supreme; but this principle would transfer the supremacy, in fact, to the states. If the controlling power of the states be established; if their supremacy as to taxation be acknowledged; what is to restrain their exercising this control in any shape they may please to give it? Their sovereignty is not confined to taxation. That is not the only mode in which it might be displayed. The question is, in truth, a question of supremacy; and if the right of the states to tax the means employed by the general government be conceded, the declaration that the constitution, and the laws made in pursuance thereof, shall be the supreme law of the land, is empty and unmeaning declamation.

\*   \*   \*

We are unanimously of opinion, that the law passed by the legislature of Maryland, imposing a tax on the Bank of the United States, is unconstitutional and void. This opinion does not deprive the states of any resources which they originally possessed. It does not extend to a tax paid by the real property of the bank, in common with other real property within the state, nor to a tax imposed on the interest which the citizens of Maryland may hold in this institution, in common with other property of the same description throughout the state. But this is a tax on the operations of the bank, and is, consequently, a tax on the operation of an instrument employed by the government of the Union to carry its powers into execution. Such a tax must be unconstitutional.

Reversed.

# *Barron v. Baltimore* (1833)

*The declaration made in* Barron v. Baltimore *(1833) that citizenship had a dual aspect—state and national—set the terms of the Supreme Court's interpretation of the Bill of Rights for nearly a century. The reasoning of the case proved persuasive even after the adoption of the Fourteenth Amendment, as the federal courts refused to extend the protections of the federal Constitution to citizens aggrieved by the actions of state or local governments.*

*Barron brought suit in a federal court claiming that the city of Baltimore had appropriated his property for a public purpose without paying him just compensation. He asserted that the Fifth Amendment to the Constitution operated as a constraint upon both state and federal governments.*

CHIEF JUSTICE JOHN MARSHALL delivered the opinion of the Court.

. . . The question presented is, we think, of great importance, but not of much difficulty. The constitution was ordained and established by the people of the United States for themselves, for their own government, and not for the government of the individual states. Each state established a constitution for itself, and in that constitution, provided such limitations and restrictions on the powers of its particular government, as its judgment dictated. The people of the United States framed such a government for the United States as they supposed best adapted to their situation and best calculated to promote their interests. The powers they conferred on this government were to be exercised by itself; and the limitations on power, if expressed in general terms, are naturally, and, we think, necessarily, applicable to the government created by the instrument. They are limitations of power granted in the instrument itself; not of distinct governments, framed by different persons and for different purposes.

If these propositions be correct, the fifth amendment must be understood as restraining the power of the general government, not as applicable to the states. In their several constitutions, they have imposed such restrictions on their respective governments, as their own wisdom suggested; such as they deemed most proper for themselves. It is a subject on which they judge exclusively, and with which others interfere no further than they are supposed to have a common interest.

\*   \*   \*

Had the people of the several states, or any of them, required changes in their constitutions; had they required additional safe-guards to liberty from the apprehended encroachments of their particular governments; the remedy was in their own hands, and could have been applied by themselves. A convention could have been assembled by the discontented state, and the required improvements could have been made by itself.

. . . Had Congress engaged in the extraordinary occupation of improving the constitutions of the several states, by affording the people additional protection from the exercise of power by their own governments, in matters which concerned themselves alone, they would have declared this purpose in plain and intelligible language.

But it is universally understood, it is a part of the history of the day, that the great revolution which established the constitution of the United States, was not effected without immense opposition. Serious fears were extensively entertained, that those powers which the patriot statesmen, who then watched over the interests of our country, deemed essential to union, and to the attainment of those unvaluable objects for which union was sought, might be exercised in a manner dangerous to liberty. In almost every convention by which the constitution was adopted, amendments to guard against the abuse of power were recommended. These amendments demanded security against the apprehended encroachments of the general government—not against those of the local governments. In compliance with a sentiment thus generally expressed, to quiet fears thus extensively entertained, amendments were proposed by the required majority in congress, and adopted by the states. These amendments contain no expression indicating an intention to apply them to the state governments. This court cannot so apply them.

We are of opinion, that the provision in the fifth amendment to the constitution, declaring that private property shall not be taken for public use, without just compensation, is intended solely as a limitation on the exercise of power by the government of the United States, and is not applicable to the legislation of the states. We are, therefore, of opinion, that there is no repugnancy between the several acts of the general assembly of Maryland, given in evidence by the defendants at the trial of this cause, in the court of that state, and the constitution of the United States. This court, therefore, has no jurisdiction of the cause, and it is dismissed.

This cause came on to be heard, on the transcript of the record from the court of appeals for the western shore of the state of Maryland, and was argued by counsel: On consideration whereof, it is the opinion of this court, that there is no repugnancy between the several acts of the general assembly of Maryland, given in evidence by the defendants at the trial of this cause in the court of that state, and the constitution of the United States; whereupon, it is ordered and adjudged by this court, that this writ of error be and the same is hereby dismissed, for the want of jurisdiction.

# *Roe v. Wade* (1973)

*One of the most significant changes in constitutional interpretation in the last three decades has been the Court's willingness to look beyond the explicit language of the Bill of Rights to find unenumerated rights, such as the right to privacy. In discovering such rights, the Court has engaged in what is known as substantive due process analysis—defining and articulating fundamental rights—distinct from its efforts to define the scope of procedural due process, when it decides what procedures the state and federal governments must follow to be fair in their treatment of citizens. The Court's move into the substantive due process area has generated much of the political discussion over the proper role of the Court in constitutional interpretation.*

*The case that has been the focal point for this debate is* Roe v. Wade, *the 1973 case that held that a woman's right to privacy protected her decision to have an abortion. The right to privacy in matters relating to contraception and childbearing had been recognized in the 1965 decision of* Griswold v. Connecticut, *and was extended in subsequent decisions culminating in* Roe. *The theoretical issue of concern here relates back to the incorporation issue: Should the Supreme Court be able to prohibit the states not only from violating the express guarantees contained in the Bill of Rights, but its implied guarantees as well?*

*Texas law prohibited abortions except for "the purpose of saving the life of the mother." The plaintiff challenged the constitutionality of the statute, claiming that it infringed upon her substantive due process right to privacy.*

JUSTICE BLACKMUN delivered the opinion of the Court.

. . . [We] forthwith acknowledge our awareness of the sensitive and emotional nature of the abortion controversy, of the vigorous opposing views, and the deep and seemingly absolute convictions that the subject inspires. One's philosophy, one's experiences, one's exposure to the raw edges of human existence, one's religious training, one's attitudes toward life and family and their values, and the moral standards one establishes and seeks to observe, are all likely to affect one's thinking [about] abortion. In addition, population growth, pollution, poverty, and racial overtones tend to complicate and not to simplify the problem. Our task, of course, is to resolve the issue by constitutional measurement, free of emotion and of predilection. We seek earnestly to do this, and, because we do, we have inquired into, and in this opinion place some emphasis upon, medical and medical-legal history and what that history reveals about man's attitudes toward the abortion procedure over the centuries.

\* \* \*

[*The Court here reviewed ancient and contemporary attitudes toward abortion, observing that restrictive laws date primarily from the late nineteenth century. The Court also reviewed the possible state interests in restricting abortions, including discouraging illicit sexual conduct, limiting access to a hazardous medical procedure, and the states' general interests in protecting fetal life. The Court addressed only the third interest as a current legitimate interest of the state.*]

. . . The Constitution does not explicitly mention any right of privacy. In a line of decisions, however, . . . the Court has recognized that a right of personal privacy, or a guarantee of certain areas or zones of privacy, does exist under the Constitution. . . . This right of privacy, whether it be founded in the Fourteenth Amendment's concept of personal liberty and restrictions upon state action, as we feel it is, or, as the District Court determined, in the Ninth Amendment's reservation of rights to the people, is broad enough to encompass a woman's decision whether or not to terminate her pregnancy. The detriment that the State would impose upon the pregnant woman by denying this choice altogether is apparent. Specific and direct harm medically diagnosable even in early pregnancy may be involved. Maternity, or additional offspring, may force upon the woman a distressful life and future. Psychological harm may be imminent. Mental and physical health may be taxed by child care. There is also the distress, for all concerned, associated with the unwanted child, and there is the problem of bringing a child into a family already unable, psychologically and otherwise, to care for it. In other cases, as in this one, the additional difficulties and continuing stigma of unwed motherhood may be involved. All these are factors the woman and her responsible physician necessarily will consider in consultation.

On the basis of elements such as these, appellants and some amici [friends of the Court] argue that the woman's right is absolute and that she is entitled to terminate her pregnancy at whatever time, in whatever way, and for whatever reason she alone chooses. With this we do not agree. Appellants' arguments that Texas either has no valid interest at all in regulating the abortion decision, or no interest strong enough to support any limitation upon the woman's sole determination, is unpersuasive. The Court's decisions recognizing a right of privacy also acknowledge that some state regulation in areas protected by that right is appropriate. As noted above, a State may properly assert important interests in safeguarding health, in maintaining medical standards, and in protecting potential life. At some point in pregnancy, these respective interests become sufficiently compelling to sustain regulation of the factors that govern the abortion decision. The privacy right involved, therefor, cannot be said to be absolute. In fact, it is not clear to us that the claim asserted by some amici that one has an unlimited right to do with one's body as one pleases bears a close relationship to the right of privacy previously articulated in the Court's decisions.

\* \* \*

We therefore conclude that the right of personal privacy includes the abortion decision, but that this right is not unqualified and must be considered against state interests in regulation.

Where certain "fundamental rights" are involved, the Court has held that regulation limiting these rights may be justified only by a "compelling state interest," and that legislative enactments must be narrowly drawn to express only the legitimate state interests at stake.

. . . The District Court held that the appellee failed to meet his burden of demonstrating that the Texas statute's infringement upon Roe's rights was necessary to support a compelling state interest. . . . Appellee argues that the State's determination to recognize and protect prenatal life from and after conception constitutes a compelling state interest. As noted above, we do not agree fully with either formulation.

The appellee and certain amici argue that the fetus is a "person" within the language and meaning of the Fourteenth Amendment. In support of this they outline at length and in detail the well-known facts of fetal development. If this suggestion of personhood is established, the appellant's case, of course, collapses, for the fetus' right to life is then guaranteed specifically by the Amendment. The appellant conceded as much on reargument. On the other hand, the appellee conceded on reargument that no case could be cited that holds that a fetus is a person within the meaning of the Fourteenth Amendment.

The Constitution does not define "person" in so many words. Section 1 of the Fourteenth Amendment contains three references to "person." The first, in defining "citizens," speaks of "persons born or naturalized in the United States." The word also appears both in the Due Process Clause and in the Equal Protection Clause. "Person" is used in other places in the Constitution. . . . But in nearly all these instances, the use of the word is such that it has application only postnatally. None indicates, with any assurance, that it has any possible pre-natal application.

All this, together with our observation, that throughout the major portion of the 19th century prevailing legal abortion practices were far freer than they are today, persuades us that the word "person," as used in the Fourteenth Amendment, does not include the unborn.

. . . The pregnant woman cannot be isolated in her privacy. She carries an embryo and, later, a fetus, if one accepts the medical definitions of the developing young in the human uterus. . . . The situation therefore is inherently different from marital intimacy, or bedroom possession of obscene material, or marriage, or procreation, or education, with which [earlier cases defining the right to privacy] were concerned. As we have intimated above, it is reasonable and appropriate for a State to decide that at some point in time another interest, that of health of the mother or that of potential human life, becomes significantly involved. The woman's privacy is no longer sole and any right of privacy she possesses must be measured accordingly.

Texas urges that, apart from the Fourteenth Amendment, life begins at conception and is present throughout pregnancy, and that, therefore, the State has a compelling interest in protecting that life from and after conception. We need not resolve the difficult question of when life begins. When those trained in the respective disciplines of medicine, philosophy, and theology are unable to arrive at any consensus, the judiciary, at this point in the development of man's knowledge, is not in a position to speculate as to the answer.

. . . In view of all this, we do not agree that, by adopting one theory of life, Texas may override the rights of the pregnant woman that are at stake. We repeat, however, that the State does have an important and legitimate interest in preserving and protecting the health of the pregnant woman, whether she be a resident of the State or a nonresident who seeks medical consultation and treatment there, and that it has still *another* important and legitimate interest in protecting the potentiality of human life. These interests are separate and distinct. Each grows in substantiality as the woman approaches term and, at a point during pregnancy, each becomes "compelling."

With respect to the State's important and legitimate interest in the health of the mother, the "compelling" point, in the light of present medical knowledge, is at approximately the end of the first trimester. This is so because of the now established medical fact . . . that until the end of the first trimester mortality in abortion is less than mortality in normal childbirth. It follows that, from and after this point, a State may regulate the abortion procedure to the extent that the regulation reasonably relates to the preservation and protection of maternal health. Examples of permissible state regulation in this area are requirements as to the qualifications of the person who is to perform the abortion; as to the licensure of that person; as to the facility in which the procedure is to be performed, that is, whether it must be a hospital or may be a clinic or some other place of less-than-hospital status; as to the licensing of the facility; and the like.

This means, on the other hand, that, for the period of pregnancy prior to this "compelling" point, the attending physician, in consultation with his patient, is free to determine, without regulation by the State, that in his medical judgment the patient's pregnancy should be terminated. If that decision is reached, the judgment may be effectuated by an abortion free of interference by the State.

With respect to the State's important and legitimate interest in potential life, the "compelling" point is at viability. This is so because the fetus then presumably has the capability of meaningful life outside the mother's womb. State regulation protective of fetal life after viability thus has both logical and biological justifications. If the State is interested in protecting fetal life after viability, it may go so far as to proscribe abortion during that period except when it is necessary to preserve the life or health of the mother.

Measured against these standards, the Texas Penal Code, in restricting legal abortions to those "procured or attempted by medical advice for the purpose of saving the life of the mother," sweeps too broadly. The statute makes no distinction between abortions performed early in pregnancy and those performed later, and it limits to a single reason, "saving" the mother's life, the legal justification for the procedure. The statute, therefore, cannot survive the constitutional attack made upon it here.

\* \* \*

Reversed.

# *Brown v. Board of Education of Topeka, Kansas* (1954)

*Brown v. Board of Education (1954) was a momentous opinion, invalidating the system of segregation that had been established under Plessy v. Ferguson (1896). However, the constitutional pronouncement only marked the beginning of the struggle for racial equality, as federal courts got more and more deeply involved in trying to prod recalcitrant state and local governments into taking steps to end racial inequalities.*

*The Brown case involved appeals from several states. In each case, the plaintiffs had been denied access to public schools designated only for white children under a variety of state laws. They challenged the Plessy v. Ferguson (1896) "separate but equal" doctrine, contending that segregated schools were by their nature unequal.*

*Chief Justice Warren first discussed the history of the Fourteenth Amendment's equal protection clause, finding it too inconclusive to be of assistance in determining how the Fourteenth Amendment should be applied to the question of public education.*

CHIEF JUSTICE WARREN writing for the majority.

. . . The doctrine of "separate but equal" did not make its appearance in this Court until 1896, in the case of Plessy v. Ferguson, involving not education but transportation. American courts have since labored with the doctrine for over a half a century. In this Court, there have been six cases involving the "separate but equal" doctrine in the field of public education.

\* \* \*

In the instant cases, [the question of the application of the separate but equal doctrine to public education] is directly presented. Here, . . . there are findings below that the Negro and white schools involved have been equalized, or are being equalized, with respect to buildings, curricula, qualifications and salaries of teachers, and other "tangible" factors. Our decision, therefore, cannot turn on merely a comparison of these tanglible factors in the Negro and white schools involved in each of the cases. We must look instead to the effect of segregation itself on public education.

In approaching this problem, we cannot turn the clock back to 1868 when the [Fourteenth] Amendment was adopted, or even to 1896 when Plessy v. Ferguson was written. We must consider public education in the light of its full development and its present place in American life throughout the Nation. Only in this way can it be determined if segregation in public schools deprives these plaintiffs of the equal protection of the laws.

Today, education is perhaps the most important function of state and local governments. Compulsory school attendance laws and the great expenditures for education both demonstrate our recognition of the importance of education to our democratic society. It is required in the performance of our most basic responsibilities, even service in the armed forces. It is the very foundation of good citizenship. Today it is a principal instrument in awakening the child to cultural values, in preparing him for later professional training, and in helping him to adjust normally to his environment. In these days, it is doubtful that any child may reasonably be expected to succeed in life if he is denied the opportunity of an education. Such an opportunity, where the state has undertaken to provide it, is a right which must be made available to all on equal terms.

We come then to the question presented: Does segregation of children in public schools solely on the basis of race, even though the physical facilities and other "tangible" factors may be equal, deprive the children of the minority group of equal educational opportunities? We believe that it does.

In *Sweatt v. Painter*, in finding that a segregated law school for Negroes could not provide them equal educational opportunities, this Court relied in large part on "those qualities which are incapable of objective measurement but which make for greatness in a law school." In McLaurin v. Oklahoma State Regents, the Court, in requiring that a Negro admitted to a white graduate school be treated like all other students, again resorted to intangible considerations: ". . . his ability to study, to engage in discussions and exchange views with other students, and, in general, to learn his profession." Such considerations apply with added force to children in grade and high schools. To separate them from others of similar age and qualifications solely because of their race generates a feeling of inferiority as to their status in the community that may affect their hearts and minds in a way unlikely ever to be undone. The effect of this separation on their educational opportunities was well stated by a finding in the Kansas case by a court which nevertheless felt compelled to rule against the Negro plaintiffs:

"Segregation of white and colored children in public schools has a detrimental effect upon the colored children. The impact is greater when it has the sanction of the law; for the policy of separating the races is usually interpreted as denoting the inferiority of the Negro group. A sense of inferiority affects the motivation of a child to learn. Segregation with the sanction of law, therefore, has a tendency to [retard] the educational and mental development of Negro children and to deprive them of some of the benefits they would receive in a racial[ly] integrated school system." Whatever may have been the extent of psychological knowledge at the time of Plessy v. Ferguson, this finding is amply supported by modern authority. Any language in Plessy v. Ferguson contrary to this finding is rejected.

We conclude that in the field of public education the doctrine of "separate but equal" has no place. Separate educational facilities are inherently unequal. Therefore, we hold that the plaintiffs and others similarly situated for whom the actions have been brought are, by reason of the segregation complained of, deprived of the equal protection of the laws guaranteed by the Fourteenth Amendment. This disposition makes unnecessary any discussion whether such segregation also violates the Due Process Clause of the Fourteenth Amendment.

Because these are class actions, because of the wide applicability of this decision, and because of the great variety of local conditions, the formulation of decrees in these cases presents problems of considerable complexity. On reargument, the consideration of appropriate relief was necessarily subordinated to the primary question—the constitutionality of segregation in public education. We have now announced that such segregation is a denial of the equal protection of the laws.

# United States v. Nixon (1974)

*The Supreme Court has had few occasions to rule on the constitutional limits of executive authority. The Court is understandably reluctant to articulate the boundaries of presidential and legislative power, given the Court's own somewhat ambiguous institutional authority. In the case that follows, however, the Court looked at one of the ways in which the Constitution circumscribes the exercise of presidential prerogative.*

*United States v. Nixon (1974) involves claims to executive authority. President Richard Nixon was implicated in a conspiracy to cover up a burglary of the Democratic Party Headquarters at the Watergate Hotel in Washington, D.C., during the 1972 reelection campaign. The Special Prosecutor assigned to investigate the break-in and file appropriate criminal charges asked the trial court to order the President to disclose a number of documents and tapes related to the cover-up in order to determine the scope of the President's involvement. The President produced edited versions of some of the materials, but refused to comply with most of the trial court's order, asserting that he was entitled to withhold the information under a claim of "executive privilege."*

CHIEF JUSTICE BURGER delivered the opinion of the Court.

In the District Court, the President's counsel argued that the court lacked jurisdiction to issue the subpoena because the matter was an intra-branch dispute between a subordinate and superior officer of the Executive Branch and hence not subject to judicial resolution. That argument has been renewed in this Court with emphasis on the contention that the dispute does not present a "case" or "controversy" which can be adjudicated in the federal courts. The President's counsel argues that the federal courts should not intrude into areas committed to the other branches of Government. He views the present dispute as essentially a "jurisdictional" dispute within the Executive Branch which he analogizes to a dispute between two congressional committees. Since the Executive Branch has exclusive authority and absolute discretion to decide whether to prosecute a case, it is contended that a President's decision is final in determining what evidence is to be used in a given criminal case.

. . . Although his counsel concedes the President has delegated certain specific powers to the Special Prosecutor, he has not "waived nor delegated to the Special Prosecutor the President's duty to claim privilege as to all materials which fall within the President's inherent authority to refuse to disclose to any executive officer." The Special Prosecutor's demand for the items therefore presents, in the view of the President's counsel, a political question since it involves a "textually demonstrable" grant of power under Art. II. . . .

The demands of and the resistance to the subpoena present an obvious controversy in the ordinary sense, but that alone is not sufficient to meet constitutional standards. In the constitutional sense, controversy means more than disagreement and conflict; rather it means the kind of controversy courts traditionally resolve. Here at issue is the production or non-production of specified evidence deemed by the Special Prosecutor to be relevant and admissible in a pending criminal case. It is sought by one official of the Government within the scope of his express authority; it is resisted by the Chief Executive on the ground of his duty to preserve the confidentiality of the communications of the President. Whatever the correct answer on the merits, these issues are "of a type which are traditionally justiciable."

\*   \*   \*

. . . We turn to the claim that the subpoena should be quashed because it demands "confidential conversations between a President and his close advisors that it would be inconsistent with the public interest to produce." The first contention is a broad claim that the separation of powers doctrine precludes judicial review of a President's claim of privilege. The second contention is that if he does not prevail on the claim of absolute privilege, the court should hold as a matter of constitutional law that the privilege prevails over the subpoena. . . .

\*   \*   \*

*[The Court discussed its authority to interpret the Constitution, concluding that it had full power to adjudicate a claim of executive privilege.]*

In support of his claim of absolute privilege, the President's counsel urges two grounds one of which is common to all governments and one of which is peculiar to our system of separation of powers. The first ground is the valid need for protection of communications between high government officials and those who advise and assist them in the performance of their manifold duties; the importance of this confidentiality is too plain to require further discussion. Human experience teaches that those who expect public dissemination of their remarks may well temper candor with a concern for appearances and for their own interests to the detriment of the decisionmaking process. Whatever the nature of the privilege of confidentiality of presidential communications in the exercise of Art. II powers the privilege can be said to derive from the supremacy of each branch within its own assigned area of constitutional duties. Certain powers and privileges flow from the nature of enumerated powers; the protection of the confidentiality of presidential communications has similar constitutional underpinnings.

The second ground asserted by the President's counsel in support of the claim of absolute privilege rests on the doctrine of separation of powers. Here it is argued that the independence of the Executive Branch within its own sphere, insulates a president from a judicial subpoena in an ongoing criminal prosecution, and thereby protects confidential presidential communications.

However, neither the doctrine of separation of powers, nor the need for confidentiality of high level communications, without more, can sustain an absolute, unqualified presidential privilege of immunity from judicial process under all circumstances. The President's need for complete candor and objectivity from advisers calls for great deference from the courts. However, when the privilege depends solely on the broad, undifferentiated claim of public interest in the confidentiality of such conversations, a confrontation with other values arises. Absent a claim of need to protect military, diplomatic or sensitive national security secrets, we find it difficult to accept the argument that even the very important interest in confidentiality of presidential communications is significantly diminished by production of such material for *in camera* inspection with all the protection that a district court will be obliged to provide.

The impediment that an absolute, unqualified privilege would place in the way of the primary constitutional duty of the judicial branch to do justice in criminal prosecutions would plainly conflict with the function of the courts under Art. III. In designing the structure of our Government and dividing and allocating the sovereign power among three coequal branches, the Framers of the Constitution sought to provide a comprehensive system, but the separate powers were not intended to operate with absolute independence. To read the Art. II powers of the President as providing an absolute privilege as against a subpoena essential to enforcement of criminal statutes on no more than a generalized claim of the public interest in confidentiality of nonmilitary and non-diplomatic discussions would upset the constitutional balance of "a workable government" and gravely impair the role of the court under Art. III.

Since we conclude that the legitimate needs of the judicial process may outweigh presidential privilege, it is necessary to resolve those competing interests in a manner that preserves the essential functions of each branch. The rights and indeed the duty to resolve that question does not free the judiciary from according high respect to the representations made on behalf of the President. The expectation of a President to the confidentiality of his conversations and correspondence, like the claim of confidentiality of judicial deliberations, for example, has all the values to which we accord deference for the privacy of all citizens and added to those values the necessity for protection of the public interest in his responsibilities against the inroads of such a privilege on the fair administration of criminal justice. The interest in preserving confidentiality is weighty indeed and entitled to great respect. However we cannot conclude that advisers will be moved to temper the candor of their remarks by the infrequent occasions of disclosure because of the possibility that such conversations will be called for in the context of a criminal prosecution.

On the other hand, the allowance of the privilege to withhold evidence that is demonstrably relevant in a criminal trial would cut deeply into the guarantee of due process of law and gravely impair the basic function of the courts. A President's acknowledged need for confidentiality in the communications of his office is general in nature, whereas the constitutional need for production of relevant evidence in a criminal proceeding is specific and central to the fair adjudication of a particular criminal case in the administration of justice. Without access to specific facts a criminal prosecution may be totally frustrated. The President's broad interest in confidentiality of communications will not be vitiated by disclosure of a limited number of conversations preliminarily shown to have some bearing on the pending criminal cases.

We conclude that when the ground for asserting privilege as to subpoenaed materials sought for use in a criminal trial is based only on the generalized interest in confidentiality, it cannot prevail over the fundamental demand of due process of law in the fair administration of criminal justice. The generalized assertion of privilege must yield to the demonstrated, specific need for evidence in a pending criminal trial.

*   *   *

In this case the President challenges a subpoena served on him as a third party requiring the production of materials for use in a criminal prosecution on the claim that he has a privilege against disclosure of confidential communications. He does not place his claim of privilege on the ground they are military or diplomatic secrets. As to these areas of Art. II duties the courts have traditionally shown the utmost deference to presidential responsibilities. No case of the Court, however, has extended this high degree of deference to a President's generalized interest in confidentiality. Nowhere in the Constitution, as we have noted earlier, is there any explicit reference to a privilege of confidentiality; yet to the extent this interest relates to the effective discharge of a President's powers, it is constitutionally based.

*   *   *

[*The Court distinguished this case from cases involving claims against the president while acting in an official capacity.*]

Mr. Chief Justice Marshall sitting as a trial judge in the *Burr* case was extraordinarily careful to point out that: "[I]n no case of this kind would a Court be required to proceed against the President as against an ordinary individual." Marshall's statement cannot be read to mean in any sense that a President is above the law, but relates to the singularly unique role under Art. II of a President's communications and activities, related to the performance of duties under that Article. Moreover, a President's communications and activities encompass a vastly wider range of sensitive material than would be true of any "ordinary individual." It is therefore necessary in the public interest to afford presidential confidentiality the greatest protection consistent with the fair administration of justice. The need for confidentiality even as to idle conversations with associates in which casual reference might be made concerning political leaders within the country or foreign statesmen is too obvious to call for further treatment. We have no doubt that the District Judge will at all times accord the presidential records that high degree of deference suggested in *United States v. Burr*, and will discharge his responsibility to see to it that until released to the Special Prosecutor no *in camera* [private] material is revealed to anyone. This burden applies with even greater force to excised material; once the decision is made to excise, the material is restored to its privileged status and should be returned under seal to its lawful custodian.

Affirmed.

# *United States v. Lopez* (1995)

*How far does Congress's authority extend with respect to the states? Since the 1930s, when a liberalization of Supreme Court doctrine cleared the way for an expansion of federal authority, Congress has relied on a loose interpretation of the Commerce Clause to justify extensive involvement in state and local affairs. (Congress can also shape what states do, for example, by placing conditions upon the receipt of federal funds). In 1990, Congress enacted the Gun-Free School Zones Act, making possession of a firearm in designated school zones a federal crime. When Alfonso Lopez, Jr., was convicted of violating the act, his lawyer challenged the constitutionality of the law, arguing that it was "invalid as beyond the power of Congress under the Commerce Clause." In a striking reversal of interpretation, the Supreme Court agreed and declared the law invalid, holding that banning guns in schools was too far removed from any effect on interstate commerce to warrant federal intervention. Critics of the decision argued that the Court's reasoning might invalidate a large body of federal crime and drug legislation that relies on the connection between regulated activity and interstate commerce. Supporters maintained that the decision marked a new era of judicial respect for federalism and state autonomy.*

CHIEF JUSTICE REHNQUIST delivered the opinion of the Court.

In the Gun-Free School Zones Act of 1990, Congress made it a federal offense "for any individual knowingly to possess a firearm at a place that the individual knows, or has reasonable cause to believe, is a school zone." The Act neither regulates a commercial activity nor contains a requirement that the possession be connected in any way to interstate commerce. We hold that the Act exceeds the authority of "Congress to regulate Commerce . . . among the several States. . . ." (U.S. Constitution Art. I, 8, cl. 3).

On March 10, 1992, respondent, who was then a 12th-grade student, arrived at Edison High School in San Antonio, Texas, carrying a concealed .38 caliber handgun and five bullets. Acting upon an anonymous tip, school authorities confronted respondent, who admitted that he was carrying the weapon. He was arrested and charged under Texas law with firearm possession on school premises. The next day, the state charges were dismissed after federal agents charged respondent by complaint with violating the Gun-Free School Zones Act of 1990.

A federal grand jury indicted respondent on one count of knowing possession of a firearm at a school zone, in violation of 922(q) [the relevant section of the Act of 1990]. Respondent moved to dismiss his federal indictment on the ground that 922(q) "is unconstitutional as it is beyond the power of Congress to legislate control over our public schools." The District Court denied the motion, concluding that 922(q) "is a constitutional exercise of Congress' well-defined power to regulate activities in and affecting commerce, and the 'business' of elementary, middle and high schools . . . affects interstate commerce." Respondent waived his right to a jury trial. The District Court conducted a bench trial, found him guilty of violating 922(q), and sentenced him to six months' imprisonment and two years' supervised release.

On appeal, respondent challenged his conviction based on his claim that 922(q) exceeded Congress' power to legislate under the Commerce Clause. The Court of Appeals for the Fifth Circuit agreed and reversed respondent's conviction. It held that, in light of what it characterized as insufficient congressional findings and legislative history, "in the full reach of its terms, is invalid as beyond the power of Congress under the Commerce Clause." Because of the importance of the issue, we granted *certiorari* and we now affirm.

We start with first principles. The Constitution creates a Federal Government of enumerated powers. As James Madison wrote, "[t]he powers delegated by the proposed Constitution to the federal government are few and defined. Those which are to remain in the State governments are numerous and indefinite." (*The Federalist*, No. 45). This constitutionally mandated division of authority was adopted by the Framers to ensure protection of our fundamental liberties. Just as the separation and independence of the coordinate branches of the Federal Government serves to prevent the accumulation of excessive power in any one branch, a healthy balance of power between the States and the Federal Government will reduce the risk of tyranny and abuse from either front.

*[For the next several pages Rehnquist reviews the evolution of interpretations of the Commerce Clause, starting with* Gibbons v. Ogden *(1824). This case established the relatively narrow interpretation of the Commerce Clause in which the Court prevented* states *from interfering with interstate commerce. Very rarely did cases concern Congress's power. The 1887 Interstate Commerce Act and the 1890 Sherman Antitrust Act expanded Congress's power to regulate intrastate commerce "where the interstate and intrastate aspects of commerce were so mingled together that full regulation of interstate commerce required incidental regulation of intrastate commerce," arguing that the Commerce Clause authorized such regulation. Several New Deal era cases,* NLRB v. Jones & Laughlin Steel Corp. *(1937),* United States v. Darby *(1941), and* Wickard v. Filburn *(1942) broadened the interpretation of the Commerce Clause.]*

*Jones & Laughlin Steel, Darby,* and *Wickard* ushered in an era of Commerce Clause jurisprudence that greatly expanded the previously defined authority of Congress under that Clause. In part, this was a recognition of the great changes that had occurred in the way business was carried on in this country. Enterprises that had once been local or at most regional in nature had become national in scope. But the doctrinal change also reflected a view that earlier Commerce Clause cases artificially had constrained the authority of Congress to regulate interstate commerce.

But even these modern-era precedents which have expanded congressional power under the Commerce Clause confirm that this power is subject to outer limits. In *Jones & Laughlin Steel*, the Court warned that the scope of the interstate commerce power "must be considered in the light of our dual system of government and may not be extended so as to embrace effects upon interstate commerce so indirect and remote that to embrace them, in view of our complex society, would effectually obliterate the distinction between what is national and what is local and create a completely centralized government." Since that time, the Court has heeded that warning and undertaken to decide whether a rational basis existed for concluding that a regulated activity sufficiently affected interstate commerce.

\*   \*   \*

Consistent with this structure, we have identified three broad categories of activity that Congress may regulate under its commerce power. First, Congress may regulate the use of the channels of interstate commerce. Second, Congress is empowered to regulate and protect the instrumentalities of interstate commerce, or persons or things in interstate commerce, even though the threat may come only from intrastate activities. Finally, Congress' commerce authority includes the power to regulate those activities having a substantial relation to interstate commerce, those activities that substantially affect interstate commerce.

Within this final category, admittedly, our case law has not been clear whether an activity must *affect* or *substantially affect* interstate commerce in order to be within Congress' power to regulate it under the Commerce Clause. We conclude, consistent with the great weight of our case law, that the proper test requires an analysis of whether the regulated activity *substantially affects* interstate commerce.

We now turn to consider the power of Congress, in the light of this framework, to enact 922(q) [The Gun-Free School Zones Act]. The first two categories of authority may be quickly disposed of: 922(q) is not a regulation of the use of the channels of interstate commerce, nor is it an attempt to prohibit the interstate transportation of a commodity through the channels of commerce; nor can 922(q) be justified as a regulation by which Congress has sought to protect an instrumentality of interstate commerce or a thing in interstate commerce. Thus, if 922(q) is to be sustained, it must be under the third category as a regulation of an activity that substantially affects interstate commerce.

First, we have upheld a wide variety of congressional Acts regulating intrastate economic activity where we have concluded that the activity substantially affected interstate commerce. Examples include the regulation of intrastate coal mining; intrastate extortionate credit transactions, restaurants utilizing substantial interstate supplies, inns and hotels catering to interstate guests, and production and consumption of home-grown wheat. These examples are by no means exhaustive, but the pattern is clear. Where economic activity substantially affects interstate commerce, legislation regulating that activity will be sustained.

Even *Wickard*, which is perhaps the most far reaching example of Commerce Clause authority over intrastate activity, involved economic activity in a way that the possession of a gun in a school zone does not. Roscoe Filburn operated a small farm in Ohio, on which, in the year involved, he raised 23 acres of wheat. It was his practice to sow winter wheat in the fall, and after harvesting it in July to sell a portion of the crop, to feed part of it to poultry and livestock on the farm, to use some in making flour for home consumption, and to keep the remainder for seeding future crops. The Secretary of Agriculture assessed a penalty against him under the Agricultural Adjustment Act of 1938 because he harvested about 12 acres more wheat than his allotment under the Act permitted. The Act was designed to regulate the volume of wheat moving in interstate and foreign commerce in order to avoid surpluses and shortages, and concomitant fluctuation in wheat prices, which had previously obtained. The Court said, in an opinion sustaining the application of the Act to Filburn's activity, "One of the primary purposes of the Act in question was to increase the market price of wheat and to that end to limit the volume thereof that could affect the market. It can hardly be denied that a factor of such volume and variability as home-consumed wheat would have a substantial influence on price and market conditions. This may arise because being in marketable condition such wheat overhangs the market and, if induced by rising prices, tends to flow into the market and check price increases. But if we assume that it is never marketed, it supplies a need of the man who grew it which would otherwise be reflected by purchases in the open market. Home-grown wheat in this sense competes with wheat in commerce" (317 U.S., at 128).

Section 922(q) is a criminal statute that by its terms has nothing to do with *commerce* or any sort of economic enterprise, however broadly one might define those terms. Section 922(q) is not an essential part of a larger regulation of economic activity, in which the regulatory scheme could be undercut unless the intra-state activity were regulated. It cannot, therefore, be sustained under our cases upholding regulations of activities that arise out of or are connected with a commercial transaction, which viewed in the aggregate, substantially affects interstate commerce.

Second, 922(q) contains no jurisdictional element which would ensure, through case-by-case inquiry, that the firearm possession in question affects interstate commerce. . . . 922(q) has no express jurisdictional element which might limit its reach to a discrete set of firearm possessions that additionally have an explicit connection with or effect on interstate commerce.

\* \* \*

The Government's essential contention, in fine, is that we may determine here that 922(q) is valid because possession of a firearm in a local school zone does indeed substantially affect interstate commerce. The Government argues that possession of a firearm in a school zone may result in violent crime and that violent crime can be expected to affect the functioning of the national economy in two ways. First, the costs of violent crime are substantial, and, through the mechanism of insurance, those costs are spread throughout the population. Second, violent crime reduces the willingness of individuals to travel to areas within the country that are perceived to be unsafe. The Government also argues that the presence of guns in schools poses a substantial threat to the educational process by threatening the learning environment. A handicapped educational process, in turn, will result in a less productive citizenry. That, in turn, would have an adverse effect on the Nation's economic well-being. As a result, the Government argues that Congress could rationally have concluded that 922(q) substantially affects interstate commerce.

We pause to consider the implications of the Government's arguments. The Government admits, under its "costs of crime" reasoning, that Congress could regulate not only all violent crime, but all activities that might lead to violent crime, regardless of how tenuously they relate to interstate commerce. Similarly, under the Government's "national productivity" reasoning, Congress could regulate any activity that it found was related to the economic productivity of individual citizens: family law (including marriage, divorce, and child custody), for example. Under the theories that the Government presents in support of 922(q), it is difficult to perceive any limitation on federal power, even in areas such as criminal law enforcement or education where States historically have been sovereign. Thus, if we were to accept the Government's arguments, we are hard-pressed to posit any activity by an individual that Congress is without power to regulate.

Although Justice Breyer argues that acceptance of the Government's rationales would not authorize a general federal police power, he is unable to identify any activity that the States may regulate but Congress may not. Justice Breyer posits that there might be some limitations on Congress' commerce power such as family law or certain aspects of education. These suggested limitations, when viewed in light of the dissent's expansive analysis, are devoid of substance.

Justice Breyer focuses, for the most part, on the threat that firearm possession in and near schools poses to the educational process and the potential economic consequences flowing from that threat. Specifically, the dissent reasons that (1) gun-related violence is a serious problem;

(2) that problem, in turn, has an adverse effect on classroom learning; and (3) that adverse effect on classroom learning, in turn, represents a substantial threat to trade and commerce. This analysis would be equally applicable, if not more so, to subjects such as family law and direct regulation of education.

For instance, if Congress can, pursuant to its Commerce Clause power, regulate activities that adversely affect the learning environment, then, a fortiori, it also can regulate the educational process directly. Congress could determine that a school's curriculum has a "significant" effect on the extent of classroom learning. As a result, Congress could mandate a federal curriculum for local elementary and secondary schools because what is taught in local schools has a significant "effect on classroom learning," and that, in turn, has a substantial effect on interstate commerce.

Justice Breyer rejects our reading of precedent and argues that "Congress . . . could rationally conclude that schools fall on the commercial side of the line." Again, Justice Breyer's rationale lacks any real limits because, depending on the level of generality, any activity can be looked upon as commercial. Under the dissent's rationale, Congress could just as easily look at child rearing as "fall[ing] on the commercial side of the line" because it provides a "valuable service" namely, to equip [children] with the skills they need to survive in life and, more specifically, in the workplace. We do not doubt that Congress has authority under the Commerce Clause to regulate numerous commercial activities that substantially affect interstate commerce and also affect the educational process. That authority, though broad, does not include the authority to regulate each and every aspect of local schools.

Admittedly, a determination whether an intrastate activity is commercial or noncommercial may in some cases result in legal uncertainty. But, so long as Congress' authority is limited to those powers enumerated in the Constitution, and so long as those enumerated powers are interpreted as having judicially enforceable outer limits, congressional legislation under the Commerce Clause always will engender "legal uncertainty." As Chief Justice Marshall stated in *McCulloch v. Maryland*, (1819), "The [federal] government is acknowledged by all to be one of enumerated powers. The principle, that it can exercise only the powers granted to it . . . is now universally admitted. But the question respecting the extent of the powers actually granted, is perpetually arising, and will probably continue to arise, as long as our system shall exist." The Constitution mandates this uncertainty by withholding from Congress a plenary police power that would authorize enactment of every type of legislation. Congress has operated within this framework of legal uncertainty ever since this Court determined that it was the judiciary's duty "to say what the law is." Any possible benefit from eliminating this "legal uncertainty" would be at the expense of the Constitution's system of enumerated powers.

*   *   *

These are not precise formulations, and in the nature of things they cannot be. But we think they point the way to a correct decision of this case. The possession of a gun in a local school zone is in no sense an economic activity that might, through repetition elsewhere, substantially affect any sort of interstate commerce. Respondent was a local student at a local school; there is no indication that he had recently moved in interstate commerce, and there is no requirement that his possession of the firearm have any concrete tie to interstate commerce.

To uphold the Government's contentions here, we would have to pile inference upon inference in a manner that would bid fair to convert congressional authority under the Commerce Clause to a general police power of the sort retained by the States. Admittedly, some of our prior cases have taken long steps down that road, giving great deference to congressional action. The broad language in these opinions has suggested the possibility of additional expansion, but we decline here to proceed any further. To do so would require us to conclude that the Constitution's enumeration of powers does not presuppose something not enumerated, and that there never will be a distinction between what is truly national and what is truly local. This we are unwilling to do.

For the foregoing reasons the judgment of the Court of Appeals is Affirmed.

# The Declaration of Independence

*In Congress, July 4, 1776*

When in the course of human events, it becomes necessary for one people to dissolve the political bands which have connected them with another, and to assume among the Powers of the earth, the separate and equal station to which the Laws of Nature and of Nature's God entitle them, a decent respect to the opinions of mankind requires that they should declare the causes which impel them to the separation.

We hold these truths to be self-evident, that all men are created equal, that they are endowed by their Creator with certain unalienable rights, that among these are Life, Liberty and the pursuit of Happiness. That to secure these rights, Governments are instituted among Men, deriving their just powers from the consent of the governed. That whenever any Form of Government becomes destructive of these ends, it is the Right of the People to alter or to abolish it, and to institute new Government, laying its foundation on such principles and organizing its powers in such form, as to them shall seem most likely to effect their Safety and Happiness. Prudence, indeed, will dictate that Governments long established should not be changed for light and transient causes; and accordingly all experience hath shown, that mankind are more disposed to suffer, while evils are sufferable, than to right themselves by abolishing the forms to which they are accustomed. But when a long train of abuses and usurpations, pursuing invariably the same Object evinces a design to reduce them under absolute Despotism, it is their right, it is their duty, to throw off such Government, and to provide new Guards for their future security.—Such has been the patient sufferance of these Colonies; and such is now the necessity which constrains them to alter their former Systems of Government. The history of the present King of Great Britain is a history of repeated injuries and usurpations, all having in direct object the establishment of an absolute Tyranny over these States. To prove this, let Facts be submitted to a candid world.

He has refused his Assent to Laws, the most wholesome and necessary for the public good.

He has forbidden his Governors to pass Laws of immediate and pressing importance, unless suspended in their operation till his Assent should be obtained; and when so suspended, he has utterly neglected to attend to them.

He has refused to pass other Laws for the accommodation of large districts of people, unless those people would relinquish the right of Representation in the Legislature, a right inestimable to them and formidable to tyrants only.

He has called together legislative bodies at places unusual, uncomfortable, and distant from the depository of their public Records, for the sole purpose of fatiguing them into compliance with his measures.

He has dissolved Representative Houses repeatedly, for opposing with manly firmness his invasions on the rights of the people.

He has refused for a long time, after such dissolutions, to cause others to be elected; whereby the Legislative powers, incapable of Annihilation, have returned to the People at large for their exercise; the State remaining in the mean time exposed to all the dangers of invasion from without, and convulsions within.

He has endeavoured to prevent the population of these States; for that purpose obstructing the Laws for Naturalization of Foreigners; refusing to pass others to encourage their migrations hither, and raising the conditions of new Appropriations of Lands.

He has obstructed the Administration of Justice, by refusing his Assent to Laws for establishing Judiciary Powers.

He has made Judges dependent on his Will alone, for the tenure of their offices, and the amount and payment of their salaries.

He has erected a multitude of New Offices, and sent hither swarms of Officers to harrass our People, and eat out their substance.

He has kept among us, in times of peace, Standing Armies without the Consent of our legislature.

He has affected to render the Military independent of and superior to the Civil Power.

He has combined with others to subject us to a jurisdiction foreign to our constitution, and unacknowledged by our laws; giving his Assent to their Acts of pretended Legislation:

For quartering large bodies of armed troops among us:

For protecting them, by a mock Trial, from Punishment for any Murders which they should commit on the Inhabitants of these States:

For cutting off our Trade with all parts of the world:

For imposing Taxes on us without our Consent:

For depriving us in many cases, of the benefits of Trial by jury:

For transporting us beyond Seas to be tried for pretended offences:

For abolishing the free System of English Laws in a neighbouring Province, establishing therein an Arbitrary government, and enlarging its Boundaries so as to render it at once an example and fit instrument for introducing the same absolute rule into these Colonies:

For taking away our Charters, abolishing our most valuable Laws, and altering fundamentally the Forms of our Governments:

For suspending our own Legislatures, and declaring themselves invested with Power to legislate for us in all cases whatsoever.

He has abdicated Government here, by declaring us out of his Protection and waging War against us.

He has plundered our seas, ravaged our Coasts, burnt our towns, and destroyed the lives of our people.

He is at this time transporting large armies of foreign mercenaries to compleat the works of death, desolation and tyranny, already begun with circumstances of Cruelty & perfidy scarcely paralleled in the most barbarous ages, and totally unworthy the Head of a civilized nation.

He has constrained our fellow Citizens taken Captive on the high Seas to bear Arms against their Country, to become the executioners of their friends and Brethren, or to fall themselves by their Hands.

He has excited domestic insurrections amongst us, and has endeavored to bring on the inhabitants of our frontiers, the merciless Indian Savages, whose known rule of warfare, is an undistinguished destruction of all ages, sexes, and conditions.

In every stage of these Oppressions we have Petitioned for Redress in the most humble terms: Our repeated Petitions have been answered only by repeated injury. A Prince, whose character is thus marked by every act which may define a Tyrant, is unfit to be the ruler of a free people.

Nor have we been wanting in attention to our British brethren. We have warned them from time to time of attempts by their legislature to extend an unwarrantable jurisdiction over us. We have reminded them of the circumstances of our emigration and settlement here. We have appealed to their native justice and magnanimity, and we have conjured them by the ties of our common kindred to disavow these usurpations, which, would inevitably interrupt our connections and correspondence. They too must have been deaf to the voice of justice and of consanguinity. We must, therefore, acquiesce in the necessity, which denounces our Separation, and hold them, as we hold the rest of mankind, Enemies in War, in Peace Friends.

WE, THEREFORE, the Representatives of the UNITED STATES OF AMERICA, in General Congress, Assembled, appealing to the Supreme Judge of the world for the rectitude of our intentions, do, in the Name, and by Authority of the good People of these Colonies, solemnly publish and declare, That these United Colonies are, and of Right ought to be FREE AND INDEPENDENT STATES; that they are Absolved from all Allegiance to the British Crown, and that all political connection between them and the State of Great Britain, is and ought to be totally dissolved; and that as Free and Independent States, they have full Power to levy War, conclude Peace, contract Alliances, establish Commerce, and to do all other

Acts and Things which Independent States may of right do. And for the support of this Declaration, with a firm reliance on the protection of Divine Providence, we mutually pledge to each other our Lives, our Fortunes and our sacred Honor.

The foregoing Declaration was, by order of Congress, engrossed, and signed by the following members:

*John Hancock*

NEW HAMPSHIRE
*Josiah Bartlett*
*William Whipple*
*Matthew Thornton*

MASSACHUSETTS BAY
*Samuel Adams*
*John Adams*
*Robert Treat Paine*
*Elbridge Gerry*

RHODE ISLAND
*Stephen Hopkins*
*William Ellery*

CONNECTICUT
*Roger Sherman*
*Samuel Huntington*
*William Williams*
*Oliver Wolcott*

NEW YORK
*William Floyd*
*Philip Livingston*
*Francis Lewis*
*Lewis Morris*

NEW JERSEY
*Richard Stockton*
*John Witherspoon*
*Francis Hopkinson*
*John Hart*
*Abraham Clark*

PENNSYLVANIA
*Robert Morris*
*Benjamin Rush*
*Benjamin Franklin*
*John Morton*
*George Clymer*
*James Smith*
*George Taylor*
*James Wilson*
*George Ross*

DELAWARE
*Caesar Rodney*
*George Read*
*Thomas M'Kean*

MARYLAND
*Samuel Chase*
*William Paca*

*Thomas Stone*
*Charles Carroll,*
   *of Carrollton*

VIRGINIA
*George Wythe*
*Richard Henry Lee*
*Thomas Jefferson*
*Benjamin Harrison*
*Thomas Nelson, Jr.*
*Francis Lightfoot Lee*
*Carter Braxton*

NORTH CAROLINA
*William Hooper*
*Joseph Hewes*
*John Penn*

SOUTH CAROLINA
*Edward Rutledge*
*Thomas Heyward, Jr.*
*Thomas Lynch, Jr.*
*Arthur Middleton*

GEORGIA
*Button Gwinnett*
*Lyman Hall*
*George Walton*

*Resolved*, That copies of the Declaration be sent to the several assemblies, conventions, and committees, or councils of safety, and to the several commanding officers of the continental troops; that it be proclaimed in each of the United States, at the head of the army.

# The Constitution of the United States of America

*Annotated with references to the* Federalist Papers; *bracketed material is by the editors of this volume.*

Federalist Paper Number and Author

[PREAMBLE]

84 (Hamilton)

We the People of the United States, in Order to form a more perfect Union, establish Justice, insure domestic Tranquility, provide for the common defence, promote the general Welfare, and secure the Blessings of Liberty to ourselves and our Posterity, do ordain and establish this Constitution for the United States of America.

## ARTICLE I

*Section 1*

[LEGISLATURE POWERS]

10, 45 (Madison)

All legislative Powers herein granted shall be vested in a Congress of the United States, which shall consist of a Senate and House of Representatives.

*Section 2*

[HOUSE OF REPRESENTATIVES, HOW CONSTITUTED, POWER OF IMPEACHMENT]

39 (Madison) 45 (Madison) 52–53, 57 (Madison)

The House of Representatives shall be composed of Members chosen every second Year by the People of the several States, and the Electors in each State shall have the Qualifications requisite for Electors of the most numerous Branch of the State Legislature.

52 (Madison), 60 (Hamilton)

No Person shall be a Representative who shall not have attained to the Age of twenty five Years, and been seven Years a Citizen of the United States, and who shall not, when elected, be an Inhabitant of that State in which he shall be chosen.

54 (Madison)

Representatives and *direct Taxes** shall be apportioned among

* [Modified by Sixteenth Amendment.]

54
(Madison)

58
(Madison)

55–56
(Madison)

the several States which may be included within this Union, according to their respective Numbers, *which shall be determined by adding to the whole Number of free Persons, including those bound to Service for a Term of Years,* and excluding Indians not taxed, *three-fifths of all other Persons.*\* The actual Enumeration shall be made within three Years after the first Meeting of the Congress of the United States, and within every subsequent Term of ten Years, in such Manner as they shall by Law direct. The Number of Representatives shall not exceed one for every thirty Thousand, but each State shall have at Least one Representative; *and until such enumeration shall be made, the State of New Hampshire shall be entitled to chuse three, Massachusetts eight, Rhode Island and Providence Plantations one, Connecticut five, New-York six, New Jersey four, Pennsylvania eight, Delaware one, Maryland six, Virginia ten, North Carolina five, South Carolina five and Georgia three.*†

When vacancies happen in the Representation from any State, the Executive Authority thereof shall issue Writs of Election to fill such Vacancies.

79
(Hamilton)

The House of Representatives shall chuse their Speaker and other Officers; and shall have the sole Power of Impeachment.

### Section 3

[THE SENATE, HOW CONSTITUTED, IMPEACHMENT TRIALS]

39, 45
(Madison),
60
(Hamilton),

62–63
(Madison)
59
(Hamilton)

68
(Hamilton)

62
(Madison),
64 (Jay)

The Senate of the United States shall be composed of two Senators from each State, *chosen by the Legislature thereof,*‡ for six Years; and each Senator shall have one Vote.

Immediately after they shall be assembled in Consequence of the first Election, they shall be divided as equally as may be into three Classes. The Seats of the Senators of the first Class shall be vacated at the Expiration of the second Year, of the second Class at the Expiration of the fourth Year, and of the third Class at the Expiration of the sixth Year, so that one third may be chosen every second Year: *and if Vacancies happen by Resignation, or otherwise, during the Recess of the Legislature of any State, the Executive thereof may make temporary Appointments until the next Meeting of the Legislature, which shall then fill such Vacancies.*§

No person shall be a Senator who shall not have attained to the Age of thirty Years, and been nine Years a Citizen of the

---

\* [Modified by Fourteenth Amendment.]
† [Temporary provision.]
‡ [Modified by Seventeenth Amendment.]
§ [Modified by Seventeenth Amendment.]

United States, and who shall not, when elected, be an Inhabitant of that State for which he shall be chosen.

The Vice-President of the United States shall be President of the Senate, but shall have no Vote, unless they be equally divided.

39<br>(Madison),<br>65–67, 79<br>(Hamilton)<br>65<br>(Hamilton)<br>84<br>(Hamilton)The Senate shall chuse their other Officers, and also a President pro tempore, in the Absence of the Vice-President, or when he shall exercise the Office of President of the United States.

The Senate shall have the sole Power to try all Impeachments. When sitting for that Purpose, they shall be on Oath or Affirmation. When the President of the United States is tried, the Chief Justice shall preside: And no Person shall be convicted without the Concurrence of two thirds of the Members present.

Judgment in Cases of Impeachment shall not extend further than to removal from Office, and disqualification to hold and enjoy any Office of honor, Trust or Profit under the United States: but the Party convicted shall nevertheless be liable and subject to Indictment, Trial, Judgment and Punishment, according to Law.

### Section 4

[ELECTION OF SENATORS AND REPRESENTATIVES]

59–61<br>(Hamilton)The Times, Places and Manner of holding Elections for Senators and Representatives, shall be prescribed in each State by the Legislature thereof; but the Congress may at any time by Law make or alter such Regulations, except as to the Place of Chusing Senators.

*The Congress shall assemble at least once in every Year, and such Meeting shall be on the first Monday in December, unless they shall by Law appoint a different Day.\**

### Section 5

[QUORUM, JOURNALS, MEETINGS, ADJOURNMENTS]

Each House shall be the Judge of the Elections, Returns and Qualifications of its own Members, and a Majority of each shall constitute a Quorum to do Business; but a smaller Number may adjourn from day to day, and may be authorized to compel the Attendance of absent Members, in such Manner, and under such Penalties as each House may provide.

Each House may determine the Rules of its Proceedings, pun-

---

\* [Modified by Twentieth Amendment.]

ish its Members for disorderly Behavior, and, with the Concurrence of two-thirds, expel a Member.

Each House shall keep a Journal of its Proceedings, and from time to time publish the same, excepting such Parts as may in their Judgment require Secrecy; and the Yeas and Nays of the Members of either House on any question shall, at the Desire of one-fifth of those Present, be entered on the Journal.

Neither House, during the Session of Congress, shall, without the Consent of the other, adjourn for more than three days, nor to any other Place than that in which the two Houses shall be sitting.

## Section 6

[COMPENSATION, PRIVILEGES, DISABILITIES]

The Senators and Representatives shall receive a Compensation for their Services, to be ascertained by Law, and paid out of the Treasury of the United States. They shall in all Cases, except Treason, Felony and Breach of the Peace, be privileged from Arrest during their Attendance at the Session of their respective Houses, and in going to and returning from the same; and for any Speech or Debate in either House, they shall not be questioned in any other Place.

55
(Madison),
76
(Hamilton)
No Senator or Representative shall, during the Time for which he was elected, be appointed to any civil Office under the authority of the United States, which shall have been created, or the Emoluments whereof shall have been increased during such time; and no Person holding any Office under the United States, shall be a Member of either House during his Continuance in Office.

## Section 7

[PROCEDURE IN PASSING BILLS AND RESOLUTIONS]

66
(Hamilton)
All bills for raising Revenue shall originate in the House of Representatives; but the Senate may propose or concur with Amendments as on other Bills.

69, 73
(Hamilton)
Every Bill which shall have passed the House of Representatives and the Senate, shall, before it become a Law, be presented to the President of the United States; If he approve he shall sign it, but if not he shall return it, with his Objections to that House in which it shall have originated, who shall enter the Objections at large on their Journal, and proceed to reconsider it. If after such Reconsideration two-thirds of that House shall agree to

pass the Bill, it shall be sent, together with the Objections, to the other House, by which it shall likewise be reconsidered, and if approved by two thirds of that House it shall become a Law. But in all such Cases the Votes of both Houses shall be determined by Yeas and Nays, and the Names of the Persons voting for and against the Bill shall be entered on the Journal of each House respectively. If any Bill shall not be returned by the President within ten Days (Sundays excepted) after it shall have been presented to him, the Same shall be a Law, in like Manner as if he had signed it, unless the Congress by their Adjournment prevent its Return, in which Case it shall not be a Law.

69, 73
(Hamilton)

Every Order, Resolution, or Vote to which the Concurrence of the Senate and House of Representatives may be necessary (except on a question of Adjournment) shall be presented to the President of the United States; and before the Same shall take Effect, shall be approved by him, or being disapproved by him, shall be repassed by two-thirds of the Senate and House of Representatives, according to the Rules and Limitations prescribed in the Case of a Bill.

*Section 8*

[POWERS OF CONGRESS]
The Congress shall have Power

30–36
(Hamilton),

To lay and collect Taxes, Duties, Imposts and Excises, to pay the Debts and provide for the common Defence and general Welfare of the United States; but all Duties, Imposts and Excises shall be uniform throughout the United States;

41
(Madison)

56
(Madison)

To borrow money on the Credit of the United States;

42, 45, 56
(Madison)

To regulate Commerce with foreign Nations, and among the several States, and with the Indian Tribes;

32
(Hamilton),

To establish an uniform Rule of Naturalization, and uniform Laws on the subject of Bankruptcies throughout the United States;

42
(Madison)
42
(Madison)

To coin Money, regulate the Value thereof, and of foreign Coin, and fix the Standard of Weights and Measures;

42
(Madison)

To provide for the Punishment of counterfeiting the Securities and current Coin of the United States;

To establish Post Offices and Post Roads;

42
(Madison)
43
(Madison)

To promote the Progress of Science and useful Arts, by securing for limited Times to Authors and Inventors the exclusive Right to their respective Writings and Discoveries;

81
(Hamilton)

To constitute Tribunals inferior to the supreme Court;

42
(Madison)

To define and Punish Piracies and Felonies committed on the high Seas, and Offenses against the Law of Nations;

41
(Madison)

To declare War, grant Letters of Marque and Reprisal, and make Rules concerning Captures on Land and Water;

23, 24, 26
(Hamilton),

To raise and support Armies, but no Appropriation of Money to that Use shall be for a longer Term than two Years;

41
(Madison)

To provide and maintain a Navy;

To make Rules for the Government and Regulation of the land and naval forces;

29
(Hamilton)

To provide for calling forth the Militia to execute the Laws of the Union, suppress Insurrections and repel Invasions;

29
(Hamilton),

56
(Madison)

To provide for organizing, arming, and disciplining the Militia, and for governing such Part of them as may be employed in the Service of the United States, reserving to the States respectively, the Appointment of the Officers, and the Authority of training the Militia according to the discipline prescribed by Congress;

32
(Hamilton),
43
(Madison)

To exercise exclusive Legislation in all Cases whatsoever, over such District (not exceeding ten Miles square) as may, by Cession of particular States, and the Acceptance of Congress, become the Seat of the Government of the United States, and to exercise like Authority over all Places purchased by the Consent of the Leg-

43
(Madison)

islature of the State in which the Same shall be, for the Erection of Forts, Magazines, Arsenals, dock-Yards, and other needful Buildings;—And

29, 33
(Hamilton)

To make all Laws which shall be necessary and proper for carrying into Execution the foregoing Powers, and all other Pow-

44
(Madison)

ers vested by this Constitution in the Government of the United States, or in any Department or Officer thereof.

## Section 9

[SOME RESTRICTIONS ON FEDERAL POWER]

42
(Madison)

*The Migration or Importation of such Persons as any of the States now existing shall think proper to admit, shall not be prohibited by the Congress prior to the Year one thousand eight hundred and eight, but a tax or duty may be imposed on such Importation, not exceeding ten dollars for each Person.\**

83, 84
(Hamilton)

The privilege of the Writ of *Habeas Corpus* shall not be suspended, unless when in Cases of Rebellion or Invasion the public Safety may require it.

84
(Hamilton)

No Bill of Attainder or ex post facto Law shall be passed.

*No Capitation, or other direct, Tax shall be laid, unless in Proportion to the Census or Enumeration herein before directed to be taken.†*

\* [Temporary provision.]
† [Modified by Sixteenth Amendment.]

No Tax or Duty shall be laid on Articles exported from any State.

32
(Hamilton)

No Preference shall be given by any Regulation of Commerce or Revenue to the Ports of one State over those of another: nor shall Vessels bound to, or from, one State, be obliged to enter, clear, or pay Duties in another.

No Money shall be drawn from the Treasury, but in Consequence of Appropriations made by Law; and a regular Statement and Account of the Receipts and Expenditures of all public Money shall be published from time to time.

39
(Madison),
84
(Hamilton)

No Title of Nobility shall be granted by the United States: And no Person holding any Office of Profit or Trust under them, shall, without the Consent of the Congress, accept of any present, Emolument, Office, or Title, of any kind whatever, from any King, Prince or foreign State.

*Section 10*

[RESTRICTIONS UPON POWERS OF STATES]

33
(Hamilton),
44
(Madison)

No State shall enter into any Treaty, Alliance, or Confederation; grant Letters of Marque and Reprisal; coin Money; emit Bills of Credit; make any Thing but gold and silver Coin a Tender in Payment of Debts; pass any Bill of Attainder, ex post facto Law, or Law impairing the Obligation of Contracts, or grant any Title of Nobility.

32
(Hamilton),

44
(Madison)

No State shall, without the Consent of the Congress, lay any Imposts or Duties on Imports or Exports, except what may be absolutely necessary for executing its inspection Laws: and the net Produce of all Duties and Imposts, laid by any State on Imports or Exports, shall be for the Use of the Treasury of the United States; and all such Laws shall be subject to the Revision and Controul of the Congress.

No State shall, without the Consent of Congress, lay any duty of Tonnage, keep Troops, or Ships of War in time of Peace, enter into any Agreement or Compact with another State, or with a foreign Power, or engage in War, unless actually invaded, or in such imminent Danger as will not admit of Delay.

# ARTICLE II

*Section 1*

[EXECUTIVE POWER, ELECTION, QUALIFICATIONS OF THE PRESIDENT]

39
(Madison),
70, 71, 84
(Hamilton)

The executive Power shall be vested in a President of the United States of America. *He shall hold his Office during the Term* *of four years, and, together with the Vice-President, chosen for the same Term, be elected, as follows:*\**

69, 71
(Hamilton)

Each State shall appoint, in such Manner as the Legislature thereof may direct, a Number of Electors, equal to the whole Number of Senators and Representatives to which the State may

39, 45
(Madison),

be entitled in the Congress: but no Senator or Representative, or Person holding an Office of Trust or Profit under the United

68, 77
(Hamilton)

States, shall be appointed an Elector.

*The electors shall meet in their respective States, and vote by ballot for two Persons, of whom one at least shall not be an Inhabitant of the same State with themselves. And they shall make a List of all the Persons voted for, and of the Number of Votes for each; which List they shall sign and certify, and transmit sealed to the Seat of the Government of the United States, directed to the President of the Senate. The*

66
(Hamilton)

*President of the Senate shall, in the Presence of the Senate and House of Representatives, open all the Certificates, and the Votes shall then be counted. The Person having the greatest Number of Votes shall be the President, if such Number be a Majority of the whole Number of Electors appointed; and if there be more than one who have such Majority, and have an equal Number of Votes, then the House of Representatives shall immediately chuse by Ballot one of them for President; and if no Person have a Majority, then from the five highest on the List the said House shall in like Manner chuse the President. But in chusing the President, the Votes shall be taken by States, the Representation from each State having one Vote; a quorum for this Purpose shall consist of a Member or Members from two-thirds of the States, and a Majority of all the States shall be necessary to a Choice. In every Case, after the Choice of the President, the Person having the greatest Number of Votes of the Electors shall be the Vice-President. But if there should remain two or more who have equal Votes, the Senate shall chuse from them by Ballot the Vice-President.‡*

The Congress may determine the Time of chusing the Electors, and the Day on which they shall give their Votes; which Day shall be the same throughout the United States.

No Person except a natural born Citizen, or a Citizen of the United States, at the time of the Adoption of this Constitution, shall be eligible to the Office of President; neither shall any Person be eligible to that Office who shall not have attained to the

64 (Jay)

Age of thirty-five Years, and been fourteen Years a Resident within the United States.

In Case of the Removal of the President from Office, or his Death, Resignation, or Inability to discharge the Powers and Du-

* [Number of terms limited to two by Twenty-second Amendment.]
‡ [Modified by Twelfth and Twentieth Amendment.]

ties of the said Office, the same shall devolve on the Vice-President, and the Congress may by Law provide for the Case of Removal, Death, Resignation or Inability, both of the President and Vice-President, declaring what Officer shall then act as President, and such Officer shall act accordingly, until the Disability be removed, or a President shall be elected.

73, 79
(Hamilton)
The President shall, at stated Times, receive for his Services, a Compensation, which shall neither be encreased nor diminished during the Period for which he shall have been elected, and he shall not receive within that Period any other Emolument from the United States, or any of them.

Before he enter on the Execution of his Office, he shall take the following Oath or Affirmation:—"I do solemnly swear (or affirm) that I will faithfully execute the Office of President of the United States, and will to the best of my Ability, preserve, protect and defend the Constitution of the United States."

*Section 2*

[POWERS OF THE PRESIDENT]

69, 74
(Hamilton)
The President shall be Commander in Chief of the Army and Navy of the United States, and of the Militia of the several States, when called into the actual Service of the United States; he may require the Opinion, in writing, of the principal Officer in each of the executive Departments, upon any Subject relating to the

74
(Hamilton)
69
(Hamilton)
74
(Hamilton)
Duties of their respective Offices, and he shall have Power to Grant Reprieves and Pardons for Offenses against the United States, except in Cases of Impeachment.

42
(Madison)
64 (Jay),
66
(Hamilton)
He shall have Power, by and with the Advice and Consent of the Senate, to make Treaties, provided two thirds of the Senators present concur; and he shall nominate, and by and with the Advice and Consent of the Senate, shall appoint Ambassadors, other public Ministers and Consuls, Judges of the Supreme

42
(Madison),
66, 69,
76, 77
(Hamilton)
Court, and all other Officers of the United States, whose Appointments are not herein otherwise provided for, and which shall be established by Law: but the Congress may by Law vest the Appointment of such inferior Officers, as they think proper, in the President alone, in the Courts of Law, or in the Heads of Departments.

67, 76
(Hamilton)
The President shall have Power to fill up all Vacancies that may happen during the Recess of the Senate, by granting Commissions which shall expire at the End of their next Session.

## Section 3

### [POWERS AND DUTIES OF THE PRESIDENT]

77
(Hamilton)
69, 77
(Hamilton)

77
(Hamilton)
69, 77
(Hamilton)
42
(Madison),
69, 77
(Hamilton)
78
(Hamilton)

He shall from time to time give to the Congress Information of the State of the Union, and recommend to their Consideration such Measures as he shall judge necessary and expedient; he may, on extraordinary Occasions, convene both Houses, or either of them, and in Case of Disagreement between them, with Respect to the Time of Adjournment, he may adjourn them to such Time as he shall think proper; he shall receive Ambassadors and other public Ministers; he shall take Care that the Laws be faithfully executed, and shall Commission all the Officers of the United States.

## Section 4

### [IMPEACHMENT]

39
(Madison),

69
(Hamilton)

The President, Vice-President and all civil Officers of the United States, shall be removed from Office on Impeachment for, and Conviction of, Treason, Bribery, or other high Crimes and Misdemeanors.

# ARTICLE III

## Section 1

### [JUDICIAL POWER, TENURE OR OFFICE]

81, 82
(Hamilton)
65
(Hamilton)
78, 79
(Hamilton)

The judicial Power of the United States, shall be vested in one Supreme Court, and in such inferior Courts as the Congress may from time to time ordain and establish. The Judges, both of the supreme and inferior Courts, shall hold their Offices during good Behavior, and shall, at stated Times, receive for their Services a Compensation, which shall not be diminished during their Continuance in Office.

## Section 2

### [JURISDICTION]

80
(Hamilton)

The judicial Power shall extend to all Cases, in Law and Equity, arising under this Constitution, the Laws of the United States, and Treaties made, or which shall be made, under their Authority;—to all Cases affecting Ambassadors, other public Ministers and Consuls;—to all Cases of admiralty and maritime Jurisdiction;—to Controversies to which the United States shall be a party;—to Controversies between two or more States;—*between a State and Citizens of another State*;—between Citizens of different States,—between Citizens of the same State claiming

Lands under Grants of different States, *and between a State*, or the Citizens thereof, *and foreign States, Citizens or Subjects*.*

81
(Hamilton)

In all Cases affecting Ambassadors, other public Ministers and Consuls, and those in which a State shall be Party, the supreme Court shall have original Jurisdiction. In all the other Cases before mentioned, the Supreme Court shall have appellate Jurisdiction, both as to Law and Fact, with such Exceptions, and under such Regulations as the Congress shall make.

83, 84
(Hamilton)

The Trial of all Crimes, except in Cases of Impeachment, shall be by Jury; and such Trial shall be held in the State where the said Crimes shall have been committed; but when not committed within any State, the Trial shall be at such Place or Places as the Congress may by Law have directed.

*Section 3*

[TREASON, PROOF, AND PUNISHMENT]

43
(Madison),

98
(Hamilton)

Treason against the United States, shall consist only in levying War against them, or in adhering to their Enemies, giving them Aid and Comfort. No Person shall be convicted of Treason unless on the Testimony of two Witnesses to the same overt Act, or on Confession in open Court.

43
(Madison),
84
(Hamilton)

The Congress shall have Power to declare the Punishment of Treason, but no Attainder of Treason shall work Corruption of Blood, or Forfeiture except during the Life of the Person attained.

ARTICLE IV

*Section 1*

[FAITH AND CREDIT AMONG STATES]

42
(Madison)

Full Faith and Credit shall be given in each State to the public Acts, Records, and judicial Proceedings of every other State. And the Congress may by general Laws prescribe the Manner in which such Acts, Records and Proceedings shall be proved, and the Effect thereof.

*Section 2*

[PRIVILEGES AND IMMUNITIES, FUGITIVES]

80
(Hamilton)

The Citizens of each State shall be entitled to all Privileges and Immunities of Citizens in the several States.

A Person charged in any State with Treason, Felony, or other Crime, who shall flee from Justice, and be found in another State, shall on demand of the executive Authority of the State from

* [Modified by Eleventh Amendment.]

which he fled, be delivered up, to be removed to the State having Jurisdiction of the Crime.

*No Person held to Service or Labour in one State, under the Laws thereof, escaping into another, shall, in Consequence of any Law or Regulation therein, be discharged from such Service or Labour, but shall be delivered up on Claim of the Party to whom such Service or Labour may be due.*\*

### Section 3

[ADMISSION OF NEW STATES]

43
(Madison)   New States may be admitted by the Congress into this Union; but no new States shall be formed or erected within the Jurisdiction of any other State; nor any State be formed by the Junction of two or more States, or Parts of States, without the Consent of the Legislatures of the States concerned as well as of the Congress.

43
(Madison)   The Congress shall have Power to dispose of and make all needful Rules and Regulations respecting the Territory or other Property belonging to the United States; and nothing in this Constitution shall be so construed as to Prejudice any Claims of the United States, or of any particular State.

### Section 4

[GUARANTEE OF REPUBLICAN GOVERNMENT]

39, 43
(Madison)   The United States shall guarantee to every State in this Union a Republican Form of Government, and shall protect each of them against Invasion; and on Application of the Legislature, or of the Executive (when the Legislature cannot be convened) against domestic Violence.

## ARTICLE V

[AMENDMENT OF THE CONSTITUTION]

39, 43
(Madison)
85
(Hamilton)   The Congress, whenever two-thirds of both Houses shall deem it necessary, shall propose Amendments to this Constitution, or, on the Application of the Legislatures of two-thirds of the several States, shall call a Convention for proposing Amendments, which, in either Case, shall be valid to all Intents and Purposes, as Part of this Constitution, when ratified by the Legislatures of three-fourths of the several States, or by Conventions in three-fourths thereof, as the one or the other Mode of Ratification may be proposed by the Congress; *Provided that no Amend-*

---

\* [Repealed by the Thirteenth Amendment.]

*ment which may be made prior to the Year One thousand eight hundred and eight shall in any Manner affect the first and fourth Clauses in the Ninth Section of the first Article;** and that no State, without its Consent, shall be deprived of its equal Suffrage in the Senate.

43
(Madison)

# ARTICLE VI

[DEBTS, SUPREMACY, OATH]

43
(Madison)

All Debts contracted and Engagements entered into, before the Adoption of this Constitution, shall be as valid against the United States under this Constitution, as under the Confederation.

27, 33
(Hamilton),
39, 44
(Madison)

This Constitution, and the Laws of the United States which shall be made in Pursuance thereof; and all Treaties made, or which shall be made, under the Authority of the United States, shall be the supreme Law of the Land; and the Judges in every State shall be bound thereby, any Thing in the Constitution or Laws of any State to the Contrary notwithstanding.

27
(Hamilton),
44
(Madison)

The Senators and Representatives before mentioned, and the Members of the several State Legislatures, and all executive and judicial Officers, both of the United States and of the several States, shall be bound by Oath or Affirmation, to support this Constitution; but no religious Test shall ever be required as a Qualification to any Office or public Trust under the United States.

# ARTICLE VII

[RATIFICATION AND ESTABLISHMENT]

39, 40, 43
(Madison)

The Ratification of the Conventions of nine States, shall be sufficient for the Establishment of this Constitution between the States so ratifying the Same.‡

Done in Convention by the Unanimous Consent of the States present the Seventeenth Day of September in the Year of our Lord one thousand seven hundred and Eighty seven and of the Independence of the United States of America the Twelfth. *In Witness* whereof We have hereunto subscribed our Names,

G:⁰ WASHINGTON—
*Presidt, and Deputy
from Virginia*

* [Temporary provision.]
‡ [The Constitution was submitted on September 17, 1787, by the Constitutional Convention, was ratified by the conventions of several states at various dates up to May 29, 1790, and became effective on March 4, 1789.]

| | | | |
|---|---|---|---|
| New Hampshire | JOHN LANGDON | Delaware | GEO READ |
| | NICHOLAS GILMAN | | GUNNING BEDFOR JUN |
| Massachusetts | NATHANIEL GORHAM | | JOHN DICKINSON |
| | RUFUS KING | | RICHARD BASSETT |
| | | | JACO: BROOM |
| Connecticut | WM SAML JOHNSON | | |
| | ROGER SHERMAN | Maryland | JAMES MCHENRY |
| | | | DAN OF ST THOS. JENIFER |
| New York | ALEXANDER HAMILTON | | DANL CARROLL |
| New Jersey | WIL: LIVINGSTON | Virginia | JOHN BLAIR— |
| | DAVID BREARLEY | | JAMES MADISON JR. |
| | WM PATERSON | | |
| | JONA: DAYTON | North Carolina | WM BLOUNT |
| | | | RICHD DOBBS SPAIGHT |
| Pennsylvania | B FRANKLIN | | HU WILLIAMSON |
| | THOMAS MIFFLIN | | |
| | ROBT MORRIS | South Carolina | J. RUTLEDGE |
| | GEO. CLYMER | | CHARLES COTESWORTH PINCKNEY |
| | THOS. FITZSIMONS | | CHARLES PINCKNEY |
| | JARED INGERSOLL | | PIERCE BUTLER |
| | JAMES WILSON | Georgia | WILLIAM FEW |
| | GOUV MORRIS | | ABR BALDWIN |

# Amendments to the Constitution

*Proposed by Congress and Ratified*
*by the Legislatures of the Several States,*
*Pursuant to Article V of the Original Constitution.*

*Amendments I–X, known as the Bill of Rights, were proposed by Congress on September 25, 1789, and ratified on December 15, 1791. Federalist Papers comments, mainly in opposition to a Bill of Rights, can be found in #84 (Hamilton).*

## AMENDMENT I

[FREEDOM OF RELIGION, OF SPEECH, AND OF THE PRESS]
Congress shall make no law respecting an establishment of religion, or prohibiting the free exercise thereof; or abridging the freedom of speech, or of the press; or the right of the people peaceably to assemble, and to petition the Government for a redress of grievances.

## AMENDMENT II

[RIGHT TO KEEP AND BEAR ARMS]
A well regulated Militia, being necessary to the security of a free State, the right of the people to keep and bear Arms, shall not be infringed.

## AMENDMENT III

[QUARTERING OF SOLDIERS]
No Soldier shall, in time of peace be quartered in any house, without the consent of the Owner, nor in time of war, but in a manner to be prescribed by law.

## AMENDMENT IV

[SECURITY FROM UNWARRANTABLE SEARCH AND SEIZURE]

The right of the people to be secure in their persons, houses, papers, and effects, against unreasonable searches and seizures, shall not be violated, and no Warrants shall issue, but upon probable cause, supported by Oath or affirmation, and particularly describing the place to be searched, and the persons or things to be seized.

## AMENDMENT V

[RIGHTS OF ACCUSED PERSONS IN CRIMINAL PROCEEDINGS]

No person shall be held to answer for a capital, or otherwise infamous crime, unless on a presentment or indictment of a Grand Jury, except in cases arising in the land or naval forces, or in the Militia, when in actual service in time of War or public danger; nor shall any person be subject for the same offence to be twice put in jeopardy of life or limb; nor shall be compelled in any Criminal Case to be a witness against himself, nor be deprived of life, liberty, or property, without due process of law; nor shall private property be taken for public use, without just compensation.

## AMENDMENT VI

[RIGHT TO SPEEDY TRIAL, WITNESSES, ETC.]

In all criminal prosecutions, the accused shall enjoy the right to a speedy and public trial, by an impartial jury of the State and district wherein the crime shall have been committed, which district shall have been previously ascertained by law, and to be informed of the nature and cause of the accusation; to be confronted with the witnesses against him; to have compulsory process for obtaining Witnesses in his favor, and to have the Assistance of Counsel for his defence.

## AMENDMENT VII

[TRIAL BY JURY IN CIVIL CASES]

In suits at common law, where the value in controversy shall exceed twenty dollars, the right of trial by jury shall be preserved, and no fact tried by a jury shall be otherwise re-examined in any Court of the United States, than according to the rules of the common law.

# Amendment VIII

[BAILS, FINES, PUNISHMENTS]
Excessive bail shall not be required, nor excessive fines imposed, nor cruel and unusual punishments inflicted.

# Amendment IX

[RESERVATION OF RIGHTS OF PEOPLE]
The enumeration in the Constitution, of certain rights, shall not be construed to deny or disparage others retained by the people.

# Amendment X

[POWERS RESERVED TO STATES OR PEOPLE]
The powers not delegated to the United States by the Constitution, nor prohibited by it to the States, are reserved to the States respectively, or to the people.

# Amendment XI

*[Proposed by Congress on March 4, 1794; declared ratified on January 8, 1798.]*

[RESTRICTION OF JUDICIAL POWER]
The Judicial power of the United States shall not be construed to extend to any suit in law or equity, commenced or prosecuted against one of the United States by Citizens of another State, or by Citizens or Subjects of any foreign State.

# Amendment XII

*[Proposed by Congress on December 9, 1803; declared ratified on September 25, 1804.]*

[ELECTION OF PRESIDENT AND VICE-PRESIDENT]
The Electors shall meet in their respective states, and vote by ballot for President and Vice-President, one of whom, at least, shall not be an inhabitant of the same state with themselves; they shall name in their ballots the person voted for as President, and in distinct ballots the person voted for as Vice-President, and they shall make distinct lists of all persons voted for as President, and of all persons voted for as Vice-President, and of the number of votes for each, which lists they shall sign and certify, and transmit sealed to the seat of the government of the United States, directed to the President of the Senate;—The President of the Senate shall, in presence of the Senate and House of Representatives, open all the certificates and the votes shall then be counted;—The

person having the greatest number of votes for President, shall be the President, if such number be a majority of the whole number of Electors appointed; and if no person have such majority, then from the persons having the highest numbers not exceeding three on the list of those voted for as President, the House of Representatives shall choose immediately, by ballot, the President. But in choosing the President, the votes shall be taken by states, the representation from each state having one vote; a quorum for this purpose shall consist of a member or members from two-thirds of the states, and a majority of all the states shall be necessary to a choice. And if the House of Representatives shall not choose a President whenever the right of choice shall devolve upon them, before the fourth day of March next following, then the Vice-President shall act as President, as in the case of the death or other constitutional disability of the President. The person having the greatest number of votes as Vice-President, shall be the Vice-President, if such number be a majority of the whole number of Electors appointed, and if no person have a majority, then from the two highest numbers on the list, the Senate shall choose the Vice-President; a quorum for the purpose shall consist of two-thirds of the whole number of Senators, and a majority of the whole number shall be necessary to a choice. But no person constitutionally ineligible to the office of President shall be eligible to that of Vice-President of the United States.

# AMENDMENT XIII

*[Proposed by Congress on January 31, 1865; declared ratified on December 18, 1865.]*

*Section 1*

[ABOLITION OF SLAVERY]

Neither slavery nor involuntary servitude, except as a punishment for crime whereof the party shall have been duly convicted, shall exist within the United States, or any place subject to their jurisdiction.

*Section 2*

[POWER TO ENFORCE THIS ARTICLE]

Congress shall have power to enforce this article by appropriate legislation.

# Amendment XIV

*[Proposed by Congress on June 13, 1866, declared ratified on July 28, 1868.]*

## Section 1

[CITIZENSHIP RIGHTS NOT TO BE ABRIDGED BY STATES]

All persons born or naturalized in the United States, and subject to the jurisdiction thereof, are citizens of the United States and of the State wherein they reside. No state shall make or enforce any law which shall abridge the privileges or immunities of citizens of the United States; nor shall any State deprive any person of life, liberty, or property, without due process of law; nor deny to any person within its jurisdiction the equal protection of the laws.

## Section 2

[APPORTIONMENT OF REPRESENTATIVES IN CONGRESS]

Representatives shall be apportioned among the several States according to their respective numbers, counting the whole number of persons in each State, excluding Indians not taxed. But when the right to vote at any election for the choice of electors for President and Vice-President of the United States, Representatives in Congress, the Executive and Judicial officers of a State, or the members of the Legislature thereof, is denied to any of the male inhabitants of such State, being twenty-one years of age, and citizens of the United States, or in any way abridged, except for participation in rebellion, or other crime, the basis of representation therein shall be reduced in the proportion which the number of such male citizens shall bear to the whole number of male citizens twenty-one years of age in such State.

## Section 3

[PERSONS DISQUALIFIED FROM HOLDING OFFICE]

No person shall be a Senator or Representative in Congress, or elector of President and Vice-President, or hold any office, civil or military, under the United States, or under any State, who, having previously taken an oath, as a member of Congress, or as an officer of the United States, or as a member of any State legislature, or as an executive or judicial officer of any State, to support the Constitution of the United States, shall have engaged in insurrection or rebellion against the same, or given aid or comfort to the enemies thereof. But Congress may by a vote of two-thirds of each House, remove such disability.

*Section 4*

[WHAT PUBLIC DEBTS ARE VALID]

The validity of the public debt of the United States, authorized by law, including debts incurred for payment of pensions and bounties for services in suppressing insurrection or rebellion, shall not be questioned. But neither the United States nor any State shall assume or pay any debt or obligation incurred in aid of insurrection or rebellion against the United States, or any claim for the loss or emancipation of any slave; but all such debts, obligations and claims shall be held illegal and void.

*Section 5*

[POWER TO ENFORCE THIS ARTICLE]

The Congress shall have power to enforce, by appropriate legislation, the provisions of this article.

# AMENDMENT XV

*[Proposed by Congress on February 26, 1869; declared ratified on March 30, 1870.]*

*Section 1*

[BLACK SUFFRAGE]

The right of citizens of the United States to vote shall not be denied or abridged by the United States or by any State on account of race, color, or previous condition of servitude.

*Section 2*

[POWER TO ENFORCE THIS ARTICLE]

The Congress shall have power to enforce this article by appropriate legislation.

# AMENDMENT XVI

*[Proposed by Congress on July 12, 1909; declared ratified on February 25, 1913.]*

[AUTHORIZING INCOME TAXES]

The Congress shall have power to lay and collect taxes on incomes, from whatever source derived, without apportionment among the several States, and without regard to any census or enumeration.

## AMENDMENT XVII

*[Proposed by Congress on May 13, 1912; declared ratified on May 31, 1913.]*

[POPULAR ELECTION OF SENATORS]

The Senate of the United States shall be composed of two Senators from each State, elected by the people thereof, for six years; and each Senator shall have one vote. The electors in each State shall have the qualifications requisite for electors of the most numerous branch of the State Legislature.

When vacancies happen in the representation of any State in the Senate, the executive authority of such State shall issue writs of election to fill such vacancies: Provided, That the Legislature of any State may empower the executive thereof to make temporary appointments until the people fill the vacancies by election as the Legislature may direct.

This amendment shall not be so construed as to affect the election or term of any Senator chosen before it becomes valid as part of the Constitution.

## AMENDMENT XVIII

*[Proposed by Congress December 18, 1917; declared ratified on January 29, 1919.]*

*Section 1*

[NATIONAL LIQUOR PROHIBITION]

*After one year from the ratification of this article, the manufacture, sale, or transportation of intoxicating liquors within, the importation thereof into, or the exportation thereof from the United States and all territory subject to the jurisdiction thereof for beverage purposes is hereby prohibited.*

*Section 2*

[POWER TO ENFORCE THIS ARTICLE]

*Congress and the several states shall have concurrent power to enforce this article by appropriate legislation.*

*Section 3*

[RATIFICATION WITHIN SEVEN YEARS]

*This article shall be inoperative unless it shall have been ratified as an amendment to the Constitution by the legislatures of the several states, as provided in the Constitution, within seven years from the date of the submission hereof to the states by Congress.**

---

* [Repealed by the Twenty-first Amendment.]

# AMENDMENT XIX

*[Proposed by Congress on June 4, 1919; declared ratified on August 26, 1920.]*

[FEMALE SUFFRAGE]

The right of the citizens of the United States to vote shall not be denied or abridged by the United States or by any state on account of sex.

Congress shall have power, by appropriate legislation, to enforce this article by appropriate legislation.

# AMENDMENT XX

*[Proposed by Congress on March 2, 1932; declared ratified on February 6, 1933.]*

*Section 1*

[TERMS OF OFFICE]

The terms of the President and Vice-President shall end at noon on the 20th day of January, and the terms of Senators and Representatives at noon on the 3rd day of January, of the years in which such terms would have ended if this article had not been ratified; and the terms of their successors shall then begin.

*Section 2*

[TIME OF CONVENING CONGRESS]

The Congress shall assemble at least once in every year, and such meeting shall begin at noon on the 3rd day of January, unless they shall by law appoint a different day.

*Section 3*

[DEATH OF PRESIDENT-ELECT]

If, at the time fixed for the beginning of the term of the President, the President-elect shall have died, the Vice-President-elect shall become President. If a President shall not have been chosen before the time fixed for the beginning of his term, or if the President-elect shall have failed to qualify, then the Vice-President-elect shall act as President until a President shall have qualified; and the Congress may by law provide for the case wherein neither a President-elect nor a Vice-President-elect shall have qualified, declaring who shall then act as President, or the manner in which one who is to act shall be selected, and such person shall act accordingly until a President or Vice-President shall have qualified.

*Section 4*

[ELECTION OF THE PRESIDENT]

The Congress may by law provide for the case of the death of any of the persons from whom the House of Representatives may choose a President whenever the right of choice shall have devolved upon them, and for the case of the death of any of the persons from whom the Senate may choose a Vice-President whenever the right of choice shall have devolved upon them.

*Section 5*

[AMENDMENT TAKES EFFECT]

Sections 1 and 2 shall take effect on the 15th day of October following ratification of this article.

*Section 6*

[RATIFICATION WITHIN SEVEN YEARS]

This article shall be inoperative unless it shall have been ratified as an amendment to the Constitution by the legislatures of three-fourths of the several States within seven years from the date of its submission.

# AMENDMENT XXI

*[Proposed by Congress on February 20, 1933; declared ratified on December 5, 1933.]*

*Section 1*

[NATIONAL LIQUOR PROHIBITION REPEALED]

The eighteenth article of amendment to the Constitution of the United States is hereby repealed.

*Section 2*

[TRANSPORTATION OF LIQUOR INTO "DRY" STATES]

The transportation or importation into any State, Territory, or Possession of the United States for delivery or use therein of intoxicating liquors, in violation of the laws thereof, is hereby prohibited.

*Section 3*

[RATIFICATION WITHIN SEVEN YEARS]

The article shall be inoperative unless it shall have been ratified as an amendment to the Constitution by conventions in the several States, as provided in the Constitution, within seven years from the date of the submission hereof to the States by the Congress.

# AMENDMENT XXII

*[Proposed by Congress on March 21, 1947; declared ratified on February 26, 1951.]*

## Section 1

[TENURE OF PRESIDENT LIMITED]
No person shall be elected to the office of the President more than twice, and no person who has held the office of President or acted as President for more than two years of a term to which some other person was elected President shall be elected to the Office of the President more than once. But this Article shall not apply to any person holding the office of President when this Article was proposed by the Congress, and shall not prevent any person who may be holding the office of President, or acting as President, during the term within which this Article becomes operative from holding the office of President or acting as President during the remainder of such term.

## Section 2

[RATIFICATION WITHIN SEVEN YEARS]
This Article shall be inoperative unless it shall have been ratified as an amendment to the Constitution by the legislatures of three-fourths of the several states within seven years from the date of its submission to the States by the Congress.

# AMENDMENT XXIII

*[Proposed by Congress on June 21, 1960; declared ratified on March 29, 1961.]*

## Section 1

[ELECTORAL COLLEGE VOTES FOR THE DISTRICT OF COLUMBIA]
The District constituting the seat of Government of the United States shall appoint in such manner as the Congress may direct:
A number of electors of President and Vice-President equal to the whole number of Senators and Representatives in Congress to which the District would be entitled if it were a State, but in no event more than the least populous State; they shall be in addition to those appointed by the States, but they shall be considered, for the purposes of the election of President and Vice-President, to be electors appointed by a State; and they shall meet in the District and perform such duties as provided by the twelfth article of amendment.

*Section 2*

[POWER TO ENFORCE THIS ARTICLE]

The Congress shall have power to enforce this article by appropriate legislation.

# AMENDMENT XXIV

*[Proposed by Congress on August 27, 1963; declared ratified on January 23, 1964.]*

*Section 1*

[ANTI-POLL TAX]

The right of citizens of the United States to vote in any primary or other election for President or Vice-President, for electors for President or Vice-President, or for Senator or Representative in Congress, shall not be denied or abridged by the United States or any State by reason of failure to pay any poll tax or other tax.

*Section 2*

[POWER TO ENFORCE THIS ARTICLE]

The Congress shall have power to enforce this article by appropriate legislation.

# AMENDMENT XXV

*[Proposed by Congress on July 7, 1965; declared ratified on February 10, 1967.]*

*Section 1*

[VICE-PRESIDENT TO BECOME PRESIDENT]

In case of the removal of the President from office or his death or resignation, the Vice-President shall become President.

*Section 2*

[CHOICE OF A NEW VICE-PRESIDENT]

Whenever there is a vacancy in the office of the Vice-President, the President shall nominate a Vice-President who shall take office upon confirmation by a majority vote of both houses of Congress.

*Section 3*

[PRESIDENT MAY DECLARE OWN DISABILITY]

Whenever the President transmits to the President pro tempore of the Senate and the Speaker of the House of Representatives his written declaration that he is unable to discharge the powers and duties of his office, and until he transmits to them a written declaration to the contrary, such powers and duties shall be discharged by the Vice-President as Acting President.

*Section 4*

[ALTERNATE PROCEDURES TO DECLARE AND TO END PRESIDENTIAL DISABILITY]

Whenever the Vice-President and a majority of either the principal officers of the executive departments or of such other body as Congress may by law provide, transmit to the President pro tempore of the Senate and the Speaker of the House of Representatives their written declaration that the President is unable to discharge the powers and duties of his office, the Vice-President shall immediately assume the powers and duties of the office as Acting President.

Thereafter, when the President transmits to the President pro tempore of the Senate and the Speaker of the House of Representatives his written declaration that no inability exists, he shall resume the powers and duties of his office unless the Vice-President and a majority of either the principal officers of the executive department or of such other body as Congress may by law provide, transmit within four days to the President pro tempore of the Senate and the Speaker of the House of Representatives their written declaration that the President is unable to discharge the powers and duties of his office. Thereupon Congress shall decide the issue, assembling within 48 hours for that purpose if not in session. If the Congress, within 21 days after receipt of the latter written declaration, or, if Congress is not in session, within 21 days after Congress is required to assemble, determines by two-thirds vote of both houses that the President is unable to discharge the powers and duties of his office, the Vice-President shall continue to discharge the same as Acting President; otherwise, the President shall resume the powers and duties of his office.

# AMENDMENT XXVI

*[Proposed by Congress on March 23, 1971; declared ratified on June 30, 1971.]*

*Section 1*

[EIGHTEEN-YEAR-OLD SUFFRAGE]

The right of citizens of the United States, who are eighteen years of age or older, to vote shall not be denied or abridged by the United States or by any State on account of age.

*Section 2*

[POWER TO ENFORCE THIS ARTICLE]

The Congress shall have power to enforce this article by appropriate legislation.

# AMENDMENT XXVII

[LIMITING CONGRESSIONAL PAY CHANGES]
*[Proposed by Congress on September 25, 1789; ratified on May 7, 1992.]*

No law varying the compensation for the services of the Senators and Representatives shall take effect until an election of Representatives shall have intervened.

# Acknowledgments

Adler, Jonathan. "A Framer's Design." National Review Online. Reprinted by permission of United Feature Syndicate, Inc.

Aizenman, Nurith. "The Case for More Regulation." Reprinted with permission from *The Washington Monthly*. Copyright by Washington Monthly Publishing LLC, 733 15th St. NW, Suite 1000, Washington, DC 20005. (202) 393–5155. Web site: www.washingtonmonthly.com.

Beard, Charles. Reprinted with the permission of Scribner, an imprint of Simon & Schuster Adult Publishing Group, from *An Economic Interpretation of the Constitution of the United States* by Charles Beard. Copyright (c) 1935 by The Macmillan Company; copyright renewed 1963 by William Beard and Miriam Vagts Beard.

Bresler, Robert. "Media Bias and the Culture Wars." from *USA Today* (July 2004). Reprinted with the permission of author, Robert J. Bresler, Professor Emeritus of Public Policy, Pennsylvania State University.

Brown, Robert. *Charles Beard and the Constitution*, Copyright (c) 1956, renewed 1984 by Princeton University Press. Reprinted by permission of Princeton University Press.

Burtless, Gary. "Growing American Inequality: Source and Remedies." from *Brookings Review*, (Winter 1999). Reprinted with the permission of The Brookings Institution, Washington, DC.

Citizens Against Government Waste. "Introduction to *The Pig Book*. May 2004. Copyright © 2004 *Congressional Book Summary* by Citizens Against Government Waste.

Clinton, Hillary. "Now Can We Talk About Health Care?" *The New York Times Magazine*, April 18, 2004. Reprinted with the permission of Senator Hillary Rodham Clinton.

Chinni, Dante. "Arsenic Flap and Sound Science." Reproduced with permission from the 6/4/2001 issue of *The Christian Science Monitor* (www.csmonitor.com) © 2001 The Christian Science Monitor. All rights reserved.

Cohn, Jonathan. "Roll Out the Barrel: The Case Against the Case Against Pork." Reprinted with the permission of *The New Republic*, Copyright (c) 2002, The New Republic, LLC.

Cunningham, Brent. "Rethinking Objective Journals." Reprinted with the permission of www.alternet.org.

de Tocqueville, Alexis. "Political Associations in the United States." From *Democracy in America*, edited by J. P. Mayer and Max Lerner, translated by George Lawrence. English translation copyright (c) 1965 by Harper & Row, Publishers, Inc. Reprinted by permission of HarperCollins Publishers Inc.

Derthick, Martha. "American Federalism: Half-Full or Half-Empty?" *Brookings Review* (Winter 2000), Vol. 18 No. 1. Reprinted with the permission of the publisher.

Faucheux, Ron. "Reelection Tips for Legislators." *Campaigns and Elections* (February 1998). Reprinted with the permission of the author.

Fiorina, Morris P. "The Decline of Collective Responsibility in American Politics." Reprinted by permission of *Daedalus*, Journal of the American Academy of Arts and Sciences, from the issue entitled, "The End of Consensus?" (Summer 1980), Vol. 109, No. 3. "What Culture Wars?" from the *Wall Street Journal*, July 14, 2004. Reprinted with the permission of the author.

Friedman, Leon. "Overruling the Court." Reprinted with permission from *The American Prospect* Vol. 12, No. 15 (August 27, 2001). The American Prospect, 5 Broad Street, Boston, MA 02102. All rights reserved.

Fund, John H. "Make Way for Election Month." *The American Spectator* (October 2004). Granted with permission.

Gallup, George. "Polling the Public." Copyright (c) 1944, 1948, 1976 by Princeton University Press. Reprinted by permission of Princeton University Press.

Gelernter, David. "The Holocaust Shrug: Why Is there So Much Indifference to the Liberation of Iraq?" *The Weekly Standard*, April 5, 2005. Reprinted with the permission of The Weekly Standard.

Gervais, Robert. "The Necessity of Free-Market Prices for Medical Care." *Journal of American Physicians and Surgeons* (Summer 2004). Published by the Association of American Physicians and Surgeons.

Gorman, Siobhan. "Intelligence—Worlds Apart." Copyright 2003 by National Journal Group, Inc. All rights reserved. Reprinted by permission.

Hacker, Jacob and Paul. "Popular Fiction" TNR Online. Reprinted by permission of The New Republic. © 2004, The New Republic, LLC.

Hartz, Louis. Excerpts from *The Liberal Tradition in America: An Interpretation of American Political Thought since the Revolution*. Copyright © 1955 and renewed 1983 by Louis Hartz, reprinted by permission of Harcourt, Inc.

Hibbing, John and Elizabeth Theiss-Morse. "Too Much of a Good Thing: More Representative Is Not Necessarily Better." *Political Science & Politics* (March 1998). Reprinted with the permission of the authors.

Hofstadt, Richard. From *The Paranoid Style in American Politics and Other Essays* by Richard Hofstadt, copyright 1952, 1964, 1965 by Richard Hofstadt. Used by permission of Alfred A. Knopf, a division of Random House, Inc.

Holt, Jim. "The Human Factor." *The New York Times Magazine*, March 28, 2004. Copyright © 2004 Jim Holt. Reprinted by permission.

John, David C. "Providing Social Security Benefits in the Future." From The Heritage Foundation, March 25, 2004. Reprinted with the permission of the publisher.

Jones, Charles. "Perspectives on the Presidency." From *The Presidency in a Separated System*. Reprinted with the permission of The Brookings Institution, Washington, DC.

Kammen, Michael. "Introduction." From *The Origins of the American Constitution*, edited by Michael Kammen, copyright © 1986 by Michael Kammen. Used by permission of Viking Penguin, a division of Penguin Group (USA) Inc.

Kennan, George. "The Sources of Soviet Conduct." Reprinted by permission of *Foreign Affairs*, Vol. 25, No. 4 (July 1947). Copyright 1947 by the Council on Foreign Relations, Inc.

Kettl, Donald. "Real-Life Federalism." *Potomac Chronicle*. Reprinted with the permission of the author, Donald Kettl, University of Wisconsin-Madison.

Key, V. O. Jr. "The Voice of the People: An Echo." From *The Responsible Electorate* by V. O. Key, Jr., edited by Milton C. Cummings, Jr., pp. 1–8. Cambridge, Mass.: The Belknap Press of Harvard University Press, Copyright © 1996 by the President and Fellows of Harvard College.

Klein, Naomi. "Baghdad Year Zero." Copyright © 2004 by Harper's Magazine. All rights reserved. Reproduced from the September issue by special permission.

King, Martin L. Jr. "Letter from a Birmingham Jail." Reprinted by arrangement with the Estate of Martin Luther King, Jr., c/o Writers House as agent for the proprietor New York, NY. Copyright 1963 Dr. Martin Luther King, Jr., Copyright renewed 1991 Coretta Scott King.

Last, Jonathan. "The Not-So-Swift Mainstream Media." *The Weekly Standard*, September 6, 2004. Reprinted with the permission of The Weekly Standard.